GIVE ME LIBERTY!

An American History

Third Edition

W · W · NORTON & COMPANY · NEW YORK · LONDON

GIVE ME LIBERTY!

AN AMERICAN HISTORY

Third Edition

by ERIC FONER

W. W. Norton & Company has been independent since its founding in 1923, when William Warder Norton and Mary D. Herter Norton first published lectures delivered at the People's Institute, the adult education division of New York City's Cooper Union. The firm soon expanded its program beyond the Institute, publishing books by celebrated academics from America and abroad. By mid-century, the two major pillars of Norton's publishing program—trade books and college texts—were firmly established. In the 1950s, the Norton family transferred control of the company to its employees, and today—with a staff of 400 and a comparable number of trade, college, and professional titles published each year—W. W. Norton & Company stands as the largest and oldest publishing house owned wholly by its employees.

Editor: Steve Forman
Editorial Assistant: Rebecca Charney
Managing Editor, College: Marian Johnson
Associate Managing Editor, College: Kim Yi
Copy Editor: JoAnn Simony
Marketing Manager: Tamara McNeill
Media Editor: Steve Hoge
Production Manager: Chris Granville
Art Director: Rubina Yeh
Designer: Antonina Krass
Photo Researchers: Patricia Marx and Stephanie Romeo
Composition and layout: TexTech and Carole Desnoes
Manufacturing: Transcon

Library of Congress Cataloging-in-Publication Data
Foner, Eric.
  Give me liberty!: An American history / Eric Foner. — 3rd ed.
    p. cm.
  Includes bibliographical references and index.
  ISBN 978-0-393-93430-4 (hardcover)
1. United States—History. 2. United States—Politics and government.
3. Democracy—United States—History. 4. Liberty—History. I. Title.

E178.F66 2010
973—dc22
                                                            2010015330

W. W. Norton & Company, Inc., 500 Fifth Avenue, New York, NY 10110
www.wwnorton.com

W. W. Norton & Company Ltd., Castle House, 75/76 Wells Street, London W1T 3QT
1 2 3 4 5 6 7 8 9 0

For my mother, Liza Foner (1909–2005), an accomplished artist who lived through most of the twentieth century and into the twenty-first

Contents

Part 1 American Colonies to 1763

Part 2 A New Nation, 1763–1840

Part 3 Slavery, Freedom, and the Crisis of the Union, 1840–1877

Part 4 Toward a Global Presence, 1870–1920

Part 5 Depression and Wars, 1920–1953

Appendix

DOCUMENTS

TABLES AND FIGURES

LIST OF MAPS, TABLES, AND FIGURES

ABOUT THE AUTHOR

ERIC FONER is DeWitt Clinton Professor of History at Columbia University, where he earned his B.A. and Ph.D. In his teaching and scholarship, he focuses on the Civil War and Reconstruction, slavery, and nineteenth-century America. Professor Foner's publications include *Free Soil, Free Labor, Free Men: The Ideology of the Republican Party before the Civil War; Tom Paine and Revolutionary America; Nothing but Freedom: Emancipation and Its Legacy; Reconstruction: America's Unfinished Revolution, 1863–1877; The Story of American Freedom;* and *Forever Free: The Story of Emancipation and Reconstruction.* His history of Reconstruction won the *Los Angeles Times* Book Award for History, the Bancroft Prize, and the Parkman Prize. He has served as president of the Organization of American Historians and the American Historical Association. In 2006 he received the Presidential Award for Outstanding Teaching from Columbia University. His most recent book is *The Fiery Trial: Abraham Lincoln and American Slavery.*

Preface

Give Me Liberty! An American History is a survey of American history from the earliest days of European exploration and conquest of the New World to the first years of the twenty-first century. It offers students a clear, concise narrative whose central theme is the changing contours of American freedom.

I am extremely gratified by the response to the first two editions of *Give Me Liberty!*, which have been used in survey courses at many hundreds of two- and four-year colleges and universities throughout the country. The comments I have received from instructors and students encourage me to think that *Give Me Liberty!* has worked well in their classrooms. Their comments have also included many valuable suggestions for revisions, which I greatly appreciate. These have ranged from corrections of typographical and factual errors to thoughts about subjects that needed more extensive treatment. In making revisions for this Third Edition, I have tried to take these suggestions into account. I have also incorporated the findings and insights of new scholarship that has appeared since the original edition was written.

The most significant changes in this Third Edition reflect my desire to place American history more fully in a global context. The book remains, of course, a survey of American, not world, history. But in the past few years, scholars writing about the American past have sought to delineate the connections and influences of the United States on the rest of the world as well as the global developments that have helped to shape the course of events here at home. They have also devoted greater attention to transnational processes—the expansion of empires, international labor migrations, the rise and fall of slavery, the globalization of economic enterprise—that cannot be understood solely within the confines of one country's national boundaries. Without in any way seeking to homogenize the history of individual nations or neglect the domestic forces that have shaped American development, the Third Edition reflects this recent emphasis in American historical writing. Small changes relating to this theme may be found throughout the book. The major additions seeking to illuminate the global context of American history are as follows:

Chapter 4 includes a brief discussion of how the Great Awakening in the American colonies took place at a time of growing religious fundamentalism in many parts of the world. Chapter 5 now devotes attention to the global impact of the American Declaration of Independence, including how both colonial peoples seeking national independence and groups who felt themselves deprived of equal rights seized upon the Declaration's language to promote their own causes. Chapter 8 discusses how the slave revolution in Saint Domingue, which established the black republic of Haiti, affected the thinking of both black and white Americans in the early 1800s. The chapter also contains a new section on the Barbary Wars, the first armed encounter between the United States and Islamic states.

In Chapter 10, I have added a new section discussing the response in the United States to the Latin American wars of independence of the early nineteenth century, and the similarities and differences between these struggles and our own War of Independence. Chapter 11 contains a new section discussing the abolition of slavery elsewhere in the Western Hemisphere and how the aftermath of emancipation in other areas affected the debate over slavery in the United States. Chapter 13 compares the California gold rush with the consequences of the discovery of gold in Australia at the same time, and also adds a discussion of the "opening" of Japan to American commerce in the 1850s. And in Chapter 14, I added to the discussion of the Civil War a comparison of its destructiveness with that of other conflicts of the era, and also an examination of how the consolidation of national power in the United States reflected a worldwide process underway at the same time in other countries. In that chapter, too, reflecting the findings of recent scholarship, there are new discussions of the war's impact on American religion and on Native Americans. Chapter 15, dealing with the era of Reconstruction, now compares the aftermath of slavery in the United States with the outcome in other places where the institution was abolished.

In Chapter 16, a new section places the westward movement in the United States in the context of the settlement of frontier regions of other countries, ranging from Argentina to Australia and South Africa, and discusses the consequences for native populations in these societies. Chapter 17 expands on the acquisition by the United States of an overseas empire as a result of the Spanish-American War, and includes a new section on the Global Color Line—the worldwide development of national policies intended to guarantee white supremacy. I have strengthened, in Chapter 19, the discussion of the aftermath of World War I by examining the impact around the world of President Woodrow Wilson's rhetoric concerning national self-determination, and the disappointment felt when the principle was not applied to the Asian and African colonies of European empires. Chapter 22 now includes a section on black internationalism—how World War II led many black Americans to identify their campaign for equal rights with the struggle for national independence of colonial peoples in other parts of the world. In Chapter 23, I have expanded the discussion of the idea of human rights to indicate some of the ambiguities of the concept as it emerged as a major theme of international debate after World War II. There is a new section in Chapter 24 on the global reaction to American racial segregation and to the stirrings in the 1950s of the civil rights movement. I have strengthened the treatment of the 1960s by adding a discussion of the global 1968—how events in the United States in that volatile year occurred at the same time as uprisings of young people in many other parts of the world.

And in Chapter 28, the book's final chapter, I have significantly expanded coverage of the last few years of American history, including the election of Barack Obama, the nation's first African-American president, the continuing controversy over the relationship between liberty and security in the context of a global war on terror, and the global economic crisis that began in 2008.

As in the Second Edition, the Voices of Freedom sections in each chapter now include two documents; I have changed a number of them to reflect the new emphasis on the global context of American history. I have also revised the end-of-chapter bibliographies to reflect current scholarship. And I now include references to websites that contain digital images and documents relating to the chapter themes.

This Third Edition also introduces some new features. Visions of Freedom, a parallel to the Voices of Freedom document excerpts that have proven useful to instructors and students, highlights in each chapter an image that illuminates an understanding of freedom. I believe that examining this theme through visual as well as written evidence helps students to appreciate how our concepts of freedom have changed over the course of American history. The Visions of Freedom feature includes a headnote and questions that encourage students to think critically about the images.

The pedagogy in the book has been revised and enhanced to give students more guidance as they move through chapters. The end-of-chapter review pages have been expanded with additional review questions, many more key terms with page references, and a new set of questions on the freedom theme. The aim of the pedagogy, as always, is to offer students guidance through the material without getting in the way of the presentation.

I have also added new images in each chapter to expand the visual representation of key ideas and personalities in the text. Taken together, I believe these changes enhance the purpose of *Give Me Liberty!*: to offer students a clear, concise, and thematically enriched introduction to American history.

Americans have always had a divided attitude toward history. On the one hand, they tend to be remarkably future-oriented, dismissing events of even the recent past as "ancient history" and sometimes seeing history as a burden to be overcome, a prison from which to escape. On the other hand, like many other peoples, Americans have always looked to history for a sense of personal or group identity and of national cohesiveness. This is why so many Americans devote time and energy to tracing their family trees and why they visit historical museums and National Park Service historical sites in ever-increasing numbers. My hope is that this book will convince readers with all degrees of interest that history does matter to them.

The novelist and essayist James Baldwin once observed that history "does not refer merely, or even principally, to the past. On the contrary, the great force of history comes from the fact that we carry it within us, . . . [that] history is literally present in all that we do." As Baldwin recognized, the force of history is evident in our own world. Especially in a political democracy like the United States, whose government is designed to rest on the consent of informed citizens, knowledge of the past is essential—not only for those of us whose profession is the teaching and writing of history, but for everyone. History, to be sure, does not offer simple lessons or immediate answers to current questions. Knowing the history of immigration to the United States, and all of the tensions, turmoil, and aspirations associated with it, for example, does not tell us what current immigration policy ought to be. But without that knowledge, we have no way of understanding which approaches have worked and which have not—essential information for the formulation of future public policy.

History, it has been said, is what the present chooses to remember about the past. Rather than a fixed collection of facts, or a group of interpretations that cannot be challenged, our understanding of history is constantly changing. There is nothing unusual in the fact that each generation rewrites history to meet its own needs, or that scholars disagree among themselves on basic questions like the causes of the Civil War or the reasons for the Great Depression. Precisely because each generation asks different questions of the past, each generation formulates different answers. The past thirty years have witnessed a remarkable expansion of the scope of historical study. The experiences of groups neglected by earlier scholars, including women, African-Americans, working people, and others, have received unprecedented attention from historians. New subfields—social history, cultural history, and family history among them—have taken their place alongside traditional political and diplomatic history.

Give Me Liberty! draws on this voluminous historical literature to present an up-to-date and inclusive account of the American past, paying due attention to the experience of diverse groups of Americans while in no way neglecting the events and processes Americans have experienced in common. It devotes serious attention to political, social, cultural, and economic history, and to their interconnections. The narrative brings together major events and prominent leaders with the many groups of ordinary people who make up American society. *Give Me Liberty!* has a rich cast of characters, from Thomas Jefferson to campaigners for woman suffrage, from Franklin D. Roosevelt to former slaves seeking to breathe meaning into emancipation during and after the Civil War.

Aimed at an audience of undergraduate students with little or no detailed knowledge of American history, *Give Me Liberty!* guides readers through the complexities of the subject without overwhelming them with excessive detail. The unifying theme of freedom that runs through the text gives shape to the narrative and integrates the numerous strands that make up the American experience. This approach builds on that of my earlier book, *The Story of American Freedom* (1998), although *Give Me Liberty!* places events and personalities in the foreground and is more geared to the structure of the introductory survey course.

Freedom, and the battles to define its meaning, has long been central to my own scholarship and undergraduate teaching, which focuses on the nineteenth century and especially the era of the Civil War and Reconstruction (1850–1877). This was a time when the future of slavery tore the nation apart and emancipation produced a national debate over what rights the former slaves, and all Americans, should enjoy as free citizens. I have found that attention to clashing definitions of freedom and the struggles of different groups to achieve freedom as they understood it offers a way of making sense of the bitter battles and vast transformations of that pivotal era. I believe that the same is true for American history as a whole.

No idea is more fundamental to Americans' sense of themselves as individuals and as a nation than freedom. The central term in our political language, freedom—or liberty, with which it is almost always used interchangeably—is deeply embedded in the record of our history and the language of everyday life. The Declaration of Independence lists liberty among mankind's inalienable rights; the Constitution announces its purpose as securing liberty's blessings. The United States fought the Civil War to bring about a new birth of freedom, World War II for the Four Freedoms, and the Cold War to defend the Free World. Americans' love of liberty has been represented by liberty poles, liberty caps, and statues of liberty, and acted out by burning stamps and burning draft cards, by running away from slavery, and by demonstrating for the right to vote. "Every man in the street, white, black, red, or yellow," wrote the educator and statesman Ralph Bunche in 1940, "knows that this is 'the land of the free' . . . 'the cradle of liberty.'"

The very universality of the idea of freedom, however, can be misleading. Freedom is not a fixed, timeless category with a single unchanging definition. Indeed, the history of the United States is, in part, a story of debates, disagreements, and struggles over freedom. Crises like the American Revolution, the Civil War, and the Cold War have permanently transformed the idea of freedom. So too have demands by various groups of Americans to enjoy greater freedom. The meaning of freedom has been constructed not only in congressional debates and political treatises, but on plantations and picket lines, in parlors and even bedrooms.

Over the course of our history, American freedom has been both a reality and a mythic ideal—a living truth for millions of Americans, a cruel mockery for others. For some, freedom has been what some scholars call a "habit of the heart," an ideal so taken for granted that it is lived out but rarely analyzed. For others, freedom is not a birthright but a distant goal that has inspired great sacrifice.

Give Me Liberty! draws attention to three dimensions of freedom that have been critical in American history: (1) the *meanings* of freedom; (2) the *social conditions* that make freedom possible; and (3) the *boundaries* of freedom that determine who is entitled to enjoy freedom and who is not. All have changed over time.

In the era of the American Revolution, for example, freedom was primarily a set of rights enjoyed in public activity—the right of a community to be governed by laws to which its representatives had consented and of individuals to engage in religious worship without governmental interference. In the nineteenth century, freedom came to be closely identified with each person's opportunity to develop to the fullest his or her innate talents. In the twentieth, the "ability to choose," in both public and private life, became perhaps the dominant understanding of freedom. This development was encouraged by the explosive growth of the consumer marketplace (a development that receives considerable attention in *Give Me Liberty!*), which offered Americans an unprecedented array of goods with which to satisfy their needs and desires. During the 1960s, a crucial chapter in the history of American freedom, the idea of personal freedom was extended into virtually every realm, from attire and "lifestyle" to relations between the sexes. Thus, over time, more and more areas of life have been drawn into Americans' debates about the meaning of freedom.

A second important dimension of freedom focuses on the social conditions necessary to allow freedom to flourish. What kinds of economic institutions and relationships best encourage individual freedom? In the colonial era and for more than a century after independence, the answer centered on economic autonomy, enshrined in the glorification of the independent small producer—the farmer, skilled craftsman, or shopkeeper—who did not have to depend on another person for his livelihood. As the industrial economy matured, new conceptions of economic freedom came to the fore: "liberty of contract" in the Gilded Age, "industrial freedom" (a say in corporate decision-making) in the Progressive era, economic security during the New Deal, and, more recently, the ability to enjoy mass consumption within a market economy.

The boundaries of freedom, the third dimension of this theme, have inspired some of the most intense struggles in American history. Although founded on the premise that liberty is an entitlement of all humanity, the United States for much of its history deprived many of its own people of freedom. Non-whites have rarely enjoyed the same access to freedom as white Americans. The belief in equal opportunity as the birthright of all Americans has coexisted with persistent efforts to limit freedom by race, gender, class, and in other ways.

Less obvious, perhaps, is the fact that one person's freedom has frequently been linked to another's servitude. In the colonial era and nineteenth century, expanding freedom for many Americans rested on the lack of freedom—slavery, indentured servitude, the subordinate position of women—for others. By the same token, it has been through battles at the boundaries—the efforts of racial minorities, women, and others to secure greater freedom—that the meaning and experience of freedom have been deepened and the concept extended into new realms.

Time and again in American history, freedom has been transformed by the demands of excluded groups for inclusion. The idea of freedom as a universal birthright owes much both to abolitionists who sought to extend the blessings of liberty to blacks and to immigrant groups who insisted on full recognition as American citizens. The principle of equal protection of the law without regard to race, which became a central element of American freedom, arose from the antislavery struggle and the Civil War and was reinvigorated by the civil rights revolution of the 1960s, which called itself the "freedom movement." The battle for the right of free speech by labor radicals and birth control advocates in the first part of the twentieth century helped to make civil liberties an essential element of freedom for all Americans.

Although concentrating on events within the United States, *Give Me Liberty!* also, as indicated above, situates American history in the context of developments in other parts of the world. Many of the forces that shaped American history, including the international migration of peoples, the development of slavery, the spread of democracy, and the expansion of capitalism, were worldwide processes not confined to the United States. Today, American ideas, culture, and economic and military power exert unprecedented influence throughout the world. But beginning with the earliest days of settlement, when European empires competed to colonize North America and enrich themselves from its trade, American history cannot be understood in isolation from its global setting.

Freedom is the oldest of clichés and the most modern of aspirations. At various times in our history, it has served as the rallying cry of the powerless and as a justification of the status quo. Freedom helps to bind our culture together and exposes the contradictions between what America claims to be and what it sometimes has been. American history is not a narrative of continual progress toward greater and greater freedom. As the abolitionist Thomas

Wentworth Higginson noted after the Civil War, "revolutions may go backward." Though freedom can be achieved, it may also be taken away. This happened, for example, when the equal rights granted to former slaves immediately after the Civil War were essentially nullified during the era of segregation. As was said in the eighteenth century, the price of freedom is eternal vigilance.

In the early twenty-first century, freedom continues to play a central role in American political and social life and thought. It is invoked by individuals and groups of all kinds, from critics of economic globalization to those who seek to secure American freedom at home and export it abroad. I hope that *Give Me Liberty!* will offer beginning students a clear account of the course of American history, and of its central theme, freedom, which today remains as varied, contentious, and ever-changing as America itself.

ACKNOWLEDGMENTS

All works of history are, to a considerable extent, collaborative books, in that every writer builds on the research and writing of previous scholars. This is especially true of a textbook that covers the entire American experience, over more than five centuries. My greatest debt is to the innumerable historians on whose work I have drawn in preparing this volume. The Suggested Reading list at the end of each chapter offers only a brief introduction to the vast body of historical scholarship that has influenced and informed this book. More specifically, however, I wish to thank the following scholars, who generously read portions of this work and offered valuable comments, criticisms, and suggestions:

For the First Edition:
  Valerie Adams, Embry-Riddle Aeronautical University
  Terry Alford, Northern Virginia Community College
  Tyler Anbinder, George Washington University
  Eric Arnesen, University of Illinois, Chicago
  Ira Berlin, University of Maryland
  Nikki Brown, Kent State University
  Jon Butler, Yale University
  Diane S. Clemens, University of California, Berkeley
  Paul G. E. Clemens, Rutgers University
  Jane Dailey, Johns Hopkins University
  Douglas Deal, State University of New York, Oswego
  Ricky Dobbs, Texas A&M University, Commerce
  Thomas Dublin, State University of New York, Binghamton
  Joel Franks, San Jose State University
  Kirsten Gardner, University of Texas at San Antonio
  Lawrence B. Glickman, University of South Carolina
  Colin Gordon, University of Iowa
  Sam Haynes, University of Texas at Arlington
  Rebecca Hill, Borough of Manhattan Community College
  Jesse Hingson, Manatee Community College
  Wallace Hutcheon, Northern Virginia Community College

Kevin Kenny, Boston College
Peter Kolchin, University of Delaware
Bruce Laurie, University of Massachusetts, Amherst
Daniel Letwin, Pennsylvania State University
Peter Mancall, University of Southern California
Louis Masur, City College, City University of New York
Alan McPherson, Howard University
Don Palm, Sacramento City College
Larry Peterson, North Dakota State University
John Recchiuti, Mount Union College
Scott Sandage, Carnegie-Mellon University
Bryant Simon, University of Georgia
Brooks Simpson, Arizona State University
Judith Stein, City College, City University of New York
George Stevens, Dutchess Community College
Thomas Sugrue, University of Pennsylvania
Alan Taylor, University of California, Davis
Daniel B. Thorp, Virginia Polytechnic Institute
Helena Wall, Pomona College
Jon Wiener, University of California, Irvine

For the Second Edition:
Marsha Ackermann, Eastern Michigan University
Valerie Adams, Embry-Riddle Aeronautical University
Omar Ali, Towson University
Ellen Baker, Columbia University
Ruth Bloch, University of California, Los Angeles
Roger Bromert, Southern Oklahoma State University
Charlotte Brooks, University at Albany, State University of New York
Barbara Calluori, Montclair State University
Robert Cassanello, University of Central Florida
Thomas Clarkin, San Antonio College
Gerard Clock, Pace University
Ronald Dufour, Rhode Island College
Mike Green, Community College of Southern Nevada
Maurine Greenwald, University of Pittsburgh
Evan Haefeli, Columbia University
Sharon A. Roger Hepburn, Radford College
Tam Hoskisson, Northern Arizona University
David Hsiung, Juniata College
Jeanette Keith, Bloomsburg University of Pennsylvania
Daniel Kotzin, Kutztown University
Robert M. S. McDonald, U.S. Military Academy
Stephen L. McIntyre, Missouri State University
Cynthia Northrup, University of Texas at Arlington
Kathleen Banks Nutter, Stony Brook University, State University
    of New York
John Paden, Rappahannock Community College
Sarah Phillips, Columbia University
Charles K. Piehl, Minnesota State University, Mankato
Ann Plane, University of California, Santa Barbara

Charles Postel, California State University, Sacramento
John Recchiuti, Mount Union College
Rob Risko, Trinity Valley Community College, Athens
Wade Shaffer, West Texas A&M University
Silvana R. Siddali, Saint Louis University
Judith Stein, The City College of the City University of New York
George Stevens, Dutchess Community College
Matthew A. Sutton, Oakland University
Timothy Thurber, Virginia Commonwealth University
David Voelker, University of Wisconson—Green Bay
Peter Way, Bowling Green State University
Richard Weiner, Indiana University—Purdue University Fort Wayne
Barbara Welke, University of Minnesota

For the Third Edition:
Vicki Arnold, Northern Virginia Community College
James Barrett, University of Illinois
Stephen Branch, College of the Canyons
Cynthia Clark, University of Texas at Arlington
Sylvie Coulibaly, Kenyon College
Ashley Cruseturner, McLennan Community College
Kevin Davis, Central Texas College
Jennifer Duffy, Western Connecticut State University
Melody Flowers, McLennan Community College
Lawrence Foster, Georgia Institute of Technology
Monica Gisolfi, University of North Carolina, Wilmington
Adam Goudsouzian, University of Memphis
Katie Graham, Diablo Valley College
Mike Green, Southern Nevada Community College
Dan Greene, Baylor University
Jennifer Gross, Jacksonville State University
Sandra Harvey, Lone Star College–CyFair
Toby Higbie, University of California, Los Angeles
Ernest Ialongo, Hostos Community College
Justin Jackson, Columbia University
Norman Love, El Paso Community College
James M. McCaffrey, University of Houston
John McCusker, Trinity University, San Antonio
Gil Montemayor, McLennan Community College
David Orique, University of Oregon
Michael Pebworth, Cabrillo College
Ray Raphael, Humboldt State University
Andrew Reiser, Dutchess Community College
Esther Robinson, Lone Star College–CyFair
Jerry Rodnitzky, University of Texas at Arlington
Diane Sager, Maple Woods Community College
Claudio Saunt, University of Georgia
James Seymour, Lone Star College–CyFair
Adam Simmons, Fayetteville State University
Andrew Slap, East Tennessee State University
Tim Solie, Minnesota State University

David Stebenne, Ohio State University
George Stevens, Dutchess Community College
Robert Tinkler, California State University, Chico
Kathleen Thomas, University of Wisconsin, Stout
Elaine Thompson, Louisiana Tech University
Doris Wagner, University of Louisville
Greg Wilson, University of Akron
William Young, Maple Woods Community College

I am particularly grateful to my colleagues in the Columbia University Department of History: Pablo Piccato, for his advice on Latin American history; Evan Haefeli and Ellen Baker, who read and made many suggestions for improvements in their areas of expertise (colonial America and the history of the West, respectively); and Sarah Phillips, who offered advice on treating the history of the environment.

I am also deeply indebted to the graduate students at Columbia University's Department of History who helped with this project. Theresa Ventura offered invaluable assistance in gathering material for the new sections placing American history in a global context. James Delbourgo conducted research for the chapters on the colonial era. Beverly Gage did the same for the twentieth century. Daniel Freund provided all-round research assistance. Victoria Cain did a superb job of locating visual images. I also want to thank my colleagues Elizabeth Blackmar and Alan Brinkley for offering advice and encouragement throughout the writing of this book.

Many thanks to Joshua Brown, director of the American Social History Project, whose website, History Matters, lists innumerable online resources for the study of American history. Bill Young at Maple Woods Community College did a superb job revising and enhancing the in-book pedagogy. Monica Gisolfi (University of North Carolina, Wilmington) and Robert Tinkler (California State University, Chico) did excellent work on the Instructor's Manual and Test Bank. Kathleen Thomas (University of Wisconsin, Stout) helped greatly in the revisions of the companion media packages.

At W. W. Norton & Company, Steve Forman was an ideal editor—patient, encouraging, always ready to offer sage advice, and quick to point out lapses in grammar and logic. I would also like to thank Steve's assistant, Rebecca Charney, for her indispensable and always cheerful help on all aspects of the project; JoAnn Simony for her careful work as manuscript editor; Stephanie Romeo and Patricia Marx for their resourceful attention to the illustrations program; Rubina Yeh and the irreplaceable Antonina Krass for their refinements of the book design; Debra Morton-Hoyt for splendid work on the covers for the Third Edition; Kim Yi for keeping the many threads of the project aligned and then tying them together; Christine D'Antonio and Chris Granville for their efficiency and care in book production; Steve Hoge for orchestrating the rich media package that accompanies the textbook; Nicole Netherton, Tamara McNeill, Steve Dunn, and Mike Wright for their alert reads of the U.S. survey market and their hard work in helping establish *Give Me Liberty!* within it; and Drake McFeely, Roby Harrington, and Julia Reidhead for maintaining Norton as an independent, employee-owned publisher dedicated to excellence in its work.

Many students may have heard stories of how publishing companies alter the language and content of textbooks in an attempt to maximize sales and avoid alienating any potential reader. In this case, I can honestly say that W. W. Norton allowed me a free hand in writing the book and, apart from the usual editorial corrections, did not try to influence its content at all. For this I thank them, while I accept full responsibility for the interpretations presented and for any errors the book may contain. Since no book of this length can be entirely free of mistakes, I welcome readers to send me corrections at ef17@columbia.edu.

My greatest debt, as always, is to my family—my wife, Lynn Garafola, for her good-natured support while I was preoccupied by a project that consumed more than its fair share of my time and energy, and my daughter, Daria, who while a ninth and tenth grader read every chapter as it was written and offered invaluable suggestions about improving the book's clarity, logic, and grammar.

Eric Foner
New York City
July 2010

GIVE ME LIBERTY!

An American History

Third Edition

Part 3

SLAVERY, FREEDOM, AND THE CRISIS OF THE UNION, 1840–1877

During the middle part of the nineteenth century, the United States confronted its greatest crisis, as the division between slave and free societies tore the country apart. A new nation emerged from the Civil War, with slavery abolished and the meaning of freedom transformed for all Americans.

Despite the hope of some of the founders that slavery might die out, the institution grew in size and economic importance as the nineteenth century progressed. Slavery expanded westward with the young republic, and the slave population grew to nearly 4 million by 1860. After the northern states abolished slavery, it became the "peculiar institution" of the South, the basis of a society growing ever more different from the rest of the country in economic structure and social values. Planters who dominated southern life also exerted enormous influence in national affairs. They developed a defense of slavery that insisted the institution was the foundation of genuine freedom for white citizens. Slaves, meanwhile, created their own semiautonomous culture that nurtured from one generation to the next their hope for liberation from bondage. Nonetheless, slavery was in some ways a national institution. Slave-grown cotton, a source of wealth to slaveowners, also provided the raw material for the North's growing textile industry and became the country's most important export.

During the 1820s and 1830s, numerous social movements arose that worked to reform American society. Their inspiration lay primarily in the Second Great Awakening, the religious revivals that swept both North and South and offered salvation to sinners and

improvement to society at large. While some reform movements were national in scope, others existed only in the North. Most notable among the latter was a new, militant movement demanding the immediate abolition of slavery and the incorporation of blacks as equal citizens of the republic. The abolitionists helped to focus discussions of freedom on the sharp contradiction between liberty and slavery. They promoted an understanding of freedom as control over one's self and participation as an equal member in social and political life. They not only helped to place the issue of slavery squarely on the national agenda but also inspired the stirrings of protest among a number of northern women, whose work in the antislavery movement led them to resent their own lack of legal rights and educational and economic opportunities.

In the 1840s, the conflict between free and slave societies moved to the center stage of American politics. It did so as a result of the nation's territorial expansion. The acquisition of a vast new area of land as the result of the Mexican War raised the question of whether slavery would be able to expand further westward. By the 1850s, this issue had destroyed the Whig Party, weakened the Democrats, and led to the creation of an entirely new party, the Republicans, dedicated to confining slavery to the states where it already existed. Exalting the superiority of northern society, based on "free labor," to southern society, based on slavery, Republicans elected Abraham Lincoln as president in 1860, even though he did not receive a single vote in most of the southern states. In response, seven slave states seceded from the Union and formed a new nation, the Confederate States of America. When southern forces fired on Fort Sumter, an enclave of Union control in Charleston Harbor, they inaugurated the Civil War, by far the bloodiest conflict in American history.

Begun as a struggle to preserve the Union, the Civil War eventually became a crusade for emancipation, which brought the nation what President Lincoln called "a new birth of freedom." The North's failure to achieve military victory in the first two years of the war, coupled with the actions of slaves who by the thousands abandoned the plantations to flee to Union lines, propelled the Lincoln administration down the road to emancipation. Although it freed few slaves on the day it was issued, January 1, 1863, Lincoln's Emancipation Proclamation proved to be the turning point of the Civil War, for it announced that, henceforth, the Union army would serve as an agent of freedom. And by authorizing, for the first time, the enlistment of black men into the Union army, the Proclamation raised the question of black citizenship in the postwar world.

The era of Reconstruction that followed the Civil War was a time of intense political and social conflict, in which the definition of freedom and the question of who was entitled to enjoy it played a central role. Former slaves claimed that freedom meant full incorporation into

PUBLISHED BY THE SUPERVISORY COMMITTEE FOR RECRUITING COLORED REGIMENTS
1210 CHESTNUT ST. PHILADELPHIA.

American society, with the same rights and opportunities whites enjoyed. They also demanded that the government guarantee them access to land, to provide an economic foundation for their freedom. Most southern whites believed that blacks should go back to work on the plantations, enjoying very few political and civil rights. Andrew Johnson, who succeeded Lincoln as president, shared their view. But the majority of northern Republicans came to believe that the emancipated slaves should enjoy the same legal rights as whites. In 1867, they granted black men in the South the right to vote. During Reconstruction, northern Republicans rewrote the laws and Constitution to incorporate the ideal of equal citizenship for all Americans, regardless of race. This was a dramatic expansion of the meaning of freedom.

In the South, Reconstruction witnessed a short-lived period in which former slaves voted and held office alongside whites, a remarkable experiment in interracial democracy. On the other hand, the former slaves failed to achieve the economic freedom they desired, since the North proved unwilling to distribute land. As a result, most former slaves, and increasing numbers of whites in the war-devastated South, found themselves confined to working as sharecroppers on land owned by others. But the genuine advances achieved during Reconstruction, such as improved access to education, exercise of political rights, and the creation of new black institutions like independent churches, produced a violent reaction by upholders of white supremacy. During the 1870s, the North retreated from its commitment to equality. In 1877, Reconstruction came to an end. Many of the rights guaranteed to the former slaves were violated in the years that followed.

Although Reconstruction only lasted from 1865 to 1877, the issues debated then forecast many of the controversies that would envelop American society in the decades that followed. The definition of American citizenship, the power of the federal government and its relationship to the states, the future of political democracy in a society marked by increasing economic inequality—all these were Reconstruction issues, and all reverberated in the Gilded Age and Progressive era that followed.

The Civil War era resolved the contradiction of the existence of slavery in a land that celebrated freedom. But just as the American Revolution left to nineteenth-century Americans the problem of slavery, the Civil War and Reconstruction left to future generations the challenge of bringing genuine freedom to the descendants of slavery.

CHAPTER 11

The Peculiar Institution

An American Slave Market, *painted in 1852 by the unknown artist Taylor, depicts the sale of slaves, including one who had attempted to run away.*

FOCUS QUESTIONS

- How did slavery shape social and economic relations in the Old South?

- What were the legal and material constraints on slaves' lives and work?

- How did family, gender, religion, and values combine to create distinct slave cultures in the Old South?

- What were the major forms of resistance to slavery?

A photograph of Frederick Douglass, the fugitive slave who became a prominent abolitionist, taken between 1847 and 1852. As a fellow abolitionist noted at the time, "The very look and bearing of Douglass are an irresistible logic against the oppression of his race."

In an age of "self-made" men, no American rose more dramatically from humble origins to national and international distinction than Frederick Douglass. Born into slavery in 1818, he became a major figure in the crusade for abolition, the drama of emancipation, and the effort during Reconstruction to give meaning to black freedom.

Douglass was the son of a slave mother and an unidentified white man, possibly his owner. As a youth in Maryland, he gazed out at the ships in Chesapeake Bay, seeing them as "freedom's swift-winged angels." In violation of Maryland law, Douglass learned to read and write, initially with the assistance of his owner's wife and then, after her husband forbade her to continue, with the help of local white children. "From that moment," he later wrote, he understood that knowledge was "the pathway from slavery to freedom." Douglass experienced slavery in all its variety, from work as a house servant and as a skilled craftsman in a Baltimore shipyard to labor as a plantation field hand. When he was fifteen, Douglass's owner sent him to a "slave breaker" to curb his independent spirit. After numerous whippings, Douglass defiantly refused to allow himself to be disciplined again. This confrontation, he recalled, was "the turning-point in my career as a slave." It rekindled his desire for freedom. In 1838, having borrowed the free papers of a black sailor, he escaped to the North.

Frederick Douglass went on to become the most influential African-American of the nineteenth century and the nation's preeminent advocate of racial equality. "He who has endured the cruel pangs of slavery," he wrote, "is the man to advocate liberty." Douglass lectured against slavery throughout the North and the British Isles, and he edited a succession of antislavery publications. He published a widely read autobiography that offered an eloquent condemnation of slavery and racism. Indeed, his own accomplishments testified to the incorrectness of prevailing ideas about blacks' inborn inferiority. Douglass was also active in other reform movements, including the campaign for women's rights. During the Civil War, he advised Abraham Lincoln on the employment of black soldiers and became an early advocate of giving the right to vote to the emancipated slaves. Douglass died in 1895, as a new system of white supremacy based on segregation and disenfranchisement was being fastened upon the South.

Throughout his career, Douglass insisted that slavery could only be overthrown by continuous resistance. "Those who profess to favor freedom, and yet deprecate agitation," he declared, "are men who want crops without plowing up the ground, they want rain without thunder and lightning, they want the ocean without the awful roar of its many waters." In effect, Douglass argued that in their desire for freedom, the slaves were truer to the nation's underlying principles than the white Americans who annually celebrated the Fourth of July while allowing the continued existence of slavery.

THE OLD SOUTH

When Frederick Douglass was born, slavery was already an old institution in America. Two centuries had passed since the first twenty Africans were landed in Virginia from a Dutch ship. After abolition in the North, slavery had become the "peculiar institution" of the South—that is, an institution unique to southern society. The Mason-Dixon Line, drawn by two surveyors in the eighteenth century to settle a boundary dispute between Maryland and Pennsylvania, eventually became the dividing line between slavery and freedom.

Despite the hope of some of the founders that slavery might die out, in fact the institution survived the crisis of the American Revolution and rapidly expanded westward. During the first thirty years of Douglass's life, the number of slaves and the economic and political importance of slavery continued to grow. On the eve of the Civil War, the slave population had risen to nearly 4 million, its high rate of natural increase more than making up for the prohibition in 1808 of further slave imports from Africa. In the South as a whole, slaves made up one-third of the total population, and in the cotton-producing states of the Deep South, around half. By the 1850s, slavery had crossed the Mississippi River and was expanding rapidly in Arkansas, Louisiana, and eastern Texas. In 1860, one-third of the nation's cotton crop was grown west of the Mississippi.

COTTON IS KING

In the nineteenth century, cotton replaced sugar as the world's major crop produced by slave labor. And although slavery survived in Brazil and the Spanish and French Caribbean, its abolition in the British empire in 1833 made the United States indisputably the center of New World slavery.

Table 11.1 GROWTH OF THE SLAVE POPULATION	
Year	*Slave Population*
1790	697,624
1800	893,602
1810	1,191,362
1820	1,538,022
1830	2,009,043
1840	2,487,355
1850	3,204,313
1860	3,953,760

An engraving from just after the Civil War shows a cotton gin in use. Black laborers bring cotton to the machine, which runs it through a series of pronged wheels, to separate the seeds from the fiber.

SLAVE POPULATION, 1860

Slave distribution
(one dot represents 200 slaves)

0   150   300 miles
0   150   300 kilometers

Rather than being evenly distributed throughout the South, the slave population was concentrated in areas with the most fertile soil and easiest access to national and international markets. By 1860, a significant percentage of the slave population had been transported from the Atlantic coast to the Deep South via the internal slave trade.

When measured by slavery's geographic extent, the numbers held in bondage, and the institution's economic importance both regionally and nationally, the Old South was the largest and most powerful slave society the modern world has known. Its strength rested on a virtual monopoly of cotton, the South's "white gold." Cotton had been grown for thousands of years in many parts of the globe. The conquistador Hernán Cortés was impressed by the high quality of woven cotton clothing worn by the Aztecs. But in the nineteenth century, cotton assumed an unprecedented role in the world economy.

Because the early industrial revolution centered on factories using cotton as the raw material to manufacture cloth, cotton had become by far the most important commodity in international trade. And three-fourths of the world's cotton supply came from the southern United States. Throughout the world, hundreds of thousands of workers loaded, unloaded, spun, and wove cotton, and thousands of manufacturers and merchants owed their wealth to the cotton trade. Textile manufacturers in places as far-flung as Massachusetts, Lancashire in Great Britain, Normandy in France, and the suburbs of Moscow depended on a regular supply of American cotton.

As early as 1803, cotton had become the most important American export. Cotton sales earned the money from abroad that allowed the United States to pay for imported manufactured goods. On the eve of the Civil War, it represented well over half of the total value of American exports. In 1860, the economic investment represented by the slave population exceeded the value of the nation's factories, railroads, and banks combined.

THE SECOND MIDDLE PASSAGE

As noted in Chapter 9, to replace the slave trade from Africa, which had been prohibited by Congress in 1808, a massive trade in slaves developed within the United States. More than 2 million slaves were sold between 1820 and 1860, a majority to local buyers but hundreds of thousands from older states to "importing" states of the Lower South. Slave trading was a visible, established business. The main business districts of southern cities contained the offices of slave traders, complete with signs reading "Negro Sales" or "Negroes Bought Here." Auctions of slaves took place at public slave markets, as in New Orleans, or at courthouses. Southern newspapers carried advertisements for slave sales, southern banks financed slave trading, southern ships and railroads carried slaves from buyers to sellers, and southern states and municipalities earned revenue by taxing the sale of slaves. Virtually every slaveowner at one time or another bought and sold slaves. The Cotton Kingdom could not have arisen without the internal slave trade, and the economies of older states like Virginia came increasingly to rely on the sale of slaves.

A slave dealer's place of business in Atlanta. The buying and selling of slaves was a regularized part of the southern economy, and such businesses were a common sight in every southern town.

SLAVERY AND THE NATION

Slavery, Henry Clay proclaimed in 1816, "forms an exception . . . to the general liberty prevailing in the United States." But Clay, like many of his contemporaries, underestimated slavery's impact on the entire nation. The "free states" had ended slavery, but they were hardly unaffected by it. The Constitution, as we have seen, enhanced the power of the South in the House of Representatives and electoral college and required all states to return fugitives from bondage. Slavery shaped the lives of all Americans, white as well as black. It helped to determine where they lived, how they worked, and under what conditions they could exercise their freedoms of speech, assembly, and the press.

Northern merchants and manufacturers participated in the slave economy and shared in its profits. Money earned in the cotton trade helped to finance industrial development and internal improvements in the North. Northern ships carried cotton to New York and Europe, northern bankers financed cotton plantations, northern companies insured slave property, and northern factories turned cotton into cloth. New York City's rise to commercial prominence depended as much on the establishment of shipping lines that gathered the South's cotton and transported it to Europe, as on the Erie Canal. The Lords of the Loom (New England's early factory owners) relied on cotton supplied by the Lords of the Lash (southern slaveowners). Northern manufacturers like Brooks Brothers supplied cheap fabrics (called "Negro cloth") to clothe the South's slaves.

An advertisement by a slave trader seeking owners wishing to sell slaves. Dealers like Griggs played a crucial role in moving slaves from the Upper South to the burgeoning Cotton Kingdom of the Gulf Coast states.

This 1860 view of New Orleans captures the size and scale of the cotton trade in the South's largest city. More than 3,500 steamboats arrived in New Orleans in 1860.

THE SOUTHERN ECONOMY

There was no single South before the Civil War. In the eight slave states of the Upper South, slaves and slaveowners made up a smaller percentage of the total population than in the seven Deep South states that stretched from South Carolina west to Texas. The Upper South had major centers of industry in Baltimore, Richmond, and St. Louis, and its economies were more diversified than those in the Deep South, which was heavily dependent on cotton. Not surprisingly, during the secession crisis of 1860–1861, the Deep South states were the first to leave the Union. Even after the war began, four Upper South states (Delaware, Maryland, Kentucky, and Missouri) refused to join the Confederacy.

Nonetheless, slavery led the South down a very different path of economic development than the North's, limiting the growth of industry, discouraging immigrants from entering the region, and inhibiting technological progress. The South did not share in the urban growth experienced by the rest of the country. Most southern cities were located on the region's periphery and served mainly as centers for gathering and shipping cotton. Southern banks existed primarily to help finance the plantations. They loaned money for the purchase of land and slaves, not manufacturing development. Southern railroads mostly consisted of short lines that brought cotton from the interior to coastal ports.

In the Cotton Kingdom, the only city of significant size was New Orleans. With a population of 168,000 in 1860, New Orleans ranked as the nation's sixth-largest city. As the gathering point for cotton grown along the Mississippi River and sugar from the plantations of southeastern Louisiana, it was the world's leading exporter of slave-grown crops. Unlike other cities with slavery (apart from St. Louis and Baltimore, on the periphery of the South), New Orleans also attracted large numbers of European immigrants. In 1860, 40 percent of its population was foreign-born. And New Orleans's rich French heritage and close connections with the Caribbean produced a local culture quite different from that of the rest of the United States, reflected in the city's distinctive music, dance, religion, and cuisine.

In 1860, the South produced less than 10 percent of the nation's manufactured goods. Many northerners viewed slavery as an obstacle to American economic progress. But as New Orleans showed, slavery and economic growth could go hand in hand. In general, the southern economy was hardly stagnant, and slavery proved very profitable for most owners. The profits produced by slavery for the South and the nation as a whole formed a powerful obstacle to abolition. Speaking of cotton, Senator James Henry Hammond of South Carolina declared, "No power on earth dares to make war upon it. Cotton is king."

PLAIN FOLK OF THE OLD SOUTH

The foundation of the Old South's economy, slavery powerfully shaped race relations, politics, religion, and the law. Its influence was pervasive: "Nothing escaped," writes one historian, "nothing and no one." This was true despite the fact that the majority of white southerners—three out of four white families—owned no slaves. Since planters monopolized the best land, most small white farmers lived outside the plantation belt in hilly areas unsuitable for cotton production. They worked the land using family labor rather than slaves or hired workers.

Many southern farmers lived lives of economic self-sufficiency remote from the market revolution. They raised livestock and grew food for their families, purchasing relatively few goods at local stores. Those residing on marginal land in isolated hill areas and the Appalachian Mountains were often desperately poor and, since nearly all the southern states lacked systems of free public education, were more often illiterate than their north-

An upcountry family, dressed in homespun, in Cedar Mountain, Virginia. Many white families in the pre–Civil War South were largely isolated from the market economy. This photograph was taken in 1862 but reflects the prewar way of life.

ern counterparts. Not until the arrival of railroads and coal mining later in the nineteenth century would such areas become integrated into the market economy. Most yeoman farmers enjoyed a comfortable standard of living, and many owned a slave or two. But even successful small farmers relied heavily on home production to supply their basic needs. Unlike northern farmers, therefore, they did not provide a market for manufactured goods. This was one of the main reasons why the South did not develop an industrial base.

Some poorer whites resented the power and privileges of the great planters. Politicians like Andrew Johnson of Tennessee and Joseph Brown of Georgia rose to power as self-proclaimed spokesmen of the common man against the "slaveocracy." But most poor whites made their peace with the planters in whose hands economic and social power was concentrated. Racism, kinship ties, common participation in a democratic political culture, and regional loyalty in the face of outside criticism all served to cement bonds between planters and the South's "plain folk." In the plantation regions, moreover, small farmers manned the slave patrols that kept a lookout for runaway slaves and those on the roads without permission. Non-slaveholders frequently rented slaves from planters and regularly elected slaveowners to public offices in the South. Like other white southerners, most small farmers believed their economic and personal freedom rested on slavery. Not until the Civil War would class tensions among the white population threaten the planters' domination.

THE PLANTER CLASS

Even among slaveholders, the planter was far from typical. In 1850, a majority of slaveholding families owned five or fewer slaves. Less than 40,000 families possessed the twenty or more slaves that qualified them as planters. Fewer than 2,000 families owned a hundred slaves or more. Nonetheless, even though the planter was not the typical slaveholder or white southerner, his values and aspirations dominated southern life. The plantation, wrote Frederick Douglass, was "a little nation by itself, with its own language, its own rules, regulations, and customs." These rules and customs set the tone for southern society.

Ownership of slaves provided the route to wealth, status, and influence. Planters not only held the majority of slaves, but they controlled the most fertile land, enjoyed the highest incomes, and dominated state and local offices and the leadership of both political parties. Small slaveholders aspired to move up into the ranks of the planter class. Those who acquired

A detail from Norman's Chart of the Lower Mississpppi River *(1858) shows slave plantations laid out so that each fronted on the river and, therefore, had easy access to the market.*

wealth almost always invested it in land and slaves. But as the price of a "prime field hand" rose from $1,000 in 1840 to $1,800 in 1860 (the latter figure equivalent to around $40,000 today), it became more and more difficult for poorer white southerners to become slaveholders.

Slavery, of course, was a profit-making system, and slaveowners kept close watch on world prices for their products, invested in enterprises such as railroads and canals, and carefully supervised their plantations. Their wives—the "plantation mistresses" idealized in southern lore for femininity, beauty, and dependence on men—were hardly idle. They cared for sick slaves, directed the domestic servants, and supervised the entire plantation when their husbands were away. The wealthiest Americans before the Civil War were planters in the South Carolina low country and the cotton region around Natchez, Mississippi. Frederick Stanton, a cotton broker turned planter in the Natchez area, owned 444 slaves and more than 15,000 acres of land in Mississippi and Louisiana.

Nonetheless, Alexis de Tocqueville observed that "the northerner loves to make money, the southerner to spend it." Many of the richest planters squandered their wealth in a lifestyle complete with lavish entertain-ments and summer vacations in Newport and Saratoga. House slaves were so numerous in Charleston, wrote one visitor to the city, that "the Charlestonians are obliged to exercise their wits to devise sufficient variety to keep them employed." On the cotton frontier, many planters lived in crude log homes. But in the older slave states, and as settled society developed in the Deep South, they constructed elegant mansions adorned with white columns in the Greek Revival style of architecture. Planters discouraged their sons from entering "lowly" trades like commerce and manufacturing, one reason why the South remained overwhelmingly agricultural.

THE PATERNALIST ETHOS

The slave plantation was deeply embedded in the world market, and planters sought to accumulate land, slaves, and profits. Many invested in railroads and banks as well as slaves. But planters' values glorified not the competitive capitalist marketplace, but a hierarchical, agrarian society in which slaveholding gentlemen took personal responsibility for the physical and moral well-being of their dependents—women, children, and slaves. "The master," wrote one planter, "as the head of the system, has a right to the obedience and labor of the slave, but the slave has also his mutual rights in the master; the right of protection, the right of counsel and guidance, the right of subsistence, the right of care and attention in sickness and old age."

This outlook, known as "paternalism" (from the Latin word for "father"), had been a feature of American slavery even in the eighteenth century. But it became more ingrained after the closing of the African slave trade in 1808, which narrowed the cultural gap between master and slave and gave owners an economic interest in the survival of their human property. Unlike the absentee planters of the West Indies, many of whom resided in Great Britain, southern slaveholders lived on their plantations and thus had year-round contact with their slaves.

The paternalist outlook both masked and justified the brutal reality of slavery. It enabled slaveowners to think of themselves as kind, responsible masters even as they bought and sold their human property—a practice at odds with the claim that slaves formed part of the master's "family." Some slaveowners tried to reform the system to eliminate its most oppressive features. The Reverend Charles C. Jones, a wealthy planter of Liberty County, Georgia, organized his neighbors to promote the religious instruction of slaves, improve slave housing, diet, and medical care, and discourage severe punishments. But even Jones believed his slaves so "degraded" and lacking in moral self-discipline that he could not contemplate an end to slavery.

THE CODE OF HONOR

As time went on, the dominant southern conception of the good society diverged more and more sharply from that of the egalitarian, competitive, individualistic North. In the South, for example, both upper- and lower-class whites adhered to a code of personal honor, in which men were expected to defend, with violence if necessary, their own reputation and that of their families. Although dueling was illegal, many prominent southerners took part in duels to avenge supposed insults. In 1826, Henry Clay and John Randolph, two of the most important southern political leaders, fought a duel with pistols after Clay took exception to criticisms by Randolph on the floor of Congress. Fortunately, each missed the other. Twenty years later, however, John H. Pleasants, editor of the *Richmond Whig*, died in a duel with the son of a rival newspaperman.

Table 11.2 SLAVEHOLDING, 1850 (IN ROUND NUMBERS)	
Number of Slaves Owned	*Slaveholders*
1	68,000
2–4	105,000
5–9	80,000
10–19	55,000
20–49	30,000
50–99	6,000
100–199	1,500
200 +	250

A pre–Civil War engraving depicting the paternalist ideal. The old slave in the foreground says, "God Bless you massa! you feed and clothe us, . . . and when too old to work, you provide for us!" The master replies, "These poor creatures are a sacred legacy from my ancestors and while a dollar is left me, nothing shall be spared to increase their comfort and happiness."

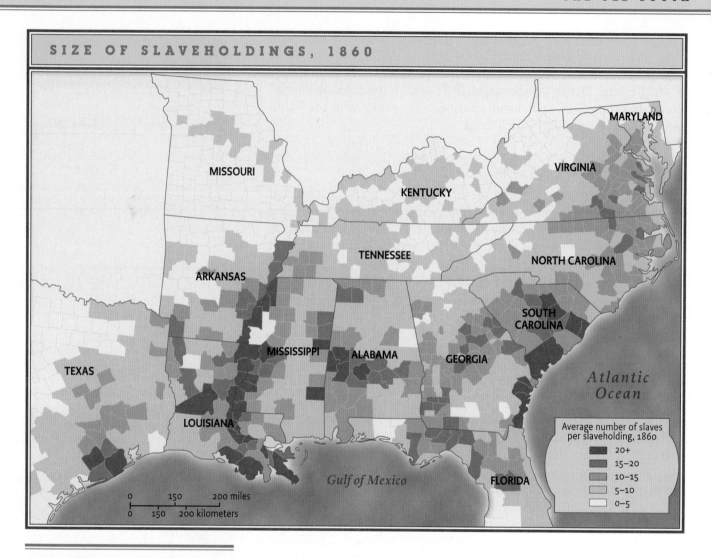

SIZE OF SLAVEHOLDINGS, 1860

Average number of slaves
per slaveholding, 1860

- 20+
- 15–20
- 10–15
- 5–10
- 0–5

Most southern slaveholders owned fewer than five slaves. The largest plantations were concentrated in coastal South Carolina and along the Mississippi River.

Just as southern men had a heightened sense of their own honor and masculinity, white southern women, even more than in the North, were confined within the "domestic circle." "A man loves his children," wrote George Fitzhugh, a Virginia lawyer and author of numerous books and articles on social issues, "because they are weak, helpless, and dependent. He loves his wife for similar reasons." As will be discussed in the next chapter, many northern women before the Civil War became part of a thriving female culture centered on voluntary religious and reform organizations. Few parallels existed in the South, and plantation mistresses often complained of loneliness and isolation.

THE PROSLAVERY ARGUMENT

Some southerners worried about their standing in the eyes of the world, especially how others viewed the intellectual life of their region. "We of the South," one wrote, "must, to Europe, continue to appear inferior to the North in intellectual cultivation." The free states outstripped the slave states in public education, the number of colleges, and in newspapers, literary journals, and other publications. Nonetheless, the life of the mind flourished in the Old South, and the region did not lack for novelists, political philosophers, scientists, and the like.

In the thirty years before the outbreak of the Civil War, however, even as northern criticism of the "peculiar institution" began to deepen, proslavery thought came to dominate southern public life. Fewer and fewer white southerners shared the view, common among the founding fathers, that slavery was, at best, a "necessary evil." "Many in the South," John C. Calhoun proclaimed in 1837, "once believed that [slavery] was a moral and political evil.... That folly and delusion are gone; we see it now in its true light, and regard it as the most safe and stable basis for free institutions in the world."

Even those who had no direct stake in slavery shared with planters a deep commitment to white supremacy. Indeed, racism—

St. John Plantation, *an 1861 painting by Marie Adrien Persac, a French-born artist who originally came to the United States to hunt buffalo. This was a Louisiana sugar plantation; the sugar mill can be seen on the extreme right. In Persac's romanticized depiction, whites enjoy themselves on horseback, while slaves appear to have little to do but watch.*

the belief that blacks were innately inferior to whites and unsuited for life in any condition other than slavery—formed one pillar of the proslavery ideology. Most slaveholders also found legitimation for slavery in biblical passages such as the injunction that servants should obey their masters. Others argued that slavery was essential to human progress. Had not the ancient republics of Greece and Rome and the great European empires of the seventeenth and eighteenth centuries rested on slave labor? Without slavery, planters would be unable to cultivate the arts, sciences, and other civilized pursuits.

Still other defenders of slavery insisted that the institution guaranteed equality for whites by preventing the growth of a class doomed to a life of unskilled labor. Like northerners, they claimed to be committed to the ideal of freedom. Slavery for blacks, they declared, was the surest guarantee of "perfect equality" among whites, liberating them from the "low, menial" jobs like factory labor and domestic service performed by wage laborers in the North. Slavery made possible the considerable degree of economic autonomy (the social condition of freedom) enjoyed not only by planters but by non-slaveholding whites. Because of slavery, claimed one congressman, white southerners were as "independent as the bird which cleaves the air." And because independence was necessary for citizenship, slavery was the "cornerstone of our republican edifice."

ABOLITION IN THE AMERICAS

American slaveowners were well aware of developments in slave systems elsewhere in the Western Hemisphere. As noted in Chapter 8, the slave revolution in Haiti sent shock waves of fear throughout the American South. White southerners were further alarmed by slave uprisings early in the nineteenth century in Barbados, British Guiana, and Jamaica. And they observed carefully the results of the wave of emancipations that swept the

VISIONS OF FREEDOM

Slavery as It Exists in America; Slavery as It Exists in England. *Published in Boston in 1850, this lithograph illustrates one aspect of proslavery thought. The artist depicts southern slaves as happy and carefree, while English workers, including children, are victims of the oppressive system of "factory slavery." The portrait at the bottom is of George Thompson, an English abolitionist who lectured against slavery in the United States. At the rear of the top image, a northerner addresses a slaveowner, suggesting that people in the North had been "deceived by false reports" about slavery and therefore had caused unnecessary "trouble" between the regions. In the bottom image, a poor woman exclaims, "Oh Dear! What wretched slaves this factory life makes me and my children."*

QUESTIONS

1. To whom do you think this image is addressed, and is the audience likely to be convinced that slaves enjoy more freedom than English laborers?

2. Why do you think the artist chose to compare the condition of slaves with that of English, not American, free laborers?

hemisphere in the first four decades of the century. In these years, slavery was abolished in most of Spanish America and in the British empire.

In most Latin American nations, the end of slavery followed the pattern established earlier in the northern United States—gradual emancipation accompanied by some kind of recognition of the owners' legal right to property in slaves. These "laws of the free womb" allowed slaveholders to retain ownership of existing slaves while freeing their slaves' children after they worked for the mother's owner for a specified number of years. Such laws, wrote one official, "respected the past and corrected only the future." Abolition was far swifter in the British empire, where Parliament in 1833 mandated almost immediate emancipation, with a seven-year transitional period of "apprenticeship." This system produced so much conflict between former master and former slave that Britain decreed complete freedom in 1838. The law appropriated 20 million pounds to compensate the owners.

The experience of emancipation in other parts of the hemisphere strongly affected debates over slavery in the United States. Southern slaveowners judged the vitality of the Caribbean economy by how much sugar and other crops it produced for the world market. Since many former slaves preferred to grow food for their own families, defenders of slavery in the United States charged that British emancipation had been a failure. Abolitionists disagreed, pointing to the rising standard of living of freed slaves, the spread of education among them, and other improvements in their lives. But the stark fact remained that, in a hemispheric perspective, slavery was a declining institution. By 1840, slavery had been outlawed in Mexico, Central America, and Chile, and only small numbers of aging slaves remained in Venezuela, Colombia, and Peru. During the European revolutions of 1848, France and Denmark emancipated their colonial slaves. At mid-century, significant New World slave systems remained only in Cuba, Puerto Rico, Brazil—and the United States.

SLAVERY AND LIBERTY

Many white southerners declared themselves the true heirs of the American Revolution. They claimed to be inspired by "the same spirit of freedom and independence" that motivated the founding generation. Like their ancestors of the 1760s and 1770s, their political language was filled with contrasts between liberty and slavery and complaints that outsiders proposed to reduce them to "slaves" by interfering with their local institutions. Southern state constitutions enshrined the idea of equal rights for free men, and the South participated fully in the movement toward political democracy for whites.

Beginning in the 1830s, however, proslavery writers began to question the ideals of liberty, equality, and democracy so widely shared elsewhere in the nation. South Carolina, the only southern state where a majority of white families owned slaves, became the home of an aggressive defense of slavery that repudiated the idea that freedom and equality were universal entitlements. The language of the Declaration of Independence—that all men were created equal and entitled to liberty—was "the most false and dangerous of all political errors," insisted John C. Calhoun. Proslavery

A plate manufactured in England to celebrate emancipation in the British empire. After a brief period of apprenticeship, the end of slavery came on August 1, 1838. At the center, a family of former slaves celebrates outside their cabin.

spokesmen returned to the older definition of freedom as a privilege rather than a universal entitlement, a "reward to be earned, not a blessing to be gratuitously lavished on all alike."

As the sectional controversy intensified after 1830, a number of southern writers and politicians came to defend slavery less as the basis of equality for whites than as the foundation of an organic, hierarchical society. Many southern clergymen, in the course of offering a religious defense of slavery, argued that inequality and hence the submission of inferior to superior—black to white, female to male, lower classes to upper classes—was a "fundamental law" of human existence. A hierarchy of "ranks and orders in human society," insisted John B. Alger, a Presbyterian minister in South Carolina, formed part of the "divine arrangement" of the world.

SLAVERY AND CIVILIZATION

The Virginia writer George Fitzhugh took the argument to its most radical conclusion, repudiating not only Jeffersonian ideals but the notion of America's special mission in the world. Far from being the natural condition of mankind, Fitzhugh wrote, "universal liberty" was the exception, an experiment carried on "for a little while" in "a corner of Europe" and the northern United States. Taking the world and its history as a whole, slavery, "without regard to race and color," was "the general, . . . normal, natural" basis of "civilized society." Indeed, wrote Fitzhugh, slaveowners and slaves shared a "community of interest" unknown in "free society." Since they lacked economic cares, he contended, "the Negro slaves of the South are the happiest, and, in some degree, the freest people in the world." White workers in both the North and South, according to Fitzhugh, would fare better having individual owners, rather than living as "slaves" of the economic marketplace.

It seems safe to assume that few non-slaveholding white southerners agreed that enslavement would offer them greater freedom than they already enjoyed. Nor was Fitzhugh entirely consistent. Sometimes, he argued that all free laborers would be better off as slaves. On other occasions, he spoke of slavery only for blacks—perpetual "children" for whom liberty would be "a curse."

Abraham Lincoln would later observe that the essential function of the proslavery argument was to serve the interests of those who benefited from a system of extreme inequality. He imagined Dr. Frederick A. Ross, a leading proslavery clergyman, considering whether he should free his slave Sambo. God's view of the subject, Lincoln noted, was not entirely clear, and "no one thinks of asking Sambo's opinion." Therefore, it fell to Dr. Ross to decide the question. "If he decides that God wills Sambo to continue a slave," Lincoln wrote, "he thereby retains his own comfortable position; but if he decides that God wills Sambo to be free, he thereby has to walk out of the shade, take off his gloves, and [work] for his own bread." Under these circumstances, it was hardly surprising that Dr. Ross found the argument that Sambo should remain a slave very persuasive.

After 1830, southern writers, newspaper editors, politicians, and clergymen increasingly devoted themselves to spreading the defense of slavery. The majority of white southerners came to believe that freedom for whites rested on the power to command the labor of blacks. In the words of the Richmond *Enquirer*, "freedom is not possible without slavery."

LIFE UNDER SLAVERY

SLAVES AND THE LAW

For slaves, the "peculiar institution" meant a life of incessant toil, brutal punishment, and the constant fear that their families would be destroyed by sale. Before the law, slaves were property. Although they had a few legal rights (all states made it illegal to kill a slave except in self-defense, and slaves accused of serious crimes were entitled to their day in court, before all-white judges and juries), these were haphazardly enforced. Slaves could be sold or leased by their owners at will and lacked any voice in the governments that ruled over them. They could not testify in court against a white person, sign contracts or acquire property, own firearms, hold meetings unless a white person was present, or leave the farm or plantation without the permission of their owner. By the 1830s, it was against the law to teach a slave to read or write.

Not all of these laws were rigorously enforced. Some members of slave-holding families taught slave children to read (although rather few, since well over 90 percent of the slave population was illiterate in 1860). In the South Carolina rice fields, owners allowed some slaves to carry shotguns, in defiance of the law, to scare off birds feasting on rice seeds. It was quite common throughout the South for slaves to gather without white supervision at crossroads villages and country stores on Sunday, their day of rest. But the extent to which authorities enforced or bent the law depended on the decisions of the individual owners.

The slave, declared a Louisiana law, "owes to his master . . . a respect without bounds, and an absolute obedience." Not only did the owner have the legal right to what Alabama's legal code called the "time, labor, and services" of his slaves, but no aspect of their lives, from the choice of marriage partners to how they spent their free time, was immune from his interference. The entire system of southern justice, from the state militia and courts down to armed patrols in each locality, was designed to enforce the master's control over the person and labor of his slaves.

In one famous case, a Missouri court considered the "crime" of Celia, a slave who had killed her master in 1855 while resisting a sexual assault. State law deemed "any woman" in such circumstances to be acting in self-defense. But Celia, the court ruled, was not a "woman" in the eyes of the law. She was a slave, whose master had complete power over her person. The court sentenced her to death. However, since Celia was pregnant, her execution was postponed until the child was born, so as not to deprive her owner's heirs of their property rights.

CONDITIONS OF SLAVE LIFE

As the nineteenth century progressed, some southern states enacted laws to prevent the mistreatment of slaves, and their material living conditions improved. Food supplies and wild game were abundant in the South, and many slaves supplemented the food provided by their owners (primarily cornmeal and pork or bacon) with chickens and vegetables they raised themselves, animals they hunted in the forests, and, not infrequently, items they stole from the plantation smokehouse. Compared with their counter-

Metal shackles, from around 1850. Slaves were shackled as a form of punishment, or to prevent escape when being transported from one place to another.

VOICES OF FREEDOM

FROM Letter by Joseph Taper to Joseph Long (1840)

No one knows how many slaves succeeded in escaping from bondage before the Civil War. Some settled in northern cities like Boston, Cincinnati, and New York. But because the Constitution required that fugitives be returned to slavery, many continued northward until they reached Canada.

One successful fugitive was Joseph Taper, a slave in Frederick County, Virginia, who in 1837 ran away to Pennsylvania with his wife and children. Two years later, learning that a "slave catcher" was in the neighborhood, the Tapers fled to Canada. In 1840, Taper wrote to a white acquaintance in Virginia recounting some of his experiences.

The biblical passage to which Taper refers reads: "And I will come near to you to judgment; and I will be a swift witness against the sorcerers, and against the adulterers, and against false swearers, and against those that oppress the hireling in his wages, the widow, and the fatherless, and that turn aside the stranger from his right, and fear not me, saith the Lord of hosts."

Dear sir,

I now take the opportunity to inform you that I am in a land of liberty, in good health. . . . Since I have been in the Queen's dominions I have been well contented, Yes well contented for Sure, man is as God intended he should be. That is, all are born free and equal. This is a wholesome law, not like the Southern laws which puts man made in the image of God, on level with brutes. O, what will become of the people, and where will they stand in the day of Judgment. Would that the 5th verse of the 3d chapter of Malachi were written as with the bar of iron, and the point of a diamond upon every oppressor's heart that they might repent of this evil, and let the oppressed go free. . . .

We have good schools, and all the colored population supplied with schools. My boy Edward who will be six years next January, is now reading, and I intend keeping him at school until he becomes a good scholar.

I have enjoyed more pleasure within one month here than in all my life in the land of bondage. . . . My wife and self are sitting by a good comfortable fire happy, knowing that there are none to molest [us] or make [us] afraid. God save Queen Victoria. The Lord bless her in this life, and crown her with glory in the world to come is my prayer,

Yours With much respect
most obt, Joseph Taper

From the Rules of Highland Plantation (1838)

A wealthy Louisiana slaveholder, Bennet H. Barrow considered himself a model of planter paternalism who, by his own standards, treated his slaves well. An advocate of rigorous plantation discipline, he drew up a series of strict rules, which he recommended to other owners.

No Negro shall leave the place at any time without my permission. . . . No Negro shall be allowed to marry out of the plantation.

No Negro shall be allowed to sell anything without my express permission. I have ever maintained the doctrine that my Negroes have no time whatever, that they are always liable to my call without questioning for a moment the propriety, of it. I adhere to this on the grounds of expediency and right. The very security of the plantation requires that a general and uniform control over the people of it should be exercised. . . . You must . . . make him as comfortable at home as possible, affording him what is essentially necessary for his happiness—you must provide for him yourself and by that means create in him a habit of perfect dependence on you. Allow it once to be understood by a Negro that he is to provide for himself, and you that moment give him an undeniable claim on you for a portion of his time to make this provision, and should you from necessity, or any other cause, encroach upon his time, disappointment and discontent are seriously felt.

If I employ a laborer to perform a certain quantum of work per day and I agree to pay him a certain amount for the performance of said work, when he has accomplished it I of course have no further claim on him for his time or services—but how different is it with a slave. . . . If I furnish my Negro with every necessary of life, without the least care on his part—if I support him in sickness, however long it may be, and pay all his expenses, though he does nothing—if I maintain him in his old age, . . . am I not entitled to an exclusive right in his time?

No rule that I have stated is of more importance than that relating to Negroes marrying out of the plantation. . . . It creates a feeling of independence, from being, of right, out of the control of the masters for a time.

Never allow any man to talk to your Negroes, nothing more injurious.

QUESTIONS

1. How does Taper's letter reverse the rhetoric, common among white Americans, which saw the United States as a land of freedom and the British empire as lacking in liberty?

2. Why does Barrow feel that his slaves owe him complete obedience?

3. What do these documents suggest about whether masters and slaves shared the same values?

parts in the West Indies and Brazil, American slaves enjoyed better diets, lower rates of infant mortality, and longer life expectancies. Many factors contributed to improving material conditions. One was the growing strength of the planters' paternalist outlook. Douglass himself noted that "not to give a slave enough to eat, is regarded as the most aggravated development of meanness, even among slaveholders." Most of the South, moreover, lies outside the geographical area where tropical diseases like malaria, yellow fever, and typhoid fever flourish, so health among all southerners was better than in the Caribbean. And with the price of slaves rising dramatically after the closing of the African slave trade, it made economic sense for owners to become concerned with the health and living conditions of their human property.

Improvements in the slaves' living conditions were meant to strengthen slavery, not undermine it. Even as the material lives of the majority of slaves improved, the South drew tighter and tighter the chains of bondage. If slaves in the United States enjoyed better health and diets than elsewhere in the Western Hemisphere, they had far less access to freedom. In Brazil, it was not uncommon for an owner to free slaves as a form of celebration— on the occasion of a wedding in the owner's family, for example—or to allow slaves to purchase their freedom. Although slavery in Brazil lasted until 1888, more than half the population of African descent was already free in 1850. (The comparable figure in the American South was well below 10 percent.) In the nineteenth-century South, more and more states set limits on voluntary manumission, requiring that such acts be approved by the legislature. "All the powers of earth," declared Abraham Lincoln in 1857, seemed to be "rapidly combining" to fasten bondage ever more securely upon American slaves. Few slave societies in history have so systematically closed off all avenues to freedom as the Old South.

FREE BLACKS IN THE OLD SOUTH

The existence of slavery helped to define the status of those blacks who did enjoy freedom. On the eve of the Civil War, nearly half a million free blacks lived in the United States, a majority in the South. Most were the descendants of slaves freed by southern owners in the aftermath of the Revolution or by the gradual emancipation laws of the northern states. Their numbers were supplemented by slaves who had been voluntarily liberated by their masters, who had been allowed to purchase their freedom, or who succeeded in running away.

When followed by "black" or "Negro," the word "free" took on an entirely new meaning. Whites defined their freedom, in part, by their distance from slavery. But among blacks, wrote Douglass, "the distinction between the slave and the free is not great." Northern free blacks, as noted in Chapter 10, generally could not vote and enjoyed few economic opportunities. Free blacks in the South could legally own property and marry and, of course, could not be bought and sold. But many regulations restricting the lives of slaves also applied to them. Free blacks had no voice in selecting public officials. Like slaves, they were prohibited from owning dogs, firearms, or liquor, and they could not strike a white person, even in self-defense. They were not allowed to testify in court or serve on juries, and they had to carry at all times a certificate of freedom. Poor free blacks who required public assistance could be bound out to labor alongside slaves. "Free negroes," declared a South Carolina judge in 1848, "belong to a degraded caste of society" and should learn to conduct themselves "as inferiors."

As noted above, nineteenth-century Brazil had a large free black population. In the West Indies, many children of white owners and female slaves gained their freedom, becoming part of a "free colored" population sharply distinguished from both whites above them and slaves below. In the absence of a white lower middle class, free blacks in Jamaica and other Caribbean islands operated shops and worked as clerks in government offices.

In the United States, a society that equated "black" and "slave" and left little room for a mulatto group between them, free blacks were increasingly considered an undesirable group, a potential danger to the slave system. By the 1850s, most southern states prohibited free blacks from entering their territory and a few states even moved to expel them altogether, offering the choice of enslavement or departure. Nonetheless, a few free blacks managed to prosper within slave society. William Johnson, a Natchez barber, acquired enough money to purchase a plantation with fifteen slaves; he hunted with upper-class whites and loaned them money. But he suffered from the legal disadvantages common to his race. He could not, for example, testify against his debtors in court when they failed to pay. In Virginia, the slaves freed and given land by the will of Richard Randolph (noted in Chapter 6) established a vibrant community they called Israel Hill. Despite the legal restrictions on free blacks in the state, they prospered as farmers and skilled craftsmen, and they learned to defend their rights in court, even winning lawsuits against whites who owed them money.

	Table 11.3 FREE BLACK POPULATION, 1860	
Region	**Free Black Population**	**Percentage of Total Black Population**
North	226,152	100%
South	261,918	6.2
Upper South	224,963	12.8
Lower South	36,955	1.5
Delaware	19,829	91.7
Washington, D.C.	11,131	77.8
Kentucky	10,684	4.5
Maryland	83,942	49.1
Missouri	3,572	3.0
North Carolina	30,463	8.4
Tennessee	7,300	2.6
Virginia	58,042	10.6
Alabama	2,690	0.6
Arkansas	144	0.1
Florida	932	1.5
Georgia	3,500	0.8
Louisiana	18,647	5.3
Mississippi	773	0.2
South Carolina	9,914	2.4
Texas	355	0.2

THE UPPER AND LOWER SOUTH

Very few free blacks (around 37,000 persons, or less than 2 percent of the area's black population) lived in the Lower South in 1860. Like William Johnson, a majority of them resided in cities. Mississippi, an overwhelmingly rural state with no real urban centers, had fewer than 800 free blacks on the eve of the Civil War. In New Orleans and Charleston, on the other hand, relatively prosperous free black communities developed, mostly composed of mixed-race descendants of unions between white men and slave women. Some became truly wealthy—Antoine Dubuclet of Louisiana, for example, owned 100 slaves. Many free blacks in these cities acquired an education and worked as skilled craftsmen such as tailors, carpenters, and mechanics. They established churches for their communities

Slaves were an ever-present part of southern daily life. In this 1826 portrait of the five children of Commodore John Daniel Daniels, a wealthy Baltimore shipowner, a young slave lies on the floor at their side, holding the soap for a game of blowing bubbles, while another hovers in the background, almost depicted as part of the room's design.

and schools for their children. Some New Orleans free blacks sent their children to France for an education. These elite free blacks did everything they could to maintain a separation from the slave population. The Brown Fellowship Society of Charleston, for example, would not even allow dark-skinned free men to join. Even in these cities, however, most free blacks were poor unskilled laborers.

In the Upper South, where the large majority of southern free blacks lived, they generally worked for wages as farm laborers. Here, where tobacco had exhausted the soil, many planters shifted to grain production, which required less year-round labor. They sold off many slaves to the Lower South and freed others. By 1860, half the African-American population of Maryland was free. Planters hired local free blacks to work alongside their slaves at harvest time. Free blacks in Virginia and Maryland were closely tied to the slave community and often had relatives in bondage. Some owned slaves, but usually these were free men who had purchased their slave wives and children but could not liberate them because the law required any slave who became free to leave the state. Overall, in the words of Willis A. Hodges, a member of a free Virginia family that helped runaways to reach the North, free blacks and slaves were "one man of sorrow."

SLAVE LABOR

First and foremost, slavery was a system of labor; "from sunup to first dark," with only brief interruptions for meals, work occupied most of the slaves' time. Large plantations were diversified communities, where slaves performed all kinds of work. The 125 slaves on one plantation, for instance, included a butler, two waitresses, a nurse, a dairymaid, a gardener, ten carpenters, and two shoemakers. Other plantations counted among their slaves engineers, blacksmiths, and weavers, as well as domestic workers from cooks to coachmen.

Slaves cut wood to provide fuel for steamboats, worked in iron and coal mines, manned the docks in southern seaports, and laid railroad track. They were set to work by local authorities to construct and repair bridges, roads, and other facilities and by the federal government to build forts and other public buildings in the South. Businessmen, merchants, lawyers, and civil servants owned slaves, and by 1860 some 200,000 worked in industry, especially in the ironworks and tobacco factories of the Upper South. In southern cities, thousands were employed as unskilled laborers and skilled artisans. Reliance on unfree labor, moreover, extended well beyond the ranks of slaveholders, for, as noted earlier, many small farmers and manufacturers rented slaves from plantation owners. A few owners gave trusted slaves extensive responsibilities. Simon Gray's owner made him the head of a riverboat crew on the Mississippi. Gray supervised both white and slave workers, sold his owner's lumber at urban markets, and handled large sums of money.

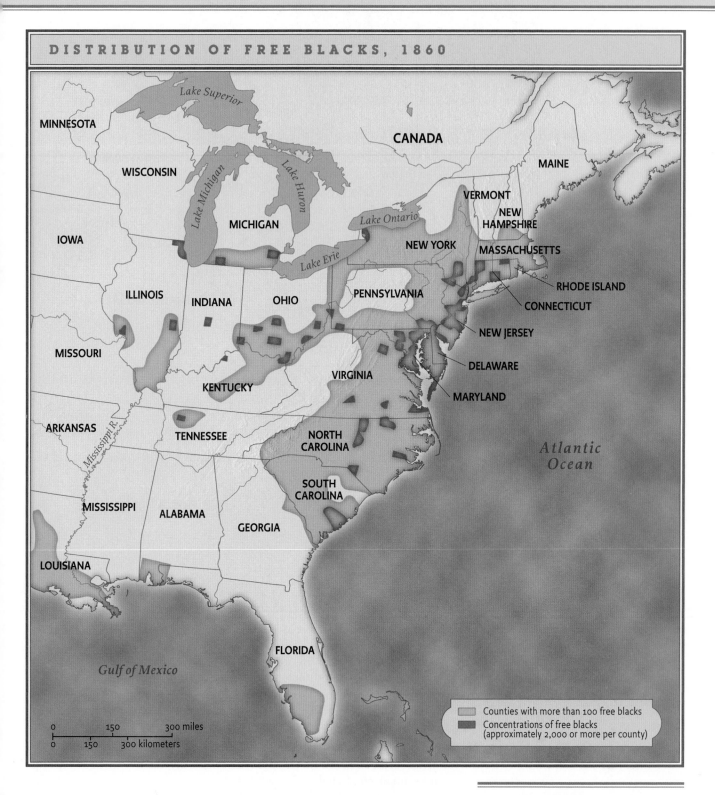

DISTRIBUTION OF FREE BLACKS, 1860

Legend:
- Counties with more than 100 free blacks
- Concentrations of free blacks (approximately 2,000 or more per county)

GANG LABOR AND TASK LABOR

Gray's experience, of course, was hardly typical. The large majority of slaves—75 percent of women and nearly 90 percent of men, according to one study—worked in the fields. The precise organization of their labor varied according to the crop and the size of the holding. On small farms, the owner often toiled side-by-side with his slaves. The largest concentration of

The nation's population in 1860 included nearly 500,000 free blacks. The majority lived in the slave states, especially Maryland and Virginia.

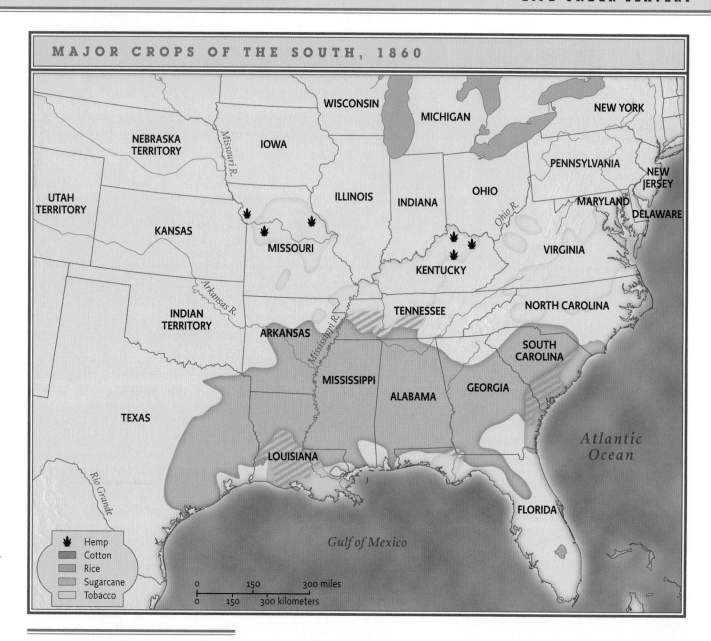

MAJOR CROPS OF THE SOUTH, 1860

Legend:
- Hemp
- Cotton
- Rice
- Sugarcane
- Tobacco

Cotton was the major agricultural crop of the South, and, indeed, the nation, but slaves also grew rice, sugarcane, tobacco, and hemp.

slaves, however, lived and worked on plantations in the Cotton Belt, where men, women, and children labored in gangs, often under the direction of an overseer and perhaps a slave "driver" who assisted him. Among slaves, overseers had a reputation for meting out harsh treatment. "The requisite qualifications for an overseer," wrote Solomon Northup, a free black who spent twelve years in slavery after being kidnapped from the North, "are utter heartlessness, brutality, and cruelty. It is his business to produce large crops, no matter [what the] cost."

The 150,000 slaves who worked in the sugar fields of southern Louisiana also labored in large gangs. Conditions here were among the harshest in the South, for the late fall harvest season required round-the-clock labor to cut and process the sugarcane before it spoiled. On the rice plantations of South Carolina and Georgia, the system of task labor, which had originated in the colonial era, prevailed. With few whites willing to venture into the malaria-infested swamps, slaves were assigned daily tasks and allowed to set their own pace of work. Once a slave's task had been completed, he or she could spend the rest of the day hunting, fishing, or cultivating garden crops.

SLAVERY IN THE CITIES

From the slaves' point of view, slavery in the different regions of the South could be "worse" in some respects and "better" in others. Slaves in the rice fields, for example, endured harsh working conditions but enjoyed more independence than other rural slaves because of the task system of labor and the absence of a large resident white population. Skilled urban craftsmen also enjoyed considerable autonomy. Most city slaves were servants, cooks, and other domestic laborers. But owners sometimes allowed those with craft skills to "hire their own time." This meant that they could make work arrangements individually with employers, with most of the wages going to the slave's owner. Many urban slaves even lived on their own. But slave-holders increasingly became convinced that, as one wrote, the growing independence of skilled urban slaves "exerts a most injurious influence upon the relation of master and servant." For this reason, many owners in the 1850s sold city slaves to the countryside and sought replacements among skilled white labor.

During his time in Baltimore, Frederick Douglass "sought my own employment, made my own contracts, and collected my own earnings." Compared to conditions on the plantation, he concluded, "I was really well off." Douglass hastened to add, however, that his favored treatment in no way lessened his desire for freedom—"it was *slavery*, not its mere incidents, that I hated."

A female slave drying cotton on a plantation in the South Carolina Sea Islands, 1862. Slave men, women, and children all worked in the cotton fields.

MAINTAINING ORDER

Slaveowners employed a variety of means in their attempts to maintain order and discipline among their human property and persuade them to labor productively. At base, the system rested on force. Masters had almost complete discretion in inflicting punishment, and rare was the slave who went through his or her life without experiencing a whipping. Josiah Henson, who escaped to the North and published an autobiography, wrote that he could never erase from his memory the traumatic experience of seeing his father brutally whipped for striking a white man. Any infraction of plantation rules, no matter how minor, could be punished by the lash. One Georgia planter recorded in his journal that he had whipped a slave "for not bringing over milk for my coffee, being compelled to take it without."

Subtler means of control supplemented violence. Owners encouraged and

In this undated photograph, men, women, and children pick cotton under the watchful eye of an overseer. Unlike sugarcane, cotton does not grow to a great height, allowing an overseer to supervise a large number of slaves.

A Public Whipping of Slaves in Lexington, Missouri, in 1856, *an illustration from the abolitionist publication* The Suppressed Book about Slavery. *Whipping was a common form of punishment for slaves.*

exploited divisions among the slaves, especially between field hands and house servants. They created systems of incentives that rewarded good work with time off or even money payments. One Virginia slaveholder gave his slaves ten cents per day for good work and reported that this made them labor "with as much steadiness and cheerfulness as whites," thereby "saving all the expense of overseers." Probably the most powerful weapon wielded by slaveowners was the threat of sale, which separated slaves from their immediate families and from the communities that, despite overwhelming odds, African-Americans created on plantations throughout the South.

SLAVE CULTURE

Slaves never abandoned their desire for freedom or their determination to resist total white control over their lives. In the face of grim realities, they succeeded in forging a semi-independent culture, centered on the family and church. This enabled them to survive the experience of bondage without surrendering their self-esteem and to pass from generation to generation a set of ideas and values fundamentally at odds with those of their masters.

Slave culture drew on the African heritage. African influences were evident in the slaves' music and dances, style of religious worship, and the use of herbs by slave healers to combat disease. (Given the primitive nature of professional medical treatment, some whites sought out slave healers instead of trained physicians.) Unlike the plantation regions of the Caribbean and Brazil, where the African slave trade continued into the nineteenth century and the black population far outnumbered the white, most slaves in the United States were American-born and lived amidst a white majority. Slave culture was a new creation, shaped by African traditions and American values and experiences.

THE SLAVE FAMILY

At the center of the slave community stood the family. On the sugar plantations of the West Indies, the number of males far exceeded that of females, the workers lived in barracks-type buildings, and settled family life was nearly impossible. The United States, where the slave population grew from natural increase rather than continued importation from Africa, had an even male-female ratio, making the creation of families far more possible. To be sure, the law did not recognize the legality of slave marriages. The master had to consent before a man and woman could "jump over the broomstick" (the slaves' marriage ceremony), and families stood in constant danger of being broken up by sale.

Nonetheless, most adult slaves married, and their unions, when not disrupted by sale, typically lasted for a lifetime. To solidify a sense of family continuity, slaves frequently named children after cousins, uncles, grandparents, and other relatives. Nor did the slave family simply mirror kinship patterns among whites. Slaves, for example, did not marry first cousins, a practice common among white southerners. Most slaves lived in two-parent families. But because of constant sales, the slave community had a significantly higher number of female-headed households than among whites, as well as families in which grandparents, other relatives, or even non-kin assumed responsibility for raising children.

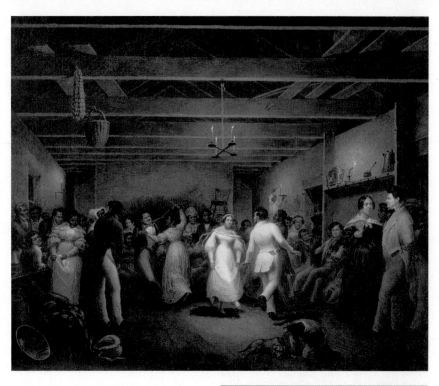

Kitchen Ball at White Sulphur Springs, Virginia, *an 1838 painting by the German-born American artist Christian Mayr. Fashionably dressed domestic slaves celebrate the wedding of a couple, dressed in white at the center.*

THE THREAT OF SALE

As noted above, the threat of sale, which disrupted family ties, was perhaps the most powerful disciplinary weapon slaveholders possessed. As the domestic slave trade expanded with the rise of the Cotton Kingdom, about one slave marriage in three in slave-selling states like Virginia was broken by sale. Many children were separated from their parents by sale. According to one estimate, at least 10 percent of the teenage slaves in the Upper South were sold in the interstate slave trade. Fear of sale permeated slave life, especially in the Upper South. "Mother, is Massa going to sell us tomorrow?" ran a line in a popular slave song. As a reflection of their paternalist responsibilities, some owners encouraged slaves to marry. Others, however, remained unaware of their slaves' family connections, and their interest in slave children was generally limited to the children's ability to work in the fields. The federal census broke down the white population by five-year age categories, but it divided slaves only once, at age ten, the point at which they became old enough to enter the plantation labor force.

Slave traders gave little attention to preserving family ties. A public notice, "Sale of Slaves and Stock," announced the 1852 auction of property belonging to a recently deceased Georgia planter. It listed thirty-six individuals ranging from an infant to a sixty-nine-year old woman and ended with the proviso: "Slaves will be sold separate, or in lots, as best suits the purchaser." Sales like this were a human tragedy. "My dear wife," a Georgia slave wrote in 1858, "I take the pleasure of writing you these few [lines] with much regret to inform you that I am sold. . . . Give my love to my father and mother and tell them good bye for me, and if we shall not meet

Sale of Slaves and Stock.

The Negroes and Stock listed below, are a Prime Lot, and belong to the ESTATE OF THE LATE LUTHER McGOWAN, and will be sold on Monday, Sept. 22nd, 1852, at the Fair Grounds, in Savannah, Georgia, at 1:00 P. M. The Negroes will be taken to the grounds two days previous to the Sale, so that they may be inspected by prospective buyers.

On account of the low prices listed below, they will be sold for cash only, and must be taken into custody within two hours after sale.

No.	Name.	Age.	Remarks.	Price.
1	Lunesta	27	Prime Rice Planter,	$1,275.00
2	Violet	16	Housework and Nursemaid,	900.00
3	Lizzie	30	Rice, Unsound,	300.00
4	Minda	27	Cotton, Prime Woman,	1,200.00
5	Adam	28	Cotton, Prime Young Man,	1,100.00
6	Abel	41	Rice Hand, Eyesight Poor,	675.00
7	Tanney	22	Prime Cotton Hand,	950.00
8	Flementina	39	Good Cook. Stiff Knee,	400.00
9	Lanney	34	Prime Cottom Man,	1,000.00
10	Sally	10	Handy in Kitchen,	675.00
11	Maccabey	35	Prime Man, Fair Carpenter,	980.00
12	Dorcas Judy	25	Seamstress, Handy in House,	800.00
13	Happy	60	Blacksmith,	575.00
14	Mowden	15	Prime Cotton Boy,	700.00
15	Bills	21	Handy with Mules,	900.00
16	Theopolis	39	Rice Hand, Gets Fits,	575.00
17	Coolidge	29	Rice Hand and Blacksmith,	1,275.00
18	Bessie	69	Infirm, Sews,	250.00
19	Infant	1	Strong Likely Boy	400.00
20	Samson	41	Prime Man, Good with Stock,	975.00
21	Callie May	27	Prime Woman, Rice,	1,000.00
22	Honey	14	Prime Girl, Hearing Poor,	850.00
23	Angelina	16	Prime Girl, House or Field,	1,000.00
24	Virgil	21	Prime Field Hand,	1,100.00
25	Tom	40	Rice Hand, Lame Leg,	750.00
26	Noble	11	Handy Boy,	900.00
27	Judge Lesh	55	Prime Blacksmith,	800.00
28	Booster	43	Fair Mason, Unsound,	600.00
29	Big Kate	37	Housekeeper and Nurse,	950.00
30	Melie Ann	19	Housework, Smart Yellow Girl,	1,250.00
31	Deacon	26	Prime Rice Hand,	1,000.00
32	Coming	19	Prime Cotton Hand,	1,000.00
33	Mabel	47	Prime Cotton Hand,	800.00
34	Uncle Tim	60	Fair Hand with Mules,	600.00
35	Abe	27	Prime Cotton Hand,	1,000.00
36	Tennes	29	Prime Rice Hand and Cocahman,	1,250.00

There will also be offered at this sale, twenty head of Horses and Mules with harness, along with thirty head of Prime Cattle. Slaves will be sold separate, or in lots, as best suits the purchaser. Sale will be held rain or shine.

A broadside advertising the public sale of slaves, along with horses, mules, and cattle, after the death of their owner. The advertisement notes that the slaves will be sold individually or in groups "as best suits the purchaser," an indication that families were likely to be broken up. The prices are based on each slave's sex, age, and skill.

Virginian Luxuries. *Originally painted on the back panel of a formal portrait, this image illustrates two "luxuries" of a Virginia slaveowner—the power to sexually abuse slave women and to whip slaves.*

in this world I hope to meet in heaven. My dear wife for you and my children my pen cannot express the grief I feel to be parted from you all."

GENDER ROLES AMONG SLAVES

In some ways, gender roles under slavery differed markedly from those in the larger society. Slave men and women experienced, in a sense, the equality of powerlessness. The nineteenth century's "cult of domesticity," which defined the home as a woman's proper sphere, did not apply to slave women, who regularly worked in the fields. Slave men could not act as the economic providers for their families. Nor could they protect their wives from physical or sexual abuse by owners and overseers (a frequent occurrence on many plantations) or determine when and under what conditions their children worked.

When slaves worked "on their own time," however, more conventional gender roles prevailed. Slave men chopped wood, hunted, and fished, while women washed, sewed, and assumed primary responsibility for the care of children. Some planters allowed their slaves small plots of land on which to grow food to supplement the rations provided by the owner; women usually took charge of these "garden plots." But whatever its internal arrangements, the family was central to the slave community, allowing for the transmission of values, traditions, and survival strategies—in a word, of slave culture—from one generation to the next.

SLAVE RELIGION

A distinctive version of Christianity also offered solace to slaves in the face of hardship and hope for liberation from bondage. Some blacks, free and slave, had taken part in the Great Awakening of the colonial era, and even more were swept into the South's Baptist and Methodist churches during the religious revivals of the late eighteenth and early nineteenth centuries. As one preacher recalled of the great camp meeting that drew thousands of worshipers to Cane Ridge, Kentucky, in 1801, no distinctions were made "as to age, sex, color, or anything of a temporary nature; old and young, male and female, black and white, had equal privilege to minister the light which they received, in whatever way the Spirit directed."

Even though the law prohibited slaves from gathering without a white person present, every plantation, it seemed, had its own black preacher. Usually the preacher was a "self-called" slave who possessed little or no formal education but whose rhetorical abilities and familiarity with the Bible made him one of the most respected members of the slave community. Especially in southern cities, slaves also worshiped in biracial congregations with white ministers, where they generally were required to sit in the back pews or in the balcony. Urban free blacks established their own churches, sometimes attended by slaves.

To masters, Christianity offered another means of social control. Many required slaves to attend services conducted by white ministers, who preached that theft was immoral and that the Bible required servants to obey their masters. One slave later recalled being told in a white minister's sermon "how good God was in bringing us over to this country from dark and benighted Africa, and permitting us to listen to the sound of the gospel." Several slaves walked out of the service during a sermon by Charles C. Jones stressing that God had commanded servants to obey their masters and that they should not try to run away. One man came up to Jones at the end and said, "the doctrine is *one-sided*."

THE GOSPEL OF FREEDOM

The slaves transformed the Christianity they had embraced, turning it to their own purposes. A blend of African traditions and Christian belief, slave religion was practiced in secret nighttime gatherings on plantations and in "praise meetings" replete with shouts, dances, and frequent emotional interchanges between the preacher and the congregation. One former slave later recalled typical secret religious gatherings: "We used to slip off into the woods in the old slave days on Sunday evening way down in the swamps to sing and pray to our own liking. We prayed for this day of freedom."

The biblical story of Exodus, in which God chose Moses to lead the enslaved Jews of Egypt into a promised land of freedom, played a central role in black Christianity. Slaves identified themselves as a chosen people, whom God in the fullness of time would deliver from bondage. At the same time, the figure of Jesus Christ represented to slaves a personal redeemer, one who truly cared for the oppressed. Slaves found other heroes and symbols in the Bible as well: Jonah, who overcame hard luck and escaped from the belly of a whale; David, who vanquished the more powerful Goliath; and Daniel, who escaped from the lion's den. And the Christian

A black preacher, as portrayed in Harper's Weekly, *February 2, 1867. Although engraved after the Civil War, the scene is the same as religious services under slavery.*

PRAYER MEETING.

Plantation Burial, *a painting from around 1860 by John Antrobus, an English artist who emigrated to New Orleans in 1850 and later married the daughter of a plantation owner. A slave preacher conducts a funeral service while black men, women, and children look on. The well-dressed white man and woman on the far right are, presumably, the plantation owner and his wife. This is a rare eyewitness depiction of black culture under slavery.*

message of brotherhood and the equality of all souls before the Creator, in the slaves' eyes, offered an irrefutable indictment of the institution of slavery.

THE DESIRE FOR LIBERTY

If their masters developed an elaborate ideology defending the South's "peculiar institution," slave culture rested on a conviction of the unjustness of bondage and the desire for freedom. "Nobody," the British political philosopher Edmund Burke had written during the American Revolution, "will be argued into slavery." Frederick Douglass called the proslavery argument "flimsy nonsense," which men would be "ashamed to remember" once slavery had been abolished. Whatever proslavery writers asserted and ministers preached, blacks thought of themselves as a working people unjustly deprived of the fruits of their labor by idle planters who lived in luxury. "We bake the bread / they give us the crust," said a line from one slave song.

Most slaves fully understood the impossibility of directly confronting the system. Their folk tales had no figures equivalent to Paul Bunyan, the powerful, larger-than-life backwoodsman popular in white folklore. Slaves' folklore, such as the Brer Rabbit stories, glorified the weak hare who outwitted stronger foes like the bear and fox, rather than challenging them directly. Their religious songs, or spirituals, spoke of lives of sorrow ("I've been 'buked and I've been scorned"), while holding out hope for ultimate liberation ("Didn't my Lord deliver Daniel?"). When they sang, "I'm bound for the land of Canaan," slaves meant not only relief from worldly woes in an afterlife but also escaping to the North or, in God's good time, witnessing the breaking of slavery's chains.

"Freedom," declared a black minister after emancipation, "burned in the black heart long before freedom was born." A fugitive who reached the North later recalled that the "desire for freedom" was the "constant theme" of conversations in the slave quarters. Even the most ignorant slave, observed Solomon Northup, could not "fail to observe the difference between their own condition and the meanest white man's, and to realize the injustice of laws which place it within [the owner's] power not only to appropriate the profits of their industry, but to subject them to unmediated and unprovoked punishment without remedy."

The world of most rural slaves was bounded by their local communities and kin. They became extremely familiar with the local landscape, crops, and population, but had little knowledge of the larger world. Nonetheless, slaves could not remain indifferent to the currents of thought unleashed by the American Revolution or to the language of freedom in the society around them. "I am in a land of liberty," wrote Joseph Taper, a Virginia slave who escaped to Canada around 1840. "Here man is as God intended he should be . . . not like the southern laws which put man, made in the image of God, on level with brutes." The social and political agenda African-Americans would put forward in the Reconstruction era that followed emancipation—stressing civil and political equality, the strengthening of the black community, and autonomy in their working lives—flowed directly out of their experience in slavery.

RESISTANCE TO SLAVERY

Confronted with federal, state, and local authorities committed to preserving slavery, and outnumbered within the South as a whole by the white population, slaves could only rarely express their desire for freedom by outright rebellion. Compared to Brazil and the West Indies, which experienced numerous uprisings, involving hundreds or even thousands of slaves, revolts in the United States were smaller and less frequent. There was no parallel, of course, to the successful slave revolution in Haiti discussed in Chapter 8 or to the unsuccessful 1831 rebellion in Jamaica that appears to have involved as many as 20,000 slaves. This does not, however, mean that slaves in the United States placidly accepted the system under which they were compelled to live. Resistance to slavery took many forms in the Old South, from individual acts of defiance to occasional uprisings. These actions posed a constant challenge to the slaveholders' self-image as benign paternalists and their belief that slaves were obedient subjects grateful for their owners' care.

FORMS OF RESISTANCE

The most widespread expression of hostility to slavery was "day-to-day resistance" or "silent sabotage"—doing poor work, breaking tools, abusing animals, and in other ways disrupting the plantation routine. Frederick Law Olmsted, a northerner who toured the South in the 1850s, took note of "gates left open, rails removed from fences by the negroes, mules lamed and implements broken, a flat boat set adrift in the river, men ordered to cart rails for a new fence, depositing them so that a double expense of labor would be required to lay them." Many slaves made believe that they were ill to avoid work (although almost no slaves reported themselves sick on Sunday, their only day of rest). Then there was the theft of food, a form of resistance so common that one southern physician diagnosed it as a hereditary disease unique to blacks. Less frequent, but more dangerous, were serious crimes committed by slaves, including arson, poisoning, and armed assaults against individual whites.

FUGITIVE SLAVES

Even more threatening to the stability of the slave system were slaves who ran away. Formidable obstacles confronted the prospective fugitive. As Solomon Northup recalled, "Every white man's hand is raised against him, the patrollers are watching for him, the hounds are ready to follow in his track." Slaves had little or no knowledge of geography, apart from understanding that following the north star led to freedom. No one knows how many slaves succeeded in reaching the North or Canada—the most common rough estimate is around 1,000 per year. Not surprisingly, most of those who succeeded lived, like Frederick Douglass, in the Upper South,

SLAVE RESISTANCE IN THE NINETEENTH-CENTURY ATLANTIC WORLD

MICHIGAN

NEW YORK

Boston • MASSACHUSETTS

New Haven • Newport

ILLINOIS

INDIANA

OHIO

PENNSYLVANIA

RHODE ISLAND

CONECTICUT

Philadelphia •

New York

MISSOURI

Baltimore •

NEW JERSEY

DELAWARE

MARYLAND

VIRGINIA

Richmond, 1800
(Gabriel's Rebellion)

KENTUCKY

Southampton County, 1831
(Nat Turner's Rebellion)

ARKANSAS

TENNESSEE

NORTH CAROLINA

SOUTH CAROLINA

Wilmington

Atlantic Ocean

MISSISSIPPI

ALABAMA

GEORGIA

Charleston, 1822
(Denmark Vesey Conspiracy)

Louisiana, 1811

Savannah

LOUISIANA

FLORIDA

Insurrection aboard the
slave ship Creole, 1841

Gulf of Mexico

Bahama Islands

Insurrection aboard the
slave ship Amistad, 1839

CUBA

Haiti, 1791–1804

HAITI

MEXICO

Jamaica, 1831

St. Kitts
Nevis ○ Antigua

Caribbean Sea

St. Vincent ○

Barbados, 1816

Trinidad

Pacific Ocean

SOUTH AMERICA

Denemarra, 1823

| | Insurrections and major conspiracies |

0   250   500 miles
0   250   500 kilometers

Instances of slave resistance occurred throughout the Western Hemisphere, on land and at sea. This map shows the location of major events in the nineteenth century.

especially Maryland, Virginia, and Kentucky, which bordered on the free states. Douglass, who escaped at age twenty, was also typical in that the large majority of fugitives were young men. Most slave women were not willing to leave children behind, and to take them along on the arduous escape journey was nearly impossible.

In the Deep South, fugitives tended to head for cities like New Orleans or Charleston, where they hoped to lose themselves in the free black community. Other escapees fled to remote areas like the Great Dismal Swamp of Virginia or the Florida Everglades, where the Seminole Indians offered refuge before they were forced to move west. Even in Tennessee, a study of newspaper advertisements for runaways finds that around 40 percent were thought to have remained in the local neighborhood, 30 percent to have headed to other locations in the South, while only 25 percent tried to reach the North.

The Underground Railroad, a loose organization of sympathetic abolitionists who hid fugitives in their homes and sent them on to the next "station," assisted some runaway slaves. A few courageous individuals made forays into the South to liberate slaves. The best known was Harriet Tubman. Born in Maryland in 1820, Tubman escaped to Philadelphia in 1849 and during the next decade risked her life by making some twenty trips back to her state of birth to lead relatives and other slaves to freedom. But most who managed to reach the North did so on their own initiative, sometimes showing remarkable ingenuity. William and Ellen Craft impersonated a sickly owner traveling with her slave. Henry "Box" Brown packed himself inside a crate and literally had himself shipped from Georgia to freedom in the North.

A typical broadside offering a reward for the capture of a runaway slave.

THE *AMISTAD*

In a few instances, large groups of slaves collectively seized their freedom. The most celebrated instance involved fifty-three slaves who in 1839 took control of the *Amistad*, a ship transporting them from one port in Cuba to another, and tried to force the navigator to steer it to Africa. The *Amistad* wended its way up the Atlantic coast, until an American vessel seized it off the coast of Long Island. President Martin Van Buren favored returning the slaves to Cuba. But abolitionists brought their case to the Supreme Court, where former president John Quincy Adams argued that since they had been recently brought from Africa in violation of international treaties banning the slave trade, the captives should be freed. The Court accepted Adams's reasoning, and most of the captives made their way back to Africa.

The *Amistad* case had no legal bearing on slaves within the United States. But it may well have inspired a similar uprising in 1841, when 135 slaves being transported by sea from Norfolk, Virginia, to New Orleans seized control of the ship *Creole* and sailed for Nassau in the British Bahamas. Their leader had the evocative name Madison Washington. To the dismay of the Tyler administration, the British gave refuge to the *Creole* slaves.

SLAVE REVOLTS

Resistance to slavery occasionally moved beyond such individual and group acts of defiance to outright rebellion. The four largest conspiracies in American history occurred within the space of thirty-one years in the early nineteenth century. The first, organized by the Virginia slave Gabriel in 1800, was discussed in Chapter 8. It was followed eleven years later by an uprising on sugar plantations upriver from New Orleans. Somewhere between 200 and 500 men and women, armed with sugarcane knives, axes, clubs, and a few guns, marched toward the city, destroying property as they proceeded. The white population along the route fled in panic to New

A lithograph depicting Joseph Cinqué, leader of the slave revolt on the Spanish ship Amistad *off the coast of Cuba in 1839. The ship was eventually seized near Long Island. After a long legal battle, the Supreme Court allowed the slaves to return to Africa.*

Orleans. Within two days, the militia and regular army troops met the rebels and dispersed them in a pitched battle, killing sixty-six. Soon afterwards, the principal leaders were executed. Captured rebels offered little explanation for their revolt other than the desire, as one put it, "to kill the white." But they seem to have been inspired by the recent success of the slave revolution in Haiti.

The next major conspiracy was organized in 1822 by Denmark Vesey, a slave carpenter in Charleston, South Carolina, who had purchased his freedom after winning a local lottery. An outspoken, charismatic leader, Vesey rebuked blacks who stepped off the city's sidewalks to allow whites to pass and took a leading role in the local African Methodist Church. His conspiracy reflected the combination of American and African influences then circulating in the Atlantic world and coming together in black culture. "He studied the Bible a great deal," recalled one of his followers, "and tried to prove from it that slavery and bondage is against the Bible." Vesey also quoted the Declaration of Independence, pored over newspaper reports of the debates in Congress regarding the Missouri Compromise, and made pronouncements like "all men had equal rights, blacks as well as whites." And he read to his co-conspirators accounts of the successful slave revolution in Haiti. The African heritage was present in the person of Vesey's lieutenant Gullah Jack, a religious "conjurer" from Angola who claimed to be able to protect the rebels against injury or death. The plot was discovered before it could reach fruition.

As in the case of many slave conspiracies, evidence about the Vesey plot is contradictory and disputed. Much of it comes from a series of trials in which the court operated in secret and failed to allow the accused to confront those who testified against them. South Carolina's governor, Thomas Bennett Jr., a number of whose slaves were among the accused, complained to Robert Y. Hayne, the state's attorney general, that the court proceedings violated "the rules which universally obtain among civilized nations." Hayne replied that to try a "free white man" under such circumstances would clearly violate his fundamental rights. But, he added, "slaves are not entitled to these rights," since "all the provisions of our constitution in favor of liberty are intended for freemen only." In the end, thirty-five slaves and free blacks, among them Vesey and three slaves belonging to the governor, were executed and an equal number banished from the state.

NAT TURNER'S REBELLION

The best known of all slave rebels was Nat Turner, a slave preacher and religious mystic in Southampton County, Virginia, who came to believe that God had chosen him to lead a black uprising. Turner traveled widely in the county conducting religious services. He told of seeing black and white angels fighting in the sky and the heavens running red with blood. Perhaps from a sense of irony, Turner initially chose July 4, 1831, for his rebellion only to fall ill on the appointed day. On August 22, he and a handful of followers marched from farm to farm assaulting the white inhabitants. Most of their victims were women and children, for many of the area's men were attending a religious revival across the border in North Carolina. By the time the militia put down the uprising, about eighty slaves had joined Turner's band, and some sixty whites had been killed. Turner was subsequently captured and, with seventeen other rebels, condemned to die. Asked before his execution whether he regretted what he had done, Turner responded, "Was not Christ crucified?"

Nat Turner's was the last large-scale rebellion in southern history. Like Gabriel's and Vesey's conspiracies, Turner's took place outside the heart of the plantation South, where slavery was most rigidly policed. Because Turner began with only a handful of followers, he faced less chance of discovery or betrayal than Gabriel or Vesey. Nonetheless, his revolt demonstrated conclusively that in a region where whites outnumbered blacks and the white community was armed and united, slaves stood at a fatal disadvantage in any violent encounter. Only an outside force could alter the balance of power within the South. Slave resistance, however, hardly disappeared. Turner's uprising, in fact, demonstrated the connection between outright rebellion and less dramatic forms of resistance. For in its aftermath, numerous reports circulated of "insubordinate" behavior by slaves on Virginia's farms and plantations.

Turner's rebellion sent shock waves through the entire South. "A Nat Turner," one white Virginian warned, "might be in any family." In the panic that followed the revolt, hundreds of innocent slaves were whipped and scores executed. For one last time, Virginia's leaders openly debated whether steps ought to be taken to do away with the "peculiar institution." "The blood of Turner and his innocent victims," declared a Richmond newspaper, "has opened the doors which have been shut for fifty years." But a proposal to commit the state to gradual emancipation and the removal of the black population from the state failed to win legislative approval. The measure gained overwhelming support in the western part of Virginia, where slaves represented less than 10 percent of the population, but it failed to win sufficient votes in the eastern counties where slavery was centered.

Instead of moving toward emancipation, the Virginia legislature of 1832 decided to fasten even more tightly the chains of bondage. New laws prohibited blacks, free or slave, from acting as preachers (a measure that proved impossible to enforce), strengthened the militia and patrol systems, banned free blacks from owning firearms, and prohibited teaching slaves

An engraving depicting Nat Turner's slave rebellion of 1831, from a book published soon after the revolt.

to read. Other southern states followed suit. In the debate's aftermath, Thomas R. Dew, a professor at the College of William and Mary in Virginia, published an influential pamphlet pointing to the absurdity of deporting the bulk of the state's labor force. The state, he insisted, faced a stark choice—retain slavery, or free the slaves and absorb them into Virginia society. Few critics of slavery were willing to accept the latter alternative.

In some ways, 1831 marked a turning point for the Old South. In that year, Parliament launched a program for abolishing slavery throughout the British empire (a process completed in 1838), underscoring the South's growing isolation in the Western world. Turner's rebellion, following only a few months after the appearance in Boston of William Lloyd Garrison's abolitionist journal, *The Liberator* (discussed in the next chapter), suggested that American slavery faced enemies both within and outside the South. The proslavery argument increasingly permeated southern intellectual and political life, while dissenting opinions were suppressed. Some states made membership in an abolitionist society a criminal offense, while mobs drove critics of slavery from their homes. The South's "great reaction" produced one of the most thoroughgoing suppressions of freedom of speech in American history. Even as reform movements arose in the North that condemned slavery as contrary to Christianity and to basic American values, and national debate over the peculiar institution intensified, southern society closed in defense of slavery.

SUGGESTED READING

BOOKS

Aptheker, Herbert. *American Negro Slave Revolts* (1943). Still the fullest account of slave rebellions in the United States.

Berlin, Ira. *Slaves without Masters: The Free Negro in the Antebellum South* (1974). A careful study of the status of free blacks, stressing differences between the Upper and Lower South.

Clinton, Catherine. *The Plantation Mistress: Woman's World in the Old South* (1982). Explores how the institution of slavery affected the lives of planters' wives and daughters.

Davis, David Brion. *Inhuman Bondage: The Rise and Fall of Slavery in the New World* (2006). Places the history of slavery in the United States firmly in a hemispheric context.

Genovese, Eugene D. *Roll, Jordan, Roll: The World the Slaves Made* (1974). A classic study of the paternalist ethos and the culture that developed under slavery.

Gutman, Herbert G. *The Black Family in Slavery and Freedom* (1976). A pioneering examination of how slaves created and sustained families under the harsh conditions of slavery.

Johnson, Walter. *Soul by Soul: Life inside the Antebellum Slave Market* (1999). Considers the operations of the New Orleans slave market as a window into slavery as a whole.

Joyner, Charles D. *Down by the Riverside: A South Carolina Slave Community* (1984). Studies slave communities in coastal South Carolina, emphasizing the blend of African and American influences.

Kolchin, Peter. *American Slavery, 1619–1877* (rev. ed., 2003). A careful, up-to-date survey of the history of slavery in North America from its beginning through emancipation.

McCurry, Stephanie. *Masters of Small Worlds: Yeoman Households, Gender Relations, and the Political Culture of Antebellum South Carolina* (1995). Studies the lives of men and women in non-slaveholding families, to explore their links with the planter class.

O'Brien, Michael. *Conjectures of Order: Intellectual Life and the American South* (2004). A comprehensive study of intellectual life in the Old South.

Rugemer, Edward B. *The Problem of Emancipation: The Caribbean Roots of the American Civil War* (2008). Explores how developments in the West Indies affected the outlook of American slaveholders.

Stevenson, Brenda. *Life in Black and White: Family and Community in the Slave South* (1996). Focusing on Virginia, an examination of how slaves adapted to the rise of the interstate slave trade.

Wade, Richard. *Slavery in the Cities: The South, 1820–1860* (1964). An examination of slavery in southern cities, and growing white fears of lack of control of the urban slave population.

Wright, Gavin. *The Political Economy of the Cotton South: Households, Markets, and Wealth in the Nineteenth Century* (1978). Presents the economic development and structure of the cotton South, by a prominent economic historian.

WEBSITES

Born in Slavery: Slave Narratives from the Federal Writers' Project: http://lcweb2.loc. gov/ammem/snhtml/snhome.html

Documenting the American South: http://docsouth.unc.edu

Gilder Lehrman Center for the Study of Slavery, Resistance, and Abolition: www.yale.edu/glc/index.htm

Slaves and the Courts, 1740–1860: http://memory.loc.gov/ammem/sthtml/sthome.html

REVIEW QUESTIONS

1. Given that by 1860 the economic investment represented by the slave population exceeded the value of the nation's factories, railroads, and banks combined, explain how important slavery was to the national economy and the emergence of the United States as a great power.

2. While some poor southern whites resented the dominance of the "slavocracy" most supported the institution and accepted the power of the planter class. Why did the "plain folk" continue to support slavery?

3. Describe the paternalistic ethos the planters embraced, and explain how it both masked and justified the brutal realities of slavery.

4. Identify the basic elements of the proslavery defense and those points aimed especially at non-southern audiences.

5. Compare slaves in the Old South with those elsewhere in the world, focusing on health, diet, and opportunities for freedom.

6. Describe the difference between gang labor and task labor for slaves, and explain how slaves' tasks varied by region across the Old South.

7. Enslaved African-Americans developed their own culture. What were the different sources of this culture, and how did it vary by region?

8. Identify the different types of resistance to slavery. Which ones were the most common, the most effective, and the most demonstrative?

FREEDOM QUESTIONS

1. In Frederick Douglass's view, how were slaves, in their desire for freedom, closer to the founding ideals than the whites who celebrated the Fourth of July but preserved slavery?

2. How did slavery affect the lives and freedoms of both black and white Americans?

3. How did the defenders of slavery handle the founding ideas that freedom and equality were natural rights?

4. What constraints were there on the rights of free blacks in the antebellum South?

5. How did slaves think of freedom, and what were the sources for their beliefs?

KEY TERMS

the "peculiar institution" (p. 417)

"Cotton Is King" (p. 417)

Lords of the Loom and Lords of the Lash (p. 419)

"plain folk" (p. 422)

southern paternalism (p. 423)

the proslavery argument (p. 424)

slave religion (p. 441)

"silent sabotage" (p. 443)

Underground Railroad (p. 445)

runaways (p. 445)

Harriet Tubman (p. 445)

Denmark Vesey's conspiracy (p. 446)

Nat Turner's Rebellion (p. 447)

REVIEW TABLE

Slave Rebellions and the Old South

Rebellion	Date	Result
Gabriel's Rebellion	1800	Virginia prohibits blacks from congregating on Sundays without white supervision and restricts masters voluntarily freeing their slaves
Denmark Vesey's conspiracy	1822	Vesey is executed in South Carolina, and the state increases restrictions on free blacks
Nat Turner's Rebellion	1831	The only large-scale rebellion in the South, it causes Virginia to further tighten its grip on slavery
Amistad	1839	Slaves aboard the ship win their freedom, increasing southern fear of federal power to attack slavery

CHAPTER 12

An Age of Reform, 1820–1840

An abolitionist banner. Antislavery organizations adopted the Liberty Bell as a symbol of their campaign to extend freedom to black Americans. Previously, the bell, forged in Philadelphia in the eighteenth century, had simply been known as the Old State House Bell.

• What were the major movements and goals of antebellum reform?

• What were the different varieties of abolitionism?

• How did abolitionism challenge barriers to racial equality and free speech?

• What were the diverse sources of the antebellum women's rights movement and its significance?

Among the many Americans who devoted their lives to the crusade against slavery, few were as selfless or courageous as Abby Kelley. Born in Massachusetts in 1811, she was educated at a Quaker boarding school in Rhode Island. As a teacher in Lynn, Massachusetts, she joined the Female Anti-Slavery Society and, like thousands of other northern women, threw herself into the abolitionist movement. In 1838, Kelley began to give public speeches about slavery. Her first lecture outside of Lynn was literally a baptism of fire. Enraged by reports that abolitionists favored "amalgamation" of the races—that is, sexual relations between whites and blacks—residents of Philadelphia stormed the meeting hall and burned it to the ground.

For two decades, Kelley traveled throughout the North, speaking almost daily in churches, public halls, and antislavery homes on "the holy cause of human rights." Her career illustrated the interconnections of the era's reform movements. In addition to abolitionism, she was active in pacifist organizations—which opposed the use of force, including war, to settle disputes—and was a pioneer in the early struggle for women's rights. "In striving to strike [the slave's] irons off," she wrote, women "found most surely that we were manacled ourselves." Kelley was not the first American woman to speak in public. But she covered more miles and gave more speeches than any other female orator. She forthrightly challenged her era's assumption that woman's "place" was in the home. More than any other individual, remarked Lucy Stone, another women's rights advocate, Kelley "earned for us all the right of free speech."

Abby Kelley's private life was as unconventional as her public career. She enjoyed a long and happy marriage to Stephen S. Foster, a strong-willed abolitionist given to interrupting Sunday sermons to denounce ministers who failed to condemn slavery. She gave birth to a daughter in 1847 but soon returned to lecturing. When criticized for not devoting herself to the care of her infant, Kelley replied: "I have done it for the sake of the mothers whose babies are sold away from them. The most precious legacy I can leave my child is a free country."

THE REFORM IMPULSE

"In the history of the world," wrote Ralph Waldo Emerson in 1841, "the doctrine of reform has never such hope as at the present hour." Abolitionism was only one of the era's numerous efforts to improve American society. During his visit in the early 1830s, Alexis de Tocqueville noted how in the absence of a powerful national government, Americans' political and

A rare photograph of an abolitionist meeting in New York State around 1850. The woman at the center wearing a bonnet may be Abby Kelley. Frederick Douglass sits immediately to her right.

social activities were organized through voluntary associations—churches, fraternal orders, political clubs, and the like. The reform impulse was part of this proliferation of voluntary groups. Americans established organizations that worked to prevent the manufacture and sale of liquor, end public entertainments and the delivery of the mail on Sunday, improve conditions in prisons, expand public education, uplift the condition of wage laborers, and reorganize society on the basis of cooperation rather than competitive individualism.

Nearly all these groups worked to convert public opinion to their cause. They sent out speakers, gathered signatures on petitions, and published pamphlets. Like Abby Kelley, many reformers were active in more than one crusade. Some reform movements, like restraining the consumption of liquor and alleviating the plight of the blind and insane, flourished throughout the nation. Others, including women's rights, labor unionism, and educational reform, were weak or nonexistent in the South, where they were widely associated with antislavery sentiment. Reform was an international crusade. Peace, temperance, women's rights, and antislavery advocates regularly crisscrossed the Atlantic to promote their cause.

Reformers adopted a wide variety of tactics to bring about social change. Some relied on "moral suasion" to convert people to their cause. Others, like opponents of the "demon rum," sought to use the power of the government to force sinners to change their ways. Some reformers decided to withdraw altogether from the larger society and establish their own cooperative settlements. They hoped to change American life by creating "heavens on earth," where they could demonstrate by example the superiority of a collective way of life. Reformers never amounted to anything like a majority of the population, even in the North, but they had a profound impact on both politics and society.

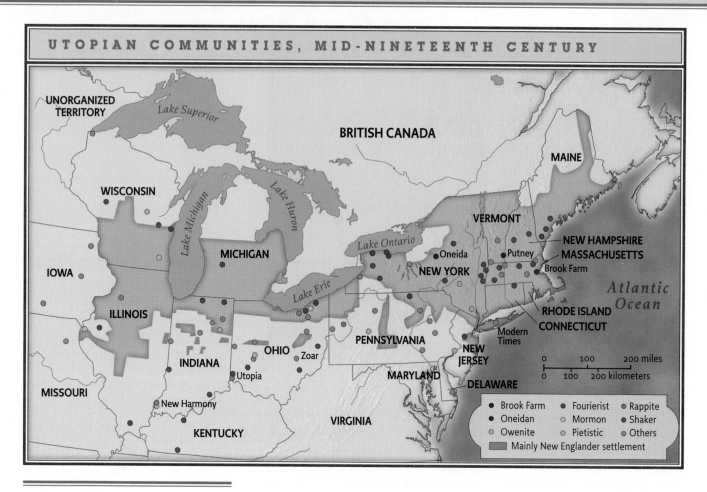

UTOPIAN COMMUNITIES, MID-NINETEENTH CENTURY

In the first half of the nineteenth century, dozens of utopian communities were established in the United States, where small groups of men and women attempted to establish a more perfect social order within the larger society.

UTOPIAN COMMUNITIES

About 100 reform communities were established in the decades before the Civil War. Historians call them "utopian" after Thomas More's sixteenth-century novel *Utopia*, an outline of a perfect society. (The word has also come to imply that such plans are impractical and impossible to realize.) These communities differed greatly in structure and motivation. Some were subject to the iron discipline of a single leader, while others operated in a democratic fashion. Most arose from religious conviction, but others were inspired by the secular desire to counteract the social and economic changes set in motion by the market revolution.

Nearly all the communities set out to reorganize society on a cooperative basis, hoping to restore social harmony to a world of excessive individualism and to narrow the widening gap between rich and poor. Through their efforts, the words "socialism" and "communism," meaning a social organization in which productive property is owned by the community rather than private individuals, entered the language of politics. Most utopian communities also tried to find substitutes for conventional gender relations and marriage patterns. Some prohibited sexual relations between men and women altogether; others allowed them to change partners at will. But nearly all insisted that the abolition of private property must be accompanied by an end to men's "property" in women.

THE SHAKERS

Religious communities attracted those who sought to find a retreat from a society permeated by sin, "a refuge from the evils of this Sodom," as the founders of Zoar, in Ohio, put it. But the Shakers, the most successful of the religious communities, also had a significant impact on the outside world. At their peak during the 1840s, cooperative Shaker settlements, which stretched from Maine to Kentucky, included more than 5,000 members. The Shakers were founded in the late eighteenth century by Mother Ann Lee, the daughter of an English blacksmith, who became a religious exhorter and claimed that Christ had directed her to emigrate with her followers to America. The first Shaker community was established in upstate New York in 1787.

God, the Shakers believed, had a "dual" personality, both male and female, and thus the two sexes were spiritually equal. Their work was deemed equally important (although each man was assigned a "sister" to take care of his washing and sewing). "Virgin purity" formed a pillar of the Shakers' faith. They completely abandoned traditional family life. Men and women lived separately in large dormitory-like structures and ate in communal dining rooms. Their numbers grew by attracting converts and adopting children from orphanages, rather than through natural increase. Numerous outsiders visited Shaker communities to observe the religious services that gave the group its name, in which men and women, separated by sex, engaged in frenzied dancing. Although they rejected the individual accumulation of private property, the Shakers proved remarkably successful economically. They were among the first to market vegetable and flower seeds and herbal medicines commercially and to breed cattle for profit. Their beautifully crafted furniture is still widely admired today.

An engraving of a Shaker dance, drawn by Benson Lossing, an artist who visited a Shaker community and reported on life there for Harper's Magazine *in 1857.*

THE MORMONS' TREK

Another migration brought thousands of members of the Church of Jesus Christ of Latter-Day Saints, or Mormons, to modern-day Utah. One of the era's numerous religious sects that hoped to create a Kingdom of God on earth, the Mormons had been founded in the 1820s by Joseph Smith, a young farmer in upstate New York. Smith claimed to have been led by an angel to a set of golden plates covered with strange writing, which he translated as the Book of Mormon. It claimed that ancient Hebrews had emigrated to the New World and become the ancestors of the American Indians.

The absolute authority Smith exercised over his followers, as well as the refusal of the Mormons to separate church and state, alarmed many neighbors. Even more outrageous to the general community was the Mormon practice of polygamy, which allows one man to have more than one wife, a repudiation of traditional Christian teaching and nineteenth-century morality. Mobs drove Smith and his followers out of New York, Ohio, and Missouri before they settled in 1839 in Nauvoo, Illinois, where they hoped to await the Second Coming of Christ. There, five years later, Smith was arrested on the charge of inciting a riot that destroyed an anti-Mormon newspaper. While in jail awaiting trial, Smith was murdered by a group of intruders. His successor as Mormon leader, Brigham Young, led more than 10,000 followers across the Great Plains and Rocky Mountains to the shores of the Great Salt Lake in present-day Utah, seeking a refuge where they could practice their faith undisturbed. The Mormons' plight revealed the limits of religious toleration in nineteenth-century America.

ONEIDA

Another influential and controversial community was Oneida, founded in 1848 in upstate New York by John Humphrey Noyes, the Vermont-born son of a U.S. congressman. After graduating from Dartmouth College, Noyes briefly studied law but soon experienced a conversion at a religious revival and decided to become a minister. Noyes took the revivalists' message that man could achieve moral perfection to an atypical extreme. He preached that he and his followers had become so perfect that they had achieved a state of complete "purity of heart," or sinlessness.

In 1836, Noyes and his followers formed a small community in Putney, Vermont. Like the Shakers, Noyes did away with private property and abandoned traditional marriage. But in contrast to Shaker celibacy, he taught that all members of his community formed a single "holy family" of equals. His community became notorious for what Noyes called "complex marriage," whereby any man could propose sexual relations to any woman, who had the right to reject or accept his invitation, which would then be registered in a public record book. The great danger was "exclusive affections," which, Noyes felt, destroyed the harmony of the community.

After being indicted for adultery by local officials, Noyes in 1848 moved his community to Oneida, where it survived until 1881. Oneida was an extremely dictatorial environment. To become a member of the community, one had to demonstrate command of Noyes's religious teachings and live according to his rules. Members carefully observed each other's conduct and publicly criticized those who violated Noyes's regulations. By the 1860s, a committee was even determining which couples would be permitted to have children—an early example of "eugenics," as the effort to improve the human race by regulating reproduction came to be known.

WORLDLY COMMUNITIES

To outside observers, utopian communities like Oneida seemed a case of "voluntary slavery." But because of their members' selfless devotion to the teachings and rules laid down by their leader, spiritually oriented communities often achieved remarkable longevity. The Shakers survived well into the twentieth century. Communities with a more worldly orientation tended to be beset by internal divisions and therefore lasted for much shorter periods.

In 1841, New England transcendentalists established Brook Farm not far from Boston, where they hoped to demonstrate that manual and intellectual labor could coexist harmoniously. They modeled the community in part on the ideas of the French social reformer Charles Fourier, who envisioned communal living and working arrangements, while retaining private property. Fourier's blueprint for "phalanxes," as he called his settlements, planned everything to the last detail, from the number of residents (2,000) to how much income would be generated by charging admission to sightseers. With leisure time devoted to music, dancing, dramatic readings, and intellectual discussion, Brook Farm was like an exciting miniature university. But it attracted mostly writers, teachers, and ministers, some of whom disliked farm labor. The novelist Nathaniel Hawthorne, a resident for a time, complained about having to shovel manure. Brook Farm disbanded after a few years, and Hawthorne offered a skeptical view of life there in his 1852 novel *The Blithedale Romance*.

THE OWENITES

The most important secular communitarian (meaning a person who plans or lives in a cooperative community) was Robert Owen, a British factory owner. Appalled by the degradation of workers in the early industrial revolution, Owen created a model factory village at New Lanark, Scotland, which combined strict rules of work discipline with comfortable housing and free public education. Around 1815, its 1,500 employees made New Lanark the largest center of cotton manufacturing in the world. Convinced that the "rich and the poor, the governors and the governed, have really but one interest," Owen promoted communitarianism as a peaceful means of ensuring that workers received the full value of their labor. In 1824, he purchased the Harmony community in Indiana—originally founded by the German Protestant religious leader George Rapp, who had emigrated to America with his followers at the beginning of the nineteenth century. Here, Owen established New Harmony, where he hoped to create a "new moral world."

"The character of man is, without a single exception, always formed for him," Owen declared. Individuals could be transformed by changing the

The Crisis, *a publication by the communitarian Robert Owen and his son, Robert Dale Owen. The cover depicts Owen's vision of a planned socialist community.*

circumstances in which they lived. In Owen's scheme, children would be removed at an early age from the care of their parents to be educated in schools where they would be trained to subordinate individual ambition to the common good. Owen also defended women's rights, especially access to education and the right to divorce. At New Harmony, he promised, women would no longer be "enslaved" to their husbands, and "false notions" about innate differences between the sexes would be abandoned.

Harmony eluded the residents of New Harmony. They squabbled about everything from the community's constitution to the distribution of property. Owen's settlement survived for only a few years, but it strongly influenced the labor movement, educational reformers, and women's rights advocates. Owen's vision resonated with the widely held American belief that a community of equals could be created in the New World.

Quite different from Owen's planned system were the short-lived secular communities founded by Josiah Warren, an early American anarchist (one who believes that all institutions that exercise power over individuals, including government, are illegitimate). At Utopia, Ohio, and Modern Times, New York, Warren established totally unregulated voluntary settlements. Like other communitarians, Warren tried to address the sources of labor unrest and women's inequality. In an attempt to solve the labor problem, he created stores where goods were exchanged according to the amount of work that had gone into producing them, thus preventing middlemen like bankers and merchants from sharing in the hard-earned income of farmers, laborers, and manufacturers. Marriage in Warren's communities was a purely voluntary arrangement, since no laws regulated personal behavior. In effect, Warren took American individualism to its logi-

The Drunkard's Progress, *an 1826 anti-liquor broadside illustrating how drinking leads a respectable man and his family to ruin.*

cal extreme. Freedom, he declared, meant "allowing each individual to be absolute despot or sovereign" over himself.

RELIGION AND REFORM

Most Americans saw the ownership of property as the key to economic independence—and, therefore, to freedom—and marriage as the foundation of the social order. Few were likely to join communities that required them to surrender both. Far more typical of the reform impulse were movements that aimed at liberating men and women either from restraints external to themselves, such as slavery and war, or from forms of internal "servitude" like drinking, illiteracy, and a tendency toward criminality. Drinkers, proclaimed one reformer, could not be considered free: they were "chained to alcohol, bound to the demon rum." Many of these reform movements drew their inspiration from the religious revivalism of the Second Great Awakening, discussed in Chapter 9. If, as the revivalist preachers maintained, God had created man as a "free moral agent," sinners could not only reform themselves but could also remake the world.

The revivals popularized the outlook known as "perfectionism," which saw both individuals and society at large as capable of indefinite improvement. Regions like upstate New York and northern Ohio became known as "burned-over districts" because of the intense revivals they experienced in the 1820s and 1830s. Such areas became fertile soil for the era's reform movements and their vision of a society freed from sin. Under the impact of the revivals, older reform efforts moved in a new, radical direction. Temperance (which literally means moderation in the consumption of liquor) was transformed into a crusade to eliminate drinking entirely. Criticism of war became outright pacifism. And, as will be related below, critics of slavery now demanded not gradual emancipation but immediate and total abolition.

A temperance banner from around 1850 depicts a young man torn between a woman in white, who illustrates female purity, and a temptress, who offers him a drink of liquor.

THE TEMPERANCE MOVEMENT

To members of the North's emerging middle-class culture, reform became a badge of respectability, an indication that individuals had taken control of their own lives and had become morally accountable human beings. The American Temperance Society, founded in 1826, directed its efforts to redeeming not only habitual drunkards but also the occasional drinker. It claimed by the 1830s to have persuaded hundreds of thousands of Americans to renounce liquor. By 1840, the consumption of alcohol per person had fallen to less than half the level of a decade earlier. (It had peaked in 1830 at seven gallons per person per year, compared to around two gallons today.) During the 1840s, the Washingtonian Society gathered reformed drinkers in "experience meetings" where they offered public testimony about their previous sins.

The temperance crusade and other reform movements aroused considerable hostility. One person's sin is another's pleasure or cherished custom. Those Americans who enjoyed Sunday recreation or a stiff drink from time to time did not think they were any less moral than those who had been reborn at a religious camp meeting, had abandoned drinking, and devoted the Sabbath to religious observances.

A German Beer Garden on Sunday Evening, *an engraving from* Harper's Weekly, *October 15, 1858. German and Irish immigrants resented efforts of temperance reformers to prohibit the sale of alcoholic beverages.*

CRITICS OF REFORM

Many Americans saw the reform impulse as an attack on their own freedom. Drinking was a prominent feature of festive celebrations and events like militia gatherings. As in the colonial era, taverns were popular meeting places for workingmen in early-nineteenth-century towns and cities, sites not only of drinking but also of political discussions, organizational meetings, and popular recreations. A "Liberty Loving Citizen" of Worcester, Massachusetts, wondered what gave one group of citizens the right to dictate to others how to conduct their personal lives.

American Catholics, their numbers growing because of Irish and German immigration, proved hostile to the reform impulse. Catholics understood freedom in ways quite different from Protestant reformers. They viewed sin as an inescapable burden of individuals and society. The perfectionist idea that evil could be banished from the world struck them as an affront to genuine religion, and they bitterly opposed what they saw as reformers' efforts to impose their own version of Protestant morality on their neighbors. While reformers spoke of man as a free moral agent, Catholics tended to place less emphasis on individual independence and more on the importance of communities centered on family and church. "Man," declared Archbishop John Hughes of New York, the nation's most prominent Catholic leader, was not an autonomous creature but "by his nature, a being of society."

REFORMERS AND FREEDOM

Reformers had to reconcile their desire to create moral order and their quest to enhance personal freedom. They did this through a vision of freedom that was liberating and controlling at the same time. On the one hand, reformers insisted that their goal was to enable Americans to enjoy genuine liberty. In a world in which personal freedom increasingly meant the opportunity to compete for economic gain and individual self-improvement, they spoke of liberating Americans from various forms of "slavery" that made it impossible to succeed—slavery to drink, to poverty, to sin.

On the other hand, reformers insisted that self-fulfillment came through self-discipline. Their definition of the free individual was the person who internalized the practice of self-control. Philip Schaff, a German minister who emigrated to Pennsylvania in 1843, wrote that "true national freedom, in the American view," was "anything but an absence of restraint." Rather, it "rests upon a moral groundwork, upon the virtue of self-possession and self-control in individual citizens." In some ways, reformers believed, American society suffered from an excess of liberty—the anarchic "natural liberty" John Winthrop had warned against in the early days of Puritan Massachusetts, as opposed to the "Christian liberty" of the morally upright citizen.

Many religious groups in the East worried that settlers in the West and immigrants from abroad lacked self-control and led lives of vice, exhibited by drinking, violations of the Sabbath, and lack of Protestant devotion. They formed the American Tract Society, the American Bible Society, and other groups that flooded eastern cities and the western frontier with copies of the gospel and pamphlets promoting religious virtue. Between 1825 and 1835, the pamphlets distributed by the Tract Society amounted to more than 500 million pages. Both their understanding of freedom and their ability to take advantage of the new printing technologies influenced the era's reform movements.

THE INVENTION OF THE ASYLUM

The tension between liberation and control in the era's reform movements was vividly evident in the proliferation of new institutions that reformers hoped could remake human beings into free, morally upright citizens. In colonial America, crime had mostly been punished by whipping, fines, or banishment. The poor received relief in their own homes, orphans lived with neighbors, and families took care of mentally ill members.

The New York House of Refuge, one of many institutions established in the 1820s and 1830s to address social ills by assisting and reforming criminals and the poor. Young boys and girls convicted of petty theft were assigned to the House of Refuge, where they performed supervised labor and received some educational instruction.

During the 1830s and 1840s, Americans embarked on a program of institution building—jails for criminals, poorhouses for the destitute, asylums for the insane, and orphanages for children without families. These institutions differed in many respects, but they shared with communitarians and religious believers in "perfectionism" the idea that social ills once considered incurable could in fact be eliminated. The way to "cure" undesirable elements of society was to place afflicted persons and impressionable youths in an environment where their character could be transformed. Prisons and asylums would eventually become overcrowded places where rehabilitating the inmates seemed less important than simply holding them at bay, away from society. At the outset, however, these institutions were inspired by the conviction that those who passed through their doors could eventually be released to become productive, self-disciplined citizens.

THE COMMON SCHOOL

The largest effort at institution building before the Civil War came in the movement to establish common schools—that is, tax-supported state school systems open to all children. In the early nineteenth century, most children were educated in locally supported schools, private academies, charity schools, or at home, and many had no access to learning at all. School reform reflected the numerous purposes that came together in the era's reform impulse. Horace Mann, a Massachusetts lawyer and Whig politician who served as director of the state's board of education, was the era's leading educational reformer. His annual reports, widely read throughout the country, combined conservatism and radicalism, liberation and social control.

Mann embraced the new industrial order of his state. But he hoped that universal public education could restore equality to a fractured society by bringing the children of all classes together in a common learning experience and equipping the less fortunate to advance in the social scale. Education would "equalize the conditions of men"—in effect, it would serve as industrial society's alternative to moving west to acquire a farm. This view of free public education as an avenue to social advancement was also shared by the early labor movement, which made the establishment of common schools one of its goals. At the same time, Mann argued that the schools would reinforce social stability by rescuing students from the influence of parents who failed to instill the proper discipline. Character building was as important a function of education as reading, writing, and arithmetic. To some extent, the schools' "silent curriculum"—obedience to authority, promptness in attendance, organizing one's day according to predetermined time periods that changed at the ringing of a bell—helped to prepare students for work in the new industrial economy.

The schools, Mann believed, were training free individuals—meaning persons who internalized self-discipline. But he encountered persistent opposition

This daguerreotype from around 1850 depicts a classroom in a school for girls presided over by a male teacher.

from parents who did not wish to surrender the moral education of their children to teachers and bureaucrats. Nonetheless, with labor organizations, factory owners, and middle-class reformers all supporting the idea, every northern state by 1860 had established tax-supported school systems for its children. The common school movement created the first real career opportunity for women, who quickly came to dominate the ranks of teachers. The South, where literate blacks were increasingly viewed as a danger to social order and planters had no desire to tax themselves to pay for education for poor white children, lagged far behind in public education. This was one of many ways in which North and South seemed to be growing apart.

THE CRUSADE AGAINST SLAVERY

Compared with drinking, Sabbath-breaking, and illiteracy, the greatest evil in American society at first appeared to attract the least attention from reformers. For many years, it seemed that the only Americans willing to challenge the existence of slavery were Quakers, slaves, and free blacks. After the antislavery impulse spawned by the Revolution died out, the slavery question faded from national life, with occasional eruptions like the Missouri controversy of 1819–1821.

COLONIZATION

Before the 1830s, those white Americans willing to contemplate an end to bondage almost always coupled calls for abolition with the "colonization" of freed slaves—their deportation to Africa, the Caribbean, or Central America. In 1816, proponents of this idea founded the American Colonization Society, which promoted the gradual abolition of slavery and the settlement of black Americans in Africa. It soon established Liberia on the coast of West Africa, an outpost of American influence whose capital, Monrovia, was named for President James Monroe.

Colonization struck many observers as totally impractical. When the English writer Harriet Martineau visited the United States in the 1830s, she was amazed that former president James Madison endorsed the idea. "How such a mind as his" could be convinced that slavery would not end unless blacks were deported from the country she could not understand. In her account of her travels, *Society in America* (1837), she called colonization a way in which "slave-owners who had scruples about holding men as property might, by sending their slaves away over sea, relieve their consciences without annoying their neighbors."

Nonetheless, numerous prominent political leaders of the Jacksonian era—including Henry Clay, John Marshall, Daniel Webster, and Jackson himself—supported the Colonization Society. Many northerners saw colonization as the only way to rid the nation of slavery. Southern supporters of colonization devoted most of their energy to persuading those African-Americans who were already free to leave the United States. Free blacks, they insisted, were a "degraded" group whose presence posed a danger to white society. Other colonizationists believed that slavery and racism were so deeply embedded in American life, that blacks could never

A pamphlet issued in 1848 by the American Colonization Society urging free blacks to emigrate to Liberia, in West Africa, and defending the Society against "certain cavilings"—that is, abolitionist criticism.

achieve equality if freed and allowed to remain in the country. Like Indian removal, colonization rested on the premise that America is fundamentally a white society.

BLACKS AND COLONIZATION

In the decades before the Civil War, several thousand black Americans did emigrate to Liberia with the aid of the Colonization Society. Some were slaves emancipated by their owners on the condition that they depart, while others left voluntarily, motivated by a desire to spread Christianity in Africa or to enjoy rights denied them in the United States. Having experienced "the legal slavery of the South and the social slavery of the North," wrote one emigrant on leaving for Liberia, he knew he could "never be a free man in this country."

But most African-Americans adamantly opposed the idea of colonization. In fact, the formation of the American Colonization Society galvanized free blacks to claim their rights as Americans. Early in 1817, some 3,000 free blacks assembled in Philadelphia for the first national black convention. Their resolutions insisted that blacks were Americans, entitled to the same freedom and rights enjoyed by whites. "We have no wish to separate from our present homes," they declared. In the years that followed, a number of black organizations removed the word "African" from their names to eliminate a possible reason for being deported from the land of their birth.

MILITANT ABOLITIONISM

The abolitionist movement that arose in the 1830s differed profoundly from its genteel, conservative predecessor. Drawing on the religious conviction that slavery was an unparalleled sin and the secular one that it contradicted the values enshrined in the Declaration of Independence, a new generation of reformers rejected the traditional approach of gradual emancipation and demanded immediate abolition. Also unlike their predecessors, they directed explosive language against slavery and slaveholders and insisted that blacks, once free, should be incorporated as equal citizens of the republic rather than being deported. White abolitionists themselves were hardly free of the racism that pervaded American society. Some, indeed, wondered whether the slaves were too "feminine" in character to revolt against oppression, which they claimed manly Anglo-Saxons would surely do. Nonetheless, nearly all abolitionists insisted that economic, civil, and political rights in the United States should be equally enjoyed without regard to race. Perfecting American society, they insisted, meant rooting out not just slavery, but racism in all its forms.

The first indication of the new spirit of abolitionism came in 1829 with the appearance of *An Appeal to the Coloured Citizens of the World* by David Walker, a free black who had been born in North Carolina and now operated a used-clothing store in Boston. A passionate indictment of slavery and racial prejudice, the *Appeal* called on black Americans to mobilize for abolition—by force if necessary—and warned whites that the nation faced divine punishment if it did not mend its sinful ways. Walker invoked the

William Lloyd Garrison, editor of The Liberator *and probably the nation's most prominent abolitionist, in a daguerreotype from around 1850.*

Bible and the Declaration of Independence, but he went beyond these familiar arguments to call on blacks to take pride in the achievements of ancient African civilizations and to claim all their rights as Americans. "Tell us no more about colonization," Walker wrote, addressing white readers, "for America is as much our country as it is yours."

The masthead of William Lloyd Garrison's The Liberator, *with engravings of scenes of slavery and freedom.*

THE EMERGENCE OF GARRISON

Walker's language alarmed both slaveholders and many white critics of slavery. When free black sailors secretly distributed the pamphlet in the South, some southern states put a price on Walker's head. Walker, however, did not create an abolitionist organization, and he died in mysterious circumstances in 1830. Not until the appearance in 1831 of *The Liberator*, William Lloyd Garrison's weekly journal published in Boston, did the new breed of abolitionism find a permanent voice. "I will be as harsh as truth," Garrison announced, "and as uncompromising as justice. On this subject, I do not wish to think, or speak, or write, with moderation. . . . I will not equivocate—I will not excuse—I will not retreat a single inch—and I will be heard."

And heard he was, partly because southerners, outraged by his inflammatory rhetoric (one editorial called slaveowners "an adulterous and perverse generation, a brood of vipers"), reprinted Garrison's editorials in their own newspapers in order to condemn them, thus providing him with instant notoriety. Some of Garrison's ideas, such as his suggestion that the North abrogate the Constitution and dissolve the Union to end its complicity in the evil of slavery, were rejected by many abolitionists. But his call for the immediate abolition of slavery echoed throughout antislavery circles. Garrison's pamphlet, *Thoughts on African Colonization*, persuaded many foes of slavery that blacks must be recognized as part of American society, not viewed as aliens to be shipped overseas. Other antislavery publications soon emerged, but *The Liberator* remained the preeminent abolitionist journal.

SPREADING THE ABOLITIONIST MESSAGE

Beginning with a handful of activists, the abolitionist movement expanded rapidly throughout the North. Antislavery leaders took advantage of the rapid development of print technology and the expansion of literacy due to common school education to spread their message. Like radical pamphlet-

5

A is an Abolitionist—
    A man who wants to free
The wretched slave—and give to all
    An equal liberty.

B is a Brother with a skin
    Of somewhat darker hue,
But in our Heavenly Father's sight,
    He is as dear as you.

C is the Cotton-field, to which
    This injured brother's driven,
When, as the white man's *slave*, he toils
    From early morn till even.

D is the Driver, cold and stern,
    Who follows, whip in hand,
To punish those who dare to rest,
    Or disobey command.

Pages from an abolitionist book for children. Abolitionists sought to convince young and old of the evils of slavery.

eers of the American Revolution and evangelical ministers of the Second Great Awakening, they recognized the democratic potential in the production of printed material. Abolitionists seized upon the recently invented steam printing press to produce millions of copies of pamphlets, newspapers, petitions, novels, and broadsides. Between the formation of the American Anti-Slavery Society in 1833 and the end of the decade, some 100,000 northerners joined local groups devoted to abolition. Most were ordinary citizens—farmers, shopkeepers, craftsmen, laborers, along with a few prominent businessmen like the merchants Arthur and Lewis Tappan of New York.

If Garrison was the movement's most notable propagandist, Theodore Weld, a young minister who had been converted by the evangelical preacher Charles G. Finney, helped to create its mass constituency. A brilliant orator, Weld trained a band of speakers who brought the abolitionist message into the heart of the rural and small-town North. Their methods were those of the revivals—fervent preaching, lengthy meetings, calls for individuals to renounce their immoral ways—and their message was a simple one: slavery was a sin. "In discussing the subject of slavery," wrote Weld, "I have always presented it as preeminently a moral question, arresting the conscience of the nation. As a question of politics and national economy, I have passed it with scarce a look or a word."

There was far more to Weld's moralistic approach than a concern for religious righteousness. Identifying slavery as a sin was essential to replacing the traditional strategies of gradual emancipation and colonization with immediate abolition. The only proper response to the sin of slavery, abolitionist speakers proclaimed, was the institution's immediate elimination. Weld also supervised the publication of abolitionist pamphlets, including his own *Slavery As It Is* (1839), a compilation of accounts of the maltreatment of slaves. Since Weld took all his examples from the southern press, they could not be dismissed as figments of the northern imagination.

SLAVERY AND MORAL SUASION

Many southerners feared that the abolitionists intended to spark a slave insurrection, a belief strengthened by the outbreak of Nat Turner's Rebellion a few months after *The Liberator* made its appearance. Yet not only was Garrison completely unknown to Turner, but nearly all abolitionists, despite their militant language, rejected violence as a means of ending slavery. Many were pacifists or "non-resistants," who believed that coercion should be eliminated from all human relationships and institutions. Their strategy was "moral suasion" and their arena the public sphere. Slaveholders must be convinced of the sinfulness of their ways, and the North of its complicity in the peculiar institution. (Some critics charged that this approach left nothing for the slaves to do in seeking their own liberation but await the nation's moral regeneration.)

Standing outside established institutions, abolitionists adopted the role of radical social critics. Among the first to appreciate the key role of public opinion in a mass democracy, they focused their efforts not on infiltrating the existing political parties, but on awakening the nation to the moral evil of slavery. Their language was deliberately provocative, calculated to seize public attention. "Slavery," said Garrison, "will not be overthrown without excitement, without a most tremendous excitement."

ABOLITIONISTS AND THE IDEA OF FREEDOM

The abolitionist crusade both reinforced and challenged common understandings of freedom in Jacksonian America. Abolitionists helped to popularize the concept, fortified by the market revolution, that personal freedom derived not from the ownership of productive property such as land

Slave Market of America, an engraving produced by the American Anti-Slavery Society in 1836, illustrates how abolitionists sought to identify their cause with American traditions, even as they mocked the nation's claim to be a "land of the free."

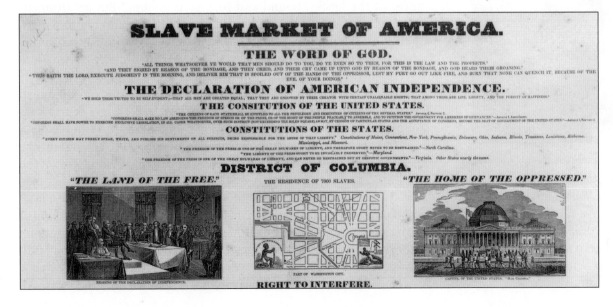

but from ownership of one's self and the ability to enjoy the fruits of one's labor. Abolitionists repudiated the idea of "wage slavery," which had been popularized by the era's labor movement. Compared with the slave, the person working for wages, they insisted, was an embodiment of freedom: the free laborer could change jobs if he wished, accumulate property, and enjoy a stable family life. Only slavery, wrote the abolitionist William Goodell, deprived human beings of their "grand central right—the inherent right of self-ownership."

On the other hand, abolitionists argued that slavery was so deeply embedded in American life that its destruction would require fundamental changes in the North as well as the South. They insisted that the inherent, natural, and absolute right to personal liberty, regardless of race, took precedence over other forms of freedom, such as the right of citizens to accumulate and hold property or self-government by local political communities.

A NEW VISION OF AMERICA

In a society in which the rights of citizenship had become more and more closely associated with whiteness, the antislavery movement sought to reinvigorate the idea of freedom as a truly universal entitlement. The origins of the idea of an American people unbounded by race lies not with the founders, who by and large made their peace with slavery, but with the abolitionists. The antislavery crusade viewed slaves and free blacks as members of the national community, a position summarized in the title of Lydia Maria Child's popular treatise of 1833, *An Appeal in Favor of That Class of Americans Called Africans.* Child's text insisted that blacks were fellow countrymen, not foreigners or a permanently inferior caste. They should no more be considered Africans than whites were Englishmen. The idea that birthplace alone, not race, should determine who was an American, later enshrined in the Fourteenth Amendment, represented a radical departure from the traditions of American life. "We do not admit," declared the *New England Magazine* in 1832, "that America is as much the country of the blacks, bound and free, as it is ours." But abolitionists maintained that the slaves, once freed, should be empowered to participate fully in the public life of the United States. Abolitionists also pioneered the modern idea that human rights took precedence over national sovereignty. They urged the United States to participate in the courts that brought together judges from Britain and other countries to punish those who violated the ban on the Atlantic slave trade. These courts were perhaps the first example of transnational human rights enforcement. But with southerners exerting powerful influence in Washington, the United States did not join the court system until 1862, in the midst of the Civil War.

The crusade against slavery, wrote Angelina Grimké, who became a leading abolitionist speaker, was the nation's preeminent "school in which human rights are . . . investigated." Abolitionists debated the Constitution's relationship to slavery. William Lloyd Garrison burned the document, calling it a covenant with the devil; Frederick Douglass came to believe that it offered no national protection to slavery. But despite this difference of opin-

One of many popular lithographs illustrating scenes from Harriet Beecher Stowe's novel Uncle Tom's Cabin, *the most widely read of all antislavery writings. This depicts the slave Eliza escaping with her child across the ice floes of the Ohio River.*

ion, abolitionists developed an alternative, rights-oriented view of constitutional law, grounded in their universalistic understanding of liberty. Seeking to define the core rights to which all Americans were entitled—the meaning of freedom in concrete legal terms—abolitionists invented the concept of equality before the law regardless of race, one all but unknown in American life before the Civil War. Abolitionist literature also helped to expand the definition of cruelty. The graphic descriptions of the beatings, brandings, and other physical sufferings of the slaves helped to popularize the idea of bodily integrity as a basic right that slavery violated.

Despite being denounced by their opponents as enemies of American principles, abolitionists consciously identified their movement with the revolutionary heritage. The Declaration of Independence was not as fundamental to public oratory in the early republic as it would later become. Abolitionists seized upon it, interpreting the document's preamble as a condemnation of slavery. The Liberty Bell, later one of the nation's most venerated emblems of freedom, did not achieve that status until abolitionists adopted it as a symbol and gave it its name, as part of an effort to identify their principles with those of the founders. (Prior to the 1830s, it was simply the Old State House Bell, used at various times to mark the death of prominent citizens, summon students at the University of Pennsylvania to their classes, and celebrate patriotic holidays.) Of course, Americans of all regions and political beliefs claimed the Revolution's legacy. Mobs that disrupted abolitionist meetings invoked the "spirit of '76," as did southern defenders of slavery. Abolitionists never represented more than a small part of the North's population. But as the slavery controversy intensified, the belief spread far beyond abolitionist circles that slavery contradicted the nation's heritage of freedom.

Harriet Beecher Stowe, author of the abolitionist novel Uncle Tom's Cabin.

BLACK AND WHITE ABOLITIONISM

BLACK ABOLITIONISTS

Blacks played a leading role in the antislavery movement. Even before the appearance of *The Liberator*, as we have seen, northern free blacks had organized in opposition to the Colonization Society. James Forten, a successful black sailmaker in Philadelphia, helped to finance *The Liberator* in its early years. As late as 1834, northern blacks, attracted by Garrison's rejection of colonization and his demand for equal rights for black Americans, made up a majority of the journal's subscribers. Several blacks served on the board of directors of the American Anti-Slavery Society, and northern-born blacks and fugitive slaves quickly emerged as major organizers and speakers.

Frederick Douglass was only one among many former slaves who published accounts of their lives in bondage; these accounts convinced thousands of northerners of the evils of slavery. Indeed, the most effective piece of antislavery literature of the entire period, Harriet Beecher Stowe's novel *Uncle Tom's Cabin*, was to some extent modeled on the autobiography of fugitive slave Josiah Henson. Serialized in 1851 in a Washington antislavery newspaper and published as a book the following year, *Uncle Tom's*

The frontispiece of the 1848 edition of David Walker's Appeal *and Henry Highland Garnet's* Address to the Slaves *depicts a black figure receiving "liberty" and "justice" from heaven.*

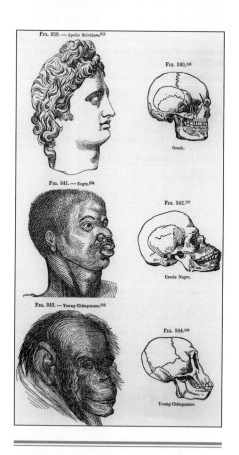

An illustration from Types of Mankind, *an 1854 book by the physicians and racial theorists Josiah C. Nott and George R. Gliddon, who argued that blacks formed a separate species, midway between whites and chimpanzees. Abolitionists sought to counter the pseudoscientific defenses of slavery and racism.*

Cabin sold more than 1 million copies by 1854, and it also inspired numerous stage versions. By portraying slaves as sympathetic men and women, and as Christians at the mercy of slaveholders who split up families and set bloodhounds on innocent mothers and children, Stowe's melodrama gave the abolitionist message a powerful human appeal.

ABOLITIONISM AND RACE

The first racially integrated social movement in American history and the first to give equal rights for blacks a central place in its political agenda, abolitionism was nonetheless a product of its time and place. Racism, as we have seen, was pervasive in nineteenth-century America, North as well as South. White abolitionists could not free themselves entirely from this prejudice. They monopolized the key decision-making posts, charged black spokesman Martin R. Delany, relegating blacks to "a mere secondary, underling position." By the 1840s, black abolitionists sought an independent role within the movement, regularly holding their own conventions. The black abolitionist Henry Highland Garnet, who as a child had escaped from slavery in Maryland with his father, proclaimed at one such gathering in 1843 that slaves should rise in rebellion to throw off their shackles. His position was so at odds with the prevailing belief in moral suasion that the published proceedings entirely omitted the speech. Not until 1848 did Garnet's speech appear in print, along with David Walker's *Appeal*, in a pamphlet partially financed by a then-obscure abolitionist named John Brown.

What is remarkable, however, is not that white abolitionists reflected the prejudices of their society, but the extent to which they managed to rise above them. "While the word 'white' is on the statute-book of Massachusetts," declared Edmund Quincy, an active associate of William Lloyd Garrison, "Massachusetts is a slave state." Defying overwhelming odds, abolitionists launched legal and political battles against racial discrimination in the North. They achieved occasional victories, such as the end of school segregation in Massachusetts in 1855. Not only did abolitionists struggle to overturn northern laws discriminating against blacks but they refused to compromise the principle that the slave was a moral being, created in the image of God. The abolitionist emblem—a portrait of a slave in chains coupled with the motto "Am I Not a Man and a Brother?"—challenged white Americans to face up to the reality that men and women no different from themselves were being held in bondage.

Most adamant in contending that the struggle against slavery required a redefinition of both freedom and Americanness were black members of the abolitionist crusade. Black abolitionists developed an understanding of freedom that went well beyond the usage of most of their white contemporaries. They worked to attack the intellectual foundations of racism, seeking to disprove pseudoscientific arguments for black inferiority. They challenged the prevailing image of Africa as a continent without civilization. Many black abolitionists called on free blacks to seek out skilled and dignified employment in order to demonstrate the race's capacity for advancement.

SLAVERY AND AMERICAN FREEDOM

At every opportunity, black abolitionists rejected the nation's pretensions as a land of liberty. Many free blacks dramatically reversed the common association of the United States with the progress of freedom. Black communities in the North devised an alternative calendar of "freedom celebrations" centered on January 1, the date in 1808 on which the slave trade became illegal, and August 1, the anniversary of West Indian emancipation, rather than July 4. (Many localities forcibly barred them from Independence Day festivities.) In doing so, they offered a stinging rebuke to white Americans' claims to live in a land of freedom. Thanks to its embrace of emancipation in the 1830s, declared a group of black abolitionists in Philadelphia, Britain had become a model of liberty and justice, while the United States remained a land of tyranny.

Even more persistently than their white counterparts, black abolitionists articulated the ideal of color-blind citizenship. "The real battleground between liberty and slavery," wrote Samuel Cornish, "is prejudice against color." (Cornish, a Presbyterian minister, had helped to establish the nation's first black newspaper, *Freedom's Journal*, in New York City in 1827. The first editor, John B. Russwurm, closed the paper after two years and moved to Liberia, explaining, "we consider it a waste of mere words to talk of ever enjoying citizenship in this country.") Black abolitionists also identified the widespread poverty of the free black population as a consequence of slavery and insisted that freedom possessed an economic dimension. It must be part of the "great work" of the antislavery crusade, insisted Charles L. Reason, "to abolish not only chattel slavery, but that other kind of slavery, which, for generation after generation, dooms an oppressed people to a condition of dependence and pauperism."

Am I Not a Man and a Brother? *The most common abolitionist depiction of a slave, this image not only presents African-Americans as unthreatening individuals seeking white assistance but also calls upon white Americans to recognize blacks as fellow men unjustly held in bondage.*

The greatest oration on American slavery and American freedom was delivered in Rochester in 1852 by Frederick Douglass. Speaking just after the annual Independence Day celebration, Douglass posed the question, "What, to the Slave, is the Fourth of July?" (see p. 481 and the Appendix for excerpts from the speech). He answered that Fourth of July festivities revealed the hypocrisy of a nation that proclaimed its belief in liberty yet daily committed "practices more shocking and bloody" than any other country on earth. Like other abolitionists, however, Douglass also laid claim to the founders' legacy. The Revolution had left a "rich inheritance of justice, liberty, prosperity, and independence," from which subsequent generations had tragically strayed. Only by abolishing slavery and freeing the "great doctrines" of the Declaration of Independence from the "narrow bounds" of race could the United States recapture its original mission.

GENTLEMEN OF PROPERTY AND STANDING

At first, abolitionism aroused violent hostility from northerners who feared that the movement threatened to disrupt the Union, interfere with profits wrested from slave labor, and overturn white supremacy. Led by "gentlemen of property and standing" (often merchants with close commercial ties to the South), mobs disrupted abolitionist meetings in northern cities. In 1835, a Boston crowd led William Lloyd Garrison through the streets with a rope around his neck. The editor barely escaped with his life. In the following year, a Cincinnati mob destroyed the printing press of James G. Birney, a former slaveholder who had been converted to abolitionism by Theodore Weld and had been forced to flee Kentucky for the North.

In 1837, antislavery editor Elijah P. Lovejoy became the movement's first martyr when he was killed by a mob in Alton, Illinois, while defending his

A New Method of Assorting the Mail, As Practised by Southern Slave-Holders, *an engraving criticizing the burning of abolitionist materials taken from the U.S. Post Office in Charleston in 1835.*

Destruction by Fire of Pennsylvania Hall, *a lithograph depicting the burning of the abolitionist meeting hall by a Philadelphia mob in 1838.*

press. A native of Maine and a Presbyterian minister, Lovejoy had begun his editorial career in the slave state of Missouri but had soon been forced to move to Illinois. His message, that "the system of Negro slavery is an awful evil and sin," won few converts in Alton, then the state's largest city, which enjoyed a flourishing trade with the South. Four times, mobs destroyed his printing press, only to see Lovejoy resume publication. The fifth attack ended in his death. In 1838, a mob in Philadelphia burned to the ground Pennsylvania Hall, which abolitionists had built to hold their meetings. Before starting the fire, however, the mob patriotically carried a portrait of George Washington to safety.

Elsewhere, crowds of southerners, with the unspoken approval of Andrew Jackson's postmaster general, Amos Kendall, burned abolitionist literature that they had removed from the mails. In 1836, when abolitionists began to flood Washington with petitions calling for emancipation in the nation's capital, the House of Representatives adopted the notorious "gag rule," which prohibited their consideration. The rule was repealed in 1844, thanks largely to the tireless opposition of former president John Quincy Adams, who since 1831 had represented Massachusetts in the House.

SLAVERY AND CIVIL LIBERTIES

Far from stemming the movement's growth, however, mob attacks and attempts to limit abolitionists' freedom of speech convinced many northerners that slavery was incompatible with the democratic liberties of white Americans. In a speech after Lovejoy's murder, Theodore Weld commented on the contrast between Americans' self-confident claims to freedom and the reality of anti-abolitionist violence: "The empty name is everywhere— *free* government, *free* men, *free* speech, *free* schools, and *free* churches. Hollow counterfeits all! . . . The substance has gone." It was the murder of Lovejoy that led Wendell Phillips, who became one of the movement's greatest orators, to associate himself with the abolitionist cause. "We commenced the present struggle," announced abolitionist William Jay, "to obtain the freedom of the slave; we are compelled to continue it to preserve our own. We are now contending . . . for the liberty of speech, of the press, and of conscience."

The abolitionist movement now broadened its appeal so as to win the support of northerners who cared little about the rights of blacks but could be convinced that slavery endangered their own cherished freedoms. The gag rule aroused considerable resentment in the North. "If the government once begins to discriminate as to what is orthodox and what heterodox in opinion," wrote the *New York Evening Post*, hardly a supporter of abolitionism, "farewell, a long farewell to our freedom."

For many years, the American public sphere excluded discussion of slavery. Tocqueville had noted that in a democracy, individual dissenters found it difficult to stand up against the overwhelming power of majority opinion. Americans valued free speech, he wrote, but he did "not know any country where, in general, less independence of mind and genuine freedom of discussion reign than in America." The fight for the right to debate slavery openly and without reprisal led abolitionists to elevate "free opinion"— freedom of speech and of the press and the right of petition—to a central place in what Garrison called the "gospel of freedom." In defending free speech, abolitionists claimed to have become custodians of the "rights of every freeman."

THE ORIGINS OF FEMINISM

THE RISE OF THE PUBLIC WOMAN

"When the true history of the antislavery cause shall be written," Frederick Douglass later recalled, "women will occupy a large space in its pages." Much of the movement's grassroots strength derived from northern women, who joined by the thousands. Most were evangelical Protestants, New England Congregationalists, or Quakers convinced, as Martha Higginson of Vermont wrote, that slavery was "a disgrace in this land of Christian light and liberty." A few became famous, but most antislavery women remain virtually unknown to history. One such activist was Lucy Colman, whose mother sang her antislavery songs when she was a child. Colman's career illustrated how the era's reform movements often overlapped. She became an abolitionist lecturer, a teacher at a school for blacks in upstate New York, an advocate of women's rights, and an opponent of capital punishment.

The public sphere was open to women in ways government and party politics were not. Long before they could vote, women circulated petitions, attended meetings, marched in parades, and delivered public lectures. They became active in the temperance movement, the building of asylums, and other reform activities. Dorothea Dix, a Massachusetts schoolteacher, for example, was the leading advocate of more humane treatment of the insane, who at the time generally were placed in jails alongside debtors and hardened criminals. Thanks to her efforts, twenty-eight states constructed

VISIONS OF FREEDOM

A Women's Rights Quilt. *Made by an unknown woman only a few years after the Seneca Falls Convention of 1848, this quilt embodies an unusual form of political expression. It includes scenes visualizing a woman engaged in various activities that violated the era's cult of domesticity, and it illustrates some of the demands of the early women's rights movement. The individual blocks show a woman driving her own buggy and a banner advocating "women's rights," another dressing to go out while her husband remains at home wearing an apron, and a third addressing a public meeting with a mixed male-female audience.*

QUESTIONS

1. Which aspects of freedom does the quiltmaker emphasize?

2. What aspects of women's rights are not depicted in the quilt?

The May Session of the Woman's Rights Convention, *a cartoon published in* Harper's Weekly, *June 11, 1859. A female orator addresses the audience of men and women, while hecklers in the balcony disrupt the proceedings.*

mental hospitals before the Civil War. In 1834, middle-class women in New York City organized the Female Moral Reform Society, which sought to redeem prostitutes from lives of sin and to protect the morality of single women. They attacked the era's sexual double standard by publishing lists of men who frequented prostitutes or abused women. By 1840, the society had been replicated in hundreds of American communities.

WOMEN AND FREE SPEECH

All these activities enabled women to carve out a place in the public sphere. But it was participation in abolitionism that inspired the early movement for women's rights. In working for the rights of the slave, not a few women developed a new understanding of their own subordinate social and legal status. The daughters of a prominent South Carolina slaveholder, Angelina and Sarah Grimké had been converted first to Quakerism and then abolitionism while visiting Philadelphia. During the 1830s, they began to deliver popular lectures that offered a scathing condemnation of slavery from the perspective of those who had witnessed its evils firsthand.

The Grimké sisters were neither the first women to lecture in public nor the first to be feverishly condemned by self-proclaimed guardians of female modesty. Frances Wright, a Scottish-born follower of reformer Robert Owen, spoke at New York's Hall of Science in the late 1820s and early 1830s, on subjects ranging from communitarianism to slavery, women's rights, and the plight of northern laborers. One New York newspaper called Wright a "female monster" for "shamefully obtruding herself upon the public." Maria Stewart, a black Bostonian, in 1832 became the first American woman to lecture to mixed male and female audiences. She, too, received intense criticism. "I have made myself contemptible in the eyes of many," Stewart wrote. "This is the land of freedom," she added, "and we claim our rights," including the right to speak in public.

Stewart left Boston in 1833 and rarely lectured again. The Grimké sisters, however, used the controversy over their speeches as a springboard for a vigorous argument against the idea that taking part in assemblies, demonstrations, and lectures was unfeminine. Outraged by the sight of females sacrificing all "modesty and delicacy" by appearing on the public lecture platform, a group of Massachusetts clergymen denounced the sisters. In reply, they forthrightly defended not only the right of women to take part in political debate but also their right to share the social and educational privileges enjoyed by men. "Since I engaged in the investigation of the rights of the slave," declared Angelina Grimké, "I have necessarily been led to a better understanding of my own." Her sister Sarah proceeded to publish *Letters on the Equality of the Sexes* (1838), a powerful call for equal rights for women and a critique of the notion of separate spheres. The book raised numerous issues familiar even today, including what later generations would call "equal pay for equal work." Why, Sarah Grimké wondered, did male teachers invariably receive higher wages than women, and a male tailor earn "two or three times as much" as a female counterpart "although the work done by each may be equally good?"

WOMEN'S RIGHTS

The Grimkés were the first to apply the abolitionist doctrine of universal freedom and equality to the status of women. When the prominent writer Catharine Beecher reprimanded the sisters for stepping outside "the domestic and social sphere," urging them to accept the fact that "heaven" had designated man "the superior" and woman "the subordinate," Angelina Grimké issued a stinging answer. "I know nothing," she wrote, "of men's rights and women's rights. My doctrine, then is, that whatever it is morally right for man to do, it is morally right for woman to do." Like their predecessors Frances Wright and Maria Stewart, the Grimké sisters soon retired from the fray, unwilling to endure the intense criticism to which they were subjected. But their writings helped to spark the movement for women's rights, which arose in the 1840s.

Elizabeth Cady Stanton and Lucretia Mott, the key organizers of the Seneca Falls Convention of 1848, were veterans of the antislavery crusade. In 1840, they had traveled to London as delegates to the World Anti-Slavery Convention, only to be barred from participating because of their sex. The Seneca Falls Convention, a gathering on behalf of women's rights held in the upstate New York town where Stanton lived, raised the issue of woman's suffrage for the first time. Stanton, the principal author, modeled the Seneca Falls Declaration of Sentiments on the Declaration of Independence (see the Appendix for the full text). But the document added "women" to Jefferson's axiom "all men are created equal," and in place of a list of injustices committed by George III, it condemned the "injuries and usurpations on the part of man toward woman." The first to be listed was denying her the right to vote. As Stanton told the convention, only the vote would make woman "free as man is free," since in a democratic society, freedom was impossible without access to the ballot. The argument was

VOICES OF FREEDOM

FROM ANGELINA GRIMKÉ,
Letter in *The Liberator* (August 2, 1837)

The daughters of a prominent South Carolina slaveholder, Angelina and Sarah Grimké became abolitionists after being sent to Philadelphia for education. In this article, Angelina Grimké explains how participation in the movement against slavery led her to a greater recognition of women's lack of basic freedoms.

Since I engaged in the investigation of the rights of the slave, I have necessarily been led to a better understanding of my own; for I have found the Anti-Slavery cause to be . . . the school in which human rights are more fully investigated, and better understood and taught, than in any other [reform] enterprise. . . . Here we are led to examine why human beings have any rights. It is because they are moral beings. . . . Now it naturally occurred to me, that if rights were founded in moral being, then the circumstance of sex could not give to man higher rights and responsibilities, than to woman. . . .

When I look at human beings as moral beings, all distinction in sex sinks to insignificance and nothingness; for I believe it regulates rights and responsibilities no more than the color of the skin or the eyes. My doctrine, then is, that whatever it is morally right for man to do, it is morally right for woman to do. . . . This regulation of duty by the mere circumstance of sex . . . has led to all that [numerous] train of evils flowing out of the anti-christian doctrine of masculine and feminine virtues. By this doctrine, man has been converted into the warrior, and clothed in sternness . . . whilst woman has been taught to lean upon an arm of flesh, to . . . be admired for her personal charms, and caressed and humored like a spoiled child, or converted into a mere drudge to suit the convenience of her lord and master. . . . It has robbed woman of . . . the right to think and speak and act on all great moral questions, just as men think and speak and act. . . .

The discussion of the wrongs of slavery has opened the way for the discussion of other rights, and the ultimate result will most certainly be . . . the letting of the oppressed of every grade and description go free.

FROM FREDERICK DOUGLASS,
Speech on July 5, 1852, Rochester, New York

One of the most prominent reform leaders of his era, Frederick Douglass escaped from slavery in 1838 and soon became an internationally known writer and orator against slavery. His speech of July 1852 condemned the hypocrisy of a nation that proclaimed its devotion to freedom while practicing slavery. It was reprinted in 1855 in his autobiography, *My Bondage and My Freedom.*

Fellow-citizens, pardon me, allow me to ask, why am I called upon to speak here to-day? What have I, or those I represent, to do with your national independence? Are the great principles of political freedom and of natural justice, embodied in that Declaration of Independence, extended to us? . . . Such is not the case. I say it with a sad sense of the disparity between us. I am not included within the pale of this glorious anniversary! Your high independence only reveals the immeasurable distance between us. . . . The rich inheritance of justice, liberty, prosperity and independence, bequeathed by your fathers, is shared by you, not by me. . . .

For the present, it is enough to affirm the equal manhood of the negro race. Is it not astonishing that, while we are ploughing, planting and reaping, using all kinds of mechanical tools, erecting houses, constructing bridges, building ships, . . . acting as clerks, merchants and secretaries . . . confessing and worshiping the Christian's God, and looking hopefully for life and immortality beyond the grave, we are called upon to prove that we are men! . . .

Would you have me argue that man is entitled to liberty? That he is the rightful owner of his body? You have already declared it. Must I argue the wrongfulness of slavery? . . . that men have a natural right to freedom? . . . To do so, would be to make myself ridiculous, and to offer an insult to your understanding. There is not a man beneath the canopy of heaven, that does not know that slavery is wrong *for him.* . . .

What, to the American slave, is your 4th of July? I answer: a day that reveals to him, more than all other days in the year, the gross injustice and cruelty to which he is the constant victim. To him, your celebration is a sham; your boasted liberty, an unholy license; your national greatness, swelling vanity; your sounds of rejoicing are empty and heartless; your denunciations of tyrants, brass fronted impudence; your shouts of liberty and equality, hollow mockery—a thin veil to cover up crimes that would disgrace a nation of savages. There is not a nation on the earth guilty of practices, more shocking and bloody, than are the people of these United States, at this very hour.

QUESTIONS

1. What consequences does Grimké believe follow from the idea of rights being founded in the individual's "moral being"?

2. How does Douglass turn the ideals proclaimed by white Americans into weapons against slavery?

3. What do these documents suggest about the language and arguments employed by abolitionists?

Portrait of feminist Margaret Fuller (1810–1850) from an undated daguerreotype.

simple and irrefutable: in the words of Lydia Maria Child, "either the theory of our government [the democratic principle that government rests on the will of the people] is *false*, or women have a right to vote."

Seneca Falls marked the beginning of the seventy-year struggle for woman's suffrage. The vote, however, was hardly the only issue raised at the convention. The Declaration of Sentiments condemned the entire structure of inequality that denied women access to education and employment, gave husbands control over the property and wages of their wives and custody of children in the event of divorce, deprived women of independent legal status after they married, and restricted them to the home as their "sphere of action." Equal rights became the rallying cry of the early movement for women's rights, and equal rights meant claiming access to all the prevailing definitions of freedom.

FEMINISM AND FREEDOM

Like abolitionism, temperance, and other reforms, women's rights was an international movement. Lacking broad backing at home, early feminists found allies abroad. "Women alone will say what freedom they want," declared an article in *The Free Woman*, a journal established in Paris in 1832. With their household chores diminished because of the availability of manufactured goods and domestic servants, many middle-class women chafed at the restrictions that made it impossible for them to gain an education, enter the professions, and in other ways exercise their talents. Whether married or not, early feminists insisted, women deserved the range of individual choices—the possibility of self-realization—that constituted the essence of freedom.

Women, wrote Margaret Fuller, had the same right as men to develop their talents, to "grow . . . to live freely and unimpeded." The daughter of a Jeffersonian congressman, Fuller was educated at home, at first under her father's supervision (she learned Latin before the age of six) and later on her own. She became part of New England's transcendentalist circle (discussed in Chapter 9) and from 1840 to 1842 edited *The Dial*, a magazine that reflected the group's views. In 1844, Fuller became literary editor of the *New York Tribune*, the first woman to achieve so important a position in American journalism.

In *Woman in the Nineteenth Century*, published in 1845, Fuller sought to apply to women the transcendentalist idea that freedom meant a quest for personal development. "Every path" to self-fulfillment, she insisted, should be "open to woman as freely as to man." Fuller singled out Abby Kelley as a "gentle hero" for continuing to speak in public despite being denounced by men for venturing "out of her sphere." Fearing that marriage to an American would inevitably mean subordination to male dictation, Fuller traveled to Europe as a correspondent for the *Tribune*. There she married an Italian patriot. Along with her husband and baby, she died in a shipwreck in 1850 while returning to the United States.

WOMEN AND WORK

Women also demanded the right to participate in the market revolution. At an 1851 women's rights convention, the black abolitionist Sojourner Truth

Woman's Emancipation, *a satirical engraving from* Harper's Monthly, *August 1851, illustrating the much-ridiculed "Bloomer" costume.*

insisted that the movement devote attention to the plight of poor and working-class women and repudiate the idea that women were too delicate to engage in work outside the home. Born a slave in New York State around 1799, Truth did not obtain her freedom until the state's emancipation law of 1827. A listener at her 1851 speech (which was not recorded at the time) later recalled that Truth had spoken of her years of hard physical labor, had flexed her arm to show her strength, and exclaimed, "and aren't I a woman?"

Although those who convened at Seneca Falls were predominantly from the middle class—no representatives of the growing number of "factory girls" and domestic servants took part—the participants rejected the identification of the home as the women's "sphere." Women, wrote Pauline Davis in 1853, "must go *to work*" to emancipate themselves from "bondage." During the 1850s, some feminists tried to popularize a new style of dress, devised by Amelia Bloomer, consisting of a loose-fitting tunic and trousers. In her autobiography, published in 1898, Elizabeth Cady Stanton recalled that women who adopted Bloomer's attire were ridiculed by the press and insulted by "crowds of boys in the streets." They found that "the physical freedom enjoyed did not compensate for the persistent persecution and petty annoyances suffered at every turn." The target of innumerable male jokes, the "bloomer" costume attempted to make a serious point—that the long dresses, tight corsets, and numerous petticoats considered to be appropriate female attire were so confining that they made it almost impossible for women to claim a place in the public sphere or to work outside the home.

In one sense, feminism demanded an expansion of the boundaries of freedom rather than a redefinition of the idea. Women, in the words of one reformer, should enjoy "the rights and liberties that every 'free white male citizen' takes to himself as God-given." But even as it sought to apply prevailing notions of freedom to women, the movement posed a fundamental challenge to some of society's central beliefs—that the capacity for independence and rationality were male traits, that the world was properly

Am I Not a Woman and a Sister?, *an illustration from* The Liberator, *1849. Identifying with the plight of the female slave enabled free women to see more clearly the inequalities they themselves faced.*

divided into public and private realms, and that issues of justice and freedom did not apply to relations within the family. In every realm of life, including the inner workings of the family, declared Elizabeth Cady Stanton, there could be "no happiness without freedom."

THE SLAVERY OF SEX

The dichotomy between freedom and slavery powerfully shaped early feminists' political language. Just as the idea of "wage slavery" enabled northern workers to challenge the inequalities inherent in market definitions of freedom, the concept of the "slavery of sex" empowered the women's movement to develop an all-encompassing critique of male authority and their own subordination. Feminists of the 1840s and 1850s pointed out that the law of marriage made nonsense of the description of the family as a "private" institution independent of public authority. When the abolitionists and women's rights activists Lucy Stone and Henry Blackwell married, they felt obliged to repudiate New York's laws that clothed the husband "with legal powers which . . . no man should possess."

Feminist abolitionists did not invent the analogy between marriage and slavery. The English writer Mary Wollstonecraft had invoked it as early as the 1790s in *A Vindication of the Rights of Woman* (discussed in Chapter 8). But the analogy between free women and slaves gained prominence as it was swept up in the accelerating debate over slavery. "Woman is a slave, from the cradle to the grave," asserted Ernestine Rose. "Father, guardian, husband—master still. One conveys her, like a piece of property, over to the other." For their part, southern defenders of slavery frequently linked slavery and marriage as natural and just forms of inequality. Eliminating the former institution, they charged, would threaten the latter.

Marriage was not, literally speaking, equivalent to slavery. The married woman, however, did not enjoy the fruits of her own labor—a central element of freedom. Beginning with Mississippi in 1839, numerous states enacted married women's property laws, shielding from a husband's creditors property brought into a marriage by his wife. Such laws initially aimed not to expand women's rights as much as to prevent families from losing their property during the depression that began in 1837. But in 1860, New York enacted a more far-reaching measure, allowing married women to sign contracts, buy and sell property, and keep their own wages. In most states, however, property accumulated after marriage, as well as wages earned by the wife, still belonged to the husband.

"SOCIAL FREEDOM"

Influenced by abolitionism, women's rights advocates turned another popular understanding of freedom—self-ownership, or control over one's own person—in an entirely new direction. The emphasis in abolitionist literature on the violation of the slave woman's body by her master helped to give the idea of self-ownership a concrete reality that encouraged application to free women as well. The law of domestic relations presupposed the husband's right of sexual access to his wife and to inflict corporal punishment on her. Courts proved reluctant to intervene in cases of physical abuse so long as it was not "extreme" or "intolerable." "Women's Rights," declared a Boston meeting in 1859, included "freedom and equal rights in the family." The demand that women should enjoy the rights to regulate their own sexual activity and procreation and to be protected by the state against violence at the hands of their husbands challenged the notion that claims for justice, freedom, and individual rights should stop at the household's door.

The issue of women's private freedom revealed underlying differences within the movement for women's rights. Belief in equality between the sexes and in the sexes' natural differences coexisted in antebellum feminist thought. Even as they entered the public sphere and thereby challenged some aspects of the era's "cult of domesticity" (discussed in Chapter 9), many early feminists accepted other elements. Allowing women a greater role in the public sphere, many female reformers argued, would bring their "inborn" maternal instincts to bear on public life, to the benefit of the entire society.

Even feminists critical of the existing institution of marriage generally refrained from raising in public the explosive issue of women's "private" freedom. The question frequently arose, however, in the correspondence of feminist leaders. "Social Freedom," Susan B. Anthony observed to Lucy Stone, "lies at the bottom of all—and until woman gets that, she must continue the slave of men in all other things." Women like Anthony, who never married, and Stone, who with her husband created their own definition of marriage, reflected the same dissatisfactions with traditional family life as the women who joined communitarian experiments. Not until the twentieth century would the demand that freedom be extended to intimate aspects of life inspire a mass movement. But the dramatic fall in the birthrate over the course of the nineteenth century suggests that many women were quietly exercising "personal freedom" in their most intimate relationships.

THE ABOLITIONIST SCHISM

Even in reform circles, the demand for a greater public role for women remained extremely controversial. Massachusetts physician Samuel Gridley Howe pioneered humane treatment of the blind and educational reform, and he was an ardent abolitionist. But Howe did not support his wife's participation in the movement for female suffrage, which, he complained, caused her to "neglect domestic relations." When organized abolitionism split into two wings in 1840, the immediate cause was a dispute over the proper role of women in antislavery work. Abby Kelley's appointment to the business committee of the American Anti-Slavery Society sparked the formation of a rival abolitionist organization, the American and Foreign Anti-Slavery Society, which believed it wrong for a woman to occupy so prominent a position. The antislavery poet John Greenleaf Whittier compared Kelley to Eve, Delilah, and Helen of Troy, women who had sown the seeds of male destruction.

Behind the split lay the fear among some abolitionists that Garrison's radicalism on issues like women's rights, as well as his refusal to support the idea of abolitionists voting or running for public office, impeded the movement's growth. Determined to make abolitionism a political movement, the seceders formed the Liberty Party, which nominated

This image appeared on the cover of the sheet music for "Get Off the Track!", a song popularized by the Hutchinson singers, who performed antislavery songs. The trains Immediate Emancipation *(with* The Liberator *as its front wheel) and* Liberty Party *pull into a railroad station. The* Herald of Freedom *and* American Standard *were antislavery newspapers. The song's lyrics praised William Lloyd Garrison and criticized various politicians, among them Henry Clay. The chorus went: "Roll it along! Through the nation / Freedom's car, Emancipation."*

James G. Birney as its candidate for president. He received only 7,000 votes (about one-third of 1 percent of the total). In 1840, antislavery northerners saw little wisdom in "throwing away" their ballots on a third-party candidate.

While the achievement of most of their demands lay far in the future, the women's rights movement succeeded in making "the woman question" a permanent part of the transatlantic discussion of social reform. As for abolitionism, although it remained a significant presence in northern public life until emancipation was achieved, by 1840 the movement had accomplished its most important work. More than 1,000 local antislavery societies were now scattered throughout the North, representing a broad constituency awakened to the moral issue of slavery. The "great duty of freedom," Ralph Waldo Emerson had declared in 1837, was "to open our halls to discussion of this question." The abolitionists' greatest achievement lay in shattering the conspiracy of silence that had sought to preserve national unity by suppressing public debate over slavery.

SUGGESTED READING

BOOKS

Bestor, Arthur E. *Backwoods Utopias: The Sectarian and Owenite Phases of Communitarian Socialism in America* (1948). An account of some of the numerous communitarian experiments in pre–Civil War America.

Boylan, Anne M. *The Origins of Women's Activism: New York and Boston, 1797–1840* (2002). Considers how middle-class urban women organized numerous associations for social improvement and thereby gained a place in the public sphere.

Burin, Eric. *Slavery and the Peculiar Solution: A History of the American Colonization Society* (2005). A history of the movement to send black Americans, free and slave, to Africa.

Bushman, Claudia L. and Richard L. Bushman. *Building the Kingdom: A History of Mormons in America* (2001). A survey of the history of American Mormons.

Goodman, Paul. *Of One Blood: Abolitionists and the Origins of Racial Equality* (1998). Explores the origins of racial egalitarianism in the movement against slavery.

Harding, Vincent. *There Is a River: The Black Struggle for Freedom in America* (1981). A study that links slave resistance and black abolitionism as phases of a common struggle for freedom.

Jeffrey, Julie R. *The Great Silent Army of Abolitionism: Ordinary Women in the Antislavery Movement* (1998). The role of women as the grassroots foot soldiers of the abolitionist movement.

Kaestle, Carl F. *Pillars of the Republic: Common Schools and American Society, 1780–1860* (1983). Surveys the movement to introduce free public education in the United States.

Kraditor, Aileen S. *Means and Ends in American Abolitionism* (1969). An influential discussion of the political strategies of Garrisonian abolitionists.

McGreevy, John T. *Catholicism and American Freedom* (2003). Contains an illuminating discussion of how Catholics responded to Protestant-based reform movements.

Nye, Russell B. *Fettered Freedom: Civil Liberties and the Slavery Controversy, 1830–1860* (1949). Examines the impact of mob activities and other violations of civil liberties on the growth of abolitionism.

Rothman, David J. *The Discovery of the Asylum: Social Order and Disorder in the New Republic* (1971). Relates the rise of prisons, orphanages, and asylums and their common characteristics.

Stewart, James B. *Holy Warriors: The Abolitionists and American Slavery* (rev. ed., 1996). A recent survey of the history of the antislavery movement.

Tyrrell, Ian. *Sobering Up: From Temperance to Prohibition in Antebellum America, 1800–1860* (1979). Traces the movement against the sale and use of liquor and how it changed in the first part of the nineteenth century.

WEBSITES

Samuel J. May Anti-Slavery Collection: http://dlxs.library.cornell.edu/m/mayanti slavery/

Women and Social Movements in the United States, 1600–2000: http://asp6new .alexanderstreet.com/wam2/wam2.index.map.aspx

REVIEW QUESTIONS

1. To what degree was antebellum reform international in scope?

2. What were the aims of prisons, asylums, and other institutions in this period of social change?

3. Why did Horace Mann believe that universal public education would return both equality and stability to a society fractured by the market revolution?

4. Why did so many prominent Americans, from both the North and South, support the colonization of freed slaves?

5. What was the strategy of "moral suasion" and why did most early abolitionists advocate this policy? How successful was it?

6. How was racism evident even in the abolitionist movement, and what steps did some abolitionists take to fight racism in American society?

7. How could antebellum women participate in the public sphere even though they were excluded from government and politics?

8. How did women's participation in the abolitionist movement enable them to raise issues of their own natural rights and freedoms?

9. How did the feminism of this period challenge traditional gender beliefs and social structures?

FREEDOM QUESTIONS

1. What freedoms did the Shakers and Mormons seek for their members?

2. Compare the limitations to freedom for slaves and white women in this period.

3. How did the physical and legal assaults on abolitionists become perceived as attacks on the liberties of all white Americans in the North?

4. How did the abolitionist movement promote the idea of freedom as universal, and thus alter the national definition of liberty?

5. Some reformers believed that government power could be a force for freedom. Other groups saw the reform movements as attacks on freedom and the community. Explain both views.

KEY TERMS

utopian communities (p. 456)

polygamy (p. 458)

secular communitarian (p. 459)

"perfectionism" (p. 461)

temperance movement (p. 461)

self-discipline (p. 462)

common school (p. 464)

public education (p. 464)

American Colonization Society
(p. 465)

American Anti-Slavery Society
(p. 468)

"moral suasion" (p. 469)

Uncle Tom's Cabin (p. 471)

"Am I Not a Man and a Brother?"
(p. 473)

"gentlemen of property and
standing" (p. 474)

gag rule (p. 476)

Dorothea Dix (p. 476)

woman suffrage (p. 479)

Woman in the Nineteenth Century
(p. 482)

Liberty Party (p. 485)

REVIEW TABLE

Reform Organizations

Society	Date	Purpose
American Colonization Society	1816	To promote the gradual abolition of slavery and the settlement of black Americans in Africa
American Temperance Society	1826	To redeem all drinkers
American Anti-Slavery Society	1833	To abolish slavery immediately
Female Moral Reform Society	1834	To redeem prostitutes from lives of sin and protect the morality of single women

CHAPTER 13

A House Divided, 1840–1861

Abraham Lincoln's nickname, "The Railsplitter," recalled his humble origins. An unknown artist created this larger-than-life portrait. The White House is visible in the distance. The painting is said to have been displayed during campaign rallies in 1860.

FOCUS QUESTIONS

- What were the major factors contributing to U.S. territorial expansion in the 1840s?

- Why did the expansion of slavery become the most divisive political issue in the 1840s and 1850s?

- What combination of issues and events fueled the creation of the Republican Party in the 1850s?

- What enabled Lincoln to emerge as president from the divisive party politics of the 1850s?

- What were the final steps on the road to secession?

In 1855, Thomas Crawford, one of the era's most prominent American sculptors, was asked to design a statue to adorn the Capitol's dome, still under construction in Washington, D.C. He proposed a statue of Freedom, a female figure wearing a liberty cap. Secretary of War Jefferson Davis of Mississippi, one of the country's largest slaveholders, objected to Crawford's plan. A familiar symbol in the colonial era, the liberty cap had fallen into disfavor among some Americans after becoming closely identified with the French Revolution. Davis's disapproval, however, rested on other grounds. Ancient Romans, he noted, regarded the cap as "the badge of the freed slave." Its use, he feared, might suggest that there was a connection between the slaves' longing for freedom and the liberty of free-born Americans. Davis ordered the liberty cap replaced with a less controversial military symbol, a feathered helmet.

Crawford died in Italy, where he had spent most of his career, in 1857. Two years later, the colossal Statue of Freedom, which weighed 15,000 pounds, was transported to the United States in several pieces and assembled at a Maryland foundry under the direction of Philip Reed, a slave craftsman. In 1863, it was installed atop the Capitol, where it can still be seen today. By the time it was put in place, the country was immersed in the Civil War and Jefferson Davis had become president of the Confederate States of America. The dispute over the Statue of Freedom

The original and final designs for Thomas Crawford's Statue of Freedom *for the dome of the Capitol building. Secretary of War Jefferson Davis of Mississippi insisted that the liberty cap in the first design, a symbol of the emancipated slave in ancient Rome, be replaced.*

offers a small illustration of how, by the mid-1850s, nearly every public question was being swept up into the gathering storm over slavery.

FRUITS OF MANIFEST DESTINY

CONTINENTAL EXPANSION

In the 1840s, slavery moved to the center stage of American politics. It did so not in the moral language or with the immediatist program of abolitionism, but as a result of the nation's territorial expansion. By 1840, with the completion of Indian removal, virtually all the land east of the Mississippi River was in white hands. The depression that began in 1837 sparked a large migration of settlers further west. Some headed to Oregon, whose Willamette Valley was reputed to be one of the continent's most beautiful and fertile regions. Until the 1840s, the American presence in the area had been limited to a few fur traders and explorers. But between 1840 and 1845, some 5,000 emigrants made the difficult 2,000-mile journey by wagon train to Oregon from jumping-off places on the banks of the Missouri River. By 1860, nearly 300,000 men, women, and children had braved disease, starvation, the natural barrier of the Rocky Mountains, and occasional Indian attacks to travel overland to Oregon and California.

During most of the 1840s, the United States and Great Britain jointly administered Oregon, and Utah was part of Mexico. This did not stop Americans from settling in either region. National boundaries meant little to those who moved west. The 1840s witnessed an intensification of the old belief that God intended the American nation to reach all the way to the Pacific Ocean. As noted in Chapter 9, the term that became a shorthand for this expansionist spirit was "manifest destiny."

A rare photograph of wagons on their way to Oregon during the 1840s.

VISIONS OF FREEDOM

American Progress. *This 1872 painting by John Gast, commissioned by the author of a travel guide to the Pacific coast, reflects the ebullient spirit of manifest destiny. A female figure descended from earlier representations of the goddess of liberty wears the star of empire and leads the movement westward while Indians retreat before her. Symbols of civilization abound: the eastern city in the upper right corner, railroads, fenced animals, stagecoaches, and telegraph wires and a "school book" held by the central figure.*

QUESTIONS

1. How does Gast explain the conquest of the West by white Americans?

2. What elements of Indian–white relations does the artist leave out?

THE MEXICAN FRONTIER: NEW MEXICO AND CALIFORNIA

Settlement of Oregon did not directly raise the issue of slavery. But the nation's acquisition of part of Mexico did. When Mexico achieved its independence from Spain in 1821 it was nearly as large as the United States and its population of 6.5 million was about two-thirds that of its northern neighbor. Mexico's northern provinces—California, New Mexico, and Texas—however, were isolated and sparsely settled outposts surrounded by Indian country. New Mexico's population at the time of Mexican independence consisted of around 30,000 persons of Spanish origin, 10,000 Pueblo Indians, and an indeterminate number of "wild" Indians—nomadic bands of Apaches, Comanches, Navajos, and Utes. With the opening in 1821 of the Santa Fe Trail linking that city with Independence, Missouri, New Mexico's commerce with the United States eclipsed trade with the rest of Mexico.

California's non-Indian population in 1821, some 3,200 missionaries, soldiers, and settlers, was vastly outnumbered by about 20,000 Indians living and working on land owned by religious missions and by 150,000 members of unsubdued tribes in the interior. In 1834, in the hope of reducing the power of the Catholic Church and attracting Mexican and foreign settlers to California, the Mexican government dissolved the great mission landholdings and emancipated Indians working for the friars. Most of the land ended up in the hands of a new class of Mexican cattle ranchers, the *Californios*, who defined their own identity in large measure against the surrounding Indian population. *Californios* referred to themselves as *gente de razón* (people capable of reason) as opposed to the *indios*, whom they called *gente sin razón* (people without reason). For the "common good," Indians were required to continue to work for the new landholders.

A watercolor of a scene on a ranch near Monterey, California, in 1849 depicts Californios *supervising the work of Native Americans.*

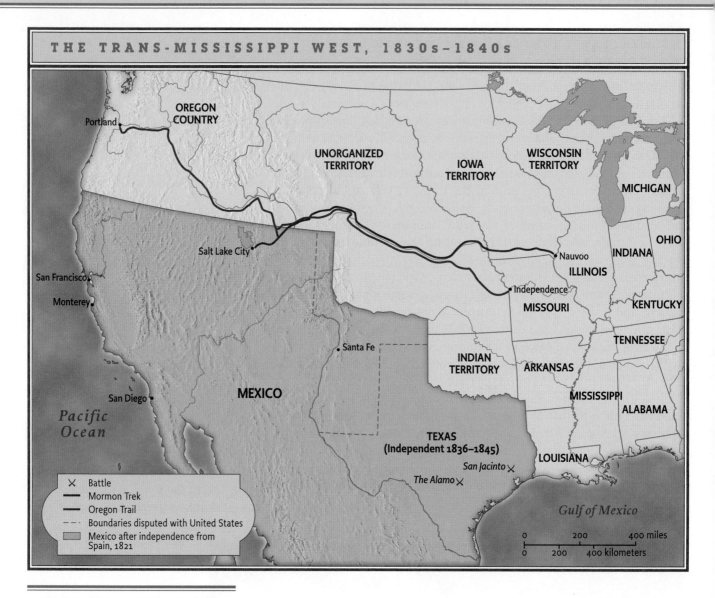

THE TRANS-MISSISSIPPI WEST, 1830s–1840s

Westward migration in the early and mid-1840s took American settlers across Indian country into the Oregon Territory, ownership of which was disputed with Great Britain. The Mormons migrated west to Salt Lake City, then part of Mexico.

By 1840, California was already linked commercially with the United States. New England ships were trading with the region, as illustrated in Richard Henry Dana's popular novel *Two Years before the Mast* (1840), an account of a young man's voyage to California and his experiences there. California also attracted a small number of American newcomers. In 1846, Alfred Robinson, who had moved from Boston, published *Life in California*. "In this age of annexation," he wondered, "why not extend the 'area of freedom' by the annexation of California?"

THE TEXAS REVOLT

The first part of Mexico to be settled by significant numbers of Americans was Texas, whose non-Indian population of Spanish origin (called *Tejanos*) numbered only about 2,000 when Mexico became independent. In order to develop the region, the Mexican government accepted an offer by Moses Austin, a Connecticut-born farmer, to colonize it with Americans. In 1820, Austin received a large land grant. He died soon afterward and his son

Stephen continued the plan, reselling land in smaller plots to American settlers at twelve cents per acre. By 1830, the population of American origin had reached around 7,000, considerably exceeding the number of *Tejanos.*

Alarmed that its grip on the area was weakening, the Mexican government in 1830 annulled existing land contracts and barred future emigration from the United States. Led by Stephen Austin, American settlers demanded greater autonomy within Mexico. Part of the area's tiny *Tejano* elite joined them. Mostly ranchers and large farmers, they had welcomed the economic boom that accompanied the settlers and had formed economic alliances with American traders. The issue of slavery further exacerbated matters. Mexico had abolished slavery, but local authorities allowed American settlers to bring slaves with them. When Mexico's ruler, General Antonio López de Santa Anna, sent an army in 1835 to impose central authority, a local committee charged that his purpose was "to give liberty to our slaves and make slaves of ourselves."

The appearance of Santa Anna's army sparked a chaotic revolt in Texas. The rebels formed a provisional government that soon called for Texan independence. On March 13, 1836, Santa Anna's army stormed the Alamo, a mission compound in San Antonio, killing its 187 American and *Tejano* defenders. "Remember the Alamo" became the Texans' rallying cry. In April, forces under Sam Houston, a former governor of Tennessee, routed Santa Anna's army at the Battle of San Jacinto and forced him to recognize Texan independence. Houston was soon elected the first president of the Republic of Texas. In 1837, the Texas Congress called for union with the United States. But fearing the political disputes certain to result from an attempt to add another slave state to the Union, Presidents Andrew Jackson and Martin Van

A flag carried at the Battle of San Jacinto during the Texas revolt of 1836 portrays a female figure displaying the rallying cry "Liberty or Death."

The plaza in San Antonio not long after the United States annexed Texas in 1845.

Buren shelved the question. Settlers from the United States nonetheless poured into the region, many of them slaveowners taking up fertile cotton land. By 1845, the population of Texas had reached nearly 150,000.

THE ELECTION OF 1844

Texas annexation remained on the political back burner until President John Tyler revived it in the hope of rescuing his failed administration and securing southern support for renomination in 1844. In April 1844, a letter by John C. Calhoun, whom Tyler had appointed secretary of state, was leaked to the press. It linked the idea of absorbing Texas directly to the goal of strengthening slavery in the United States. Some southern leaders, indeed, hoped that Texas could be divided into several states, thus further enhancing the South's power in Congress. Late that month, Henry Clay and former president Van Buren, the prospective Whig and Democratic candidates for president and two of the party system's most venerable leaders, met at Clay's Kentucky plantation. They agreed to issue letters rejecting immediate annexation on the grounds that it might provoke war with Mexico. Clay and Van Buren were reacting to the slavery issue in the traditional manner—by trying to keep it out of national politics.

Clay went on to receive the Whig nomination, but for Van Buren the letters proved to be a disaster. At the Democratic convention, southerners bent on annexation deserted Van Buren's cause, and he failed to receive the two-thirds majority necessary for nomination. The delegates then turned to the little-known James K. Polk, a former governor of Tennessee whose main assets were his support for annexation and his close association with Andrew Jackson, still the party's most popular figure. Like nearly all the presidents before him, Polk was a slaveholder. He owned substantial cotton plantations in Tennessee and Mississippi, where conditions were so brutal that only half of the slave children lived to the age of fifteen, and adults frequently ran away. To soothe injured feelings among northern Democrats over the rejection of Van Buren, the party platform called not only for the "reannexation" of Texas (implying that Texas had been part of the Louisiana Purchase and therefore once belonged to the United States) but also the "reoccupation" of all of Oregon. "Fifty-four forty or fight"—American control of Oregon all the way to its northern boundary at north latitude 54°40′—became a popular campaign slogan. But the bitterness of the northern Van Burenites over what they considered to be a betrayal on the part of the South would affect American politics for years to come.

Polk was the first "dark horse" candidate for president—that is, one whose nomination was completely unexpected. In the fall, he defeated Clay in an extremely close election. Polk's margin in the popular vote was less than 2 percent. Had not James G. Birney, running again as the Liberty Party candidate, received 16,000 votes in New York, mostly from antislavery Whigs, Clay would have been elected. In March 1845, only days before Polk's inauguration, Congress declared Texas part of the United States.

THE ROAD TO WAR

James K. Polk may have been virtually unknown, but he assumed the presidency with a clearly defined set of goals: to reduce the tariff, reestablish the independent Treasury system, settle the dispute over ownership of Oregon, and bring California into the Union. Congress soon enacted the first two goals, and the third was accomplished in an agreement with Great Britain dividing Oregon at the forty-ninth parallel. Many northerners were bitterly disappointed by this compromise, considering it a betrayal of Polk's campaign promise not to give up any part of Oregon without a fight. But the president secured his main objectives, the Willamette Valley and the magnificent harbor of Puget Sound.

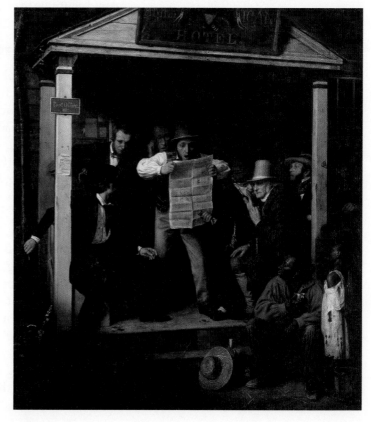

War News from Mexico, *an 1848 painting by Richard C. Woodville, shows how Americans received war news through the popular press.*

Acquiring California proved more difficult. Polk dispatched an emissary to Mexico offering to purchase the region, but the Mexican government refused to negotiate. By the spring of 1846, Polk was planning for military action. In April, American soldiers under Zachary Taylor moved into the region between the Nueces River and the Rio Grande, land claimed by both countries on the disputed border between Texas and Mexico. This action made conflict with Mexican forces inevitable. When fighting broke out, Polk claimed that the Mexicans had "shed blood upon American soil" and called for a declaration of war.

THE WAR AND ITS CRITICS

The Mexican War was the first American conflict to be fought primarily on foreign soil and the first in which American troops occupied a foreign capital. Inspired by the expansionist fervor of manifest destiny, a majority of Americans supported the war. They were convinced, as Herman Melville put it in his novel *White-Jacket* (1850), that since Americans "bear the ark of Liberties" for all mankind, "national selfishness is unbounded philanthropy . . . to the world." But a significant minority in the North dissented, fearing that far from expanding the "great empire of liberty," the administration's real aim was to acquire new land for the expansion of slavery. Ulysses S. Grant, who served with distinction in Mexico, later called the war "one of the most unjust ever waged by a stronger nation against a weaker nation," an indication that the United States was beginning to behave like "European monarchies," not a democratic republic. Henry David Thoreau was jailed in Massachusetts in 1846 for refusing to pay taxes as a protest against the war. Defending his action, Thoreau wrote an important essay, "On Civil Disobedience," which inspired such later advocates of nonviolent resistance to unjust laws as Martin Luther King Jr. "Under a government which imprisons any unjustly," wrote Thoreau, "the true place of a just man is also a prison."

Among the war's critics was Abraham Lincoln, who had been elected to Congress in 1846 from Illinois. Like many Whigs, Lincoln questioned whether the Mexicans had actually inflicted casualties on American soil, as Polk claimed, and in 1847 he introduced a resolution asking the president to specify the precise "spot" where blood had first been shed. But Lincoln was also disturbed by Polk's claiming the right to initiate an invasion of Mexico. "Allow the president to invade a neighboring country whenever he shall deem it necessary to repel an invasion," he declared, "and you allow him to make war at pleasure. . . . If today he should choose to say he thinks it necessary to invade Canada to prevent the British from invading us, how could you stop him?" Lincoln's stance proved unpopular in Illinois. He had already agreed to serve only one term in Congress, but when Democrats captured his seat in 1848, many blamed the result on Lincoln's criticism of the war. But the concerns he raised regarding the president's power to "make war at pleasure" would continue to echo in the twentieth and twenty-first centuries.

COMBAT IN MEXICO

More than 60,000 volunteers enlisted and did most of the fighting. Combat took place on three fronts. In June 1846, a band of American insurrectionists proclaimed California freed from Mexican control and named Captain John C. Frémont, head of a small scientific expedition in the West, its ruler. Their aim was California's incorporation into the United States, but for the moment they adopted a flag depicting a large bear as the symbol of the area's independence. A month later, the U.S. Navy sailed into Monterey and San Francisco Harbors, raised the American flag, and put an end to the "bear flag republic." At almost the same time, 1,600 American troops under General Stephen W. Kearney occupied Sante Fe without resistance and then set out for southern California, where they helped to put down a Mexican uprising against American rule.

The bulk of the fighting occurred in central Mexico. In February 1847, Taylor defeated Santa Anna's army at the Battle of Buena Vista. When the Mexican government still refused to negotiate, Polk ordered American forces under Winfield Scott to march inland from the port of Vera Cruz toward Mexico City. Scott's forces routed Mexican defenders and in September occupied the country's capital. In February 1848, the two governments agreed to the Treaty of Guadalupe Hidalgo, which confirmed the annexation of Texas and ceded California and present-day New Mexico,

THE MEXICAN WAR, 1846–1848

The Mexican War was the first in which an American army invaded another country and occupied its capital. As a result of the war, the United States acquired a vast new area in the modern-day Southwest.

Arizona, Nevada, and Utah to the United States. In exchange, the United States paid Mexico $15 million. The Mexican Cession, as the land annexed from Mexico was called, established the present territorial boundaries on the North American continent except for the Gadsden Purchase, a parcel of additional land bought from Mexico in 1853, and Alaska, acquired from Russia in 1867.

The Mexican War is only a footnote in most Americans' historical memory. Unlike other wars, few public monuments celebrate the conflict. Mexicans, however, regard the war (or "the dismemberment," as it is called in that country) as a central event of their national history and a source of continued resentment over a century and a half after it was fought. As the

A map of the United States from 1848 reveals how the size of the country had grown during the past four years: Texas (its western boundary still unfixed) had been annexed in 1845; the dispute with Great Britain over Oregon was settled in 1846; and the Mexican Cession—the area of present-day Arizona, New Mexico, Utah, Nevada, and California—was added in 1848 at the end of the Mexican War.

Mexican negotiators of 1848 complained, it was unprecedented to launch a war because a country refused to sell part of its territory to a neighbor.

RACE AND MANIFEST DESTINY

With the end of the Mexican War, the United States absorbed half a million square miles of Mexico's territory, one-third of that nation's total area. A region that for centuries had been united was suddenly split in two, dividing families and severing trade routes. An estimated 75,000 to 100,000 Spanish-speaking Mexicans and more than 150,000 Indians inhabited the Mexican Cession. The Treaty of Guadalupe Hidalgo guaranteed to "male citizens" of the area "the free enjoyment of their liberty and property" and "all the rights" of Americans—a provision designed to protect the property of large Mexican landowners in California. As to Indians whose homelands and hunting grounds suddenly became part of the United States, the treaty referred to them only as "savage tribes" whom the United States must prevent from launching incursions into Mexico across the new border.

The spirit of manifest destiny gave a new stridency to ideas about racial superiority. During the 1840s, territorial expansion came to be seen as proof of the innate superiority of the "Anglo-Saxon race" (a mythical construct defined largely by its opposites: blacks, Indians, Hispanics, and Catholics). "*Race*," declared John L. O'Sullivan's *Democratic Review*, was the "key" to the "history of nations" and the rise and fall of empires.

"Race" in the mid-nineteenth century was an amorphous notion involving color, culture, national origin, class, and religion. Newspapers, magazines, and scholarly works popularized the link between American freedom and the supposedly innate liberty-loving qualities of Anglo-Saxon Protestants. The annexation of Texas and conquest of much of Mexico became triumphs of civilization, progress, and liberty over the tyranny of the Catholic Church and the innate incapacity of "mongrel races." Indeed, calls by some expansionists for the United States to annex all of Mexico failed in part because of fear that the nation could not assimilate its large non-white Catholic population, supposedly unfit for citizenship in a republic.

REDEFINING RACE

The imposition of the American system of race relations proved detrimental to many inhabitants of the newly acquired territories. Texas had already demonstrated as much. Mexico had abolished slavery and declared persons of Spanish, Indian, and African origin equal before the law. The Texas constitution adopted after independence not only included protections for slavery but also denied civil rights to Indians and persons of African origin. Only whites were permitted to purchase land, and the entrance of free blacks into the state was prohibited altogether. "Every privilege dear to a free man is taken away," one free black resident of Texas complained.

Local circumstances affected racial definitions in the former Mexican territories. Texas defined "Spanish" Mexicans, especially those who occupied important social positions, as white. The residents of New Mexico of both Mexican and Indian origin, on the other hand, were long deemed "too Mexican" for democratic self-government. With white migration lagging, Congress did not allow New Mexico to become a state until 1912.

GOLD-RUSH CALIFORNIA

California had a non-Indian population of less than 15,000 when the Mexican War ended. For most of the 1840s, ten times as many Americans emigrated to Oregon as to California. But this changed dramatically after January 1848, when gold was discovered in the foothills of the Sierra Nevada Mountains at a sawmill owned by the Swiss immigrant Johann A. Sutter. A mania for gold spread throughout the world, fanned by newspaper accounts of instant wealth acquired by early migrants. By ship and land, newcomers poured into California. The non-Indian population rose to 200,000 by 1852 and more than 360,000 eight years later.

California's gold-rush population was incredibly diverse. Experienced miners flooded in from Mexico and South America. Tens of thousands of Americans who had never seen a mine arrived from the East, and from overseas came Irish, Germans, Italians, and Australians. Nearly

The gold rush brought thousands of fortune seekers, from nearly every corner of the globe, to California.

A contemporary depiction of mining operations during the California gold rush shows Native Americans, Mexicans, and numerous other miners all searching for gold.

25,000 Chinese landed between 1849 and 1852, almost all of them young men who had signed long-term labor contracts with Chinese merchants, who in turn leased them to mining and railroad companies and other employers. San Francisco, a town of 1,000 in 1848, became the gateway to the *El Dorado* of northern California. By 1850, it had 30,000 residents and had become perhaps the world's most racially and ethnically diverse city. Unlike farming frontiers settled by families, most of the gold-rush migrants were young men. Women played many roles in western mining communities, running restaurants and boardinghouses and working as laundresses, cooks, and prostitutes. But as late as 1860, California's male population outnumbered females by nearly three to one.

CALIFORNIA AND THE BOUNDARIES OF FREEDOM

As early surface mines quickly became exhausted, they gave way to underground mining that required a large investment of capital. This economic development worsened conflicts among California's many racial and ethnic groups engaged in fierce competition for gold. The law was very fragile in gold-rush California. In 1851 and 1856, "committees of vigilance" took control of San Francisco, sweeping aside established courts to try and execute those accused of crimes. White miners organized extralegal groups that expelled "foreign miners"—Mexicans, Chileans, Chinese, French, and American Indians—from areas with gold. The state legislature imposed a tax of twenty dollars per month on foreign miners, driving many of them from the state.

California would long remain in the American imagination a place of infinite opportunity, where newcomers could start their lives anew. But the boundaries of freedom there were tightly drawn. The state constitution of 1850 limited voting and the right to testify in court to whites, excluding Indians, Asians, and the state's few blacks (who numbered only 962 persons). California landowners who claimed Spanish descent or had intermarried with American settlers were deemed to be white. But with land titles derived from Mexican days challenged in court, many sold out to newcomers from the East.

For California's Indians, the gold rush and absorption into the United States proved to be disastrous. Gold seekers overran Indian communities. Miners, ranchers, and vigilantes murdered thousands of Indians. Determined to reduce the native population, state officials paid millions in bounties to private militias that launched attacks on the state's Indians. Although California was a free state, thousands of Indian children, declared orphans or vagrants by local courts, were bought and sold as slaves. By 1860, California's Indian population, nearly 150,000 when the Mexican War ended, had been reduced to around 30,000.

THE OTHER GOLD RUSH

In a remarkable coincidence, the California gold rush took place almost simultaneously with another located halfway around the world. In 1851, gold was discovered in Australia, then a collection of British colonies. During the 1850s, California and Australia together produced 80 percent of the world's gold. Like California, Australia attracted gold-seekers from across the globe. The population of Victoria, the colony where gold was found, grew from 77,000 in 1851 to 411,000 six years later. Like San Francisco, the Australian city of Melbourne rose to prominence on the basis of its proximity to the gold fields.

As in California, the gold rush was a disaster for the aboriginal peoples (as native Australians are called), whose population, already declining, fell precipitously. In Australia, like California, significant numbers of Chinese miners took part in the gold rush, only to face persistent efforts by miners of European origin to drive them from the fields. Indeed, Australians frequently modeled anti-Chinese legislation—especially their tax on foreign miners—on measures that had been pioneered in California.

OPENING JAPAN

The Mexican War ended with the United States in possession of the magnificent harbors of San Diego and San Francisco, long seen as jumping off points for trade with the Far East. In the 1850s, the United States took the lead in opening Japan, a country that had closed itself to nearly all foreign contact for more than two centuries. In 1853 and 1854, American warships under the command of Commodore Matthew Perry (the younger brother of Oliver Perry, a hero of the War of 1812) sailed into Tokyo Harbor. Perry, who had been sent by President Millard Fillmore to negotiate a trade treaty, demanded that the Japanese deal with him. Alarmed by European intrusions into China and impressed by Perry's armaments as well as a musical pageant he presented that included a blackface minstrel show, Japanese leaders agreed to do so. In 1854, they opened two ports to American shipping. Two years later, Townsend Harris, a mer-

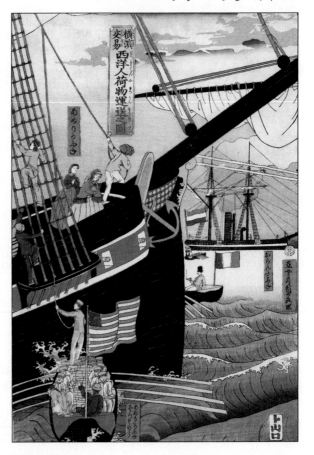

Transportation of Cargo by Westerners at the Port of Yokohama, 1861, by the Japanese artist Utagawa Sadahide, depicts ships in port, including an American one on the left, eight years after Commodore Perry's first voyage to Japan.

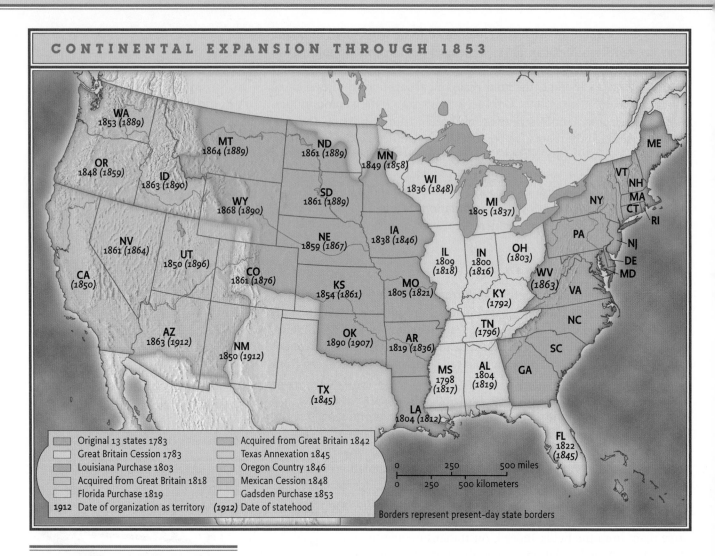

CONTINENTAL EXPANSION THROUGH 1853

Legend:
- Original 13 states 1783
- Great Britain Cession 1783
- Louisiana Purchase 1803
- Acquired from Great Britain 1818
- Florida Purchase 1819
- Acquired from Great Britain 1842
- Texas Annexation 1845
- Oregon Country 1846
- Mexican Cession 1848
- Gadsden Purchase 1853
- **1912** Date of organization as territory   **(1912)** Date of statehood

Borders represent present-day state borders

By 1853, with the Gadsden Purchase, the present boundaries of the United States in North America, with the exception of Alaska, had been created.

chant from New York City, arrived as the first American consul (and, according to some accounts, was the inspiration for Puccini's great opera, *Madame Butterfly*, about an American who marries and then abandons a Japanese woman). Harris persuaded the Japanese to allow American ships into additional ports and to establish full diplomatic relations between the two countries. As a result, the United States acquired refueling places on the route to China—seen as Asia's most important trading partner. And Japan soon launched a process of modernization that transformed it into the region's major military power.

A DOSE OF ARSENIC

Victory over Mexico added more than 1 million square miles to the United States—an area larger than the Louisiana Purchase. But the acquisition of this vast territory raised the fatal issue that would disrupt the political system and plunge the nation into civil war—whether slavery should be allowed to expand into the West. Events soon confirmed Ralph Waldo Emerson's prediction that if the United States gobbled up part of Mexico, "it will be as the man who swallows arsenic. . . . Mexico will poison us."

THE WILMOT PROVISO

Before 1846, the status of slavery in all parts of the United States had been settled, either by state law or by the Missouri Compromise, which determined slavery's status in the Louisiana Purchase. The acquisition of new land reopened the question of slavery's expansion. The divisive potential of this issue became clear in 1846, when Congressman David Wilmot of Pennsylvania proposed a resolution prohibiting slavery from all territory acquired from Mexico. Party lines crumbled as every northerner, Democrat and Whig alike, supported what came to be known as the Wilmot Proviso, while nearly all southerners opposed it. The measure passed the House, where the more populous North possessed a majority, but failed in the Senate, with its even balance of free and slave states. The Proviso, said one newspaper, "as if by magic, brought to a head the great question that is about to divide the American people."

In 1848, opponents of slavery's expansion organized the Free Soil Party and nominated Martin Van Buren for president and Charles Francis Adams, the son of John Quincy Adams, as his running mate. Democrats nominated Lewis Cass of Michigan, who proposed that the decision on whether to allow slavery should be left to settlers in the new territories (an idea later given the name "popular sovereignty"). Van Buren was motivated in part by revenge against the South for jettisoning him in 1844. But his campaign struck a chord among northerners opposed to the expansion of slavery, and he polled some 300,000 votes, 14 percent of the northern total. Victory in 1848 went to the Whig candidate, Zachary Taylor, a hero of the Mexican War and a Louisiana sugar planter. But the fact that a former president and the son of another abandoned their parties to run on a Free Soil platform showed that antislavery sentiment had spread far beyond abolitionist ranks. "Antislavery," commented Senator William H. Seward of New York, "is at length a respectable element in politics."

THE FREE SOIL APPEAL

The Free Soil position had a popular appeal in the North that far exceeded the abolitionists' demand for immediate emancipation and equal rights for blacks. While Congress possessed no constitutional power to abolish slavery within a state, well-known precedents existed for keeping territories (areas that had not yet entered the Union as states) free from slavery. Congress had done this in 1787 in the Northwest Ordinance and again in the Missouri Compromise of 1820–1821. Many northerners had long resented what they considered southern domination of the federal government. The idea of preventing the creation of new slave states appealed to those who favored policies, such as the protective tariff and government aid to internal improvements, that the majority of southern political leaders opposed.

For thousands of northerners, moreover, the ability to move to the new western territories held out the promise of economic betterment. The depression of the early 1840s had reinforced the traditional equation of land ownership with economic freedom. The labor movement promoted access to western land as a way of combating unemployment and low wages in the East. "Freedom of the soil," declared George Henry Evans, the editor of a pro-labor newspaper, offered the only alternative to permanent economic dependence for American workers.

Such views merged easily with opposition to the expansion of slavery. If slave plantations were to occupy the fertile lands of the West, northern migration would be effectively blocked. The term "free soil" had a double meaning. The Free Soil platform of 1848 called both for barring slavery from western territories and for the federal government to provide free homesteads to settlers in the new territories. Unlike abolitionism, the "free soil" idea also appealed to the racism so widespread in northern society. Wilmot himself insisted that his controversial Proviso was motivated not by "morbid sympathy for the slaves" but to advance "the cause and rights of the free white man," in part by preventing him from having to compete with "black labor."

To white southerners, the idea of barring slavery from territory acquired from Mexico seemed a violation of their equal rights as members of the Union. Southerners had fought and died to win these territories; surely they had a right to share in the fruits of victory. To single out slavery as the one form of property barred from the West would be an affront to the South and its distinctive way of life. A majority of slaves in 1848 lived in states that had not even existed when the Constitution was adopted. Many older plantation areas already suffered from soil exhaustion. Just as northerners believed westward expansion essential to their economic well-being, southern leaders became convinced that slavery must expand or die. Moreover, the admission of new free states would overturn the delicate political balance between the sections and make the South a permanent minority. Southern interests would not be secure in a Union dominated by non-slaveholding states.

CRISIS AND COMPROMISE

In world history, the year 1848 is remembered as the "springtime of nations," a time of democratic uprisings against the monarchies of Europe and demands by ethnic minorities for national independence. American principles of liberty and self-government appeared to be triumphing in the Old World. The Chartist movement in Great Britain organized massive demonstrations in support of a proposed Charter that demanded democratic reforms. The French replaced their monarchy with a republic. Hungarians proclaimed their independence from Austrian rule. Patriots in Italy and Germany, both divided into numerous states, demanded national unification. But the revolutionary tide receded. Chartism faded away. In France, the Second Republic was soon succeeded by the reign of Emperor Napoleon III. Revolts in Budapest, Rome, and other cities were crushed. Would their own experiment in self-government, some Americans wondered, suffer the same fate as the failed revolutions of Europe?

With the slavery issue appearing more and more ominous, established party leaders moved to resolve differences between the sections. Some disputes were of long standing, but the immediate source of controversy arose from the acquisition of new lands after the Mexican War. In 1850, California asked to be admitted to the Union as a free state. Many southerners opposed the measure, fearing that it would upset the sectional balance in Congress. Senator Henry Clay offered a plan with four main provisions

Senator Daniel Webster of Massachusetts in a daguerreotype from 1850, the year his speech in support of the Compromise of 1850 contributed to its passage.

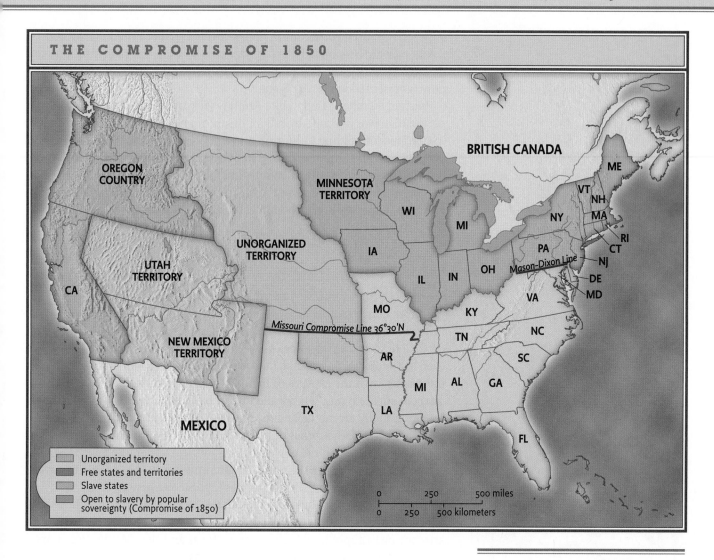

THE COMPROMISE OF 1850

- Unorganized territory
- Free states and territories
- Slave states
- Open to slavery by popular sovereignty (Compromise of 1850)

that came to be known as the Compromise of 1850. California would enter the Union as a free state. The slave trade, but not slavery itself, would be abolished in the nation's capital. A stringent new law would allow southerners to reclaim runaway slaves. And the status of slavery in the remaining territories acquired from Mexico would be left to the decision of the local white inhabitants. The United States would also agree to pay off the massive debt Texas had accumulated while independent.

The Compromise of 1850 attempted to settle issues arising from the acquisition of territory from Mexico by admitting California as a free state and providing that the status of slavery in Utah and New Mexico would be determined by the settlers.

THE GREAT DEBATE

In the Senate debate on the Compromise, the divergent sectional positions received eloquent expression. Powerful leaders spoke for and against compromise. Daniel Webster of Massachusetts announced his willingness to abandon the Wilmot Proviso and accept a new fugitive slave law if this were the price of sectional peace. John C. Calhoun, again representing South Carolina, was too ill to speak. A colleague read his remarks rejecting the very idea of compromise. Slavery, Calhoun insisted, must be protected by the national government and extended into all the new territories. The North must yield or the Union could not survive. William H. Seward of New

York also opposed compromise. To southerners' talk of their constitutional rights, Seward responded that a "higher law" than the Constitution condemned slavery—the law of morality. Here was the voice of abolitionism, now represented in the U.S. Senate.

President Zachary Taylor, like Andrew Jackson a southerner but a strong nationalist, was alarmed by talk of disunion. He accused southern leaders in Congress of holding California hostage to their own legislative aims and insisted that all Congress needed to do was admit California to the Union. But Taylor died suddenly of an intestinal infection on July 9, 1850. His successor, Millard Fillmore of New York, threw his support to Clay's proposals. Fillmore helped to break the impasse in Congress and secure adoption of the Compromise of 1850.

THE FUGITIVE SLAVE ISSUE

For one last time, political leaders had removed the dangerous slavery question from congressional debate. The new Fugitive Slave Act, however, made further controversy inevitable. The law allowed special federal commissioners to determine the fate of alleged fugitives without benefit of a jury trial or even testimony by the accused individual. It prohibited local authorities from interfering with the capture of fugitives and required individual citizens to assist in such capture when called upon by federal agents. Thus, southern leaders, usually strong defenders of states' rights and local autonomy, supported a measure that brought federal agents into communities throughout the North, armed with the power to override local law enforcement and judicial procedures to secure the return of runaway slaves. The security of slavery was more important to them than states'-rights consistency.

The fugitive slave issue affected all the free states, not just those that bordered on the South. Slave catchers, for example, entered California attempting to apprehend fugitives from Texas and New Mexico who hoped to reach freedom in British Columbia. The issue drew into politics individuals like Ralph Waldo Emerson, who, although antislavery, had previously remained aloof from the abolitionist crusade. Emerson and others influenced by transcendentalism viewed the Fugitive Slave Act as a dangerous example of how a government doing the bidding of the South could override an individual's ability to act according to his conscience—the foundation, for Emerson, of genuine freedom.

During the 1850s, federal tribunals heard more than 300 cases and ordered 157 fugitives returned to the South, many at the government's expense. But the law further widened sectional divisions. In a series of dramatic confrontations, fugitives, aided by abolitionist allies, violently resisted recapture. A large crowd in 1851 rescued the escaped slave Jerry from jail in Syracuse, New York, and spirited him off to Canada. In the same year, an owner who attempted to recapture a fugitive was killed in Christiana, Pennsylvania. Later in the decade, Margaret Garner, a Kentucky slave who had escaped with her family to Ohio, killed her own young daughter rather than see her returned to slavery by federal marshals. (At the end of the twentieth century, this incident would become the basis for Toni Morrison's celebrated novel *Beloved*.)

In the North, several thousand fugitives and free-born blacks, worried

An 1855 broadside depicting the life of Anthony Burns, a runaway slave captured in Boston and returned to the South in 1854 by federal officials enforcing the Fugitive Slave Act.

that they might be swept up in the stringent provisions of the Fugitive Slave Act, fled to safety in Canada. The sight of so many refugees seeking liberty in a foreign land challenged the familiar image of the United States as an asylum for freedom. "Families are separating," reported a Toronto newspaper in October 1850, "leaving their homes, and flying in all directions to seek in Canada, under the British flag, the protection denied to them in the free republic."

DOUGLAS AND POPULAR SOVEREIGNTY

At least temporarily, the Compromise of 1850 seemed to have restored sectional peace and party unity. In the 1852 presidential election, Democrat Franklin Pierce won a sweeping victory over the Whig Winfield Scott on a platform that recognized the Compromise as a final settlement of the slavery controversy. Pierce received a broad popular mandate, winning 254 electoral votes to Scott's 42. Yet his administration turned out to be one of the most disastrous in American history. It witnessed the collapse of the party system inherited from the Age of Jackson.

In 1854, the old political order finally succumbed to the disruptive pressures of sectionalism. Early in that year, Illinois senator Stephen A. Douglas introduced a bill to provide territorial governments for Kansas and Nebraska, located within the Louisiana Purchase. With Calhoun, Clay, and Webster (the "great triumvirate") all having died between 1850 and 1852, Douglas, although only forty-one, saw himself as the new leader of the Senate. A strong believer in western development, he hoped that a transcontinental railroad could be constructed through Kansas or Nebraska. But he feared that this could not be accomplished unless formal governments had been established in these territories. Southerners in Congress, however, seemed adamant against allowing the organization of new free territories that might further upset the sectional balance. Douglas hoped to satisfy them by applying the principle of popular sovereignty, whereby the status of slavery would be determined by the votes of local settlers, not Congress. To Douglas, popular sovereignty embodied the idea of local self-government and offered a middle ground between the extremes of North and South. It was a principle on which all parts of the Democratic Party could unite, and which might enable him to capture the presidential nomination in 1856 to succeed the ineffectual Pierce.

THE KANSAS-NEBRASKA ACT

Unlike the lands taken from Mexico, Kansas and Nebraska lay in the nation's heartland, directly in the path of westward migration. Slavery, moreover, was prohibited there under the terms of the Missouri Compromise, which Douglas's bill repealed. In response to Douglas's proposal, a group of antislavery congressmen issued the *Appeal of the Independent Democrats*. Written by two abolitionists from Ohio—Congressman Joshua Giddings and Senator Salmon P. Chase—the *Appeal* proved to be one of the most effective pieces of political persuasion in American history. It arraigned Douglas's bill as a "gross violation of a sacred pledge," part and parcel of "an atrocious

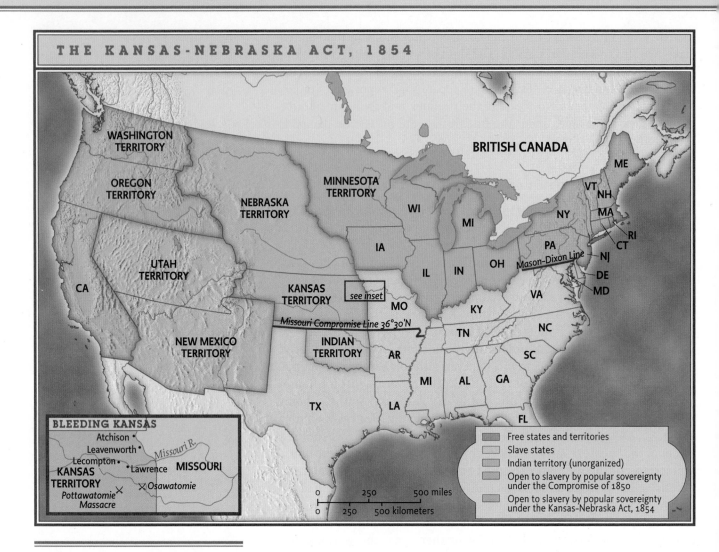

THE KANSAS-NEBRASKA ACT, 1854

Legend:
- Free states and territories
- Slave states
- Indian territory (unorganized)
- Open to slavery by popular sovereignty under the Compromise of 1850
- Open to slavery by popular sovereignty under the Kansas-Nebraska Act, 1854

BLEEDING KANSAS (inset)
Atchison · Leavenworth · Lecompton · Lawrence · Osawatomie · Pottawatomie Massacre · KANSAS TERRITORY · MISSOURI · Missouri R.

The Kansas-Nebraska Act opened a vast area in the nation's heartland to the possible spread of slavery by repealing the Missouri Compromise and providing that settlers would determine the status of slavery in these territories.

plot" to convert free territory into a "dreary region of despotism, inhabited by masters and slaves." It helped to convince millions of northerners that southern leaders aimed at nothing less than extending their peculiar institution throughout the West.

Thanks to Douglas's energetic leadership, the Kansas-Nebraska Act became law. But it shattered the Democratic Party's unity. Even as Congress debated, protest meetings sprang up throughout the North. Fearing that the bill's unpopularity among their constituents would harm their chances for reelection, half the northern Democrats in the House cast negative votes. Loyalty to Pierce, Douglas, and their party led the other half to support the measure. It is difficult to think of a piece of legislation in American history that had a more profound impact on national life. In the wake of the bill's passage, American politics underwent a profound reorganization. During the next two years, the Whig Party, unable to develop a unified response to the political crisis, collapsed. From a region divided between the two parties, the South became solidly Democratic. Most northern Whigs, augmented by thousands of disgruntled Democrats, joined a new organization, the Republican Party, dedicated to preventing the further expansion of slavery.

THE RISE OF THE REPUBLICAN PARTY

THE NORTHERN ECONOMY

The disruptive impact of slavery on the traditional parties was the immediate cause of political transformation in the mid-1850s. But the rise of the Republican Party also reflected underlying economic and social changes, notably the completion of the market revolution and the beginning of mass immigration from Europe. The period from 1843, when prosperity returned, to 1857, when another economic downturn hit, witnessed explosive economic growth, especially in the North. The catalyst was the completion of the railroad network. From 5,000 miles in 1848, railroad track mileage grew to 30,000 by 1860, with most of the construction occurring in Ohio, Illinois, and other states of the Old Northwest. Four great trunk railroads now linked eastern cities with western farming and commercial centers. The railroads completed the reorientation of the Northwest's trade from the South to the East. As late as 1850, most western farmers still shipped their produce down the Mississippi River. Ten years later, however, railroads transported nearly all their crops to the East, at a fraction of the previous cost. By 1860, for example, 60 million bushels of wheat were passing through Buffalo on their way to market in eastern cities and abroad. The economic integration of the Northwest and Northeast created the groundwork for their political unification in the Republican Party.

By 1860, the North had become a complex, integrated economy, with eastern industrialists marketing manufactured goods to the commercial farmers of the West, while residents of the region's growing cities consumed the food westerners produced. Northern society stood poised between old and new ways. The majority of the population still lived not in large cities but in small towns and rural areas, where the ideal of economic independence—owning one's own farm or shop—still lay within reach. Yet the majority of the northern workforce no longer labored in agriculture, and the industrial revolution was spreading rapidly.

An 1853 broadside for one section of the Illinois Central Railroad. One of the most important new lines of the 1850s, the Illinois Central opened parts of the Old Northwest to settlement and commercial agriculture, and it helped to cement Chicago's place as the region's foremost city.

The Lackawanna Valley, *an 1855 painting by George Inness commissioned by the president of the Delaware, Lackawanna, and Western Railroad. In the background is the roundhouse at Scranton, Pennsylvania. Like* The Mill on the Brandywine *in Chapter 9, the scene emphasizes the harmony of technological progress and nature. The factory on the right is almost entirely hidden by trees. Yet the tree stumps in the foreground suggest some regret that the natural environment is giving way to progress.*

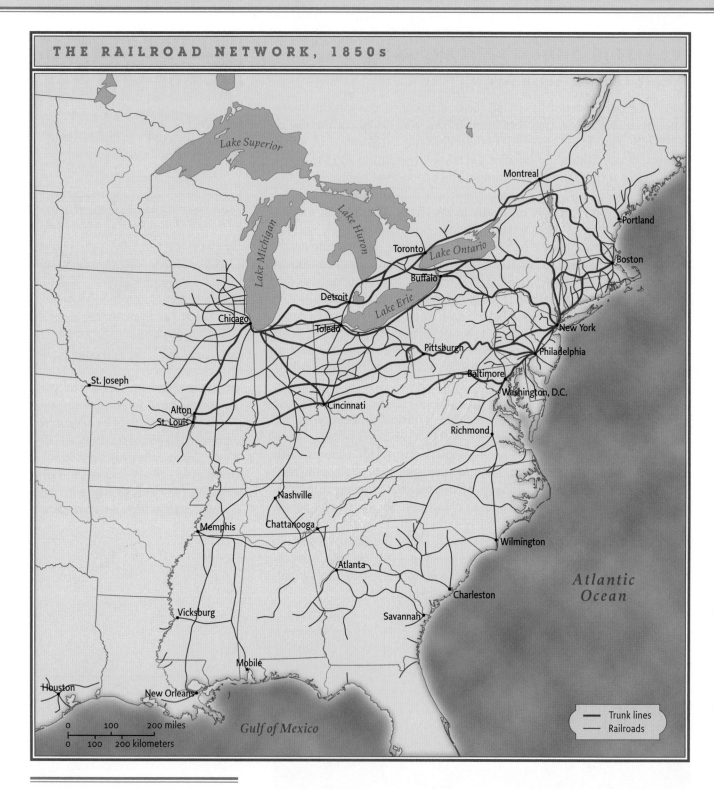

THE RAILROAD NETWORK, 1850s

The rapid expansion of the railroad network in the 1850s linked the Northeast and Old Northwest in a web of commerce. The South's rail network was considerably less developed, accounting for only 30 percent of the nation's track mileage.

Two great areas of industrial production had arisen. One, along the Atlantic coast, stretched from Boston to Philadelphia and Baltimore. A second was centered on or near the Great Lakes, in inland cities like Buffalo, Cleveland, Pittsburgh, and Chicago. Driven by railroad expansion, coal mining and iron manufacturing were growing rapidly. Chicago, the old Northwest's major rail center and the jumping-off place for settlers heading for the Great Plains, had become a complex manufacturing center, producing 5,000 reapers each year, along with barbed wire, windmills, and prefabricated "balloon frame" houses, all of which facilitated further western settlement. New York City by 1860 had become the nation's preeminent financial, commercial, and manufacturing center. Although the southern economy was also growing and the continuing expansion of cotton production brought wealth to slaveholders, the South did not share in these broad economic changes.

THE RISE AND FALL OF THE KNOW-NOTHINGS

As noted in Chapter 9, nativism—hostility to immigrants, especially Catholics—emerged as a local political movement in the 1840s. But in 1854, with the party system in crisis, it burst on the national political scene with the sudden appearance of the American, or Know-Nothing, Party (so called because it began as a secret organization whose members, when asked about its existence, were supposed to respond, "I know nothing"). The party trumpeted its dedication to reserving political office for native-born Americans and to resisting the "aggressions" of the Catholic Church, such as its supposed efforts to undermine public school systems. The Know-Nothings swept the 1854 state elections in Massachusetts, electing the governor, all of the state's congressmen, and nearly every member of the state legislature. They captured the mayor's office in cities like Philadelphia, Chicago, and San Francisco as well. In many states, nativists emerged as a major component of victorious "anti-Nebraska" coalitions of voters opposed to the Kansas-Nebraska Act. In the North, the Know-Nothings' appeal combined anti-Catholic and antislavery sentiment, with opposition to the sale of liquor often added to the equation. After all, most Catholics, as noted in the previous chapter, vigorously opposed the reform move-

George Catlin's 1827 painting Five Points *depicts a working-class immigrant neighborhood in New York City that gained a reputation for crime, drinking, and overcrowding.*

ments inspired by evangelical Protestantism, especially antislavery and temperance. The 1854 elections, said one observer, revealed "a deep seated feeling in favor of human freedom and also a fine determination that hereafter none but Americans shall rule America."

Despite severe anti-Irish discrimination in jobs, housing, and education, however, it is remarkable how little came of demands that immigrants be barred from the political nation. All European immigrants benefited from being white. During the 1850s, free blacks found immigrants pushing them out of even the jobs as servants and common laborers previously available to them. The newcomers had the good fortune to arrive after white male suffrage had become the norm and automatically received the right to vote. Even as New England states sought to reduce immigrant political power (Massachusetts and Connecticut made literacy a voting requirement, and Massachusetts mandated a two-year waiting period between becoming a naturalized citizen and voting), western states desperate for labor allowed immigrants to vote well before they became citizens. In a country where the suffrage had become essential to understandings of freedom, it is significant that many white male immigrants could vote almost from the moment they landed in America, while non-whites, whose ancestors had lived in the country for centuries, could not.

Political Chart of the United States, *an 1856 chart graphically illustrating the division between slave and free states and providing statistics to demonstrate the superiority of free to slave society. The image underscores the Republican contention that it is essential to prevent slavery from spreading into the western territories. John C. Frémont, Republican presidential candidate, is pictured at the top.*

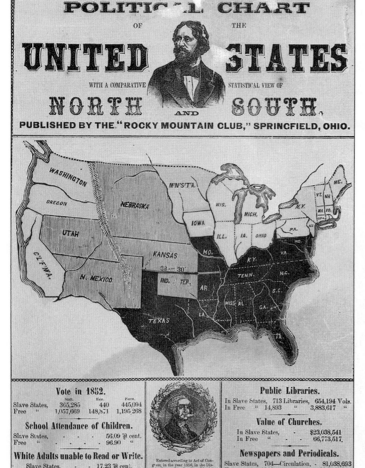

THE FREE LABOR IDEOLOGY

By 1856, it was clear that the Republican Party—a coalition of antislavery Democrats, northern Whigs, Free Soilers, and Know-Nothings opposed to the further expansion of slavery—would become the major alternative to the Democratic Party in the North. Republicans managed to convince most northerners that the Slave Power, as they called the South's proslavery political leadership, posed a more immediate threat to their liberties and aspirations than "popery" and immigration. The party's appeal rested on the idea of "free labor." In Republican hands, the antithesis between "free society" and "slave society" coalesced into a comprehensive worldview that glorified the North as the home of progress, opportunity, and freedom.

The defining quality of northern society, Republicans declared, was the opportunity it offered each laborer to move up to the status of landowning farmer or independent craftsman, thus achieving the economic independence essential to freedom. Slavery, by contrast, spawned a social order consisting of degraded slaves, poor whites with no hope of advancement, and idle aristocrats. The struggle over the territories was a contest about which of two antagonistic labor systems would dominate the West and, by implication, the nation's future. If slavery were to spread into the West, northern free laborers would be barred, and their chances for social advancement severely diminished. Slavery,

Republicans insisted, must be kept out of the territories so that free labor could flourish.

To southern claims that slavery was the foundation of liberty, Republicans responded with the rallying cry "freedom national"—meaning not abolition, but ending the federal government's support of slavery. Under the banner of free labor, northerners of diverse backgrounds and interests rallied in defense of the superiority of their own society. Republicans acknowledged that some northern laborers, including most Irish immigrants, were locked into jobs as factory workers and unskilled laborers and found it extremely difficult to rise in the social scale. But Republicans concluded that it was their "dependent nature"—a lack of Protestant, middle-class virtues—that explained the plight of the immigrant poor.

Republicans were not abolitionists—they focused on preventing the spread of slavery, not attacking it where it existed. Nonetheless, many party leaders viewed the nation's division into free and slave societies as an "irrepressible conflict," as Senator William H. Seward of New York put it in 1858, that eventually would have to be resolved. These "two systems" of society, Seward insisted, were "incompatible" within a single nation. The market revolution, Seward argued, by drawing the entire nation closer together in a web of transportation and commerce, heightened the tension between freedom and slavery. The United States, he predicted, "must and will, sooner or later, become either entirely a slaveholding nation, or entirely a free-labor nation."

BLEEDING KANSAS AND THE ELECTION OF 1856

Their free labor outlook, which resonated so effectively with deeply held northern values, helps to explain the Republicans' rapid rise to prominence. But dramatic events in 1855 and 1856 also fueled the party's growth. When Kansas held elections in 1854 and 1855, hundreds of proslavery Missourians crossed the border to cast fraudulent ballots. President Franklin Pierce recognized the legitimacy of the resulting proslavery legislature and replaced the territorial governor, Andrew H. Reeder of Pennsylvania, when he dissented. Settlers from free states soon established a rival government, and a sporadic civil war broke out in Kansas in which some 200 persons eventually lost their lives. In one incident, in May 1856, a proslavery mob attacked the free-soil stronghold of Lawrence, burning public buildings and pillaging private homes.

"Bleeding Kansas" seemed to discredit Douglas's policy of leaving the decision on slavery up to the local population, thus aiding the Republicans. The party also drew strength from an unprecedented incident in the halls of Congress. South Carolina representative Preston Brooks, wielding a gold-tipped cane, beat

A contemporary print denounces South Carolina congressman Preston S. Brooks's assault on Massachusetts senator Charles Sumner in May 1856. The attack on the floor of the Senate was in retaliation for Sumner's speech accusing Senator Andrew P. Butler (Brooks's distant cousin) of having taken "the harlot slavery" as his mistress.

SOUTHERN CHIVALRY — ARGUMENT versus CLUB'S.

Liberty, the Fair Maid of Kansas, in the Hands of the "Border Ruffians," *a cartoon blaming the Democratic Party for violence in Kansas in 1856. Leading Democrats surround the maid of liberty—from left to right, Secretary of State William L. Marcy, Democratic presidential candidate James Buchanan, President Franklin Pierce, Lewis Cass, the party's candidate for president in 1848, and Stephen A. Douglas, author of the Kansas-Nebraska Act, shown scalping an Indian.*

the antislavery senator Charles Sumner of Massachusetts unconscious after Sumner delivered a denunciation of "The Crime against Kansas." Many southerners applauded Brooks, sending him canes emblazoned with the words "Hit him again!"

In the election of 1856, the Republican Party chose as its candidate John C. Frémont and drafted a platform that strongly opposed the further expansion of slavery. Stung by the northern reaction to the Kansas-Nebraska Act, the Democrats nominated James Buchanan, who had been minister to Great Britain in 1854 and thus had no direct connection with that divisive measure. The Democratic platform endorsed the principle of popular sovereignty as the only viable solution to the slavery controversy. Meanwhile, the Know-Nothings presented ex-president Millard Fillmore as their candidate. Frémont outpolled Buchanan in the North, carrying eleven of sixteen free states—a remarkable achievement for an organization that had existed for only two years. But Buchanan won the entire South and the key northern states of Illinois, Indiana, and Pennsylvania, enough to ensure his victory. Fillmore carried only Maryland. But he ran well among former Whig voters in the Upper South and more conservative areas of the North, who were reluctant to join the Democrats but feared Republican victory might threaten the Union.

The 1856 election returns made starkly clear that parties had reoriented themselves along sectional lines. One major party had been destroyed, another seriously weakened, and a new one had arisen, devoted entirely to the interests of the North.

THE EMERGENCE OF LINCOLN

The final collapse of the party system took place during the administration of a president who epitomized the old political order. Born during George Washington's presidency, James Buchanan had served in Pennsylvania's legislature, in both houses of Congress, and as secretary of state under James K. Polk. A staunch believer in the Union, he committed himself to pacifying inflamed sectional emotions. Few presidents have failed more disastrously in what they set out to accomplish.

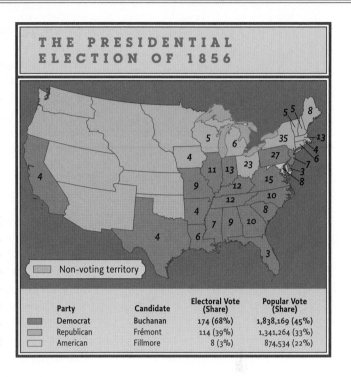

THE PRESIDENTIAL ELECTION OF 1856

Non-voting territory

Party	Candidate	Electoral Vote (Share)	Popular Vote (Share)
Democrat	Buchanan	174 (68%)	1,838,169 (45%)
Republican	Frémont	114 (39%)	1,341,264 (33%)
American	Fillmore	8 (3%)	874,534 (22%)

THE DRED SCOTT DECISION

Even before his inauguration, Buchanan became aware of an impending Supreme Court decision that held out the hope of settling the slavery controversy once and for all. This was the case of Dred Scott. During the 1830s, Scott had accompanied his owner, Dr. John Emerson of Missouri, to Illinois, where slavery had been prohibited by the Northwest Ordinance of 1787 and by state law, and to Wisconsin Territory, where it was barred by the Missouri Compromise. After returning to Missouri, Scott sued for his freedom, claiming that residence on free soil had made him free.

The Dred Scott decision, one of the most famous—or infamous—rulings in the long history of the Supreme Court, was announced in March 1857, two days after Buchanan's inauguration. The justices addressed three questions. Could a black person be a citizen and therefore sue in federal court? Did residence in a free state make Scott free? Did Congress possess the power to prohibit slavery in a territory? All nine justices issued individual opinions. But essentially, the Court divided 6-3 (with Justice Robert C. Grier of Pennsylvania, at Buchanan's behind-the-scenes urging, joining a southern majority). Speaking for the majority, Chief Justice Roger B. Taney declared that only white persons could be citizens of the United States. The nation's founders, Taney insisted, believed that blacks "had no rights which the white man was bound to respect." Descended from different ancestors and lacking a history of freedom, blacks, he continued, could never be part of the nation's "political family."

The case could have ended there, since Scott had no right to sue, but inspired by the idea of resolving the slavery issue, Taney pressed on. Scott, he declared, remained a slave. Illinois law had no effect on him after his return to Missouri. As for his residence in Wisconsin, Congress possessed no power under the Constitution to bar slavery from a territory. The Missouri Compromise, recently repealed by the Kansas-Nebraska Act, had

Dred Scott as painted in 1857, the year the Supreme Court ruled that he and his family must remain in slavery. (Collection of the New York Historical Society)

been unconstitutional and so was any measure interfering with southerners' right to bring slaves into the western territories. The decision in effect declared unconstitutional the Republican platform of restricting slavery's expansion. It also seemed to undermine Douglas's doctrine of popular sovereignty. For if Congress lacked the power to prohibit slavery in a territory, how could a territorial legislature created by Congress do so? The Court, a Georgia newspaper exulted, "covers every question regarding slavery and settles it in favor of the South."

THE DECISION'S AFTERMATH

Perhaps the person least directly affected by the Dred Scott decision was the plaintiff himself, for a new master immediately emancipated Scott and his wife, Harriet. Both died on the eve of the Civil War, having enjoyed their freedom for only a few years. The impact on the party system was more far-reaching. Among the decision's casualties was the reputation of the Court itself, which, in the North, sank to the lowest level in all of American history. Rather than abandoning their opposition to the expansion of slavery, Republicans now viewed the Court as controlled by the Slave Power.

Slavery, announced President Buchanan, henceforth existed in all the territories, "by virtue of the Constitution." In 1858, his administration attempted to admit Kansas as a slave state under the Lecompton Constitution, which had been drafted by a pro-southern convention and never submitted to a popular vote. Outraged by this violation of popular sovereignty, Douglas formed an unlikely alliance with congressional Republicans to block the attempt. Kansas remained a territory; it would join the Union as a free state on the eve of the Civil War. The Lecompton battle convinced southern Democrats that they could not trust their party's most popular northern leader.

LINCOLN AND SLAVERY

The depth of Americans' divisions over slavery were brought into sharp focus in 1858 in one of the most storied election campaigns in the nation's history. Seeking reelection to the Senate as both a champion of popular sovereignty and the man who had prevented the administration from forcing slavery on the people of Kansas, Douglas faced an unexpectedly strong challenge from Abraham Lincoln, then little known outside of Illinois. Born into a modest farm family in Kentucky in 1809, Lincoln had moved as a youth to frontier Indiana and then Illinois. Although he began running for public office at the age of twenty-one, until the mid-1850s his career hardly seemed destined for greatness. He had served four terms as a Whig in the state legislature and one in Congress from 1847 to 1849.

Lincoln reentered politics in 1854 as a result of the Kansas-Nebraska Act. He once said that he "hated slavery as much as any abolitionist." Unlike abolitionists, however, Lincoln was willing to compromise with the South to preserve the Union. "I hate to see the poor creatures hunted down," he once wrote of fugitive slaves, "but I bite my lip and keep silent." But on one question he was inflexible—stopping the expansion of slavery.

Lincoln developed a critique of slavery and its expansion that gave voice to the central values of the emerging Republican Party and the millions of northerners whose loyalty it commanded. His speeches combined the moral fervor of the abolitionists with the respect for order and the Constitution of more conservative northerners. "I hate it," he said in 1854 of the prospect of slavery's expansion, "because of the monstrous injustice of slavery itself. I hate it because it deprives our republican example of its just influence in the world—enables the enemies of free institutions, with plausibility, to taunt us as hypocrites—causes the real friends of freedom to doubt our sincerity." If slavery were allowed to expand, he warned, the "love of liberty" would be extinguished and with it America's special mission to be a symbol of democracy for the entire world.

Even though Lincoln lived in a society firmly in the grasp of the market revolution and worked on occasion as an attorney for the Illinois Central Railroad, one of the nation's largest corporations, his America was the world of the small producer. In a sense, his own life personified the free labor ideology and the opportunities northern society offered to laboring men. During the 1850s, property-owning farmers, artisans, and shopkeepers far outnumbered wage earners in Illinois. Lincoln was fascinated and disturbed by the writings of proslavery ideologues like George Fitzhugh (discussed in Chapter 11), and he rose to the defense of northern society. "I want every man to have the chance," said Lincoln, "and I believe a black man is entitled to it, in which he *can* better his condition." Blacks might not be the equal of whites in all respects, but in their "natural right" to the fruits of their labor, they were "my equal and the equal of all others."

Abraham Lincoln in 1858, the year of the Lincoln-Douglas debates.

THE LINCOLN-DOUGLAS CAMPAIGN

The campaign against Douglas, the North's preeminent political leader, created Lincoln's national reputation. Accepting his party's nomination for the Senate in June 1858, Lincoln etched sharply the differences between them. "A house divided against itself," he announced, "cannot stand. I believe this government cannot endure, permanently half *slave* and half *free*." Lincoln's point was not that civil war was imminent, but that Americans must choose between favoring and opposing slavery. There could be no middle ground. Douglas's policy of popular sovereignty, he insisted, reflected a moral indifference that could only result in the institution's spread throughout the entire country.

The Lincoln-Douglas debates, held in seven Illinois towns and attended by tens of thousands of listeners, remain classics of American political oratory. Clashing definitions of freedom lay at their heart. To Lincoln, freedom meant opposition to slavery. The nation needed to rekindle the spirit of the founding fathers, who, he claimed, had tried to place slavery on the path to "ultimate extinction." Douglas argued that the essence of freedom lay in local self-government and individual self-determination. A large and diverse nation could only survive by respecting the right of each locality to determine its own institutions. In response to a question posed by Lincoln during the Freeport debate, Douglas insisted that popular sovereignty was not incompatible with the Dred Scott decision. Although territorial legislatures could no longer exclude slavery directly, he argued, if the people

Stephen A. Douglas in a daguerreotype from around 1853.

VOICES OF FREEDOM

FROM THE LINCOLN-DOUGLAS DEBATES (1858)

The most famous political campaign in American history, the 1858 race for the U.S. Senate between Senator Stephen A. Douglas (a former Illinois judge) and Abraham Lincoln was highlighted by seven debates in which they discussed the politics of slavery and contrasting understandings of freedom.

DOUGLAS: Mr. Lincoln says that this government cannot endure permanently in the same condition in which it was made by its framers—divided into free and slave states. He says that it has existed for about seventy years thus divided, and yet he tells you that it cannot endure permanently on the same principles and in the same relative conditions in which our fathers made it. . . . One of the reserved rights of the states, was the right to regulate the relations between master and servant, on the slavery question.

Now, my friends, if we will only act conscientiously upon this great principle of popular sovereignty which guarantees to each state and territory the right to do as it pleases on all things local and domestic instead of Congress interfering, we will continue to be at peace one with another.

LINCOLN: Judge Douglas says, "Why can't this Union endure permanently, half slave and half free?" "Why can't we let it stand as our fathers placed it?" That is the exact difficulty between us. . . . I say when this government was first established it was the policy of its founders to prohibit the spread of slavery into the new territories of the United States, where it had not existed. But Judge Douglas and his friends have broken up that policy and placed it upon a new basis by which it is to become national and perpetual. All I have asked or desired anywhere is that it should be placed back again upon the basis that the founders of our government originally placed it—restricting it from the new territories. . . .

Judge Douglas assumes that we have no interest in them—that we have no right to interfere. . . . Do we not wish for an outlet for our surplus population, if I may so express myself? Do we not feel an interest in getting to that outlet with such institutions as we would like to have prevail there? Now irrespective of the moral aspect of this question as to whether there is a right or wrong in enslaving a negro, I am still in favor of our new territories being in such a condition that white men may find a home. I am in favor of this not merely for our own people, but as an outlet for *free white people everywhere*, the world over—in which Hans and Baptiste and Patrick, and all other men from all the world, may find new homes and better their conditions in life.

DOUGLAS: For one, I am opposed to negro citizenship in any and every form. I believe this government was made on the white basis. I believe it was made by white men, for the benefit of white men and their posterity forever . . . I do not believe that the Almighty made the negro capable of self-government. I say to you, my fellow-citizens, that in my opinion the signers of the Declaration of Independence had no reference to the negro whatever when they declared all men to be created equal. They desired to express by that phrase, white men, men of European birth and European descent . . . when they spoke of the equality of men.

LINCOLN: I have no purpose to introduce political and social equality between the white and the black races. There is a physical difference between the two, which in my judgment will probably forever forbid their living together upon the footing of perfect equality, and inasmuch as it becomes a necessity that there must be a difference, I, as well as Judge Douglas, am in favor of the race to which I belong, having the superior position. . . . But I hold that notwithstanding all this, there is no reason in the world why the negro is not entitled to all the natural rights enumerated in the Declaration of Independence, the right to life, liberty, and the pursuit of happiness. I hold that he is as much entitled to these as the white man. I agree with Judge Douglas he is not my equal in many respects—certainly not in color, perhaps not in moral or intellectual endowment. But in the right to eat the bread, without leave of anybody else, which his own hand earns, *he is my equal and the equal of Judge Douglas, and the equal of every living man.*

DOUGLAS: He tells you that I will not argue the question whether slavery is right or wrong. I tell you why I will not do it. . . . I hold that the people of the slaveholding states are civilized men as well as ourselves, that they bear consciences as well as we, and that they are accountable to God and their posterity and not to us. It is for them to decide therefore the moral and religious right of the slavery question for themselves within their own limits. . . . He says that he looks forward to a time when slavery shall be abolished everywhere. I look forward to a time when each state shall be allowed to do as it pleases.

LINCOLN: I suppose that the real difference between Judge Douglas and his friends, and the Republicans, is that the Judge is not in favor of making any difference between slavery and liberty . . . and consequently every sentiment he utters discards the idea that there is any wrong in slavery. . . . That is the real issue. That is the issue that will continue in this country when these poor tongues of Judge Douglas and myself shall be silent. It is the eternal struggle between these two principles—right and wrong—throughout the world.

QUESTIONS

1. How do Lincoln and Douglas differ on what rights black Americans are entitled to enjoy?

2. Why does Lincoln believe the nation cannot exist forever half slave and half free, whereas Douglas believes it can?

3. How does each of the speakers balance the right of each state to manage its own affairs against the right of every person to be free?

wished to keep slaveholders out all they needed to do was refrain from giving the institution legal protection.

In a critique not only of the antislavery movement but of the entire reform impulse deriving from religious revivalism, Douglas insisted that politicians had no right to impose their own moral standards on society as a whole. "I deny the right of Congress," he declared, "to force a good thing upon a people who are unwilling to receive it." If a community wished to own slaves, it had a right to do so. Of course, when Douglas spoke of the "people," he meant whites alone. He spent much of his time in the debates attempting to portray Lincoln as a dangerous radical whose positions threatened to degrade white Americans by reducing them to equality with blacks. The United States government, Douglas proclaimed, had been created "by white men for the benefit of white men and their posterity for ever."

Lincoln shared many of the racial prejudices of his day. He opposed giving Illinois blacks the right to vote or serve on juries and spoke frequently of colonizing blacks overseas as the best solution to the problems of slavery and race. Yet, unlike Douglas, Lincoln did not use appeals to racism to garner votes. And he refused to exclude blacks from the human family. No less than whites, they were entitled to the inalienable rights of the Declaration of Independence, which applied to "all men, in all lands, everywhere," not merely to Europeans and their descendants.

The Illinois election returns revealed a state sharply divided, like the nation itself. Southern Illinois, settled from the South, voted strongly Democratic, while the rapidly growing northern part of the state was firmly in the Republican column. Until the adoption of the Seventeenth Amendment in the early twentieth century, each state's legislature chose its U.S. senators. In 1858, Republican candidates for the legislature won more votes statewide than Democrats. But because the apportionment of seats, based on the census of 1850, did not reflect the growth of northern Illinois since then, the Democrats emerged with a narrow margin in the legislature. Douglas was reelected. His victory was all the more remarkable because elsewhere in the North Republicans swept to victory in 1858. Resentment over the administration's Kansas policy split the Democratic Party, sometimes producing two Democratic candidates (pro-Douglas and pro-Buchanan) running against a single Republican. Coupled with the impact of the economic recession that began in 1857, this helped to produce Republican victories even in Indiana and Pennsylvania, which Democrats had carried two years earlier.

JOHN BROWN AT HARPERS FERRY

An armed assault by the abolitionist John Brown on the federal arsenal at Harpers Ferry, Virginia, further heightened sectional tensions. Brown had a long career of involvement in antislavery activities. In the 1830s and 1840s, he had befriended fugitive slaves and, although chronically in debt, helped to finance antislavery publications. Like other abolitionists, Brown was a deeply religious man. But his God was not the forgiving Jesus of the revivals, who encouraged men to save themselves through conversion, but the vengeful Father of the Old Testament. During the civil war in Kansas,

John Brown in an 1847 portrait by Augustus Washington, a black photographer.

An 1835 painting of the federal arsenal at Harpers Ferry, Virginia (now West Virginia). John Brown's raid on Harpers Ferry in October 1859 helped to bring on the Civil War.

Brown traveled to the territory. In May 1856, after the attack on Lawrence, he and a few followers murdered five proslavery settlers at Pottawatomie Creek. For the next two years, he traveled through the North and Canada, raising funds and enlisting followers for a war against slavery.

On October 16, 1859, with twenty-one men, seven of them black, Brown seized Harpers Ferry. Militarily, the plan made little sense. Brown's band was soon surrounded and killed or captured by a detachment of federal soldiers headed by Colonel Robert E. Lee. Placed on trial for treason to the state of Virginia, Brown conducted himself with dignity and courage, winning admiration from millions of northerners who disapproved of his violent deeds. When Virginia's governor, Henry A. Wise, spurned pleas for clemency and ordered Brown executed, he turned Brown into a martyr to much of the North. Henry David Thoreau pronounced him "a crucified hero." Since Brown's death, radicals of both the left and right have revered Brown as a man willing to take action against an institution he considered immoral. Black leaders have long hailed him as a rare white person willing to sacrifice himself for the cause of racial justice.

To the South, the failure of Brown's assault seemed less significant than the adulation he seemed to arouse from much of the northern public. His raid and execution further widened the breach between the sections. Brown's last letter was a brief, prophetic statement: "I, John Brown, am quite certain that the crimes of this guilty land will never be purged away but with blood."

THE RISE OF SOUTHERN NATIONALISM

With the Republicans continuing to gain strength in the North, Democrats might have been expected to put a premium on party unity as the election of 1860 approached. By this time, however, a sizable group of southerners now viewed their region's prospects as more favorable outside the Union than within it. Throughout the 1850s, influential writers and political leaders kept up a drumbeat of complaints about the South's problems. The sky-high price of slaves made it impossible for many planters' sons and upwardly mobile small farmers to become planters in their own right. Many white southerners felt that the opportunity was eroding for economic independence through ownership of land and slaves—liberty as they understood it. The North, secessionists charged, reaped the benefits of the cotton trade, while southerners fell deeper and deeper into debt. To remain in the Union meant to accept "bondage" to the North. But an independent South could become the foundation of a slave empire ringing the Caribbean and embracing Cuba, other West Indian islands, Mexico, and parts of Central America.

More and more southerners were speaking openly of southward expansion. In 1854, Pierre Soulé of Louisiana, the American ambassador to Spain, had persuaded the ministers to Britain and France to join him in signing the Ostend Manifesto, which called on the United States to purchase or seize Cuba, where slavery was still legal, from Spain. Meanwhile, the military adventurer William Walker led a series of "filibustering" expeditions (the term derived from the Spanish word for pirate, *filibustero*) in Central America.

Born in Tennessee, Walker had headed to California to join the gold rush. Failing to strike it rich, he somehow decided to try to become the leader of a Latin American country. In 1853, he led a band of men who "captured" Baja California—a peninsula owned by Mexico south of California—and named himself president of an independent republic. The arrival of Mexican naval vessels forced Walker and his men to beat a hasty retreat. Walker next decided to establish himself as ruler of Nicaragua in Central America, and to open that country to slavery. Nicaragua at the time was engaged in a civil war, and one faction invited Walker to assist it by bringing 300 armed men. In 1855, Walker captured the city of Granada and in the following year proclaimed himself president. The administration of Franklin Pierce recognized Walker's government, but neighboring countries sent in troops, who forced Walker to flee. His activities represented clear violations of American neutrality laws. But Walker won acclaim in the South, and when federal authorities placed him on trial in New Orleans in 1858, the jury acquitted him.

By the late 1850s, southern leaders were bending every effort to strengthen the bonds of slavery. "Slavery is our king," declared a South Carolina politician in 1860. "Slavery is our truth, slavery is our divine right." New state laws further restricted access to freedom. One in Louisiana stated simply: "After the passage of this act, no slave shall be emancipated in this state." Some southerners called for the reopening of the African slave trade, hoping that an influx of new slaves would lower the price, thereby increasing the number of whites with a vested interest in the peculiar institution. By early 1860, seven states of the Deep South had gone on record demanding that the Democratic Platform pledge to protect slavery in all the territories that had not yet been admitted to the Union as states. Virtually no northern politician could accept this position. For southern leaders to insist on it would guarantee the destruction of the Democratic Party as a national institution. But southern nationalists, known as "fire-eaters," hoped to split the party and the country and form an independent Southern Confederacy.

THE DEMOCRATIC SPLIT

When the Democratic convention met in April 1860, Douglas's supporters commanded a majority but not the two-thirds required for a presidential nomination. Because of his fight against Kansas's Lecompton Constitution and his refusal to support congressional laws imposing slavery on all the territories, Douglas had become unacceptable to political leaders of the Deep South. They were still determined to bring Kansas into the Union as a slave state. When the convention adopted a platform reaffirming the doctrine of popular sovereignty, delegates from the seven slave states of the Lower South walked out and the gathering recessed in confusion. Six weeks later, it reconvened, replaced the bolters with Douglas supporters, and nominated him for president. In response, southern Democrats placed their own ticket in the field, headed by John C. Breckinridge of Kentucky. Breckinridge insisted that slavery must be protected in the western territories.

The Democratic Party, the last great bond of national unity, had been shattered. National conventions had traditionally been places where party managers, mindful of the need for unity in the fall campaign, reconciled their differences. But in 1860, neither northern nor southern Democrats were interested in conciliation. Southern Democrats no longer trusted their northern counterparts. Douglas's backers, for their part, would not accept a platform that doomed their party to certain defeat in the North.

THE NOMINATION OF LINCOLN

Meanwhile, Republicans gathered in Chicago and chose Lincoln as their standard-bearer. Although he entered the convention with fewer delegates than William H. Seward, Lincoln did not suffer from Seward's political liabilities. Former Know-Nothings, a majority of whom had by now joined Republican ranks, bitterly resented Seward's efforts as governor of New York to channel state funds to Catholic schools. Seward had a not entirely deserved reputation for radicalism as a result of his "higher law" and "irrepressible conflict" speeches, discussed earlier.

Lincoln's devotion to the Union appealed to moderate Republicans, and his emphasis on the moral dimension of the sectional controversy made him acceptable to Republicans from abolitionist backgrounds. Having never associated with the Know-Nothings, he could appeal to immigrant voters, and nativists preferred him to the hated Seward. Most important, coming from Illinois, Lincoln was better positioned to carry the pivotal "doubtful states" essential for Republican victory. On the third ballot, he was nominated. The party platform denied the validity of the Dred Scott decision, reaffirmed Republicans' opposition to slavery's expansion, and added economic planks designed to appeal to a broad array of northern voters—free homesteads in the West, a protective tariff, and government aid in building a transcontinental railroad.

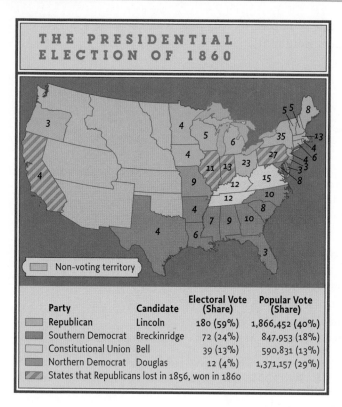

THE PRESIDENTIAL ELECTION OF 1860

Non-voting territory

Party	Candidate	Electoral Vote (Share)	Popular Vote (Share)
Republican	Lincoln	180 (59%)	1,866,452 (40%)
Southern Democrat	Breckinridge	72 (24%)	847,953 (18%)
Constitutional Union	Bell	39 (13%)	590,831 (13%)
Northern Democrat	Douglas	12 (4%)	1,371,157 (29%)
States that Republicans lost in 1856, won in 1860			

THE ELECTION OF 1860

In effect, two presidential campaigns took place in 1860. In the North, Lincoln and Douglas were the combatants. In the South, the Republicans had no presence and three candidates contested the election—Douglas, Breckinridge, and John Bell of Tennessee, the candidate of the hastily organized Constitutional Union Party. A haven for Unionist former Whigs, this new party adopted a platform consisting of a single pledge—to preserve "the Constitution as it is [that is, with slavery] and the Union as it was [without sectional discord]."

The most striking thing about the election returns was their sectional character. Lincoln carried all of the North except New Jersey, receiving 1.8 million popular votes (54 percent of the regional total and 40 percent of the national) and 180 electoral votes (a clear majority). Breckinridge captured most of the slave states, although Bell carried three Upper South states and about 40 percent of the southern vote as a whole. Douglas placed first only in Missouri, but his 1.3 million popular votes were second in number only to Lincoln's. Douglas was the only candidate with significant support in all parts of the country, a vindication, in a sense, of his long effort to transcend sectional divisions. But his failure to carry either section suggested that a traditional political career based on devotion to the Union was no longer possible. Without a single vote in ten southern states, Lincoln was elected the nation's sixteenth president. He failed to secure a majority of the national popular vote. But because of the North's superiority in population, Lincoln would still have carried the electoral college and thus been elected president even if the votes of his three opponents had all been cast for a single candidate.

THE IMPENDING CRISIS

THE SECESSION MOVEMENT

In the eyes of many white southerners, Lincoln's victory placed their future at the mercy of a party avowedly hostile to their region's values and interests. Those advocating secession did not believe Lincoln's administration would take immediate steps against slavery in the states. But if, as seemed quite possible, the election of 1860 marked a fundamental shift in power, the beginning of a long period of Republican rule, who could say what the North's antislavery sentiment would demand in five years, or ten? Slaveowners, moreover, feared Republican efforts to extend their party into the South by appealing to non-slaveholders. Rather than accept permanent minority status in a nation governed by their opponents, Deep South political leaders boldly struck for their region's independence. At stake, they believed, was not a single election, but an entire way of life.

An 1860 engraving of a mass meeting in Savannah, Georgia, shortly after Lincoln's election as president, which called for the state to secede from the Union. The banner on the obelisk at the center reads, "Our Motto State's Rights, Equality of the States, Don't Tread on Me"—the last a slogan from the American Revolution.

In the months that followed Lincoln's election, seven states stretching from South Carolina to Texas seceded from the Union. These were the states of the Cotton Kingdom, where slaves represented a larger part of the total population than in the Upper South. First to secede was South Carolina, the state with the highest percentage of slaves in its population and a long history of political radicalism. On December 20, 1860, the legislature unanimously voted to leave the Union. Its *Declaration of the Immediate Causes of Secession* placed the issue of slavery squarely at the center of the crisis. The North had "assumed the right of deciding upon the propriety of our domestic institutions." Lincoln was a man "whose opinions and purposes are hostile to slavery." Experience had proved "that slaveholding states cannot be safe in subjection to nonslaveholding states." Secessionists equated their movement with the struggle for American independence. Proslavery ideologue George Fitzhugh, however, later claimed that southern secession was even more significant than the "commonplace affair" of 1776, since the South rebelled not merely against a particular government but against the erroneous modern idea of freedom based on "human equality" and "natural liberty."

THE SECESSION CRISIS

As the Union unraveled, President Buchanan seemed paralyzed. He denied that a state could secede, but he also insisted that the federal government had no right to use force against it. Other political leaders struggled to find a formula to resolve the crisis. Senator John J. Crittenden of Kentucky, a slave state on the border between North and South, offered the most widely supported compromise plan of the secession winter. Embodied in a series of unamendable constitutional amendments, Crittenden's proposal would

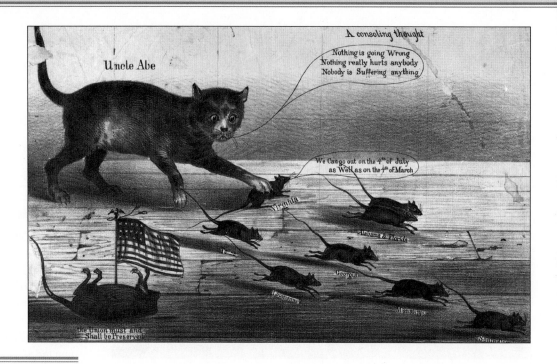

A Richmond, Virginia, cartoonist in April 1861 depicts Lincoln as a cat seeking to catch the southern states as mice fleeing the Union, which lies dead on the left.

have guaranteed the future of slavery in the states where it existed, and extended the Missouri Compromise line to the Pacific Ocean, dividing between slavery and free soil all territories "now held, or hereafter acquired." The seceding states rejected the compromise as too little, too late. But many in the Upper South and North saw it as a way to settle sectional differences and prevent civil war.

Crittenden's plan, however, foundered on the opposition of Abraham Lincoln. Willing to conciliate the South on issues like the return of fugitive slaves, Lincoln took an unyielding stand against the expansion of slavery. Here, he informed one Republican leader, he intended to "hold firm, as with a chain of steel." A fundamental principle of democracy, Lincoln believed, was at stake. "We have just carried an election," he wrote, "on principles fairly stated to the people. Now we are told in advance that the government shall be broken up unless we surrender to those we have beaten, before we take the offices. . . . If we surrender, it is the end of us and the end of the government." Lincoln, moreover, feared that Crittenden's reference to land "hereafter acquired" offered the South a thinly veiled invitation to demand the acquisition of Cuba, Mexico, and other territory suited to slavery.

Before Lincoln assumed office on March 4, 1861, the seven seceding states formed the Confederate States of America, adopted a constitution, and chose as their president Jefferson Davis of Mississippi. With a few alterations—the president served a single six-year term; cabinet members, as in Britain, could sit in Congress—the Confederate constitution was modeled closely on that of the United States. It departed from the federal Constitution, however, in explicitly guaranteeing slave property both in the states and in any territories the new nation acquired. The "cornerstone" of the Confederacy, announced Davis's vice president, Alexander H. Stephens of Georgia, was "the great truth that the negro is not equal to the white man, that slavery, subordination to the superior race, is his natural and normal condition."

Inauguration of Mr. Lincoln, *a photograph taken on March 4, 1861. The unfinished dome of the Capitol building symbolizes the precarious state of the Union at the time Lincoln assumed office.*

AND THE WAR CAME

Even after rejecting the Crittenden Compromise, Lincoln did not believe war inevitable. When he became president, eight slave states of the Upper South remained in the Union. Here, slaves and slaveholders made up a considerably lower proportion of the population than in the Deep South, and large parts of the white population did not believe Lincoln's election justified dissolving the Union. Even within the Confederacy, whites had divided over secession, with considerable numbers of non-slaveholding farmers in opposition. In time, Lincoln believed, secession might collapse from within.

In his inaugural address, delivered on March 4, 1861, Lincoln tried to be conciliatory. He rejected the right of secession but denied any intention of interfering with slavery in the states. He said nothing of retaking the forts, arsenals, and customs houses the Confederacy had seized, although he did promise to "hold" remaining federal property in the seceding states. But Lincoln also issued a veiled warning: "In your hands, my dissatisfied fellow countrymen, and not in mine, is the momentous issue of civil war."

In his first month as president, Lincoln walked a tightrope. He avoided any action that might drive more states from the Union, encouraged southern Unionists to assert themselves within the Confederacy, and sought to quiet a growing clamor in the North for forceful action against secession. Knowing that the risk of war existed, Lincoln strove to ensure that if hostilities did break out, the South, not the Union, would fire the first shot. And that is precisely what happened on April 12, 1861, at Fort Sumter, an enclave of Union control in the harbor of Charleston, South Carolina.

A few days earlier, Lincoln had notified South Carolina's governor that he intended to replenish the garrison's dwindling food supplies. Viewing Fort Sumter's presence as an affront to southern nationhood, and perhaps

Bombardment of Fort Sumter, *a lithograph by Nathaniel Currier and James Ives depicting the beginning of the Civil War.*

hoping to force the wavering Upper South to join the Confederacy, Jefferson Davis ordered batteries to fire on the fort. On April 14, its commander surrendered. The following day, Lincoln proclaimed that an insurrection existed in the South and called for 75,000 troops to suppress it. Civil war had begun. Within weeks, Virginia, North Carolina, Tennessee, and Arkansas joined the Confederacy. "Both sides deprecated war," Lincoln later said, "but one of them would *make* war rather than let the nation survive; and the other would *accept* war rather than let it perish. And the war came."

In 1842, Henry Wadsworth Longfellow published *Poems on Slavery*, a collection that included a work entitled simply "The Warning." In it, Longfellow compared the American slave to the mighty biblical figure of Samson, who after being blinded and chained, managed to destroy the temple of his tormentors:

> There is a poor, blind Samson in this land,
> Shorn of his strength, and bound in bonds of steel,
> Who may, in some grim revel, raise his hand,
> And shake the pillars of this Commonweal,
> Till the vast Temple of our liberties
> A shapeless mass of wreck and rubbish lies.

In 1861, Longfellow's warning came to pass. The Union created by the founders lay in ruins. The struggle to rebuild it would bring about a new birth of American freedom.

SUGGESTED READING

BOOKS

Anbinder, Tyler. *Nativism and Slavery: The Northern Know-Nothings and the Politics of the 1850s* (1992). A detailed study of the relationship between nativism and antislavery politics in the North.

Cronon, William. *Nature's Metropolis: Chicago and the Great West* (1992). An influential account of the rise of Chicago and the city's relationship to its agricultural hinterland.

Current, Richard N. *Lincoln and the First Shot* (1963). Examines the decisions and strategy of both Lincoln and Jefferson Davis that produced the firing on Fort Sumter that began the Civil War.

Davis, William C. *Lone Star Rising: The Revolutionary Birth of the Texas Republic* (2004). An up-to-date history of the Texas war for independence.

Earle, Jonathan H. *Jacksonian Antislavery and the Politics of Free Soil, 1824–1854* (2004). Emphasizes the role of northern Jacksonians in antislavery politics.

Foner, Eric. *Free Soil, Free Labor, Free Men: The Ideology of the Republican Party before the Civil War* (1970). A discussion of the basic ideas that united Republicans in the 1850s, especially their "free labor ideology."

Goodman, David. *Gold Seeking: Victoria and California in the 1850s* (1994). A comparative history of the two gold rushes.

Haas, Lisbeth. *Conquests and Historical Identities in California, 1769–1936* (1995). Contains a detailed description of how California's acquisition by the United States affected the state's diverse population groups.

Johannsen, Robert W. *To the Halls of Montezuma: The Mexican War in the American Imagination* (1985). A history of the Mexican War and how it was remembered after its conclusion.

Levine, Bruce. *Half Slave and Half Free: The Roots of the Civil War* (1992). A survey of the coming of the Civil War, stressing irreconcilable differences between North and South.

Potter, David M. *The Impending Crisis, 1848–1861* (1976). Still the standard account of the nation's history in the years before the Civil War.

Sinha, Manisha. *The Counterrevolution of Slavery: Politics and Ideology in Antebellum South Carolina* (2002). A detailed study of how a vigorous defense of slavery developed in South Carolina, which justified the decision for secession.

Stampp, Kenneth. *And the War Came: The North and the Secession Crisis, 1860–61* (1950). An examination of Northern actions and attitudes during the secession crisis.

Stephanson, Anders. *Manifest Destiny: American Expansionism and the Empire of Right* (1995). Considers how the idea of an American mission to spread freedom and democracy has affected American foreign policy throughout the country's history.

WEBSITES

Getting the Message Out: National Campaign Materials, 1840–1860: http://dig.lib.niu.edu/message/

Gold Rush!: www.museumca.org/goldrush/

The Mexican-American War and the Media: www.history.vt.edu/MxAmWar/INDEX.HTM#

The Oregon Trail: www.isu.edu/~trinmich/Oregontrail.html

Uncle Tom's Cabin and American Culture: http://jefferson.village.virginia.edu/utc/

REVIEW QUESTIONS

1. Explain the justifications for the doctrine of manifest destiny, including material and idealistic motivations.

2. What economic forces promoted continental expansion in the 1830s and 1840s?

3. Why did many Americans criticize the Mexican War? How did they see expansion as a threat to American liberties?

4. How did the concept of "race" develop by the mid-nineteenth century, and how did it enter into the manifest destiny debate?

5. Explain the factors behind the creation of the Republican Party.

6. What three questions did the Supreme Court address in the Dred Scott case? Assess the Court's arguments.

7. Based on the Lincoln-Douglas debates, how did the views of both men differ on the expansion of slavery, equal rights, and the role of the national government?

8. What were the international implications of southern nationalism?

9. Explain how sectional voting patterns in the 1860 presidential election allowed southern "fire-eaters" to justify secession.

FREEDOM QUESTIONS

1. How did Americans argue that conquering Texas and other parts of Mexico was "extending the area of freedom"?

2. Explain how both northerners and southerners believed winning the struggle over the expansion of slavery was the key to preserving their freedoms and to preventing their domination by the other section of the nation.

3. According to the Republican Party, how was "free labor" the key to preserving American freedoms, and the free society threatened by the Slave Power?

4. How did southern nationalists justify independence as "freedom" from northern "bondage"?

KEY TERMS

REVIEW TABLE

Road Toward War

Event	Date	Explanation	Result
Compromise of 1850	1850	Southerners are concerned that congressional balance would be disrupted by California's request for free-state status	California becomes a free state; the Fugitive Slave Act is passed; and slavery in the New Mexico territory is to be decided by locals
Kansas-Nebraska Act	1854	A bill that provides for slavery to be decided by popular sovereignty	"Bleeding Kansas"—civil war in Kansas over the issue of slavery in 1856
Dred Scott decision	1857	Supreme Court rules that only white persons are citizens and that Congress possesses no power to bar slavery from a territory	It in effect declared unconstitutional the Republican platform of restricting slavery's expansion
John Brown and Harpers Ferry	1859	Brown raids a federal arsenal to launch a slave rebellion and is executed for his crime	Brown becomes a martyr to many in the North
1860 Election	1860	Abraham Lincoln wins with no votes in the South, ending decades of southern control of the presidency	Seven southern states secede from the Union before Lincoln is inaugurated

CHAPTER 14

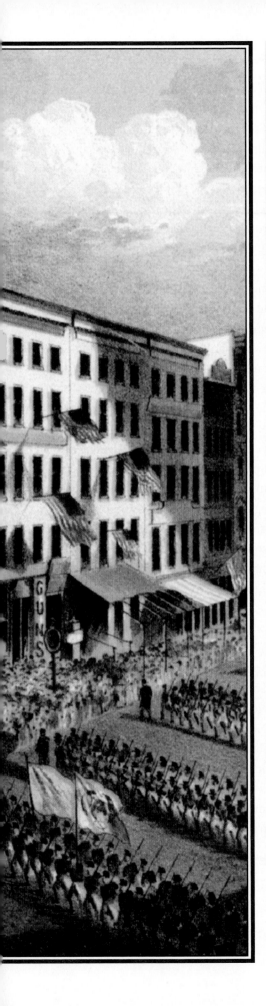

A New Birth of Freedom: The Civil War, 1861–1865

Departure of the 7th Regiment, *a lithograph from 1861 illustrating the departure of a unit of the New York State militia for service in the Civil War. A contemporary writer captured the exuberant spirit of the early days of the war: "New York was certainly raving mad with excitement. The ladies laughed, smiled, sighed, sobbed, and wept. The men cheered and shouted as never men cheered and shouted before."*

FOCUS QUESTIONS

• Why is the Civil War considered the first modern war?

• How did a war to preserve the Union become a war to end slavery?

• How did the Civil War transform the national economy and create a stronger nation-state?

• How did the war effort and leadership problems affect the society and economy of the Confederacy?

• What were the military and political turning points of the war?

• What were the most important wartime "rehearsals for Reconstruction"?

L ike hundreds of thousands of other Americans, Marcus M. Spiegel volunteered in 1861 to fight in the Civil War. Born into a Jewish family in Germany in 1829, Spiegel took part in the failed German revolution of 1848. In the following year he emigrated to Ohio, where he married the daughter of a local farmer. When the Civil War broke out, the nation's 150,000 Jews represented less than 1 percent of the total population. But Spiegel shared wholeheartedly in American patriotism. He went to war, he wrote to his brother-in-law, to defend "the flag that was ever ready to protect you and me and every one who sought its protection from oppression."

Spiegel rose to the rank of colonel in the 120th Ohio Infantry and saw action in Virginia, Mississippi, and Louisiana. He corresponded frequently with his wife, Caroline. "I have seen and learned much," he wrote in 1863. "I have seen men dying of disease and mangled by the weapons of death; I have witnessed hostile armies arrayed against each other, the charge of infantry, [and] cavalry hunting men down like beasts." But he never wavered in his commitment to the "glorious cause" of preserving the Union and its heritage of freedom.

What one Pennsylvania recruit called "the magic word *Freedom*" shaped how many Union soldiers understood the conflict. The war's purpose, wrote Samuel McIlvaine, a sergeant from Indiana, was to preserve the American nation as "the beacon light of liberty and freedom to the human race." But as the war progressed, prewar understandings of liberty gave way to something new. Millions of northerners who had not been abolitionists became convinced that preserving the Union as an embodiment of liberty required the destruction of slavery.

Marcus Spiegel's changing views mirrored the transformation of a struggle to save the Union into a war to end slavery. Spiegel was an ardent Democrat. He shared the era's racist attitudes and thought Lincoln's Emancipation Proclamation a serious mistake. Yet as the Union army penetrated the heart of the Deep South, Spiegel became increasingly opposed to slavery. "Since I am here," he wrote to his wife from Louisiana in January 1864, "I have learned and seen . . . the horrors of slavery. You know it takes me long to say anything that sounds antidemocratic [opposed to Democratic Party policies], but . . . never hereafter will I either speak or vote in favor of slavery."

Marcus Spiegel was killed in a minor engagement in Louisiana in May 1864, one of 620,000 Americans to perish in the Civil War.

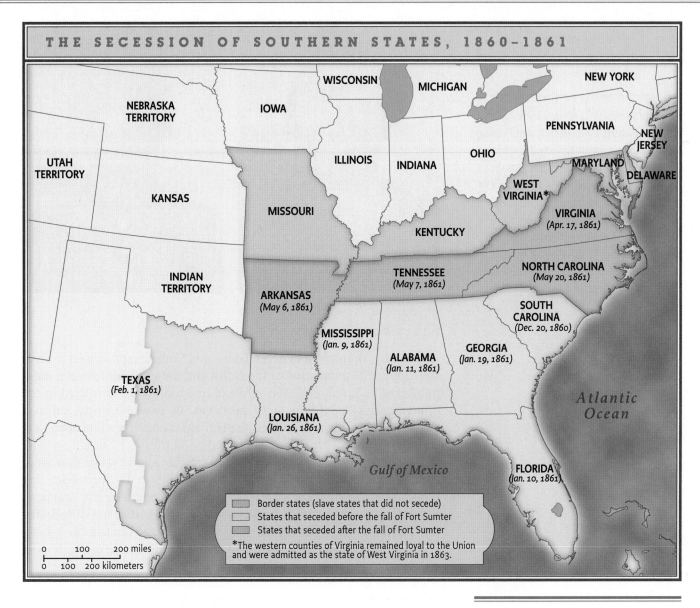

THE SECESSION OF SOUTHERN STATES, 1860–1861

Border states (slave states that did not secede)
States that seceded before the fall of Fort Sumter
States that seceded after the fall of Fort Sumter

*The western counties of Virginia remained loyal to the Union and were admitted as the state of West Virginia in 1863.

By the time secession ran its course, eleven slave states had left the Union.

THE FIRST MODERN WAR

The American Civil War is often called the first modern war. Never before had mass armies confronted each other on the battlefield with the deadly weapons created by the industrial revolution. The resulting casualties dwarfed anything in the American experience. Beginning as a battle of army versus army, the war became a conflict of society against society, in which the distinction between military and civilian targets often disappeared. In a war of this kind, the effectiveness of political leadership, the ability to mobilize economic resources, and a society's willingness to keep up the fight despite setbacks are as crucial to the outcome as success or failure on individual battlefields.

Sergeant James W. Travis, Thirty-eighth Illinois Infantry, Union army, and Private Edwin Francis Jemison, Second Louisiana Regiment, Confederate army, two of the nearly 3 million Americans who fought in the Civil War. Before going off to war, many soldiers sat for photographs like these, reproduced on small cards called cartes de visite, *which they distributed to friends and loved ones. Jemison was killed in the Battle of Malvern Hill in July 1862.*

THE TWO COMBATANTS

Almost any comparison between Union and Confederacy seemed to favor the Union. The population of the North and the loyal border slave states numbered 22 million in 1860, while only 9 million persons lived in the Confederacy, 3.5 million of them slaves. In manufacturing, railroad mileage, and financial resources, the Union far outstripped its opponent. On the other hand, the Union confronted by far the greater task. To restore the shattered nation, it had to invade and conquer an area larger than western Europe. Confederate soldiers were highly motivated fighters defending their homes and families. Like Washington's forces during the American Revolution, southern armies could lose most of the battles and still win the war if their opponent tired of the struggle. "No people," Confederate general P. G. T. Beauregard later claimed, "ever warred for independence with more relative advantages than the Confederacy."

On both sides, the outbreak of war stirred powerful feelings of patriotism. Recruits rushed to enlist, expecting a short, glorious war. Later, as enthusiasm waned, both sides resorted to a draft. The Confederacy in the spring of 1862 passed the first draft law in American history, and the North soon followed. By 1865, more than 2 million men had served in the Union army and 900,000 in the Confederate army. Each was a cross section of its society: the North's was composed largely of farm boys, shopkeepers, artisans, and urban workers, while the South's consisted mostly of non-slaveholding small farmers, with slaveowners dominating the officer corps.

Few recruits had any military experience. Fifteen years had passed since the Mexican War. Ideas about war were highly romantic, based on novels, magazine articles, and lithographs of soldiers covering themselves with glory. One private wrote home in 1862 that his notion of combat had come from the pictures of battles he had seen: "they would all be in a line, all standing in a nice level field fighting, a number of ladies taking care of the wounded, etc. But it isn't so." Nor were the recruits ready for military regimentation. "It comes rather hard at first to be deprived of liberty," wrote an Illinois soldier. Initially, the constant round of drilling, ditch digging, and other chores were only occasionally interrupted by fierce bursts of fighting

on the battlefield. According to one estimate, during the first two years of the
war the main Union force, the Army of
the Potomac, spent only thirty days in
actual combat.

THE TECHNOLOGY OF WAR

Neither the soldiers nor their officers
were prepared for the way technology
had transformed warfare. The Civil War
was the first major conflict in which the
railroad transported troops and supplies
and the first to see railroad junctions such

as Atlanta and Petersburg become major military objectives. The famous sea
battle between the Union vessel *Monitor* and the Confederate *Merrimac* in
1862 was the first demonstration of the superiority of ironclads over wooden
ships, revolutionizing naval warfare. The war saw the use of the telegraph for
military communication, the introduction of observation balloons to view
enemy lines, and even primitive hand grenades and submarines.

Perhaps most important, a revolution in arms manufacturing had
replaced the traditional musket, accurate at only a short range, with the
more modern rifle, deadly at 600 yards or more because of its grooved (or
"rifled") barrel. This development changed the nature of combat, emphasizing the importance of heavy fortifications and elaborate trenches and
giving those on the defensive—usually southern armies—a significant
advantage over attacking forces. "My men," said Confederate general
Thomas "Stonewall" Jackson, "sometimes fail to drive the enemy from his
position, but to hold one, never." The war of rifle and trench produced the
appalling casualty statistics of Civil War battles. The 620,000 who perished
in the war represent the equivalent, in terms of today's population, of more

Battle of the Iron-clads *Monitor and
Merrimac*, painted in 1877 by William
Torgerson, depicts the first clash between
ironclad ships, which took place off the
coast of Virginia on March 9, 1862.
Precursors of modern battleships,
ironclads were among the numerous
technological advances introduced during
the Civil War. The masts of a wooden
naval vessel are visible on the horizon.

Confederate dead at Spotsylvania,
Virginia, the site of a bloody battle in
1864.

A surgeon's kit used in the Civil War, containing amputation instruments, knives, and tourniquets. With medical knowledge and practices primitive at best, far more men died from wounds, infections, and disease than in battle.

than 6 million men. These figures do not include the thousands of civilians who became victims of battles or who perished in disease-ridden camps for runaway slaves or in conflicts between Unionist and Confederate families that raged in parts of the South. The death toll in the Civil War nearly equals the total number of Americans who died in all the nation's other wars, from the Revolution to the war in Iraq.

Nor was either side ready for other aspects of modern warfare. Medical care remained primitive. "I believe the doctors kill more than they cure," wrote an Alabama private in 1862. Diseases like measles, dysentery, malaria, and typhus swept through army camps, killing more men than did combat. The Civil War was the first war in which large numbers of Americans were captured by the enemy and held in dire conditions in military prisons. Some 50,000 men died in these prisons, victims of starvation and disease, including 13,000 Union soldiers at Andersonville, Georgia.

Everywhere in the world, war was becoming more destructive. The scale of Civil War bloodshed was unique in American history, but not in the nineteenth-century world. The Taiping Rebellion in China (1850–1864) resulted in 23 million deaths. The War of the Triple Alliance in South America (1864–1870), which pitted Argentina, Brazil, and Uruguay against Paraguay, caused the death of half of Paraguay's prewar population of around 525,000. Napoleon III's military destruction of the Paris Commune in 1871 resulted in the death of more than 20,000 of his fellow countrymen in a single city.

THE PUBLIC AND THE WAR

Another modern feature of the Civil War was that both sides were assisted by a vast propaganda effort to mobilize public opinion. In the Union, an

Confederate prisoners of war at Camp Douglas, Chicago, in 1864.

outpouring of lithographs, souvenirs, sheet music, and pamphlets issued by patriotic organizations and the War Department reaffirmed northern values, tarred the Democratic Party with the brush of treason, and accused the South of numerous crimes against Union soldiers and loyal civilians. Comparable items appeared in the Confederacy.

At the same time, the war's brutal realities were brought home with unprecedented immediacy to the public at large. War correspondents accompanied the armies, and newspapers reported the results of battles on the following day and quickly published long lists of casualties. The infant art of photography carried images of war into millions of American living rooms. Beginning in 1862, when photographers entered the battlefield to take shocking pictures of the dead at Antietam, the camera, in the words of one journalist, "brought the bodies and laid them in our door-yards." Mathew Brady, who organized a corps of photographers to cover the war, found the conflict a passport to fame and wealth. For photography itself, it was a turning point in its growth as an art and business enterprise.

MOBILIZING RESOURCES

The outbreak of the war found both sides unprepared. In 1861, there was no national railroad gauge (the distance separating the two tracks), so trains built for one line could not run on another. There was no national banking system, no tax system capable of raising the enormous funds needed to finance the war, and not even accurate maps of the southern states. Soon after the firing on Fort Sumter, Lincoln proclaimed a naval blockade of the South, part of the so-called Anaconda Plan, which aimed to strangle the South economically. But the navy charged with patrolling the 3,500-mile coastline consisted of only ninety vessels, fewer than half of them steam-powered. Not until late in the war did the blockade become effective.

Then there was the problem of purchasing and distributing the food, weapons, and other supplies required by the soldiers. The Union army eventually became the best-fed and best-supplied military force in history. By the war's third year, on the other hand, southern armies were suffering from acute shortages of food, uniforms, and shoes. Yet the chief of the Confederacy's Ordnance Bureau, Josiah Gorgas (a transplanted northerner), proved brilliantly resourceful in arming southern troops. Under his direc-

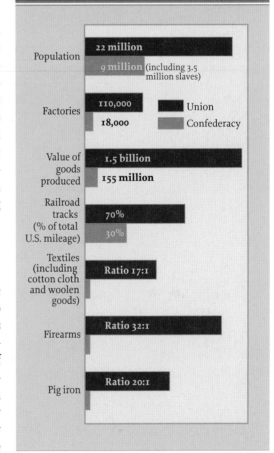

Figure 14.1 RESOURCES FOR WAR: UNION VERSUS CONFEDERACY

	Union	Confederacy
Population	22 million	9 million (including 3.5 million slaves)
Factories	110,000	18,000
Value of goods produced	1.5 billion	155 million
Railroad tracks (% of total U.S. mileage)	70%	30%
Textiles (including cotton cloth and woolen goods)	Ratio 17:1	
Firearms	Ratio 32:1	
Pig iron	Ratio 20:1	

In nearly every resource for warfare, the Union enjoyed a distinct advantage. But this did not make Union victory inevitable; as during the War of Independence, the stronger side sometimes loses.

Union army wagons crossing the Rapidan River in Virginia in May 1864. Supplying Civil War armies required an immense mobilization of economic resources.

tion, the Confederate government imported weapons from abroad and established arsenals of its own to turn out rifles, artillery, and ammunition.

MILITARY STRATEGIES

Each side tried to find ways to maximize its advantages. Essentially, the Confederacy adopted a defensive strategy, with occasional thrusts into the North. General Robert E. Lee, the leading southern commander, was a brilliant battlefield tactician who felt confident of his ability to fend off attacks by larger Union forces. He hoped that a series of defeats would weaken the North's resolve and lead it eventually to abandon the conflict and recognize southern independence.

Lincoln's early generals found it impossible to bring the Union's advantages in manpower and technology to bear on the battlefield. In April 1861, the regular army numbered little more than 15,000 men, most of whom were stationed west of the Mississippi River. Its officers had been trained to lead small, professional forces into battle, not the crowds of untrained men who assembled in 1861. The North also suffered from narrowness of military vision. Its generals initially concentrated on occupying southern territory and attempting to capture Richmond, the Confederate capital. They attacked sporadically and withdrew after a battle, thus sacrificing the North's manpower superiority and allowing the South to concentrate its smaller forces when an engagement impended.

Well before his generals did, Lincoln realized that simply capturing and occupying territory would not win the war, and that defeating the South's armies, not capturing its capital, had to be the North's battlefield objective. And when he came to adopt the policy of emancipation, Lincoln acknowledged what Confederate vice president Alexander H. Stephens had already affirmed: slavery was the "cornerstone" of the Confederacy. To win the war, therefore, the Union must make the institution that lay at the economic and social foundation of southern life a military target.

THE WAR BEGINS

In the East, most of the war's fighting took place in a narrow corridor between Washington and Richmond—a distance of only 100 miles—as a succession of Union generals led the Army of the Potomac (as the main northern force in the East was called) toward the Confederate capital, only to be turned back by southern forces. The first significant engagement, the first Battle of Bull Run, took place in northern Virginia on July 21, 1861. It ended with the chaotic retreat of the Union soldiers, along with the sightseers and politicians who had come to watch the battle. Almost 800 men died at Bull Run, a toll eclipsed many times in the years to come, but more Americans than had been killed in any previous battle in the nation's history. The encounter disabused both sides of the idea that the war would be a brief lark.

In the wake of Bull Run, George B. McClellan, an army engineer who had recently won a minor engagement with Confederate troops in western Virginia, assumed command of the Union's Army of the Potomac. A brilliant organizer, McClellan succeeded in welding his men into a superb fighting force. He seemed reluctant, however, to commit them to battle,

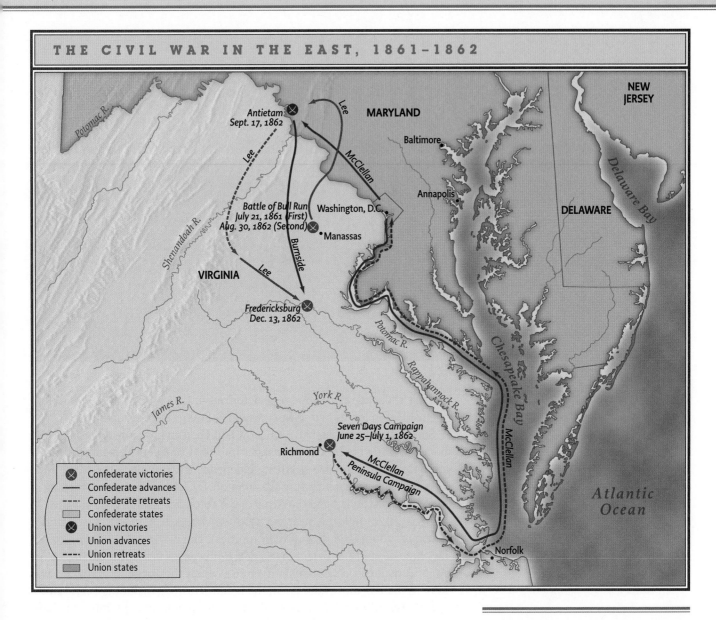

THE CIVIL WAR IN THE EAST, 1861–1862

During the first two years of the war, most of the fighting took place in Virginia and Maryland.

since he tended to overestimate the size of enemy forces. And as a Democrat, he hoped that compromise might end the war without large-scale loss of life or a weakening of slavery. Months of military inactivity followed.

THE WAR IN THE EAST, 1862

Not until the spring of 1862, after a growing clamor for action by Republican newspapers, members of Congress, and an increasingly impatient Lincoln, did McClellan lead his army of more than 100,000 men into Virginia. Here they confronted the smaller Army of Northern Virginia under the command of the Confederate general Joseph E. Johnston, and after he was wounded, Robert E. Lee. A brilliant battlefield tactician, Lee had been offered a command in the Union army but chose to fight for the Confederacy because of his devotion to Virginia. In the Seven Days' Campaign, a series of engagements in June 1862 on the peninsula south of Richmond, Lee blunted McClellan's attacks and forced him to withdraw back to the vicinity of Washington, D.C. In

The Battle of Antietam, *a painting of a Union advance by Captain James Hope of the Second Vermont Volunteers. More than 4,000 men died on September 17, 1862, when the Battle of Antietam was fought.*

August 1862, Lee again emerged victorious at the second Battle of Bull Run against Union forces under the command of General John Pope.

Successful on the defensive, Lee now launched an invasion of the North. He hoped to bring the border slave states into the Confederacy, persuade Britain and France to recognize southern independence, influence the North's fall elections, and perhaps capture Washington, D.C. At the Battle of Antietam, in Maryland, McClellan and the Army of the Potomac repelled Lee's advance. In a single day of fighting, nearly 4,000 men were killed and 18,000 wounded (2,000 of whom later died of their injuries). The dead, one survivor recalled, lay three deep in the field, mowed down "like grass before the scythe." More Americans died on September 17, 1862, when the Battle of Antietam was fought, than on any other day in the nation's history, including Pearl Harbor and D-Day in World War II and the terrorist attacks of September 11, 2001. Indeed, more American soldiers perished at Antietam than in all the other wars fought by the United States in the nineteenth century combined.

Since Lee was forced to retreat, the North could claim Antietam as a victory. It was to be the Union's last success in the East for some time. In December 1862, the Union suffered one of its most disastrous defeats of the war when General Ambrose E. Burnside, who had replaced McClellan as the head of the Army of the Potomac, assaulted Lee's army, which was entrenched on heights near Fredericksburg, Virginia. "It was not a fight," wrote one Union soldier to his mother, "it was a massacre."

THE WAR IN THE WEST

While the Union accomplished little in the East in the first two years of the war, events in the West followed a different course. Here, the architect of early success was Ulysses S. Grant. A West Point graduate who had resigned from the army in 1854 in part because of allegations of excessive drinking, Grant had been notably unsuccessful in civilian life. When the war broke out, he was working as a clerk in his brother's leather store in Galena, Illinois. But after being commissioned as a colonel in an Illinois regiment, Grant quickly displayed the daring, the logical mind, and the grasp of strategy he would demonstrate throughout the war.

In February 1862, Grant won the Union's first significant victory when he captured Forts Henry and Donelson in Tennessee. In April, naval forces under Admiral David G. Farragut steamed into New Orleans, giving the

Most of the Union's victories in the first two years of the war occurred in the West, especially at Shiloh and New Orleans.

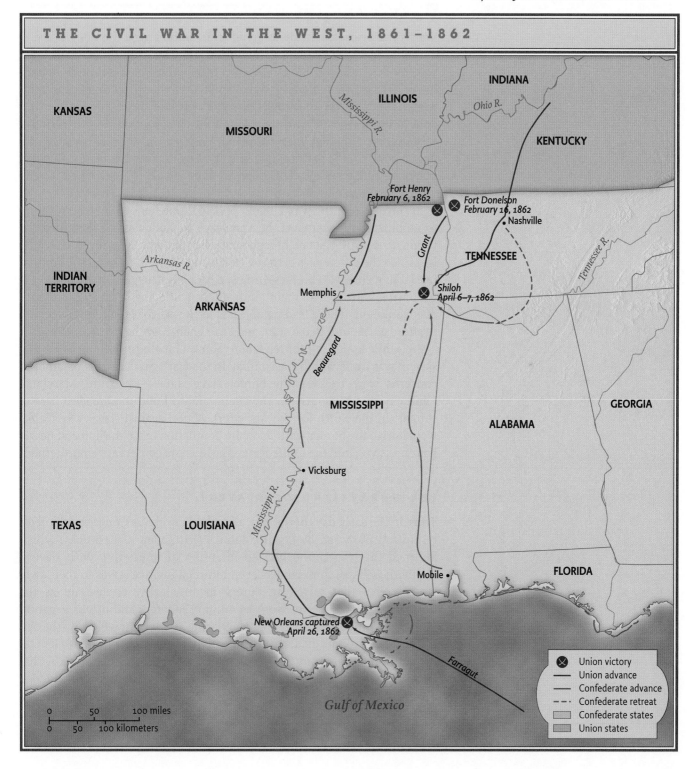

THE CIVIL WAR IN THE WEST, 1861–1862

Union control of the South's largest city and the rich sugar plantation parishes to its south and west. At the same time, Grant withstood a surprise Confederate attack at Shiloh, Tennessee. But Union momentum in the West then stalled.

THE COMING OF EMANCIPATION

SLAVERY AND THE WAR

War, it has been said, is the midwife of revolution. And the Civil War produced far-reaching changes in American life. The most dramatic of these was the destruction of slavery, the central institution of southern society. Between 1831, when the British abolished slavery in their empire, and 1888, when emancipation came to Brazil, some 6 million slaves gained their freedom in the Western Hemisphere. Of these, nearly 4 million, two-thirds of the total, lived in the southern United States. In numbers, scale, and the economic power of the institution of slavery, American emancipation dwarfed that of any other country (although far more people were liberated in 1861 when Czar Alexander II abolished serfdom in the Russian empire).

At the outset of the war, Lincoln invoked time-honored northern values to mobilize public support. In a message to Congress, he identified the Union cause with the fate of democracy for the "whole family of man." He identified the differences between North and South in terms of the familiar free labor ideology: "This is essentially a people's struggle. On the side of the Union, it is a struggle for maintaining in the world, that form and substance of government, whose leading object is to elevate the condition of men . . . to afford all, an unfettered start, and a fair chance, in the race of life."

But while appealing to free labor values, Lincoln initially insisted that slavery was irrelevant to the conflict. In the war's first year, his paramount concerns were to keep the border slave states—Delaware, Maryland, Kentucky, and Missouri—in the Union and to build the broadest base of support in the North for the war effort. Action against slavery, he feared, would drive the border, with its white population of 2.6 million and nearly 500,000 slaves, into the Confederacy and alienate conservative northerners.

THE UNRAVELING OF SLAVERY

Thus, in the early days of the war, a nearly unanimous Congress adopted a resolution proposed by Senator John J. Crittenden of Kentucky, which affirmed that the Union had no intention of interfering with slavery. Northern military commanders even returned fugitive slaves to their owners, a policy that raised an outcry in antislavery circles. Yet as the Confederacy set slaves to work as military laborers and blacks began to escape to Union lines, the policy of ignoring slavery unraveled. By the end of 1861, the military had adopted the plan, begun in Virginia by General Benjamin F. Butler, of treating escaped blacks as contraband of war—that is, property of military value subject to confiscation. Butler's order added a word to the war's vocabulary. Escaping slaves became known as "the contrabands." They were housed by the army in "contraband camps" and educated in new "contraband schools."

Meanwhile, slaves themselves took actions that helped propel a reluctant white America down the road to emancipation. Whatever the policies of the administration, blacks saw the outbreak of fighting as heralding the long-awaited end of bondage. Well before Lincoln made emancipation a war aim, blacks, in the North and the South, were calling the conflict the "freedom war." In 1861 and 1862, as the federal army occupied Confederate territory, slaves by the thousands headed for Union lines. Unlike fugitives before the war, these runaways included large numbers of women and children, as entire families abandoned the plantations. Not a few passed along military intelligence and detailed knowledge of the South's terrain. "The most valuable and reliable information of the enemy's movements in our vicinity that we have been able to get," noted the Union general Daniel E. Sickles, "derived from Negroes who came into our lines." In southern Louisiana, the arrival of the Union army in 1862 led slaves to sack plantation houses and refuse to work unless wages were paid. Slavery there, wrote a northern reporter, "is forever destroyed and worthless, no matter what Mr. Lincoln or anyone else may say on the subject."

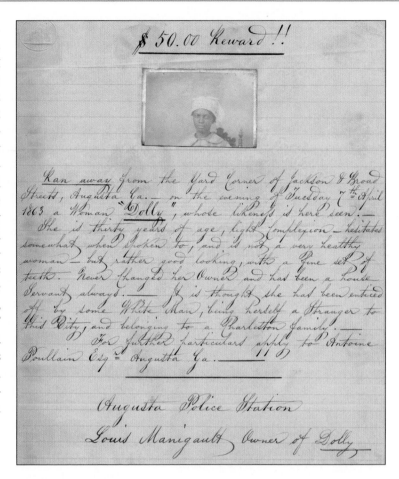

An 1863 advertisement for a runaway domestic slave circulated by Louis Manigault, a member of a prominent Georgia and South Carolina planter family. Manigault blamed an unknown white man for enticing her away, but she most likely escaped with a male slave who had begun to court her. Slaves fled to Union lines from the first days of the Civil War.

STEPS TOWARD EMANCIPATION

At first, blacks' determination to seize the opportunity presented by the war proved a burden to the army and an embarrassment to the administration. But the failure of traditional strategies to produce victory strengthened the hand of antislavery northerners. Since slavery stood at the foundation of the southern economy, they insisted, emancipation was necessary to weaken the South's ability to sustain the war.

The most uncompromising opponents of slavery before the war, abolitionists and Radical Republicans, quickly concluded that the institution must become a target of the Union war effort. "It is plain," declared Thaddeus Stevens, a Radical Republican congressman from Pennsylvania, "that nothing approaching the present policy will subdue the rebels." Outside of Congress, few pressed the case for emancipation more eloquently than Frederick Douglass. From the outset, he insisted that it was futile to "separate the freedom of the slave from the victory of the government." "Fire must be met with water," Douglass declared, "darkness with light, and war for the destruction of liberty must be met with war for the destruction of slavery."

These appeals won increasing support in a Congress frustrated by lack of military success. In March 1862, Congress prohibited the army from returning fugitive slaves. Then came abolition in the District of Columbia (with monetary compensation for slaveholders) and the territories, followed in July by the Second Confiscation Act, which liberated slaves of disloyal owners in Union-occupied territory, as well as slaves who escaped to Union lines.

Throughout these months, Lincoln struggled to retain control of the emancipation issue. In August 1861, John C. Frémont, commanding Union forces in Missouri, a state racked by a bitter guerrilla war between pronorthern and pro-southern bands, decreed the freedom of its slaves. Fearful of the order's impact on the border states, Lincoln swiftly rescinded it. In November, the president proposed that the border states embark on a program of gradual emancipation with the federal government paying owners for their loss of property. He also revived the idea of colonization. In August 1862, Lincoln met at the White House with a delegation of black leaders and urged them to promote emigration from the United States. "You and we are different races," he declared. "It is better for us both to be separated." As late as December, the president signed an agreement with a shady entrepreneur to settle former slaves on an island off the coast of Haiti.

LINCOLN'S DECISION

Sometime during the summer of 1862, Lincoln concluded that emancipation had become a political and military necessity. Many factors contributed to his decision—lack of military success, hope that emancipated slaves might help meet the army's growing manpower needs, changing northern public opinion, and the calculation that making slavery a target of the war effort would counteract sentiment in Britain for recognition of the Confederacy. But on the advice of Secretary of State William H. Seward, Lincoln delayed his announcement until after a Union victory, lest it seem an act of desperation. On September 22, 1862, five days after McClellan's army forced Lee to retreat at Antietam, Lincoln issued the Preliminary Emancipation Proclamation. It warned that unless the South laid down its arms by the end of 1862, he would decree abolition.

The initial northern reaction was not encouraging. In the fall elections of 1862, Democrats made opposition to emancipation the centerpiece of their campaign, warning that the North would be "Africanized"—inundated by freed slaves who would compete for jobs and seek to marry white women. The Republicans suffered sharp reverses. They lost control of the legislatures of Indiana and Illinois and the governorship of New York, and saw their majorities dangerously reduced in other states. In his annual message to Congress, early in December, Lincoln tried to calm northerners' racial fears, reviving the ideas of gradual emancipation and colonization. He concluded, however, on a higher note: "Fellow citizens, we cannot escape history.... The fiery trial through which we pass, will light us down, in honor or dishonor, to the latest generation.... In giving freedom to the slave, we assure freedom to the free—honorable alike in what we give, and what we preserve."

Abe Lincoln's Last Card, *an engraving from the British magazine* Punch, *October 18, 1862, portrays the Preliminary Emancipation Proclamation as the last move of a desperate gambler.*

THE EMANCIPATION PROCLAMATION

On January 1, 1863, after greeting visitors at the annual White House New Year's reception, Lincoln retired to his study to sign the Emancipation Proclamation. The document did not liberate all the slaves—indeed, on the day it was issued, it applied to very few. Because its legality derived from the president's authority as military commander-in-chief to combat the South's rebellion, the Proclamation exempted areas firmly under Union control (where the war, in effect, had already ended). Thus, it did not apply to the loyal border slave states that had never seceded or to areas of the Confederacy occupied by Union soldiers, such as Tennessee and parts of Virginia and Louisiana. But the vast majority of the South's slaves—more than 3 million men, women, and children—it declared "henceforward shall be free." Since most of these slaves were still behind Confederate lines, however, their liberation would have to await Union victories.

Despite its limitations, the Proclamation set off scenes of jubilation among free blacks and abolitionists in the North and "contrabands" and slaves in the South. "Sound the loud timbrel o'er Egypt's dark sea," intoned a black preacher at a celebration in Boston. "Jehovah hath triumphed, his people are free." By making the Union army an agent of emancipation and wedding the goals of Union and abolition, the Proclamation sounded the eventual death knell of slavery.

Not only did the Emancipation Proclamation alter the nature of the Civil War and the course of American history, but it also represented a turning point in Lincoln's own thinking. It contained no reference to compensation to slaveholders or to colonization of the freed people. For the first time, it committed the government to enlisting black soldiers in the Union army. Lincoln now became in his own mind the Great Emancipator—that is, he assumed the role that history had thrust upon him, and he tried to live up

Freed Negroes Celebrating President Lincoln's Decree of Emancipation, *a fanciful engraving from the French periodical* Le Monde Illustré, *March 21, 1863.*

VISIONS OF FREEDOM

Freedom to the Slave. *This hand-colored lithograph from 1863 celebrates the promise of emancipation and also links the American flag—the symbol of nationality—with freedom by placing a liberty cap atop it. On the left are symbols of freedom including a school, a church, a plow, and a black man reading a newspaper. A broken chain lies in the right foreground. The image conveys the optimism inspired by the Emancipation Proclamation. But many former slaves would never fully enjoy the kinds of freedom imagined in this lithograph.*

QUESTIONS

1. What does the image tell us about how emancipation was achieved?

2. In what ways does the artist suggest that freedom differed from life under slavery?

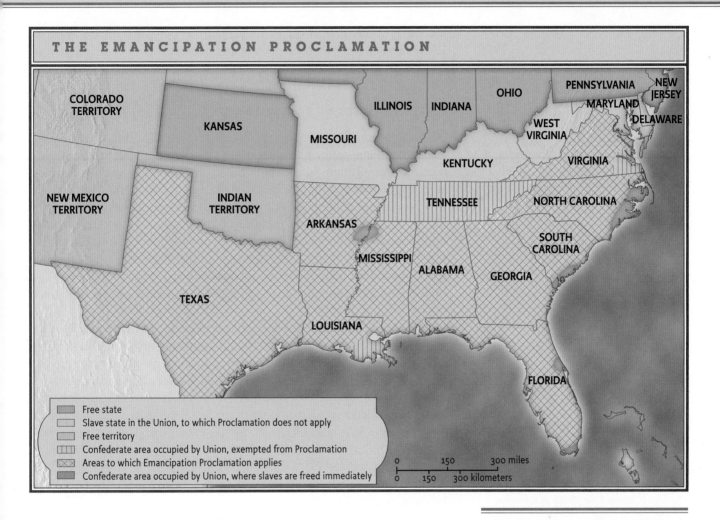

THE EMANCIPATION PROCLAMATION

Legend:
- Free state
- Slave state in the Union, to which Proclamation does not apply
- Free territory
- Confederate area occupied by Union, exempted from Proclamation
- Areas to which Emancipation Proclamation applies
- Confederate area occupied by Union, where slaves are freed immediately

0   150   300 miles
0   150   300 kilometers

to it. He would later refuse suggestions that he rescind or modify the Proclamation in the interest of peace. Were he to do so, he told one visitor, "I should be damned in time and eternity."

Like the end of slavery in Haiti and mainland Latin America, abolition in the United States came about as the result of war. But emancipation in the United States differed from its counterparts elsewhere in the Western Hemisphere—it was immediate, not gradual, and offered no compensation to slaveholders for their loss of property (with the exception of those in Washington, D.C.) It also foretold the inevitable end of slavery in Cuba, Puerto Rico, and Brazil. Not until 1888, however, when Brazil abolished the institution, did slavery come to an end in the entire Western Hemisphere.

The Civil War, which was begun to preserve the prewar Union, now portended a far-reaching transformation in southern life and a redefinition of American freedom. Decoupling emancipation from colonization meant that the freed slaves would become part of American life. A new system of labor, politics, and race relations would have to replace the shattered institution of slavery. "Up to now," wrote the socialist thinker Karl Marx, observing events from London, "we have witnessed only the first act of the Civil War—the constitutional waging of war. The second act, the revolutionary waging of war, is at hand." The evolution of

With the exception of a few areas, the Emancipation Proclamation applied only to slaves in parts of the Confederacy not under Union control on January 1, 1863. Lincoln did not "free the slaves" with a stroke of his pen, but the Proclamation did change the nature of the Civil War.

Lincoln's emancipation policy displayed the hallmarks of his wartime leadership—his capacity for growth and his ability to develop broad public support for his administration.

ENLISTING BLACK TROOPS

Of the Proclamation's provisions, few were more radical in their implications than the enrollment of blacks into military service. Since sailor had been one of the few occupations open to free blacks before the war, Secretary of the Navy Gideon Welles had already allowed African-Americans to serve on Union warships. But as during the American Revolution, when George Washington initially excluded blacks from the Continental army, blacks in the Civil War had to fight for the right to fight on land. Early in the war, Harry Jarvis, a Virginia slave, escaped to Fortress Monroe and offered to enlist in the Union army. General Benjamin F. Butler, Jarvis later recalled, "said *it wasn't a black man's war*. I told him it *would* be a black man's war before they got through."

At the outset, the Union army refused to accept northern black volunteers. The administration feared that whites would not be willing to fight alongside blacks, and that enlisting black soldiers would alienate the border slave states that remained in the Union. By the end of 1861, however, the army was employing escaped slaves as cooks, laundresses, and laborers. Preliminary steps to enlist combat troops were taken in a few parts of the South in 1862. White abolitionist Thomas Wentworth Higginson was sent to the South Carolina Sea Islands, which the Union navy had seized early in the war, to enroll slaves in the First South Carolina Volunteers. But only after the Emancipation Proclamation did the recruitment of black soldiers begin in earnest.

This widely reprinted recruiting poster urged African-American men to join the Union army after Congress and the president changed the policy of allowing only whites to serve.

COME AND JOIN US BROTHERS.

PUBLISHED BY THE SUPERVISORY COMMITTEE FOR RECRUITING COLORED REGIMENTS
1210 CHESTNUT ST. PHILADELPHIA.

By the end of the war, more than 180,000 black men had served in the Union army, and 24,000 in the navy. One-third died in battle, or of wounds or disease. Fifteen black soldiers and eight sailors received the Medal of Honor, the highest award for military valor. Some black units won considerable notoriety, among them the Fifty-fourth Massachusetts Volunteers, a company of free blacks from throughout the North commanded by Robert Gould Shaw, a young reformer from a prominent Boston family. The bravery of the Fifty-fourth in the July 1863 attack on Fort Wagner, South Carolina, where nearly half the unit, including Shaw, perished, helped to dispel widespread doubts about blacks' ability to withstand the pressures of the Civil War battlefield. (The exploits of Shaw and the Fifty-fourth Massachusetts were popularized in the 1989 film *Glory*.)

Photographs of four anonymous black Civil War soldiers, including a sergeant (with three stripes on his uniform).

Most black soldiers were emancipated slaves who joined the army in the South. After Union forces in 1863 seized control of the rich plantation lands of the Mississippi Valley, General Lorenzo Thomas raised fifty regiments of black soldiers—some 76,000 men in all. Another large group hailed from the border states exempted from the Emancipation Proclamation, where enlistment was, for most of the war, the only route to freedom. Here black military service undermined slavery, for Congress expanded the Emancipation Proclamation to liberate black soldiers and their families.

THE BLACK SOLDIER

For black soldiers themselves, military service proved to be a liberating experience. "No negro who has ever been a soldier," wrote a northern official in 1865, "can again be imposed upon; they have learned what it is to be free and they will infuse their feelings into others." Service in the army established men as community leaders and opened a door to political advancement. Out of the army came many of the leaders of the Reconstruction era. At least 130 former soldiers served in political office after the Civil War. In time, the memory of black military service would fade from white America's collective memory. Of the hundreds of Civil War monuments that still dot the northern landscape, fewer than a dozen contain an image of a black soldier. But well into the twentieth century, it remained a point of pride in black families throughout the United States that their fathers and grandfathers had fought for freedom.

The Union navy treated black sailors pretty much the same as white sailors. Conditions on ships made racial segregation impossible. Black and white sailors lived and dined together in the same quarters. They received equal pay and had the same promotion opportunities. Within the army, however, black soldiers received treatment that was anything but equal to their white counterparts. Organized into segregated units under sometimes abusive white officers, they initially received lower pay (ten dollars per month, compared to sixteen dollars for white soldiers). They were disproportionately assigned to labor rather than combat, and they could not rise to the rank of commissioned officer until the very end of the war. If captured by Confederate forces, they faced the prospect of sale into slavery or immediate execution. In a notorious incident in 1864, 200 of 262 black soldiers died when southern troops under the command of Nathan B. Forrest overran Fort Pillow in Tennessee. Some of those who perished were killed after surrendering.

Nonetheless, black soldiers played a crucial role not only in winning the Civil War but in defining the war's consequences. "Once let a black man get upon his person the brass letters U.S.," wrote Frederick Douglass in urging blacks to enlist, "and there is no power on earth which can deny that he has earned the right to citizenship in the United States." As Douglass predicted, thanks in part to black military service many Republicans in the last two years of the war came to believe that emancipation must bring with it equal protection of the laws regardless of race. One of the first acts of the federal government to recognize this principle was the granting of retroactive equal pay to black soldiers early in 1865. Racism was hardly eliminated from national life. But, declared George William Curtis, the editor of *Harper's Weekly*, the war and emancipation had transformed a government "for white men" into one "for mankind."

The service of black soldiers affected Lincoln's own outlook. He insisted that they must be treated the same as whites when captured and suspended prisoner-of-war exchanges when the Confederacy refused to include black troops. In 1864, Lincoln, who before the war had never supported suffrage for African-Americans, urged the governor of Union-occupied Louisiana to work for the partial enfranchisement of blacks, singling out soldiers as especially deserving. At some future time, he observed, they might again be called upon to "keep the *jewel of Liberty* in the family of freedom."

THE SECOND AMERICAN REVOLUTION

"Old things are passing away," wrote a black resident of California in 1862, "and eventually old prejudices must follow. The revolution has begun, and time alone must decide where it is to end." The changing status of black Americans was only one dramatic example of what some historians call the Second American Revolution—the transformation of American government and society brought about by the Civil War.

LIBERTY AND UNION

Never was freedom's contested nature more evident than during the Civil War. "We all declare for liberty," Lincoln observed in 1864, "but in using the same *word* we do not all mean the same *thing*." To the North, he continued, freedom meant for "each man" to enjoy "the product of his labor." To southern whites, it conveyed mastership—the power to do "as they please with other men, and the product of other men's labor." The Union's triumph consolidated the northern understanding of freedom as the national norm.

The attack on Fort Sumter crystallized in northern minds the direct conflict between freedom and slavery that abolitionists had insisted upon

The illustration accompanying The American Flag, *a piece of patriotic Civil War sheet music, exemplifies how the war united the ideals of liberty and nationhood.*

for decades. The war, as Frederick Douglass recognized as early as 1862, merged "the cause of the slaves and the cause of the country." "Liberty and Union," he continued, "have become identical." As during the American Revolution, religious and secular understandings of freedom joined in a celebration of national destiny. "As He died to make men holy, let us die to make men free," proclaimed the popular song "Battle Hymn of the Republic," written by Julia Ward Howe and published in 1862. Emancipation offered proof of the progressive nature and global significance of the country's history. For the first time, wrote the *Chicago Tribune*, the United States could truly exist as "our fathers designed it—the home of freedom, the asylum of the oppressed, the seat of justice, the land of equal rights under the law."

LINCOLN'S VISION

But it was Lincoln himself who linked the conflict with the deepest beliefs of northern society. It is sometimes said that the American Civil War was part of a broader nineteenth-century process of nation building. Throughout the world, powerful, centralized nation-states developed in old countries, and new nations emerged where none had previously existed. The Civil War took place as modern states were consolidating their power and reducing local autonomy. The Meiji Restoration in Japan saw the emperor reclaim power from local lords, or shoguns. Argentina in the 1850s adopted a new constitution that abolished slavery, established universal male suffrage, and gave the national government the right to intervene in local affairs. As in the United States, economic development quickly followed national unification. Japan soon emerged as a major economic power, and Argentina embarked on a policy of railroad construction, centralization of banking, industrial development, and the encouragement of European immigration, which soon made it the world's sixth largest economy.

Lincoln has been called the American equivalent of Giuseppe Mazzini or Otto von Bismarck, who during this same era created nation-states in Italy and Germany from disunited collections of principalities. But Lincoln's nation was different from those being constructed in Europe. They were based on the idea of unifying a particular people with a common ethnic, cultural, and linguistic heritage. To Lincoln, the American nation embodied a set of universal ideas, centered on political democracy and human liberty. The United States represented to the world the principle that government should rest on popular consent and that all men should be free. These ideals, Lincoln declared, allowed immigrants from abroad, who could not "trace their connection by blood" to the nation's birth, nonetheless to become fully American.

Lincoln summarized his conception of the war's meaning in November 1863 in brief remarks at the dedication of a military cemetery at the site of the war's greatest battle. The Gettysburg Address is considered his finest speech (see the Appendix for the full text). In less than three minutes, he identified the nation's mission with the principle that "all men are created equal," spoke of the war as bringing about a "new birth of freedom," and defined the essence of democratic government. The sacrifices of Union soldiers, he declared, would ensure that "government of the people, by the people, for the people, shall not perish from the earth."

Lincoln and the Female Slave, *by the free black artist David B. Bowser. Working in Philadelphia, Bowser painted flags for a number of black Civil War regiments. Lincoln confers freedom on a kneeling slave, an image that downplays blacks' role in their own emancipation.*

The Eagle's Nest, *an 1861 antisecession cartoon promising "annihilation to traitors." The eggs representing seceding states have become rotten and are hatching monsters.*

FROM UNION TO NATION

The mobilization of the Union's resources for modern war brought into being a new American nation-state with greatly expanded powers and responsibilities. The United States remained a federal republic with sovereignty divided between the state and national governments. But the war forged a new national self-consciousness, reflected in the increasing use of the word "nation"—a unified political entity—in place of the older "Union" of separate states. In his inaugural address in 1861, Lincoln used the word "Union" twenty times, while making no mention of the "nation." By 1863, "Union" does not appear at all in the 269-word Gettysburg Address, while Lincoln referred five times to the "nation."

"Liberty, . . . true liberty," the writer Francis Lieber proclaimed, "requires a country." This was the moral of one of the era's most popular works of fiction, Edward Everett Hale's short story "The Man Without a Country," published in 1863. Hale's protagonist, Philip Nolan, in a fit of anger curses the land of his birth. As punishment, he is condemned to live on a ship, never to set foot on American soil or hear the name "the United States" spoken. He learns that to be deprived of national identity is to lose one's sense of self.

THE WAR AND AMERICAN RELIGION

The upsurge of patriotism, and of national power, was reflected in many aspects of American life. Even as the war produced unprecedented casualties, the northern Protestant clergy strove to provide it with a religious justification and to reassure their congregations that the dead had not died in vain. The religious press now devoted more space to military and political developments than to spiritual matters. In numerous wartime sermons, Christianity and patriotism were joined in a civic religion that saw the war as God's mechanism for ridding the United States of slavery and enabling it to become what it had never really been—a land of freedom. Lincoln, one of the few American presidents who never joined a church, shrewdly marshaled religious symbolism to generate public support, declaring days of Thanksgiving after northern victories and encouraging northern clergymen to support Republican candidates for office.

Religious beliefs also enabled Americans to cope with the unprecedented mass death the war involved. Of course, equating death with eternal life is a central tenet of Christianity. But the war led to what one historian calls a "transformation of heaven," as Americans imagined future celestial family reunions that seemed more and more like gatherings in middle-class living rooms. Some Americans could not wait until their own deaths to see the departed. Spiritualism—belief in the ability to communicate with the dead—grew in popularity. Mary Todd Lincoln held seances in the White House to experience again the presence of her young son Willie, who succumbed to disease in 1862.

Coping with death also required unprecedented governmental action, from notifying next of kin to accounting for the dead and missing. Both the Union and Confederacy established elaborate systems for gathering statistics and maintaining records of dead and wounded soldiers, an effort supplemented by private philanthropic organizations. After the war ended, the federal government embarked on a program to locate and re-bury hundreds of thousands of Union soldiers in national military cemeteries. Between 1865 and 1871, the government reinterred more than 300,000 Union (but not Confederate) soldiers—including black soldiers, who were buried, as they had fought, in segregated sections of military cemeteries.

LIBERTY IN WARTIME

This intense new nationalism made criticism of the war effort—or of the policies of the Lincoln administration—seem to Republicans equivalent to treason. Although there had been sporadic persecution of opponents of the Mexican War, the Civil War presented, for the first time since the Revolution, the issue of the limits of wartime dissent. During the conflict, declared the Republican *New York Times*, "the safety of the nation is the supreme law." Arbitrary arrests numbered in the thousands. They included opposition newspaper editors, Democratic politicians, individuals who discouraged enlistment in the army, and ordinary civilians like the Chicago man briefly imprisoned for calling the president a "damned fool." With the Constitution unclear as to who possessed the power to suspend the writ of habeas corpus (thus allowing prisoners to be held without charge),

This image adorned a printed version of a popular Civil War song, "The Dying Soldier." It illustrates how Americans sought solace in religion in the face of the war's enormous death toll. At the left, an angel receives the dying soldier, while at the right his wife, mother, or sweetheart prays for his soul.

VOICES OF FREEDOM

FROM SPEECH *OF* ALEXANDER H. STEPHENS,
Vice President of the Confederacy (March 21, 1861)

A Whig leader in Georgia, Alexander H. Stephens opposed secession until his state voted to leave the Union. He then accepted the vice presidency of the Confederacy, and in a speech in Savannah in March 1861 he explained the basic premises of the new government.

The [Confederate] Constitution has put at rest forever all the agitating questions relating to our peculiar institutions—African slavery as it exists among us—the proper status of the negro in our form of civilization. This was the immediate cause of the late rupture and present revolution. . . . The prevailing ideas entertained by [Jefferson] and most of the leading statesmen at the time of the formation of the old Constitution, were, that the enslavement of the African was in violation of the laws of nature; that it was wrong in principle, socially, morally and politically. . . .

These ideas, however, were fundamentally wrong. They rested on the assumption of the equality of races. This was an error. . . . Our new Government is founded upon exactly the opposite ideas; its foundations are laid, its cornerstone rests, upon the great truth that the negro is not equal to the white man; that slavery, subordination to the superior race, is his natural and moral condition. This, our new Government, is the first, in the history of the world, based upon this great physical, philosophical, and moral truth. . . .

It is the first Government ever instituted upon principles in strict conformity to nature, and the ordination of Providence, in furnishing the materials of human society. Many Governments have been founded upon the principles of certain classes; but the classes thus enslaved, were of the same race, and in violation of the laws of nature. Our system commits no such violation of nature's laws. The negro by nature, or by the curse against Canaan, is fitted for that condition which he occupies in our system. . . . The substratum of our society is made of the material fitted by nature for it, and by experience we know that it is the best, not only for the superior but for the inferior race, that it should be so.

FROM ABRAHAM LINCOLN,
Address at Sanitary Fair, Baltimore (April 18, 1864)

Abraham Lincoln's speech at a Sanitary Fair (a grand bazaar that raised money for the care of Union soldiers) offers a dramatic illustration of the contested meaning of freedom during the Civil War.

The world has never had a good definition of the word liberty, and the American people, just now, are much in want of one. We all declare for liberty; but in using the same *word* we do not all mean the same *thing*. With some the word liberty may mean for each man to do as he pleases with himself, and the product of his labor; while with others the same word may mean for some men to do as they please with other men, and the product of other men's labor. Here are two, not only different, but incompatible things, called by the same name—liberty. And it follows that each of the things is, by the respective parties, called by two different and incompatible names—liberty and tyranny.

The shepherd drives the wolf from the sheep's throat, for which the sheep thanks the shepherd as a *liberator*, while the wolf denounces him for the same act as the destroyer of liberty, especially as the sheep was a black one. Plainly the sheep and the wolf are not agreed upon a definition of the word liberty; and precisely the same difference prevails today among us human creatures, even in the North, and all professing to love liberty. Hence we behold the process by which thousands are daily passing from under the yoke of bondage, hailed by some as the advance of liberty, and bewailed by others as the destruction of all liberty. Recently, as it seems, the people of Maryland have been doing something to define liberty [abolishing slavery in the state]; and thanks to them that, in what they have done, the wolf's dictionary, has been repudiated.

QUESTIONS

1. Why does Stephens argue that slavery in the South differs from slavery as it has existed in previous societies?

2. What does Lincoln identify as the essential difference between northern and southern definitions of freedom?

3. How do Lincoln and Stephens differ in their definition of liberty and whether it applies to African-Americans?

Lincoln claimed the right under the presidential war powers and twice suspended the writ throughout the entire Union for those accused of "disloyal activities."

The courts generally gave the administration a free hand. They refused to intervene when a military court convicted Clement L. Vallandigham, a leading Ohio Democrat known for his blistering antiwar speeches, of treason. On Lincoln's order, Vallandigham was banished to the Confederacy. In 1861, Chief Justice Roger B. Taney had ordered the president to release John Merryman, a civilian who had been arrested by military authorities in Maryland, but the president ignored him. Not until 1866, after the fighting had ended, did the Supreme Court, in the case *Ex parte Milligan*, declare it unconstitutional to bring accused persons before military tribunals where civil courts were operating. The Constitution, declared Justice David Davis, is not suspended in wartime—it remains "a law for rulers and people, equally in time of war and peace."

Lincoln was not a despot. Most of those arrested were quickly released, the Democratic press continued to flourish, and contested elections were held throughout the war. But the policies of the Lincoln administration offered proof—to be repeated during later wars—of the fragility of civil liberties in the face of assertive patriotism and wartime demands for national unity.

THE NORTH'S TRANSFORMATION

Even as he invoked traditional values, Lincoln presided over far-reaching changes in northern life. The effort to mobilize the resources of the Union greatly enhanced the power not only of the federal government but also of a rising class of capitalist entrepreneurs. Unlike the South, which suffered economic devastation, the North experienced the war as a time of prosperity.

Nourished by wartime inflation and government contracts, the profits of industry boomed. New England mills worked day and night to supply the army with blankets and uniforms, and Pennsylvania coal mines and ironworks rapidly expanded their production. Mechanization proceeded apace in many industries, especially those like boot and shoe production and meatpacking that supplied the army's ever-increasing needs. Agriculture also flourished, for even as farm boys by the hundreds of thousands joined the army, the frontier of cultivation pushed westward, with machinery and immigrants replacing lost labor. Wisconsin furnished 90,000 men to the Union army, yet its population, grain production, and farm income continued to grow.

GOVERNMENT AND THE ECONOMY

As in contemporary Germany and Japan, the new American nation-state that emerged during the Civil War was committed to rapid economic development. Congress adopted policies that promoted economic growth and permanently altered the nation's financial system. With the South now unrepresented, the lawmakers adopted policies long advocated by many northerners. To spur agricultural development, the Homestead Act offered 160 acres of free public land to settlers in the West. It took effect on January 1, 1863, the same day as the Emancipation Proclamation, and like the Proclamation, tried to implement a vision of freedom. By the 1930s,

Sheet music for two of the best-known patriotic songs written during the Civil War.

more than 400,000 families had acquired farms under its provisions. In addition, the Land Grant College Act assisted the states in establishing "agricultural and mechanic colleges."

BUILDING THE TRANSCONTINENTAL RAILROAD

Congress also made huge grants of money and land for internal improvements, including up to 100 million acres to the Union Pacific and Central Pacific, two companies chartered in 1862 and charged with building a railroad from the Missouri River to the Pacific coast. (These were the first corporate charters issued by the federal government since the Second Bank of the United States in 1816.)

When first proposed by entrepreneur Asa Whitney in 1846, the idea of a transcontinental railroad had been considered by Congress "too gigantic" and "entirely impracticable." And, indeed, the project was monumental. The Central Pacific progressed only twenty miles a year for the first three years of construction because the Sierra Nevada range was almost impassable. It required some 20,000 men to lay the tracks across prairies and mountains, a substantial number of them immigrant Chinese contract laborers, called "coolies" by many Americans. Hundreds of Chinese workers died blasting tunnels and building bridges through this treacherous terrain. When it was completed in 1869, the transcontinental railroad, which ran from Omaha, Nebraska, to San Francisco, expanded the national market, facilitated the spread of settlement and investment in the West, and heralded the doom of the Plains Indians.

THE WAR AND NATIVE AMERICANS

One of Lincoln's first orders as president was to withdraw federal troops from the West so that they could protect Washington, D.C. Recognizing that this would make it impossible for the army to keep white interlopers from intruding on Indian land, as treaties required it to do, Indian leaders begged Lincoln to reverse this decision, but to no avail. Inevitably, conflict flared in the West between Native Americans and white settlers, with disastrous results. During the Civil War, the Sioux killed hundreds of white farmers in Minnesota before being subdued by the army. After a military court sentenced more than 300 Indians to death, Lincoln commuted the sentences of all but 38. But their hanging in December 1862 remains the largest official execution in American history. In 1864, a unit of Colorado soldiers under the command of Colonel John Chivington attacked a village of Cheyenne and Arapaho Indians at Sand Creek, killing perhaps 400 men, women, and children.

The Union army also launched a campaign against the Navajo in the Southwest, destroying their orchards and sheep and forcing 8,000 people to move to a reservation set aside by the government. The Navajo's Long Walk became as central to their historical experience as the Trail of Tears to the Cherokee (see Chapter 10). Unlike the eastern Indians, however, the Navajo were eventually allowed to return to a portion of their lands.

Ironically, the Confederacy, although defending slavery, treated Native Americans more fairly than the Union. The Confederate Constitution provided for Indian tribes to elect representatives to Congress, and the Davis

A Union soldier stands guard over a group of Indians during the Navajo's Long Walk, in which the army removed them from their New Mexico homeland to a reservation hundreds of miles away.

administration removed state jurisdiction over Indian reservations, allowing them complete self-government. Some tribes that owned slaves, like the Cherokee, sided with the Confederacy. After 1865, they were forced to cede much of their land to the federal government and to give some land to their former slaves (the only slaveowners required to do so).

A NEW FINANCIAL SYSTEM

The need to pay for the war produced dramatic changes in financial policy. To raise money, the government increased the tariff to unprecedented heights (thus promoting the further growth of northern industry), imposed new taxes on the production and consumption of goods, and enacted the nation's first income tax. It also borrowed more than $2 billion by selling interest-bearing bonds, thus creating an immense national debt. And it printed more than $400 million worth of paper money, called "greenbacks," declared to be legal tender—that is, money that must be accepted for nearly all public and private payments and debts. To rationalize the banking system, Congress established a system of nationally chartered banks, which were required to purchase government bonds and were given the right to issue bank notes as currency. A heavy tax drove money issued by state banks out of existence. Thus, the United States, whose money supply before the war was a chaotic mixture of paper notes issued by state and local banks, now had essentially two kinds of national paper currency—greenbacks printed directly by the federal government, and notes issued by the new national banks.

Along with profitable contracts to supply goods for the military effort, wartime economic policies greatly benefited northern manufacturers, railroad men, and financiers. Numerous Americans who would take the lead in reshaping the nation's postwar economy created or consolidated their fortunes during the Civil War, among them iron and steel entrepreneur Andrew Carnegie, oil magnate John D. Rockefeller, financiers Jay Gould and J. P. Morgan, and Philip D. Armour, who earned millions supplying beef to the Union army. These and other "captains of industry" managed to escape military service, sometimes by purchasing exemptions or hiring substitutes, as allowed by the draft law.

Taken together, the Union's economic policies vastly increased the power and size of the federal government. The federal budget for 1865 exceeded $1 billion—nearly twenty times that of 1860. With its new army of clerks, tax collectors, and other officials, the government became the nation's largest employer. And while much of this expansion proved temporary, the government would never return to its weak and fragmented condition of the prewar period.

WOMEN AND THE WAR

For many northern women, the conflict opened new doors of opportunity. Women took advantage of the wartime labor shortage to move into jobs in factories and into certain largely male professions, particularly nursing. The expansion of the activities of the national government opened new jobs for women as clerks in government offices. Many of these wartime gains were short-lived, but in white-collar government jobs, retail sales, and nursing, women found a permanent place in the workforce.

Some northern women took a direct part in military campaigns. Clara Barton, a clerk in the Patent Office in Washington, D.C., when the war began, traveled with the Army of Northern Virginia, helping to organize supply lines and nursing wounded soldiers. Barton worked alone rather than as a part of the Department of Female Nurses, and she never received compensation from the government.

Hundreds of thousands of northern women took part in organizations that gathered money and medical supplies for soldiers and sent books, clothing, and food to freedmen. The United States Sanitary Commission emerged as a centralized national relief agency to coordinate donations on the northern home front. Although control at the national level remained in male hands, patriotic women did most of the grassroots work. Women played the leading role in organizing Sanitary Fairs—

Filling Cartridges at the U. S. Arsenal of Watertown, Massachusetts, *an engraving from* Harper's Weekly, *September 21, 1861. Both men and women were drawn to work in the booming war-related industries of the North.*

A female nurse photographed between two wounded Union soldiers in a Nashville military hospital in 1862. Many northern women served the army as nurses during the war.

Whimsical potholders expressing hope for a better life for emancipated slaves were sold at the Chicago Sanitary Fair of 1865, to raise money for soldiers' aid.

Camp of Thirty-first Pennsylvania Infantry, Near Washington, D.C., *an 1862 photograph by the Mathew Brady studio. Many women worked for the army as laundresses. Some accompanied their husbands and even brought their children.*

grand bazaars that displayed military banners, uniforms, and other relics of the war and sold goods to raise money for soldiers' aid. New York City's three-week fair of 1864 attracted a crowd of 30,000 and raised more than $1 million.

Many men understood women's war work as an extension of their "natural" capacity for self-sacrifice. But the very act of volunteering to work in local soldiers' aid societies brought many northern women into the public sphere and offered them a taste of independence. The suffrage movement suspended operations during the war to devote itself to the Union and emancipation. But women's continuing lack of the vote seemed all the more humiliating as their involvement in war work increased.

From the ranks of this wartime mobilization came many of the leaders of the postwar movement for women's rights. Mary Livermore, the wife of a Chicago minister, for example, toured military hospitals to assess their needs, cared for injured and dying soldiers, and organized two Sanitary Fairs. She emerged from the war with a deep resentment of women's legal and political subordination and organized her state's first woman suffrage convention. Women, she had concluded, must "think and act for themselves." After the war, Clara Barton not only became an advocate of woman suffrage but, as president of the American National Red Cross, lobbied for the United States to endorse the First Geneva Convention of 1864, which mandated the humane treatment of battlefield casualties. Largely as a result of Barton's efforts, the Senate ratified the convention in 1882. (Subsequent Geneva Conventions in the twentieth century would deal with the treatment of prisoners of war and civilians during wartime.)

The Riots in New York: The Mob Lynching a Negro in Clarkson Street, *an engraving from the British magazine* Illustrated London News, *August 8, 1863, reveals how the New York City draft riots escalated from an attempt to obstruct the draft into an assault on the city's black population.*

THE DIVIDED NORTH

Despite Lincoln's political skills, the war and his administration's policies divided northern society. Republicans labeled those opposed to the war Copperheads, after a poisonous snake that strikes without warning. Mounting casualties and rapid societal changes divided the North. Disaffection was strongest among the large southern-born population of states like Ohio, Indiana, and Illinois and working-class Catholic immigrants in eastern cities.

As the war progressed, it heightened existing social tensions and created new ones. The growing power of the federal government challenged traditional notions of local autonomy. The Union's draft law, which allowed individuals to provide a substitute or buy their way out of the army, caused widespread indignation. Workers resented manufacturers and financiers who reaped large profits while their own real incomes dwindled because of inflation. The war witnessed the rebirth of the northern labor movement, which organized numerous strikes for higher wages. The prospect of a sweeping change in the status of blacks called forth a racist reaction in many parts of the North. Throughout the war, the Democratic Party subjected Lincoln's policies to withering criticism, although it remained divided between "War Democrats," who supported the military effort while criticizing emancipation and the draft, and those who favored immediate peace.

On occasion, dissent degenerated into outright violence. In July 1863, the introduction of the draft provoked four days of rioting in New York City. The mob, composed largely of Irish immigrants, assaulted symbols of the new order being created by the war—draft offices, the mansions of wealthy Republicans, industrial establishments, and the city's black population, many of whom fled to New Jersey or took refuge in Central Park. Only the arrival of Union troops quelled the uprising, but not before more than 100 persons had died.

THE CONFEDERATE NATION

LEADERSHIP AND GOVERNMENT

The man charged with the task of rallying public support for the Confederacy proved unequal to the task. Born in 1808 in Kentucky, within eight months and 100 miles of Lincoln's birth, Jefferson Davis had moved to Mississippi as a youth, attended West Point, and acquired a large plantation. Aloof, stubborn, and humorless, he lacked Lincoln's common touch and political flexibility. Although known before the war as the "Cicero of the Senate" for his eloquent speeches, Davis, unlike Lincoln, proved unable to communicate the war's meaning effectively to ordinary men and women. Moreover, the Confederacy's lack of a party system proved to be a political liability. Like the founders of the American republic, southern leaders saw parties as threats to national unity. As a result, Davis lacked a counterpart to the well-organized Republican Party, which helped to mobilize support for the Lincoln administration.

Under Davis, the Confederate nation became far more centralized than the Old South had been. The government raised armies from scratch, took control of southern railroads, and built manufacturing plants. But it failed to find an effective way of utilizing the South's major economic resource, cotton. In the early part of the war, the administration tried to suppress cotton production, urging planters to grow food instead and banning cotton exports. This, it was hoped, would promote economic self-sufficiency and force Great Britain, whose textile mills could not operate without southern cotton, to intervene on the side of the Confederacy.

The centrality of slavery to the Confederacy is illustrated by the paper money issued by state governments and private banks, which frequently juxtaposed scenes of slaves at work with other revered images. The ten-dollar note of the Eastern Bank of Alabama depicts slaves working in the field and at a port, along with an idealized portrait of southern white womanhood. Alabama's five-dollar bill includes an overseer directing slaves in the field, and a symbol of liberty.

"King Cotton diplomacy" turned out to be ineffective. Large crops in 1859 and 1860 had created a huge stockpile in English warehouses. By the time distress hit the manufacturing districts in 1862, the government of Prime Minister Palmerston had decided not to intervene, partly because Britain needed northern wheat almost as much as southern cotton. But the Confederate policy had far-reaching global consequences. Recognizing their overdependence on southern cotton, other nations moved to expand production. Britain promoted cultivation of the crop in Egypt and India, and Russia did the same in parts of Central Asia. As a result, the resumption of American cotton production after the war led directly to a worldwide crisis of overproduction that drove down the price of cotton, impoverishing farmers around the world.

Nor did Davis deal effectively with obstructionist governors like Joseph E. Brown of Georgia, who denounced the Confederate draft as "a dangerous usurpation" of states' rights and individual liberty. All in all, Davis was so inferior to Lincoln as a wartime leader that one historian has suggested that had the North and South exchanged presidents, the South would have won the war.

A drawing by Langdon Cheves III, the teenage grandson of a prominent South Carolina political leader, depicts a Confederate killing a Yankee officer.

THE INNER CIVIL WAR

As the war progressed, social change and internal turmoil engulfed much of the Confederacy. At the outset, most white southerners rallied to the Confederate cause. No less fervently than northern troops, southern soldiers spoke of their cause in the language of freedom. "We are fighting for our liberty," wrote one volunteer, without any sense of contradiction, "against tyrants of the North . . . who are determined to destroy slavery." But public disaffection eventually became an even more serious problem for the Confederacy than for the Union.

Even as it waged a desperate struggle for independence, the South found itself increasingly divided. One grievance was the draft. Like the Union, the Confederacy allowed individuals to provide a substitute. Because of the accelerating disintegration of slavery, it also exempted one white male for every twenty slaves on a plantation (thus releasing many overseers and planters' sons from service). The "twenty-negro" provision convinced many yeomen that the struggle for southern independence had become "a rich man's war and a poor man's fight."

ECONOMIC PROBLEMS

Economic deprivation also sparked disaffection. As the blockade tightened, areas of the Confederacy came under Union occupation, and production by

An engraving in the New York Illustrated News *depicts the bread riot that took place in Mobile, Alabama, in the fall of 1863.*

slaves declined, shortages arose of essential commodities such as salt, corn, and meat. The war left countless farms, plantations, businesses, and railroads in ruins. The economic crisis, which stood in glaring contrast to the North's boom, was an unavoidable result of the war. But Confederate policies exaggerated its effects. War requires sacrifice, and civilian support for war depends, in part, on the belief that sacrifice is being fairly shared. Many non-slaveholders, however, became convinced that they were bearing an unfair share of the war's burdens.

Like the Union, the Confederacy borrowed heavily to finance the war. Unlike federal lawmakers, however, the planter-dominated Confederate Congress proved unwilling to levy heavy taxes that planters would have to pay. It relied on paper money, of which it issued $1.5 billion, far more than the North's greenbacks. Congress also authorized military officers to seize farm goods to supply the army, paying with increasingly worthless Confederate money. Small farmers deeply resented this practice, known as "impressment." "The Rebel army treated us a heap worse than [Union general William T.] Sherman did," a Georgia farmer later recalled. "I had hogs, and a mule, and a horse, and they took them all." Numerous yeoman families, many of whom had gone to war to preserve their economic independence, sank into poverty and debt. Food riots broke out in many places, including Richmond, Virginia, and Mobile, Alabama, where in 1863 large crowds of women plundered army food supplies.

In 1862, Joshua B. Moore, a slaveholder in northern Alabama, commented on how slavery threatened the Confederate war effort: "Men who have no interest in it," he wrote, "are not going to fight through a long war to save it—never. They will tire of it and quit." As the war progressed, desertion became what one officer called a "crying evil" for the southern armies. By the war's end, more than 100,000 men had deserted, almost entirely from among "the poorest class of nonslaveholders whose labor is indispensable to the daily support of their families." Men, another official noted, "cannot be expected to fight for the government that permits their wives and children to starve."

SOUTHERN UNIONISTS

By 1864, organized peace movements had appeared in several southern states, and secret societies such as the Heroes of America were actively promoting disaffection. Confederate military tribunals imprisoned hundreds of Unionists. Others were violently driven from their homes, and a few were executed by the army or civilian authorities. But southerners loyal to the Union made a significant contribution to northern victory. By the end of the war, an estimated 50,000 white southerners had fought in the Union armies.

One of the most celebrated Union heroes of the war was Elizabeth Van Lew of Richmond, who had persuaded her mother to free the family's slaves when her father died in 1843. During the war she frequently visited Libby Prison in the Confederate capital, bringing supplies to Union prisoners of war and helping some of them to escape. With the aid of Mary Elizabeth Bowser, a former slave of the Van Lew family who worked as a servant in the southern White House, Van Lew passed information about Confederate plans to Union forces.

WOMEN AND THE CONFEDERACY

Even more than in the North, the war placed unprecedented burdens on southern white women. Left alone on farms and plantations, they were often forced to manage business affairs and discipline slaves, previously the responsibility of men. As in the North, women mobilized to support soldiers in the field and stepped out of their traditional "sphere" to run commercial establishments and work in arms factories. In Richmond, "government girls" staffed many of the clerkships in the new Confederate bureaucracy. Rose Greenhow, the widow of a former American diplomat, headed an espionage ring in Washington, D.C., that passed valuable information about Union troop movements to the Confederacy early in the war. Even after her arrest and jailing, she managed to smuggle out intelligence until she was exiled to Richmond in 1862. Jefferson Davis rewarded Greenhow with $2,500 for her services.

Southern women's self-sacrificing devotion to the cause became legendary. But as the war went on and the death toll mounted, increasing numbers of women came to believe that the goal of independence was not worth the cost. The growing disaffection of southern white women, conveyed in letters to loved ones at the front, contributed to the decline in civilian morale and encouraged desertion from the army.

BLACK SOLDIERS FOR THE CONFEDERACY

The growing shortage of white manpower eventually led Confederate authorities to a decision no one could have foreseen when the war began: they authorized the arming of slaves to fight for the South. As early as September 1863, a Mississippi newspaper had argued for freeing and enlisting able-bodied black men. "Let them," it wrote, "be declared free, placed in the ranks, and told to fight for their homes and country." But many slaveholders fiercely resisted this idea, and initially, the Confederate Senate rejected it. Not until March 1865, after Robert E. Lee had endorsed the plan, did the Confederate Congress authorize the arming of slaves.

The war ended before the recruitment of black soldiers actually began. But the Confederate army did employ numerous blacks, nearly all of them slaves, as laborers. This later led to some confusion over whether blacks actually fought for the Confederacy—apart from a handful who "passed" for white, none in fact did. But the South's decision to raise black troops illustrates how the war undermined not only slavery but also the proslavery ideology. "The day you make soldiers of them is the beginning of the end of the revolution," declared Howell Cobb, a Georgia planter and politician. "If slaves make good soldiers, our whole theory of slavery is wrong."

TURNING POINTS

GETTYSBURG AND VICKSBURG

Despite the accelerating demise of slavery and the decline of morale in the South, the war's outcome remained very much in doubt for much of its third and fourth years. In April 1863, "Fighting Joe" Hooker, who had succeeded Ambrose E. Burnside as the Union commander in the East, brought the Army of the Potomac into central Virginia to confront Lee. Outnumbered two to one, Lee repelled Hooker's attack at Chancellorsville, although he lost his ablest lieutenant, "Stonewall" Jackson, mistakenly killed by fire from his own soldiers.

Lee now gambled on another invasion of the North, although his strategic objective remains unclear. Perhaps he believed a defeat on its own territory would destroy the morale of the northern army and public. In any event, the two armies, with Union soldiers now under the command of

In July 1863, the Union won major victories at Gettysburg and Vicksburg.

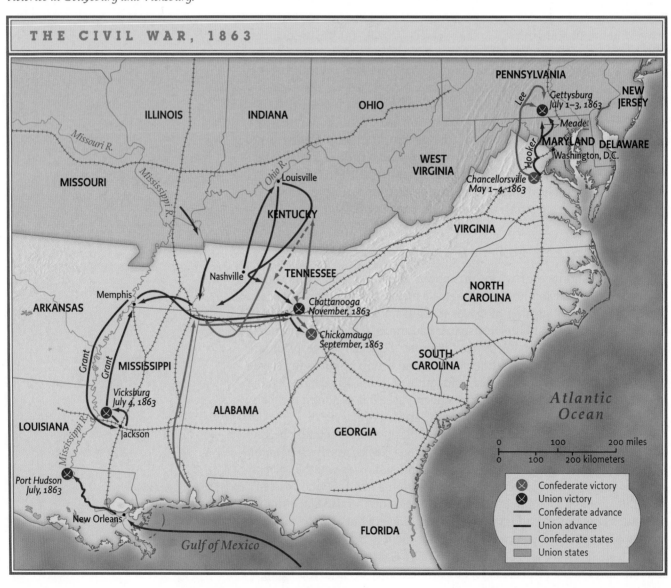

THE CIVIL WAR, 1863

General George G. Meade, met at Gettysburg, Pennsylvania, on the first three days of July 1863. With 165,000 troops involved, Gettysburg remains the largest battle ever fought on the North American continent. Lee found himself in the unusual position of confronting entrenched Union forces. After two days of failing to dislodge them, he decided to attack the center of the Union line. On July 3, Confederate forces, led by Major General George E. Pickett's crack division, marched across an open field toward Union forces. Withering artillery and rifle fire met the charge, and most of Pickett's soldiers never reached Union lines. Of the 14,000 men who made the advance—the flower of Lee's army—fewer than half returned. Later remembered as "the high tide of the Confederacy," Pickett's Charge was also Lee's greatest blunder. His army retreated to Virginia, never again to set foot on northern soil.

On the same day that Lee began his retreat from Gettysburg, the Union achieved a significant victory in the West. Late in 1862, Grant had moved into Mississippi toward the city of Vicksburg. From its heights, defended by miles of trenches and earthworks, the Confederacy commanded the central Mississippi River. When direct attacks failed, as did an attempt to divert the river by digging a canal, Grant launched a siege. On July 4, 1863, Vicksburg surrendered, and with it John C. Pemberton's army of 30,000 men, a loss the Confederacy could ill afford. The entire Mississippi Valley now lay in Union hands. The simultaneous defeats at Gettysburg and Vicksburg dealt a heavy blow to southern morale. "Today absolute ruin seems our portion," one official wrote in his diary. "The Confederacy totters to its destruction."

1864

Nearly two years, however, would pass before the war ended. Brought east to take command of Union forces, Grant in 1864 began a war of attrition against Lee's army in Virginia. That is, he was willing to accept high numbers of casualties, knowing that the North could replace its manpower losses while the South could not. Grant understood that to bring the North's manpower advantage into play, he must attack continuously "all along the line," thereby preventing the enemy from concentrating its forces or retreating to safety after an engagement.

In May 1864, the 115,000-man Army of the Potomac crossed the Rapidan River to do battle with Lee's forces in Virginia. A month of the war's bloodiest fighting followed. Grant and Lee first encountered each other in the Wilderness, a wild, shrub-covered region where, one participant recalled, "it was as though Christian men had turned to fiends, and hell itself had usurped the place of earth." Grant's army suffered 18,000 casualties, while Lee's far smaller forces incurred 7,500. Previous Union generals had broken off engagements after losses of this magnitude. But Grant continued to press forward, attacking again at Spotsylvania and then at Cold Harbor. At the end of six weeks of fighting, Grant's casualties stood at 60,000—almost the size of Lee's entire army—while Lee had lost 30,000 men. The sustained fighting in Virginia was a turning point in modern warfare. With daily combat and a fearsome casualty toll, it had far more in common with the trench warfare of World War I (discussed in Chapter 19) than the almost gentlemanly fighting with which the Civil War began.

Generals Robert E. Lee and Ulysses S. Grant, leaders of the opposing armies in the East, 1864–1865.

Grant had become the only Union general to maintain the initiative against Lee, but at a cost that led critics to label him a "butcher of men." Victory still eluded him. Grant attempted to capture Petersburg, which controlled the railway link to Richmond, but Lee got to Petersburg first, and Grant settled in for a prolonged siege. Meanwhile, General William T. Sherman, who had moved his forces into Georgia from Tennessee, encountered dogged resistance from Confederate troops. Not until September 1864 did he finally enter Atlanta, seizing Georgia's main railroad center.

As casualty rolls mounted in the spring and summer of 1864, northern morale sank to its lowest point of the war. Lincoln for a time believed he would be unable to win reelection. In May, hoping to force Lincoln to step aside, Radical Republicans nominated John C. Frémont on a platform calling for a constitutional amendment to abolish slavery, federal protection of the freedmen's rights, and confiscation of the land of leading Confederates. The Democratic candidate for president, General George B. McClellan, was hampered from the outset of the campaign by a platform calling for an immediate cease-fire and peace conference—a plan that even war-weary northerners viewed as equivalent to surrender. In the end, Frémont withdrew, and buoyed by Sherman's capture of Atlanta, Lincoln won a sweeping victory. He captured every state but Kentucky, Delaware, and New Jersey. The result ensured that the war would continue until the Confederacy's defeat.

REHEARSALS FOR RECONSTRUCTION AND THE END OF THE WAR

As the war drew toward a close and more and more parts of the Confederacy came under Union control, federal authorities found themselves presiding over the transition from slavery to freedom. In South Carolina, Louisiana, and other parts of the South, debates took place over issues—access to land, control of labor, and the new structure of political power—that would reverberate in the postwar world.

THE SEA ISLAND EXPERIMENT

The most famous "rehearsal for Reconstruction" took place on the Sea Islands just off the coast of South Carolina. The war was only a few months old when, in November 1861, the Union navy occupied the islands. Nearly the entire white population fled, leaving behind some 10,000 slaves. The navy was soon followed by other northerners—army officers, Treasury agents, prospective investors in cotton land, and a group known as Gideon's Band, which included black and white reformers and teachers committed to uplifting the freed slaves. Each of these groups, in addition to the islands' black population, had its own view of how the transition to freedom should be organized. And journalists reported every development on the islands to an eager reading public in the North.

Convinced that education was the key to making self-reliant, productive citizens of the former slaves, northern-born teachers like Charlotte Forten, a member of one of Philadelphia's most prominent black families, and Laura M. Towne, a white native of Pittsburgh, devoted themselves to teaching the freed blacks. Towne, who in 1862 helped to establish Penn school on

Long Abraham Lincoln a Little Longer, Harper's Weekly's *comment on Lincoln's reelection in 1864. At six feet four inches, Lincoln was the tallest American president.*

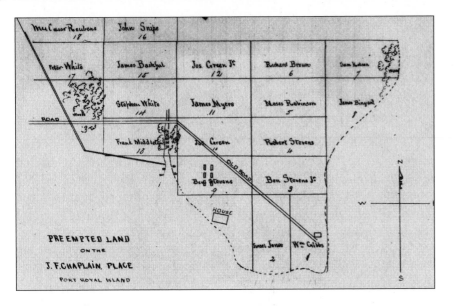

Diagram of plots selected by former slaves on Port Royal Island, South Carolina, January 25, 1864. Taking advantage of a sale of abandoned property, eighteen blacks (seventeen men and one woman) selected plots on a Sea Island plantation for purchase.

St. Helena Island, remained there as a teacher until her death in 1901. Like many of the Gideonites, Towne and Forten assumed that blacks needed outside guidance to appreciate freedom. But they sympathized with the former slaves' aspirations, central to which was the desire for land.

Other northerners, however, believed that the transition from slave to free labor meant not giving blacks land but enabling them to work for wages in more humane conditions than under slavery. When the federal government put land on the islands up for sale, most was acquired not by former slaves but by northern investors bent upon demonstrating the superiority of free wage labor and turning a tidy profit at the same time. By 1865, the Sea Island experiment was widely held to be a success. Black families were working for wages, acquiring education, and enjoying better shelter and clothing and a more varied diet than under slavery. But the experiment also bequeathed to postwar Reconstruction the contentious issue of whether land ownership should accompany black freedom.

WARTIME RECONSTRUCTION IN THE WEST

A very different rehearsal for Reconstruction, involving a far larger area and population than the Sea Islands, took place in Louisiana and the Mississippi Valley. After the capture of Vicksburg, the Union army established regulations for plantation labor. Military authorities insisted that the emancipated slaves must sign labor contracts with plantation owners who took an oath of loyalty. But, unlike before the war, they would be paid wages and provided with education, physical punishment was prohibited, and their families were safe from disruption by sale.

Neither side was satisfied with the new labor system. Blacks resented having to resume working for whites and being forced to sign labor contracts. Planters complained that their workers were insubordinate. Without the whip, they insisted, discipline could not be enforced. But only occasionally did army officers seek to implement a different vision of freedom. At Davis Bend, Mississippi, site of the cotton plantations of Jefferson Davis and his brother Joseph, General Grant decided to establish a "negro para-

Teachers in the Freedmen's Schools in Norfolk, 1863, *a photograph of a group of black and white teachers who brought education to former slaves in a Union-occupied part of Virginia.*

dise." Here, rather than being forced to labor for white owners, the emancipated slaves saw the land divided among themselves. In addition, a system of government was established that allowed the former slaves to elect their own judges and sheriffs.

THE POLITICS OF WARTIME RECONSTRUCTION

As the Civil War progressed, the future political status of African-Americans emerged as a key dividing line in public debates. Events in Union-occupied Louisiana brought the issue to national attention. Hoping to establish a functioning civilian government in the state, Lincoln in 1863 announced his Ten-Percent Plan of Reconstruction. He essentially offered an amnesty and full restoration of rights, including property except for slaves, to nearly all white southerners who took an oath affirming loyalty to the Union and support for emancipation. When 10 percent of the voters of 1860 had taken the oath, they could elect a new state government, which would be required to abolish slavery. Lincoln's plan offered no role to blacks in shaping the post-slavery order. His leniency toward southern whites seems to have been based on the assumption that many former slaveholders would come forward to accept his terms, thus weakening the Confederacy, shortening the war, and gaining white support for the ending of slavery.

Another group now stepped onto the stage of politics—the free blacks of New Orleans, who saw the Union occupation as a golden opportunity to press for equality before the law and a role in government for themselves. Their complaints at being excluded under Lincoln's Reconstruction plan won a sympathetic hearing from Radical Republicans in Congress. By the summer of 1864, dissatisfaction with events in Louisiana helped to inspire the Wade-Davis Bill, named for two leading Republican members of Congress. This bill required a majority (not one-tenth) of white male southerners to pledge support for the Union before Reconstruction could begin in any state, and it guaranteed blacks equality before the law, although not the right to vote. The bill passed Congress only to die when Lincoln refused to sign it and Congress adjourned. As the war drew to a close, it was clear that while slavery was dead, no agreement existed as to what social and political system should take its place.

VICTORY AT LAST

After Lincoln's reelection, the war hastened to its conclusion. In November 1864, Sherman and his army of 60,000 set out from Atlanta on their March to the Sea. Cutting a sixty-mile-wide swath through the heart of Georgia, they destroyed railroads, buildings, and all the food and supplies they could not use. His aim, Sherman wrote, was "to whip the rebels, to humble their pride, to follow them to their innermost recesses, and make them fear and dread us." Here was modern war in all its destructiveness, even though few civilians were physically harmed. In January 1865, after capturing Savannah, Sherman moved into South Carolina, bringing even greater destruction. Anarchy reigned on the plantations as slaves drove off remaining overseers, destroyed planters' homes, plundered smokehouses and storerooms, and claimed the land for themselves.

General William T. Sherman
photographed in 1864.

On January 31, 1865, Congress approved the Thirteenth Amendment, which abolished slavery throughout the entire Union—and in so doing, introduced the word "slavery" into the Constitution for the first time. In March, in his second inaugural address, Lincoln called for reconciliation: "with malice toward none, with charity for all, ... let us ... bind up the nation's wounds." Yet he also leveled a harsh judgment on the nation's past.

The military defeat of the Confederacy came in the East, with Sherman's March to the Sea, Grant's occupation of Richmond, and the surrender of Robert E. Lee's army.

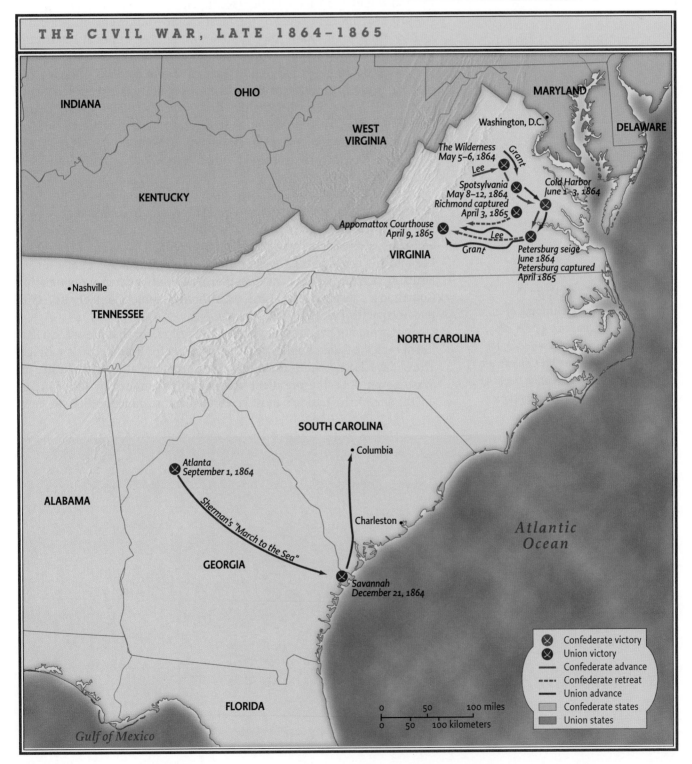

THE CIVIL WAR, LATE 1864–1865

INDIANA

OHIO

MARYLAND

KENTUCKY

WEST VIRGINIA

Washington, D.C.

DELAWARE

The Wilderness
May 5–6, 1864

Grant

Lee

Spotsylvania
May 8–12, 1864

Cold Harbor
June 1–3, 1864

Richmond captured
April 3, 1865

Appomattox Courthouse
April 9, 1865

Lee

VIRGINIA

Grant

Petersburg seige
June 1864
Petersburg captured
April 1865

• Nashville

TENNESSEE

NORTH CAROLINA

SOUTH CAROLINA

• Columbia

Atlanta
September 1, 1864

ALABAMA

Sherman's "March to the Sea"

Charleston •

*Atlantic
Ocean*

GEORGIA

Savannah
December 21, 1864

FLORIDA

Gulf of Mexico

| 0 | 50 | 100 miles |
| 0 | 50 | 100 kilometers |

Confederate victory
Union victory
Confederate advance
Confederate retreat
Union advance
Confederate states
Union states

Unlike the northern clergy, who were sure of what God intended, Lincoln suggested that man does not know God's will—a remarkably modest statement on the eve of Union victory. Perhaps, Lincoln suggested, God had brought on the war to punish the entire nation, not just the South, for the sin of slavery. And if God willed that the war continue until all the wealth created by 250 years of slave labor had been destroyed, and "every drop of blood drawn with the lash shall be paid by another drawn with the sword," this too would be an act of justice (see the Appendix for the full text).

April 1865 brought some of the most momentous events in American history. On April 2, Grant finally broke through Lee's lines at Petersburg, forcing the Army of Northern Virginia to abandon the city and leaving Richmond defenseless. The following day, Union soldiers occupied the southern capital. At the head of one black army unit marched its chaplain, Garland H. White, a former fugitive from slavery. Called upon by a large crowd to make a speech, White, as he later recalled, proclaimed "for the first time in that city freedom to all mankind." Then the "doors of all the slave pens were thrown open and thousands came out shouting and praising God, and Father, or Master Abe."

On April 4, heedless of his own safety, Lincoln walked the streets of Richmond accompanied only by a dozen sailors. At every step he was besieged by former slaves, some of whom fell on their knees before the embarrassed president, who urged them to remain standing. Meanwhile, Lee and his army headed west, only to be encircled by Grant's forces. Realizing that further resistance was useless, Lee surrendered at Appomattox Courthouse, Virginia, on April 9. Although some Confederate units remained in the field, the Civil War was over.

Lincoln did not live to savor victory. On April 11, in what proved to be his last speech, he called publicly for the first time for limited black suffrage. Three days later, while attending a performance at Ford's Theatre in Washington, D.C., the president was mortally wounded by John Wilkes Booth, one of the nation's most celebrated actors. Lincoln died the next

The Evacuation of Richmond, *a Currier and Ives lithograph from 1865, dramatically depicts the last days of the Civil War. Residents flee the Confederate capital as fires set by retreating troops to destroy ammunition supplies consume parts of the city.*

The ruins of Richmond, in an 1865 photograph by Alexander Gardner.

morning. A train carried the president's body to its final resting place in Illinois on a winding 1,600-mile journey that illustrated how tightly the railroad now bound the northern states. Grieving crowds lined the train route, and solemn processions carried the president's body to lie in state in major cities so that mourners could pay their respects. It was estimated that 300,000 persons passed by the coffin in Philadelphia, 500,000 in New York, and 200,000 in Chicago. On May 4, 1865, Lincoln was laid to rest in Springfield.

THE WAR AND THE WORLD

In 1877, soon after retiring as president, Ulysses S. Grant embarked with his wife on a two-year tour of the world. At almost every location, he was greeted as a modern-day hero. What did America in the aftermath of the Civil War represent to the world? In England, the son of the duke of Wellington greeted Grant as a military genius, the primary architect of victory in one of the greatest wars in human history, and a fitting successor to his own father, the general who had vanquished Napoleon. In Newcastle, parading English workers hailed him as the man whose military prowess had saved the world's leading experiment in democratic government, and as a "Hero of Freedom," whose commander-in-chief, Abraham Lincoln, had vindicated the principles of free labor by emancipating America's slaves. In Berlin, Otto von Bismarck, the chancellor of Germany, welcomed Grant as a nation-builder, who had accomplished on the battlefield something—national unity—that Bismarck was attempting to create for his own people. "You had to save the Union," Bismarck commented, "just as we had to save Germany."

A redesign of the American flag proposed in 1863 illustrates the linkage of nationalism and freedom that was solidified by the Civil War. The thirty-five stars forming the word "FREE" include the eleven Confederate states.

THE WAR IN AMERICAN HISTORY

The Civil War laid the foundation for modern America, guaranteeing the Union's permanence, destroying slavery, and shifting power in the nation from the South to the North (and, more specifically, from slaveowning planters to northern capitalists). It dramatically increased the power of the federal government and accelerated the modernization of the northern economy. And it placed on the postwar agenda the challenge of defining and protecting African-American freedom.

Paradoxically, both sides lost something they had gone to war to defend. Slavery was the cornerstone of the Confederacy, but the war led inexorably to slavery's destruction. In the North, the war hastened the transformation of Lincoln's America—the world of free labor, of the small shop and independent farmer—into an industrial giant. Americans, in the words of the abolitionist Wendell Phillips, would "never again ... see the republic in which we were born."

Late in May 1865, a little over a month after Lincoln's death, some 200,000 veterans paraded through Washington, D.C., for the Grand Review of the Union armies, a final celebration of the nation's triumph. The scene inspired the poet Bret Harte to imagine a very different parade—a "phantom army" of the Union dead:

> The martyred heroes of Malvern Hill,
> Of Gettysburg and Chancellorsville,
> The men whose wasted figures fill
> The patriot graves of the nation ...
> And marching beside the others,
> Came the dusky martyrs of Pillow's fight.

To Harte, the war's meaning ultimately lay in the sacrifices of individual soldiers. He included in his reverie the black troops, including those massacred at Fort Pillow. Blacks, Harte seemed to be saying, had achieved equality in death. Could the nation give it to them in life?

Here was the problem that confronted the United States as the postwar era known as Reconstruction began. "Verily," as Frederick Douglass declared, "the work does not *end* with the abolition of slavery, but only *begins*."

SUGGESTED READING

BOOKS

Ayers, Edward L. *In the Presence of Mine Enemies: War in the Heart of America, 1859–1863* (2003). A study of the experiences of Americans in two counties—one in Pennsylvania, one in Virginia—in the early years of the Civil War.

Berlin, Ira, ed. *Slaves No More: Three Essays on Emancipation and the Civil War* (1992). A careful account of the causes and consequences of emancipation during the war.

Faust, Drew G. *This Republic of Suffering* (2008). A powerful account of how the experience of mass death affected American culture, religion, and politics.

Freehling, William W. *The South vs. the South: How Anti-Confederate Southerners Shaped the Course of the Civil War* (2001). An examination of internal disunion within the Confederacy and how it affected the struggle for southern independence.

Glatthaar, Joseph T. *Forged in Battle: The Civil War Alliance of Black Soldiers and White Officers* (1990). Relates the complex experience of black Civil War soldiers and their officers.

Lawson, Melinda. *Patriot Fires: Forging a New Nationalism in the Civil War North* (2002). Considers how both public and private groups, in order to mobilize support for the war effort, promoted a new idea of American nationalism.

McPherson, James M. *Battle Cry of Freedom: The Civil War Era* (1988). The standard account of the coming of the war, its conduct, and its consequences.

Mitchell, Reid. *Civil War Soldiers* (1988). A look at the Civil War from the point of view of the experience of ordinary soldiers.

Neely, Mark E. *The Fate of Liberty: Abraham Lincoln and Civil Liberties* (1991). Explores how the Lincoln administration did and did not meet the challenge of preserving civil liberties while fighting the war.

Quarles, Benjamin. *Lincoln and the Negro* (1962). A judicious account of the evolution of Lincoln's policies regarding slavery, emancipation, and the rights of African-Americans.

Richardson, Heather C. *Greatest Nation of the Earth: Republican Economic Policies during the Civil War* (1997). Considers the far-reaching impact of the economic measures adopted by the Union during the war.

Rose, Willie Lee. *Rehearsal for Reconstruction: The Port Royal Experiment* (1964). Traces the unfolding of the issues of Reconstruction in the Sea Islands of South Carolina in the midst of the war.

Rubin, Anne S. *Shattered Nation: The Rise and Fall of the Confederacy, 1861–1868* (2005). An up-to-date account of the Confederate experience.

Silber, Nina. *Daughters of the Union: Northern Women Fight the Civil War* (2005). Examines the participation of northern women in the war effort and how this did and did not alter their lives.

Stout, Harry S. *Upon the Altar of the Nation: A Moral History of the Civil War* (2006). Examines the role of religion in mobilizing support for the war effort.

WEBSITES

A House Divided: America in the Age of Lincoln: www.digitalhistory.uh.edu/ahd/index.html

Civil War Women: http://library.duke.edu/specialcollections/collections/digitized/civil-war-women/

The American Civil War Homepage: http://sunsite.utk.edu/civil-war/

The Valley of the Shadow: Two Communities in the American Civil War: http://valley.vcdh.virginia.edu

REVIEW QUESTIONS

1. What made the American Civil War the first modern war?

2. Explain how the North won the war by considering its material resources, military strategy, and effective political and military leadership.

3. Describe how President Lincoln's war aims evolved between 1861 and 1863, changing from simply preserving the Union to also ending slavery.

4. How did the Emancipation Proclamation, northern military successes, and actions by the slaves themselves combine to finally end slavery?

5. What role did blacks play in both winning the Civil War and in defining the war's consequences?

6. What major policies did the wartime Congress pass that transformed the nation's economic and financial systems?

7. How was the American Civil War part of a global trend toward more destructive and deadly wars?

8. Compare the end of slavery in the United States to emancipation elsewhere in the world.

9. In what ways did the outcome of the Civil War change the United States's status in the world?

FREEDOM QUESTIONS

1. How did Lincoln's Gettysburg Address express the new connection between freedom, liberty, and nation?

2. Explain how both northern and southern soldiers could claim they were fighting for "freedom" and "liberty."

3. Explain how both northern and southern governments restricted liberties during the war. How were such actions justified?

4. Describe how the Civil War permanently altered the national definition of freedom and linked it to the survival of the nation

KEY TERMS

REVIEW TABLE

Rehearsals for Reconstruction

Event	Explanation	Result
Sea Island experiment, 1861–1865	Union takes islands and northerners bring their ideas for education, land distribution, and employment for blacks	Black families work for wages, get an education, and enjoy better food and shelter than under slavery
"Negro paradise"	General Grant seizes the cotton plantations of Jefferson Davis and his brother	Grant divides the land among the freed slaves, rather than have them work for white owners
Ten-Percent Plan	Lincoln's lenient plan toward the South, which offered no role for blacks	Rejected by many black southerners and the Radical Republicans in Congress
Wade-Davis Bill	Stricter reconstruction plan that guarantees blacks equality before the law	Pocket vetoed by Lincoln

Chapter 15

FROM THE PLANTATION TO THE

"What Is Freedom?": Reconstruction, 1865–1877

From the Plantation to the Senate, *an 1883 lithograph celebrating African-American progress during Reconstruction. Among the black leaders pictured at the top are Reconstruction congressmen Benjamin S. Turner, Josiah T. Walls, and Joseph H. Rainey; Hiram Revels of Mississippi, the first African-American senator; religious leader Richard Allen; and abolitionists Frederick Douglass and William Wells Brown. At the center, emancipated slaves work in a cotton field. At the bottom, children attend school and a black family stands outside their home.*

FOCUS QUESTIONS

• What visions of freedom did the former slaves and slaveholders pursue in the postwar South?

• What were the sources, goals, and competing visions for Reconstruction?

• What were the social and political effects of Radical Reconstruction in the South?

• What were the main factors, in both the North and South, for the abandonment of Reconstruction?

On the evening of January 12, 1865, less than a month after Union forces captured Savannah, Georgia, twenty leaders of the city's black community gathered for a discussion with General William T. Sherman and Secretary of War Edwin M. Stanton. Mostly Baptist and Methodist ministers, the group included several men who within a few years would assume prominent positions during the era of Reconstruction that followed the Civil War. Ulysses S. Houston, pastor of the city's Third African Baptist Church, and James Porter, an episcopal religious leader who had operated a secret school for black children before the war, in a few years would win election to the Georgia legislature. James D. Lynch, who had been born free in Baltimore and educated in New Hampshire, went on to serve as secretary of state of Mississippi.

The conversation revealed that the black leaders brought out of slavery a clear definition of freedom. Asked what he understood by slavery, Garrison Frazier, a Baptist minister chosen as the group's spokesman, responded that it meant one person's "receiving by irresistible power the work of another man, and not by his consent." Freedom he defined as "placing us where we could reap the fruit of our own labor, and take care of ourselves." The way to accomplish this was "to have land, and turn it and till it by our own labor." Frazier insisted that blacks possessed "sufficient intelligence" to maintain themselves in freedom and enjoy the equal protection of the laws.

Sherman's meeting with the black leaders foreshadowed some of the radical changes that would take place during the era known as Reconstruction (meaning, literally, the rebuilding of the shattered nation). In the years following the Civil War, former slaves and their white allies, North and South, would seek to redefine the meaning and boundaries of American freedom. Previously an entitlement of whites, freedom would be expanded to include black Americans. The laws and Constitution would be rewritten to guarantee African-Americans, for the first time in the nation's history, recognition as citizens and equality before the law. Black men would be granted the right to vote, ushering in a period of interracial democracy throughout the South. Black schools, churches, and other institutions would flourish, laying the foundation for the modern African-American community. Many of the advances of Reconstruction would prove temporary, swept away during a campaign of violence in the South, and the North's retreat from the ideal of equality. But Reconstruction laid the foundation for future struggles to extend freedom to all Americans.

All this, however, lay in the future in January 1865. Four days after the meeting, Sherman responded to the black delegation by issuing Special Field Order 15. This set aside the Sea Islands and a large area along the South Carolina and Georgia coasts for the settlement of black families on forty-acre plots of land. He also offered them broken-down mules that the army could no longer use. In Sherman's order lay the origins of the phrase, "forty acres and a mule," that would reverberate across the South in the next few years. By June, some 40,000 freed slaves had been settled on "Sherman land." Among the emancipated slaves, Sherman's order raised hopes that the end of slavery would be accompanied by the economic independence that they, like other Americans, believed essential to genuine freedom.

THE MEANING OF FREEDOM

With the end of the Civil War, declared an Illinois congressman in 1865, the United States was a "new nation," for the first time "wholly free." The destruction of slavery, however, made the definition of freedom the central question on the nation's agenda. "What is freedom?" asked Congressman James A. Garfield in 1865. "Is it the bare privilege of not being chained? If this is all, then freedom is a bitter mockery, a cruel delusion." Did freedom mean simply the absence of slavery, or did it imply other rights for the former slaves, and if so, which ones: equal civil rights, the vote, ownership of property? During Reconstruction, freedom became a terrain of conflict, its substance open to different, often contradictory interpretations. Out of the conflict over the meaning of freedom arose new kinds of relations between black and white southerners, and a new definition of the rights of all Americans.

BLACKS AND THE MEANING OF FREEDOM

African-Americans' understanding of freedom was shaped by their experiences as slaves and their observation of the free society around them. To begin with, freedom meant escaping the numerous injustices of slavery—punishment by the lash, the separation of families, denial of access to education, the sexual exploitation of black women by their owners—and sharing in the rights and opportunities of American citizens. "If I cannot do like a white man," Henry Adams, an emancipated slave in Louisiana, told his former master in 1865, "I am not free."

Blacks relished the opportunity to demonstrate their liberation from the regulations, significant and trivial, associated with slavery. They openly held mass meetings and religious services free of white supervision, and they acquired dogs, guns, and liquor, all barred to them under slavery. No longer required to obtain a pass from their owners to travel, former slaves throughout the South left the plantations in search of better jobs, family members, or simply a taste of personal liberty. Many moved to southern towns and cities, where, it seemed, "freedom was free-er."

Family Record, *a lithograph marketed to former slaves after the Civil War, centers on an idealized portrait of a middle-class black family, with scenes of slavery and freedom.*

A post–Civil War photograph of an unidentified black family, seated before their humble home, possibly a former slave cabin.

Mother and Daughter Reading, Mt. Meigs, Alabama, *an 1890 photograph by Rudolph Eickemeyer. During Reconstruction and for years thereafter, former slaves exhibited a deep desire for education, and learning took place outside of school as well as within.*

FAMILIES IN FREEDOM

With slavery dead, institutions that had existed before the war, like the black family, free blacks' churches and schools, and the secret slave church, were strengthened, expanded, and freed from white supervision. The family was central to the postemancipation black community. Former slaves made remarkable efforts to locate loved ones from whom they had been separated under slavery. One northern reporter in 1865 encountered a freedman who had walked more than 600 miles from Georgia to North Carolina, searching for the wife and children from whom he had been sold away before the war. Meanwhile, widows of black soldiers successfully claimed survivors' pensions, forcing the federal government to acknowledge the validity of prewar relationships that slavery had attempted to deny.

But while Reconstruction witnessed the stabilization of family life, freedom subtly altered relationships within the family. Emancipation increased the power of black men and brought to many black families the nineteenth-century notion that men and women should inhabit separate "spheres." Immediately after the Civil War, planters complained that freedwomen had "withdrawn" from field labor and work as house servants. Many black women preferred to devote more time to their families than had been possible under slavery, and men considered it a badge of honor to see their wives remain at home. Eventually, the dire poverty of the black community would compel a far higher proportion of black women than white women to go to work for wages.

CHURCH AND SCHOOL

At the same time, blacks abandoned white-controlled religious institutions to create churches of their own. On the eve of the Civil War, 42,000 black Methodists worshiped in biracial South Carolina churches; by the end of Reconstruction, only 600 remained. The rise of the independent black church, with Methodists and Baptists commanding the largest followings, redrew the religious map of the South. As the major institution independent of white control, the church played a central role in the black community. A place of worship, it also housed schools, social events, and political gatherings. Black ministers came to play a major role in politics. Some 250 held public office during Reconstruction.

Another striking example of the freedpeople's quest for individual and community improvement was their desire for education. Education, declared a Mississippi freedman, was "the next best thing to liberty." The thirst for learning sprang from many sources—a desire to read the Bible, the need to prepare for the economic marketplace, and the opportunity, which arose in 1867, to take part in politics. Blacks of all ages flocked to the schools established by northern missionary societies, the Freedmen's

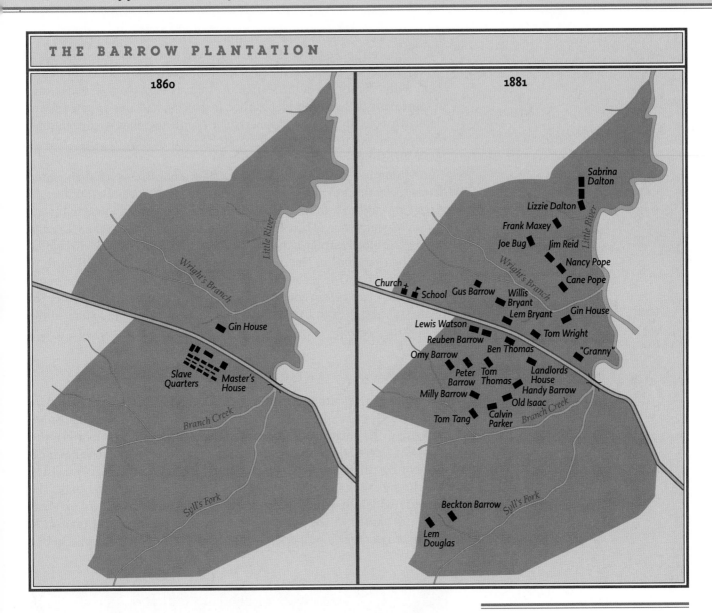

THE BARROW PLANTATION

1860

1881

Two maps of the Barrow plantation illustrate the effects of emancipation on rural life in the South. In 1860, slaves lived in communal quarters near the owner's house. Twenty years later, former slaves working as sharecroppers lived scattered across the plantation and had their own church and school.

Bureau, and groups of ex-slaves themselves. Northern journalist Sidney Andrews, who toured the South in 1865, was impressed by how much education also took place outside of the classroom: "I had occasion very frequently to notice that porters in stores and laboring men in warehouses, and cart drivers on the streets, had spelling books with them, and were studying them during the time they were not occupied with their work." Reconstruction also witnessed the creation of the nation's first black colleges, including Fisk University in Tennessee, Hampton Institute in Virginia, and Howard University in the nation's capital.

POLITICAL FREEDOM

In a society that had made political participation a core element of freedom, the right to vote inevitably became central to the former slaves' desire for empowerment and equality. As Frederick Douglass put it soon after the South's surrender in 1865, "Slavery is not abolished until the black man has the ballot." In a "monarchial government," Douglass explained, no "special" disgrace applied to those denied the right to vote. But in a democracy, "where universal suffrage is the rule," excluding any group meant branding them with "the stigma of inferiority." As soon as the Civil War ended, and in some parts of the South even earlier, free blacks and emancipated slaves claimed a place in the public sphere. They came together in conventions, parades, and petition drives to demand the right to vote and, on occasion, to organize their own "freedom ballots."

Anything less than full citizenship, black spokesmen insisted, would betray the nation's democratic promise and the war's meaning. Speakers at black conventions reminded the nation of Crispus Attucks, who fell at the Boston Massacre, and of black soldiers' contribution to the War of 1812 and during "the bloody struggle through which we have just passed." To demonstrate their patriotism, blacks throughout the South organized Fourth of July celebrations. For years after the Civil War, white southerners would "shut themselves within doors" on Independence Day, as a white resident of Charleston recorded in her diary, while former slaves commemorated the holiday themselves.

LAND, LABOR, AND FREEDOM

Like rural people throughout the world, former slaves' ideas of freedom were directly related to land ownership. Only land, wrote Merrimon Howard, a freedman from Mississippi, would enable "the poor class to enjoy the sweet boon of freedom." On the land they would develop independent communities free of white control. Many former slaves insisted that through their unpaid labor, they had acquired a right to the land. "The property which they hold," declared an Alabama black convention, "was nearly all earned by the sweat of *our* brows." In some parts of the South, blacks in 1865 seized property, insisting that it belonged to them. On one

Winslow Homer's 1876 painting, A Visit from the Old Mistress, *depicts an imaginary meeting between a southern white woman and her former slaves. Their stance and gaze suggest the tensions arising from the birth of a new social order. Homer places his subjects on an equal footing, yet maintains a space of separation between them. He exhibited the painting to acclaim at the Paris Universal Exposition in 1878.*

Tennessee plantation, former slaves claimed to be "joint heirs" to the estate and, the owner complained, took up residence "in the rooms of my house."

In its individual elements and much of its language, former slaves' definition of freedom resembled that of white Americans—self-ownership, family stability, religious liberty, political participation, and economic autonomy. But these elements combined to form a vision very much their own. For whites, freedom, no matter how defined, was a given, a birthright to be defended. For African-Americans, it was an open-ended process, a transformation of every aspect of their lives and of the society and culture that had sustained slavery in the first place. Although the freedpeople failed to achieve full freedom as they understood it, their definition did much to shape national debate during the turbulent era of Reconstruction.

MASTERS WITHOUT SLAVES

Most white southerners reacted to military defeat and emancipation with dismay, not only because of the widespread devastation but also because they must now submit to northern demands. "The demoralization is complete," wrote a Georgia girl. "We are whipped, there is no doubt about it." The appalling loss of life, a disaster without parallel in the American experience, affected all classes of southerners. Nearly 260,000 men died for the Confederacy—more than one-fifth of the South's adult male white population. The widespread destruction of work animals, farm buildings, and machinery ensured that economic revival would be slow and painful. In 1870, the value of property in the South, not counting that represented by slaves, was 30 percent lower than before the war.

Planter families faced profound changes in the war's aftermath. Many lost not only their slaves but their life savings, which they had patriotically invested in now-worthless Confederate bonds. Some, whose slaves departed the plantation, for the first time found themselves compelled to do physical labor. General Braxton Bragg returned to his "once prosperous" Alabama home to find "*all, all* was lost, except my debts." Bragg and his wife, a woman "raised in affluence," lived for a time in a slave cabin.

Southern planters sought to implement an understanding of freedom quite different from that of the former slaves. As they struggled to accept the reality of emancipation, most planters defined black freedom in the narrowest manner. As journalist Sidney Andrews discovered late in 1865, "The whites seem wholly unable to comprehend that freedom for the negro means the same thing as freedom for them. They readily enough admit that the government has made him free, but appear to believe that they have the right to exercise the same old control." Southern leaders sought to revive

The Great Labor Question from a Southern Point of View, *a cartoon by the artist Winslow Homer, published in* Harper's Weekly, *July 29, 1865. Homer satirizes the attitudes of many white southerners. While blacks labor in the fields, an idle planter warns a former slave, "My boy, we've toiled and taken care of you long enough—now you've got to work!"*

the antebellum definition of freedom as if nothing had changed. Freedom still meant hierarchy and mastery; it was a privilege not a right, a carefully defined legal status rather than an open-ended entitlement. Certainly, it implied neither economic autonomy nor civil and political equality. "A man may be free and yet not independent," Mississippi planter Samuel Agnew observed in his diary in 1865. A Kentucky newspaper summed up the stance of much of the white South: the former slave was "*free*, but free only to labor."

THE FREE LABOR VISION

Along with former slaves and former masters, the victorious Republican North tried to implement its own vision of freedom. Central to its definition was the antebellum principle of free labor, now further strengthened as a definition of the good society by the Union's triumph. In the free labor vision of a reconstructed South, emancipated blacks, enjoying the same opportunities for advancement as northern workers, would labor more productively than they had as slaves. At the same time, northern capital and migrants would energize the economy. The South would eventually come to resemble the "free society" of the North, complete with public schools, small towns, and independent farmers. Unified on the basis of free labor, proclaimed Carl Schurz, a refugee from the failed German revolution of 1848 who rose to become a leader of the Republican Party, America would become "a republic, greater, more populous, freer, more prosperous, and more powerful" than any in history.

With planters seeking to establish a labor system as close to slavery as possible, and former slaves demanding economic autonomy and access to land, a long period of conflict over the organization and control of labor followed on plantations throughout the South. It fell to the Freedmen's Bureau, an agency established by Congress in March 1865, to attempt to establish a working free labor system.

THE FREEDMEN'S BUREAU

Under the direction of O. O. Howard, a graduate of Bowdoin College in Maine and a veteran of the Civil War, the Bureau took on responsibilities that can only be described as daunting. The Bureau was an experiment in government social policy that seems to belong more comfortably to the New Deal of the 1930s or the Great Society of the 1960s (see Chapters 21 and 25, respectively) than to nineteenth-century America. Bureau agents were supposed to establish schools, provide aid to the poor and aged, settle disputes between whites and blacks and among the freedpeople, and secure for former slaves and white Unionists equal treatment before the courts. "It is not . . . in your power to fulfill one-tenth of the expectations of those who framed the Bureau," General William T. Sherman wrote to Howard. "I fear you have Hercules' task."

The Bureau lasted from 1865 to 1870. Even at its peak, there were fewer than 1,000 agents in the entire South. Nonetheless, the Bureau's achievements in some areas, notably education and health care, were striking. While the Bureau did not establish schools itself, it coordinated and helped to finance the activities of northern societies committed to black education.

By 1869, nearly 3,000 schools, serving more than 150,000 pupils in the South, reported to the Bureau. Bureau agents also assumed control of hospitals established by the army during the war, and expanded the system into new communities. They provided medical care and drugs to both black and white southerners. In economic relations, however, the Bureau's activities proved far more problematic.

The Freedmen's Bureau, *an engraving from* Harper's Weekly, *July 25, 1868, depicts the Bureau agent as a promoter of racial peace in the violent postwar South.*

THE FAILURE OF LAND REFORM

The idea of free labor, wrote one Bureau agent, was "the noblest principle on earth." All that was required to harmonize race relations in the South was fair wages, good working conditions, and the opportunity to improve the laborer's situation in life. But blacks wanted land of their own, not jobs on plantations. One provision of the law establishing the Bureau gave it the authority to divide abandoned and confiscated land into forty-acre plots for rental and eventual sale to the former slaves.

In the summer of 1865, however, President Andrew Johnson, who had succeeded Lincoln, ordered nearly all land in federal hands returned to its former owners. A series of confrontations followed, notably in South Carolina and Georgia, where the army forcibly evicted blacks who had settled on "Sherman land." When O. O. Howard, head of the Freedmen's Bureau, traveled to the Sea Islands to inform blacks of the new policy, he was greeted with disbelief and protest. A committee of former slaves drew up petitions to Howard and President Johnson. "We want Homesteads," they declared, "we were promised Homesteads by the government." Land, the freedmen insisted, was essential to the meaning of freedom. Without it, they declared, "we have not bettered our condition" from the days of slavery—"you will see, this is not the condition of really free men."

Because no land distribution took place, the vast majority of rural freedpeople remained poor and without property during Reconstruction. They

A black family in the cotton fields after the Civil War, photographed in 1867.

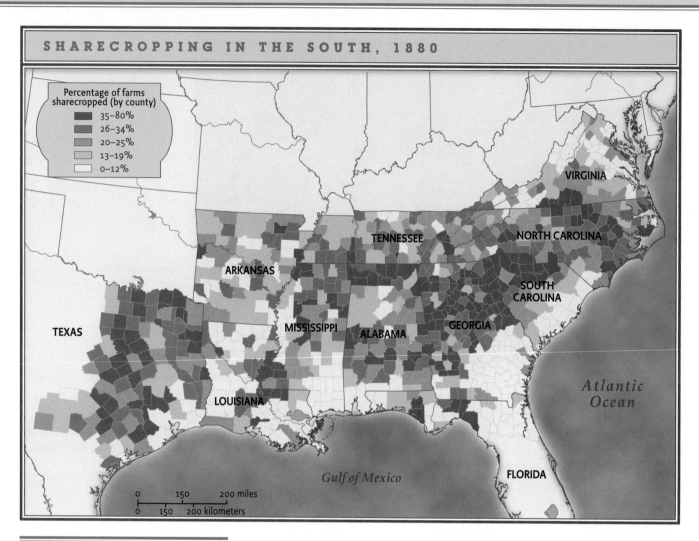

SHARECROPPING IN THE SOUTH, 1880

Percentage of farms
sharecropped (by county)
35–80%
26–34%
20–25%
13–19%
0–12%

By 1880, sharecropping had become the dominant form of agricultural labor in large parts of the South. The system involved both white and black farmers.

had no alternative but to work on white-owned plantations, often for their former owners. Far from being able to rise in the social scale through hard work, black men were largely confined to farm work, unskilled labor, and service jobs, and black women to positions in private homes as cooks and maids. Their wages remained too low to allow for any accumulation. By the turn of the century, a significant number of southern African-Americans had managed to acquire small parcels of land. But the failure of land reform produced a deep sense of betrayal that survived among the former slaves and their descendants long after the end of Reconstruction. "No sir," Mary Gaffney, an elderly ex-slave, recalled in the 1930s, "we were not given a thing but freedom."

TOWARD A NEW SOUTH

Out of the conflict on the plantations, new systems of labor emerged in the different regions of the South. The task system, under which workers were assigned daily tasks, completion of which ended their responsibilities for that day, survived in the rice kingdom of South Carolina and Georgia. Closely supervised wage labor predominated on the sugar plantations of southern Louisiana. Sharecropping came to dominate the Cotton Belt and much of the Tobacco Belt of Virginia and North Carolina.

Sharecropping initially arose as a compromise between blacks' desire for land and planters' demand for labor discipline. The system allowed each black family to rent a part of a plantation, with the crop divided between worker and owner at the end of the year. Sharecropping guaranteed the planters a stable resident labor force. Former slaves preferred it to gang labor because it offered them the prospect of working without day-to-day white supervision. But as the years went on, sharecropping became more and more oppressive. Sharecroppers' economic opportunities were severely limited by a world market in which the price of farm products suffered a prolonged decline.

THE WHITE FARMER

The plight of the small farmer was not confined to blacks in the postwar South. Wartime devastation set in motion a train of events that permanently altered the independent way of life of white yeomen, leading to what they considered a loss of freedom. Before the war, most small farmers had concentrated on raising food for their families and grew little cotton. With much of their property destroyed, many yeomen saw their economic condition worsened by successive crop failures after the war. To obtain supplies from merchants, farmers were forced to take up the growing of cotton and pledge a part of the crop as collateral (property the creditor can seize if a debt is not paid). This system became known as the "crop lien." Since interest rates were extremely high and the price of cotton fell steadily, many farmers found themselves still in debt after marketing their portion of the crop at year's end. They had no choice but to

Farmers with Cotton in the Courthouse Square, *an 1880 photograph of Marietta, Georgia. After the Civil War, more and more white farmers began growing cotton to support their families, permanently altering their formerly self-sufficient way of life.*

VOICES OF FREEDOM

FROM

Petition of Committee in Behalf of the Freedmen to Andrew Johnson (1865)

In the summer of 1865, President Andrew Johnson ordered land that had been distributed to freed slaves in South Carolina and Georgia returned to its former owners. A committee of freedmen drafted a petition asking for the right to obtain land. Johnson did not, however, change his policy.

We the freedmen of Edisto Island, South Carolina, have learned from you through Major General O. O. Howard . . . with deep sorrow and painful hearts of the possibility of [the] government restoring these lands to the former owners. We are well aware of the many perplexing and trying questions that burden your mind, and therefore pray to god (the preserver of all, and who has through our late and beloved President [Lincoln's] proclamation and the war made us a free people) that he may guide you in making your decisions and give you that wisdom that cometh from above to settle these great and important questions for the best interests of the country and the colored race.

Here is where secession was born and nurtured. Here is where we have toiled nearly all our lives as slaves and treated like dumb driven cattle. This is our home, we have made these lands what they were, we are the only true and loyal people that were found in possession of these lands. We have been always ready to strike for liberty and humanity, yea to fight if need be to preserve this glorious Union. Shall not we who are freedmen and have always been true to this Union have the same rights as are enjoyed by others? . . . Are not our rights as a free people and good citizens of these United States to be considered before those who were found in rebellion against this good and just government? . . .

[Are] we who have been abused and oppressed for many long years not to be allowed the privilege of purchasing land but be subject to the will of these large land owners? God forbid. Land monopoly is injurious to the advancement of the course of freedom, and if government does not make some provision by which we as freedmen can obtain a homestead, we have not bettered our condition. . . .

We look to you . . . for protection and equal rights with the privilege of purchasing a homestead— a homestead right here in the heart of South Carolina.

FROM a Sharecropping Contract (1866)

Few former slaves were able to acquire land in the post–Civil War South. Most ended up as sharecroppers, working on white-owned land for a share of the crop at the end of the growing season. This contract, typical of thousands of others, originated in Tennessee. The laborers signed with an X, as they were illiterate.

Thomas J. Ross agrees to employ the Freedmen to plant and raise a crop on his Rosstown Plantation. . . . On the following Rules, Regulations and Remunerations.

The said Ross agrees to furnish the land to cultivate, and a sufficient number of mules & horses and feed them to make and house said crop and all necessary farming utensils to carry on the same and to give unto said Freedmen whose names appear below one half of all the cotton, corn and wheat that is raised on said place for the year 1866 after all the necessary expenses are deducted out that accrues on said crop. Outside of the Freedmen's labor in harvesting, carrying to market and selling the same the said Freedmen . . . covenant and agrees to and with said Thomas J. Ross that for and in consideration of one half of the crop before mentioned that they will plant, cultivate, and raise under the management control and Superintendence of said Ross, in good faith, a cotton, corn and oat crop under his management for the year 1866. And we the said Freedmen agrees to furnish ourselves & families in provisions, clothing, medicine and medical bills and all, and every kind of other expenses that we may incur on said plantation for the year 1866 free of charge to said Ross. Should the said Ross furnish us any of the above supplies or any other kind of expenses, during said year, are to settle and pay him out of the net proceeds of our part of the crop the retail price of the county at time of sale or any price we may agree upon—The said Ross shall keep a regular book account, against each and every one or the head of every family to be adjusted and settled at the end of the year.

We furthermore bind ourselves to and with said Ross that we will do good work and labor ten hours a day on an average, winter and summer. . . . We further agree that we will lose all lost time, or pay at the rate of one dollar per day, rainy days excepted. In sickness and women lying in childbed are to lose the time and account for it to the other hands out of his or her part of the crop. . . .

We furthermore bind ourselves that we will obey the orders of said Ross in all things in carrying out and managing said crop for said year and be docked for disobedience. All is responsible for all farming utensils that is on hand or may be placed in care of said Freedmen for the year 1866 to said Ross and are also responsible to said Ross if we carelessly, maliciously maltreat any of his stock for said year to said Ross for damages to be assessed out of our wages.

Samuel (X) Johnson, Thomas (X) Richard, Tinny (X) Fitch, Jessie (X) Simmons, Sophe (X) Pruden, Henry (X) Pruden, Frances (X) Pruden, Elijah (X) Smith

---

QUESTIONS

1. Why do the black petitioners believe that owning land is essential to the enjoyment of freedom?

2. In what ways does the contract limit the freedom of the laborers?

3. What do these documents suggest about competing definitions of black freedom in the aftermath of slavery?

continue to plant cotton to obtain new loans. By the mid-1870s, white farmers, who cultivated only 10 percent of the South's cotton crop in 1860, were growing 40 percent, and many who had owned their land had fallen into dependency as sharecroppers, who now rented land owned by others.

Both black and white farmers found themselves caught in the sharecropping and crop-lien systems. A far higher percentage of black than white farmers in the South rented land rather than owned it. But every census from 1880 to 1940 counted more white than black sharecroppers. The workings of sharecropping and the crop-lien system are illustrated by the case of Matt Brown, a Mississippi farmer who borrowed money each year from a local merchant. He began 1892 with a debt of $226 held over from the previous year. By 1893, although he produced cotton worth $171, Brown's debt had increased to $402, because he had borrowed $33 for food, $29 for clothing, $173 for supplies, and $112 for other items. Brown never succeeded in getting out of debt. He died in 1905; the last entry under his name in the merchant's account book is a coffin.

THE URBAN SOUTH

Even as the rural South stagnated economically, southern cities experienced remarkable growth after the Civil War. As railroads penetrated the interior, they enabled merchants in market centers like Atlanta to trade directly with the North, bypassing coastal cities that had traditionally monopolized southern commerce. A new urban middle class of merchants, railroad promoters, and bankers reaped the benefits of the spread of cotton production in the postwar South.

Thus, Reconstruction brought about profound changes in the lives of southerners, black and white, rich and poor. In place of the prewar world of master, slave, and self-sufficient yeoman, the postwar South was peopled by new social classes—landowning employers, black and white sharecroppers, cotton-producing white farmers, wage-earning black laborers, and urban entrepreneurs. Each of these groups turned to Reconstruction politics in an attempt to shape to its own advantage the aftermath of emancipation.

AFTERMATHS OF SLAVERY

The United States, of course, was not the only society to confront the problem of the transition from slavery to freedom. Indeed, many parallels exist between the debates during Reconstruction and struggles that followed slavery in other parts of the Western Hemisphere over the same issues of land, control of labor, and political power. In every case, former planters (or, in Haiti, where the planter class had been destroyed, the government itself) tried to encourage or require former slaves to go back to work on plantations to grow the same crops as under slavery. Planters elsewhere held the same stereotypical views of black laborers as were voiced by their counterparts in the United States—former slaves were supposedly lazy, lacking in ambition, and thought that freedom meant an absence of labor.

For their part, former slaves throughout the hemisphere tried to carve out as much independence as possible, both in their daily lives and in their labor. They attempted to reconstruct family life by withdrawing women and children from field labor (in the West Indies, women turned to marketing their families' crops to earn income). Wherever possible, former slaves acquired land of their own and devoted more time to growing food for their families than crops for the international market. On small Caribbean islands like Barbados, where no unoccupied land existed, former slaves had no alternative but to return to plantation labor. Elsewhere, the plantations either fell to pieces, as in Haiti, or continued operating with a new labor force composed of indentured servants from India and China, as in Jamaica, Trinidad, and British Guiana. As slavery ended between the years 1838 and 1865, more than 100,000 Indian laborers were introduced into the British Caribbean—a process that could not have taken place without the consolidation of British control over India as part of its nineteenth-century empire. Southern planters in the United States brought in a few Chinese laborers in an attempt to replace freedmen, but since the federal government opposed such efforts, the Chinese remained only a tiny proportion of the southern workforce.

But if struggles over land and labor united its postemancipation experience with that of other societies, in one respect the United States was unique. Only in the United States were former slaves, within two years of the end of slavery, granted the right to vote and, thus, given a major share of political power. Few anticipated this development when the Civil War ended. It came about as the result of one of the greatest political crises of American history—the battle between President Andrew Johnson and Congress over Reconstruction. The struggle resulted in profound changes in the nature of citizenship, the structure of constitutional authority, and the meaning of American freedom.

Chinese laborers at work on a Louisiana plantation during Reconstruction.

THE MAKING OF RADICAL RECONSTRUCTION

ANDREW JOHNSON

To Lincoln's successor, Andrew Johnson, fell the task of overseeing the restoration of the Union. Born in poverty in North Carolina, as a youth Johnson worked as a tailor's apprentice. After moving to Tennessee, he achieved success through politics. Beginning as an alderman (a town official), he rose to serve in the state legislature, the U.S. Congress, and for two terms as governor of Tennessee. Johnson identified himself as the champion of his state's "honest yeomen" and a foe of large planters, whom he described as a "bloated, corrupted aristocracy." A strong defender of the Union, he became the only senator from a seceding state to remain at his post in Washington, D.C., when the Civil War began in 1861. When northern forces occupied Tennessee, Abraham Lincoln named him military governor. In 1864, Republicans nominated him to run for vice president as a symbol of the party's hope of extending its organization into the South.

In personality and outlook, Johnson proved unsuited for the responsibilities he shouldered after Lincoln's death. A lonely, stubborn man, he was intolerant of criticism and unable to compromise. He lacked Lincoln's political skills and keen sense of public opinion. A fervent believer in states' rights, Johnson insisted that since secession was illegal, the southern states had never actually left the Union or surrendered the right to govern their own affairs. Moreover, while Johnson had supported emancipation once Lincoln made it a goal of the war effort, he held deeply racist views. African-Americans, Johnson believed, had no role to play in Reconstruction.

THE FAILURE OF PRESIDENTIAL RECONSTRUCTION

A little over a month after Lee's surrender at Appomattox, and with Congress out of session until December, Johnson in May 1865 outlined his plan for reuniting the nation. He issued a series of proclamations that began the period of Presidential Reconstruction (1865–1867). Johnson offered a pardon (which restored political and property rights, except for slaves) to nearly all white southerners who took an oath of allegiance. He excluded Confederate leaders and wealthy planters whose prewar property had been valued at more than $20,000. This exemption suggested at first that Johnson planned a more punitive Reconstruction than Lincoln had intended. Most of those exempted, however, soon received individual pardons from the president. Johnson also appointed provisional governors and ordered them to call state conventions, elected by whites alone, that would establish loyal governments in the South. Apart from the requirement that they abolish slavery, repudiate secession, and refuse to pay the Confederate debt—all unavoidable consequences of southern defeat—he granted the new governments a free hand in managing local affairs.

At first, most northerners believed Johnson's policy deserved a chance to succeed. The conduct of the southern governments elected under his program, however, turned most of the Republican North against the president. By and large, white voters returned prominent Confederates and members of the old elite to power. Reports of violence directed against former slaves and northern visitors in the South further alarmed Republicans.

THE BLACK CODES

But what aroused the most opposition to Johnson's Reconstruction policy were the Black Codes, laws passed by the new southern governments that attempted to regulate the lives of the former slaves. These laws granted blacks certain rights, such as legalized marriage, ownership of property, and limited access to the courts. But they denied them the rights to testify against whites, to serve on juries or in state militias, or to vote. And in response to planters' demands that the freedpeople be required to work on the plantations, the Black Codes declared that those who failed to sign yearly labor contracts could be arrested and hired out to white landowners. Some states limited the occupations open to blacks and barred them from acquiring land, and others provided that judges could assign black children to work for their former owners without the consent of the parents. "We are not permitted to own the land whereon to build a schoolhouse or a church," complained a black convention in Mississippi. "Where is justice? Where is freedom?"

Clearly, the death of slavery did not automatically mean the birth of freedom. But the Black Codes so completely violated free labor principles that they called forth a vigorous response from the Republican North. Wars—especially civil wars—often generate hostility and bitterness. But few groups of rebels in history have been treated more leniently than the defeated Confederates. A handful of southern leaders were arrested but most were quickly released. Only one was executed—Henry Wirz, the commander of Andersonville prison, where thousands of Union prisoners of war had died. Most of the Union army was swiftly demobilized. What motivated the North's turn against Johnson's policies was not a desire to "punish" the white South, but the inability of the South's political leaders to accept the reality of emancipation. "We must see to it," announced

Selling a Freeman to Pay His Fine at Monticello, Florida, *an engraving from* Frank Leslie's Illustrated Newspaper, *January 19, 1867. Under the Black Codes enacted by southern legislatures immediately after the Civil War, blacks convicted of "vagrancy"—often because they refused to sign contracts to work on plantations—were fined and, if unable to pay, auctioned off to work for the person who paid the fine.*

Thaddeus Stevens, leader of the Radical Republicans in the House of Representatives during Reconstruction.

Republican senator William Stewart of Nevada, "that the man made free by the Constitution of the United States is a freeman indeed."

THE RADICAL REPUBLICANS

When Congress assembled in December 1865, Johnson announced that with loyal governments functioning in all the southern states, the nation had been reunited. In response, Radical Republicans, who had grown increasingly disenchanted with Johnson during the summer and fall, called for the dissolution of these governments and the establishment of new ones with "rebels" excluded from power and black men guaranteed the right to vote. Radicals tended to represent constituencies in New England and the "burned-over" districts of the rural North that had been home to religious revivalism, abolitionism, and other reform movements. Although they differed on many issues, Radicals shared the conviction that Union victory created a golden opportunity to institutionalize the principle of equal rights for all, regardless of race.

The Radicals fully embraced the expanded powers of the federal government born during the Civil War. Traditions of federalism and states' rights, they insisted, must not obstruct a sweeping national effort to protect the rights of all Americans. The most prominent Radicals in Congress were Charles Sumner, a senator from Massachusetts, and Thaddeus Stevens, a lawyer and iron manufacturer who represented Pennsylvania in the House of Representatives. Before the Civil War, both had been outspoken foes of slavery and defenders of black rights. Early in the Civil War, both had urged Lincoln to free and arm the slaves, and both in 1865 favored black suffrage in the South. "The same national authority," declared Sumner, "that destroyed slavery must see that this other pretension [racial inequality] is not permitted to survive."

Thaddeus Stevens's most cherished aim was to confiscate the land of disloyal planters and divide it among former slaves and northern migrants to the South. "The whole fabric of southern society," he declared, "*must* be changed. Without this, this Government can never be, as it has never been, a true republic." But his plan to make "small independent landholders" of the former slaves proved too radical even for many of his Radical colleagues. Congress, to be sure, had already offered free land to settlers in the West in the Homestead Act of 1862. But this land had been in the possession of the federal government, not private individuals (although originally, of course, it had been occupied by Indians). Most congressmen believed too deeply in the sanctity of property rights to be willing to take land from one group of owners and distribute it to others. Stevens's proposal failed to pass.

THE ORIGINS OF CIVIL RIGHTS

With the South unrepresented, Republicans enjoyed an overwhelming majority in Congress. But the party was internally divided. Most Republicans were moderates, not Radicals. Moderates believed that Johnson's plan was flawed, but they desired to work with the president to modify it. They feared that neither northern nor southern whites would accept black suffrage. Moderates and Radicals joined in refusing to seat the southerners recently elected to Congress, but moderates broke with the Radicals by leaving the Johnson governments in place.

Early in 1866, Senator Lyman Trumbull of Illinois proposed two bills, reflecting the moderates' belief that Johnson's policy required modification. The first extended the life of the Freedmen's Bureau, which had originally been established for only one year. The second, the Civil Rights Bill, was described by one congressman as "one of the most important bills ever presented to the House for its action." It defined all persons born in the United States as citizens and spelled out rights they were to enjoy without regard to race. Equality before the law was central to the measure—no longer could states enact laws like the Black Codes discriminating between white and black citizens. So were free labor values. According to the law, no state could deprive any citizen of the right to make contracts, bring lawsuits, or enjoy equal protection of one's person and property. These, said Trumbull, were the "fundamental rights belonging to every man as a free man." The bill made no mention of the right to vote for blacks. In constitutional terms, the Civil Rights Bill represented the first attempt to give concrete meaning to the Thirteenth Amendment, which had abolished slavery, to define in law the essence of freedom.

To the surprise of Congress, Johnson vetoed both bills. Both, he said, would centralize power in the national government and deprive the states of the authority to regulate their own affairs. Moreover, he argued, blacks did not deserve the rights of citizenship. By acting to secure their rights, Congress was discriminating "against the white race." The vetoes made a breach between the president and nearly the entire Republican Party inevitable. Congress failed by a single vote to muster the two-thirds majority necessary to override the veto of the Freedmen's Bureau Bill (although later in 1866, it did extend the Bureau's life to 1870). But in April 1866, the Civil Rights Bill became the first major law in American history to be passed over a presidential veto.

President Andrew Johnson, in an 1868 lithograph by Currier and Ives. Because of Johnson's stubborn opposition to the congressional Reconstruction policy, one disgruntled citizen drew a crown on his head with the words, "I am King."

THE FOURTEENTH AMENDMENT

Congress now proceeded to adopt its own plan of Reconstruction. In June, it approved and sent to the states for ratification the Fourteenth Amendment, which placed in the Constitution the principle of citizenship for all persons born in the United States, and which empowered the federal government to protect the rights of all Americans. The amendment prohibited the states from abridging the "privileges and immunities" of citizens or denying them the "equal protection of the law." This broad language opened the door for future Congresses and the federal courts to breathe meaning into the guarantee of legal equality.

In a compromise between the radical and moderate positions on black suffrage, the amendment did not grant blacks the right to vote. But it did provide that if a state denied the vote to any group of men, that state's representation in Congress would be reduced. (This provision did not apply when states barred women from voting.) The abolition of slavery threatened to increase southern political power, since now all blacks, not merely three-fifths as in the case of slaves, would be counted in determining a state's representation in Congress. The Fourteenth Amendment offered the leaders of the white South a choice—allow black men to vote and keep their

A Democratic Party broadside from the election of 1866 in Pennsylvania uses racist imagery to argue that government assistance aids lazy former slaves at the expense of hardworking whites.

state's full representation in the House of Representatives, or limit the vote to whites and sacrifice part of their political power.

The Fourteenth Amendment produced an intense division between the parties. Not a single Democrat in Congress voted in its favor, and only 4 of 175 Republicans were opposed. Radicals, to be sure, expressed their disappointment that the amendment did not guarantee black suffrage. (It was far from perfect, Stevens told the House, but he intended to vote for it, "because I live among men and not among angels.") Nonetheless, by writing into the Constitution the principle that equality before the law regardless of race is a fundamental right of all American citizens, the amendment made the most important change in that document since the adoption of the Bill of Rights.

THE RECONSTRUCTION ACT

The Fourteenth Amendment became the central issue of the political campaign of 1866. Johnson embarked on a speaking tour of the North, called by journalists the "swing around the circle," to urge voters to elect members of Congress committed to his own Reconstruction program. Denouncing his critics, the president made wild accusations that the Radicals were plotting to assassinate him. His behavior further undermined public support for his policies, as did riots that broke out in Memphis and New Orleans, in which white policemen and citizens killed dozens of blacks.

In the northern congressional elections that fall, Republicans opposed to Johnson's policies won a sweeping victory. Nonetheless, at the president's urging, every southern state but Tennessee refused to ratify the Fourteenth Amendment. The intransigence of Johnson and the bulk of the white South pushed moderate Republicans toward the Radicals. In March 1867, over Johnson's veto, Congress adopted the Reconstruction Act, which temporarily divided the South into five military districts and called for the creation of new state governments, with black men given the right to vote. Thus began the period of Radical Reconstruction, which lasted until 1877.

A variety of motives combined to produce Radical Reconstruction—demands by former slaves for the right to vote, the Radicals' commitment to the idea of equality, widespread disgust with Johnson's policies, the desire to fortify the Republican Party in the South, and the determination to keep ex-Confederates from office. But the conflict between President Johnson and Congress did not end with the passage of the Reconstruction Act.

IMPEACHMENT AND THE ELECTION OF GRANT

In March 1867, Congress adopted the Tenure of Office Act, barring the president from removing certain officeholders, including cabinet members, without the consent of the Senate. Johnson considered this an unconstitutional restriction on his authority. In February 1868, he removed Secretary of War Edwin M. Stanton, an ally of the Radicals. The House of Representatives responded by approving articles of impeachment—that is, it presented charges against Johnson to the Senate, which had to decide whether to remove him from office.

That spring, for the first time in American history, a president was placed on trial before the Senate for "high crimes and misdemeanors." By this point, virtually all Republicans considered Johnson a failure as president. But some moderates disliked Benjamin F. Wade, a Radical who, as temporary president of the Senate, would become president if Johnson were removed. Others feared that conviction would damage the constitutional separation of powers between Congress and the executive. Johnson's lawyers assured moderate Republicans that, if acquitted, he would stop interfering with Reconstruction policy. The final tally was 35-19 to convict Johnson, one vote short of the two-thirds necessary to remove him. Seven Republicans had joined the Democrats in voting to acquit the president.

A few days after the vote, Republicans nominated Ulysses S. Grant, the Union's most prominent military hero, as their candidate for president. Grant's Democratic opponent was Horatio Seymour, the former governor of New York. Reconstruction became the central issue of the bitterly fought 1868 campaign. Republicans identified their opponents with secession and treason, a tactic known as "waving the bloody shirt." Democrats denounced Reconstruction as unconstitutional and condemned black suffrage as a violation of America's political traditions. They appealed openly to racism. Seymour's running mate, Francis P. Blair Jr., charged Republicans with placing the South under the rule of "a semi-barbarous race" who longed to "subject the white women to their unbridled lust."

A Democratic ribbon from the election of 1868, with Horatio Seymour and Francis P. Blair Jr., the party's candidates for president and vice president. The ribbon illustrates the explicit appeals to racism that marked the campaign.

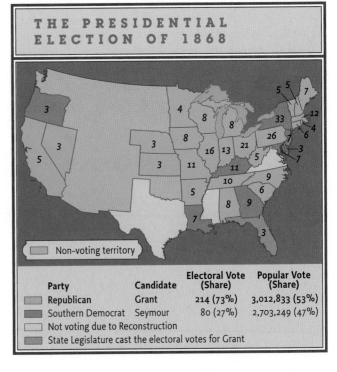

THE FIFTEENTH AMENDMENT

Grant won the election of 1868, although by a margin—300,000 of 6 million votes cast—that many Republicans

The Fifteenth Amendment, *an 1870 lithograph marking the ratification of the constitutional amendment prohibiting states from denying citizens the right to vote because of race. Surrounding an image of a celebration parade are portraits of Abraham Lincoln; President Ulysses S. Grant and his vice president, Schuyler Colfax; abolitionists John Brown, Martin R. Delany, and Frederick Douglass; and Hiram Revels, the first black to serve in the U.S. Senate. At the bottom are scenes of freedom—education, family, political representation, and church life.*

found uncomfortably slim. The result led Congress to adopt the era's third and final amendment to the Constitution. In February 1869, it approved the Fifteenth Amendment, which prohibited the federal and state governments from denying any citizen the right to vote because of race. Bitterly opposed by the Democratic Party, it was ratified in 1870.

Although the Fifteenth Amendment opened the door to suffrage restrictions not explicitly based on race—literacy tests, property qualifications, and poll taxes—and did not extend the right to vote to women, it marked the culmination of four decades of abolitionist agitation. As late as 1868, even after Congress had enfranchised black men in the South, only eight northern states allowed African-American men to vote. With the Fifteenth Amendment, the American Anti-Slavery Society disbanded, its work, its members believed, now complete. "Nothing in all history," exclaimed veteran abolitionist William Lloyd Garrison, equaled "this wonderful, quiet, sudden transformation of four millions of human beings from . . . the auction-block to the ballot-box."

THE "GREAT CONSTITUTIONAL REVOLUTION"

The laws and amendments of Reconstruction reflected the intersection of two products of the Civil War era—a newly empowered national state, and the idea of a national citizenry enjoying equality before the law. What Republican leader Carl Schurz called the "great Constitutional revolution" of Reconstruction transformed the federal system and with it, the language of freedom so central to American political culture.

Before the Civil War, American citizenship had been closely linked to race. The first Congress, in 1790, had limited to whites the right to become a naturalized citizen when immigrating from abroad. No black person, free or slave, the Supreme Court had declared in the *Dred Scott* decision of 1857, could be a citizen of the United States. The laws and amendments of Reconstruction repudiated the idea that citizenship was an entitlement of whites alone. The principle of equality before the law, moreover, did not apply only to the South. The Reconstruction amendments voided many northern laws discriminating on the basis of race. And, as one congressman noted, the amendments expanded the liberty of whites as well as blacks, including "the millions of people of foreign birth who will flock to our shores."

The new amendments also transformed the relationship between the federal government and the states. The Bill of Rights had linked civil liberties to the autonomy of the states. Its language—"Congress shall make no law"—reflected the belief that concentrated national power posed the greatest threat to freedom. The authors of the Reconstruction amendments assumed that rights required national power to enforce them. Rather than a threat to liberty, the federal government, in Charles Sumner's words, had become "the custodian of freedom."

The Reconstruction amendments transformed the Constitution from a document primarily concerned with federal-state relations and the rights of property into a vehicle through which members of vulnerable minorities could stake a claim to freedom and seek protection against misconduct by all levels of government. In the twentieth century, many of the Supreme Court's most important decisions expanding the rights of American citizens were based on the Fourteenth Amendment, perhaps most notably the 1954 *Brown* ruling that outlawed school segregation (see Chapter 24).

BOUNDARIES OF FREEDOM

Reconstruction redrew the boundaries of American freedom. Lines of exclusion that limited the privileges of citizenship to white men had long been central to the practice of American democracy. Only in an unparalleled crisis could they have been replaced, even temporarily, by the vision

Uncle Sam's Thanksgiving Dinner, *an engraving by Thomas Nast from* Harper's Weekly, *November 20, 1868, shortly after the election of Ulysses S. Grant, graphically illustrates how the boundaries of freedom had expanded during Reconstruction. The guests include, among others, African-Americans, Asian-Americans, and Native Americans, men and women, all enjoying a harmonious feast. The table's centerpiece contains the slogan, "universal suffrage."*

of a republic of equals embracing black Americans as well as white. That the United States was a "white man's government" had been a widespread belief before the Civil War. It is not difficult to understand why Andrew Johnson, in one of his veto messages, claimed that federal protection of blacks' civil rights violated "all our experience as a people."

Reconstruction Republicans' belief in universal rights also had its limits. In his remarkable "Composite Nation" speech of 1869, Frederick Douglass condemned prejudice against immigrants from China. America's destiny, he declared, was to transcend race by serving as an asylum for people "gathered here from all corners of the globe by a common aspiration for national liberty." A year later, Charles Sumner moved to strike the word "white" from naturalization requirements. Senators from the western states objected. At their insistence, the naturalization law was amended to make Africans eligible to obtain citizenship when migrating from abroad. But Asians remained ineligible. The racial boundaries of nationality had been redrawn, but not eliminated. The juxtaposition of the amended naturalization law and the Fourteenth Amendment created a significant division in the Asian-American community. Well into the twentieth century, Asian immigrants could not become citizens, but their native-born children automatically did so.

THE RIGHTS OF WOMEN

"The contest with the South that destroyed slavery," wrote the Philadelphia lawyer Sidney George Fisher in his diary, "has caused an immense increase in the popular passion for liberty and equality." But advocates of women's rights encountered the limits of the Reconstruction commitment to equality. Women activists saw Reconstruction as the moment to claim their own emancipation. No less than blacks, proclaimed Elizabeth Cady Stanton, women had arrived at a "transition period, from slavery to freedom." The rewriting of the Constitution, declared suffrage leader Olympia Brown, offered the opportunity to sever the blessings of freedom from sex as well as race and to "bury the black man and the woman in the citizen."

The destruction of slavery led feminists to search for ways to make the promise of free labor real for women. Every issue of the new women's rights journal, *The Agitator*, edited by Mary Livermore, who had led fund-raising efforts for aid to Union soldiers during the war, carried stories complaining of the limited job opportunities and unequal pay for females who entered the labor market. Other feminists debated how to achieve "liberty for married women." Demands for liberalizing divorce laws (which generally required evidence of adultery, desertion, or extreme abuse to termi-

A Delegation of Advocates of Woman Suffrage Addressing the House Judiciary Committee, *an engraving from* Frank Leslie's Illustrated Newspaper, *February 4, 1871. The group includes Elizabeth Cady Stanton, seated just to the right of the speaker, and Susan B. Anthony, at the table on the extreme right.*

nate a marriage) and for recognizing "woman's control over her own body" (including protection against domestic violence and access to what later generations would call birth control) moved to the center of many feminists' concerns. "Our rotten marriage institution," one Ohio woman wrote, "is the main obstacle in the way of woman's freedom."

FEMINISTS AND RADICALS

Talk of woman suffrage and redesigning marriage found few sympathetic male listeners. Even Radical Republicans insisted that Reconstruction was the "Negro's hour" (the hour, that is, of the black male). The Fourteenth Amendment for the first time introduced the word "male" into the Constitution, in its clause penalizing a state for denying any group of men the right to vote. The Fifteenth Amendment outlawed discrimination in voting based on race but not gender. These measures produced a bitter split both between feminists and Radical Republicans, and within feminist circles.

Some leaders, like Stanton and Susan B. Anthony, opposed the Fifteenth Amendment because it did nothing to enfranchise women. They denounced their former abolitionist allies and moved to sever the women's rights movement from its earlier moorings in the antislavery tradition. On occasion, they appealed to racial and ethnic prejudices, arguing that native-born white women deserved the vote more than non-whites and immigrants. "Patrick and Sambo and Hans and Yung Tung, who do not know the difference between a monarchy and a republic," declared Stanton, had no right to be "making laws for [feminist leader] Lucretia Mott." But other abolitionist-feminists, like Abby Kelley and Lucy Stone, insisted that despite their limitations, the Reconstruction amendments represented steps in the direction of truly universal suffrage and should be supported. The result was a split in the movement and the creation in 1869 of two hostile women's rights organizations—the National Woman Suffrage Association, led by Stanton, and the American Woman Suffrage Association, with Lucy Stone as president. They would not reunite until the 1890s.

Thus, even as it rejected the racial definition of freedom that had emerged in the first half of the nineteenth century, Reconstruction left the gender boundary largely intact. When women tried to use the rewritten legal code and Constitution to claim equal rights, they found the courts unreceptive. Myra Bradwell invoked the idea of free labor in challenging an Illinois statute limiting the practice of law to men, but the Supreme Court in 1873 rebuffed her claim. Free labor principles, the justices declared, did not apply to women, since "the law of the Creator" had assigned them to "the domestic sphere."

Despite their limitations, the Fourteenth and Fifteenth Amendments and the Reconstruction Act of 1867 marked a radical departure in American and world history. Alone among the nations that abolished slavery in the nineteenth century, the United States, within a few years of emancipation, clothed its former slaves with citizenship rights equal to those of whites. "We have cut loose from the whole dead past," wrote Timothy Howe, a Republican senator from Wisconsin, "and have cast our anchor out a hundred years" into the future. The Reconstruction Act of 1867 inaugurated America's first real experiment in interracial democracy.

Electioneering at the South, *an engraving from* Harper's Weekly, *July 25, 1868, depicts a speaker at a political meeting in the rural South. Women as well as men took part in these grassroots gatherings.*

RADICAL RECONSTRUCTION IN THE SOUTH

"THE TOCSIN OF FREEDOM"

Among the former slaves, the passage of the Reconstruction Act inspired an outburst of political organization. At mass political meetings—community gatherings attended by men, women, and children—African-Americans staked their claim to equal citizenship. Blacks, declared an Alabama meeting, deserved "exactly the same rights, privileges and immunities as are enjoyed by white men. We ask for nothing more and will be content with nothing less."

These gatherings inspired direct action to remedy long-standing grievances. Hundreds took part in sit-ins that integrated horse-drawn public streetcars in cities across the South. Plantation workers organized strikes for higher wages. Speakers, male and female, fanned out across the South. Frances Ellen Watkins Harper, a black veteran of the abolitionist movement, embarked on a two-year tour, lecturing on "Literacy, Land, and Liberation." James D. Lynch, a member of the group that met with General Sherman in 1865, organized Republican meetings. He became known, in the words of a white contemporary, as "a great orator, fluid and graceful," who "stirred the emotions" of his listeners "as no other man could do."

Determined to exercise their new rights as citizens, thousands joined the Union League, an organization closely linked to the Republican Party, and the vast majority of eligible African-Americans registered to vote. James K. Green, a former slave in Hale County, Alabama, and a League organizer, went on to serve eight years in the Alabama legislature. In the 1880s, Green looked back on his political career. Before the war, he declared, "I was entirely ignorant; I knew nothing more than to obey my master; and there were thousands of us in the same attitude. . . . But the tocsin [warning bell] of freedom sounded and knocked at the door and we walked out like free men and shouldered the responsibilities."

By 1870, all the former Confederate states had been readmitted to the Union, and in a region where the Republican Party had not existed before the war, nearly all were under Republican control. Their new state constitutions, drafted in 1868 and 1869 by the first public bodies in American history with substantial black representation, marked a considerable improvement over those they replaced. The constitutions greatly expanded public responsibilities. They established the region's first state-funded systems of free public education, and they created new penitentiaries, orphan asylums, and homes for the insane. The constitutions guaranteed equality of civil and political rights and abolished practices of the antebellum era such as whipping as a punishment for crime, property qualifications for officeholding, and imprisonment for debt. A few states initially barred former Confederates from voting, but this policy was quickly abandoned by the new state governments.

THE BLACK OFFICEHOLDER

Throughout Reconstruction, black voters provided the bulk of the Republican Party's support. But African-Americans did not control Reconstruction politics, as their opponents frequently charged. The highest offices remained almost entirely in white hands, and only in South Carolina, where blacks made up 60 percent of the population, did they form a majority of the legislature. Nonetheless, the fact that some 2,000 African-Americans occupied public offices during Reconstruction represented a fundamental shift of power in the South and a radical departure in American government.

African-Americans were represented at every level of government. Fourteen were elected to the national House of Representatives. Two blacks

The First Vote, *an engraving from* Harper's Weekly, *November 16, 1867, depicts the first biracial elections in southern history. The voters represent key sources of the black political leadership that emerged during Reconstruction—the artisan carrying his tools, the well-dressed city person (probably free before the war), and the soldier.*

Black and white members of the Mississippi Senate, 1874–1875, shortly before the end of Reconstruction in the state. The woman in the bottom row is a postmistress.

The Operations of the Registration Laws and Negro Suffrage in the South, *an engraving in* Frank Leslie's Illustrated *Newspaper, November 30, 1867, shows blacks and whites for the first time serving together on a southern jury.*

served in the U.S. Senate during Reconstruction, both representing Mississippi. Hiram Revels, who had been born free in North Carolina, was educated in Illinois, and served as a chaplain in the wartime Union army, in 1870 became the first black senator in American history. The second, Blanche K. Bruce, a former slave, was elected in 1875. Since then, only four African-Americans—Edward W. Brooke of Massachusetts (who served 1967–1978), Carol Moseley Braun of Illinois (1993–1998), Barack Obama of Illinois (2005–2008) and Roland Burris (2009–) have held seats in the Senate.

Pinckney B. S. Pinchback of Louisiana, the Georgia-born son of a white planter and a free black woman, served briefly during the winter of 1872–1873 as America's first black governor. More than a century would pass before L. Douglas Wilder of Virginia, elected in 1989, became the second. Some 700 blacks sat in state legislatures during Reconstruction, and scores held local offices ranging from justice of the peace to sheriff, tax assessor, and policeman. The presence of black officeholders and their white allies made a real difference in southern life, ensuring that blacks accused of crimes would be tried before juries of their peers and enforcing fairness in such aspects of local government as road repair, tax assessment, and poor relief.

In South Carolina and Louisiana, homes of the South's wealthiest and best-educated free black communities, most prominent Reconstruction officeholders had never experienced slavery. In addition, a number of black Reconstruction officials, like Pennsylvania-born Jonathan J. Wright, who served on the South Carolina Supreme Court, had come from the North after the Civil War. The majority, however, were former slaves who had established their leadership in the black community by serving in the Union army, working as ministers, teachers, or skilled craftsmen, or engaging in Union League organizing. Among the most celebrated black officeholders was Robert Smalls, who had worked as a slave on the Charleston docks before the Civil War and who won national fame in 1862 by secretly guiding the *Planter,* a Confederate vessel, out of the harbor and delivering it to Union forces. Smalls became a powerful political leader on the South Carolina Sea Islands and was elected to five terms in Congress.

VISIONS OF FREEDOM

The Shackle Broken—by the Genius of Freedom.
This 1874 lithograph depicts the progress of black freedom during the Civil War and Reconstruction. At the center, Robert B. Elliott, a black congressman from South Carolina, delivers a celebrated speech supporting the bill that became the Civil Rights Act of 1875.

QUESTIONS

1. What does the artist suggest about the foundations of blacks' claim to equal rights, and what they anticipated as the results of freedom?

2. What aspects of freedom does the artist include that are absent in the Visions of Freedom image in Chapter 14?

Emancipation, *an 1865 lithograph, is unusual because along with the familiar images of Lincoln and emancipated slaves, it also portrays a poor white family, suggesting that all Americans will benefit from the end of slavery and Reconstruction.*

CARPETBAGGERS AND SCALAWAGS

The new southern governments also brought to power new groups of whites. Many Reconstruction officials were northerners who for one reason or another had made their homes in the South after the war. Their opponents dubbed them "carpetbaggers," implying that they had packed all their belongings in a suitcase and left their homes in order to reap the spoils of office in the South. Some carpetbaggers were undoubtedly corrupt adventurers. The large majority, however, were former Union soldiers who decided to remain in the South when the war ended, before there was any prospect of going into politics. Others were investors in land and railroads who saw in the postwar South an opportunity to combine personal economic advancement with a role in helping to substitute, as one wrote, "the civilization of freedom for that of slavery." Teachers, Freedmen's Bureau officers, and others who came to the region genuinely hoping to assist the former slaves represented another large group of "carpetbaggers."

Most white Republicans, however, had been born in the South. Former Confederates reserved their greatest scorn for these "scalawags," whom they considered traitors to their race and region. Some southern-born Republicans were men of stature and wealth, like James L. Alcorn, the owner of one of Mississippi's largest plantations and the state's first Republican governor.

Most "scalawags," however, were non-slaveholding white farmers from the southern upcountry. Many had been wartime Unionists, and they now cooperated with the Republicans in order to prevent "rebels" from returning to power. Others hoped Reconstruction governments would help them recover from wartime economic losses by suspending the collection of debts and enacting laws protecting small property holders from losing their homes to creditors. In states like North Carolina, Tennessee, and Arkansas, Republicans initially commanded a significant minority of the white vote. Even in the Deep South, the small white Republican vote was important, because the population remained almost evenly divided between blacks (almost all of whom voted for the party of Lincoln) and whites (overwhelmingly Democratic).

SOUTHERN REPUBLICANS IN POWER

In view of the daunting challenges they faced, the remarkable thing is not that Reconstruction governments in many respects failed, but how much they did accomplish. Perhaps their greatest achievement lay in establishing the South's first state-supported public schools. The new educational systems served both black and white children, although generally in schools segregated by race. Only in New Orleans were the public schools integrated during Reconstruction, and only in South Carolina did the state university admit black students (elsewhere, separate colleges were established). By the 1870s, in a region whose prewar leaders had made it illegal for slaves to learn and had done little to provide education for poorer whites, more than half the children, black and white, were attending public schools. The new governments also pioneered civil rights legislation. Their laws made it illegal for railroads, hotels, and other institutions to discriminate on the basis of race. Enforcement varied considerably from locality to locality, but Reconstruction established for the first time at the state

Black students outside a schoolhouse in a post–Civil War photograph. The teacher is seated at the far right.

level a standard of equal citizenship and a recognition of blacks' right to a share of public services.

Republican governments also took steps to strengthen the position of rural laborers and promote the South's economic recovery. They passed laws to ensure that agricultural laborers and sharecroppers had the first claim on harvested crops, rather than merchants to whom the landowner owed money. South Carolina created a state Land Commission, which by 1876 had settled 14,000 black families and a few poor whites on their own farms.

THE QUEST FOR PROSPERITY

Rather than land distribution, however, the Reconstruction governments pinned their hopes for southern economic growth and opportunity for African-Americans and poor whites alike on regional economic development. Railroad construction, they believed, was the key to transforming the South into a society of booming factories, bustling towns, and diversified agriculture. "A free and living republic," declared a Tennessee Republican, would "spring up in the track of the railroad." Every state during Reconstruction helped to finance railroad construction, and through tax reductions and other incentives tried to attract northern manufacturers to invest in the region. The program had mixed results. Economic development in general remained weak. With abundant opportunities existing in the West, few northern investors ventured to the Reconstruction South.

To their supporters, the governments of Radical Reconstruction presented a complex pattern of disappointment and accomplishment. A revitalized southern economy failed to materialize, and most African-Americans remained locked in poverty. On the other hand, biracial democratic government, a thing unknown in American history, for the first time functioned effectively in many parts of the South. Public facilities were rebuilt and expanded, school systems established, and legal codes purged of racism. The conservative elite that had dominated southern government from colonial

Murder of Louisiana, *an 1873 cartoon, illustrates the intensity of the opposition to Reconstruction. President Ulysses S. Grant, depicted as an emperor advised by Attorney General George H. Williams in the form of the devil, prepares to sacrifice the state on the "altar of radicalism." The victim, held by two black men, has already had her heart cut out by Republican governor William P. Kellogg. The other southern states, with South Carolina kneeling in chains, look on.*

times to 1867 found itself excluded from political power, while poor whites, newcomers from the North, and former slaves cast ballots, sat on juries, and enacted and administered laws. "We have gone through one of the most remarkable changes in our relations to each other," declared a white South Carolina lawyer in 1871, "that has been known, perhaps, in the history of the world." It is a measure of how far change had progressed that the reaction against Reconstruction proved so extreme.

THE OVERTHROW OF RECONSTRUCTION

RECONSTRUCTION'S OPPONENTS

The South's traditional leaders—planters, merchants, and Democratic politicians—bitterly opposed the new governments. They denounced them as corrupt, inefficient, and examples of "black supremacy." "Intelligence, virtue, and patriotism" in public life, declared a protest by prominent southern Democrats, had given way to "ignorance, stupidity, and vice." Corruption did exist during Reconstruction, but it was confined to no race, region, or party. The rapid growth of state budgets and the benefits to be gained from public aid led in some states to a scramble for influence that produced bribery, insider dealing, and a get-rich-quick atmosphere. Southern frauds, however, were dwarfed by those practiced in these years by the Whiskey Ring, which involved high officials of the Grant administration, and by New York's Tweed Ring, controlled by the Democrats, whose thefts ran into the tens of millions of dollars. (These are discussed in the next chapter.) The rising taxes needed to pay for schools and other new public facilities and to assist railroad development were another cause of opposition to Reconstruction. Many poor whites who had initially supported the Republican Party turned against it when it became clear that their economic situation was not improving.

The most basic reason for opposition to Reconstruction, however, was that most white southerners could not accept the idea of former slaves voting, holding office, and enjoying equality before the law. In order to restore white supremacy in southern public life and to ensure planters a disciplined, reliable labor force, they believed, Reconstruction must be overthrown. Opponents launched a campaign of violence in an effort to end Republican rule. Their actions posed a fundamental challenge both for Reconstruction governments in the South and for policymakers in Washington, D.C.

"A REIGN OF TERROR"

The Civil War ended in 1865, but violence remained widespread in large parts of the postwar South. In the early years of Reconstruction, violence was mostly local and unorganized. Blacks were assaulted and murdered for refusing to give way to whites on city sidewalks, using "insolent" language, challenging end-of-year contract settlements, and attempting to buy land. The violence that greeted the advent of Republican governments after 1867, however, was far more pervasive and more directly motivated by politics. In wide areas of the South, secret societies sprang up with the aim of preventing blacks from voting and destroying the organization of the Republican Party by assassinating local leaders and public officials.

The most notorious such organization was the Ku Klux Klan, which in effect served as a military arm of the Democratic Party in the South. From its founding in 1866 in Tennessee, the Klan was a terrorist organization. It quickly spread into nearly every southern state. Led by planters, merchants, and Democratic politicians, men who liked to style themselves the South's "respectable citizens," the Klan committed some of the most brutal criminal acts in American history. In many counties, it launched what one victim called a "reign of terror" against Republican leaders, black and white.

The Klan's victims included white Republicans, among them wartime Unionists and local officeholders, teachers, and party organizers. William Luke, an Irish-born teacher in a black school, was lynched in 1870. But African-Americans—local political leaders, those who managed to acquire land, and others who in one way or another defied the norms of white supremacy—bore the brunt of the violence. In York County, South Carolina, where nearly the entire white male population joined the Klan (and women participated by sewing the robes and hoods Klansmen wore as disguises), the organization committed eleven murders and hundreds of whippings.

On occasion, violence escalated from assaults on individuals to mass terrorism and even local insurrections. In Meridian, Mississippi, in 1871, some thirty blacks were murdered in cold blood, along with a white Republican judge. The bloodiest act of violence during Reconstruction took place in Colfax, Louisiana, in 1873, where armed whites assaulted the town with a small cannon. Hundreds of former slaves were murdered, including fifty members of a black militia unit after they had surrendered.

Unable to suppress the Klan, the new southern

A Prospective Scene in the City of Oaks, a cartoon in the September 1, 1868, issue of the Independent Monitor, *a Democratic newspaper published in Tuscaloosa, Alabama. The cartoon sent a warning to the Reverend A. S. Lakin, who had moved from Ohio to become president of the University of Alabama, and Dr. N. B. Cloud, a southern-born Republican serving as Alabama's superintendent of public education. The Ku Klux Klan forced both men from their positions.*

Two Members of the Ku Klux Klan in Their Disguises, *from* Harper's Weekly, *December 19, 1868. The Klan did not adopt its familiar white robes until after Reconstruction.*

governments appealed to Washington for help. In 1870 and 1871, Congress adopted three Enforcement Acts, outlawing terrorist societies and allowing the president to use the army against them. These laws continued the expansion of national authority during Reconstruction. They defined crimes that aimed to deprive citizens of their civil and political rights as federal offenses rather than violations of state law. In 1871, President Grant dispatched federal marshals, backed up by troops in some areas, to arrest hundreds of accused Klansmen. Many Klan leaders fled the South. After a series of well-publicized trials, the Klan went out of existence. In 1872, for the first time since the Civil War, peace reigned in most of the former Confederacy.

THE LIBERAL REPUBLICANS

Despite the Grant administration's effective response to Klan terrorism, the North's commitment to Reconstruction waned during the 1870s. Many Radicals, including Thaddeus Stevens, who died in 1868, had passed from the scene. Within the Republican Party, their place was taken by politicians less committed to the ideal of equal rights for blacks. Northerners increasingly felt that the South should be able to solve its own problems without constant interference from Washington. The federal government had freed the slaves, made them citizens, and given them the right to vote. Now, blacks should rely on their own resources, not demand further assistance.

In 1872, an influential group of Republicans, alienated by corruption within the Grant administration and believing that the growth of federal power during and after the war needed to be curtailed, formed their own party. They included Republican founders like Lyman Trumbull and prominent editors and journalists such as E. L. Godkin of *The Nation.* Calling themselves Liberal Republicans, they nominated Horace Greeley, editor of the *New York Tribune,* for president.

The Old Plantation Home, *a lithograph from 1872 produced by the prominent firm of Currier and Ives in New York City, illustrates how a nostalgic image of slavery as a time of carefree happiness for African-Americans was being promoted even as Reconstruction took place.*

The Liberals' alienation from the Grant administration initially had little to do with Reconstruction. They claimed that corrupt politicians had come to power in the North by manipulating the votes of immigrants and workingmen, while men of talent and education like themselves had been pushed aside. Democratic criticisms of Reconstruction, however, found a receptive audience among the Liberals. As in the North, they became convinced, the "best men" of the South had been excluded from power while "ignorant" voters controlled politics, producing corruption and misgovernment. Power in the South should be returned to the region's "natural leaders." During the campaign of 1872, Greeley repeatedly called on Americans to "clasp hands across the bloody chasm" by putting the Civil War and Reconstruction behind them.

Changes in graphic artist Thomas Nast's depiction of blacks in Harper's Weekly *mirrored the evolution of Republican sentiment in the North.* And Not This Man? *August 5, 1865, shows the black soldier as an upstanding citizen deserving of the vote.* Colored Rule in a Reconstructed (?) State, *March 14, 1874, suggests that Reconstruction legislatures had become travesties of democratic government.*

Greeley had spent most of his career, first as a Whig and then as a Republican, denouncing the Democratic Party. But with the Republican split presenting an opportunity to repair their political fortunes, Democratic leaders endorsed Greeley as their candidate. Many rank and file Democrats, unable to bring themselves to vote for Greeley, stayed at home on election day. As a result, Greeley suffered a devastating defeat by Grant, whose margin of more than 700,000 popular votes was the largest in a nineteenth-century presidential contest. But Greeley's campaign placed on the northern agenda the one issue on which the Liberal reformers and the Democrats could agree—a new policy toward the South.

THE NORTH'S RETREAT

The Liberal attack on Reconstruction, which continued after 1872, contributed to a resurgence of racism in the North. Journalist James S. Pike, a leading Greeley supporter, in 1874 published *The Prostrate State*, an influential account of a visit to South Carolina. The book depicted a state engulfed by political corruption, drained by governmental extravagance, and under the control of "a mass of black barbarism." The South's problems, he insisted, arose from "Negro government." The solution was to restore leading whites to political power. Newspapers that had long supported Reconstruction now began to condemn black participation in southern government. They expressed their views visually as well. Engravings depicting the former slaves as heroic Civil War veterans, upstanding citizens, or victims of violence were increasingly replaced by caricatures presenting them as little more than unbridled animals. Resurgent racism offered a convenient explanation for the alleged "failure" of Reconstruction.

Other factors also weakened northern support for Reconstruction. In 1873, the country plunged into a severe economic depression. Distracted by economic problems, Republicans were in no mood to devote further attention to the South. The depression dealt the South a severe blow and further weakened the prospect that Republicans could revitalize the region's economy. Democrats made substantial gains throughout the nation in the elections of 1874. For the first time since the Civil War, their party took control of the House of Representatives. Before the new Congress met, the old one enacted a final piece of Reconstruction legislation, the Civil Rights Act of 1875. This outlawed racial discrimination in places of public accommodation like hotels and theaters. But it was clear that the northern public was retreating from Reconstruction.

The Supreme Court whittled away at the guarantees of black rights Congress had adopted. In the *Slaughterhouse Cases* (1873), butchers excluded from a state-sponsored monopoly in Louisiana went to court, claiming that their right to equality before the law guaranteed by the Fourteenth Amendment had been violated. The justices rejected their claim, ruling that the amendment had not altered traditional federalism. Most of the rights of citizens, it declared, remained under state control. Three years later, in *United States v. Cruikshank*, the Court gutted the Enforcement Acts by throwing out the convictions of some of those responsible for the Colfax Massacre of 1873.

THE TRIUMPH OF THE REDEEMERS

By the mid-1870s, Reconstruction was clearly on the defensive. Democrats had already regained control of states with substantial white voting majorities such as Tennessee, North Carolina, and Texas. The victorious Democrats called themselves Redeemers, since they claimed to have "redeemed" the white South from corruption, misgovernment, and northern and black control.

In those states where Reconstruction governments survived, violence again erupted. This time, the Grant administration showed no desire to intervene. In contrast to the Klan's activities—conducted at night by disguised men—the violence of 1875 and 1876 took place in broad daylight, as if to underscore Democrats' conviction that they had nothing to fear from Washington. In Mississippi, in 1875, white rifle clubs drilled in public and openly assaulted and murdered Republicans. When Governor Adelbert Ames, a Maine-born Union general, frantically appealed to the federal government for assistance, President Grant responded that the northern public was "tired out" by southern problems. On election day, armed Democrats destroyed ballot boxes and drove former slaves from the polls. The result was a Democratic landslide and the end of Reconstruction in Mississippi. "A revolution has taken place," wrote Ames, "and a race are disfranchised—they are to be returned to . . . an era of second slavery."

Similar events took place in South Carolina in 1876. Democrats nominated for governor former Confederate general Wade Hampton. Hampton promised to respect the rights of all citizens of the state, but his supporters, inspired by Democratic tactics in Mississippi, launched a wave of intimidation. Democrats intended to carry the election, one planter told a black official, "if we have to wade in blood knee-deep."

Of Course He Wants to Vote the Democratic Ticket, a cartoon from Harper's Weekly, October 21, 1876, comments on the campaign of terror launched by South Carolina Democrats in an attempt to carry the election of 1876.

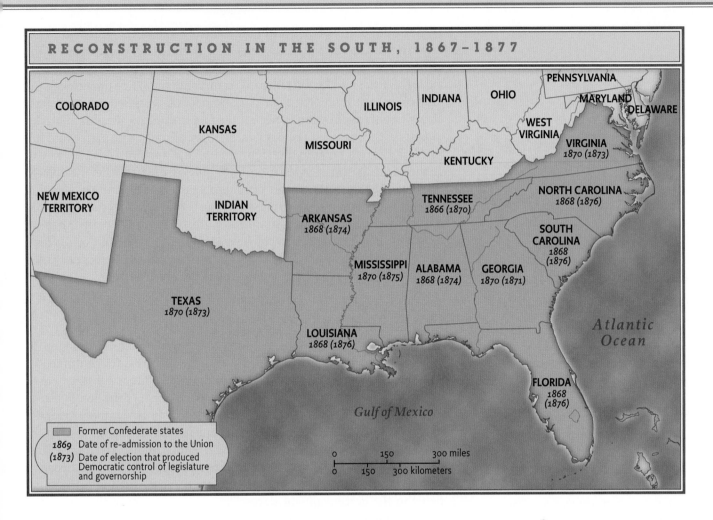

RECONSTRUCTION IN THE SOUTH, 1867–1877

COLORADO

KANSAS

ILLINOIS INDIANA OHIO

PENNSYLVANIA

MARYLAND

DELAWARE

WEST VIRGINIA

MISSOURI

KENTUCKY

VIRGINIA 1870 (1873)

NEW MEXICO TERRITORY

INDIAN TERRITORY

ARKANSAS 1868 (1874)

TENNESSEE 1866 (1870)

NORTH CAROLINA 1868 (1876)

SOUTH CAROLINA 1868 (1876)

TEXAS 1870 (1873)

MISSISSIPPI 1870 (1875)

ALABAMA 1868 (1874)

GEORGIA 1870 (1871)

LOUISIANA 1868 (1876)

Atlantic Ocean

FLORIDA 1868 (1876)

Gulf of Mexico

Former Confederate states
1869 Date of re-admission to the Union
(1873) Date of election that produced Democratic control of legislature and governorship

0   150   300 miles
0   150   300 kilometers

THE DISPUTED ELECTION AND BARGAIN OF 1877

Events in South Carolina directly affected the outcome of the presidential campaign of 1876. To succeed Grant, the Republicans nominated Governor Rutherford B. Hayes of Ohio. Democrats chose as his opponent New York's governor, Samuel J. Tilden. By this time, only South Carolina, Florida, and Louisiana remained under Republican control. The election turned out to be so close that whoever captured these states—which both parties claimed to have carried—would become the next president.

Unable to resolve the impasse on its own, Congress in January 1877 appointed a fifteen-member Electoral Commission, composed of senators, representatives, and Supreme Court justices. Republicans enjoyed an 8-7 majority on the commission, and to no one's surprise, the members decided by that margin that Hayes had carried the disputed southern states and had been elected president. Even as the commission deliberated, however, behind-the-scenes negotiations took place between leaders of the two parties. Hayes's representatives agreed to recognize

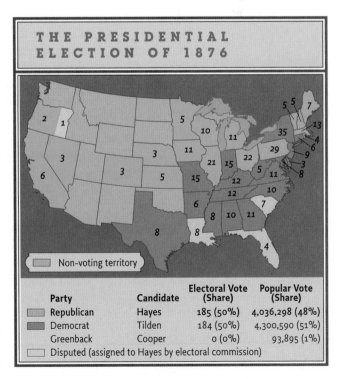

THE PRESIDENTIAL ELECTION OF 1876

Non-voting territory

Party	Candidate	Electoral Vote (Share)	Popular Vote (Share)
Republican	Hayes	185 (50%)	4,036,298 (48%)
Democrat	Tilden	184 (50%)	4,300,590 (51%)
Greenback	Cooper	0 (0%)	93,895 (1%)
Disputed (assigned to Hayes by electoral commission)			

Is This a Republican Form of Government?, *a cartoon by Thomas Nast in* Harper's Weekly, *September 2, 1876, illustrates his conviction that the overthrow of Reconstruction meant that the United States was not prepared to live up to its democratic ideals or protect the rights of black citizens threatened by violence.*

Democratic control of the entire South and to avoid further intervention in local affairs. They also pledged that Hayes would place a southerner in the cabinet position of postmaster general and that he would work for federal aid to the Texas and Pacific railroad, a transcontinental line projected to follow a southern route. For their part, Democrats promised not to dispute Hayes's right to office and to respect the civil and political rights of blacks.

Thus was concluded the Bargain of 1877. Not all of its parts were fulfilled. But Hayes became president, and he did appoint David M. Key of Tennessee as postmaster general. Hayes quickly ordered federal troops to stop guarding the state houses in Louisiana and South Carolina, allowing Democratic claimants to become governor. (Contrary to legend, Hayes did not remove the last soldiers from the South—he simply ordered them to return to their barracks.) But the Texas and Pacific never did get its land grant. Of far more significance, the triumphant southern Democrats failed to live up to their pledge to recognize blacks as equal citizens.

THE END OF RECONSTRUCTION

As a historical process—the nation's adjustment to the destruction of slavery—Reconstruction continued well after 1877. Blacks continued to vote and, in some states, hold office into the 1890s. But as a distinct era of national history—when Republicans controlled much of the South, blacks exercised significant political power, and the federal government accepted the responsibility for protecting the fundamental rights of all American citizens—Reconstruction had come to an end. Despite its limitations, Reconstruction was a remarkable chapter in the story of American freedom. Nearly a century would pass before the nation again tried to bring equal rights to the descendants of slaves. The civil rights era of the 1950s and 1960s would sometimes be called the Second Reconstruction.

Even while it lasted, however, Reconstruction revealed some of the tensions inherent in nineteenth-century discussions of freedom. The policy of granting black men the vote while denying them the benefits of land ownership strengthened the idea that the free citizen could be a poor, dependent laborer. Reconstruction placed on the national agenda a problem that would dominate political discussion for the next half-century—how, in a modern society, to define the economic essence of freedom.

SUGGESTED READING

BOOKS

Carter, Dan T. *When the War Was Over: The Failure of Self-Reconstruction in the South, 1865–1867* (1985). A careful study of the South during the period of Presidential Reconstruction.

DuBois, Ellen C. *Feminism and Suffrage: The Emergence of an Independent Women's Movement in America, 1848–1869* (1978). Explores how the split over the exclusion of women from the Fourteenth and Fifteenth Amendments gave rise to a movement for woman suffrage no longer tied to the abolitionist tradition.

Edwards, Laura. *Gendered Strife and Confusion: The Political Culture of Reconstruction* (1997). Considers how issues relating to gender relations affected the course of southern Reconstruction.

Fields, Barbara J. *Slavery and Freedom on the Middle Ground: Maryland during the Nineteenth Century* (1985). A study of slavery and emancipation in a key border state.

Foner, Eric. *Nothing but Freedom: Emancipation and Its Legacy* (1983). Includes a comparison of the emancipation experience in different parts of the Western Hemisphere.

Foner, Eric. *Reconstruction: America's Unfinished Revolution, 1863–1877* (1988). A comprehensive account of the Reconstruction era.

Hahn, Steven. *A Nation under Our Feet: Black Political Struggles in the Rural South from Slavery to the Great Migration* (2003). A detailed study of black political activism, stressing nationalist consciousness and emigration movements.

Hyman, Harold M. *A More Perfect Union: The Impact of the Civil War and Reconstruction on the Constitution* (1973). Analyzes how the laws and constitutional amendments of Reconstruction changed the Constitution and the rights of all Americans.

Jung, Moon-Ho. *Coolies and Cane: Race, Labor, and Sugar in the Age of Emancipation* (2006). Tells the story of Chinese laborers brought to work in the sugar fields after the end of slavery.

Litwack, Leon F. *Been in the Storm So Long: The Aftermath of Slavery* (1979). A detailed look at the immediate aftermath of the end of slavery and the variety of black and white responses to emancipation.

Rable, George C. *But There Was No Peace: The Role of Violence in the Politics of Reconstruction* (1984). The only full-scale study of violence in the Reconstruction South.

Richardson, Heather C. *West from Appomattox* (2007). An account that fully integrates the West into the history of the Reconstruction era.

Rodrigue, John C. *Reconstruction in the Cane Fields: From Slavery to Free Labor in Louisiana's Sugar Parishes, 1862–1880* (2001). A study of how an often-neglected part of the South experienced the aftermath of slavery.

Summers, Mark W. *Railroads, Reconstruction, and the Gospel of Prosperity: Aid under the Radical Republicans, 1865–1877* (1984). A detailed look at southern governments' efforts to promote economic development, and the political corruption that sometimes accompanied it.

Trefousse, Hans L. *The Radical Republicans: Lincoln's Vanguard for Racial Justice* (1969). An account of the political history of the Radical Republicans, from the pre–Civil War period through the end of Reconstruction.

WEBSITES

After Slavery: Race, Labor, and Politics in the Post-Emancipation Carolinas: www.afterslavery.com

America's Reconstruction: People and Politics after the Civil War: www.digitalhistory.uh.edu/reconstruction/index.html

Freedmen and Southern Society Project: www.history.umd.edu/Freedmen/

The Andrew Johnson Impeachment Trial: www.law.umkc.edu/faculty/projects/ftrials/impeach/impeachmt.htm

REVIEW QUESTIONS

1. In 1865, former Confederate general Robert Richardson remarked that "the emancipated slaves own nothing, because nothing but freedom has been given to them." Explain whether this would be an accurate assessment of Reconstruction twelve years later.

2. The women's movement split into two separate national organizations in part because the Fifteenth Amendment did not give women the vote. Explain why the two groups split.

3. Explain how important black families, churches, schools, and other institutions were to the development of African-American culture and political activism in this period.

4. Why did ownership of land and control of labor become major points of contention between former slaves and whites in the South?

5. By what methods did southern whites seek to limit African-American civil rights and liberties?

6. How did the failure of land reform and continued poverty lead to new forms of servitude for both blacks and whites?

7. What caused the confrontation between President Johnson and Congress over Reconstruction policies?

8. What national issues and attitudes combined to bring an end to Reconstruction by 1877?

9. By 1877, how did the condition of former slaves in the United States compare with that of freedmen around the globe?

FREEDOM QUESTIONS

1. After the Civil War, how did the definitions of freedom change for the nation, for the freedmen, and for southern whites?

2. Identify and explain the key elements of freedom according to the former slaves.

3. In the text we see that "Reconstruction redrew the boundaries of American freedom." How did these boundaries expand for some citizens but remain closed or restricted for others?

KEY TERMS

black families (p. 588)

the Freedmen's Bureau (p. 588)

sharecropping (p. 594)

crop-lien system (p. 598)

Black Codes (p. 601)

Civil Rights Bill of 1866 (p. 603)

Fourteenth Amendment (p. 603)

"swing around the circle" (p. 604)

"waving the bloody shirt" (p. 605)

Fifteenth Amendment (p. 605)

literacy tests (p. 606)

Bradwell v. Illinois (p. 609)

carpetbaggers and scalawags
    (p. 614)

Enforcement Acts (p. 618)

Civil Rights Act of 1875 (p. 620)

Slaughterhouse Cases (p. 620)

Redeemers (p. 620)

Bargain of 1877 (p. 622)

REVIEW TABLE

Reconstruction Constitutional Amendments

Amendment	Date Ratified	Provisions
Thirteenth	1865	Ends slavery
Fourteenth	1868	Guarantees federal protection of citizenship and equal rights under the law
Fifteenth	1870	Prohibits voting restrictions based on race, color, or previous conditions of servitude

Part 4

TOWARD A GLOBAL PRESENCE, 1870–1920

Between the era of Reconstruction and the end of World War I, the United States underwent a profound social and economic revolution that affected all aspects of Americans' lives. By 1900, the country had emerged as the world's major industrial power and, thanks to the Spanish-American War of 1898, the possessor of a small overseas empire. Giant new corporations now dominated the economy. They introduced new forms of labor control and new methods of mass production, manufacturing a seemingly endless array of industrial and consumer goods. Immigrants arrived from abroad in unprecedented numbers, providing labor for the expanding economy and fueling the growth of the nation's cities. In 1920, residents of cities for the first time outnumbered those living in rural areas.

In the first two decades of the twentieth century, the United States became a major participant in world affairs. It repeatedly sent troops to direct the affairs of Caribbean and Central American countries. During World War I, President Woodrow Wilson not only dispatched American soldiers, for the first time, to fight in Europe but also called for continuous American involvement in the creation and preservation of a peaceful, economically interconnected world order.

These changes increased the economic opportunities of many Americans. The middle class of clerks, managers, and other white-collar workers expanded significantly. Economic growth drew large numbers of women into the workforce. When the outbreak of World War I cut off immigration from Europe, hundreds of thousands of blacks moved from southern farms to jobs in northern cities, gaining access to the industrial economy and changing the country's racial configuration.

What is sometimes called "the second industrial revolution" also led to an era of persistent and often violent labor conflict. To many Americans, social life seemed increasingly polarized between those at the top, who reaped most of the benefits of economic expansion, and workers struggling to make ends meet on low wages and living in desperate conditions in city slums. Democracy itself seemed threatened by the political influence of the large corporations and the corrupt activities of city bosses. In the early twentieth century, increasing numbers of Americans concluded that only the reform of politics and increased government intervention in economic life could curb the powers of the new corporations, ensure safe working conditions, and provide economic security for ordinary men and women.

Throughout these years, divergent views of the country's course of development, and the proper role of government in shaping and reshaping it, found expression in debates over American freedom. Many Americans held to a traditional understanding of freedom as the absence of external restraints on free individuals operating in a competitive marketplace. In this view, known as "liberty of contract," any government interference with economic relationships represented an infringement on property rights and, therefore, on freedom.

Others turned to collective action, economic and political, to try to reverse what they considered a decline of traditional freedoms. Workers flocked into unions that promised not only higher wages but also "industrial freedom"—a share in basic economic decision making. During the 1890s, millions of farmers joined the Populist movement in an attempt to reverse their declining economic prospects and rescue the government from what they saw as control by powerful corporate interests. In the Progressive era of the early twentieth century, urban reformers sought to expand economic and political freedom by increasing workers' rights, weakening the power of city bosses, and using the power of the state and national governments to regulate corporate behavior.

In many cities and states, and at the national level under Presidents Theodore Roosevelt, William Howard Taft, and Woodrow Wilson, government took on new roles in Progressive America. It sought to protect workers, especially women and children, from economic hardship, established agencies to determine rules for corporate behavior, and set aside parks and forests to preserve them from commercial exploitation. To Progressives, freedom was a positive idea, the effective power to achieve personal and social goals. At the same time, the expansion of the consumer economy and the new freedoms for women offered by city life encouraged the growth of an idea of personal freedom based on individual fulfillment, including self-determination in the most intimate areas of life.

Even as definitions of freedom expanded, the number of Americans who enjoyed genuine freedom contracted. In the 1890s and the early twentieth century, the political leaders of the white South imposed on the region's African-Americans a comprehensive system of second-class citizenship that rested on racial segregation, denial of the right to vote, lack of economic opportunities, and the ever-present threat of violence. Many native-born Americans considered immigrants, especially the large numbers arriving from southern and eastern Europe, as unfit for American citizenship. They sought to restrict their numbers and to force those already here to "Americanize" themselves by abandoning traditional cultures for mainstream values.

The country's emergence as a world power intensified these debates over freedom. To its supporters, the new American empire represented a continuation of the country's traditional self-image of promoting liberty and democracy throughout the world. President Wilson envisioned American involvement in World War I as a crusade not for national aggrandizement, but to "make the world safe for democracy." Yet critics of the acquisition of foreign colonies questioned whether an empire could still be considered a democracy. This question gained new urgency during World War I. On the one hand, the war ushered in the final success of the long struggle for woman suffrage, the greatest expansion of democracy in American history. On the other, the federal government and private patriotic organizations embarked on the most extensive campaign in American history to stifle criticism of administration policies and the economic status quo. By 1920, the United States was the world's foremost economic and military power. But the role it would play in world affairs in the future, and the fate of freedom at home, remained unresolved.

CHAPTER 16

America's Gilded Age, 1870–1890

A quilt created by a Sioux woman who lived on a reservation in South Dakota around 1900, possibly as a gift for a nearby white family. It depicts scenes of traditional daily life among the Indians, including hunting buffalo and cooking game. The bird's eggs at the top left corner have hatched at the bottom right.

FOCUS QUESTIONS

• What factors combined to make the United States a mature industrial society after the Civil War?

• How was the West transformed economically and socially in this period?

• Was the Gilded Age political system effective in meeting its goals?

• How did the economic development of the Gilded Age affect American freedom?

• How did reformers of the period approach the problems of an industrial society?

An immense crowd gathered in New York Harbor on October 28, 1886, for the dedication of *Liberty Enlightening the World*, a fitting symbol for a nation now wholly free. The idea for the statue originated in 1865 with Édouard de Laboulaye, a French educator and the author of several books on the United States, as a response to the assassination of Abraham Lincoln. The statue, de Laboulaye hoped, would celebrate both the historic friendship between France and the United States and the triumph, through the Union's victory in the Civil War, of American freedom. Measuring more than 150 feet from torch to toe and standing atop a huge pedestal, the edifice was the tallest man-made structure in the Western Hemisphere. It exceeded in height, newspapers noted with pride, the Colossus of Rhodes, a wonder of the ancient world.

In time, the Statue of Liberty, as it came to be called, would become Americans' most revered national icon. For over a century it has stood as a symbol of freedom. The statue has offered welcome to millions of immigrants—the "huddled masses yearning to breathe free" celebrated in a poem by Emma Lazarus inscribed on its base in 1903. In the years since its dedication, the statue's familiar image has been reproduced by folk artists in every conceivable medium and has been used by advertisers to promote everything from cigarettes and lawn mowers to war bonds. As its use by Chinese students demanding democracy in the Tiananmen Square protests of 1989 showed, it has become a powerful international symbol as well.

The year of the statue's dedication, 1886, also witnessed the "great upheaval," a wave of strikes and labor protests that touched every part of the nation. Six months before the unveiling of the Statue of Liberty, police had killed four striking workers who attempted to prevent strikebreakers

The dedication of the Statue of Liberty, October 28, 1886.

from entering a Chicago factory. This was only one of many violent clashes that accompanied labor unrest between the end of Reconstruction in 1877 and the turn of the twentieth century. The 600 dignitaries (598 of them men) who gathered on what is now called Liberty Island for the dedication hoped the Statue of Liberty would inspire renewed devotion to the nation's political and economic system. But for all its grandeur, the statue could not conceal the deep social divisions and fears about the future of American freedom that accompanied the country's emergence as the world's leading industrial power. Nor did the celebrations address the crucial questions that moved to the center stage of American public life during the 1870s and 1880s and remained there for decades to come: What are the social conditions that make freedom possible, and what role should the national government play in defining and protecting the liberty of its citizens?

The Strike, *an 1886 painting by the German-born artist Robert Koehler, who had grown up in a working-class family in Milwaukee. Koehler depicts a confrontation between a factory owner, dressed in a silk top hat, and angry workers. A woman and her children, presumably members of a striker's family, watch from the side while another woman, at the center, appears to plead for restraint. The threat of violence hangs in the air, and a striker in the lower right-hand corner reaches for a stone. The painting was inspired by events in Pittsburgh during the Great Railroad Strike of 1877, although Koehler was living in New York City at the time.*

THE SECOND INDUSTRIAL REVOLUTION

Between the end of the Civil War and the early twentieth century, the United States underwent one of the most rapid and profound economic revolutions any country has ever experienced. There were numerous causes for this explosive economic growth. The country enjoyed abundant natural resources, a growing supply of labor, an expanding market for manufactured goods, and the availability of capital for investment. In addition, the federal government actively promoted industrial and agricultural

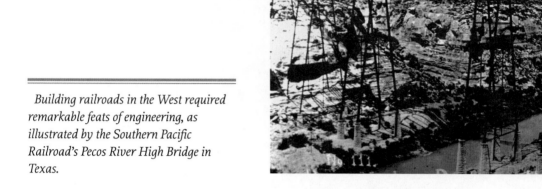

Building railroads in the West required remarkable feats of engineering, as illustrated by the Southern Pacific Railroad's Pecos River High Bridge in Texas.

development. It enacted high tariffs that protected American industry from foreign competition, granted land to railroad companies to encourage construction, and used the army to remove Indians from western lands desired by farmers and mining companies.

THE INDUSTRIAL ECONOMY

The rapid expansion of factory production, mining, and railroad construction in all parts of the country except the South signaled the transition from Lincoln's America—a world centered on the small farm and artisan workshop—to a mature industrial society. Americans of the late nineteenth century marveled at the triumph of the new economy. "One can hardly believe," wrote the philosopher John Dewey, "there has been a revolution in history so rapid, so extensive, so complete."

By 1913, the United States produced one-third of the world's industrial output—more than the total of Great Britain, France, and Germany combined. Small-scale craft production still flourished in many trades, and armies of urban workers, male and female, toiled in their own homes or in the households of others as outworkers and domestics. But half of all industrial workers now labored in plants with more than 250 employees. On the eve of the Civil War, the first industrial revolution, centered on the textile industry, had transformed New England into a center of manufacturing. But otherwise, the United States was still primarily an agricultural nation. By 1880, for the first time, the Census Bureau found a majority of the workforce engaged in non-farming jobs. The traditional dream of economic independence seemed obsolete. By 1890, two-thirds of Americans worked for wages, rather than owning a farm, business, or craft shop. Drawn to factories by the promise of employment, a new working class emerged in these years. Between 1870 and 1920, almost 11 million Americans moved from farm to city, and another 25 million immigrants arrived from overseas.

Most manufacturing now took place in industrial cities. New York, with its new skyscrapers and hundreds of thousands of workers in all sorts of manufacturing establishments, symbolized dynamic urban growth. After merging

Table 16.1 INDICATORS OF ECONOMIC CHANGE, 1870–1920			
	1870	*1900*	*1920*
Farms (millions)	2.7	5.7	6.4
Land in farms (million acres)	408	841	956
Wheat grown (million bushels)	254	599	843
Employment (millions)	14	28.5	44.5
In manufacturing (millions)	2.5	5.9	11.2
Percentage in workforce[a]			
Agricultural	52		27
Industry[b]	29		44
Trade, service, administration[c]	20		27
Railroad track (thousands of miles)	53	258	407
Steel produced (thousands of tons)	0.8	11.2	46
GNP (billions of dollars)	7.4	18.7	91.5
Per capita (in 1920 dollars)	371	707	920
Life expectancy at birth (years)	42	47	54

[a] Percentages are rounded and do not total 100.
[b] Includes manufacturing, transportation, mining, construction.
[c] Includes trade, finance, public administration.

with Brooklyn in 1898, its population exceeded 3.4 million. The city financed industrialization and westward expansion, its banks and stock exchange funneling capital to railroads, mines, and factories. But the heartland of the second industrial revolution was the region around the Great Lakes, with its factories producing iron and steel, machinery, chemicals, and packaged foods. Pittsburgh had become the world's center of iron and steel manufacturing. Chicago, by 1900 the nation's second-largest city, with 1.7 million inhabitants, was home to factories producing steel and farm machinery and giant stockyards where cattle were processed into meat products for shipment east in refrigerated rail cars. Smaller industrial cities also proliferated, often concentrating on a single industry—cast-iron stoves in Troy, New York, silk in Paterson, New Jersey, furniture in Grand Rapids, Michigan.

RAILROADS AND THE NATIONAL MARKET

The railroad made possible what is sometimes called the "second industrial revolution." Spurred by private investment and massive grants of land and money by federal, state, and local governments, the number of miles of railroad track in the United States tripled between 1860 and 1880 and tripled again by 1920, opening vast new areas to commercial farming and creating a truly national market for manufactured goods. In 1886, the railroads adopted a standard national gauge (the distance separating the two tracks), making it possible for the first time for trains of one company to travel on any other company's track. By the 1890s, five transcontinental lines trans-

Figure 16.1   RAILROAD MILEAGE BUILT, 1830–1975

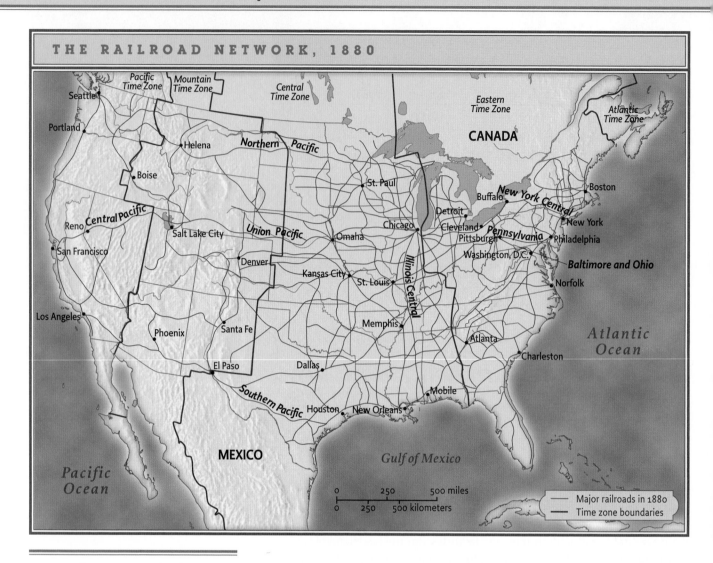

THE RAILROAD NETWORK, 1880

By 1880, the transnational rail network made possible the creation of a truly national market for goods.

ported the products of western mines, farms, ranches, and forests to eastern markets and carried manufactured goods to the West. The railroads reorganized time itself. In 1883, the major companies divided the nation into the four time zones still in use today. Indeed, the centrality of railroads to the national market meant that when railroads experienced financial crises, the entire economy suffered.

The growing population formed an ever-expanding market for the mass production, mass distribution, and mass marketing of goods, essential elements of a modern industrial economy. The spread of national brands like Ivory soap and Quaker Oats symbolized the continuing integration of the economy. So did the growth of national chains, most prominently the Atlantic and Pacific Tea Company, better known as A & P grocery stores. Based in Chicago, the national mail-order firms Montgomery Ward and Sears, Roebuck & Co. sold clothing, jewelry, farm equipment, and numerous other goods to rural families throughout the country.

THE SPIRIT OF INNOVATION

A remarkable series of technological innovations spurred rapid communication and economic growth. The opening of the Atlantic cable in 1866

(Left) Travel became globalized in the second half of the nineteenth century. This advertisement promotes an around-the-world route by railroad and steamboat, beginning in Chicago. *(Right)* The cover of the 1897 Sears, Roebuck & Co. catalog. One of the country's largest mail-order companies, Sears, Roebuck processed 100,000 orders per day at the end of the nineteenth century. The cornucopia at the center suggests the variety of items one could order by mail: furniture, a piano, a bicycle, and farm tools.

made it possible to send electronic telegraph messages instantaneously between the United States and Europe. During the 1870s and 1880s, the telephone, typewriter, and handheld camera came into use.

Scientific breakthroughs poured forth from research laboratories in Menlo Park and Orange, New Jersey, created by the era's greatest inventor, Thomas A. Edison. Born in Ohio in 1847, Edison had little formal education, but as a teenager he read popular books on science and began doing chemistry experiments. During the course of his life, Edison helped to establish entirely new industries that transformed private life, public entertainment, and economic activity, including the phonograph, light-bulb, motion picture, and a system for generating and distributing electric power. He opened the first electric generating station in Manhattan in 1882 to provide power to streetcars, factories, and private homes, and he established, among other companies, the forerunner of General Electric to market electrical equipment. The spread of electricity was essential to industrial and urban growth, providing a more reliable and flexible source of power than water or steam. However, it was not Edison but another inventor, Nikola Tesla, an ethnic Serb born in modern-day Croatia who emigrated to the United States at the age of twenty-eight, who developed an electric motor using the system of alternating current that overcame many of the challenges of using electricity for commercial and industrial purposes.

Thomas Edison's laboratory at Menlo Park, New Jersey, and some of the employees of the great inventor.

COMPETITION AND CONSOLIDATION

Economic growth was dramatic but highly volatile. The combination of a market flooded with goods and the federal monetary policies (discussed later) that removed money from the national economy led to a relentless fall in prices. The world economy suffered prolonged downturns in the 1870s and 1890s. Indeed, before the 1930s, the years from 1873 to 1897 were known throughout the world as the Great Depression.

Businesses engaged in ruthless competition. Railroads and other companies tried various means of bringing order to the chaotic marketplace. They formed "pools" that divided up markets between supposedly competing firms and fixed prices. They established "trusts"—legal devices whereby the affairs of several rival companies were managed by a single director. Such efforts to coordinate the economic activities of independent companies generally proved short-lived, disintegrating as individual firms continued their intense pursuit of profits.

To avoid cutthroat competition, more and more corporations battled to control entire industries. Many companies fell by the wayside or were gobbled up by others. The process of economic concentration culminated between 1897 and 1904, when some 4,000 firms vanished into larger corporations that served national markets and exercised an unprecedented degree of control over the marketplace. By the time the wave of mergers had been completed, giant corporations like U.S. Steel (created by financier J. P. Morgan in 1901 by combining eight large steel companies into the first billion-dollar economic enterprise), Standard Oil, and International Harvester (a manufacturer of agricultural machinery) dominated major parts of the economy.

THE RISE OF ANDREW CARNEGIE

In an era without personal or corporate income taxes, some business leaders accumulated enormous fortunes and economic power. Under the aggressive leadership of Thomas A. Scott, the Pennsylvania Railroad—for a time the nation's largest corporation—forged an economic empire that stretched across the continent and included coal mines and oceangoing steamships. With an army of professional managers to oversee its far-flung activities, the railroad pioneered modern techniques of business organization.

Another industrial giant was Andrew Carnegie, who emigrated with his family from his native Scotland at the age of thirteen and as a teenager worked in a Pennsylvania textile factory. During the 1850s, Scott hired Carnegie as his private telegraph operator and, by the eve of the Civil War, had promoted him to one of the Pennsylvania Railroad's major management positions. During the depression that began in 1873, Carnegie set out to establish a "vertically integrated" steel company—that is, one that controlled every phase of the business from raw materials to transportation, manufacturing, and distribution. By the 1890s, he dominated the steel industry and had accumulated a fortune worth hundreds of millions of dollars. Carnegie's complex of steel factories at Homestead, Pennsylvania, were the most technologically advanced in the world.

Carnegie's father, an immigrant Scottish weaver who had taken part in popular efforts to open the British political system to working-class participation, had instilled in his son a commitment to democracy and social equality. From his mother, Carnegie learned that life was a ceaseless struggle in which one must strive to get ahead or sink beneath the waves. His life reflected the tension between these elements of his upbringing. Believing that the rich had a moral obligation to promote the advancement of society, Carnegie denounced the "worship of money" and distributed much of his wealth to various philanthropies, especially the creation of public libraries in towns throughout the country. But he ran his companies with a dictatorial hand. His factories operated nonstop, with two twelve-hour shifts every day of the year except the Fourth of July.

THE TRIUMPH OF JOHN D. ROCKEFELLER

If any single name became a byword for enormous wealth, it was John D. Rockefeller, who began his working career as a clerk for a Cleveland merchant and rose to dominate the oil industry. He drove out rival firms through cutthroat competition, arranging secret deals with railroad companies, and fixing prices and production quotas. Rockefeller began with "horizontal" expan-

The Electricity Building at the Chicago World's Fair of 1893, painted by Childe Hassam. The electric lighting at the fair astonished visitors and illustrated how electricity was changing the visual landscape.

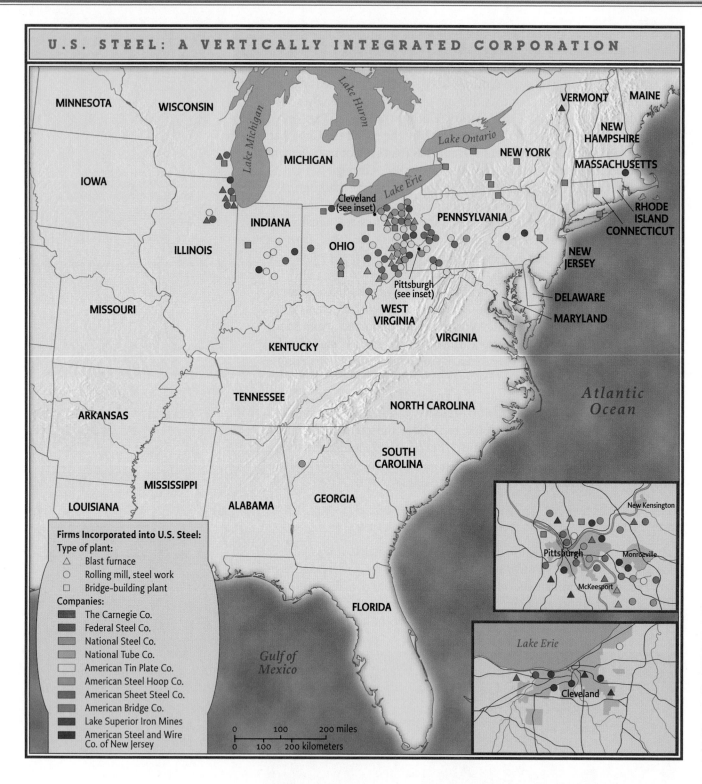

U.S. STEEL: A VERTICALLY INTEGRATED CORPORATION

Firms Incorporated into U.S. Steel:
Type of plant:
△ Blast furnace
○ Rolling mill, steel work
□ Bridge-building plant
Companies:
- The Carnegie Co.
- Federal Steel Co.
- National Steel Co.
- National Tube Co.
- American Tin Plate Co.
- American Steel Hoop Co.
- American Sheet Steel Co.
- American Bridge Co.
- Lake Superior Iron Mines
- American Steel and Wire Co. of New Jersey

sion—buying out competing oil refineries. But like Carnegie, he soon established a vertically integrated monopoly, which controlled the drilling, refining, storage, and distribution of oil. By the 1880s, his Standard Oil Company controlled 90 percent of the nation's oil industry. Like Carnegie, Rockefeller gave much of his fortune away, establishing foundations to promote education and medical research. And like Carnegie, he bitterly fought his employees' efforts to organize unions.

These and other industrial leaders inspired among ordinary Americans a combination of awe, admiration, and hostility. Depending on one's point of view, they were "captains of industry," whose energy and vision pushed the economy forward, or "robber barons," who wielded power without any accountability in an unregulated marketplace. Most rose from modest backgrounds and seemed examples of how inventive genius and business sense enabled Americans to seize opportunities for success. But their dictatorial attitudes, unscrupulous methods, repressive labor policies, and exercise of power without any democratic control led to fears that they were undermining political and economic freedom. Concentrated wealth degraded the political process, declared Henry Demarest Lloyd in *Wealth against Commonwealth* (1894), an exposé of how Rockefeller's Standard Oil Company made a mockery of economic competition and political democracy by manipulating the market and bribing legislators. "Liberty and monopoly," Lloyd concluded, "cannot live together."

Next!, a cartoon from the magazine Puck, *September 7, 1904, depicts the Standard Oil Company as an octopus with tentacles wrapped around the copper, steel, and shipping industries, as well as a state house and Congress. One tentacle reaches for the White House.*

WORKERS' FREEDOM IN AN INDUSTRIAL AGE

Striking as it was, the country's economic growth distributed its benefits very unevenly. For a minority of workers, the rapidly expanding industrial system created new forms of freedom. In some industries, skilled workers commanded high wages and exercised considerable control over the production process. A worker's economic independence now rested on technical skill rather than ownership of one's own shop and tools as in earlier times. What was known as "the miner's freedom" consisted of elaborate work rules that left skilled underground workers free of managerial supervision on the job. Through their union, skilled iron- and steelworkers fixed output quotas and controlled the training of apprentices in the technique of iron rolling. These workers often knew more about the details of production than their employers did.

Such "freedom," however, applied only to a tiny portion of the industrial labor force and had little bearing on the lives of the growing army of semiskilled workers who tended machines in the new factories. For most workers, economic insecurity remained a basic fact of life. During the depressions of the 1870s and 1890s, millions of workers lost their jobs or were forced to accept reductions of pay. The "tramp" became a familiar figure on the social landscape as thousands of men took to the roads in search of work. Many industrial workers labored sixty-hour weeks with no pensions, compensation for injuries, or protections against unemployment. Although American workers received higher wages than their counterparts in Europe, they also experienced more dangerous working conditions. Between 1880 and 1900, an average of 35,000 workers perished each year in factory and mine accidents, the highest rate in the industrial world. Most strikes for higher wages

A turn-of-the-century photograph of the Casino Grounds, Newport, Rhode Island, an exclusive country club for rich socialites of the Gilded Age.

The opening image in Matthew Smith's book, Sunshine and Shadow in New York *(1868), contrasts the living conditions of the city's rich and poor.*

failed, as employers found it easy to call on the unemployed to take the strikers' jobs, and to bring in public and private police forces to intimidate workers.

Much of the working class remained desperately poor and to survive needed income from all family members. In 1888, the Chicago *Times* published a series of articles by reporter Nell Cusack under the title "City Slave Girls," exposing wretched conditions among the growing number of women working for wages in the city's homes, factories, and sweatshops. The articles unleashed a flood of letters to the editor from women workers. One woman singled out domestic service—still the largest employment category for women—as "a slave's life," with "long hours, late and early, seven days in the week, bossed and ordered about as before the war."

SUNSHINE AND SHADOW: INCREASING WEALTH AND POVERTY

At the other end of the economic spectrum, the era witnessed an unprecedented accumulation of wealth. Class divisions became more and more visible. In frontier days, all classes in San Francisco, for example, lived near the waterfront. In the late nineteenth century, upper-class families built mansions on Nob Hill and Van Ness Avenue (known as "millionaire's row"). In eastern cities as well, the rich increasingly resided in their own exclusive neighborhoods and vacationed among members of their own class at exclusive resorts like Newport, Rhode Island. The growing urban middle class of professionals, office workers, and small businessmen moved to new urban and suburban neighborhoods linked to central business districts by streetcars and commuter railways. "Passion for money," wrote the novelist Edith Wharton in *The House of Mirth* (1905) dominated society. Wharton's book traced the difficulties of Lily Bart, a young woman of modest means pressured by her mother and New York high society to "barter" her beauty for marriage to a rich husband in a world where "to be poor ... amounted to disgrace."

By 1890, the richest 1 percent of Americans received the same total income as the bottom half of the population and owned more property than the remaining 99 percent. Many of the wealthiest Americans consciously pursued an aristocratic lifestyle, building palatial homes, attending exclusive social clubs, schools, and colleges, holding fancy-dress balls, and marrying into each other's families. In 1899, the economist and social historian Thorstein Veblen published *The Theory of the Leisure Class*, a devastating critique of an upper-class culture focused on "conspicuous consumption"—that is, spending money not on needed or even desired goods, but simply to demonstrate the possession of wealth. One of the era's most widely publicized spectacles was an elaborate costume ball organized in 1897 by Mrs. Bradley Martin, the daughter of a New York railroad financier. The theme was the royal court of prerevolutionary France. The Waldorf-Astoria Hotel was decorated to look like the palace of Versailles, the guests wore the dress of the French nobility, and the hostess bedecked herself with the actual jewels of Queen Marie Antoinette.

Not that far from the Waldorf, much of the working class lived in desperate conditions. Matthew Smith's 1868 best-seller *Sunshine and Shadow in New York* opened with an engraving that contrasted department store magnate Alexander T. Stewart's two-million-dollar mansion with housing in the city's slums. Two decades later, Jacob Riis, in *How the Other Half Lives* (1890), offered a shocking account of living conditions among the urban poor, complete with photographs of apartments in dark, airless, overcrowded tenement houses.

Baxter Street Court, 1890, one of numerous photographs by Jacob Riis depicting living conditions in New York City's slums.

THE TRANSFORMATION OF THE WEST

Nowhere did capitalism penetrate more rapidly or dramatically than in the trans-Mississippi West, whose "vast, trackless spaces," as the poet Walt Whitman called them, were now absorbed into the expanding economy. At the close of the Civil War, the frontier of settlement did not extend far beyond the Mississippi River. To the west lay millions of acres of fertile and mineral-rich land roamed by giant herds of buffalo whose meat and hides provided food, clothing, and shelter for a population of more than 250,000 Indians.

In 1893, the historian Frederick Jackson Turner gave a celebrated lecture, "The Significance of the Frontier in American History," in which he argued that on the western frontier the distinctive qualities of American culture were forged: individual freedom, political democracy, and economic mobility. The West, he added, acted as a "safety valve," drawing off those dissatisfied with their situation in the East and therefore counteracting the threat of social unrest. Turner's was one of the most influential interpretations of American history ever developed. But his lecture summarized attitudes toward the West that had been widely shared among Americans long before 1893. Ever since the beginning of colonial settlement in British North America, the West—a region whose definition shifted as the popula-

The family of David Hilton on their Nebraska homestead in 1887. The Hiltons insisted on being photographed with their organ, away from the modest sod house in which they lived, to better represent their aspiration for prosperity.

tion expanded—had been seen as a place of opportunity for those seeking to improve their condition in life.

Many Americans did indeed experience the westward movement in the way Turner described it. From farmers moving into Ohio, Indiana, and Illinois in the decades after the American Revolution to prospectors who struck it rich in the California gold rush of the mid-nineteenth century, millions of Americans and immigrants from abroad found in the westward movement a path to economic opportunity. But Turner offered only a partial account of western history. Most settlers moved west in family groups or as members of immigrant communities, not as lone pioneers. Turner seemed to portray the West as an empty space before the coming of white settlers. In fact, of course, it was already inhabited by Native Americans, whose dispossession was essential to the opening of land for settlement by others. Moreover, the West was hardly a uniform paradise of small, independent farmers. Beginning in the eighteenth century, for example, California was the site of forced Indian labor on missions established by members of religious orders, a system that helped establish the pattern of large agricultural land holdings in that region. Landlords, railroads, and mining companies in the West also utilized Mexican migrant and indentured labor, Chinese working on long-term contracts, and, until the the end of the Civil War, African-American slaves.

A DIVERSE REGION

The West, of course, was hardly a single area. West of the Mississippi River lay a variety of regions, all marked by remarkable physical beauty—the "vast, trackless" Great Plains, the Rocky Mountains, the desert of the Southwest, the Sierra Nevada, and the valleys and coastline of California and the Pacific Northwest. It would take many decades before individual settlers and corporate business enterprises penetrated all these areas. But the process was far advanced by the end of the nineteenth century.

The political and economic incorporation of the American West was part of a global process. In many parts of the world, indigenous inhabitants— the Mapuche in Chile, the Zulu in South Africa, aboriginal peoples in Australia, American Indians—were pushed aside (often after fierce resistance) as centralizing governments brought large interior regions under their control. In the United States, the incorporation of the West required the active intervention of the federal government, which acquired Indian land by war and treaty, administered land sales, regulated territorial politics, and distributed land and money to farmers, railroads, and mining companies.

In the twentieth century, the construction of federally financed irrigation systems and dams would open large areas to commercial farming. Ironically, the West would become known (not least to its own inhabitants) as a place of rugged individualism and sturdy independence. But without active governmental assistance, the region could never have been settled and developed.

FARMING ON THE MIDDLE BORDER

Even as sporadic Indian wars raged, settlers poured into the West. Territorial and state governments eager for population, and railroad companies anxious to sell land they had acquired from the government, flooded European countries and eastern cities with promotional literature promising easy access to land. More land came into cultivation in the thirty years after the Civil War than in the previous two and a half centuries of American history. Hundreds of thousands of families acquired farms under the Homestead Act, and even more purchased land from speculators and from railroad companies that had been granted immense tracts of public land by the federal government. A new agricultural empire producing wheat and corn for national and international markets arose on the Middle Border (Minnesota, the Dakotas, Nebraska, and Kansas), whose population rose from 300,000 in 1860 to 5 million in 1900. The farmers were a diverse group, including native-born easterners, blacks escaping the post-Reconstruction South, and immigrants from Canada, Germany, Scandinavia, and Great Britain. Although ethnic diversity is generally associated with eastern cities, in the late nineteenth century the most multicultural state in the Union was North Dakota.

Despite the promises of promotional pamphlets, farming on the Great Plains was not an easy task. Difficulties came in many forms—from the poisonous rattlesnakes that lived in the tall prairie grass to the blizzards and droughts that periodically afflicted the region. Much of the burden fell on women. Farm families generally invested in the kinds of labor-saving machinery that would bring in cash, not machines that would ease women's burdens in the household (like the back-breaking task of doing laundry). While husbands and sons tended to devote their labor to cash

RES. & RANCH OF H. P. GRAY, EAST OF LEMORE, TULARE CO. CAL.

An engraving from the early 1880s of a California farm adjacent to the Southern Pacific Railroad. Having been granted vast tracts of land by the federal government, the railroad encouraged settlement along its lines.

crops, farm wives cared for animals, grew crops for food, and cooked and cleaned. A farm woman in Arizona described her morning chores in her diary: "Get up, turn out my chickens, draw a pail of water . . . make a fire, put potatoes to cook, brush and sweep half inch of dust off floor, feed three litters of chickens, then mix biscuits, get breakfast, milk, besides work in the house, and this morning had to go half mile after calves." On far-flung homesteads, many miles from schools, medical care, and sources of entertainment, farm families suffered from loneliness and isolation—a problem especially severe for women when their husbands left, sometimes for weeks at a time, to market their crops.

BONANZA FARMS

John Wesley Powell, the explorer and geologist who surveyed the Middle Border in the 1870s, warned that because of the region's arid land and limited rainfall, development there required large-scale irrigation projects. The model of family farming envisioned by the Homestead Act of 1862 could not apply: no single family could do all the work required on irrigated farms—only cooperative, communal farming could succeed, Powell maintained.

Despite the emergence of a few "bonanza farms" that covered thousands of acres and employed large numbers of agricultural wage workers, family farms still dominated the trans-Mississippi West. Even small farmers, however, became increasingly oriented to national and international markets, specializing in the production of single crops for sale in faraway places. At the same time, railroads brought factory-made goods to rural people, replacing items previously produced in farmers' homes. Farm families became more and more dependent on loans to purchase land, machinery, and industrial products, and more and more vulnerable to the ups and downs of prices for agricultural goods in the world market. Agriculture reflected how the international economy was becoming more integrated. The combination of economic depressions and expanding agricultural pro-

"California Harvest Scene—Dr. Glenn's Farm in Colusa County," an engraving from 1876, illustrates the large scale of operations and heavy investment in machinery common on western "bonanza" farms.

duction in places like Argentina, Australia, and the American West pushed prices of farm products steadily downward. From Italy and Ireland to China, India, and the American South, small farmers throughout the world suffered severe difficulties in the last quarter of the nineteenth century. Many joined the migration to cities within their countries or the increasing international migration of labor.

LARGE-SCALE AGRICULTURE IN CALIFORNIA

The future of western farming ultimately lay with giant agricultural enterprises relying heavily on irrigation, chemicals, and machinery—investments far beyond the means of family farmers. A preview of the agricultural future was already evident in California, where, as far back as Spanish and Mexican days, landownership had been concentrated in large units. In the late nineteenth century, California's giant fruit and vegetable farms, owned by corporations like the Southern Pacific Railroad, were tilled not by agricultural laborers who could expect to acquire land of their own, but by migrant laborers from China, the Philippines, Japan, and Mexico, who tramped from place to place following the ripening crops. "California is not a country of farms, but ... of plantations and estates," wrote the young journalist Henry George in 1871, urging the government to take action against "land monopoly" and to "give all men an equal chance" to achieve economic independence.

THE COWBOY AND THE CORPORATE WEST

The two decades following the Civil War also witnessed the golden age of the cattle kingdom. The Kansas Pacific Railroad's stations at Abilene, Dodge City, and Wichita, Kansas, became destinations for the fabled drives of millions of cattle from Texas. A collection of white, Mexican, and black men who conducted the cattle drives, the cowboys became symbols of a life of freedom on the open range. Their exploits would later serve as the theme of many a Hollywood movie, and their clothing inspired fashions that remain popular today. But there was nothing romantic about the life of the cowboys, most of whom were low-paid wage workers. (Texas cowboys even went on strike for higher pay in 1883.) The days of the long-distance cattle drive ended in the mid-1880s, as farmers enclosed more and more of the open range with barbed-wire fences, making it difficult to graze cattle on the grasslands of the Great Plains, and two terrible winters destroyed millions of cattle. When the industry recuperated, it was reorganized in large, enclosed ranches close to rail connections.

The West was more than a farming empire. By 1890, a higher percentage of its population lived in cities than was the case in other regions. The economic focus of California's economy remained San Francisco, a major manufacturing and trading center. The explosive growth of southern California began in the 1880s, first with tourism, heavily promoted by railroad companies, followed by the discovery of oil in Los Angeles in 1892. Large corporate enterprises appeared throughout the West. The lumber industry, dominated by small-scale producers in 1860, came under the control of corporations that acquired large tracts of forest and employed armies of loggers. Western mining, from Michigan iron ore and copper to gold and silver in California,

In the late 1800s, California tried to attract immigrants by advertising its pleasant climate and the availability of land, although large-scale corporate farms were coming to dominate the state's agriculture.

Nevada, and Colorado, fell under the sway of companies that mobilized eastern and European investment to introduce advanced technology. Gold and silver rushes took place in the Dakotas in 1876, Idaho in 1883, and Alaska at the end of the century. But as in California after 1848, the independent prospector working a surface mine with his pick and shovel quickly gave way to deep-shaft corporate mining employing wage workers.

A similar process occurred in New Mexico, where traditional life based on sheep farming on land owned in common by Mexican villagers had continued more or less unchanged after the United States acquired the area in the Mexican War. Railroads reached the area in the 1870s, bringing with them eastern mining companies and commercial ranchers and farmers. Because courts only recognized Mexican-era land titles to individual plots of land, communal landholdings were increasingly made available for sale to newcomers. By 1880, three-quarters of New Mexico's sheep belonged to just twenty families. Unable to continue as sheep raisers, more and more Hispanic residents went to work for the new mines and railroads.

THE SUBJUGATION OF THE PLAINS INDIANS

The incorporation of the West into the national economy spelled the doom of the Plains Indians and their world. Their lives had already undergone profound transformations. In the eighteenth century, the spread of horses, originally introduced by the Spanish, led to a wholesale shift from farming and hunting on foot to mounted hunting of buffalo. New Indian groups migrated to the Great Plains to take advantage of the horse, coalescing into the great tribes of the nineteenth century—the Cheyenne, Comanche, Crow, Kiowa, and Sioux. Persistent warfare took place between the more established tribes and newcomers, including Indians removed from the East, who sought access to their hunting grounds.

Most migrants on the Oregon and California Trails before the Civil War

Albert Bierstadt's 1863 painting, The Rocky Mountains, Lander's Peak, *depicts Indians as an integral part of the majestic landscape of the West.*

Hunters shooting buffalo as the Kansas-Pacific Railroad cuts across the West, 1870s.

encountered little hostility from Indians, often trading with them for food and supplies. But as settlers encroached on Indian lands, bloody conflict between the army and Plains tribes began in the 1850s and continued for decades.

In 1869, President Ulysses S. Grant announced a new "peace policy" in the West, but warfare soon resumed. Drawing on methods used to defeat the Confederacy, Civil War generals like Philip H. Sheridan set out to destroy the foundations of the Indian economy—villages, horses, and especially the buffalo. Hunting by mounted Indians had already reduced the buffalo population—estimated at 30 million in 1800—but it was army campaigns and the depredations of hunters seeking buffalo hides that rendered the vast herds all but extinct. By 1886, an expedition from the Smithsonian Institution in Washington had difficulty finding twenty-five "good specimens." "A cold wind blew across the prairie when the last buffalo fell," said the Sioux leader Sitting Bull, "a death-wind for my people."

"LET ME BE A FREE MAN"

The army's relentless attacks broke the power of one tribe after another. In 1877, troops commanded by former Freedmen's Bureau commissioner O. O. Howard pursued the Nez Percé Indians on a 1,700-mile chase across the Far West. The Nez Percé (whose name was given them by Lewis and Clark in 1805 and means "pierced noses" in French) were seeking to escape to Canada after fights with settlers who had encroached on tribal lands in Oregon and Idaho. After four months, Howard forced the Indians to surrender, and they were removed to Oklahoma.

Two years later, the Nez Percé leader, Chief Joseph, delivered a speech in Washington to a distinguished audience that included President Rutherford B. Hayes. Condemning the policy of confining Indians to reservations, Joseph adopted the language of freedom and equal rights before the law so powerfully reinforced by the Civil War and Reconstruction. "Treat all men alike," he pleaded. "Give them the same law. . . . Let me be a free man—free to travel, free to stop, free to work, free to trade where I

Chief Joseph of the Nez Percé Indians in 1877, the year he surrendered to the U.S. Army.

VOICES OF FREEDOM

FROM CHIEF JOSEPH OF THE NEZ PERCÉ INDIANS, Speech in Washington, D.C. (1879)

Chief Joseph, leader of the Nez Percé Indians, led his people on a 1,700-mile trek from their homes in Oregon and Idaho through the Far West in 1877 in an unsuccessful effort to escape to Canada. Two years later, he addressed an audience in Washington, D.C., that included President Rutherford B. Hayes, appealing for the freedom and equal rights enshrined in the law after the Civil War.

My friends, I have been asked to show you my heart. I am glad to have a chance to do so. I want the white people to understand my people. Some of you think an Indian is like a wild animal. This is a great mistake. I will tell you all about our people, and then you can judge whether an Indian is a man or not. . . . I will tell you in my way how the Indian sees things. The white man has more words to tell you how they look to him, but it does not require many words to speak the truth. . . .

I have heard talk and talk, but nothing is done. Good words do not last long unless they amount to something. Words do not pay for my dead people. They do not pay for my country, now overrun by white men . . . . Good words will not get my people a home where they can live in peace and take care of themselves. I am tired of talk that comes to nothing. It makes my heart sick when I remember all the . . . broken promises. . . .

If the white man wants to live in peace with the Indian he can live in peace. There need be no trouble. Treat all men alike. Give them the same law. Give them all an even chance to live and grow. All men were made by the same Great Spirit Chief. They are all brothers. The earth is the mother of all people, and all people should have equal rights upon it. You might as well expect the rivers to run backward as that any man who was born a free man should be contented when penned up and denied liberty to go where he pleases. . . .

When I think of our condition my heart is heavy. I see men of my race treated as outlaws and driven from country to country, or shot down like animals. I know that my race must change. We cannot hold our own with the white men as we are. We only ask an even chance to live as other men live. . . .

Let me be a free man—free to travel, free to stop, free to work, free to trade where I choose, free to choose my own teachers, free to follow the religion of my fathers, free to think and talk and act for myself— and I will obey every law, or submit to the penalty.

FROM IRA STEWARD,

"A Second Declaration of Independence" (1879)

At a Fourth of July celebration in Chicago in 1879, Ira Steward, the most prominent labor leader associated with the movement for the eight-hour day, invoked the legacy of the Declaration of Independence and the abolition of slavery during the Civil War to discuss labor's grievances.

Resolved, That the practical question for an American Fourth of July is not between freedom and slavery, but between wealth and poverty. For if it is true that laborers ought to have as little as possible of the wealth they produce, South Carolina slaveholders were right and the Massachusetts abolitionists were wrong. Because, when the working classes are denied everything but the barest necessities of life, they have no decent use for liberty. . . .

Slavery is . . . the child of poverty, instead of poverty the child of slavery: and freedom is the child of wealth, instead of wealth the child of freedom. The only road, therefore, to universal freedom is the road that leads to universal wealth.

Resolved, That while the Fourth of July was heralded a hundred years ago in the name of Liberty, we now herald this day in behalf of the great economic measure of Eight Hours, or shorter day's work for wageworkers everywhere . . . because more leisure, rest and thought will cultivate habits, customs, and expenditures that mean higher wages: and the world's highest paid laborers now furnish each other with vastly more occupations or days' work than the lowest paid workers can give to one another. . . . [And] if the worker's power to buy increases with his power to do, granaries and warehouses will empty their pockets, and farms and factories fill up with producers. . . .

And we call to the workers of the whole civilized world, especially those of France, Germany, and Great Britain, to join hands with the laborers of the United States in this mighty movement. . . .

On the . . . issue of eight hours, therefore, or less hours, we join hands with all, regardless of politics, nationality, color, religion, or sex; knowing no friends or foes except as they aid or oppose this long-postponed and world-wide movement.

And for the soundness of our political economy, as well as the rectitude of our intentions, we confidently and gladly appeal to the wiser statesmanship of the civilized world.

QUESTIONS

1. What are Chief Joseph's complaints about the treatment of his people?

2. Why does Ira Steward appeal to other countries for assistance and understanding?

3. In what ways do the definitions of freedom in the two documents agree and disagree?

choose, free to . . . think and talk and act for myself." The government eventually transported the surviving Nez Percé to another reservation in Washington Territory. Until his death in 1904, Joseph would unsuccessfully petition successive presidents for his people's right to return to their beloved Oregon homeland.

Indians occasionally managed to inflict costly delay and even defeat on army units. The most famous Indian victory took place in June 1876 at Little Bighorn, when General George A. Custer and his entire command of 250 men perished. The Sioux and Cheyenne warriors, led by Sitting Bull and Crazy Horse, were defending tribal land in the Black Hills of the Dakota Territory. Reserved for them in an 1868 treaty "for as long as the grass shall grow," their lands had been invaded by whites after the discovery of gold. In the Southwest, Cochise, Geronimo, and other leaders of the Apache, who had been relocated by the government a number of times, led bands that crossed and recrossed the border with Mexico, evading the army and occasionally killing civilians. They would not surrender until the mid-1880s.

Another casualty was the Comanche empire, centered in modern-day New Mexico and Colorado. Beginning in the mid-eighteenth century, the Comanche dominated much of the Great Plains and Southwest. The Comanche had subordinated local Indian groups to their power, imposed a toll on trade routes like the Santa Fe Trail, and dealt for a time as an equal with the Spanish, French, and American governments. Their power was not finally broken until the 1870s.

These events delayed only temporarily the onward march of white soldiers, settlers, and prospectors. Between the end of the Civil War and 1890, eight new western states entered the Union (Nebraska, Colorado, North and South Dakota, Montana, Washington, Idaho, and Wyoming). Railroads now crisscrossed the Great Plains, farmers and cattlemen exploited land formerly owned by Indians, and the Plains tribes had been concentrated on

The Battle of the Little Bighorn, June 25–26, 1876, in which General George A. Custer and his entire command were killed, as drawn by Red Horse, a Sioux chief.

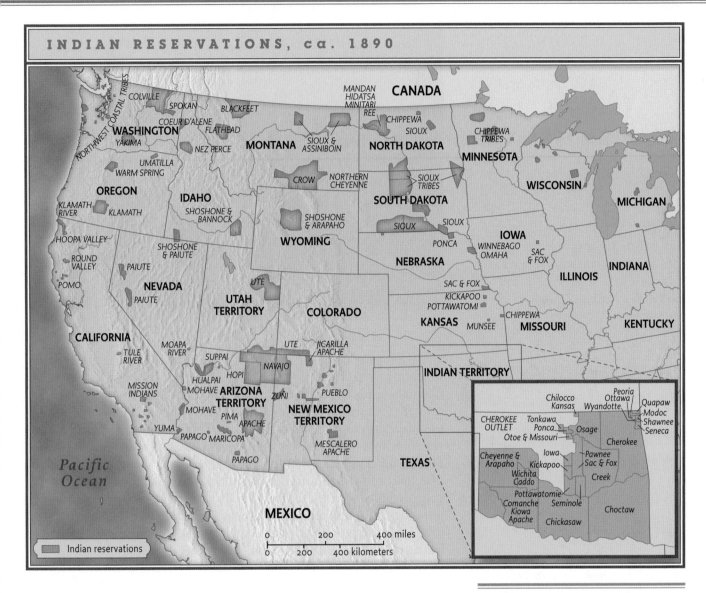

INDIAN RESERVATIONS, ca. 1890

Indian reservations

By 1890, the vast majority of the remaining Indian population had been removed to reservations scattered across the western states.

reservations, where they lived in poverty, preyed upon by unscrupulous traders and government agents. A strong opponent of the reservation system, Sitting Bull escaped to Canada after the army defeated the Sioux, but he returned and was imprisoned in 1881. He was released in 1883 and for a time became part of Buffalo Bill's Wild West Show, a popular traveling extravaganza complete with mock Indian attacks and shooting and riding exhibitions. For most Americans, Indians were now simply objects of curiosity or entertainment.

REMAKING INDIAN LIFE

"The life my people want is a life of freedom," Sitting Bull declared. The Indian idea of freedom, however, which centered on preserving their cultural and political autonomy and control of ancestral lands, conflicted with the interests and values of most white Americans. Nearly all officials believed that the federal government should persuade or force the Plains Indians to surrender most of their land and to exchange their religion, com-

Boys from the Lakota tribe on their arrival (left) *and during their stay at Carlisle, a boarding school that aimed to "civilize" Indians, by J. N. Choate, a local photographer.*

munal property, nomadic way of life, and gender relations for Christian worship, private ownership, and small farming on reservations with men tilling the fields and women working in the home.

In 1871, Congress eliminated the treaty system that dated back to the revolutionary era, by which the federal government negotiated agreements with Indians as if they were independent nations. This step was supported by railroad companies that found tribal sovereignty an obstacle to construction and by Republicans who believed that it contradicted the national unity born of the Civil War. The federal government pressed forward with its assault on Indian culture. The Bureau of Indian Affairs established boarding schools where Indian children, removed from the "negative" influences of their parents and tribes, were dressed in non-Indian clothes, given new names, and educated in white ways.

THE DAWES ACT

The crucial step in attacking "tribalism" came in 1887 with the passage of the Dawes Act, named for Senator Henry L. Dawes of Massachusetts, chair of the Senate's Indian Affairs Committee. The Act broke up the land of nearly all tribes into small parcels to be distributed to Indian families, with the remainder auctioned off to white purchasers. Indians who accepted the farms and "adopted the habits of civilized life" would become full-fledged American citizens. The policy proved to be a disaster, leading to the loss of much tribal land and the erosion of Indian cultural traditions. Whites, however, benefited enormously. On the Nez Percé reservation, for example, 172,000 acres were divided into farms for Indians, but white ranchers and land speculators purchased 500,000 acres. When the government made 2 million acres of Indian land available in Oklahoma, 50,000 white settlers poured into the territory to claim farms on the single day of

An 1893 photograph depicts the land rush when a portion of Cherokee land in the Oklahoma Territory was opened to white settlement under the provisions of the Dawes Act.

April 22, 1889. Further land rushes followed in the 1890s. In the half century after the passage of the Dawes Act, Indians lost 86 million of the 138 million acres of land in their possession in 1887.

INDIAN CITIZENSHIP

Many laws and treaties in the nineteenth century offered Indians the right to become an American citizen if they left the tribal setting and assimilated into American society. But tribal identity was the one thing nearly every Indian wished to maintain, and very few took advantage of these offers. Thus, few Indians were recognized as American citizens. Western courts ruled that the citizenship rights guaranteed by the Fourteenth and Fifteenth Amendments did not apply to them, and in *Elk v. Wilkins* (1884) the U.S. Supreme Court agreed, even though John Elk had left his tribe in Oklahoma and lived among white settlers in Nebraska. The Court questioned whether any Indian had achieved the degree of "civilization" required of American citizens.

By 1900, roughly 53,000 Indians had become American citizens by accepting land allotments under the Dawes Act. The following year, Congress granted citizenship to 100,000 residents of Indian Territory (in present-day Oklahoma). The remainder would have to wait until 1919 (for those who fought in World War I) and 1924, when Congress made all Indians American citizens.

THE GHOST DANCE AND WOUNDED KNEE

Some Indians sought solace in the Ghost Dance, a religious revitalization campaign reminiscent of the pan-Indian movements led by earlier prophets like Neolin and Tenskwatawa (discussed in Chapters 4 and 8). Its leaders foretold a day when whites disappear, the buffalo would return, and Indians could once again practice their ancestral customs "free from misery, death, and disease." Large numbers of Indians gathered for days of singing, dancing, and religious observances. Fearing a general uprising, the government sent troops to the reservations. On December 29, 1890, soldiers opened fire on Ghost Dancers encamped near Wounded Knee Creek in South Dakota, killing between 150 and 200 Indians, mostly women and children.

The Wounded Knee massacre marked the end of four centuries of armed conflict between the continent's native population and European settlers and their descendants. By 1900, the Indian population had fallen to 250,000, the lowest point in American history. A children's book about Indians published around this time stated flatly, "the Indian pictured in these pages no longer exists." Yet despite everything, Indians survived, and in the twentieth century their numbers once again would begin to grow.

SETTLER SOCIETIES AND GLOBAL WESTS

The conquest of the American West was part of a global process whereby settlers moved boldly into the interior of regions in temperate climates around

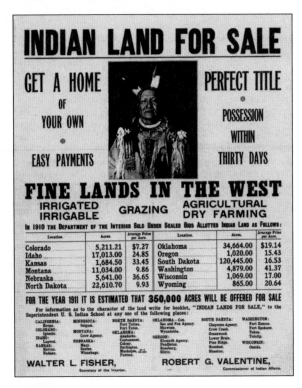

A 1911 poster advertising the federal government's sale of land formerly possessed by Indians. Under the Dawes Act of 1887, Indian families were allotted individual farms and the remaining land on reservations, so-called surplus land, was made available to whites.

the world, bringing their familiar crops and livestock and establishing mining and other industries. Countries such as Argentina, Australia, Canada, and New Zealand, as well as the United States, are often called "settler societies," because immigrants from overseas quickly outnumbered and displaced the original inhabitants—unlike in India and most parts of colonial Africa, where fewer Europeans ventured and those who did relied on the labor of the indigenous inhabitants. South Africa combined the characteristics of these two forms of Western expansion. The descendants of European immigrants grew to a substantial population and fully controlled politics and the economy, but they still remained far fewer in number than the native Africans, who did most of the work in the region's mines and rural areas.

In the late nineteenth century, even as the population of the American West grew dramatically, the Argentine military occupied the Pampas, opening a vast area for cattle raising and wheat cultivation. In 1885, Canada marked the completion of its first transcontinental railroad, although the more severe climate limited the number of western settlers to a much smaller population than in the American West (and as a result, the displacement of Indians did not produce as much conflict and bloodshed). In many settler societies, native peoples were subjected to cultural reconstruction similar to policies in the United States. In Australia, the government gathered the Aboriginal populations—their numbers devastated by disease—in "reserves" reminiscent of American Indian reservations. Australia went further than the United States in the forced assimilation of surviving Aboriginal peoples. The government removed large numbers of children from their families to be adopted by whites—a policy only abandoned in the 1970s and for which the prime minister formally apologized in 2008 in a national moment of reconciliation called Sorry Day.

POLITICS IN A GILDED AGE

The era from 1870 to 1890 is the only period of American history commonly known by a derogatory name—the Gilded Age, after the title of an 1873 novel by Mark Twain and Charles Dudley Warner. "Gilded" means covered with a layer of gold, but it also suggests that the glittering surface covers a core of little real value and is therefore deceptive. Twain and Warner were referring not only to the remarkable expansion of the economy in this period but also to the corruption caused by corporate dominance of politics and to the oppressive treatment of those left behind in the scramble for wealth. "Get rich, dishonestly if we can, honestly if we must," was the era's slogan, according to *The Gilded Age*.

THE CORRUPTION OF POLITICS

As they had earlier in the nineteenth century, Americans during the Gilded Age saw their nation as an island of political democracy in a world still dominated by undemocratic governments. In Europe, only France and Switzerland enjoyed universal male suffrage. Even in Britain, which prided itself on its tradition of political liberty, most of the working class could not

The Bosses of the Senate, *a cartoon from* Puck, *January 23, 1889, shows well-fed monopolists towering over the obedient senators. Above them, a sign rewrites the closing words of Lincoln's Gettysburg Address: "This is the Senate of the Monopolists, by the Monopolists, and for the Monopolists."*

vote until the passage of the Reform Act of 1884. As late as the eve of World War I, the House of Lords, an unelected body of hereditary aristocrats, could veto any legislation passed by the House of Commons.

Nonetheless, the power of the new corporations, seemingly immune to democratic control, raised disturbing questions for the American understanding of political freedom as popular self-government. Political corruption was rife. "The galleries and lobbies of every legislature," observed an Illinois Republican leader, "are thronged with men seeking to procure an advantage" for one corporation or another. In Pennsylvania's legislature, the "third house" of railroad lobbyists supposedly exerted as much influence as the elected chambers. In the West, many lawmakers held stock or directorships in lumber companies and railroads that received public aid.

Urban politics fell under the sway of corrupt political machines like New York's Tweed Ring, which plundered the city of tens of millions of dollars. "Boss" William M. Tweed's organization reached into every neighborhood. He forged close ties with railroad men and labor unions, and he won support from the city's immigrant poor by fashioning a kind of private welfare system that provided food, fuel, and jobs in hard times. A combination of political reformers and businessmen tired of paying tribute to the ring ousted Tweed in the early 1870s, although he remained popular among the city's poor, who considered him an urban Robin Hood.

At the national level, many lawmakers supported bills aiding companies in which they had invested money or from which they received stock or salaries. The most notorious example of corruption came to light during Grant's presidency. This was Crédit Mobilier, a corporation formed by an inner ring of Union Pacific Railroad stockholders to oversee the line's government-assisted construction. Essentially, it enabled the participants to sign contracts with themselves, at an exorbitant profit, to build the new line. The arrangement was protected by the distribution of stock to influential politicians, including Speaker of the House Schuyler Colfax, who was elected vice president in 1868. In another example of corruption, the Whiskey Ring of the Grant administration united Republican officials, tax collectors, and whiskey manufacturers in a massive scheme that defrauded the federal government of millions of tax dollars.

THE POLITICS OF DEAD CENTER

In national elections, party politics bore the powerful imprint of the Civil War. Republicans controlled the industrial North and Midwest and the agrarian West and were particularly strong among members of revivalist churches, Protestant immigrants, and blacks. Organizations of Union veterans formed a bulwark of Republican support. Every Republican candidate for president from 1868 to 1900 had fought in the Union army. (In the 1880 campaign, all four candidates—Republican James A. Garfield, Democrat Winfield Scott Hancock, Prohibitionist Neal Dow, and James B. Weaver of the Greenback-Labor Party, discussed later—had been Union generals during the war.) By 1893, a lavish system of pensions for Union soldiers and their widows and children consumed more than 40 percent of the federal budget. Democrats, after 1877, dominated the South and did well among Catholic voters, especially Irish-Americans, in the nation's cities.

The parties were closely divided. In three of the five presidential elections between 1876 and 1892, the margin separating the major candidates was less than 1 percent of the popular vote. Twice, in 1876 and 1888, the candidate with an electoral-college majority trailed in the popular vote. The congressional elections of 1874, when Democrats won control of the House of Representatives, ushered in two decades of political stalemate. A succession of one-term presidencies followed: Rutherford B. Hayes (elected in 1876), James A. Garfield (succeeded after his assassination in 1881 by Chester A. Arthur), Grover Cleveland in 1884, Benjamin Harrison in 1888, and Cleveland, elected for the second time, in 1892. Only for brief periods did the same party control the White House and both houses of Congress. More than once, Congress found itself paralyzed as important bills shuttled back and forth between House and Senate, and special sessions to complete legislation became necessary. Gilded Age presidents made little effort to mobilize public opinion or exert executive leadership. Their staffs were quite small. Grover Cleveland himself answered the White House doorbell.

In some ways, American democracy in the Gilded Age seemed remarkably healthy. Elections were closely contested, party loyalty was intense, and 80 percent or more of eligible voters turned out to cast ballots. It was an era of massive party rallies and spellbinding political oratory. James G. Blaine was among the members of Congress tainted by the Crédit Mobilier scandal, but Robert G. Ingersoll's speech before the Republican national convention of 1876 nearly secured Blaine's nomination for president by depicting him as a "plumed knight" who had raised his "shining lance" against the country's enemies.

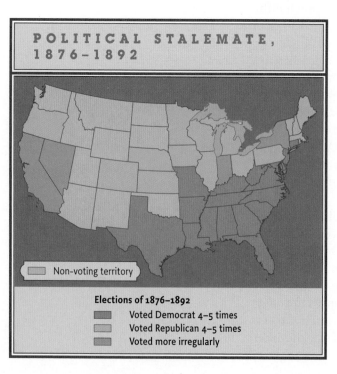

POLITICAL STALEMATE, 1876–1892

Non-voting territory

Elections of 1876–1892

Voted Democrat 4–5 times
Voted Republican 4–5 times
Voted more irregularly

GOVERNMENT AND THE ECONOMY

The nation's political structure, however, proved ill equipped to deal with the problems created by the economy's rapid growth. Despite its expanded scope and powers arising from the Civil War, the federal government remained remarkably small by modern standards. Activities from education to medical care, business regulation, civil and criminal prosecutions, and many others were almost entirely under the control of local and state governments or private institutions. The federal workforce in 1880 numbered 100,000 (today, it exceeds 2.5 million).

Nationally, both parties came under the control of powerful political managers with close ties to business interests. Republicans strongly supported a high tariff to protect American industry, and throughout the 1870s they pursued a fiscal policy based on reducing federal spending, repaying much of the national debt, and withdrawing greenbacks—the paper money issued by the Union during the Civil War—from circulation. Democrats opposed the high tariff, but the party's national leadership remained closely linked to New York bankers and financiers and resisted demands from debt-ridden agricultural areas for an increase in the money supply. In 1879, for the first time since the war, the United States returned to the gold standard—that is, paper currency became exchangeable for gold at a fixed rate.

By reducing competition from foreign manufactured goods and leaving the banks, not the government, in control of issuing money, Republican economic policies strongly favored the interests of eastern industrialists and bankers. These policies worked to the disadvantage of southern and western farmers, who had to pay a premium for manufactured goods while the prices they received for their produce steadily declined.

A political cartoon shows Grover Cleveland leading the Democratic Party in an assault against Republican high taxes.

REFORM LEGISLATION

Gilded Age national politics did not entirely lack accomplishments. Inspired in part by President Garfield's assassination by a disappointed office seeker, the Civil Service Act of 1883 created a merit system for federal employees, with appointment via competitive examinations rather than political influence. Although it applied at first to only 10 percent of the more than 100,000 government workers, the act marked the first step in establishing a professional civil service and removing officeholding from the hands of political machines. (However, since funds raised from political appointees had helped to finance the political parties, civil service reform had the unintended result of increasing politicians' dependence on donations from business interests.)

In 1887, in response to public outcries against railroad practices, Congress established the Interstate Commerce Commission (ICC) to ensure that the rates railroads charged farmers and merchants to transport their goods were "reasonable" and did not offer more favorable treatment to some shippers over others. The ICC was the first federal agency intended to regulate economic activity, but since it lacked the power to establish rates on its own—it could only sue companies in court—it had little impact on railroad practices. Three years later, Congress passed the Sherman Antitrust Act, which banned combinations and practices that restrained free trade. But the language was so vague that the act proved almost impossible to enforce. Weak as they were, these laws helped to establish the precedent that the national government could regulate the economy to promote the public good.

POLITICAL CONFLICT IN THE STATES

The nation had to weather the effects of drastic economic change and periodic economic crises without leadership from Washington. At the state and local level, however, the Gilded Age was an era of political ferment and conflict over the proper uses of governmental authority. In the immediate aftermath of the Civil War, state governments in the North, like those in the Reconstruction South, greatly expanded their responsibility for public health, welfare, and education, and cities invested heavily in public works such as park construction and improved water and gas services. Those who suffered from economic change called on the activist state created by the war to redress their own grievances.

Third parties enjoyed significant if short-lived success in local elections. The Greenback-Labor Party proposed that the federal government stop taking "greenback" money out of circulation. This, it argued, would make more funds available for investment and give the government, not private bankers, control of the money supply. It also condemned the use of militias and private police against strikes. In the late 1870s, the party controlled local government in a number of industrial and mining communities and contributed to the election of twenty-one members of Congress independent of the two major parties.

The policies of railroad companies produced a growing chorus of protest, especially in the West. Farmers and local merchants complained of excessively high freight rates, discrimination in favor of large producers and shippers, and high fees charged by railroad-controlled grain warehouses. Critics of the railroads came together in the Patrons of Husbandry, or Grange, which moved to establish cooperatives for storing and marketing farm output in the hope of forcing the carriers "to take our produce at a fair price." Founded in 1867, the Grange claimed more than 700,000 members by the mid-1870s. Its members called on state governments to establish fair freight rates and warehouse charges. In several states, the Grange succeeded in having commissions established to investigate—and, in some cases, regulate—railroad practices.

At the same time, the labor movement, revitalized during the Civil War, demanded laws establishing eight hours as a legal day's work. Seven northern legislatures passed such laws, but since most lacked strong means of enforcement they remained dead letters. But the efforts of farmers and workers to use the power of the state to

Laying Tracks at Union Square for a Railroad, *an 1890 painting, depicts one of the era's many public works assisted by state and local governments.*

counteract the inequalities of the Gilded Age inspired a far-reaching debate on the relationship between political and economic freedom in an industrial society.

FREEDOM IN THE GILDED AGE

THE SOCIAL PROBLEM

As the United States matured into an industrial economy, Americans struggled to make sense of the new social order. Debates over political economy engaged the attention of millions of Americans, reaching far beyond the tiny academic world into the public sphere inhabited by self-educated workingmen and farmers, reformers of all kinds, newspaper editors, and politicians. This broad public discussion produced thousands of books, pamphlets, and articles on such technical issues as land taxation and currency reform, as well as widespread debate over the social and ethical implications of economic change.

Many Americans sensed that something had gone wrong in the nation's social development. Talk of "better classes," "respectable classes," and "dangerous classes" dominated public discussion, and bitter labor strife seemed to have become the rule. During the Gilded Age, Congress and a number of states established investigating committees to inquire into the relations between labor and capital. Their hearings produced powerful evidence of distrust between employees and employers. In 1881, the Massachusetts Bureau of Labor Statistics reported that virtually every worker it interviewed in Fall River, the nation's largest center of textile production, complained of overwork, poor housing, and tyrannical employers. For their part, manufacturers claimed their workingmen were "the scum of the English and Irish," whose complaints reflected nothing more than a "hereditary feeling of discontent."

FREEDOM, INEQUALITY, AND DEMOCRACY

The appearance of what Massachusetts cotton manufacturer Edward Atkinson called "a permanent factory population" living on the edge of poverty alongside a growing class of millionaires posed a sharp challenge to traditional definitions of freedom. Did America's promise still lie in the opportunity it offered ordinary citizens to achieve economic autonomy? "The great curse of the Old World—the division of society into classes," declared *The Nation*, had come to America. It became increasingly difficult to view wage labor as a temporary resting place on the road to economic independence, or the West as a haven for the dispossessed small producers of the East.

Given the vast expansion of the nation's productive capacity, many Americans viewed the concentration of wealth as inevitable, natural, and justified by progress. By the turn of the century, advanced economics taught that wages were determined by the iron law of supply and demand and that wealth rightly flowed not to those who worked the hardest but to men with business skills and access to money. The close link between freedom and equality, forged in the Revolution and reinforced during the Civil

War, appeared increasingly out of date. The task of social science, wrote iron manufacturer Abram Hewitt, was to devise ways of making "men who are equal in liberty" content with the "inequality in . . . distribution" inevitable in modern society.

Among the first to take up this challenge were the self-styled "liberal" reformers. (Their beliefs were quite different from those called liberals in modern America, who advocate that an activist government try to address social needs.) This group of editors and professionals broke with the Republican Party in 1872 and helped to bring about a change in northern opinion regarding Reconstruction. But their program was not confined to the South. Like the men who led the movement for a new constitution in the 1780s, Gilded Age reformers feared that with lower-class groups seeking to use government to advance their own interests, democracy was becoming a threat to individual liberty and the rights of property. Some urged a return to the long-abandoned principle that voting should be limited to property owners. During the 1830s, Alexis de Tocqueville had reported that opponents of democracy "hide their heads." By the 1870s, wrote one observer, "expressions of doubt and distrust in regard to universal suffrage are heard constantly . . . [at] the top of our society."

SOCIAL DARWINISM IN AMERICA

The idea of the natural superiority of some groups to others, which before the Civil War had been invoked to justify slavery in an otherwise free society, now reemerged in the vocabulary of modern science to explain the success and failure of individuals and social classes. In 1859, the British scientist Charles Darwin published *On the Origin of Species*. One of the most influential works of science ever to appear, it expounded the theory of evolution whereby plant and animal species best suited to their environment took the place of those less able to adapt.

In a highly oversimplified form, language borrowed from Darwin, such as "natural selection," "the struggle for existence," and "the survival of the fittest," entered public discussion of social problems in the Gilded Age. According to what came to be called Social Darwinism, evolution was as natural a process in human society as in nature, and government must not interfere. Especially misguided, in this view, were efforts to uplift those at the bottom of the social order, such as laws regulating conditions of work or public assistance to the poor. The giant industrial corporation, Social Darwinists believed, had emerged because it was better adapted to its environment than earlier forms of enterprise. To restrict its operations by legislation would reduce society to a more primitive level.

Even the depressions of the 1870s and 1890s did not shake the widespread view that the poor were essentially responsible for their own fate. Charity workers and local governments spent much time and energy distinguishing the "deserving" poor (those, like widows and orphans, destitute through no fault of their own) from the "undeserving," a far larger number. Failure to advance in society was widely thought to indicate a lack of character, an absence of self-reliance and determination in the face of adversity. As late as 1900, half the nation's largest cities offered virtually no public relief, except to persons living in poorhouses. To improve their lot,

VISIONS OF FREEDOM

Detail from Capital and Labor. Capital and Labor, *a cotton textile from around 1870, illustrates the free labor ideal, with an employer and employee shaking hands and laborers enjoying dignity at work and a "happy home." One image and its caption ("The Two Powers in Accord") illustrates the idea of a harmony of interests between worker and employer, a key tenet of free-labor thought. Others stress the dignity of the workingman, based partly on his skill and partly on his ability to provide a comfortable home for his family. The portrait of American industry here stands in stark contrast to the widespread labor strife of the Gilded Age.*

QUESTIONS

1. Why did many Americans in the Gilded Age worry that this vision of harmony no longer described American life?

2. Give some examples of how the images here misrepresent the realities of the period.

according to the philosophy of Social Darwinism, workers should practice personal economy, keep out of debt, and educate their children in the principles of the marketplace, not look to the government for aid.

The era's most influential Social Darwinist was Yale professor William Graham Sumner. For Sumner, freedom meant "the security given to each man" that he can acquire, enjoy, and dispose of property "exclusively as he chooses," without interference from other persons or from government. Freedom thus defined required frank acceptance of inequality. Society faced two and only two alternatives: "liberty, inequality, survival of the fittest; not-liberty, equality, survival of the unfittest." In 1883, Sumner published *What Social Classes Owe to Each Other*. His answer, essentially, was nothing: "In a free state," no one was entitled to claim "help from, and cannot be charged to [offer] help to, another." Government, Sumner believed, existed only to protect "the property of men and the honor of women," not to upset social arrangements decreed by nature.

LIBERTY OF CONTRACT

The growing influence of Social Darwinism helped to popularize an idea that would be embraced by the business and professional classes in the last quarter of the nineteenth century—a "negative" definition of freedom as limited government and an unrestrained free market. Central to this social vision was the idea of contract. "The laws of contract," wrote one reformer, "are the foundation of civilization." Labor contracts reconciled freedom and authority in the workplace. So long as labor relations were governed by contracts freely arrived at by independent individuals, neither the government nor unions had a right to interfere with working conditions, and Americans had no grounds to complain of a loss of freedom.

Demands by workers that the government enforce an eight-hour day, provide relief to the unemployed, or in other ways intervene in the economy struck liberals as an example of how the misuse of political power posed a threat to liberty. "The right of each man to labor as much or as little as he chooses, and to enjoy his own earnings, is the very foundation stone of . . . freedom," wrote Chicago newspaper editor Horace White. The principle of free labor, which originated as a celebration of the independent small producer in a society of broad equality and social harmony, was transformed into a defense of the unrestrained operations of the capitalist marketplace.

THE COURTS AND FREEDOM

In elevating liberty of contract from one element of freedom to its very essence, the courts played a significant role. The Fourteenth Amendment had empowered the federal government to overturn state laws that violated citizens' rights. By the 1880s, liberty of contract, not equality before the law for former slaves, came to be defined as the amendment's true meaning. State and federal courts regularly struck down state laws regulating economic enterprise as an interference with the right of the free laborer to choose his employment and working conditions, and of the entrepreneur to utilize his property as he saw fit. For decades, the courts viewed state regulation of business—especially laws establishing maximum hours of work and safe working conditions—as an insult to free labor.

The Ironworkers' Noontime, *painted in 1880–1881 by Thomas Anshutz, an artist born in West Virginia, whose family owned iron factories. Unlike artists who depicted factories and workers earlier in the century, Anshutz does not try to reconcile nature and industry (there are no reminders of the natural environment). Nor does he emphasize the dignity of labor. The workers seem dwarfed by the factory, and some seem exhausted.*

At first, the Supreme Court was willing to accept laws regulating enterprises that represented a significant "public interest." In *Munn v. Illinois*, an 1877 decision, it upheld the constitutionality of an Illinois law that established a state board empowered to eliminate railroad rate discrimination and set maximum charges. Nine years later, however, in *Wabash v. Illinois*, the Court essentially reversed itself, ruling that only the federal government, not the states, could regulate railroads engaged in interstate commerce, as all important lines were. The decision led directly to the passage of the Interstate Commerce Act of 1887. But on virtually every occasion when cases brought by the ICC against railroads made their way to the Supreme Court, the company emerged victorious.

The courts generally sided with business enterprises that complained of a loss of economic freedom. In 1885, the New York Court of Appeals invalidated a state law that prohibited the manufacture of cigars in tenement dwellings on the grounds that such legislation deprived the worker of the "liberty" to work "where he will." Although women still lacked political rights, they were increasingly understood to possess the same economic "liberty," defined in this way, as men. On the grounds that it violated women's freedom, the Illinois Supreme Court in 1895 declared unconstitutional a state law that outlawed the production of garments in sweatshops and established a forty-eight-hour work week for women and children. In the same year, in *United States v. E. C. Knight Co.*, the U.S. Supreme Court ruled that the Sherman Antitrust Act of 1890, which barred combinations in restraint of trade, could not be used to break up a sugar refining monopoly, since the Constitution empowered Congress to regulate commerce, but not manufacturing. Their unwillingness to allow regulation of the economy, however, did not prevent the courts from acting to impede labor organization. The Sherman Act, intended to prevent business mergers that stifled competition, was used by judges primarily to issue injunctions prohibiting strikes on the grounds that they illegally interfered with the freedom of trade.

In a 1905 case that became almost as notorious as *Dred Scott* and gave the name "Lochnerism" to the entire body of liberty of contract decisions, the Supreme Court in *Lochner v. New York* voided a state law establishing ten hours per day or sixty per week as the maximum hours of work for bakers. The law, wrote Associate Justice Rufus Peckham for the 5-4 majority, "interfered with the right of contract between employer and employee" and therefore infringed upon individual freedom. By this time, the Court was invoking "liberty" in ways that could easily seem absurd. In one case, it overturned as a violation of "personal liberty" a Kansas law prohibiting "yellow-dog" contracts, which made nonmembership in a union a condition of employment. In another, it struck down state laws requiring payment of coal miners in money rather than paper usable only at company-owned stores. Workers, observed mine union leader John P. Mitchell, could not but feel that "they are being guaranteed the liberties they do not want and denied the liberty that is of real value to them."

LABOR AND THE REPUBLIC

"THE OVERWHELMING LABOR QUESTION"

As Mitchell's remark suggests, public debate in the late nineteenth century more than at almost any other moment in American history divided along class lines. The shift from the slavery controversy to what one politician called "the overwhelming labor question" was dramatically illustrated in 1877, the year of both the end of Reconstruction and also the first national labor walkout—the Great Railroad Strike. When workers protesting a pay cut paralyzed rail traffic in much of the country, militia units tried to force them back to work. After troops fired on strikers in Pittsburgh, killing twenty people, workers responded by burning the city's railroad yards, destroying millions of dollars in property. General strikes paralyzed Chicago and St. Louis. The strike revealed both a strong sense of solidarity among workers and the close ties between the Republican Party and the new class of industrialists. President Rutherford B. Hayes, who a few months earlier had ordered federal troops in the South to end their involvement in local politics, ordered the army into the North. The workers, the president wrote in his diary, were "put down by force."

"The days are over," declared the *New York Times*, "in which this country could rejoice in its freedom from the elements of social strife which have long abounded in the old countries." In the aftermath of 1877, the federal government constructed armories in major cities to ensure that troops would be on hand in the event of further labor difficulties. Henceforth, national power would be used not to protect beleaguered former slaves, but to guarantee the rights of property.

THE KNIGHTS OF LABOR AND THE "CONDITIONS ESSENTIAL TO LIBERTY"

The 1880s witnessed a new wave of labor organizing. At its center stood the Knights of Labor. The Knights were the first group to try to organize unskilled workers as well as skilled, women alongside men, and blacks as well as whites (although even the Knights excluded the despised Asian immigrants on the West Coast). The group reached a peak membership of

Ruins of the Pittsburgh Round House, *a photograph published in the July 1895 issue of* Scribner's Magazine, *shows the widespread destruction of property during the Great Railroad Strike of July 1877.*

nearly 800,000 in 1886 and involved millions of workers in strikes, boy-cotts, political action, and educational and social activities.

Caught between nostalgia for the era of small production and acknowl-edgment of the factory's triumph, labor reformers of the Gilded Age put for-ward a wide array of programs, from the eight-hour day to public employment in hard times, currency reform, anarchism, socialism, and the creation of a vaguely defined "cooperative commonwealth." All these ideas arose from the conviction that the social conditions of the 1880s needed drastic change. Americans, declared Terence V. Powderly, head of the Knights of Labor, were not "the free people that we imagine we are."

The labor movement launched a sustained assault on the understanding of freedom grounded in Social Darwinism and liberty of contract. Because of unrestrained economic growth and political corruption, the Knights charged, ordinary Americans had lost control of their economic livelihoods and their own government. Reaching back across the divide of the Civil War, labor defined employers as a new "slave power." Concentrated capital, warned George E. McNeill, a shoemaker and factory worker who became one of the movement's most eloquent writers, had become "a greater power than that of the state." "Extremes of wealth and poverty," he warned, threat-ened the very existence of democratic government. The remedy was to "engraft republican principles into our industrial system" by guaranteeing a basic set of economic rights for all Americans.

Labor raised the question whether meaningful freedom could exist in a situation of extreme economic inequality. On July 4, 1886, the Federated Trades of the Pacific Coast rewrote the Declaration of Independence. Workers, the new Declaration claimed, had been subjected not to oppres-sive government but to "the unjust domination of a special class." It went on to list among mankind's inalienable rights, "Life and the means of liv-ing, Liberty and the conditions essential to liberty."

An engraving from Frank Leslie's Illustrated Newspaper, *October 16, 1886, shows black delegate Frank J. Farrell introducing Terence V. Powderly, leader of the Knights of Labor, at the labor organization's national convention in Richmond, Virginia. The Knights were among the few nineteenth-century labor groups to recruit black members.*

MIDDLE-CLASS REFORMERS

Dissatisfaction with social conditions in the Gilded Age extended well beyond aggrieved workers. Supreme Court justice John Marshall Harlan in the late 1880s spoke of a "deep feeling of unease," a widespread fear that the country "was in real danger of another kind of slavery that would result from the aggregation of capital in the hands of a few individuals." Alarmed by fear of class warfare and the growing power of concentrated capital, social thinkers offered numerous plans for change. In the last quarter of the century, more than 150 utopian or cataclysmic novels appeared, predicting that social conflict would end either in a new, harmonious social order or in total catastrophe. One popular novel of the era, *Caesar's Column* (1891) by Ignatius Donnelly, ended with civilized society destroyed in a savage civil war between labor and capital.

Of the many books proposing more optimistic remedies for the unequal distribution of wealth, the most popular were *Progress and Poverty* (1879) by Henry George, *The Cooperative Commonwealth* (1884) by Laurence Gronlund, and Edward Bellamy's *Looking Backward* (1888). All three were among the century's greatest best-sellers, their extraordinary success testi-fying to what George called "a wide-spread consciousness . . . that there is something *radically* wrong in the present social organization." All three

The Great Labor Parade of September 1, *from* Frank Leslie's Illustrated Newspaper, September 13, *1884*. *A placard illustrates how the labor movement identified Gilded Age employers with the Slave Power of the pre–Civil War era.*

writers, though in very different ways, sought to reclaim an imagined golden age of social harmony and American freedom.

PROGRESS AND POVERTY

Although it had no direct impact on government policy, *Progress and Poverty* probably commanded more public attention than any book on economics in American history. An antislavery newspaper editor in California in the 1850s and 1860s, Henry George had witnessed firsthand the rapid monopolization of land in the state. His book began with a famous statement of "the problem" suggested by its title—the growth of "squalor and misery" alongside material progress. His solution was the "single tax," which would replace other taxes with a levy on increases in the value of real estate. The single tax would be so high that it would prevent speculation in both urban and rural land. No one knows how many of Henry George's readers actually believed in this way of solving the nation's ills. But millions responded to his clear explanation of economic relationships and his stirring account of how the "social distress" long thought to be confined to the Old World had made its appearance in the New.

Freedom lay at the heart of George's analysis. The "proper name" for the political movement spawned by his book, he once wrote, was "freedom men," who would "do for the question of industrial slavery" what the Republican Party had done for the slavery of blacks. George rejected the traditional equation of liberty with ownership of land (since the single tax in effect made land the "common property" of the entire society). In other ways, however, his definition of freedom was thoroughly in keeping with mainstream thought. Despite calling for a single massive public intervention in the economy, George saw government as a "repressive power," whose functions in the "co-operative society" of the future would be limited to enhancing the quality of life—building "public baths, museums, libraries, gardens," and the like.

THE COOPERATIVE COMMONWEALTH

Quite different in outlook was *The Cooperative Commonwealth*, the first book to popularize socialist ideas for an American audience. Its author, Laurence Gronlund, was a lawyer who had emigrated from Denmark in 1867. Socialism—the belief that private control of economic enterprises should be replaced by government ownership in order to ensure a fairer distribution of the benefits of the wealth produced—became a major political force in western Europe in the late nineteenth century. In the United States, however, where access to private property was widely considered essential to individual freedom, socialist beliefs were largely confined to immigrants, whose writings, frequently in foreign languages, attracted little attention.

Gronlund began the process of socialism's Americanization. While Karl Marx, the nineteenth century's most influential socialist theorist, had predicted that socialism would come into being via a working-class revolution, Gronlund portrayed it as the end result of a process of peaceful evolution, not violent upheaval. He thus made socialism seem more acceptable to middle-class Americans who desired an end to class conflict and the restoration of social harmony.

BELLAMY'S UTOPIA

Not until the early twentieth century would socialism become a significant presence in American public life. As Gronlund himself noted, the most important result of *The Cooperative Commonwealth* was to prepare an audience for Edward Bellamy's *Looking Backward*, which promoted socialist ideas while "ignoring that name" (Bellamy wrote of nationalism, not socialism). Bellamy lived virtually his entire life in the small industrial city of Chicopee Falls, Massachusetts. In *Looking Backward*, his main character falls asleep in the late nineteenth century only to awaken in the year 2000, in a world where cooperation has replaced class strife, "excessive individualism," and cutthroat competition. Inequality has been banished and with it the idea of liberty as a condition to be achieved through individual striving free of governmental restraint. Freedom, Bellamy insisted, was a social condition, resting on interdependence, not autonomy.

From today's vantage point, Bellamy's utopia—with citizens obligated to labor for years in an Industrial Army controlled by a single Great Trust—seems a chilling social blueprint. Yet the book inspired the creation of hundreds of nationalist clubs devoted to bringing into existence the world of 2000 and left a profound mark on a generation of reformers and intellectuals. Bellamy held out the hope of retaining the material abundance made possible by industrial capitalism while eliminating inequality. In proposing that the state guarantee economic security to all, Bellamy offered a far-reaching expansion of the idea of freedom. "I am aware that you called yourself free in the nineteenth century," a resident of the year 2000 tells Bellamy's Rip Van Winkle. But "the meaning of the word could not then have been at all what it is at present," or it could not have been applied to a

Edward Bellamy, author of the utopian novel Looking Backward.

society in which so many lived in a state of "galling personal dependence upon others as to the very means of life."

A SOCIAL GOSPEL

By 1888, when *Looking Backward* appeared, Social Darwinism and the laissez-faire definition of freedom were under attack from many quarters, including the labor movement and middle-class writers like George and Bellamy, as well as clergymen shocked by the inequities in the emerging industrial order. Most of the era's Protestant preachers concentrated on attacking individual sins like drinking and Sabbath-breaking and saw nothing immoral about the pursuit of riches. Their Gospel of Wealth gave a moral underpinning to the "liberty of contract" outlook. But the outlines of what came to be called the Social Gospel were taking shape in the writings of Walter Rauschenbusch, a Baptist minister in New York City, Washington Gladden, a Congregational clergyman in Columbus, Ohio, and others. They insisted that freedom and spiritual self-development required an equalization of wealth and power and that unbridled competition mocked the Christian ideal of brotherhood.

The Social Gospel movement originated as an effort to reform Protestant churches by expanding their appeal in poor urban neighborhoods and making them more attentive to the era's social ills. The movement's adherents established missions and relief programs in urban areas that attempted to alleviate poverty, combat child labor, and encourage the construction of better working-class housing. They worked with the Knights of Labor and other groups demanding health and safety laws. Some suggested that a more cooperative organization of the economy should replace competitive capitalism. Within American Catholicism, as well, a group of priests and bishops emerged who attempted to alter the Church's traditional hostility to movements for social reform and its isolation from contemporary currents of social thought. With most of its parishioners working men and women, they argued, the Church should lend its support to the labor movement. These developments suggested the existence of widespread dissatisfaction with the "liberty of contract" understanding of freedom.

THE HAYMARKET AFFAIR

The year of the dedication of the Statue of Liberty, 1886, also witnessed an unprecedented upsurge in labor activity. Inspired by a successful strike by western railroad unions against lines controlled by the powerful financier Jay Gould, workers flooded into the Knights of Labor. Its membership, only 100,000 in 1885, rose more than sevenfold in the following year. On May 1, 1886, some 350,000 workers in cities across the country demonstrated for an eight-hour day. Having originated in the United States, May 1, or May Day as it came to be called, soon became an annual date of parades, picnics, and protests, celebrated around the world by organized labor.

The most dramatic events of 1886 took place in Chicago, a city with a large and vibrant labor movement that brought together native-born and immigrant workers, whose outlooks ranged from immigrant socialism and anarchism to American traditions of equality and anti-monopoly. In 1885, the iron moulders union—one of the most powerful organizations of skilled industrial workers in the country—had organized a strike against a wage reduction at the great McCormick plant that produced agricultural machinery. The company brought in strikebreakers and private police, who battled in the streets with the strikers. Fearing chaos, the mayor and prominent business leaders persuaded the company to settle on the union's terms. But in February 1886, after the company installed new machinery that reduced its dependence on the iron moulders' traditional skills, it announced that henceforth the factory would operate on a nonunion basis. The result was a bitter, prolonged strike.

This time, Chicago's city government sided with the company. On May 3, 1886, four strikers were killed by police when they attempted to prevent strikebreakers from entering the factory. The next day, a rally was held in Haymarket Square to protest the killings. Near the end of the speeches, someone—whose identity has never been determined—threw a bomb into the crowd, killing a policeman. The panicked police opened fire, shooting several bystanders and a number of their own force. Soon after, police raided the offices of labor and radical groups and arrested of their leaders. Employers took the opportunity to paint the labor movement as a dangerous and un-American force, prone to violence and controlled by foreign-born radicals. The McCormick strike was defeated and the union local destroyed. Eight anarchists were charged with plotting and carrying out the bombing. Even though the evidence against them was extremely weak, a jury convicted the "Haymarket martyrs." Four were hanged, one committed suicide in prison, and the remaining three were imprisoned until John Peter Altgeld, a pro-labor governor of Illinois, commuted their sentences in 1893.

Seven of the eight men accused of plotting the Haymarket bombing were foreign-born—six Germans and an English immigrant. The last was Albert Parsons, a native of Alabama who had served in the Confederate army in the Civil War and edited a Republican newspaper in Texas during Reconstruction. Fearing violence because of his political views and the fact that his wife, Lucy Parsons, was black, Albert Parsons moved to Chicago during the 1870s. Having survived the Ku Klux Klan in Reconstruction Texas, Parsons perished on the Illinois gallows for a crime that he, like the other "Haymarket martyrs," did not commit.

LABOR AND POLITICS

The Haymarket affair took place amid an outburst of independent labor political activity. One study has identified more than 100 local political tickets associated with the Knights of Labor between 1886 and 1888, from

A cartoon from the 1880s depicts radicals as foreigners attempting to destroy the foundations of American society. A caterpillar labeled "comunism" gnaws at the leaf "capital" beneath which are the fruits of American society—among them education, industry, business, law, order, and peace.

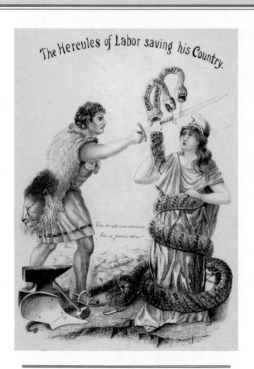

In this pro-labor cartoon from 1888, a workingman rescues liberty from the stranglehold of monopolies and the pro-business major parties.

Anniston, Alabama, to Whitewater, Wisconsin. Their major aim was to end the use of public and private police forces and court injunctions against strikes and labor organizations. At least sixty achieved some kind of electoral success. In Kansas City, a coalition of black and Irish-American workers and middle-class voters elected Tom Hanna as mayor. He proceeded to side with unions rather than employers in industrial disputes.

The most celebrated labor campaign took place in New York City, where in 1886, somewhat to his own surprise, Henry George found himself thrust into the role of labor's candidate for mayor. George's aim in running was to bring attention to the single tax on land. The labor leaders who organized the United Labor Party had more immediate goals in mind, especially stopping the courts from barring strikes and jailing unionists for conspiracy. George ran a spirited campaign, speaking at factories, immigrant associations, and labor parades and rallies. A few days after the dedication of the Statue of Liberty, New Yorkers flocked to the polls to elect their mayor. Nearly 70,000 voted for George, who finished second, eclipsing the total of the Republican candidate, Theodore Roosevelt, and coming close to defeating Democrat Abram Hewitt.

In a political system that within living memory had witnessed the disappearance of the Whig Party, the rise and fall of the Know-Nothings, and the emergence of the Republicans, the events of 1886 suggested that labor might be on the verge of establishing itself as a permanent political force. In fact, that year marked the high point of the Knights of Labor. Facing increasing employer hostility and with a poorly organized structure that could not assimilate the great spurt in new members, the Knights soon declined. The major parties, moreover, proved remarkably resourceful in appealing to labor voters.

Thus, America's Gilded Age witnessed deep and sometimes violent divisions over the definition of freedom in a rapidly industrializing society. The battle between upholders of Social Darwinism and laissez-faire, who saw freedom as the right of individuals to pursue their economic interests without outside restraint, and those who believed in collective efforts to create "industrial freedom" for ordinary Americans, would continue for many decades. In the early twentieth century, reformers would turn to new ways of addressing the social conditions of freedom and new means of increasing ordinary Americans' political and economic liberty. But before this, in the 1890s, the nation would face its gravest crisis since the Civil War, and the boundaries of freedom would once again be redrawn.

SUGGESTED READING

BOOKS

Bensel, Richard F. *The Political Economy of American Industrialization, 1877–1900* (2000). A study of the policies and political divisions that contributed to and resulted from the second industrial revolution.

Blackhawk, Ned. *Violence Over the Land: Indians and Empires in the Early American West* (2006). A history of the long conflict between Native Americans and the federal government for control of the trans-Mississippi West.

Chandler, Alfred. *The Visible Hand: The Managerial Revolution in American Business* (1977). Examines how railroads pioneered techniques of modern business management that other corporations then adopted.

De Leon, Arnoldo. *Racial Frontiers: Africans, Chinese, and Mexicans in Western America, 1848–1890* (2002). Emphasizes the diversity of the West's population and the different experiences of its racial minorities.

Deutsch, Sarah. *No Separate Refuge: Culture, Class, and Gender on the Anglo-Hispanic Frontier in the American Southwest, 1880–1940* (1987). A careful analysis of the changing experience of people of Hispanic origin in the Southwest during these years.

Fink, Leon. *Workingmen's Democracy: The Knights of Labor and American Politics* (1983). Examines the rise of the Knights of Labor and their forays into local politics in the mid-1880s.

Hamalainen, Pekka. *The Comanche Empire* (2008). The rise and fall of Comanche domination over much of the southwestern United States.

Hofstadter, Richard. *Social Darwinism in American Thought* (1944). A classic study of a major tendency in American thought during the Gilded Age.

Isenberg, Andrew C. *The Destruction of the Bison: An Environmental History, 1750–1920* (2000). Examines the numerous causes for the decimation of buffalo herds, from climate change to commercial hunting.

Jeffrey, Julie R. *Frontier Women: "Civilizing" the West? 1840–1880* (rev. ed., 1998). A study, based on letters and diaries, of the experience of women on the western frontier.

Keller, Morton. *Affairs of State: Public Life in Late Nineteenth-Century America* (1977). A comprehensive account of the activities of government during the Gilded Age.

Morgan, H. Wayne. *From Hayes to McKinley: National Party Politics, 1877–1896* (1969). The standard narrative of national politics during these years.

Shannon, Fred A. *The Farmer's Last Frontier: Agriculture 1860–1897* (1945). Remains an excellent introduction to the experience of farmers in the last four decades of the nineteenth century.

Sproat, John G. *"The Best Men": Liberal Reformers in the Gilded Age* (1968). Traces the origins, outlook, and political impact of reformers dissatisfied with the corruption of national politics.

Thomas, John L. *Alternative Americas: Henry George, Edward Bellamy, Henry Demarest Lloyd and the Adversary Tradition* (1983). A thorough exposition of the thought of three critics of Gilded Age society.

Trachtenberg, Alan. *The Incorporation of America: Culture and Society in the Gilded Age* (1982). An influential survey of how economic change affected American life during the Gilded Age.

WEBSITES

Indian Peoples of the Northern Great Plains: www.lib.montana.edu/digital/nadb/
The Dramas of Haymarket: www.chicagohistory.org/dramas/overview/over.htm
Western History Photography Collection: http://photoswest.org/presearch.html

REVIEW QUESTIONS

1. The American economy thrived because of federal involvement, not the lack of it. How did the federal government actively promote industrial and agricultural development in this period?

2. Describe the importance of the nation's railroads in the rise of America's second industrial revolution.

3. How did the development of an urban, industrial society exacerbate inequalities in U.S. society and promote class violence?

4. Describe the involvement of American family farmers in the global economy after 1870 and its effects on their independence.

5. According to *The Gilded Age* by Mark Twain and Charles Dudley Warner, the era's slogan was "Get rich, dishonestly if we can, honestly if we must." Explain how this was true of the politics of the era.

6. How successfully did third parties lead movements for reform at the state level?

7. Explain how social thinkers misapplied Charles Darwin's ideas to justify massive disparities in wealth and power and to deny government a role in equalizing opportunity.

8. How do the ideas of Henry George, Edward Bellamy, and other authors conflict with Social Darwinism?

9. Compare William Graham Sumner's comments in *What Social Classes Owe to Each Other* to those of the Federated Trades of the Pacific Coast's "rewrite" of the Declaration of Independence. What two positions are laid out?

FREEDOM QUESTIONS

1. How would the elite differ from the urban and rural poor on the following questions: What social conditions make freedom possible, and what role should the government play in defining and protecting the liberties of its citizens?

2. How did Native American ideas of freedom differ from those of settlers and government officials in this period?

3. How did the creation of a poor population of factory workers threaten traditional American ideas about freedom, equality, and democracy?

4. Explain how the courts, by embracing Social Darwinism and a "negative" idea of freedom through the liberty of contract ideal, eroded the freedoms of workers and others.

KEY TERMS

"great upheaval" of 1886 (p. 632)

standard gauge (p. 635)

railroad time zones (p. 636)

vertical integration (p. 639)

Standard Oil Company (p. 640)

"captains of industry" v. "robber barons" (p. 641)

"The Significance of the Frontier in American History" (p. 643)

bonanza farming (p. 646)

Dawes Act (p. 654)

Ghost Dance (p. 655)

greenbacks (p. 659)

Civil Service Act of 1883 (p. 659)

Interstate Commerce Commission (p. 659)

Patrons of Husbandry (p. 660)

iron law of supply and demand (p. 661)

Social Darwinism (p. 662)

liberty of contract (p. 664)

Lochner v. New York (p. 666)

Great Railroad Strike of 1877 (p. 666)

Knights of Labor (p. 666)

Social Gospel (p. 670)

REVIEW TABLE

Landmarks in Indian Relations, 1876–1890

Event	Date	Outcome
Battle at Little Bighorn	1876	General Custer's army is massacred
Chief Joseph's trek toward freedom	1877	Nez Percé tribe is captured and placed on a reservation
Dawes Act	1887	Indian lands are divided into small family plots, and the rest is sold off
Massacre at Wounded Knee	1890	Final defeat, ending the Indian Wars

CHAPTER 17

Freedom's Boundaries, at Home and Abroad, 1890–1900

A Trifle Embarrassed, *a cartoon from the magazine* Puck *in 1898, depicts Uncle Sam and a female figure of liberty standing at the gate of a Foundling [Orphan] Asylum and being presented with orphans representing Puerto Rico, Hawaii, Cuba, and the Philippines. These were the territories acquired by the United States during the Spanish-American War (all but Cuba remained American possessions). The artist seems to question whether the United States is prepared to assume the role of imperial power.*

FOCUS QUESTIONS

• What were the origins and the significance of Populism?

• How did the liberties of blacks after 1877 give way to legal segregation across the South?

• In what ways did the boundaries of American freedom grow narrower in this period?

• How did the United States emerge as an imperial power in the 1890s?

One of the most popular songs of 1892 bore the title "Father Was Killed by a Pinkerton Man." It was inspired by an incident during a bitter strike at Andrew Carnegie's steelworks at Homestead, Pennsylvania, the nineteenth century's most widely publicized confrontation between labor and capital. The strike pitted one of the nation's leading industrial corporations against a powerful union, the Amalgamated Association, which represented the skilled iron- and steelworkers among the complex's 3,800 employees.

Homestead's twelve steel mills were the most profitable and technologically advanced in the world. The union contract gave the Amalgamated Association a considerable say in their operation, including the right to approve the hiring of new workers and to regulate the pace of work. To Carnegie and Henry Clay Frick, his local supervisor, the union's power increasingly seemed an intolerable infringement on management's rights. In 1892, they decided to operate the plant on a nonunion basis. Frick surrounded the factory with a fence topped by barbed wire, constructed barracks to house strikebreakers, and fired the entire workforce. Henceforth, only workers who agreed not to join the union could work at Homestead. In response, the workers, including the unskilled laborers not included in the Amalgamated Association, blockaded the steelworks and mobilized support from the local community. The battle memorialized in song took place on July 6, 1892, when armed strikers confronted 300 private policemen from the Pinkerton Detective Agency. Seven workers and three Pinkerton agents were killed, and the Pinkertons were forced to retreat. Four days later, the governor of Pennsylvania dispatched 8,000 militiamen to open the complex on management's terms. The strikers held out until November, but the union's defeat was now inevitable. In the end, the Amalgamated Association was destroyed.

The Carnegie corporation's tactics and the workers' solidarity won the strikers widespread national sympathy. "Ten thousand Carnegie libraries," declared the *St. Louis Post-Dispatch*, "would not compensate the country for the evils resulting from Homestead." The strike became an international cause célèbre as well. British newspapers pointed out that their country restricted the use of private police forces far more severely than the United States. Britons, they claimed, understood economic liberty better than Americans.

Homestead demonstrated that neither a powerful union nor public opinion could influence the conduct of the largest corporations. The writer Hamlin Garland, who visited Homestead two years after the strike, found the workforce sullen and bitter. He described a town "as squalid and unlovely as could be imagined," with dingy houses over which hung dense clouds of black smoke. It was "American," he wrote, "only in the sense in which [it] represents the American idea of business."

In fact, two American ideas of freedom collided at Homestead—the employers' definition, based on the idea that property rights, unrestrained by union rules or public regulation, sustained the public good, and the workers' conception, which stressed economic security and independence from what they considered the "tyranny" of employers. The strife at Homestead also reflected broader battles over American freedom during the 1890s. Like the Homestead workers, many Americans came to believe that they were being denied economic independence and democratic self-government, long central to the popular understanding of freedom.

Andrew Carnegie's ironworks at Homestead, Pennsylvania.

During the 1890s, millions of farmers joined the Populist movement in an attempt to reverse their declining economic prospects and to rescue the government from what they saw as control by powerful corporate interests. The 1890s witnessed the imposition of a new racial system in the South that locked African-Americans into the status of second-class citizenship, denying them many of the freedoms white Americans took for granted. Increasing immigration produced heated debates over whether the country should reconsider its traditional self-definition as a refuge for foreigners seeking greater freedom on American shores. At the end of the 1890s, in the Spanish-American War, the United States for the first time acquired overseas possessions and found itself ruling over subject peoples from Puerto Rico to the Philippines. Was the democratic republic, many Americans wondered, becoming an empire like those of Europe? Rarely has the country experienced at one time so many debates over both the meaning of freedom and freedom's boundaries.

THE POPULIST CHALLENGE

THE FARMERS' REVOLT

Even as labor unrest crested, a different kind of uprising was ripening in the South and the trans-Mississippi West, a response to falling agricultural prices and growing economic dependency in rural areas. Like industrial workers, small farmers faced increasing economic insecurity. In the South, the sharecropping system, discussed in Chapter 15, locked millions of tenant farmers, white and black, into perpetual poverty. The interruption of cotton exports during the Civil War had led to the rapid expansion of production in India, Egypt, and Brazil. The glut of cotton on the world market led to declining prices (from 11 cents a pound in 1881 to 4.6 cents in 1894), throwing millions of small farmers deep into debt and threatening them with the loss of their land. In the West, farmers who had mortgaged their property to purchase seed, fertilizer, and equipment faced the prospect of losing their farms when unable to repay their bank loans. Farmers increasingly believed that their plight derived from the high freight rates charged by railroad companies, excessive interest rates for loans from merchants and bankers, and the fiscal policies of the federal government (discussed in the previous chapter) that reduced the supply of money and helped to push down farm prices.

Through the Farmers' Alliance, the largest citizens' movement of the nineteenth century, farmers sought to remedy their condition. Founded in Texas in the late 1870s, the Alliance spread to forty-three states by 1890. The farmers' alternatives, said J. D. Fields, a Texas Alliance leader, were "success and freedom, or failure and servitude." At first, the Alliance remained aloof from politics, attempting to improve rural conditions by the cooperative financing and marketing of crops. Alliance "exchanges" would loan money to farmers and sell their produce. But it soon became clear that farmers on their own could not finance this plan, and banks refused to extend loans to the exchanges. The Alliance therefore proposed that the federal government establish warehouses where farmers could store their crops until they were sold. Using the crops as collateral, the government would then issue loans to farmers at low interest rates, thereby ending their dependence on bankers and merchants. Since it would have to be enacted by Congress, the "subtreasury plan," as this proposal was called, led the Alliance into politics.

THE PEOPLE'S PARTY

In the early 1890s, the Alliance evolved into the People's Party (or Populists), the era's greatest political insurgency. The party did not just appeal to farmers. It sought to speak for all the "producing classes" and achieved some of its greatest successes in states like Colorado and Idaho, where it won the support of miners and industrial workers. It attracted veterans of the Knights of Labor by condemning the use of court injunctions and private police forces against strikers. But its major base lay in the cotton and wheat belts of the South and West.

Building on the Farmers' Alliance network of local institutions, the Populists embarked on a remarkable effort of community organization and education. To spread their message they published numerous pamphlets on political and economic questions, established more than 1,000 local newspapers, and sent traveling speakers throughout rural America. Wearing "a huge black sombrero and a black Prince Albert coat," Texas Populist orator "Cyclone" Davis traveled the Great Plains accompanied by the writings of Thomas Jefferson, which he quoted to demonstrate the evils of banks and large corporations. At great gatherings on the western plains, similar in some ways to religious revival meetings, and in small-town southern country stores, one observer wrote, "people commenced to think

A group of Kansas Populists, perhaps on their way to a political gathering, in a photograph from the 1890s.

who had never thought before, and people talked who had seldom spoken. . . . Little by little they commenced to theorize upon their condition."

Here was the last great political expression of the nineteenth-century vision of America as a commonwealth of small producers whose freedom rested on the ownership of productive property and respect for the dignity of labor. "Day by day," declared the *People's Party Paper* of Georgia in 1893, "the power of the individual sinks. Day by day the power of the classes, or the corporations, rises. . . . In all essential respects, the republic of our fathers is dead."

But although the Populists used the familiar language of nineteenth-century radicalism, they were hardly a backward-looking movement. They embraced the modern technologies that made large-scale cooperative enterprise possible—the railroad, the telegraph, and the national market—while looking to the federal government to regulate them in the public interest. They promoted agricultural education and believed farmers should adopt modern scientific methods of cultivation. They believed the federal government could move beyond partisan conflict to operate in a businesslike manner to promote the public good—a vision soon to be associated with the Progressive movement and, many years later, politicians like Jimmy Carter and Barack Obama.

THE POPULIST PLATFORM

The Populist platform of 1892, adopted at the party's Omaha convention, remains a classic document of American reform (see the Appendix for the full text). Written by Ignatius Donnelly, a Minnesota editor and former Radical Republican congressman during Reconstruction, it spoke of a nation "brought to the verge of moral, political, and material ruin" by political corruption and economic inequality. "The fruits of the toil of millions," the platform declared, "are boldly stolen to build up colossal fortunes . . . while their possessors despise the republic and endanger liber-

Tom Watson, the Georgia Populist leader, on the cover of the party's "campaign book" for 1892.

ty." The platform put forth a long list of proposals to restore democracy and economic opportunity, many of which would be adopted during the next half-century: the direct election of U.S. senators, government control of the currency, a graduated income tax, a system of low-cost public financing to enable farmers to market their crops, and recognition of the right of workers to form labor unions. In addition, Populists called for public ownership of the railroads to guarantee farmers inexpensive access to markets for their crops. A generation would pass before a major party offered so sweeping a plan for political action to create the social conditions of freedom.

THE POPULIST COALITION

In some southern states, the Populists made remarkable efforts to unite black and white small farmers on a common political and economic program. The obstacles to such an alliance were immense—not merely the heritage of racism and the political legacy of the Civil War, but the fact that many white Populists were landowning farmers while most blacks were tenants and agricultural laborers. Unwelcome in the southern branches of the Farmers' Alliance, black farmers formed their own organization, the Colored Farmers' Alliance. In 1891, it tried to organize a strike of cotton pickers on plantations in South Carolina, Arkansas, and Texas. The action was violently suppressed by local authorities and landowners, some of them sympathetic to the white Alliance but unwilling to pay higher wages to their own laborers.

In general, southern white Populists' racial attitudes did not differ significantly from those of their non-Populist neighbors. Nonetheless, recognizing the need for allies to break the Democratic Party's stranglehold on power in the South, some white Populists insisted that black and white

In a cartoon from Tom Watson's People's Party Paper, *February 25, 1892, northern and southern Civil War veterans bury their past antagonism and unite in the Populist campaign.*

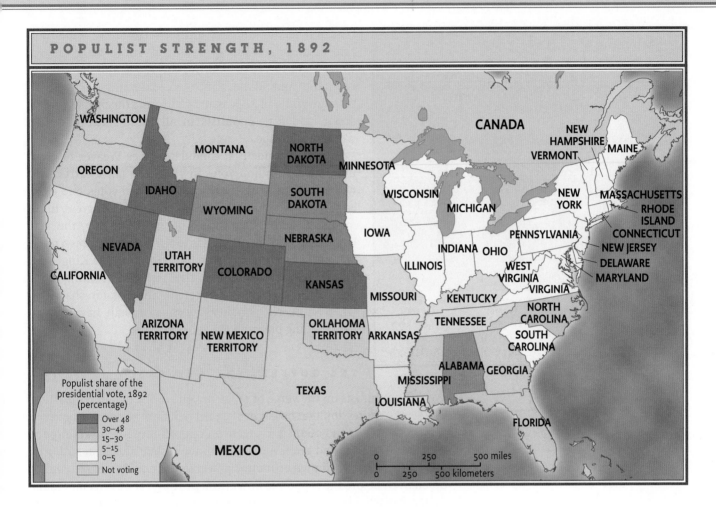

POPULIST STRENGTH, 1892

Populist share of the presidential vote, 1892 (percentage)

- Over 48
- 30–48
- 15–30
- 5–15
- 0–5
- Not voting

farmers shared common grievances and could unite for common goals. Tom Watson, Georgia's leading Populist, worked the hardest to forge a black-white alliance. "You are kept apart," he told interracial audiences, "that you may be separately fleeced of your earnings. . . . This race antagonism perpetuates a monetary system which beggars both." While many blacks refused to abandon the party of Lincoln, others were attracted by the Populist appeal. In 1894, a coalition of white Populists and black Republicans won control of North Carolina, bringing to the state a "second Reconstruction" complete with increased spending on public education and a revival of black officeholding. In most of the South, however, Democrats fended off the Populist challenge by resorting to the tactics they had used to retain power since the 1870s—mobilizing whites with warnings about "Negro supremacy," intimidating black voters, and stuffing ballot boxes on election day.

The Populist movement also engaged the energies of thousands of reform-minded women from farm and labor backgrounds. Some, like Mary Elizabeth Lease, a former homesteader and one of the first female lawyers in Kansas, became prominent organizers, campaigners, and strategists. Lease was famous for her speeches urging farmers to "raise less corn and more hell" (although she apparently never actually uttered those exact words, which would have been considered inappropriate for a woman in public). "We fought England for our liberty," Lease declared,

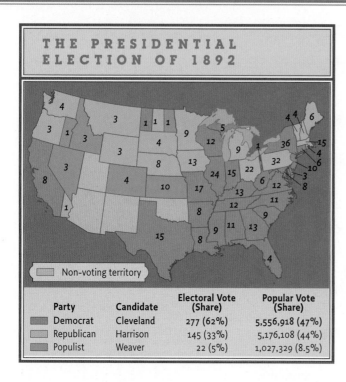

**THE PRESIDENTIAL
ELECTION OF 1892**

Non-voting territory

Party	Candidate	Electoral Vote (Share)	Popular Vote (Share)
Democrat	Cleveland	277 (62%)	5,556,918 (47%)
Republican	Harrison	145 (33%)	5,176,108 (44%)
Populist	Weaver	22 (5%)	1,027,329 (8.5%)

"and put chains on four million blacks. We wiped out slavery and . . . began a system of white wage slavery worse than the first." During the 1890s, referendums in Colorado and Idaho approved extending the vote to women, while in Kansas and California the proposal went down in defeat. Populists in all these states endorsed women's suffrage.

Populist presidential candidate James Weaver received more than 1 million votes in 1892. The party carried five western states, with twenty-two electoral votes, and elected three governors and fifteen members of Congress. In his inaugural address in 1893, Lorenzo Lewelling, the new Populist governor of Kansas, anticipated a phrase made famous seventy years later by Martin Luther King Jr.: "I have a dream. . . . In the beautiful vision of a coming time I behold the abolition of poverty. A time is foreshadowed when . . . liberty, equality, and justice shall have permanent abiding places in the republic."

THE GOVERNMENT AND LABOR

Were the Populists on the verge of replacing one of the two major parties? The severe depression that began in 1893 led to increased conflict between capital and labor and seemed to create an opportunity for expanding the Populist vote. Time and again, employers brought state or federal authority to bear to protect their own economic power or put down threats to public order. Even before the economic downturn, in 1892, the governor of Idaho declared martial law and sent militia units and federal troops into the mining region of Coeur d'Alene to break a strike. In May 1894, the federal government deployed soldiers to disperse Coxey's Army—a band of several hundred unemployed men led by Ohio businessman Jacob Coxey, who marched to Washington demanding economic relief.

Coxey's Army on the march in 1894.

Federal troops pose atop a railroad engine after being sent to Chicago to help suppress the Pullman strike of 1894.

DEBS AND THE PULLMAN STRIKE

Also in 1894, workers in the company-owned town of Pullman, Illinois, where railroad sleeping cars were manufactured, called a strike to protest a reduction in wages. The American Railway Union, whose 150,000 members included both skilled and unskilled railroad laborers, announced that its members would refuse to handle trains with Pullman cars. When the boycott crippled national rail service, President Grover Cleveland's attorney general, Richard Olney (himself on the board of several railroad companies), obtained a federal court injunction ordering the strikers back to work. Federal troops and U.S. marshals soon occupied railroad centers like Chicago and Sacramento. Violent clashes between troops and workers erupted from Maine to California, leaving thirty-four persons dead.

The strike collapsed when the union's leaders, including its charismatic president, Eugene V. Debs, were jailed for contempt of court for violating the judicial order. In the case of *In re Debs*, the Supreme Court unanimously confirmed the sentences and approved the use of injunctions against striking labor unions. On his release from prison in November 1895, more than 100,000 persons greeted Debs at a Chicago railroad depot. Hailing the crowd of well-wishers as "lovers of liberty," Debs charged that concentrated economic power, now aligned with state and national governments, was attempting to "wrest from the weak" their birthright of freedom.

POPULISM AND LABOR

In 1894, Populists made determined efforts to appeal to industrial workers. Populist senators supported the demand of Coxey's Army for federal unemployment relief, and Governor Davis Waite of Colorado, who had edited a labor newspaper before his election, sent the militia to protect striking miners against company police. In the state and congressional elections of that year, as the economic depression deepened, voters by the millions abandoned the Democratic Party of President Cleveland.

In rural areas, the Populist vote increased in 1894. But urban workers did not rally to the Populists, whose core issues—the subtreasury plan and lower mortgage interest rates—had little meaning for them and whose demand for higher prices for farm goods would raise the cost of food and reduce the value of workers' wages. Moreover, the revivalist atmosphere of many Populist gatherings and the biblical cadences of Populist speeches were alien to the largely immigrant and Catholic industrial working class. Urban working-class voters in 1894 instead shifted en masse to the Republicans, who claimed that raising tariff rates (which Democrats had recently reduced) would restore prosperity by protecting manufacturers and industrial workers from the competition of imported goods and cheap foreign labor. In one of the most decisive shifts in congressional power in American history, the Republicans gained 117 seats in the House of Representatives.

BRYAN AND FREE SILVER

In 1896, Democrats and Populists joined to support William Jennings Bryan for the presidency. A thirty-six-year-old congressman from Nebraska, Bryan won the Democratic nomination after delivering to the national convention an electrifying speech that crystallized the farmers' pride and grievances. "Burn down your cities and leave our farms," Bryan proclaimed, "and your cities will spring up again as if by magic; but destroy our farms and grass will grow in the streets of every city in the country." Bryan called for the "free coinage" of silver—the unrestricted minting of silver money. In language ringing with biblical imagery, Bryan condemned the gold standard: "You shall not press down upon the brow of labor this crown of thorns. You shall not crucify mankind upon a cross of gold."

At various points in the nineteenth century, from debates over "hard" versus "soft" money in the Jacksonian era to the greenback movement after the Civil War, the "money question" had played a central role in American politics. Bryan's demand for "free silver" was the latest expression of the view that increasing the amount of currency in circulation would raise the prices farmers received for their crops and make it easier to pay off their debts. His nomination wrested control of the Democratic Party from long-dominant leaders like President Grover Cleveland, who were closely tied to eastern businessmen.

There was more to Bryan's appeal, however, than simply free silver. A devoutly religious man, he was strongly influenced by the Social Gospel movement (discussed in the previous chapter) and tried to apply the teachings of Jesus Christ to uplifting the "little people" of the United States. He championed a vision of the government helping ordinary Americans that anticipated provisions of the New Deal of the 1930s, including a progressive income tax, banking regulation, and the right of workers to form unions.

Many Populists were initially cool to Bryan's campaign. Their party had been defrauded time and again by Democrats in the South. Veteran Populists feared that their broad program was in danger of being reduced to "free silver." But realizing that they could not secure victory alone, the party's leaders endorsed Bryan's candidacy. Bryan broke with tradition and embarked on a nationwide speaking tour, seeking to rally farmers and workers to his cause.

A cartoon from the magazine Judge, *September 14, 1896, condemns William Jennings Bryan and his "cross of gold" speech for defiling the symbols of Christianity. Bryan tramples on the Bible while holding his golden cross; a vandalized church is visible in the background.*

A Republican cartoon, entitled Dubious, *from the 1896 campaign, suggests that Bryan's platform would reduce the United States to the status of poor countries that utilized silver money.*

THE CAMPAIGN OF 1896

Republicans met the silverite challenge head on, insisting that gold was the only "honest" currency. Abandoning the gold standard, they insisted, would destroy business confidence and prevent recovery from the depression by making creditors unwilling to extend loans, since they could not be certain of the value of the money in which they would be repaid. The party nominated for president Ohio governor William McKinley, who as a congressman in 1890 had shepherded to passage the strongly protectionist McKinley Tariff.

The election of 1896 is sometimes called the first modern presidential campaign because of the amount of money spent by the Republicans and the efficiency of their national organization. Eastern bankers and industrialists, thoroughly alarmed by Bryan's call for monetary inflation and his fiery speeches denouncing corporate arrogance, poured millions of dollars into Republican coffers. (McKinley's campaign raised some $10 million; Bryan's around $300,000.) While McKinley remained at his Ohio home, where he addressed crowds of supporters from his front porch, his political manager Mark Hanna created a powerful national political machine that flooded the country with pamphlets, posters, and campaign buttons.

The results revealed a nation as divided along regional lines as in 1860. Bryan carried the South and West and received 6.5 million votes. McKinley swept the more populous industrial states of the Northeast and Midwest, attracting 7.1 million. The Republican candidate's electoral margin was even greater: 271 to 176. The era's bitter labor strife did not carry over into the electoral arena; indeed, party politics seemed to mute class conflict rather than to reinforce it. Industrial America, from financiers

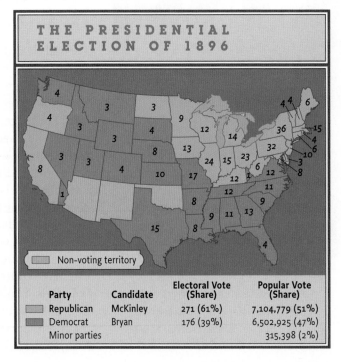

THE PRESIDENTIAL ELECTION OF 1896

| Non-voting territory |

Party	Candidate	Electoral Vote (Share)	Popular Vote (Share)
Republican	McKinley	271 (61%)	7,104,779 (51%)
Democrat	Bryan	176 (39%)	6,502,925 (47%)
Minor parties			315,398 (2%)

and managers to workers, now voted solidly Republican, a loyalty reinforced when prosperity returned after 1897.

According to some later critics, the popular children's classic *The Wonderful Wizard of Oz*, published by L. Frank Baum in 1900, offered a commentary on the election of 1896 and its aftermath. In this interpretation, the Emerald City (where everything is colored green, for money) represents Washington, D.C., and the Wizard of Oz, who remains invisible in his palace and rules by illusion, is President McKinley. The only way to get to the city is via a Yellow Brick Road (the color of gold). The Wicked Witches of the East and West represent oppressive industrialists and mine owners. In the much-beloved film version made in the 1930s, Dorothy, the all-American girl from the heartland state of Kansas, wears ruby slippers. But in the book her shoes are silver, supposedly representing the money preferred by ordinary people.

Whatever Baum's symbolism, one thing was clear. McKinley's victory shattered the political stalemate that had persisted since 1876 and created one of the most enduring political majorities in American history. During McKinley's presidency, Republicans placed their stamp on economic policy by passing the Dingley Tariff of 1897, raising rates to the highest level in history, and the Gold Standard Act of 1900. Not until 1932, in the midst of another economic depression, would the Democrats become the nation's majority party. The election of 1896 also proved to be the last presidential election with extremely high voter turnout (in some states, over 90 percent of those eligible). From then on, with the South solidly Democratic and the North overwhelmingly Republican, few states witnessed vigorous two-party campaigns. Voter participation began a downhill trend, although it rose again from the mid-1930s through the 1960s. Today, only around half the electorate casts ballots.

THE SEGREGATED SOUTH

THE REDEEMERS IN POWER

The failure of Populism in the South opened the door for the full imposition of a new racial order. The coalition of merchants, planters, and business entrepreneurs who dominated the region's politics after 1877 called themselves Redeemers, since they claimed to have redeemed the region from the alleged horrors of misgovernment and "black rule." On achieving power, they had moved to undo as much as possible of Reconstruction. State budgets were slashed, taxes, especially on landed property, reduced, and public facilities like hospitals and asylums closed. Hardest hit were the new public school systems. Louisiana spent so little on education that it became the only state in the Union in which the percentage of whites unable to read and write actually increased between 1880 and 1900. Black schools, however, suffered the most, as the gap between expenditures for black and white pupils widened steadily. "What I want here is Negroes who can make cotton," declared one planter, "and they don't need education to help them make cotton."

New laws authorized the arrest of virtually any person without employment and greatly increased the penalties for petty crimes. "They send [a man] to the penitentiary if he steals a chicken," complained a former slave

A group of Florida convict laborers. Southern states notoriously used convicts for public labor, or leased them out to work in dire conditions for private employers.

in North Carolina. As the South's prison population rose, the renting out of convicts became a profitable business. Every southern state placed at least a portion of its convicted criminals, the majority of them blacks imprisoned for minor offenses, in the hands of private businessmen. Railroads, mines, and lumber companies competed for this new form of cheap, involuntary labor. Conditions in labor camps were often barbaric, with disease rife and the death rates high. "One dies, get another" was the motto of the system's architects. The Knights of Labor made convict labor a major issue in the South. In 1892, miners in Tennessee burned the stockade where convict workers were housed and shipped them out of the region. Tennessee abolished the convict lease system three years later but replaced it with a state-owned coal mine using prison labor that reaped handsome profits for decades.

Coal miners, in a photograph by Lewis Hine. Mining was one occupation in which blacks and whites often worked side by side.

THE FAILURE OF THE NEW SOUTH DREAM

During the 1880s, Atlanta editor Henry Grady tirelessly promoted the promise of a New South, an era of prosperity based on industrial expansion and agricultural diversification. In fact, while planters, merchants, and industrialists prospered, the region as a whole sank deeper and deeper into poverty. Some industry did develop, including mining in the Appalachians, textile production in the Carolinas and Georgia, and furniture and cigarette manufacturing in certain southern cities. The new upcountry cotton factories offered jobs to entire families of poor whites from the surrounding countryside. But since the main attractions for investors were the South's low wages and taxes and the availability of convict labor, these enterprises made little contribution to regional economic development. With the exception of Birmingham, Alabama, which by 1900 had developed into an important center for the manufacture of iron and steel, southern cities were mainly export centers for cotton, tobacco, and rice, with little industry or skilled labor. Overall, the region remained dependent on the North for capital and manufactured goods. In 1900, southern per capita income amounted to only 60 percent of the national average. As late as the 1930s, President Franklin D. Roosevelt would declare the South the nation's "number one" economic problem.

BLACK LIFE IN THE SOUTH

As the most disadvantaged rural southerners, black farmers suffered the most from the region's condition. In the Upper South, economic development offered some opportunities—mines, iron furnaces, and tobacco factories employed black laborers, and a good number of black farmers managed to acquire land. In the rice kingdom of coastal South Carolina and Georgia, planters found themselves unable to acquire the capital necessary to repair irrigation systems and machinery destroyed by the war. By the turn of the century, most of the great plantations had fallen to pieces, and many blacks

Black women washing laundry, one of the few jobs open to them in the New South.

acquired land and took up self-sufficient farming. In most of the Deep South, however, African-Americans owned a smaller percentage of the land in 1900 than they had at the end of Reconstruction.

In southern cities, the network of institutions created after the Civil War—schools and colleges, churches, businesses, women's clubs, and the like—served as the foundation for increasingly diverse black urban communities. They supported the growth of a black middle class, mostly professionals like teachers and physicians, or businessmen like undertakers and shopkeepers serving the needs of black customers. But the labor market was rigidly divided along racial lines. Black men were excluded from supervisory positions in factories and workshops and white-collar jobs such as clerks in offices. A higher percentage of black women than white worked for wages, but mainly as domestic servants. They could not find employment among the growing numbers of secretaries, typists, and department store clerks.

Even after the demise of the Knights of Labor, some local unions, mainly of dockworkers and mine laborers, had significant numbers of black members. But in most occupations, the few unions that existed in the South excluded blacks, forming yet another barrier to their economic advancement.

THE KANSAS EXODUS

Overall, one historian has written, the New South was "a miserable landscape dotted only by a few rich enclaves that cast little or no light upon the poverty surrounding them." Trapped at the bottom of a stagnant economy, some blacks sought a way out through emigration from the South. In 1879 and 1880, an estimated 40,000 to 60,000 African-Americans migrated to Kansas, seeking political equality, freedom from violence, access to education, and economic opportunity. The name participants gave to this migration—the Exodus, derived from the biblical account of the Jews

KANSAS STATE
HISTORICAL SOCIETY.

Ho for Kansas!

Brethren, Friends, & Fellow Citizens:
I feel thankful to inform you that the

REAL ESTATE
AND
Homestead Association,
Will Leave Here the

15th of April, 1878,

In pursuit of Homes in the Southwestern Lands of America, at Transportation Rates, cheaper than ever was known before.

For full information inquire of
Benj. Singleton, better known as old Pap,
NO. 5 NORTH FRONT STREET.
Beware of Speculators and Adventurers, as it is a dangerous thing to fall in their hands.
Nashville, Tenn., March 18, 1878.

An 1878 poster seeking recruits for the Kansas Exodus.

Benjamin "Pap" Singleton (on the left), who helped to organize the "Exodus" of 1879, superimposed on a photograph of a boat carrying African-Americans emigrating from the South to Kansas.

escaping slavery in Egypt—indicated that its roots lay in deep longings for the substance of freedom. Those promoting the Exodus, including former fugitive slave Benjamin "Pap" Singleton, the organizer of a real estate company, distributed flyers and lithographs picturing Kansas as an idyllic land of rural plenty. Lacking the capital to take up farming, however, most black migrants ended up as unskilled laborers in towns and cities. But few chose to return to the South. In the words of one minister active in the movement, "We had rather suffer and be free."

Despite deteriorating prospects in the South, most African-Americans had little alternative but to stay in the region. The real expansion of job opportunities was taking place in northern cities. But most northern employers refused to offer jobs to blacks in the expanding industrial economy, preferring to hire white migrants from rural areas and immigrants from Europe. Not until the outbreak of World War I in Europe in 1914 cut off immigration did northern employers open industrial jobs to blacks, setting in motion the Great Migration discussed in Chapter 19. Until then, the vast majority of African-Americans remained in the South.

THE DECLINE OF BLACK POLITICS

Neither black voting nor black officeholding came to an abrupt end in 1877. Blacks continued to cast ballots in large numbers, although Democrats solidified their control of state and local affairs by redrawing district lines and substituting appointive for elective officials in counties with black majorities. A few blacks even served in Congress in the 1880s and 1890s. Nonetheless, political opportunities became more and more restricted. Not until the 1990s would the number of black legislators in the South approach the level seen during Reconstruction.

For black men of talent and ambition, other avenues—business, the law, the church—increasingly seemed to offer greater opportunities for personal advancement and community service than politics. The banner of political leadership passed to black women activists. The National Association of Colored Women, founded in 1896, brought together local and regional women's clubs to press for both women's rights and racial uplift. Most female activists emerged from the small urban black middle class and preached the necessity of "respectable" behavior as part and parcel of the struggle for equal rights. They aided poor families, offered lessons in home life and childrearing, and battled gambling and drinking in black communities. Some poor blacks resented middle-class efforts to instruct them in proper behavior. But by insisting on the right of black women to be considered as "respectable" as their white counterparts, the women reformers challenged the racial ideology that consigned all blacks to the status of degraded second-class citizens.

For nearly a generation after the end of Reconstruction, despite fraud and violence, black southerners continued to cast ballots. In some states, the Republican Party remained competitive. In Virginia, a coalition of mostly black Republicans and anti-Redeemer Democrats formed an alliance known as the Readjuster movement (the name derived from their plan to scale back, or "readjust," the state debt). They governed the state between 1879 and 1883. Tennessee and Arkansas also witnessed the formation of biracial political coalitions that challenged Democratic Party rule. Despite the limits of the Populists' interracial alliance, the threat of a biracial political insurgency frightened the ruling Democrats and contributed greatly to the disenfranchisement movement. In North Carolina, for example, the end of the Populist-Republican coalition government in 1898—accomplished by a violent campaign that culminated in a riot in Wilmington in which scores of blacks were killed—was quickly followed by the elimination of black voting.

THE ELIMINATION OF BLACK VOTING

Between 1890 and 1906, every southern state enacted laws or constitutional provisions meant to eliminate the black vote. Since the Fifteenth Amendment prohibited the use of race as a qualification for the suffrage, how were such measures even possible? Southern legislatures drafted laws that on paper appeared color-blind, but that were actually designed to end black voting. The most popular devices were the poll tax (a fee that each citizen had to pay in order to retain the right to vote), literacy tests, and the requirement that a prospective voter demonstrate to election officials an "understanding" of the state constitution. Six southern states also adopted a "grandfather clause," exempting from the new requirements descendants of persons eligible to vote before the Civil War (when only whites, of course, could cast ballots in the South). The racial intent of the grandfather clause was so clear that the Supreme Court in 1915 invalidated such laws for violating the Fifteenth Amendment. The other methods of limiting black voting, however, remained on the books.

Some white leaders presented disenfranchisement as a "good government" measure—a means of purifying politics by ending the fraud, violence, and manipulation of voting returns regularly used against Republicans and Populists. But ultimately, as a Charleston newspaper declared, the aim was to make clear that the white South "does not desire or intend ever to include black men among its citizens." Democrats persistently raised the threat of "Negro domination" to justify the denial of the right to vote. Although election officials often allowed whites who did not meet the new qualifications to register, numerous poor and illiterate whites also lost the right to vote, a result welcomed by many planters and urban reformers. Louisiana, for example, reduced the number of blacks registered to vote from 130,000 in 1894 to 1,342 a decade later. But 80,000 white voters also lost the right. Disenfranchisement led directly to the rise of a generation of southern "demagogues," who mobilized white voters by extreme appeals to racism. Tom Watson, who as noted before had tried to forge an interracial Populist coalition in the 1890s, reemerged early in the twentieth century as a power in Georgia public life through vicious speeches whipping up prejudice against blacks, Jews, and Catholics.

As late as 1940, only 3 percent of adult black southerners were registered to vote. The elimination of black and many white voters, which reversed the nineteenth-century trend toward more inclusive suffrage, could not have been accomplished without the approval of the North. In 1891, the Senate defeated a proposal for federal protection of black voting rights in the South. Apart from the grandfather clause, the Supreme Court gave its approval to disenfranchisement laws. According to the Fourteenth Amendment, any state that deprived male citizens of the franchise was supposed to lose part of its representation in Congress. But like much of the Constitution, this provision was consistently violated so far as African-Americans were concerned. As a result, southern congressmen wielded far greater power on the national scene than their tiny electorates warranted. As for blacks, for decades thereafter, they would regard "the loss of suffrage as being the loss of freedom."

THE LAW OF SEGREGATION

Along with disenfranchisement, the 1890s saw the widespread imposition of segregation in the South. Laws and local customs requiring the separation of the races had numerous precedents. They had existed in many parts

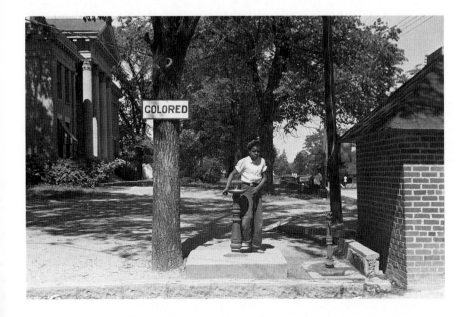

African-Americans of all ages were required to abide by segregation laws. Here, in a twentieth-century photograph, a youth is about to drink from a "colored" water fountain.

of the pre–Civil War North. Southern schools and many other institutions had been segregated during Reconstruction. In the 1880s, however, southern race relations remained unsettled. Some railroads, theaters, and hotels admitted blacks and whites on an equal basis while others separated them by race or excluded blacks altogether.

In 1883, in the *Civil Rights Cases*, the Supreme Court invalidated the Civil Rights Act of 1875, which had outlawed racial discrimination by hotels, theaters, railroads, and other public facilities. The Fourteenth Amendment, the Court insisted, prohibited unequal treatment by state authorities, not private businesses. In 1896, in the landmark decision in *Plessy v. Ferguson*, the Court gave its approval to state laws requiring separate facilities for blacks and whites. The case arose in Louisiana, where the legislature had required railroad companies to maintain a separate car or section for black passengers. A Citizens Committee of black residents of New Orleans came together to challenge the law. To create a test case, Homer Plessy, a light-skinned African-American, refused a conductor's order to move to the "colored only" part of his railroad car and was arrested.

To argue the case before the Supreme Court, the Citizens Committee hired Albion W. Tourgée, who as a judge in North Carolina during Reconstruction had waged a courageous battle against the Ku Klux Klan. "Citizenship is national and knows no color," he insisted, and racial segregation violated the Fourteenth Amendment's guarantee of equal protection before the law. But in an 8-1 decision, the Court upheld the Louisiana law, arguing that segregated facilities did not discriminate so long as they were "separate but equal." The lone dissenter, John Marshall Harlan, reprimanded the majority with an oft-quoted comment: "Our constitution is color-blind." Segregation, he insisted, sprang from whites' conviction that they were the "dominant race" (a phrase used by the Court's majority), and it violated the principle of equal liberty. To Harlan, freedom for the former slaves meant the right to participate fully and equally in American society.

SEGREGATION AND WHITE DOMINATION

As Harlan predicted, states reacted to the *Plessy* decision by passing laws mandating racial segregation in every aspect of southern life, from schools to hospitals, waiting rooms, toilets, and cemeteries. Some states forbade taxi drivers to carry members of different races at the same time. Despite the "thin disguise" (Harlan's phrase) of equality required by the Court's "separate but equal" doctrine, facilities for blacks were either nonexistent or markedly inferior. In 1900, no public high school for blacks existed in the entire South. Black elementary schools, one observer reported, occupied buildings "as bad as stables."

More than a form of racial separation, segregation was one part of an all-encompassing system of white domination, in which each component—disenfranchisement, unequal economic status, inferior education—reinforced the others. The point was not so much to keep the races apart as to ensure that when they came into contact with each other, whether in politics, labor relations, or social life, whites held the upper hand. For example, many blacks could be found in "whites-only" railroad cars. But they entered as servants and nurses, not as paying customers entitled to equal treatment.

An elaborate social etiquette developed, with proper behavior differentiated by race. One sociologist who studied the turn-of-the-century South reported that in places of business, blacks had to stand back and wait until whites had been served. They could not raise their voices or in other ways act assertively in the presence of whites, and they had to "give way" on the streets. In shops, whites but not blacks were allowed to try on clothing.

Segregation affected other groups as well as blacks. In some parts of Mississippi where Chinese laborers had been brought in to work the fields after the Civil War, three separate school systems—white, black, and Chinese—were established. In California, black, Hispanic, and American Indian children were frequently educated alongside whites, but state law required separate schools for those of "mongolian or Chinese descent." In Texas and California, although Mexicans were legally considered "white," they found themselves barred from many restaurants, places of entertainment, and other public facilities.

THE RISE OF LYNCHING

Those blacks who sought to challenge the system, or who refused to accept the demeaning behavior that was a daily feature of southern life, faced not only overwhelming political and legal power but also the threat of violent reprisal. In every year between 1883 and 1905, more than fifty persons, the vast majority of them black men, were lynched in the South—that is, murdered by a mob. Lynching continued well into the twentieth century. By mid-century, the total number of victims since 1880 had reached nearly 5,000. Some lynchings occurred secretly at night; others were advertised

Part of the crowd of 10,000 that watched the 1893 lynching of Henry Smith in Paris, Texas. Smith was accused of raping and murdering a four-year-old girl. The word "justice" was painted on the platform.

Table 17.1 STATES WITH OVER 200 LYNCHINGS, 1889-1918

State	Number of Lynchings
Georgia	386
Mississippi	373
Texas	335
Louisiana	313
Alabama	276
Arkansas	214

in advance and attracted large crowds of onlookers. Mobs engaged in activities that shocked the civilized world. In 1899, Sam Hose, a plantation laborer who killed his employer in self-defense, was brutally murdered near Newman, Georgia, before 2,000 onlookers, some of whom arrived on a special excursion train from Atlanta. A crowd including young children watched as his executioners cut off Hose's ears, fingers, and genitals, burned him alive, and then fought over pieces of his bones as souvenirs. Law enforcement authorities made no effort to prevent the lynching or to bring those who committed the crime to justice.

Like many victims of lynchings, Hose was accused after his death of having raped a white woman. Many white southerners considered preserving the purity of white womanhood a justification for extralegal vengeance. Yet in nearly all cases, as activist Ida B. Wells argued in a newspaper editorial after a Memphis lynching in 1892, the charge of rape was a "bare lie." Born a slave in Mississippi in 1862, Wells had become a schoolteacher and editor. Her essay condemning the lynching of three black men in Memphis led a mob to destroy her newspaper, the *Memphis Free Press*, while she was out of the city. Wells moved to the North, where she became the nation's leading antilynching crusader. She bluntly insisted that given the conditions of southern blacks, the United States had no right to call itself the "land of the free."

Although many countries have witnessed outbreaks of violence against minority racial, ethnic, or religious groups, widespread lynching of individuals over so long a period was a phenomenon unknown elsewhere. Canada, for example, has experienced only one lynching in its history—in 1884, when a mob from the United States crossed the border into British Columbia to lynch an Indian teenager who had fled after being accused of murder.

Years later, black writer Blyden Jackson recalled growing up in early-twentieth-century Louisville, Kentucky, a city in many ways typical of the New South. It was a divided society. There was the world "where white folks lived . . . the Louisville of the downtown hotels, the lower floors of the big movie houses . . . the inner sanctums of offices where I could go only as a humble client or a menial custodian." Then there was the black world, "the homes, the people, the churches, and the schools," where "everything was black." "I knew," Jackson later recalled, "that there were two Louisvilles and . . . two Americas."

THE POLITICS OF MEMORY

As the white North and South moved toward reconciliation in the 1880s and 1890s, one cost was the abandonment of the dream of racial equality spawned by the Civil War and written into the laws and Constitution during Reconstruction. In popular literature and memoirs by participants, at veterans' reunions and in public memorials, the Civil War came to be remembered as a tragic family quarrel among white Americans in which blacks had played no significant part. It was a war of "brother against brother" in which both sides fought gallantly for noble causes—local rights on the part of the South, preservation of the Union for the North. Slavery increasingly came to be viewed as a minor issue, not the war's fundamental cause, and Reconstruction as a regrettable period of "Negro rule" when former slaves had power thrust upon them by a vindictive North. This outlook gave legitimacy to southern efforts to eliminate black voting, lest the region once again suffer the alleged "horrors" of Reconstruction.

Southern governments erected monuments to the Lost Cause, school history textbooks emphasized happy slaves and the evils of Reconstruction, and the role of black soldiers in winning the war was all but forgotten. In fact, when a group of black veterans attempted to participate in a Florida ceremony commemorating the fiftieth anniversary of the outbreak of the Civil War in 1911, a white mob tore the military insignias off their jackets and drove them away.

REDRAWING THE BOUNDARIES

The effective nullification of the laws and amendments of Reconstruction and the reduction of blacks to the position of second-class citizens reflected nationwide patterns of thought and policy. As the nineteenth century drew to a close, American society seemed to be fracturing along lines of both class and race. The result, commented economist Simon Patten, was a widespread obsession with redrawing the boundary of freedom by identifying and excluding those unworthy of the blessings of liberty. "The South," he wrote, "has its negro, the city has its slums. . . . The friends of American institutions fear the ignorant immigrant, and the workingman dislikes the Chinese." As Patten suggested, many Americans embraced a more and more restricted definition of nationhood. The new exclusiveness was evident in the pages of popular periodicals, filled with derogatory imagery depicting blacks and other "lesser" groups as little more than savages and criminals incapable of partaking in American freedom.

A cartoon from the magazine Judge *illustrates anti-immigrant sentiment. A tide of newcomers representing the criminal element of other countries washes up on American shores, to the consternation of Uncle Sam.*

THE HIGH TIDE OF IMMIGRATION—A NATIONAL MENACE.

THE NEW IMMIGRATION AND THE NEW NATIVISM

The 1890s witnessed a major shift in the sources of immigration to the United States. Despite the prolonged depression, 3.5 million newcomers entered the United States during the decade, seeking jobs in the industrial centers of the North and Midwest. Over half arrived not from Ireland, England, Germany, and Scandinavia, the traditional sources of immigration, but from southern and eastern Europe, especially Italy and the Russian and Austro-Hungarian empires. The "new immigrants" were widely described by native-born Americans as members of distinct "races," whose lower level of civilization explained everything from their willingness to work for substandard wages to their supposed inborn tendency toward criminal behavior. They were "beaten men from beaten races," wrote economist Francis Amasa Walker, representing "the worst failures in the struggle for existence." American cities, said an Ohio newspaper, were being overrun by foreigners who "have no true appreciation of the meaning of liberty" and therefore posed a danger to democratic government.

Founded in 1894 by a group of Boston professionals, the Immigration Restriction League called for reducing immigration by barring the illiterate from entering the United States. Such a measure was adopted by Congress early in 1897 but was vetoed by President Cleveland. Like the South, northern and western states experimented with ways to eliminate undesirable voters. Nearly all the states during the 1890s adopted the secret or "Australian" ballot, meant both to protect voters' privacy and to limit the participation of illiterates (who could no longer receive help from party officials at polling places). Several states ended the nineteenth-century practice of allowing immigrants to vote before becoming citizens and adopted stringent new residency and literacy requirements. None of these measures approached the scope of black disenfranchisement in the South or the continued denial of voting rights to women. But suffrage throughout the country was increasingly becoming a privilege, not a right.

CHINESE EXCLUSION AND CHINESE RIGHTS

The boundaries of nationhood, expanded so dramatically in the aftermath of the Civil War, slowly contracted. Leaders of both parties expressed vicious opinions regarding immigrants from China—they were "odious, abominable, dangerous, revolting," declared Republican leader James G. Blaine. Between 1850 and 1870, nearly all Chinese immigrants had been unattached men, brought in by labor contractors to work in western gold fields, railroad construction, and factories. In the early 1870s, entire Chinese families began to immigrate, leading Congress in 1875 to exclude Chinese women from entering the country. California congressman Horace Page, the bill's author, insisted that it was intended to preserve the health of white citizens by barring Chinese prostitutes. But immigration authorities enforced the Page law so as to keep out as well the wives and daughters of arriving men and of those already in the country.

Beginning in 1882, Congress temporarily excluded immigrants from China from entering the country altogether. Although non-whites had long been barred from becoming naturalized citizens, this was the first

Chinese agricultural laborers in southern California around 1880.

Result of an anti-Chinese riot in Seattle, Washington.

time that race had been used to exclude an entire group of people from entering the United States. Congress renewed the restriction ten years later and made it permanent in 1902.

At the time of exclusion, 105,000 persons of Chinese descent lived in the United States. Nearly all of them resided on the West Coast, where they suffered intense discrimination and periodic mob violence. In the late-nineteenth-century West, thousands of Chinese immigrants were expelled from towns and mining camps, and mobs assaulted Chinese residences and businesses. Drawing on the legislation of the Reconstruction era, Chinese victims sued local governments for redress when their rights were violated and petitioned Congress for indemnity. Their demands for equal rights forced the state and federal courts to define the reach of the Fourteenth Amendment. For example, between 1871 and 1885, San Francisco provided no public education for Chinese children. In 1885, the California Supreme Court, in *Tape v. Hurley*, ordered the city to admit Chinese students to public schools. The state legislature responded by passing a law authorizing segregated education, and the city established a school for Chinese. But Joseph and Mary Tape, who had lived in the United States since the 1860s, insisted that their daughter be allowed to attend her neighborhood school like other children. "Is it a disgrace to be born a Chinese?" Mary Tape wrote. "Didn't God make us all!" But her protest failed. Not until 1947 did California repeal the law authorizing separate schools for the Chinese.

The U.S. Supreme Court also considered the status of Chinese-Americans. In *Yick Wo v. Hopkins* (1886), the Court unanimously ordered San Francisco to grant licenses to Chinese-operated laundries, which the city government had refused to do. To deny a person the opportunity to earn a living, the Court declared, was "intolerable in any country where freedom prevails." Twelve years later, in *United States v. Wong Kim Ark*, the Court ruled that the

Booker T. Washington, advocate of industrial education and economic self-help.

Fourteenth Amendment awarded citizenship to children of Chinese immigrants born on American soil.

Yet the Justices also affirmed the right of Congress to set racial restrictions on immigration. And in its decision in *Fong Yue Ting* (1893), the Court authorized the federal government to expel Chinese aliens without due process of law. In his dissent, Justice David J. Brewer acknowledged that the power was now directed against a people many Americans found "obnoxious." But "who shall say," he continued, "it will not be exercised tomorrow against other classes and other people?" Brewer proved to be an accurate prophet. In 1904, the Court cited *Fong Yue Ting* in upholding a law barring anarchists from entering the United States, demonstrating how restrictions on the rights of one group can become a precedent for infringing on the rights of others.

Exclusion profoundly shaped the experience of Chinese-Americans, long stigmatizing them as incapable of assimilation and justifying their isolation from mainstream society. Congress for the first time also barred groups of whites from entering the country, beginning in 1875 with prostitutes and convicted felons, and in 1882 adding "lunatics" and those likely to become a "public charge." "Are we still a [place of refuge] for the oppressed of all nations?" wondered James B. Weaver, the Populist candidate for president in 1892.

THE EMERGENCE OF BOOKER T. WASHINGTON

The social movements that had helped to expand the nineteenth-century boundaries of freedom now redefined their objectives so that they might be realized within the new economic and intellectual framework. Prominent black leaders, for example, took to emphasizing economic self-help and individual advancement into the middle class as an alternative to political agitation.

Symbolizing the change was the juxtaposition, in 1895, of the death of Frederick Douglass with Booker T. Washington's widely praised speech at the Atlanta Cotton Exposition that urged blacks to adjust to segregation and abandon agitation for civil and political rights. Born a slave in 1856, Washington had studied as a young man at Hampton Institute, Virginia. He adopted the outlook of Hampton's founder, General Samuel Armstrong, who emphasized that obtaining farms or skilled jobs was far more important to African-Americans emerging from slavery than the rights of citizenship. Washington put this view into practice when he became head of Tuskegee Institute in Alabama, a center for vocational education (education focused on training for a job rather than broad learning).

In his Atlanta speech, Washington repudiated the abolitionist tradition that stressed ceaseless agitation for full equality. He urged blacks not to try to combat segregation: "In all the things that are purely social we can be as separate as the fingers, yet one as the hand in all things essential to mutual progress." Washington advised his people to seek the assistance of white employers who, in a land racked by labor turmoil, would prefer a docile, dependable black labor force to unionized whites. Washington's ascendancy rested in large part on his success in channeling aid from wealthy northern whites to Tuskegee and to black politicians and newspapers who backed his program. But his support in the black community also arose from a widespread sense that in the world of the late nineteenth century, frontal assaults on white power were impossible and that blacks should concentrate on building up their segregated communities.

THE RISE OF THE AFL

Within the labor movement, the demise of the Knights of Labor and the ascendancy of the American Federation of Labor (AFL) during the 1890s reflected a similar shift away from a broadly reformist past to more limited goals. As the Homestead and Pullman strikes demonstrated, direct confrontations with the large corporations were likely to prove suicidal. Unions, declared Samuel Gompers, the AFL's founder and longtime president, should not seek economic independence, pursue the Knights' utopian dream of creating a "cooperative commonwealth," or form independent parties with the aim of achieving power in government. Rather, the labor movement should devote itself to negotiating with employers for higher wages and better working conditions for its members. Like Washington, Gompers spoke the language of the era's business culture. Indeed, the AFL policies he pioneered were known as "business unionism." Gompers embraced the idea of "freedom of contract," shrewdly turning it into an argument against interference by judges with workers' right to organize unions.

During the 1890s, union membership rebounded from its decline in the late 1880s. But at the same time, the labor movement became less and less inclusive. Abandoning the Knights' ideal of labor solidarity, the AFL restricted membership to skilled workers—a small minority of the labor force—effectively excluding the vast majority of unskilled workers and, therefore, nearly all blacks, women, and new European immigrants. AFL membership centered on sectors of the economy like printing and building construction that were dominated by small competitive businesses with workers who frequently were united by craft skill and ethnic background. AFL unions had little presence in basic industries like steel and rubber, or in the large-scale factories that now dominated the economy.

THE WOMEN'S ERA

Changes in the women's movement reflected the same combination of expanding activities and narrowing boundaries. The 1890s launched what would later be called the "women's era"—three decades during which women, although still denied the vote, enjoyed larger opportunities than in the past for economic independence and played a greater and greater role in public life. By now, nearly every state had adopted laws giving married women control over their own wages and property and the right to sign separate contracts and make separate wills. Nearly 5 million women worked for wages in 1900. Although most were young, unmarried, and concentrated in traditional jobs such as domestic service and the garment industry, a generation of college-educated women was beginning to take its place in better-paying clerical and professional positions.

Through a network of women's clubs, temperance associations, and social reform organizations, women exerted a growing influence on public affairs. Founded in 1874, the Women's Christian Temperance Union (WCTU) grew to become the era's largest female organization, with a

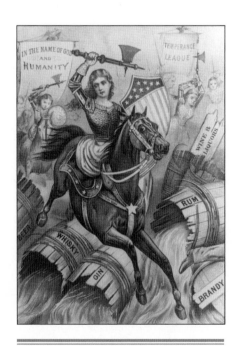

Woman's Holy War, a lithograph from *1874, the year the Women's Christian Temperance Union was founded, portrays an advocate of prohibition as an armed crusader against hard liquor.*

A drawing for the 1896 meeting of the National American Woman Suffrage Association depicts Elizabeth Cady Stanton (with the Woman's Bible, which she wrote, on her lap) and Susan B. Anthony seated on either side of George Washington. They, in turn, are flanked by Utah and Wyoming, which as territories had been the first parts of the United States to give women the right to vote. Although the image might lead viewers to assume that Stanton and Anthony had joined Washington in heaven, they were both still alive in 1896.

membership by 1890 of 150,000. Under the banner of Home Protection, it moved from demanding the prohibition of alcoholic beverages (blamed for leading men to squander their wages on drink and treat their wives abusively) to a comprehensive program of economic and political reform, including the right to vote. Women, insisted Frances Willard, the group's president, must abandon the idea that "weakness" and dependence were their nature and join assertively in movements to change society. "A wider freedom is coming to the women of America," she declared in an 1895 speech to male and female strikers in a Massachusetts shoe factory. "Too long has it been held that woman has no right to enter these movements. So much for the movements. Politics is the place for woman."

At the same time, the center of gravity of feminism shifted toward an outlook more in keeping with prevailing racial and ethnic norms. The earlier "feminism of equal rights," which claimed the ballot as part of a larger transformation of women's status, was never fully repudiated. The movement continued to argue for women's equality in employment, education, and politics. But with increasing frequency, the native-born, middle-class women who dominated the suffrage movement claimed the vote as educated members of a "superior race."

A new generation of suffrage leaders suggested that educational and other voting qualifications did not conflict with the movement's aims, so long as they applied equally to men and women. Immigrants and former slaves had been enfranchised with "ill-advised haste," declared Carrie Chapman Catt, president of the National American Woman Suffrage Association (created in 1890 to reunite the rival suffrage organizations formed after the Civil War). Indeed, Catt suggested, extending the vote to native-born white women would help to counteract the growing power of the "ignorant foreign vote" in the North and the dangerous potential for a second Reconstruction in the South. Elitism within the movement was reinforced when many advocates of suffrage blamed the "slum vote" for the defeat of a women's suffrage referendum in California. In 1895, the same year that Booker T. Washington delivered his Atlanta address, the National American Woman Suffrage Association held its annual convention in that segregated city. Like other American institutions, the organized movement for women's suffrage had made its peace with nativism and racism.

BECOMING A WORLD POWER

THE NEW IMPERIALISM

In the last years of the 1890s, the narrowed definition of nationhood was projected abroad, as the United States took its place as an imperial power on the international stage. In world history, the last quarter of the nineteenth century is known as the age of imperialism, when rival European empires carved up large parts of the world among themselves. For most of this period, the United States remained a second-rate power. In 1880, the sultan of Turkey decided to close three foreign embassies to reduce expenses. He chose those in Sweden, Belgium, and the United States. In that year, the American navy was smaller than Denmark's or Chile's. When European powers met at the Berlin Congress of 1884–1885 to divide most of Africa among themselves, the United States attended because of its relationship with Liberia but did not sign the final agreement.

Throughout the nineteenth century, large empires dominated much of the globe. Some were land-based, like the Russian, Ottoman, and Chinese empires, and others included territories on several continents linked by sea, such as the British, French, and Spanish. After 1870, a "new imperialism" arose, dominated by European powers and Japan. Belgium, Great Britain, and France consolidated their hold on colonies in Africa, and newly unified Germany acquired colonies there as well. The British and Russians sought to increase their influence in Central Asia, and all the European powers struggled to dominate parts of China. By the early twentieth century, most of Asia, Africa, the Middle East, and the Pacific had been divided among these empires. The justification for this expansion of imperial power was that it would bring modern "civilization" to the supposedly backward peoples of the non-European world. The natives, according to their colonial occupiers, would be instructed in Western values, labor practices, and the Christian religion. Eventually, they would be accorded the right of self-government, although no one could be sure how long this would take. In the meantime, "empire" was another word for "exploitation."

AMERICAN EXPANSIONISM

Territorial expansion, of course, had been a feature of American life from well before independence. But the 1890s marked a major turning point in America's relationship with the rest of the world. Americans were increasingly aware of themselves as an emerging world power. "We are a great imperial Republic destined to exercise a controlling influence upon the actions of mankind and to affect the future of the world," proclaimed Henry Watterson, an influential newspaper editor.

Until the 1890s, American expansion had taken place on the North American continent. Ever since the Monroe Doctrine (see Chapter 10), to be sure, many Americans had considered the Western Hemisphere an American sphere of influence. There was persistent talk of acquiring Cuba, and President Grant had sought to annex the Dominican Republic, only to see the Senate reject the idea. The last territorial acquisition before the 1890s had been Alaska, purchased from Russia by Secretary of State William H. Seward in 1867, to much derision from those who could not see the purpose of American ownership of "Seward's icebox." Seward, however, was mostly interested in the Aleutian Islands, a part of Alaska that stretched much of the way to Asia (see the map on p. 711) and that, he believed, could be the site of coaling stations for merchant ships plying the Pacific.

Most Americans who looked overseas were interested in expanded trade, not territorial possessions. The country's agricultural and industrial production could no longer be entirely absorbed at home. By 1890, companies like Singer Sewing Machines and John D. Rockefeller's Standard Oil Company aggressively marketed their products abroad. Especially during economic downturns, business leaders insisted on the necessity of greater access to foreign customers.

THE LURE OF EMPIRE

One group of Americans who spread the nation's influence overseas were religious missionaries, thousands of whom ventured abroad in the late nineteenth century to spread Christianity, prepare the world for the second coming of Christ, and uplift the poor. Inspired by Dwight Moody, a Methodist evangelist, the Student Volunteer Movement for Foreign Missions sent more than 8,000 missionaries to "bring light to heathen worlds" across the globe. Missionary work offered employment to those with few opportunities at home, including blacks and women, who made up a majority of the total.

A small group of late-nineteenth-century thinkers actively promoted American expansionism, warning that the country must not allow itself to be shut out of the scramble for empire. In *Our Country* (1885), Josiah Strong, a prominent Congregationalist clergyman, sought to update the idea of manifest destiny. Having demonstrated their special aptitude for liberty and self-government on the North American continent, Strong announced, Anglo-Saxons should now spread their institutions and values to "inferior races" throughout the world. The economy would benefit, he insisted, since one means of civilizing "savages" was to turn them into consumers of American goods.

Naval officer Alfred T. Mahan, in *The Influence of Sea Power upon History* (1890), argued that no nation could prosper without a large fleet of ships engaged in international trade, protected by a powerful navy operating from overseas bases. Mahan published his book in the same year that the census bureau announced that there was no longer a clear line separating settled from unsettled land. Thus, the frontier no longer existed. "Americans," wrote Mahan, "must now begin to look outward." His arguments influenced the outlook of James G. Blaine, who served as secretary of state during Benjamin Harrison's presidency (1889–1893). Blaine urged the president to try to acquire Hawaii, Puerto Rico, and Cuba as strategic naval bases.

Although independent, Hawaii was already closely tied to the United States through treaties that exempted imports of its sugar from tariff duties and provided for the establishment of an American naval base at Pearl Harbor. Hawaii's economy was dominated by American-owned sugar plantations that employed a workforce of native islanders and Chinese, Japanese, and Filipino laborers under long-term contracts. Early in 1893, a group of American planters organized a rebellion that overthrew the Hawaii government of Queen Liliuokalani. On the eve of leaving office, Harrison submitted a treaty of annexation to the Senate. After determining that a majority of Hawaiians did not favor the treaty, Harrison's successor, Grover Cleveland, withdrew it. In July 1898, in the midst of the Spanish-American War, the United States finally annexed the Hawaiian Islands. In 1993, the U.S. Congress passed, and President Bill Clinton signed, a resolution expressing regret to native Hawaiians for "the overthrow of the Kingdom of Hawaii . . . with the participation of agents and citizens of the United States."

The depression that began in 1893 heightened the belief that a more aggressive foreign policy was necessary to stimulate American exports. Fears of economic and ethnic disunity fueled an assertive nationalism. In the face of social conflict and the new immigration, government and private organizations in the 1890s promoted a unifying patriotism. These were the years when rituals like the Pledge of Allegiance and the practice of standing for the playing of "The Star-Spangled Banner" came into existence. Americans had long honored the Stars and Stripes, but the "cult of the flag," including an official Flag Day, dates to the 1890s. New, mass-circulation newspapers also promoted nationalistic sentiments. By the late 1890s, papers like William Randolph Hearst's *New York Journal* and Joseph Pulitzer's *New York World*—dubbed the "yellow press" by their critics after the color in which Hearst printed a popular comic strip—were selling a million copies each day by mixing sensational accounts of crime and political corruption with aggressive appeals to patriotic sentiments.

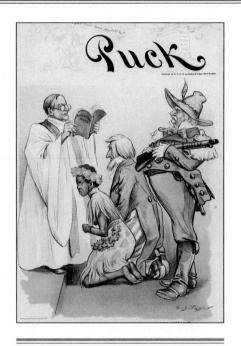

A cartoon in Puck, *December 1, 1897, imagines the annexation of Hawaii by the United States as a shotgun wedding. The minister, President McKinley, reads from a book entitled* Annexation Policy. *The Hawaiian bride appears to be looking for a way to escape. Most Hawaiians did not support annexation.*

THE "SPLENDID LITTLE WAR"

All these factors contributed to America's emergence as a world power in the Spanish-American War of 1898. But the immediate origins of the war lay not at home but in the long Cuban struggle for independence from Spain. Ten years of guerrilla war had followed a Cuban revolt in 1868. The movement for independence resumed in 1895. As reports circulated of widespread suffering caused by the Spanish policy of rounding up civilians and moving them into detention camps, the Cuban struggle won growing support in the United States.

The destruction of the battleship Maine *in Havana Harbor (later found to have been an accident) provided the occasion for patriotic pageants like "Remember the Maine," by William H. West's Big Minstrel Jubilee.*

Demands for intervention escalated after February 15, 1898, when an explosion—probably accidental, a later investigation concluded—destroyed the American battleship *Maine* in Havana Harbor, with the loss of nearly 270 lives. The yellow press blamed Spain and insisted on retribution. After Spain rejected an American demand for a cease-fire on the island and eventual Cuban independence, President McKinley in April asked Congress for a declaration of war. The purpose, declared Senator Henry Teller of Colorado, was to aid Cuban patriots in their struggle for "liberty and freedom." To underscore the government's humanitarian intentions, Congress adopted the Teller Amendment, stating that the United States had no intention of annexing or dominating the island.

Secretary of State John Hay called the Spanish-American conflict a "splendid little war." It lasted only four months and resulted in fewer than 400 American combat deaths. Having shown little interest in imperial expansion before 1898, McKinley now embraced the idea. The war's most decisive engagement, in fact, took place not in Cuba but at Manila Bay, a strategic harbor in the Philippine Islands in the distant Pacific Ocean. Here, on May 1, the American navy under Admiral George Dewey defeated a Spanish fleet. Soon afterward, soldiers went ashore, becoming the first American army units to engage in combat outside the Western Hemisphere. July witnessed another naval victory off Santiago, Cuba, and the landing of American troops on Cuba and Puerto Rico.

ROOSEVELT AT SAN JUAN HILL

The most highly publicized land battle of the war took place in Cuba. This was the charge up San Juan Hill, outside Santiago, by Theodore Roosevelt's

Rough Riders. An ardent expansionist, Roosevelt had long believed that a war would reinvigorate the nation's unity and sense of manhood, which had suffered, he felt, during the 1890s. A few months shy of his fortieth birthday when war broke out, Roosevelt resigned his post as assistant secretary of the navy to raise a volunteer cavalry unit, which rushed to Cuba to participate in the fighting. Roosevelt envisioned his unit as a cross section of American society and enrolled athletes from Ivy League colleges, western cowboys, representatives of various immigrant groups, and even some American Indians. But with the army still segregated, he excluded blacks from his regiment. Ironically, when the Rough Riders reached the top of San Juan Hill, they found that black units had preceded them— a fact Roosevelt omitted in his reports of the battle, which were widely reproduced in the popular press. His heroic exploits made Roosevelt a national hero. He was elected governor of New York that fall and in 1900 became McKinley's vice president.

Charge of the Rough Riders at San Juan Hill, *a painting by Frederic Remington, depicts the celebrated unit, commanded by Theodore Roosevelt, in action in Cuba during the Spanish-American War of 1898. Roosevelt, on horseback, leads the troops. Remington had been sent to the island the previous year by publisher William Randolph Hearst to provide pictures of Spanish atrocities during the Cuban war for independence in the hope of boosting the New York Journal's circulation.*

AN AMERICAN EMPIRE

With the backing of the yellow press, the war quickly escalated from a crusade to aid the suffering Cubans to an imperial venture that ended with the United States in possession of a small overseas empire. McKinley became convinced that the United States could neither return the Philippines to Spain nor grant them independence, for which he believed the inhabitants unprepared. In an interview with a group of Methodist ministers, the president spoke of receiving a divine revelation that Americans had a duty to "uplift and civilize" the Filipino people and to train them for self-government. In the treaty with Spain that ended the war, the United States acquired the Philippines, Puerto Rico, and the Pacific island of Guam. As for Cuba, before recognizing its independence, McKinley forced the island's new government to approve the Platt Amendment to the new Cuban constitution (drafted by Senator Orville H. Platt of Connecticut), which authorized the United States to intervene militarily whenever it saw fit. The United States also acquired a permanent lease on naval stations in Cuba, including what is now the facility at Guantánamo Bay.

The Platt Amendment passed the Cuban Congress by a single vote. Cuban patriots were terribly disappointed. José Martí had fomented revolution in Cuba from exile in the United States and then traveled to the island to take part in the uprising, only to be killed in a battle with Spanish soldiers in 1895. "To change masters is not to be free," Martí had written. And the memory of the betrayal of 1898 would help to inspire another Cuban revolution half a century later.

American interest in its new possessions had more to do with trade than gaining wealth from natural resources or large-scale American settlement. Puerto Rico and Cuba were gateways to Latin America, strategic outposts from which American naval and commercial power could be projected throughout the hemisphere. The Philippines, Guam, and Hawaii lay astride shipping routes to the markets of Japan and China. In 1899, soon after the end of the Spanish-American War, Secretary of State John Hay announced the Open Door policy, demanding that European powers that had recently

In both the Caribbean and the Pacific, the United States achieved swift victories over Spain in the Spanish-American War.

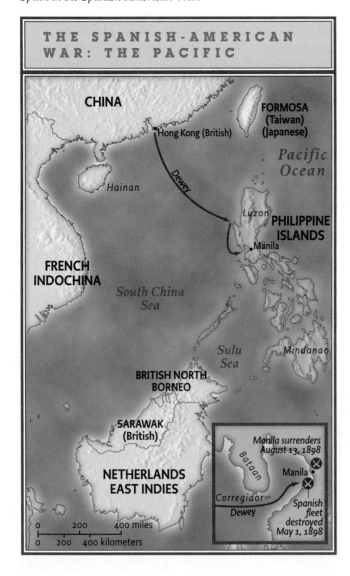

THE SPANISH-AMERICAN WAR: THE PACIFIC

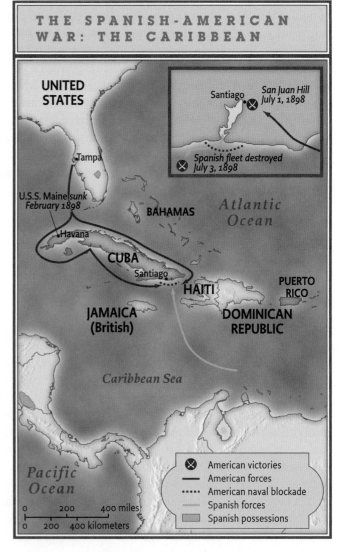

THE SPANISH-AMERICAN WAR: THE CARIBBEAN

VISIONS OF FREEDOM

"CIVILIZATION BEGINS AT HOME."

Civilization Begins at Home. *This cartoon from the New York World, a Democratic newspaper, was published in November 1898, not long after the end of the Spanish-American War. It depicts a figure representing justice urging President William McKinley to turn his attention from the Philippines to domestic problems in the United States.*

QUESTIONS

1. What problems within the United States does the cartoonist draw attention to, and what point is he trying to make?

2. What position does the cartoonist appear to take on the question of annexing the Philippines?

In this cartoon comment on the American effort to suppress the movement for Philippine independence, Uncle Sam tries to subdue a knife-wielding insurgent.

Emilio Aguinaldo, leader of the Philippine War against American occupation, in a more dignified portrayal than in the cartoon above.

divided China into commercial spheres of influence grant equal access to American exports. The Open Door referred to the free movement of goods and money, not people. Even as the United States banned the immigration of Chinese into this country, it insisted on access to the markets and investment opportunities of Asia. Such economic ambitions could easily lead to military intervention. When Chinese nationalists in the 1900 Boxer Rebellion killed thousands of Christian Chinese and beseiged foreign embassies in Beijing, the United States contributed over 3,000 soldiers to the international force that helped to suppress the rebellion.

THE PHILIPPINE WAR

Many Cubans, Filipinos, and Puerto Ricans had welcomed American intervention as a way of breaking Spain's long hold on these colonies. Large planters looked forward to greater access to American markets, and local elites hoped that the American presence would fend off radical changes proposed by rebellious nationalist movements. Nationalists and labor leaders admired America's democratic ideals and believed that American participation in the destruction of Spanish rule would lead to social reform and political self-government.

But the American determination to exercise continued control, direct or indirect, led to a rapid change in local opinion, nowhere more so than in the Philippines. Filipinos had been fighting a war against Spain since 1896. After Dewey's victory at Manila Bay, their leader, Emilio Aguinaldo, established a provisional government with a constitution modeled on that of the United States. But once McKinley decided to retain possession of the islands, the Filipino movement turned against the United States. The result was a second war, far longer (it lasted from 1899 to 1903) and bloodier (it cost the lives of well more than 100,000

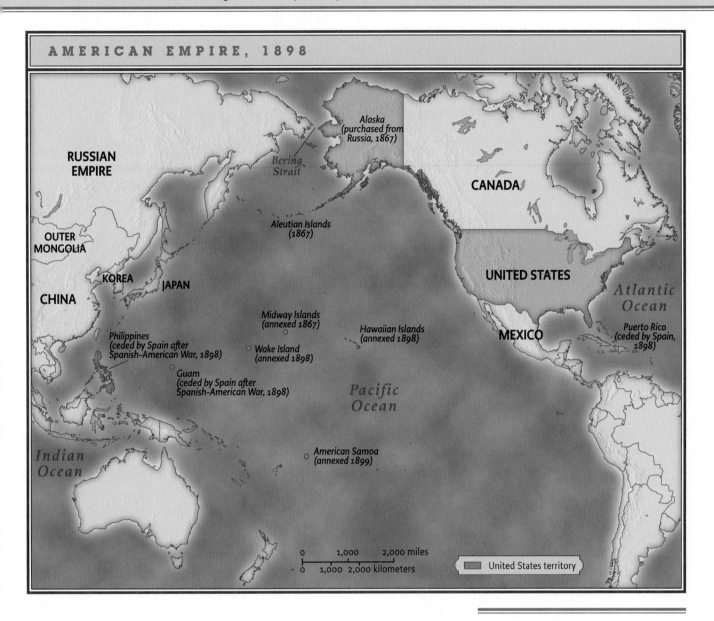

AMERICAN EMPIRE, 1898

Alaska (purchased from Russia, 1867)

Bering Strait

RUSSIAN EMPIRE

CANADA

OUTER MONGOLIA

Aleutian Islands (1867)

KOREA　JAPAN

CHINA

UNITED STATES

Atlantic Ocean

Midway Islands (annexed 1867)

Hawaiian Islands (annexed 1898)

MEXICO

Puerto Rico (ceded by Spain, 1898)

Philippines (ceded by Spain after Spanish-American War, 1898)

Wake Island (annexed 1898)

Guam (ceded by Spain after Spanish-American War, 1898)

Pacific Ocean

Indian Ocean

American Samoa (annexed 1899)

0　1,000　2,000 miles
0　1,000　2,000 kilometers

United States territory

As a result of the Spanish-American War, the United States became the ruler of a far-flung overseas empire.

Filipinos and 4,200 Americans) than the Spanish-American conflict. Today, this is perhaps the least remembered of all American wars. At the time, however, it was closely followed and widely debated in the United States. Press reports of atrocities committed by American troops—the burning of villages, torture of prisoners of war, and rape and execution of civilians—tarnished the nation's self-image as liberators. "We do not intend to free the people of the Philippines," complained Mark Twain. "We have gone there to conquer."

The McKinley administration justified its policies on the grounds that its aim was to "uplift and civilize and Christianize" the Filipinos (although most residents of the islands were already Roman Catholics). William Howard Taft, who became governor-general of the Philippines in 1901, believed it might take a century to raise Filipinos to the condition where they could appreciate "what Anglo-Saxon liberty is."

Once in control of the Philippines, the colonial administration took seriously the idea of modernizing the islands. It expanded railroads and

VOICES OF FREEDOM

From Interview with President McKinley (1899)

In 1899, soon after the end of the Spanish-American War, President William McKinley met with a group of Methodist Church leaders to discuss his decision to annex the Philippines. McKinley offered a defense of American empire as being in the best interests of Americans and Filipinos.

Before you go I would like to say just a word about the Philippine business. I have been criticized a good deal about the Philippines, but don't deserve it. The truth is I didn't want the Philippines, and when they came to us, as a gift from the gods, I did not know what to do with them. When the Spanish War broke out [Admiral] Dewey was at Hong Kong, and I ordered him to go to Manila and to capture or destroy the Spanish fleet, and he had to; because, if defeated, he had no place to refit on that side of the globe, and if the Dons [Spanish] were victorious they would likely cross the Pacific and ravage our Oregon and California coasts. And so he had to destroy the Spanish fleet, and did it! But that was as far as I thought then.

When I next realized that the Philippines had dropped into our laps I confess I did not know what to do with them. I sought counsel from all sides—Democrats as well as Republicans—but got little help. I thought first we would take only Manila; then Luzon; then other islands perhaps also. I walked the floor of the White House night after night until midnight; and I am not ashamed to tell you, gentlemen, that I went down on my knees and prayed [to] Almighty God for light and guidance more than one night. And one night late it came to me this way—I don't know how it was, but it came: (1) That we could not give them back to Spain—that would be cowardly and dishonorable; (2) that we could not turn them over to France and Germany—our commercial rivals in the Orient—that would be bad business and discreditable; (3) that we could not leave them to themselves—they were unfit for self-government—and they would soon have anarchy and misrule over there worse than Spain's was; and (4) that there was nothing left for us to do but to take them all, and to educate the Filipinos, and uplift and civilize and Christianize them, and by God's grace do the very best we could by them, as our fellow-men for whom Christ also died. And then I went to bed, and went to sleep, and slept soundly, and the next morning I sent for the chief engineer of the War Department (our map-maker), and I told him to put the Philippines on the map of the United States (pointing to a large map on the wall of his office), and there they are, and there they will stay while I am President!

FROM "Aguinaldo's Case against the United States" (1899)

Emilio Aguinaldo, who led the Filipino armed struggle for independence against Spain and then another war against the United States when President McKinley decided to annex the Philippines, explained his reasons for opposing American imperialism in an article in the widely read magazine, the *North American Review*. He contrasted American traditions of self-government with the refusal to grant this right to the Philippines.

We Filipinos have all along believed that if the American nation at large knew exactly, as we do, what is daily happening in the Philippine Islands, they would rise en masse, and demand that this barbaric war should stop [and] . . . she would cease to be the laughing stock of other civilized nations, as she became when she abandoned her traditions and set up a double standard of government—government by consent in America, government by force in the Philippine Islands. . . .

You have been deceived all along the line. You have been greatly deceived in the personality of my countrymen. You went to the Philippines under the impression that their inhabitants were ignorant savages. . . . We have been represented by your popular press as if we were Africans or Mohawk Indians. . . .

You repeat constantly the dictum that we cannot govern ourselves. . . . With equal reason, you might have said the same thing some fifty or sixty years ago of Japan; and, little over a hundred years ago, it was extremely questionable, when you, also, were rebels against the English Government, if you could govern yourselves. . . . Now, the moral of all this obviously is: Give us the chance; treat us exactly as you demanded to be treated at the hands of England when you rebelled against her autocratic methods.

Now, here is a unique spectacle—the Filipinos fighting for liberty, the American people fighting them to give them liberty. . . . You entered into an alliance with our chiefs at Hong Kong and at Singapore, and you promised us your aid and protection in our attempt to form a government on the principles and after the model of the government of the United States. . . . In combination with our forces, you compelled Spain to surrender. . . . Joy abounded in every heart, and all went well . . . until . . . the Government at Washington . . . commenc[ed] by ignoring all promises that had been made and end[ed] by ignoring the Philippine people, their personality and rights, and treating them as a common enemy. . . . In the face of the world you emblazon humanity and Liberty upon your standard, while you cast your political constitution to the winds and attempt to trample down and exterminate a brave people whose only crime is that they are fighting for their liberty.

QUESTIONS

1. How persuasive is McKinley's account of how and why he decided to annex the Philippines?

2. Why does Aguinaldo think that the United States is betraying its own values?

3. How do these documents reflect different definitions of liberty in the wake of the Spanish-American War?

harbors, brought in American schoolteachers and public health officials, and sought to modernize agriculture (although efforts to persuade local farmers to substitute corn for rice ran afoul of Filipino climate and cultural traditions). The United States, said President McKinley, had an obligation to its "little brown brothers." Yet in all the new possessions, American policies tended to serve the interests of land-based local elites—native-born landowners in the Philippines, American sugar planters in Hawaii and Puerto Rico—and such policies bequeathed enduring poverty to the majority of the rural population. Under American rule, Puerto Rico, previously an island of diversified small farmers, became a low-wage plantation economy controlled by absentee corporations. By the 1920s, its residents were among the poorest in the entire Caribbean.

CITIZENS OR SUBJECTS?

American rule also brought with it American racial attitudes. In an 1899 poem, the British writer Rudyard Kipling urged the United States to take up the "white man's burden" of imperialism. American proponents of empire agreed that the domination of non-white peoples by whites formed part of the progress of civilization. Among the soldiers sent to the Philippines to fight Aguinaldo were a number of black regiments. Their letters from the front suggested that American atrocities arose from white troops applying to the Filipino population the same "treatment for colored peoples" practiced at home. "Is America any better than Spain?" wondered George W. Prioleau, a black cavalryman who had fought at San Juan Hill.

America's triumphant entry into the ranks of imperial powers sparked an intense debate over the relationship among political democracy, race, and American citizenship. The American system of government had no provision for permanent colonies. The right of every people to self-government was one of the main principles of the Declaration of Independence. The idea of an "empire of liberty" assumed that new territories would eventually be admitted as equal states and their residents would be American citizens. In the aftermath of the Spanish-American War, however, nationalism, democracy, and American freedom emerged more closely identified than ever with notions of Anglo-Saxon superiority.

Leaders of both parties, while determined to retain the new overseas possessions, feared that people of what one congressman called "an alien race and foreign tongue" could not be incorporated into the Union. The Foraker Act of 1900 declared Puerto Rico an "insular territory," different from previous territories in the West. Its 1 million inhabitants were defined as citizens of Puerto Rico, not the United States, and denied a future path to statehood. Filipinos occupied a similar status. In a series of cases decided between 1901 and 1904 and known collectively as the Insular Cases, the Supreme Court held that the Constitution did not fully apply to the territories recently acquired by the United States—a significant limitation of the scope of American freedom. Congress, the Court

William Howard Taft, the rotund American governor-general of the Philippines, astride a local water buffalo.

Some of the 1,200 Filipinos exhibited at the 1904 Louisiana Purchase Exposition in St. Louis. The federal government displayed the Filipinos in a "native" setting in order to win public support for the annexation of the Philippines.

declared, must recognize the "fundamental" personal rights of residents of the Philippines and Puerto Rico. But otherwise it could govern them as it saw fit for an indefinite period of time. Thus, two principles central to American freedom since the War of Independence—no taxation without representation, and government based on the consent of the governed—were abandoned when it came to the nation's new possessions.

In the twentieth century, the territories acquired in 1898 would follow different paths. Hawaii, which had a sizable population of American missionaries and planters, became a traditional territory. Its population, except for Asian immigrant laborers, became American citizens, and it was admitted as a state in 1959. After nearly a half-century of American rule, the Philippines achieved independence in 1946. Until 1950, the U.S. Navy administered Guam, which remains today an "unincorporated" territory. As for Puerto Rico, it is sometimes called "the world's oldest colony," because ever since the Spanish conquered the island in 1493 it has lacked full self-government. Congress extended American citizenship to Puerto Ricans in 1917. Puerto Rico today remains in a kind of political limbo, poised on the brink of statehood or independence. The island has the status of a commonwealth. It elects its own government but lacks a voice in Congress (and in the election of the U.S. president) and key issues such as defense and environmental policy are controlled by the United States.

DRAWING THE GLOBAL COLOR LINE

Just as American ideas about liberty and self-government had circulated around the world in the Age of Revolution, American racial attitudes had a global impact in the age of empire. The turn of the twentieth century was a time of worldwide concern about immigration, race relations, and the "white man's burden," all of which inspired a global sense of fraternity

School Begins, an *1899 cartoon from* Puck, *suggests doubts about the project of "civilizing" non-whites in new American possessions. Uncle Sam lectures four unkempt black children, labeled "Philippines," "Hawaii," "Porto Rico," and "Cuba," while neatly dressed pupils representing various states study quietly. In the background, an American Indian holds a book upside down, while a black man washes the window. A Chinese student, apparently hoping for instruction, waits at the door.*

among "Anglo-Saxon" nations. Chinese exclusion in the United States strongly influenced anti-Chinese laws adopted in Canada, and American segregation and disenfranchisement became models for Australia and South Africa as they formed new governments; they read in particular the proceedings of the Mississippi constitutional convention of 1890, which pioneered ways to eliminate black voting rights.

One "lesson" these countries learned from the United States was that the "failure" of Reconstruction demonstrated the impossibility of multiracial democracy. The extremely hostile account of Reconstruction by the British writer James Bryce in his widely read book *The American Commonwealth* (published in London in 1888) circulated around the world. Bryce called African-Americans "children of nature" and insisted that giving them the right to vote had been a terrible mistake, which had produced all kinds of corruption and misgovernment. His book was frequently cited by the founders of the Australian Commonwealth (1901) to justify their "white Australia" policy, which barred the further immigration of Asians. The Union of South Africa, inaugurated in 1911, saw its own policy of racial separation—later known as apartheid—as following in the footsteps of segregation in the United States. South Africa, however, went much further, enacting laws that limited skilled jobs to whites and dividing the country into areas where black Africans could and could not live. Even American proposals that did not become law, such as the literacy test for immigrants vetoed by President Cleveland, influenced measures adopted overseas. The United States, too, learned from other countries. The Gentleman's Agreement that limited Japanese immigration early in the twentieth century (see Chapter 19) followed a similar arrangement between Japan and Canada.

"REPUBLIC OR EMPIRE?"

The emergence of the United States as an imperial power sparked intense debate. Opponents formed the Anti-Imperialist League. It united writers and social reformers who believed American energies should be directed at home, businessmen fearful of the cost of maintaining overseas outposts, and racists who did not wish to bring non-white populations into the United States. Among its prominent members were E. L. Godkin, the editor of *The Nation*, the novelist William Dean Howells, and the labor leader George E. McNeill. The League held meetings throughout the country and published pamphlets called Liberty Tracts, warning that empire was incompatible with democracy. America's historic mission, the League declared, was to "help the world by an example of successful self-government," not to conquer other peoples. A "republic of free men," anti-imperialists proclaimed, should assist the people of Puerto Rico and the Philippines in their own "struggles for liberty," rather than subjecting them to colonial rule.

In 1900, Democrats again nominated William Jennings Bryan to run against McKinley. The Democratic platform opposed the Philippine War for placing the United States in the "un-American" position of "crushing with military force" another people's desire for "liberty and self-government." George S. Boutwell, president of the Anti-Imperialist League, declared that the most pressing question in the election was the nation's future character— "republic or empire?"

But without any sense of contradiction, proponents of an imperial foreign policy also adopted the language of freedom. Anti-imperialists were the real "infidels to the gospel of liberty," claimed Senator Albert Beveridge of Indiana, because America ventured abroad not for material gain or national power, but to bring "a new day of freedom" to the peoples of the world. America's was a "benevolent" imperialism, rooted in a national mission to uplift backward cultures and spread liberty across the globe. Beveridge did not, however, neglect more practical considerations. American trade, he insisted, "henceforth must be with Asia. The Pacific is our ocean. . . . Where shall we turn for consumers of our surplus? Geography answers the question. China is our natural customer." And the Philippines held the key to "the commercial situation of the entire East." Riding the wave of patriotic sentiment inspired by the war, and with the economy having recovered from the depression of 1893–1897, McKinley in 1900 repeated his 1896 triumph.

At the dawn of the twentieth century, the United States seemed poised to take its place among the world's great powers. Writers at home and overseas confidently predicted that American influence would soon span the globe. In his 1902 book *The New Empire*, Brooks Adams, a grandson of John Quincy Adams, predicted that because of its economic power, the United States would soon "outweigh any single empire, if not all empires combined." Years would pass before this prediction was fulfilled. But in 1900, many features that would mark American life for much of the twentieth century were already apparent. The United States had surpassed Britain, France, and Germany in industrial production. The merger movement of 1897–1904 (discussed in the previous chapter) left broad sections of the economy under the control of giant corporations. The political system had stabilized. The white North and South had achieved reconciliation, while

A Republican campaign poster from the election of 1900 links prosperity at home and benevolent imperialism abroad as achievements of William McKinley's first term in office.

rigid lines of racial exclusion—the segregation of blacks, Chinese exclusion, Indian reservations—limited the boundaries of freedom and citizenship.

Yet the questions central to nineteenth-century debates over freedom—the relationship between political and economic liberty, the role of government in creating the conditions of freedom, and the definition of those entitled to enjoy the rights of citizens—had not been permanently answered. Nor had the dilemma of how to reconcile America's role as an empire with traditional ideas of freedom. These were the challenges bequeathed by the nineteenth century to the first generation of the twentieth.

SUGGESTED READING

BOOKS

Aleinikoff, Alexander. *Semblances of Sovereignty: The Constitution, the State, and American Citizenship* (2002). Includes a careful discussion of the citizenship status of American minorities and residents of overseas possessions.

Blight, David. *Race and Reunion: The Civil War in American Memory* (2001). Examines how a memory of the Civil War that downplayed the issue of slavery played a part in sectional reconciliation and the rise of segregation.

Brands, H. W. *The Reckless Decade: America in the 1890s* (2002). A lively account of the decade.

Factor, Robert L. *The Black Response to America: Men, Ideals, and Organization from Frederick Douglass to the NAACP* (1970). Discusses black social and political thought, including that of Booker T. Washington and his critics.

Goodwyn, Lawrence. *The Populist Moment: A Short History of the Agrarian Revolt in America* (1978). A sympathetic account of the rise and fall of Populism.

Higginbotham, Evelyn. *Righteous Discontent: The Women's Movement in the Black Baptist Church, 1880–1920* (1993). Explains how black women developed ways of exerting their influence in public life even as black men were losing the right to vote.

Kraditor, Aileen S. *The Ideas of the Woman Suffrage Movement, 1890–1920* (1962). A careful examination of various tendencies in the movement for the right to vote for women.

Krause, Paul. *The Battle for Homestead, 1880–1892: Politics, Culture, and Steel* (1992). An account of the era's most celebrated conflict between capital and labor.

LaFeber, Walter. *The New Empire: An Interpretation of American Expansion, 1860–1898* (1963). A classic examination of the forces that led the United States to acquire an overseas empire.

Lake, Marilyn, and Henry Reynolds. *Drawing the Global Color Line* (2008). Traces the global transmission of ideas about white supremacy in the late nineteenth century.

Linn, Brian M. *The Philippine War, 1899–1902* (2000). A detailed history of America's "forgotten war."

McClain, Charles J. *In Search of Equality: The Chinese Struggle against Discrimination in Nineteenth-Century America* (1994). Explores how Chinese-Americans worked to combat the discrimination to which they were subjected and to assert their rights.

McMillen, Neil R. *Dark Journey: Black Mississippians in the Age of Jim Crow* (1989). A powerful account of black life in the segregation era and the boundaries within which it operated.

Perez, Louis A. *The War of 1898: The United States and Cuba in History and Historiography* (1998). Presents the Cuban side of the Spanish-American War, including a detailed discussion of the Cuban movement for independence and how American intervention affected it.

Postel, Charles. *The Populist Vision* (2007). A history of the Populist movement that stresses how it anticipated many public policies of the twentieth century.

Sanders, Elizabeth. *Roots of Reform: Farmers, Workers, and the American State, 1877–1917* (1999). Emphasizes the role of farmers' movements in putting forth many of the proposals associated with political reform in the late nineteenth and early twentieth centuries.

Woodward, C. Vann. *Origins of the New South, 1877–1913* (1951). A classic treatment of the New South, emphasizing how its rulers failed to meet the needs of most southerners, white as well as black.

WEBSITES

1896: The Presidential Campaign: http://projects.vassar.edu/1896/1896home.html

The Chinese in California, 1850–1925: http://lcweb2.loc.gov/ammem/award 99/cubhtml/cichome.html

The History of Jim Crow: www.jimcrowhistory.org

The World of 1898: The Spanish-American War: www.loc.gov/rr/hispanic/1898

REVIEW QUESTIONS

1. What economic issues gave rise to the Populist Party, and what political and economic changes did the party advocate?

2. How did employers use state and federal forces to protect their own economic interests, and what were the results?

3. Why is the election of 1896 called the first modern presidential election?

4. Who were the Redeemers, and how did they change society and politics in the New South?

5. Using political, economic, and social examples, explain how the freedoms of Southern blacks were reduced after 1877.

6. How does the politics of memory, focusing on the Civil War and Reconstruction, demonstrate how whites removed blacks from a significant role in U.S. history?

7. What ideas and interests motivated the United States to create an empire in the late nineenth century?

8. Compare the arguments for and against U.S. imperialism. Be sure to consider the views of President McKinley and Emilio Aguinaldo.

9. Explain the impact of American racial attitudes and practices on other nations during the age of empire.

FREEDOM QUESTIONS

1. Describe the debate sparked by the Spanish-American War over the relationships between political democracy, race, citizenship, and freedom.

2. Since the Age of Jackson, the meanings of freedom included economic independence and democratic self-government. Why did workers, farmers, and women feel excluded from these freedoms between 1877 and 1900?

3. Explain Eugene V. Debs's argument that the government was being used to deprive workers of their birthright of freedom.

4. How did political leaders and the courts justify the erosion of black rights in the name of freedom?

5. What restrictions were placed on the freedoms of post–Civil War immigrants, and how were these limitations justified?

KEY TERMS

agricultural expansion and decline (pp. 679–680)

the People's Party (p. 680)

Coxey's Army (p. 684)

"free coinage" of silver (p. 686)

Kansas Exodus (p. 690)

elimination of black voting (p. 692)

Civil Rights Cases (p. 694)

Plessy v. Ferguson (p. 694)

"separate but equal" (p. 694)

lynching (p. 695)

politics of memory (p. 696)

Immigration Restriction League (p. 698)

Yick Wo v. Hopkins (p. 699)

United States v. Wong Kim Ark (p. 699)

Fong Yue Ting (p. 700)

Alfred T. Mahan (p. 704)

U.S.S. Maine (p. 706)

Platt Amendment (p. 708)

Emilio Aguinaldo (p. 710)

Foraker Act (p. 714)

Anti-Imperialist League (p. 717)

REVIEW TABLE

Facing the Limits of Freedom

Group Affected	Challenge Faced	Response	Explanation
Family farmers	Low crop prices, high costs, loss of family farms	Farmers Alliance, Populist Party	Advocated federal government restore democracy and economic opportunity for all
Blacks	Jim Crow laws; lynching	Booker T. Washington's "Atlanta Compromise"	Advocated a policy of accommodation and vocational education
Labor	Viewed as radical	Samuel Gompers's "business unionism"	Concentrated on wages, hours, not social reform
Women	Denied the right to vote	Organizations like the Women's Christian Temperance Union	Allowed women to exert more influence on public affairs
Chinese	1882 Chinese Exclusion Act	United States v. Wong Kim Ark	Decision held that the Fourteenth Amendment awarded citizenship to American-born children of Chinese immigrants
Filipinos	Controlled and denied rights by colonial powers	Wars against Spain and the United States	Wanted independence from foreign powers

CHAPTER 18

The Progressive Era, 1900–1916

A rare color photograph from around 1900 shows the teeming street life of Mulberry Street, on New York City's densely populated Lower East Side. The massive immigration of the early twentieth century transformed the life of urban centers throughout the country and helped to spark the Progressive movement.

FOCUS QUESTIONS

- Why was the city such a central element in Progressive America?

- How did the labor and women's movements challenge the nineteenth-century meanings of American freedom?

- In what ways did Progressivism include both democratic and anti-democratic impulses?

- How did the Progressive presidents foster the rise of the nation-state?

It was late afternoon on March 25, 1911, when fire broke out at the Triangle Shirtwaist Company. The factory occupied the top three floors of a ten-story building in the Greenwich Village neighborhood of New York City. Here some 500 workers, mostly young Jewish and Italian immigrant women, toiled at sewing machines producing ladies' blouses, some earning as little as three dollars per week. Those who tried to escape the blaze discovered that the doors to the stairwell had been locked—the owners' way, it was later charged, of discouraging theft and unauthorized bathroom breaks. The fire department rushed to the scene with high-pressure hoses. But their ladders reached only to the sixth floor. As the fire raged, onlookers watched in horror as girls leapt from the upper stories. By the time the blaze had been put out, 46 bodies lay on the street and 100 more were found inside the building.

The Triangle Shirtwaist Company was typical of manufacturing in the nation's largest city, a beehive of industrial production in small, crowded factories. New York was home to 30,000 manufacturing establishments with more than 600,000 employees—more industrial workers than the entire state of Massachusetts. Triangle had already played a key role in the era's labor history. When 200 of its workers tried to join the International Ladies' Garment Workers Union (ILGWU), the owners responded by firing them. This incident helped to spark a general walkout of female garment workers in 1909—the Uprising of the 20,000. Among the strikers' demands was better safety in clothing factories. The impoverished immigrants forged an alliance with middle- and upper-class female supporters, including members of the Women's Trade Union League, which had been founded in 1903 to help bring women workers into unions. Alva Belmont, the ex-wife of railroad magnate William Vanderbilt, contributed several of her cars to a parade in support of the striking workers. By the time the walkout ended early in 1911, the ILGWU had won union contracts with more than 300 firms. But the Triangle Shirtwaist Company was not among them.

The Triangle fire was not the worst fire disaster in American history (seven years earlier, over 1,000 people had died in a blaze on the *General Slocum* excursion boat in New York Harbor). But it had an unrivaled impact on public consciousness. More than twenty years later, Franklin D. Roosevelt would refer to it in a press conference as an example of why the government needed to regulate industry. In its wake, efforts to organize the city's workers accelerated, and the state legislature passed new factory inspection laws and fire safety codes.

Triangle focused attention on the social divisions that plagued American society during the first two decades of the twentieth century, a period known as the Progressive era. These were years when economic expansion produced millions of new jobs and brought an unprecedented array of goods within reach of American consumers. Cities expanded rapidly—by 1920, for the first time, more Americans lived in towns and

Policemen stare up as the Triangle fire of 1911 rages, while the bodies of factory workers who plunged to their deaths to escape the blaze lie on the sidewalk.

cities than in rural areas. Yet severe inequality remained the most visible feature of the urban landscape, and persistent labor strife raised anew the question of government's role in combating social inequality. The fire and its aftermath also highlighted how traditional gender roles were changing as women took on new responsibilities in the workplace and in the making of public policy.

The word "Progressive" came into common use around 1910 as a way of describing a broad, loosely defined political movement of individuals and groups who hoped to bring about significant change in American social and political life. Progressives included forward-looking businessmen who realized that workers must be accorded a voice in economic decision making, and labor activists bent on empowering industrial workers. Other major contributors to Progressivism were members of female reform organizations who hoped to protect women and children from exploitation, social scientists who believed that academic research would help to solve social problems, and members of an anxious middle class who feared that their status was threatened by the rise of big business.

Everywhere in early-twentieth-century America the signs of economic and political consolidation were apparent—in the power of a small directorate of Wall Street bankers and corporate executives, the manipulation of democracy by corrupt political machines, and the rise of new systems of managerial control in workplaces. In these circumstances, wrote Benjamin P. DeWitt, in his 1915 book *The Progressive Movement*, "the individual could not hope to compete . . . . Slowly, Americans realized that they were not free."

As this and the following chapter will discuss, Progressive reformers responded to the perception of declining freedom in varied, contradictory ways. The era saw the expansion of political and economic freedom

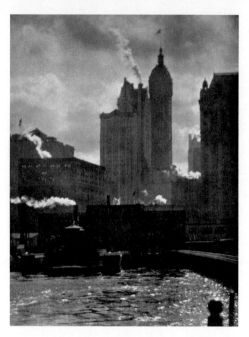

City of Ambition, *1910, by the photographer Alfred Stieglitz, captures the stark beauty of New York City's new skyscrapers.*

through the reinvigoration of the movement for woman suffrage, the use of political power to expand workers' rights, and efforts to improve democratic government by weakening the power of city bosses and giving ordinary citizens more influence on legislation. It witnessed the flowering of understandings of freedom based on individual fulfillment and personal self-determination—the ability to participate fully in the ever-expanding consumer marketplace and, especially for women, to enjoy economic and sexual freedoms long considered the province of men. At the same time, many Progressives supported efforts to limit the full enjoyment of freedom to those deemed fit to exercise it properly. The new system of white supremacy born in the 1890s became fully consolidated in the South. Growing numbers of native-born Americans demanded that immigrants abandon their traditional cultures and become fully "Americanized." And efforts were made at the local and national levels to place political decision making in the hands of experts who did not have to answer to the electorate. Even as the idea of freedom expanded, freedom's boundaries contracted in Progressive America.

AN URBAN AGE AND A CONSUMER SOCIETY

FARMS AND CITIES

The Progressive era was a period of explosive economic growth, fueled by increasing industrial production, a rapid rise in population, and the continued expansion of the consumer marketplace. In the first decade of the twentieth century, the economy's total output rose by about 85 percent. For the last time in American history, farms and cities grew together. As farm prices recovered from their low point during the depression of the 1890s, American agriculture entered what would later be remembered as its "golden age." The expansion of urban areas stimulated demand for farm goods. Farm families poured into the western Great Plains. More than 1 million claims for free government land were filed under the Homestead Act of 1862—more than in the previous forty years combined. Between 1900 and 1910, the combined population of Texas and Oklahoma rose by nearly 2 million people, and Kansas, Nebraska, and the Dakotas added 800,000. Irrigation transformed the Imperial Valley of California and parts of Arizona into major areas of commercial farming.

But it was the city that became the focus of Progressive politics and of a new mass-consumer society. Throughout the industrialized world, the number of great cities multiplied. The United States counted twenty-one cities whose population exceeded

	Table 18.1 RISE OF THE CITY, 1880–1920	
Year	**Urban Population (percentage)**	**Number of Cities with 100,000+ Population**
1880	20%	12
1890	28	15
1900	38	18
1910	50	21
1920	68	26

100,000 in 1910, the largest of them New York, with 4.7 million residents. The twenty-three square miles of Manhattan Island were home to over 2 million people, more than lived in thirty-three of the states. Fully a quarter of them inhabited the Lower East Side, an immigrant neighborhood more densely populated than Bombay or Calcutta in India.

The stark urban inequalities of the 1890s continued into the Progressive era. Immigrant families in New York's downtown tenements often had no electricity or indoor toilets. Three miles to the north stood the mansions of Fifth Avenue's Millionaire's Row. According to one estimate, J. P. Morgan's financial firm directly or indirectly controlled 40 percent of all financial and industrial capital in the United States. Alongside such wealth, reported the Commission on Industrial Relations, established by Congress in 1912, more than one-third of the country's mining and manufacturing workers lived in "actual poverty."

The city captured the imagination of artists, writers, and reformers. The glories of the American landscape had been the focal point of nineteenth-century painters (exemplified by the Hudson River school, which produced canvases celebrating the wonders of nature). The city and its daily life now

The mansion of Cornelius Vanderbilt II on New York City's Fifth Avenue, in a 1920 photograph. Designed in the style of a French château, it took up the entire block. Today, the Bergdorf Goodman department store occupies the site.

Six O'Clock, Winter, *a 1912 painting by John Sloan, depicts a busy city street with an elevated railroad overhead. Sloan was one of a group of painters dubbed the Ashcan School because of their focus on everyday city life.*

became their preoccupation. Painters like George W. Bellows and John Sloan and photographers such as Alfred Stieglitz and Edward Steichen captured the electric lights, crowded bars and theaters, and soaring skyscrapers of the urban landscape. With its youthful, exuberant energies, the city seemed an expression of modernity itself.

THE MUCKRAKERS

Others saw the city as a place where corporate greed undermined traditional American values. At a time when more than 2 million children under the age of fifteen worked for wages, Lewis Hine photographed child laborers to draw attention to persistent social inequality. A new generation of journalists writing for mass-circulation national magazines exposed the ills of industrial and urban life. *The Shame of the Cities* by Lincoln Steffens (published as a series in *McClure's Magazine* in 1901–1902 and in book form in 1904) showed how party bosses and business leaders profited from political corruption. *McClure's* also hired Ida Tarbell to expose the arrogance and economic machinations of John D. Rockefeller's Standard Oil Company. Published in two volumes in 1904, her *History of the Standard Oil Company* was the most substantial product of what Theodore Roosevelt disparaged as "muckraking"—the use of journalistic skills to expose the underside of American life.

Major novelists of the era took a similar unsparing approach to social ills. Theodore Dreiser's *Sister Carrie* (1900) traced a hopeful young woman's descent into prostitution in Chicago's harsh urban environment. Perhaps the era's most influential novel was Upton Sinclair's *The Jungle* (1906), whose description of unsanitary slaughterhouses and the sale of rotten meat stirred public outrage and led directly to the passage of the Pure Food and Drug Act and the Meat Inspection Act of 1906.

IMMIGRATION AS A GLOBAL PROCESS

If one thing characterized early-twentieth-century cities, it was their immigrant character. The "new immigration" from southern and eastern Europe

Two photographs by Lewis Hine, who used his camera to chronicle the plight of child laborers: a young spinner in a southern cotton factory and "breaker" boys who worked in a Pennsylvania coal mine.

(discussed in Chapter 17) had begun around 1890 but reached its peak during the Progressive era. Between 1901 and the outbreak of World War I in Europe in 1914, some 13 million immigrants came to the United States, the majority from Italy, Russia, and the Austro-Hungarian empire. In fact, Progressive-era immigration formed part of a larger process of worldwide migration set in motion by industrial expansion and the decline of traditional agriculture. Poles emigrated not only to Pittsburgh and Chicago but to work in German factories and Scottish mines. Italians sought jobs in Belgium, France, and Argentina as well as the United States. As many as 750,000 Chinese migrated to other countries each year.

During the years from 1840 to 1914 (when immigration to the United States would be virtually cut off, first by the outbreak of World War I and then by legislation), perhaps 40 million persons emigrated to the United States and another 20 million to other parts of the Western Hemisphere, including Canada, Argentina, Brazil, and the Caribbean. This population flow formed one part of a massive shifting of peoples throughout the world, much of which took place in Asia. Millions of persons migrated to Southeast Asia and the South Pacific, mainly from India and China. Millions more moved from Russia and northern Asia to Manchuria, Siberia, and Central Asia.

The century between 1815, when the Napoleonic Wars in Europe and the War of 1812 in the United States ended, and the outbreak of World War I in 1914, witnessed a series of massive shifts in the world's population. The 35 million people who crossed the Atlantic to North America formed the largest migration stream, but millions of migrants also moved to South America, eastern Russia, and various parts of Asia.

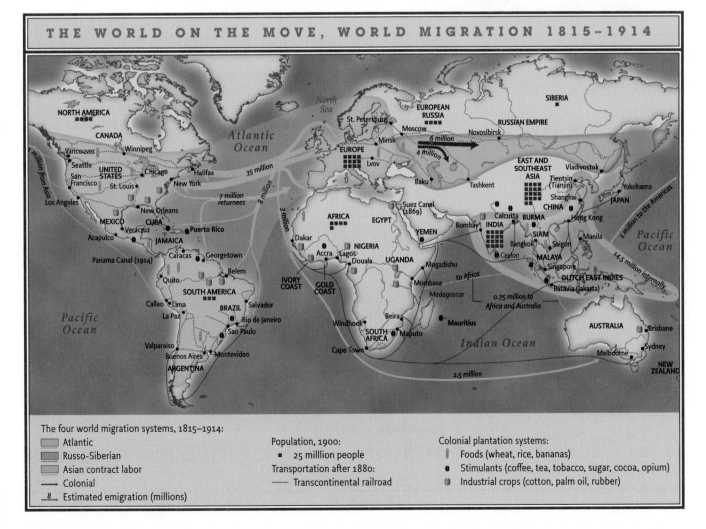

THE WORLD ON THE MOVE, WORLD MIGRATION 1815–1914

The four world migration systems, 1815–1914:

- ▬ Atlantic
- ▬ Russo-Siberian
- ▬ Asian contract labor
- ⟶ Colonial
- _8_ Estimated emigration (millions)

Population, 1900:
- ■ 25 milllion people

Transportation after 1880:
- ------ Transcontinental railroad

Colonial plantation systems:
- ▯ Foods (wheat, rice, bananas)
- ● Stimulants (coffee, tea, tobacco, sugar, cocoa, opium)
- ▯ Industrial crops (cotton, palm oil, rubber)

An illustration in the 1912 publication
The New Immigration *depicts the
various "types" entering the United States.*

Numerous causes inspired this massive uprooting of population. Rural southern and eastern Europe and large parts of Asia were regions marked by widespread poverty and illiteracy, burdensome taxation, and declining economies. Political turmoil at home, like the revolution that engulfed Mexico after 1911, also inspired emigration. Not all of these immigrants could be classified as "free laborers," however. Large numbers of Chinese, Mexican, and Italian migrants, including many who came to the United States, were bound to long-term labor contracts. These contracts were signed with labor agents, who then provided the workers to American employers. But all the areas attracting immigrants were frontiers of one kind or another—agricultural, mining, or industrial—with expanding job opportunities.

Most European immigrants to the United States entered through Ellis Island. Located in New York Harbor, this became in 1892 the nation's main facility for processing immigrants. Millions of Americans today trace their ancestry to an immigrant who passed through Ellis Island. The less fortunate, who failed a medical examination or were judged to be anarchists, prostitutes, or in other ways undesirable, were sent home.

At the same time, an influx of Asian and Mexican newcomers was taking place in the West. After the exclusion of immigrants from China in the late nineteenth century, a small number of Japanese arrived, primarily to work as agricultural laborers in California's fruit and vegetable fields and on Hawaii's sugar plantations. By 1910, the population of Japanese origin had grown to 72,000. Between 1910 and 1940, Angel Island in San Francisco Bay—the "Ellis Island of the West"—served as the main entry point for immigrants from Asia.

Far larger was Mexican immigration. Between 1900 and 1930, some 1 million Mexicans (more than 10 percent of that country's population)

*Italian Family on Ferry Boat, Leaving
Ellis Island, a 1905 photograph by Lewis
Hine. The family of immigrants has just
passed through the inspection process at
the gateway to the United States.*

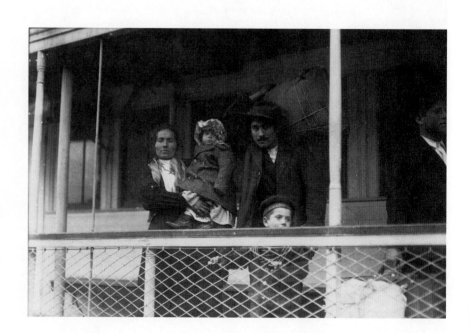

entered the United States—a number exceeded by only a few European countries. Many Mexicans entered through El Paso, Texas, the main southern gateway into the United States. Many ended up in the San Gabriel Valley of California, where citrus growers searching for cheap labor had earlier experimented with Native American, South Asian, Chinese, and Filipino migrant workers.

By 1910, one-seventh of the American population was foreign-born, the highest percentage in the country's history. More than 40 percent of New York City's population had been born abroad. In Chicago and smaller industrial cities like Providence, Milwaukee, and San Francisco, the figure exceeded 30 percent. Although many newcomers moved west to take part in the expansion of farming, most clustered in industrial centers. By 1910, nearly three-fifths of the workers in the twenty leading manufacturing and mining industries were foreign-born.

THE IMMIGRANT QUEST FOR FREEDOM

Like their nineteenth-century predecessors, the new immigrants arrived imagining the United States as a land of freedom, where all persons enjoyed equality before the law, could worship as they pleased, enjoyed economic opportunity, and had been emancipated from the oppressive social hierarchies of their homelands. "America is a free country," one Polish immigrant wrote home. "You don't have to be a serf to anyone." Agents sent abroad by the American government to investigate the reasons for large-scale immigration reported that the main impetus was a desire to share in the "freedom and prosperity enjoyed by the people of the United States." Freedom, they added, was largely an economic ambition—a desire to escape from "hopeless poverty" and achieve a standard of living impossible at home. While some of the new immigrants, especially Jews fleeing religious persecution in the Russian empire, thought of themselves as permanent emigrants, the majority initially planned to earn enough money to return home and purchase land. Groups like Mexicans and Italians included many "birds of passage," who remained only temporarily in the United States. In 1908, a year of economic downturn in the United States, more Italians left the country than entered.

The new immigrants clustered in close-knit "ethnic" neighborhoods with their own shops, theaters, and community organizations, and often continued to speak their native tongues. As early as 1900, more than 1,000 foreign-language newspapers were published in the United

Table 18.2 IMMIGRANTS AND THEIR CHILDREN AS PERCENTAGE OF POPULATION, TEN MAJOR CITIES, 1920	
City	*Percentage*
New York City	76%
Cleveland	72
Boston	72
Chicago	71
Detroit	65
San Francisco	64
Minneapolis	63
Pittsburgh	59
Seattle	55
Los Angeles	45

A community settlement map for Chicago in 1900 illustrates the immigrant and racial neighborhoods in the nation's second largest city.

An immigrant from Mexico, arriving around 1912 in a cart drawn by a donkey.

States. Churches were pillars of these immigrant communities. In New York's East Harlem, even anti-clerical Italian immigrants, who resented the close alliance in Italy between the Catholic Church and the oppressive state, participated eagerly in the annual festival of the Madonna of Mt. Carmel. After Italian-Americans scattered to the suburbs, they continued to return each year to reenact the festival.

Although most immigrants earned more than was possible in the impoverished regions from which they came, they endured low wages, long hours, and dangerous working conditions. In the mines and factories of Pennsylvania and the Midwest, eastern European immigrants performed low-wage unskilled labor, while native-born workers dominated skilled and supervisory jobs. The vast majority of Mexican immigrants became poorly paid agricultural, mine, and railroad laborers, with little prospect of upward economic mobility. "My people are not in America," remarked one Slavic priest, "they are under it."

CONSUMER FREEDOM

Cities, however, were also the birthplace of a mass-consumption society that added new meaning to American freedom. There was, of course, nothing unusual in the idea that the promise of American life lay, in part, in the enjoyment by the masses of citizens of goods available in other countries only to the well-to-do. Not until the Progressive era, however, did the advent of large downtown department stores, chain stores in urban neighborhoods, and retail mail-order houses for farmers and small-town resi-

In Hester Street, *painted in 1905, George Luks, a member of the Ashcan School of urban artists, captures the colorful street life of an immigrant neighborhood in New York City.*

VISIONS OF FREEDOM

Movie, 5 Cents. *In this 1907 painting, the artist John Sloan depicts the interior of a movie house. By this time, millions of people each week were flocking to see silent motion pictures. The audience includes different classes and races, as well as couples and women attending alone.*

QUESTIONS

1. What does the nature of the audience suggest about movie theaters as places of a new social freedom?

2. Does the painting help explain why some critics complained that movies promoted immorality?

Women at work in a shoe factory, 1908.

dents make available to consumers throughout the country the vast array of goods now pouring from the nation's factories. By 1910, Americans could purchase, among many other items, electric sewing machines, washing machines, vacuum cleaners, and record players. Low wages, the unequal distribution of income, and the South's persistent poverty limited the consumer economy, which would not fully come into its own until after World War II. But it was in Progressive America that the promise of mass consumption became the foundation for a new understanding of freedom as access to the cornucopia of goods made available by modern capitalism.

Leisure activities also took on the characteristics of mass consumption. Amusement parks, dance halls, and theaters attracted large crowds of city dwellers. The most popular form of mass entertainment at the turn of the century was vaudeville, a live theatrical entertainment consisting of numerous short acts typically including song and dance, comedy, acrobats, magicians, and trained animals. In the 1890s, brief motion pictures were already being introduced into vaudeville shows. As the movies became longer and involved more sophisticated plot narratives, separate theaters developed. By 1910, 25 million Americans per week, mostly working-class urban residents, were attending "nickelodeons"—motion-picture theaters whose five-cent admission charge was far lower than at vaudeville shows.

THE WORKING WOMAN

The new visibility of women in urban public places—at work, as shoppers, and in places of entertainment like cinemas and dance halls—indicated that traditional gender roles were changing dramatically in Progressive America. As the Triangle fire revealed, more and more women were working for wages. Black women still worked primarily as domestics or in southern cotton fields. Immigrant women were largely confined to low-paying factory employment. But for native-born white women, the kinds of jobs available expanded enormously. By 1920, around 25 percent of employed women were office workers or telephone operators, and only 15 percent worked in domestic service, the largest female job category of the nineteenth century. Female work was no longer confined to young, unmarried white women and adult black women. In 1920, of 8 million women working for wages, one-quarter were married and living with their husbands.

Table 18.3 PERCENTAGE OF WOMEN 14 YEARS AND OLDER IN THE LABOR FORCE			
Year	All Women	Married Women	Women as % of Labor Force
1900	20.4%	5.6%	18%
1910	25.2	10.7	24
1920	23.3	9.0	24
1930	24.3	11.7	25

The working woman—immigrant and native, working-class and professional—became a symbol of female emancipation. Women faced special limitations on their economic freedom, including wage discrimination and exclusion from many jobs. Yet almost in spite of themselves, union leader Abraham Bisno remarked, young immigrant working women developed a sense of independence: "They acquired the *right to a personality*," something alien to the highly patriarchal family structures of the old country. "We enjoy our independence and freedom" was the assertive statement of the Bachelor Girls Social Club, a group of female mail-order clerks in New York.

The growing number of younger women who desired a lifelong career, wrote Charlotte Perkins Gilman in her influential book *Women and Economics* (1898), offered evidence of a "spirit of personal independence" that pointed to a coming transformation of both economic and family life. Gilman's writings reinforced the claim that the road to woman's freedom lay through the workplace. In the home, she argued, women experienced not fulfillment but oppression, and the housewife was an unproductive parasite, little more than a servant to her husband and children. By condemning women to a life of domestic drudgery, prevailing gender norms made them incapable of contributing to society or enjoying freedom in any meaningful sense of the word.

The desire to participate in the consumer society produced remarkably similar battles within immigrant families of all nationalities between parents and their self-consciously "free" children, especially daughters. Contemporaries, native and immigrant, noted how "the novelties and frivolities of fashion" appealed to young working women, who spent part of their meager wages on clothing and makeup and at places of entertainment. Daughters considered parents who tried to impose curfews or to prevent them from going out alone to dances or movies as old-fashioned and not sufficiently "American." Immigrant parents found it very difficult to adapt to what one Mexican mother called "this terrible freedom in this United States." "The Mexican girls," she told a sociologist studying immigrant life in Los Angeles, "seeing American girls with freedom, they want it too."

THE RISE OF FORDISM

If any individual exemplified the new consumer society, it was Henry Ford. The son of an immigrant Irish farmer, Ford had worked as an apprentice in Michigan machine shops and later as an engineer for the Edison Illuminating Company. Ford did not invent the automobile, but he developed the techniques of production and marketing that brought it within the reach of ordinary Americans. In 1905, he established the Ford Motor Company, one of dozens of small automobile manufacturing firms that emerged in these years. Three years later, he introduced the Model T, a simple, light vehicle sturdy enough to navigate the country's poorly maintained roads. While early European models like the Mercedes aimed at an elite market and were superior in craftsmanship, Ford concentrated on standardizing output and lowering prices.

In 1913, Ford's factory in Highland Park, Michigan, adopted the method of production known as the moving assembly line, in which car frames were brought to workers on a continuously moving conveyor belt. The process enabled Ford to expand output by greatly reducing the time it took

Table 18.4 PERCENTAGE OF WOMEN WORKERS IN VARIOUS OCCUPATIONS		
Occupation	*1900*	*1920*
Professional, technical	8.2%	11.7%
Clerical	4.0	18.7
Sales workers	4.3	6.2
Unskilled and semiskilled manufacturing	23.7	20.2
Household workers	28.7	15.7

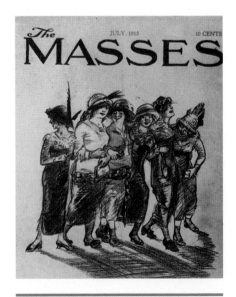

The Return from Toil, *a drawing by John Sloan for the radical magazine* The Masses, *pictures working women not as downtrodden but as independent-minded, stylish, and self-confident.*

The assembly line at the Ford Motor Company factory in Highland Park, Michigan, around 1915.

to produce each car. In 1914, he raised wages at his factory to the unheard of level of five dollars per day (more than double the pay of most industrial workers), enabling him to attract a steady stream of skilled laborers. Labor conditions in the Ford plant were not as appealing as the wages, however: assembly-line work was monotonous (the worker repeated the same basic motions for the entire day), and Ford used spies and armed detectives to prevent unionization. When other businessmen criticized him for endangering profits by paying high wages, Ford replied that workers must be able to afford the goods being turned out by American factories. Ford's output rose from 34,000 cars, priced at $700 each, in 1910, to 730,000 Model T's that sold at a price of $316 (well within the reach of many workers) in 1916. The economic system based on mass production and mass consumption came to be called Fordism.

THE PROMISE OF ABUNDANCE

As economic production shifted from capital goods (steel, railroad equipment, etc.) to consumer products, the new advertising industry perfected ways of increasing sales, often by linking goods with the idea of freedom. Numerous products took "liberty" as a brand name or used an image of the Statue of Liberty as a sales device. The department-store magnate Edward Filene called consumerism a "school of freedom," since shoppers made individual choices on basic questions of living. Economic abundance would eventually come to define the "American way of life," in which personal fulfillment was to be found through acquiring material goods.

The promise of abundance shifted the quest for freedom to the realm of private life, but it also inspired political activism. Exclusion from the world of mass consumption would come to seem almost as great a denial of the

Table 18.5 SALES OF PASSENGER CARS	
Year	Number of Cars (in thousands)
1900	4.1
1905	24.2
1910	181.0
1915	895.9
1920	1,905.5
1925	3,735.1

One day's output of Model T Fords, in a 1913 photograph. The assembly line made mass production like this possible.

rights of citizenship as being barred from voting once had been. The desire for consumer goods led many workers to join unions and fight for higher wages. The argument that monopolistic corporations artificially raised prices at the expense of consumers became a weapon against the trusts. "Consumers' consciousness," wrote Walter Lippmann, who emerged in these years as one of the nation's most influential social commentators, was growing rapidly, with the "high cost of living" as its rallying cry.

AN AMERICAN STANDARD OF LIVING

The maturation of the consumer economy gave rise to concepts—a "living wage" and an "American standard of living"—that offered a new language for criticizing the inequalities of wealth and power in Progressive America. Father John A. Ryan's influential book *A Living Wage* (1906) described a decent standard of living (one that enabled a person to participate in the consumer economy) as a "natural and absolute" right of citizenship. Ryan had grown up in Minnesota in a family sympathetic to Henry George, the Knights of Labor, and the Populists. His book sought to translate into American terms Pope Leo XIII's powerful statement of 1894, *Rerum Novarum*, which criticized the divorce of economic life from ethical considerations, endorsed the right of workers to organize unions, and repudiated competitive individualism in favor of a more cooperative vision of the good society. Ryan's insistence that economic relationships should be governed by moral standards had a powerful influence on social thought among American Catholics.

The popularity of the idea of an American standard of living reflected, in part, the emergence of a mass-consumption society during the Progressive era. For the first time in the nation's history, mass consumption came to occupy a central place in descriptions of American society and its future. In the

One of the numerous advertisements of the early twentieth century that invoked the Statue of Liberty to market consumer goods, in this case a brand of crackers.

Picturesque America, *a 1909 cartoon by Harry Grant Dart, offers a satirical comment on how advertising was threatening to overwhelm public life. Dart also includes a political comment— "He would rather advertise than be president"—on Senator Robert LaFollette of Wisconsin, pictured at the top right delivering a speech.*

Gilded Age, social theorists like Henry George had wondered why economic progress produced both increased wealth and abject misery. The Progressive generation was strongly influenced by the more optimistic writings of Simon W. Patten, a prophet of prosperity. Patten announced the end of the "reign of want" and the advent of a society of abundance and leisure. In the dawning "new civilization," he proclaimed, Americans would enjoy economic equality in a world in which "every one is independent and free."

VARIETIES OF PROGRESSIVISM

For most Americans, however, Patten's "new civilization" lay far in the future. The more immediate task, in the Progressives' view, was to humanize industrial capitalism and find common ground in a society still racked by labor conflict and experiencing massive immigration from abroad. Some Progressives proposed to return to a competitive marketplace populated by small producers. Others accepted the permanence of the large corporation and looked to the government to reverse the growing concentration of wealth and to ensure social justice. Still others would relocate freedom from the economic and political worlds to a private realm of personal fulfillment and unimpeded self-expression. But nearly all Progressives agreed that freedom must be infused with new meaning to deal with the economic and social conditions of the early twentieth century. The "old democracy," wrote Walter Weyl, associate editor of *The New Republic*, a weekly magazine that became the "bible" of Progressive intellectuals, provided no answer to the problems of a world in which the "chief restrictions upon liberty" were economic, not political.

INDUSTRIAL FREEDOM

In Progressive America, complaints of a loss of freedom came not only from the most poorly paid factory workers but from better-off employees as well. Large firms in the automobile, electrical, steel, and other industries sought to implement greater control over the work process. Efficiency expert Frederick W. Taylor pioneered what he called "scientific management"—a program that sought to streamline production and boost profits by systematically controlling costs and work practices. Through scientific study, the "one best way" of producing goods could be determined and implemented. The role of workers was to obey the detailed instructions of supervisors. Not surprisingly, many skilled workers saw the erosion of their traditional influence over the work process as a loss of freedom. "Men and women," complained Samuel Gompers, whose American Federation of Labor (AFL) represented such skilled workers, "cannot live during working hours under autocratic conditions, and instantly become sons and daughters of freedom as they step outside the shop gates."

The great increase in the number of white-collar workers—the army of salespeople, bookkeepers, salaried professionals, and corporate managers that sprang up with the new system of management—also undermined the experience of personal autonomy. For although they enjoyed far higher social status and incomes than manual workers, many, wrote one commentator, were the kind of individuals who "under former conditions, would have been . . . managing their own businesses," not working for someone else.

These developments helped to place the ideas of "industrial freedom" and "industrial democracy," which had entered the political vocabulary in the Gilded Age, at the center of political discussion during the Progressive era. Lack of "industrial freedom" was widely believed to lie at the root of the much-discussed "labor problem." Since in an industrial age the prospect of managing one's own business seemed increasingly remote, many Progressives believed that the key to increasing industrial freedom lay in empowering workers to participate in economic decision making via strong unions. Louis D. Brandeis, an active ally of the labor movement whom President Woodrow Wilson appointed to the Supreme Court in 1916, maintained that unions embodied an essential principle of freedom—the right of people to govern themselves. The contradiction between "political liberty" and "industrial slavery," Brandeis insisted, was America's foremost social problem. Workers deserved a voice not only in establishing wages and working conditions but also in making such managerial decisions as the relocation of factories, layoffs, and the distribution of profits.

THE SOCIALIST PRESENCE

Economic freedom was also a rallying cry of American socialism, which reached its greatest influence during the Progressive era. Founded in 1901, the Socialist Party brought together surviving late-nineteenth-century radicals such as Populists and followers of Edward Bellamy, with a portion of the labor movement. The party called for immediate reforms such as free college education, legislation to improve the condition of laborers, and, as an ultimate goal, democratic control over the economy through public ownership of railroads and factories. It was the task of socialism, said western labor leader John O'Neill, to "gather together the shards of liberty"—the fragments of the American heritage of freedom—scattered by a government controlled by capitalist millionaires.

By 1912, the Socialist Party claimed 150,000 dues-paying members, published hundreds of newspapers, enjoyed substantial support in the American Federation of Labor, and had elected scores of local officials. Socialism flourished in diverse communities throughout the country. On the Lower East Side of New York City, it arose from the economic exploitation of immigrant workers and Judaism's tradition of social reform. Here, a vibrant socialist culture developed, complete with Yiddish-language newspapers and theaters, as well as large public meetings and street demonstrations. In 1914, the district elected socialist Meyer London to Congress. Another center of socialist strength was Milwaukee, where Victor Berger, a German-born teacher and newspaper editor, mobilized local AFL unions into a potent political force that elected Emil Seidel mayor in 1910. Seidel's administration provided aid to the unemployed, forced the police to recognize the rights of strikers, and won the respect of middle-class residents for its honesty and freedom from machine domination. Socialism also made

Roller skaters with socialist leaflets during a New York City strike in 1916. A "scab" is a worker who crosses the picket line during a strike.

VOICES OF FREEDOM

FROM CHARLOTTE PERKINS GILMAN, Women and Economics (1898)

Women and Economics, by the prolific feminist social critic and novelist Charlotte Perkins Gilman, influenced the new generation of women aspiring to greater independence. It insisted that how people earned a living shaped their entire lives, and that therefore women must free themselves from the home to achieve genuine freedom.

It is not motherhood that keeps the housewife on her feet from dawn till dark; it is house service, not child service. Women work longer and harder than most men. . . . A truer spirit is the increasing desire of young girls to be independent, to have a career of their own, at least for a while, and the growing objection of countless wives to the pitiful asking for money, to the beggary of their position. More and more do fathers give their daughters, and husbands their wives, a definite allowance,—a separate bank account,—something . . . all their own.

The spirit of personal independence in the women of today is sure proof that a change has come . . . . The radical change in the economic position of women is advancing upon us. . . . The growing individualization of democratic life brings inevitable change to our daughters as well as to our sons. . . . One of its most noticeable features is the demand in women not only for their own money, but for their own work for the sake of personal expression. Few girls today fail to manifest some signs of this desire for individual expression. . . .

Economic independence for women necessarily involves a change in the home and family relation. But, if that change is for the advantage of individual and race, we need not fear it. It does not involve a change in the marriage relation except in withdrawing the element of economic dependence, nor in the relation of mother to child save to improve it. But it does involve the exercise of human faculty in women, in social service and exchange rather than in domestic service solely. . . . [Today], when our still developing social needs call for an ever-increasing . . . freedom, the woman in marrying becomes the house-servant, or at least the housekeeper, of the man. . . . When women stand free as economic agents, they will [achieve a] much better fulfilment of their duties as wives and mothers and [contribute] to the vast improvement in health and happiness of the human race.

From John Mitchell, "The Workingman's Conception of Industrial Liberty" (1910)

During the Progressive era, the idea of "industrial liberty" moved to the center of political discussion. Progressive reformers and labor leaders like John Mitchell, head of the United Mine Workers, condemned the prevailing idea of liberty of contract in favor of a broader definition of economic freedom.

While the Declaration of Independence established civil and political liberty, it did not, as you all know, establish industrial liberty. . . . Liberty means more than the right to choose the field of one's employment. He is not a free man whose family must buy food today with the money that is earned tomorrow. He is not really free who is forced to work unduly long hours and for wages so low that he can not provide the necessities of life for himself and his family; who must live in a crowded tenement and see his children go to work in the mills, the mines, and the factories before their bodies are developed and their minds trained. To have freedom a man must be free from the harrowing fear of hunger and want; he must be in such a position that by the exercise of reasonable frugality he can provide his family with all of the necessities and the reasonable comforts of life. He must be able to educate his children and to provide against sickness, accident, and old age. . . .

A number of years ago the legislatures of several coal producing States enacted laws requiring employers to pay the wages of their workmen in lawful money of the United States and to cease the practice of paying wages in merchandise. From time immemorial it had been the custom of coal companies to conduct general supply stores, and the workingmen were required, as a condition of employment, to accept products in lieu of money in return for services rendered. This system was a great hardship to the workmen. . . . The question of the constitutionality of this legislation was carried into the courts and by the highest tribunal it was declared to be an invasion of the workman's liberty to deny him the right to accept merchandise in lieu of money as payment of his wages. . . . [This is] typical of hundreds of instances in which laws that have been enacted for the protection of the workingmen have been declared by the courts to be unconstitutional, on the grounds that they invaded the liberty of the working people. . . . Is it not natural that the workingmen should feel that they are being guaranteed the liberties they do not want and denied the liberty that is of real value to them? May they not exclaim, with Madame Roland [of the French Revolution], "O Liberty! Liberty! How many crimes are committed in thy name!"

===

QUESTIONS

1. What does Gilman see as the main obstacles to freedom for women?

2. What does Mitchell believe will be necessary to establish "industrial liberty"?

3. How do the authors differ in their view of the relationship of the family to individual freedom?

SOCIALIST TOWNS AND CITIES, 1900–1920

Although the Socialist Party never won more than 6 percent of the vote nationally, it gained control of numerous small and medium-sized cities between 1900 and 1920.

inroads among tenant farmers in old Populist areas like Oklahoma, and in the mining regions of Idaho and Montana.

THE GOSPEL OF DEBS

No one was more important in spreading the socialist gospel or linking it to ideals of equality, self-government, and freedom than Eugene V. Debs, the railroad union leader who, as noted in the previous chapter, had been jailed during the Pullman Strike of 1894. For two decades, Debs criss-crossed the country preaching that control of the economy by a democratic government held out the hope of uniting "political equality and economic freedom." As a champion of the downtrodden, Debs managed to bridge the cultural divide among New York's Jewish immigrants, prairie socialists of the West, and native-born intellectuals attracted to the socialist ideal. "While there is a lower class," proclaimed Debs, "I am in it, . . . while there is a soul in prison, I am not free."

Throughout the Atlantic world of the early twentieth century, socialism was a rising presence. Debs would receive more than 900,000 votes for president (6 percent of the total) in 1912. In that year, the socialist *Appeal to Reason*, published in Girard, Kansas, with a circulation of 700,000, was the largest weekly newspaper in the country, and socialist Max Hayes polled one-third of the vote when he challenged Samuel Gompers for the presidency of the AFL. In western Europe, socialism experienced even more pronounced growth. In the last elections before the outbreak of World War I in 1914, socialists in France, Germany, and Scandinavia won between one-sixth and one-third of the vote. "Socialism is coming," declared the *Appeal to Reason*. "It is coming like a prairie fire and nothing can stop it."

One Big Union, *the emblem of the Industrial Workers of the World.*

AFL AND IWW

Socialism was only one example of widespread discontent in Progressive America. The labor strife of the Gilded Age continued into the early twentieth century. Having survived the depression of the 1890s, the American Federation of Labor saw its membership triple to 1.6 million between 1900 and 1904. At the same time, it sought to forge closer ties with forward-looking corporate leaders willing to deal with unions as a way to stabilize employee relations. AFL president Gompers joined with George Perkins of the J. P. Morgan financial empire and Mark Hanna, who had engineered McKinley's election, in the National Civic Federation, which accepted the right of collective bargaining for "responsible" unions. It helped to settle hundreds of industrial disputes and encouraged improvements in factory safety and the establishment of pension plans for long-term workers. Most employers nonetheless continued to view unions as an intolerable interference with their authority, and resisted them stubbornly.

The AFL mainly represented the most privileged American workers—skilled industrial and craft laborers, nearly all of them white, male, and native-born. In 1905, a group of unionists who rejected the AFL's exclusionary policies formed the Industrial Workers of the World (IWW). Part trade union, part advocate of a workers' revolution that would seize the means of production and abolish the state, the IWW made solidarity its guiding principle, extending "a fraternal hand to every wage-worker, no matter what his religion, fatherland, or trade." The organization sought to mobilize those excluded from the AFL—the immigrant factory-labor force, migrant timber and agricultural workers, women, blacks, and even the despised Chinese on the West Coast. The IWW's most prominent leader was William "Big Bill" Haywood, who had worked in western mines as a youth. Dubbed by critics "the most dangerous man in America," Haywood became a national figure in 1906 when he was kidnapped and spirited off to Idaho, accused of instigating the murder of a former anti-union governor. Defended by labor lawyer Clarence Darrow, Haywood was found not guilty.

THE NEW IMMIGRANTS ON STRIKE

The Uprising of the 20,000 in New York's garment industry, mentioned earlier, was one of a series of mass strikes among immigrant workers that placed labor's demand for the right to bargain collectively at the forefront

Striking New York City garment workers carrying signs in multiple languages, 1913.

of the reform agenda. These strikes demonstrated that while ethnic divisions among workers impeded labor solidarity, ethnic cohesiveness could also be a basis of unity, so long as strikes were organized on a democratic basis. The IWW did not originate these confrontations but was sometimes called in by local unionists to solidify the strikers. IWW organizers printed leaflets, posters, and banners in multiple languages and insisted that each nationality enjoy representation on the committee coordinating a walkout. It drew on the sense of solidarity within immigrant communities to persuade local religious leaders, shopkeepers, and officeholders to support the strikes.

The labor conflict that had the greatest impact on public consciousness took place in Lawrence, Massachusetts. The city's huge woolen mills employed 32,000 men, women, and children representing twenty-five nationalities. They worked six days per week and earned an average of sixteen cents per hour. When the state legislature in January 1912 enacted a fifty-four-hour limit to the workweek, employers reduced the weekly take-home pay of those who had been laboring longer hours. Workers spontaneously went on strike, and called on the IWW for assistance.

In February, Haywood and a group of women strikers devised the idea of sending strikers' children out of the city for the duration of the walkout. Socialist families in New York City agreed to take them in. The sight of the children, many of whom appeared pale and half-starved, marching up Fifth Avenue from the train station led to a wave of sympathy for the strikers. "I have worked in the slums of New York," wrote one observer, "but I have never found children who were so uniformly ill-nourished, ill-fed, and ill-clothed." A few days later, city officials ordered that no more youngsters could leave Lawrence. When a group of mothers and children gathered at the railroad station in defiance of the order, club-wielding police drove them away, producing outraged headlines around the world. The governor of Massachusetts soon intervened, and the strike was settled on the workers' terms. A banner carried by the Lawrence strikers gave a new slogan to the labor movement: "We want bread and roses, too"—a declaration that workers sought not only higher wages but the opportunity to enjoy the finer things of life.

Another highly publicized labor uprising took place in New Orleans, where a 1907 strike of 10,000 black and white dockworkers prevented employers' efforts to eliminate their unions and reduce their wages. This was a remarkable expression of interracial solidarity at a time when segregation had become the norm throughout the South. Other strikes proved less successful. A six-month walkout of 25,000 silk workers in Paterson, New Jersey, in 1913 failed despite publicity generated by the Paterson pageant, in which the strikers reenacted highlights of their struggle before a sympathetic audience at New York's Madison Square Garden.

A strike against the Rockefeller-owned Colorado Fuel and Iron Company was also unsuccessful. Mostly recent immigrants from Europe and Mexico, the strikers demanded recognition of the United Mine Workers of America, wage increases, an eight-hour workday, and the right to shop and live in places not owned by the company. When the walkout began, in September 1913, the mine owners evicted 11,000 strikers and their families from company housing. They moved into tent colonies, which armed militia units soon surrounded. On April 20, 1914, the militia attacked the largest tent city, at Ludlow, and burned it to the ground, killing an estimated twenty to thirty men, women, and children. Seven months after the Ludlow Massacre, the strike was called off.

LABOR AND CIVIL LIBERTIES

The fiery organizer Mary "Mother" Jones, who at the age of eighty-three had been jailed after addressing the Colorado strikers, later told a New York audience that the union "had only the Constitution; the other side had the bayonets." Yet the struggle of workers for the right to strike and of labor radicals against restraints on open-air speaking made free speech a significant public issue in the early twentieth century. By and large, the courts rejected their claims. But these battles laid the foundation for the rise of civil liberties as a central component of freedom in twentieth-century America.

State courts in the Progressive era regularly issued injunctions prohibiting strikers from speaking, picketing, or distributing literature during labor disputes. Like the abolitionists before them, the labor movement, in the name of freedom, demanded the right to assemble, organize, and spread their views. The investigations of the Commission on Industrial Relations revealed the absence of free speech in many factory communities, with labor organizers prohibited from speaking freely under threat of either violence from private police or suppression by local authorities. "I don't think we live in a free country or enjoy civil liberties," Clarence Darrow told the commission.

The IWW's battle for civil liberties breathed new meaning into the idea of freedom of expression. Lacking union halls, its organizers relied on songs, street theater, impromptu organizing meetings, and street corner gatherings to spread their message and attract support. In response to IWW activities, officials in Los Angeles, Spokane, Denver, and more than a dozen other cities limited or prohibited outdoor meetings. To arouse popular support, the IWW filled the jails with members who defied local law by speaking in public. Sometimes, prisoners

The New York shirtwaist strike of 1909 inspired workers in other cities. Here women in Rochester, New York, boldly hold aloft a strike banner.

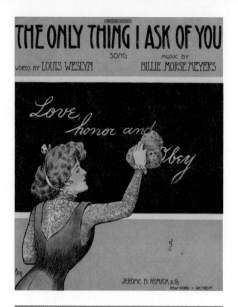

A sheet music cover, with a modern woman erasing the word "obey" from marriage vows.

Isadora Duncan brought a new freedom to an old art form.

were brutally treated, as in Spokane, where three died and hundreds were hospitalized after being jailed for violating a local law requiring prior approval of the content of public speeches. In nearly all the free-speech fights, however, the IWW eventually forced local officials to give way. "Whether they agree or disagree with its methods or aims," wrote one journalist, "all lovers of liberty everywhere owe a debt to this organization for ... [keeping] alight the fires of freedom."

THE NEW FEMINISM

During the Progressive era, the word "feminism" first entered the political vocabulary. One organization, the Feminist Alliance, constructed apartment houses with communal kitchens, cafeterias, and daycare centers, to free women from the constraints of the home. In 1914, a mass meeting at New York's Cooper Union debated the question "What is Feminism?" The meeting was sponsored by Heterodoxy, a women's club located in Greenwich Village that brought together female professionals, academics, and reformers. Feminism, said one speaker, meant women's emancipation "both as a human being and a sex-being." Feminists' forthright attack on traditional rules of sexual behavior added a new dimension to the discussion of personal freedom.

Heterodoxy was part of a new radical "bohemia" (a social circle of artists, writers, and others who reject conventional rules and practices). Its definition of feminism merged issues like the vote and greater economic opportunities with open discussion of sexuality. In New York's Greenwich Village and counterparts in Chicago, San Francisco, and other cities, a "lyrical left" came into being in the prewar years. Its members formed discussion clubs, attended experimental theaters, and published magazines. They confidently expected to preside over the emancipation of the human spirit from the prejudices of the nineteenth century.

One symbol of the new era was Isadora Duncan, who brought from California a new, expressive dance based on the free movement of a body liberated from the constraints of traditional technique and costume. "I beheld the dance I had always dreamed of," wrote the novelist Edith Wharton on seeing a Duncan performance, "satisfying every sense as a flower does, or a phrase of Mozart's." Another sign of artistic revolution was the Armory Show of 1913, an exhibition that exposed New Yorkers to new cubist paintings from Europe by artists previously unknown in the United States, like Pablo Picasso.

The lyrical left made freedom the key to its vision of society. At the famed salon in heiress Mabel Dodge's New York living room, a remarkable array of talented radicals gathered to discuss with equal passion labor unrest, modern trends in the arts, and sexual liberation. Although many Progressives frequented the Dodge salon, there was a world of difference between the exuberant individualism of the lyrical left and most Progressives' preoccupation with order and efficiency. "What [women] are really after," explained Crystal Eastman, is "*freedom.*" A graduate of New York University Law School, Eastman had taken a leading role both in the suffrage movement and in investigating industrial accidents. But her definition of freedom went beyond the vote, beyond "industrial democracy," to encompass emotional and sexual self-determination.

THE RISE OF PERSONAL FREEDOM

During the Progressive era, as journalist William M. Reedy jested, it struck "sex o'clock" in America. The founder of psychiatry, Sigmund Freud, lectured at Clark University in Worcester, Massachusetts, in 1909, and discovered that his writings on infantile sexuality, repression, and the irrational sources of human behavior were widely known "even in prudish America." Issues of intimate personal relations previously confined to private discussion blazed forth in popular magazines and public debates.

For the generation of women who adopted the word "feminism" to express their demand for greater liberty, free sexual expression and reproductive choice emerged as critical definitions of women's emancipation. Greenwich Village became a center of sexual experimentation. The aura of tolerance attracted many homosexuals to the area, and although organized demands for gay rights lay far in the future, the gay community became an important element of the Village's lifestyle. But new sexual attitudes spread far beyond bohemia; they flourished among the young, unmarried, self-supporting women who made sexual freedom a hallmark of their oft-proclaimed personal independence.

THE BIRTH-CONTROL MOVEMENT

The growing presence of women in the labor market reinforced demands for access to birth control, an issue that gave political expression to changing sexual behavior. In the nineteenth century, the right to "control one's body" generally meant the ability to refuse sexual advances, including those of a woman's husband. Now, it suggested the ability to enjoy an active sexual life without necessarily bearing children. Emma Goldman, who had emigrated to the United States from Lithuania at the age of sixteen, toured the country lecturing on subjects from anarchism to the need for more enlightened attitudes toward homosexuality. She regularly included the right to birth control in her speeches and distributed pamphlets with detailed information about various contraceptive devices. "I demand freedom for both sexes," she proclaimed, "freedom of action, freedom in love and freedom in motherhood." Goldman constantly ran afoul of the law. By one count, she was arrested more than forty times for dangerous or "obscene" statements or simply to keep her from speaking.

By forthrightly challenging the laws banning contraceptive information and devices, Margaret Sanger, one of eleven children of an Irish-American working-class family, placed the issue of birth control at the heart of the new feminism. In 1911, she began a column on sex education, "What Every Girl Should Know," for *The Call*, a New York socialist newspaper. Postal officials barred one issue, containing a column on venereal disease, from the mails. The next issue of *The Call* included a blank page with the headline: "What Every Girl Should Know—Nothing; by order of the U. S. Post Office."

By 1914, the intrepid Sanger was openly advertising birth-control devices in her own journal, *The Woman Rebel*. "No woman can call herself free," she proclaimed, "who does not own and control her own body [and] can choose consciously whether she will or will not be a mother." In 1916, Sanger opened a clinic in a working-class neighborhood of Brooklyn and began distributing contraceptive devices to poor Jewish and Italian

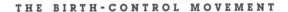

The much-beloved and much-feared Emma Goldman, with a poster advertising a series of her lectures, illustrating the remarkable variety of topics on which she spoke.

Mothers with baby carriages wait outside Margaret Sanger's birth-control clinic in Brownsville, Brooklyn, 1916.

women, an action for which she was sentenced to a month in prison. Few Progressives rallied to her defense. But for a time, the birth-control issue became a crossroads where the paths of labor radicals, cultural modernists, and feminists intersected. The IWW and Socialist Party distributed Sanger's writings. Like the IWW free-speech fights and Goldman's persistent battle for the right to lecture, Sanger's travail was part of a rich history of dissent in the Progressive era that helped to focus enlightened opinion on the ways local authorities and national obscenity legislation set rigid limits to Americans' freedom of expression.

NATIVE AMERICAN PROGRESSIVISM

Many groups participated in the Progressive impulse. Founded in 1911, the Society of American Indians was a reform organization typical of the era. It brought together Indian intellectuals to promote discussion of the plight of Native Americans in the hope that public exposure would be the first step toward remedying injustice. Because many of the Society's leaders had been educated at government-sponsored boarding schools, the Society united Indians of many tribal backgrounds. It created a pan-Indian public space independent of white control.

Many of these Indian intellectuals were not unsympathetic to the basic goals of federal Indian policy, including the transformation of communal landholdings on reservations into family farms. But Carlos Montezuma, a founder of the Society of American Indians, became an outspoken critic. Born in Arizona, he had been captured as a child by members of a neighboring tribe and sold to a traveling photographer, who brought him to Chicago. There Montezuma attended school and eventually obtained a medical degree.

In 1916, Montezuma established a newsletter, *Wassaja* (meaning "signaling"), that condemned federal paternalism toward the Indians and called for the abolition of the Bureau of Indian Affairs. Convinced that outsiders exerted too much power over life on the reservations, he insisted that self-determination was the only way for Indians to escape poverty and marginalization: "We must free ourselves.... We must be independent."

But he also demanded that Indians be granted full citizenship and all the constitutional rights of other Americans. Montezuma's writings had little influence at the time on government policy, but Indian activists would later rediscover him as a forerunner of Indian radicalism.

THE POLITICS OF PROGRESSIVISM

EFFECTIVE FREEDOM

Progressivism was an international movement. In the early twentieth century, cities throughout the world experienced similar social strains arising from rapid industrialization and urban growth. In 1850, London and Paris were the only cities whose population exceeded 1 million. By 1900, there were twelve—New York, Chicago, and Philadelphia in the United States, and others in Europe, Latin America, and Asia. Facing similar social problems, reformers across the globe exchanged ideas and envisioned new social policies. Sun Yat-Sen, the Chinese leader, was influenced by the writings of Henry George and Edward Bellamy. The mayor of Osaka, Japan, called for a new "social economy" that replaced competition with cooperation.

As governments in Britain, France, and Germany instituted old age pensions, minimum wage laws, unemployment insurance, and the regulation of workplace safety, American reformers came to believe they had much to learn from the Old World. The term "social legislation," meaning governmental action to address urban problems and the insecurities of working-class life, originated in Germany but soon entered the political vocabulary of the United States.

Progressives believed that the modern era required a fundamental rethinking of the functions of political authority, whether the aim was to combat the power of the giant corporations, protect consumers, civilize the marketplace, or guarantee industrial freedom at the workplace. Drawing on the reform programs of the Gilded Age and the example of European legislation, Progressives sought to reinvigorate the idea of an activist, socially conscious government. Even in South Carolina, with its strong tradition of belief in local autonomy, Governor Richard I. Manning urged his constituents to modify their view of government as "a threat to individual liberty," to see it instead as "a means for solving the ills of the body politic."

Progressives could reject the traditional assumption that powerful government posed a threat to freedom, because their understanding of freedom was itself in flux. "Effective freedom," wrote the philosopher John Dewey, was far different from the "highly formal and limited concept of liberty" as protection from outside restraint. Freedom was a positive, not a negative, concept—the "power to do specific things." As such, it depended on "the *distribution* of powers that exists at a given time." Thus, freedom inevitably became a political question. "Freedom," wrote Dewey's brilliant young admirer, the writer Randolph Bourne, "means a democratic cooperation in determining the ideals and purposes and industrial and social institutions of a country."

STATE AND LOCAL REFORMS

Throughout the Western world, social legislation proliferated in the early twentieth century. In the United States, with a political structure more decentralized than in European countries, state and local governments

Children at play at the Hudson-Bank Gymnasium, built in 1898 in a New York immigrant neighborhood by the Outdoor Recreation League, one of many Progressive era groups that sought to improve life in urban centers.

enacted most of the era's reform measures. In cities, Progressives worked to reform the structure of government to reduce the power of political bosses, establish public control of "natural monopolies" like gas and water works, and improve public transportation. They raised property taxes in order to spend more money on schools, parks, and other public facilities.

Gilded Age mayors Hazen Pingree and Samuel "Golden Rule" Jones pioneered urban Progressivism. A former factory worker who became a successful shoe manufacturer, Pingree served as mayor of Detroit from 1889 to 1897. He battled the business interests that had dominated city government, forcing gas and telephone companies to lower their rates, and established a municipal power plant. Jones had instituted an eight-hour day and paid vacations at his factory that produced oil drilling equipment. As mayor of Toledo, Ohio, from 1897 to 1905, he founded night schools and free kindergartens, built new parks, and supported the right of workers to unionize.

Since state legislatures defined the powers of city government, urban Progressives often carried their campaigns to the state level. Pingree became governor of Michigan in 1896, in which post he continued his battle against railroads and other corporate interests. Hiram Johnson, who as public prosecutor had secured the conviction for bribery of San Francisco political boss Abraham Ruef, was elected governor of California in 1910. Having promised to "kick the Southern Pacific [Railroad] out of politics," he secured passage of the Public Utilities Act, one of the country's strongest railroad-regulation measures, as well as laws banning child labor and limiting the working hours of women.

The most influential Progressive administration at the state level was that of Robert M. La Follette, who made Wisconsin a "laboratory for democracy." After serving as a Republican member of Congress, La Follette became convinced that an alliance of railroad and lumber companies controlled state politics. Elected governor in 1900, he instituted a series of measures known as the Wisconsin Idea, including nominations of candidates for office through primary elections rather than by political bosses, the taxation of corporate wealth, and state regulation of railroads and public utilities. To staff his administration, he drew on nonpartisan faculty members from the University of Wisconsin.

PROGRESSIVE DEMOCRACY

"We are far from free," wrote Randolph Bourne in 1913, "but the new spirit of democracy is the angel that will free us." Progressives hoped to reinvigorate democracy by restoring political power to the citizenry and civic harmony to a divided society. Alarmed by the upsurge in violent class conflict and the unrestricted power of corporations, they believed that political reforms could help to create a unified "people" devoted to greater democracy and social reconciliation. Yet increasing the responsibilities of government made it all the more important to identify who was entitled to political participation and who was not.

The Progressive era saw a host of changes implemented in the political process, many seemingly contradictory in purpose. The electorate was simultaneously expanded and contracted, empowered and removed from direct influence on many functions of government. Democracy was enhanced by the Seventeenth Amendment—which provided that U.S. senators be chosen by popular vote rather than by state legislatures—by widespread adoption of the popular election of judges, and by the use of primary elections among party members to select candidates for office. Several states, including California under Hiram Johnson, adopted the initiative and referendum (the former allowed voters to propose legislation, the latter to vote directly on it) and the recall, by which officials could be removed from office by popular vote. The era culminated with a constitutional amendment enfranchising women—the largest expansion of democracy in American history.

But the Progressive era also witnessed numerous restrictions on democratic participation, most strikingly the disenfranchisement of blacks in the South, a process, as noted in Chapter 17, supported by many white southern Progressives as a way of ending election fraud. To make city government more honest and efficient, many localities replaced elected mayors with appointed nonpartisan commissions or city managers—a change that insulated officials from machine domination but also from popular control. New literacy tests and residency and registration requirements, common in northern as well as southern states, limited the right to vote among the poor. Taken as a whole, the electoral changes of the Progressive era represented a significant reversal of the idea that voting was an inherent right of American citizenship. And, as will be noted in the next chapter, most white Progressives proved remarkably indifferent to the plight of African-Americans. In the eyes of many Progressives, the "fitness" of voters, not their absolute numbers, defined a functioning democracy.

GOVERNMENT BY EXPERT

"He didn't believe in democracy; he believed simply in government." The writer H. L. Mencken's quip about Theodore Roosevelt came uncomfortably close to the mark for many Progressive advocates of an empowered state. Most Progressive thinkers were highly uncomfortable with the real world of politics, which seemed to revolve around the pursuit of narrow class, ethnic, and regional interests. Robert M. La Follette's reliance on college professors to staff important posts in his administration reflected a larger Progressive faith in expertise. The government could best exercise intelligent control over society through a democracy run by impartial experts who were in many respects unaccountable to the citizenry.

This impulse toward order, efficiency, and centralized management—all in the name of social justice—was an important theme of Progressive reform. The title of Walter Lippmann's influential 1914 work of social commentary, *Drift and Mastery,* posed the stark alternatives facing the nation.

A staff member greets an immigrant family at Hull House, the settlement house established in Chicago by Jane Addams.

"Drift" meant continuing to operate according to the outmoded belief in individual autonomy. "Mastery" required applying scientific inquiry to modern social problems. The new generation of educated professionals, Lippmann believed, could be trusted more fully than ordinary citizens to solve America's deep social problems. Political freedom was less a matter of direct participation in government than of qualified persons devising the best public policies.

JANE ADDAMS AND HULL HOUSE

But alongside this elitist politics, Progressivism also included a more democratic vision of the activist state. As much as any other group, organized women reformers spoke for the more democratic side of Progressivism. Still barred from voting and holding office in most states, women nonetheless became central to the political history of the Progressive era. Women challenged the barriers that excluded them from formal political participation and developed a democratic, grassroots vision of Progressive government. In so doing, they placed on the political agenda new understandings of female freedom. The immediate catalyst was a growing awareness among women reformers of the plight of poor immigrant communities and the emergence of the condition of women and child laborers as a major focus of public concern.

The era's most prominent female reformer was Jane Addams, who had been born in 1860, the daughter of an Illinois businessman. After graduating from college, Addams, who never married, resented the prevailing expectation that a woman's life should be governed by what she called the "family claim"—the obligation to devote herself to parents, husband, and children. In 1889, she founded Hull House in Chicago, a "settlement house" devoted to improving the lives of the immigrant poor. Hull House was modeled on Toynbee Hall, which Addams had visited after its establishment in a working-class neighborhood of London in 1884. Unlike previous reformers, who had aided the poor from afar, settlement house workers moved into poor neighborhoods. They built kindergartens and playgrounds for children, established employment bureaus and health clinics, and showed female victims of domestic abuse how to gain legal protection. By 1910, more than 400 settlement houses had been established in cities throughout the country.

"SPEARHEADS FOR REFORM"

Addams was typical of the Progressive era's "new woman." By 1900, there were more than 80,000 college-educated women in the United States. Many found a calling in providing social services, nursing, and education to poor families in the growing cities. The efforts of middle-class women to uplift the poor, and of laboring women to uplift themselves, helped to shift the center of gravity of politics toward activist government. Women like Addams discovered that even well-organized social work was not enough to alleviate the problems of inadequate housing, income, and health. Government action was essential. Hull House instigated an array of reforms in Chicago, soon adopted elsewhere, including stronger building and sanitation codes, shorter working hours and safer labor conditions, and the right of labor to organize.

Female activism spread throughout the country. Ironically, the exclusion of blacks from jobs in southern textile mills strengthened the region's movement against child labor. Reformers portrayed child labor as a menace to white supremacy, depriving white children of educations they would need as adult members of the dominant race. These reformers devoted little attention to the condition of black children. Women's groups in Alabama were instrumental in the passage of a 1903 state law restricting child labor. By 1915, every southern state had followed suit. But with textile mill owners determined to employ children and many poor families dependent on their earnings, these laws were enforced only sporadically.

Visiting nurse on a New York City rooftop, 1908. Efforts to uplift the immigrant poor offered new opportunities for professional employment to many women during the Progressive era.

The settlement houses have been called "spearheads for reform." They produced prominent Progressive figures like Julia Lathrop, the first woman to head a federal agency (the Children's Bureau, established in 1912 to investigate the conditions of mothers and children and advocate their interests). Florence Kelley, the daughter of Civil War–era Radical Republican congressman William D. Kelley and a veteran of Hull House, went on to mobilize women's power as consumers as a force for social change. In the Gilded Age, the writer Helen Campbell had brilliantly exposed the contradiction of a market economy in which fashionable women wore clothing produced by poor women in wretched sweatshops. "Emancipation on the one side," she pointedly observed, "has meant no corresponding emancipation for the other." A generation later, under Kelley's leadership, the National Consumers' League became the nation's leading advocate of laws governing the working conditions of women and children. Freedom of choice in the marketplace, Kelley insisted, enabled socially conscious consumers to "unite with wage earners" by refusing to purchase goods produced under exploitative conditions.

THE CAMPAIGN FOR WOMAN SUFFRAGE

After 1900, the campaign for women's suffrage moved beyond the elitism of the 1890s to engage a broad coalition ranging from middle-class members of women's clubs to unionists, socialists, and settlement house workers. For the first time, it became a mass movement. Membership in the National American Woman Suffrage Association grew from 13,000 in 1893 to more than 2 million by 1917. The group campaigned throughout the country for the right to vote and began to enjoy some success. By 1900, more than half the states allowed women to vote in local elections dealing with school issues, and Wyoming, Colorado, Idaho, and Utah had adopted full women's suffrage.

Cynics charged that Wyoming legislators used suffrage to attract more female migrants to their predominantly male state, while Utah hoped to

In this 1912 woman suffrage parade in New York City, a mother wheels a baby carriage to counteract the charge that allowing women to vote would undermine the family.

enhance the political power of husbands in polygamous marriages banned by law but still practiced by some Mormons. In Colorado and Idaho, however, the success of referendums in the 1890s reflected the power of the Populist Party, a strong supporter of votes for women. Between 1910 and 1914, seven more western states enfranchised women. In 1913, Illinois became the first state east of the Mississippi River to allow women to vote in presidential elections.

These campaigns, which brought women aggressively into the public sphere, were conducted with a new spirit of militancy. They also made effective use of the techniques of advertising, publicity, and mass entertainment characteristic of modern consumer society. California's successful 1911 campaign utilized automobile parades, numerous billboards and electric signs, and countless suffrage buttons and badges. Nonetheless, state campaigns were difficult, expensive, and usually unsuccessful. The movement increasingly focused its attention on securing a national constitutional amendment giving women the right to vote.

MATERNALIST REFORM

Ironically, the desire to exalt women's role within the home did much to inspire the reinvigoration of the suffrage movement. Many of the era's experiments in public policy arose from the conviction that the state had an obligation to protect women and children. Female reformers helped to launch a mass movement for direct government action to improve the living standards of poor mothers and children. Laws providing for mothers' pensions (state aid to mothers of young children who lacked male support) spread rapidly after 1910. The pensions tended to be less than generous, and local eligibility requirements opened the door to unequal treatment (white widows benefited the most, single mothers were widely discriminated against, and black women were almost entirely excluded). "Maternalist" reforms like mothers' pensions rested on the assumption that the government should encourage women's capacity for bearing and raising children

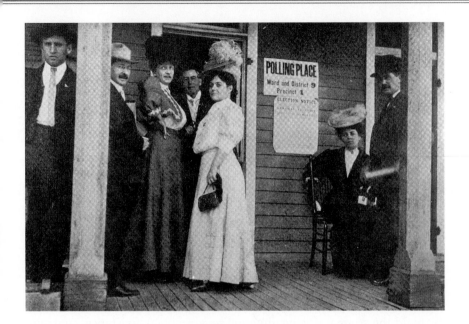

In 1893, Colorado became the first state to allow women to vote. Here well-dressed women wait to vote alongside men in a 1907 election in Denver.

and enable them to be economically independent at the same time. Both feminists and believers in conventional domestic roles supported such measures. The former hoped that these laws would subvert women's dependence on men, the latter that they would strengthen traditional families and the mother-child bond.

Other Progressive legislation recognized that large numbers of women did in fact work outside the home, but defined them as a dependent group (like children) in need of state protection in ways male workers were not. In 1908, in the landmark case of *Muller v. Oregon*, Louis D. Brandeis filed a famous brief citing scientific and sociological studies to demonstrate that because they had less strength and endurance than men, long hours of labor were dangerous for women, while their unique ability to bear children gave the government a legitimate interest in their working conditions. Persuaded by Brandeis's argument, the Supreme Court unanimously upheld the constitutionality of an Oregon law setting maximum working hours for women.

Thus, three years after the notorious *Lochner* decision invalidating a New York law limiting the working hours of male bakers (discussed in Chapter 16), the Court created the first large breach in "liberty of contract" doctrine. But the cost was high: at the very time that women in unprecedented numbers were entering the labor market and earning college degrees, Brandeis's brief and the Court's opinion solidified the view of women workers as weak, dependent, and incapable of enjoying the same economic rights as men. By 1917, thirty states had enacted laws limiting the hours of labor of female workers. Many women derived great benefit from these laws; others saw them as an infringement on their freedom.

While the maternalist agenda built gender inequality into the early foundations of the welfare state, the very use of government to regulate working conditions called into question basic assumptions concerning liberty of contract. Although not all reformers were willing to take the step, it was easy to extend the idea of protecting women and children to demand that government better the living and working conditions of men as well,

Louis D. Brandeis, Progressive reformer and advocate of the labor movement, was appointed to the Supreme Court in 1916 by President Woodrow Wilson.

by insuring them against the impact of unemployment, old age, ill health, and disability. Brandeis himself insisted that government should concern itself with the health, income, and future prospects of all its citizens.

THE IDEA OF ECONOMIC CITIZENSHIP

Brandeis envisioned a different welfare state from that of the maternalist reformers, one rooted less in the idea of healthy motherhood than in the notion of universal economic entitlements, including the right to a decent income and protection against unemployment and work-related accidents. For him, the right to assistance derived from citizenship itself, not some special service to the nation (as in the case of mothers) or upstanding character (which had long differentiated the "deserving" from the "undeserving" poor).

This vision, too, enjoyed considerable support in the Progressive era. By 1913, twenty-two states had enacted workmen's compensation laws to benefit workers, male or female, injured on the job. This legislation was the first wedge that opened the way for broader programs of social insurance. To avoid the stigma of depending on governmental assistance, contributions from workers' own wages funded these programs in part, thus distinguishing them from charity dispensed by local authorities to the poor. But state minimum wage laws and most laws regulating working hours applied only to women. Women and children may have needed protection, but interference with the freedom of contract of adult male workers was still widely seen as degrading. The establishment of a standard of living and working conditions beneath which no American should be allowed to fall would await the coming of the New Deal.

THE PROGRESSIVE PRESIDENTS

Despite the ferment of Progressivism on the city and state levels, the most striking political development of the early twentieth century was the rise of the national state. The process of nationalization was occurring throughout American life. National corporations dominated the economy; national organizations like the American Medical Association came into being to raise the incomes and respect of professions. The process was even reflected in the consolidation of local baseball teams into the American and National Leagues and the advent in 1903 of the World Series. Only energetic national government, Progressives believed, could create the social conditions of freedom.

Despite creative experiments in social policy at the city and state levels, the tradition of localism seemed to most Progressives an impediment to a renewed sense of national purpose. Poverty, economic insecurity, and lack of industrial democracy were national problems that demanded national solutions. The democratic national state, wrote *New Republic* editor Herbert Croly, offered an alternative to control of Americans' lives by narrow interests that manipulated politics or by the all-powerful corporations. Croly proposed a new synthesis of American political traditions. To achieve the "Jeffersonian ends" of democratic self-determination and individual freedom, he insisted, the country needed to employ the "Hamiltonian means" of government intervention in the economy. Each in his own way, the

Progressive presidents—Theodore Roosevelt, William Howard Taft, and Woodrow Wilson—tried to address this challenge.

THEODORE ROOSEVELT

In September 1901, the anarchist Leon Czolgosz assassinated William McKinley while the president visited the Pan-American Exposition in Buffalo, New York. At the age of forty-two, Vice President Theodore Roosevelt became the youngest man ever to hold the office of president. Roosevelt was an impetuous, energetic individual with a penchant for what he called the "strenuous life" of manly adventure. In many ways, he became the model for the twentieth-century president, an official actively and continuously engaged in domestic and foreign affairs. (The foreign policies of the Progressive presidents will be discussed in the next chapter.) Roosevelt regarded the president as "the steward of the public welfare." He moved aggressively to set the political agenda.

President Theodore Roosevelt addressing a crowd in Evanston, Illinois, in 1902.

When the British writer H. G. Wells visited the United States soon after the turn of the century, he found that "the steady trend towards concentration" had become "the cardinal topic of thought and discussion in the American mind." Roosevelt's program, which he called the Square Deal, attempted to confront the problems caused by economic consolidation by distinguishing between "good" and "bad" corporations. The former, among which he included U.S. Steel and Standard Oil, served the public interest. The latter were run by greedy financiers interested only in profit, and had no right to exist.

Soon after assuming office, Roosevelt shocked the corporate world by announcing his intention to prosecute under the Sherman Antitrust Act the Northern Securities Company. Created by financier J. P. Morgan, this "holding company" owned the stock and directed the affairs of three major western railroads. It monopolized transportation between the Great Lakes and the Pacific. Morgan was outraged. "Wall Street is paralyzed," quipped one newspaper, "at the thought that a President of the United States should sink to enforce the law." In 1904, the Supreme Court ordered Northern Securities dissolved, a major victory for the antitrust movement.

ROOSEVELT AND ECONOMIC REGULATION

Roosevelt also believed that the president should be an honest broker in labor disputes, rather than automatically siding with employers as his predecessors had usually done. When a strike paralyzed the West Virginia and Pennsylvania coalfields in 1902, he summoned union and management leaders to the White House. By threatening a federal takeover of the mines, he persuaded the owners to allow the dispute to be settled by a commission he himself would appoint.

Reelected in 1904, Roosevelt pushed for more direct federal regulation of the economy. Appealing to the public for support, he condemned the misuse of the "vast power conferred by vast wealth." He proposed to strengthen the Interstate Commerce Commission, which the Supreme Court had essentially limited to collecting economic statistics. By this time, journalistic exposés, labor unrest, and the agitation of Progressive reformers had created significant public support for Roosevelt's regulatory program. In 1906,

Putting the Screws on Him, a 1904 cartoon, depicts President Theodore Roosevelt squeezing ill-gotten gains out of the trusts.

Congress passed the Hepburn Act, giving the ICC the power to examine rail-roads' business records and to set reasonable rates, a significant step in the development of federal intervention in the corporate economy. That year, as has been noted, also saw the Pure Food and Drug Act, which established a federal agency to police the quality and labeling of food and drugs, and the Meat Inspection Act. Many businessmen supported these measures, recognizing that they would benefit from greater public confidence in the quality and safety of their products. But they were alarmed by Roosevelt's calls for federal inheritance and income taxes and the regulation of all inter-state businesses.

THE CONSERVATION MOVEMENT

A dedicated outdoorsman who built a ranch in North Dakota in the 1880s, Roosevelt also moved to preserve parts of the natural environment from economic exploitation. If the United States lagged behind Europe in many areas of social policy, it led the way in the conservation of national resources. The first national park, Yellowstone in Wyoming, had been created in 1872—partly to preserve an area of remarkable natural beauty, and partly at the urging of the Northern Pacific Railroad, which was anxious to pro-mote western tourism. In the 1890s, the Scottish-born naturalist John Muir organized the Sierra Club to help preserve forests, which he called "God's first temples," from uncontrolled logging by timber companies and other intrusions of civilization. Congress in that decade authorized the president to withdraw "forest reserves" from economic development.

It was under Roosevelt that conservation became a concerted federal pol-icy. Relying for advice on Gifford Pinchot, the head of the U.S. Forest Service, he ordered that millions of acres be set aside as wildlife preserves and encouraged Congress to create new national parks. The creation of parks like Yellowstone, Yosemite, and Glacier required the removal of Indians who hunted and fished there as well as the reintroduction of animals that had previously disappeared. City dwellers who visited the national parks did not realize that these were to a considerable extent artificially cre-ated and managed environments, not primordial nature.

In some ways, conservation was a typical Progressive reform. Manned by experts, the government could stand above political and economic battles, serving the public good while preventing "special interests" from causing irreparable damage to the environment. The aim was less to end the eco-nomic utilization of natural resources than to develop responsible, scien-tific plans for their use. Pinchot halted timber companies' reckless assault on the nation's forests. But unlike Muir, he believed that development and conservation could go hand in hand and that logging, mining, and grazing on public lands should be controlled, not eliminated. Conservation also reflected the Progressive thrust toward efficiency and control—in this case, control of nature itself.

In the view of Progressive conservationists, the West's scarcest resource—water—cried out for regulation. Governments at all levels moved to control the power of western rivers, building dams and irrigation projects to regu-larize their flow, prevent waste, and provide water for large-scale agriculture and urban development. With such projects came political conflict, as cities like Los Angeles and San Francisco battled with rural areas for access to water. After secretly buying up large tracts of land in the Owens Valley east of the city, for example, the City of Los Angeles constructed a major aqueduct between 1908 and 1913, over the vigorous objections of the valley's residents. By the 1920s, so much water had been diverted to the city that the once thriving farming and ranching businesses of Owens Valley could no longer operate.

TAFT IN OFFICE

Having served nearly eight years as president, Roosevelt did not run again in 1908. His chosen successor was William Howard Taft, a federal judge from Ohio who had served as governor of the Philippines after the Spanish-American War. Taft defeated William Jennings Bryan, making his third unsuccessful race for the White House. Taft's inaugural address expressed the Progressive view of the state: "The scope of a modern government . . . has been widened far beyond the principles laid down by the old 'laissez-faire' school of political writers."

Theodore Roosevelt and the conservationist John Muir at Glacier Point, Yosemite Valley, California, in 1906. Yosemite was set aside as a national park in 1890.

Although temperamentally more conservative than Roosevelt, Taft pursued antitrust policy even more aggressively. He persuaded the Supreme Court in 1911 to declare John D. Rockefeller's Standard Oil Company (one of Roosevelt's "good" trusts) in violation of the Sherman Antitrust Act and to order its breakup into separate marketing, producing, and refining companies. The government also won a case against American Tobacco, which the Court ordered to end pricing policies that were driving smaller firms out of business. In these decisions, the justices announced a new standard for judging large corporations—the "rule of reason"—which in effect implemented Roosevelt's old distinction between good and bad trusts. Big businesses were not, in and of themselves, antitrust violators, unless they engaged in policies that stifled competition.

Taft supported the Sixteenth Amendment to the Constitution, which authorized Congress to enact a graduated income tax (one whose rate of taxation is higher for wealthier citizens). It was ratified shortly before he left office. A 2 percent tax on incomes over $4,000 had been included in a tariff enacted in 1894 but had been quickly declared unconstitutional by the Supreme Court as a "communistic threat to property." The movement to resurrect the income tax united southern and western farmers who wished to reduce government dependence on revenue from the tariff, which they believed discriminated against nonindustrial states, and Progressives who believed that taxation should be based on the ability to pay. A key step in the modernization of the federal government, the income tax provided a reliable and flexible source of revenue for a national state whose powers, responsibilities, and expenditures were growing rapidly.

Despite these accomplishments, Taft seemed to gravitate toward the more conservative wing of the Republican Party. Only a few months after taking office, he signed the Payne-Aldrich Tariff, which reduced rates on imported goods but not nearly as much as reformers wished. Taft's rift with Progressives grew deeper when Richard A. Ballinger, the new secretary of the interior, concluded that Roosevelt had exceeded his authority in placing land in forest reserves. Ballinger decided to return some of this land to the public domain, where mining and lumber companies would have access to it. Gifford Pinchot accused Ballinger of colluding with business interests and

Eugene V. Debs, the Socialist Party candidate, speaking in Chicago during the 1912 presidential campaign.

repudiating the environmental goals of the Roosevelt administration. When Taft fired Pinchot in 1910, the breach with party Progressives became irreparable. In 1912, Roosevelt challenged Taft for the Republican nomination. Defeated, Roosevelt launched an independent campaign as the head of the new Progressive Party.

THE ELECTION OF 1912

All the crosscurrents of Progressive era thinking about what *McClure's Magazine* called "the problem of the relation of the State and the corporation" came together in the presidential campaign of 1912. The four-way contest between Taft, Roosevelt, Democrat Woodrow Wilson, and Socialist Eugene V. Debs became a national debate on the relationship between political and economic freedom in the age of big business. At one end of the political spectrum stood Taft, who stressed that economic individualism could remain the foundation of the social order so long as government and private entrepreneurs cooperated in addressing social ills. At the other end was Debs. Relatively few Americans supported the Socialist Party's goal of abolishing the "capitalistic system" altogether, but its immediate demands—including public ownership of the railroads and banking system, government aid to the unemployed, and laws establishing shorter working hours and a minimum wage—summarized forward-looking Progressive thought.

But it was the battle between Wilson and Roosevelt over the role of the federal government in securing economic freedom that galvanized public attention in 1912. The two represented competing strands of Progressivism. Both believed government action necessary to preserve individual freedom, but they differed over the dangers of increasing the government's power and the inevitability of economic concentration. Though representing a party thoroughly steeped in states' rights and laissez-faire ideology, Wilson was deeply imbued with Progressive ideas. "Freedom today," he declared, "is something more than being let alone. The program of a government of freedom must in these days be positive, not negative merely." As governor of New Jersey, Wilson had presided over the implementation of a system of workmen's compensation and state regulation of utilities and railroads.

NEW FREEDOM AND NEW NATIONALISM

Strongly influenced by Louis D. Brandeis, with whom he consulted frequently during the campaign, Wilson insisted that democracy must be reinvigorated by restoring market competition and freeing government from domination by big business. Wilson feared big government as much as he feared the power of the corporations. The New Freedom, as he called his program, envisioned the federal government strengthening antitrust laws, protecting the right of workers to unionize, and actively encouraging small businesses—creating, in other words, the conditions for the renewal of economic competition without increasing government regulation of the economy. Wilson warned that corporations were as likely to corrupt government as to be managed by it, a forecast that proved remarkably accurate.

To Roosevelt's supporters, Wilson seemed a relic of a bygone era; his program, they argued, served the needs of small businessmen but ignored the inevitability of economic concentration and the interests of professionals, consumers, and labor. Wilson and Brandeis spoke of the "curse of bigness." What the nation actually needed, Walter Lippmann countered, was frank acceptance of the benefits of bigness, coupled with the intervention of government to counteract its abuses. Lippmann was expressing the core of the New Nationalism, Roosevelt's program of 1912. Only the "controlling and directing power of the government," Roosevelt insisted, could restore "the liberty of the oppressed." He called for heavy taxes on personal and corporate fortunes and federal regulation of industries, including railroads, mining, and oil.

The Progressive Party platform offered numerous proposals to promote social justice. Drafted by a group of settlement-house activists, labor reformers, and social scientists, the platform laid out a blueprint for a modern, democratic welfare state, complete with woman suffrage, federal supervision of corporate enterprise, national labor and health legislation for women and children, an eight-hour day and "living wage" for all workers, and a national system of social insurance covering unemployment, medical care, and old age. Described by Roosevelt as the "most important document" since the end of the Civil War, the platform brought together many of the streams of thought and political experiences that flowed into Progressivism. Roosevelt's campaign helped to give freedom a modern social and economic content and established an agenda that would define political liberalism for much of the twentieth century.

WILSON'S FIRST TERM

The Republican split ensured a sweeping victory for Wilson, who won about 42 percent of the popular vote, although Roosevelt humiliated Taft by winning about 27 percent to the president's 23 percent. In office, Wilson proved himself a strong executive leader. He established an office at the Capitol so that he could confer regularly with members of Congress about pending legislation, and he was the first president to hold regular press conferences in order to influence public opinion directly and continuously. He delivered messages personally to Congress rather than sending them in written form like all his predecessors since John Adams.

With Democrats in control of Congress, Wilson moved aggressively to implement his version of Progressivism. The first significant measure of his presidency was the Underwood Tariff, which substantially reduced duties on imports and, to make up for lost revenue, imposed a graduated income tax on the richest 5 percent of Americans. There followed the Clayton Act of 1914, which exempted labor unions from antitrust laws and barred courts from issuing injunctions curtailing the right to strike. In 1916 came the Keating-Owen Act outlawing child labor in the manufacture of goods sold in interstate commerce, the Adamson Act establishing an eight-hour workday on the

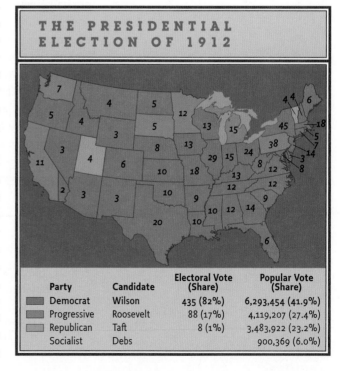

THE PRESIDENTIAL ELECTION OF 1912

Party	Candidate	Electoral Vote (Share)	Popular Vote (Share)
Democrat	Wilson	435 (82%)	6,293,454 (41.9%)
Progressive	Roosevelt	88 (17%)	4,119,207 (27.4%)
Republican	Taft	8 (1%)	3,483,922 (23.2%)
Socialist	Debs		900,369 (6.0%)

nation's railroads, and the Warehouse Act, reminiscent of the Populist sub-treasury plan, which extended credit to farmers when they stored their crops in federally licensed warehouses.

THE EXPANDING ROLE OF GOVERNMENT

Some of Wilson's policies seemed more in tune with Roosevelt's New Nationalism than the New Freedom of 1912. He abandoned the idea of aggressive trust-busting in favor of greater government supervision of the economy. Wilson presided over the creation of two powerful new public agencies. In 1913, Congress created the Federal Reserve System, consisting of twelve regional banks. They were overseen by a central board appointed by the president and empowered to handle the issuance of currency, aid banks in danger of failing, and influence interest rates so as to promote economic growth. The law was a delayed response to the Panic of 1907, when the failure of several financial companies threatened a general collapse of the banking system. With the federal government lacking a modern central bank, it had been left to J. P. Morgan to assemble the funds to prop up threatened financial institutions. Morgan's actions highlighted the fact that in the absence of federal regulation of banking, power over finance rested entirely in private hands.

A second expansion of national power occurred in 1914, when Congress established the Federal Trade Commission (FTC) to investigate and prohibit "unfair" business activities such as price-fixing and monopolistic practices. Both the Federal Reserve and FTC were welcomed by many business leaders as a means of restoring order to the economic marketplace and warding off more radical measures for curbing corporate power. But they reflected the remarkable expansion of the federal role in the economy during the Progressive era.

By 1916, the social ferment and political mobilizations of the Progressive era had given birth to a new American state. With new laws, administrative agencies, and independent commissions, government at the local, state, and national levels had assumed the authority to protect and advance "industrial freedom." Government had established rules for labor relations, business behavior, and financial policy, protected citizens from market abuses, and acted as a broker among the groups whose conflicts threatened to destroy social harmony. But a storm was already engulfing Europe that would test the Progressive faith in empowered government as the protector of American freedom.

SUGGESTED READING

BOOKS

Bodnar, John. *The Transplanted: A History of Immigrants in Urban America* (1985). A comprehensive account of American immigration.

Cameron, Ardis. *Radicals of the Worst Sort: Laboring Women in Lawrence, Massachusetts, 1860–1912* (1993). Describes the lives of working women in Lawrence and their role in the strike of 1912.

Cott, Nancy F. *The Grounding of Modern Feminism* (1987). A careful study of feminist ideas in the Progressive era.

Dawley, Alan. *Struggles for Justice: Social Responsibility and the Liberal State* (1991). Examines the varieties of Progressive reform and various efforts to use the power of government for social betterment.

Diner, Steven. *A Very Different Age: Americans of the Progressive Era* (1998). A survey of the main trends of the Progressive period.

Glickman, Lawrence B. *A Living Wage: Workers and the Making of American Consumer Society* (1997). Traces the origins and development of the idea that workers are entitled to a "living wage."

Hofstadter, Richard. *The Age of Reform: From Bryan to F. D. R.* (1955). A classic account of the ideas of reformers from Populism to the New Deal.

Johnston, Robert D. *The Radical Middle Class: Populist Democracy and the Question of Capitalism in Progressive Era Portland* (2003). Analyzes how Progressivism operated in one important city.

Maddox, Lucy. *Citizen Indians: Native American Intellectuals, Race, and Reform* (2005). A study of the Society of American Indians and other manifestations of Indian Progressivism.

Montgomery, David. *The Fall of the House of Labor: The Workplace, the State, and American Labor Activism, 1865–1925* (1987). An account of the labor battles of the era and the gradual decline of labor's power, especially at the workplace.

Orsi, Robert A. *The Madonna of 115th Street: Faith and Community in Italian Harlem, 1880–1950* (1985). An influential study of a single immigrant community and the role of religion in binding it together.

Peiss, Kathy. *Cheap Amusements: Working Women and Leisure in Turn-of-the-Century New York* (1986). Explores the rise of mass entertainment and how it affected women's lives in Progressive America.

Recchiuti, John L. *Civic Engagement: Social Science and Progressive-Era Reform in New York City* (2006). Examines the influence of a group of reform-minded scholars on the politics of the Progressive era.

Rodgers, Daniel T. *Atlantic Crossings: Social Politics in a Progressive Age* (1998). A comprehensive study of the flow of Progressive ideas and policies back and forth across the Atlantic.

Stansell, Christine. *American Moderns: Bohemian New York and the Creation of a New Century* (2000). A colorful account of the Greenwich Village radicals who expanded the idea of personal freedom in the Progressive era.

Stromquist, Shelton. *Re-Inventing "The People": The Progressive Movement, the Class Problem, and the Origins of Modern Liberalism* (2006). Discusses how the desire to re-create social harmony in an age of labor conflict shaped Progressivism.

WEBSITES

Evolution of the Conservation Movement, 1860–1920: http://lcweb2.loc.gov/ammem/amrvhtml/conshome.html

Immigration to the United States, 1789–1930: http://ocp.hul.harvard.edu/ immigration/

Triangle Shirtwaist Factory Fire: www.ilr.cornell.edu/trianglefire/

Urban Experience in Chicago: Hull House and Its Neighborhoods: www.uic.edu/jaddams/hull/urbanexp/index.htm

Votes for Women: http://memory.loc.gov/ammem/naw/nawshome.html

REVIEW QUESTIONS

1. Identify the main groups and ideas that drove the Progressive movement.

2. Explain how immigration to the United States in this period was part of a global movement of peoples.

3. Describe how Fordism transformed American industrial and consumer society.

4. Socialism was a rising force across the globe in the early twentieth century. How successful was the movement in the United States?

5. Explain why the Industrial Workers of the World (IWW) grew so rapidly and aroused so much opposition.

6. What did striking workers mean when they declared that they wanted "bread and roses, too"?

7. What did Progressive era feminists want to change in society, and how did their actions help to spearhead broader reforms?

8. Explain how and why Progressivism was an international movement.

9. How did each Progressive era president view the role of the federal government?

10. How democratic was the Progressive movement?

FREEDOM QUESTIONS

1. Immigrants came to the United States in search of freedom and economic opportunity. Describe to what extent they achieved and were denied these goals.

2. Explain the concept of "consumer freedom" and its connections to the growing women's movement and the new urban society.

3. How did workers and employers differ in their idea of "industrial freedom"?

4. How did the struggles of the Industrial Workers of the World and suffrage advocates promote a broader defense of freedom of expression?

5. Assess the record of the Progressive movement in promoting the expansion of freedom and democracy.

KEY TERMS

muckrakers (p. 728)

child labor (p. 728)

Ellis Island and Angel Island (p. 730)

Mexican immigration (p. 730)

Fordism (p. 736)

American standard of living (p. 737)

Rerum Novarum (p. 737)

"scientific management" (p. 738)

Industrial Workers of the World (p. 743)

"New Feminism" (p. 746)

birth-control movement (p. 747)

Society of American Indians (p. 748)

"effective freedom" (p. 749)

maternalist reform (p. 754)

Muller v. Oregon (p. 755)

workmen's compensation laws (p. 756)

coal miners' strike of 1902 (p. 757)

Pure Food and Drug Act (p. 758)

Roosevelt and conservation (p. 758)

Federal Reserve System (p. 762)

Federal Trade Commission (p. 762)

REVIEW TABLE

Key Federal Legislation

Act	Date	Purpose
Hepburn Act	1906	To give the Interstate Commerce Commission the power to oversee railroad practices and rates
Pure Food and Drug Act	1906	To police the quality and labeling of food and drugs
Federal Reserve System	1913	To regulate interest rates and promote national economic growth
Federal Trade Commission	1914	To investigate and prohibit "unfair" business activities
Clayton Act	1914	To exempt labor unions from antitrust laws and allow unions the right to strike
Keating-Owen Act	1916	To outlaw child labor in manufacturing goods sold in interstate commerce
Adamson Act	1916	To establish an eight-hour work day on the nation's railroads

Appendix

DOCUMENTS

TABLES AND FIGURES

The Declaration of Independence (1776)

When in the course of human events, it becomes necessary for one people to dissolve the political bands which have connected them with another, and to assume among the Powers of the earth, the separate and equal station to which the Laws of Nature and of Nature's God entitle them, a decent respect to the opinions of mankind requires that they should declare the causes which impel them to the separation.

We hold these truths to be self-evident, that all men are created equal, that they are endowed by their Creator with certain unalienable rights, that among these are Life, Liberty, and the pursuit of Happiness. That to secure these rights, Governments are instituted among Men, deriving their just powers from the consent of the governed. That whenever any Form of Government becomes destructive of these ends, it is the Right of the People to alter or to abolish it, and to institute new Government, laying its foundation on such principles and organizing its powers in such form, as to them shall seem most likely to effect their Safety and Happiness. Prudence, indeed, will dictate that Governments long established should not be changed for light and transient causes; and accordingly all experience hath shown, that mankind are more disposed to suffer, while evils are sufferable, than to right themselves by abolishing the forms to which they are accustomed. But when a long train of abuses and usurpations, pursuing invariably the same Object evinces a design to reduce them under absolute Despotism, it is their right, it is their duty, to throw off such Government, and to provide new Guards for their future security.—Such has been the patient sufferance of these Colonies; and such is now the necessity which constrains them to alter their former Systems of Government. The history of the present King of Great Britain is a history of repeated injuries and usurpations, all having in direct object the establishment of an absolute Tyranny over these States. To prove this, let Facts be submitted to a candid world.

He has refused his Assent to Laws, the most wholesome and necessary for the public good.

He has forbidden his Governors to pass Laws of immediate and pressing importance, unless suspended in their operation till his Assent should be obtained; and when so suspended, he has utterly neglected to attend to them.

He has refused to pass other Laws for the accommodation of large districts of people, unless those people would relinquish the right of Representation in the Legislature, a right inestimable to them and formidable to tyrants only.

He has called together legislative bodies at places unusual, uncomfortable, and distant from the depository of their public Records, for the sole purpose of fatiguing them into compliance with his measures.

He has dissolved Representative Houses repeatedly, for opposing with manly firmness his invasions on the rights of the people.

He has refused for a long time, after such dissolutions, to cause others to be elected; whereby the Legislative powers, incapable of Annihilation, have returned to the People at large for their exercise; the State remaining in the mean time exposed to all dangers of invasion from without, and convulsions within.

He has endeavoured to prevent the population of these States; for that purpose obstructing the Laws of Naturalization of Foreigners; refusing to pass others to encourage their migrations hither, and raising the conditions of new Appropriations of Lands.

He has obstructed the Administration of Justice, by refusing his Assent to Laws for establishing Judiciary powers.

He has made Judges dependent on his Will alone, for the tenure of their offices, and the amount and payment of their salaries.

He has erected a multitude of New Offices, and sent hither swarms of Officers to harass our People, and eat out their substance.

He has kept among us, in times of peace, Standing Armies without the Consent of our legislatures.

He has affected to render the Military independent of and superior to the Civil Power.

He has combined with others to subject us to a jurisdiction foreign to our constitution, and unacknowledged by our laws; giving his Assent to their Acts of pretended Legislation:

For quartering large bodies of armed troops among us:

For protecting them, by a mock Trial, from Punishment for any Murders which they should commit on the Inhabitants of these States:

For cutting off our Trade with all parts of the world:

For imposing taxes on us without our Consent:

For depriving us of many cases, of the benefits of Trial by jury:

For transporting us beyond Seas to be tried for pretended offences:

For abolishing the free System of English Laws in a neighbouring Province, establishing therein an Arbitrary government, and enlarging its Boundaries so as to render it at once an example and fit instrument for introducing the same absolute rule into these Colonies:

For taking away our Charters, abolishing our most valuable Laws, and altering fundamentally the Forms of our Governments:

For suspending our own Legislatures, and declaring themselves invested with Power to legislate for us in all cases whatsoever.

He has abdicated Government here, by declaring us out of his Protection and waging War against us.

He has plundered our seas, ravaged our Coasts, burnt our towns, and destroyed the lives of our people.

He is at this time transporting large armies of foreign mercenaries to compleat the works of death, desolation, and tyranny, already begun with circumstances of Cruelty & perfidy scarcely paralleled in the most barbarous ages, and totally unworthy the Head of a civilized nation.

He has constrained our fellow Citizens taken Captive on the high Seas to bear Arms against their Country, to become the executioners of their friends and Brethren, or to fall themselves by their Hands.

He has excited domestic insurrections amongst us, and has endeavoured to bring on the inhabitants of our frontiers, the merciless Indian Savages, whose known rule of warfare, is an undistinguished destruction of all ages, sexes, and conditions.

In every stage of these Oppressions We have Petitioned for Redress in the most humble terms: Our repeated Petitions have been answered only by repeated injury. A Prince, whose character is thus marked by every act which may define a Tyrant, is unfit to be the ruler of a free people.

Nor have We been wanting in attention to our British brethren. We have warned them from time to time of attempts by their legislature to extend an unwarrantable jurisdiction over us. We have reminded them of the circumstances of our emigration and settlement here. We have appealed to their native justice and magnanimity, and we have conjured them by the ties of our common kindred to disavow these usurpations, which, would inevitably interrupt our connections and correspondence. They too must have been deaf to the voice of justice and of consanguinity. We must, therefore, acquiesce in the necessity, which denounces our Separation, and hold them, as we hold the rest of mankind, Enemies in War, in Peace Friends.

WE, THEREFORE, the Representatives of the UNITED STATES OF AMERICA, in General Congress, Assembled, appealing to the Supreme Judge of the world for the rectitude of our intentions, do, in the Name, and by Authority of the good People of these Colonies, solemnly publish and declare, That these United Colonies are, and of Right ought to be FREE AND INDEPENDENT STATES; that they are Absolved from all Allegiance to the British Crown, and that all political connection between them and the State of Great Britain, is and ought to be totally dissolved; and that as Free and Independent States, they have full Power to levy War, conclude Peace, contract Alliances, establish Commerce, and to do all other Acts and Things which Independent States may of right do. And for the support of this Declaration, with a firm reliance on the Protection of Divine Providence, we mutually pledge to each other our Lives, our Fortunes, and our sacred Honor.

The foregoing Declaration was, by order of Congress, engrossed, and signed by the following members:

John Hancock

NEW HAMPSHIRE
Josiah Bartlett
William Whipple
Matthew Thornton

MASSACHUSETTS BAY
Samuel Adams
John Adams
Robert Treat Paine
Elbridge Gerry

RHODE ISLAND
Stephen Hopkins
William Ellery

CONNECTICUT
Roger Sherman
Samuel Huntington
William Williams
Oliver Wolcott

NEW YORK
William Floyd
Philip Livingston
Francis Lewis
Lewis Morris

NEW JERSEY
Richard Stockton
John Witherspoon
Francis Hopkinson
John Hart
Abraham Clark

PENNSYLVANIA
Robert Morris
Benjamin Rush
Benjamin Franklin
John Morton
George Clymer
James Smith
George Taylor
James Wilson
George Ross

DELAWARE
Caesar Rodney
George Read
Thomas M'Kean

MARYLAND
Samuel Chase
William Paca
Thomas Stone
Charles Carroll, of Carrollton

VIRGINIA
George Wythe
Richard Henry Lee
Thomas Jefferson
Benjamin Harrison
Thomas Nelson, Jr.
Francis Lightfoot Lee
Carter Braxton

NORTH CAROLINA
William Hooper
Joseph Hewes
John Penn

SOUTH CAROLINA
Edward Rutledge
Thomas Heyward, Jr.
Thomas Lynch, Jr.
Arthur Middleton

GEORGIA
Button Gwinnett
Lyman Hall
George Walton

Resolved, That copies of the Declaration be sent to the several assemblies, conventions, and committees, or councils of safety, and to the several commanding officers of the continental troops; that it be proclaimed in each of the United States, at the head of the army.

The Constitution of the United States (1787)

We the People of the United States, in order to form a more perfect Union, establish Justice, insure domestic Tranquility, provide for the common defence, promote the general Welfare, and secure the Blessings of Liberty to ourselves and our Posterity, do ordain and establish this Constitution for the United States of America.

ARTICLE. I.

Section. 1. All legislative Powers herein granted shall be vested in a Congress of the United States, which shall consist of a Senate and House of Representatives.

Section. 2. The House of Representatives shall be composed of Members chosen every second Year by the People of the several States, and the Electors in each State shall have the Qualifications requisite for Electors of the most numerous Branch of the State Legislature.

No Person shall be a Representative who shall not have attained to the Age of twenty five Years, and been seven Years a Citizen of the United States, and who shall not, when elected, be an Inhabitant of that State in which he shall be chosen.

Representatives and direct Taxes shall be apportioned among the several States which may be included within this Union, according to their respective Numbers, which shall be determined by adding to the whole Number of free Persons, including those bound to Service for a Term of Years, and excluding Indians not taxed, three fifths of all other Persons. The actual Enumeration shall be made within three Years after the first Meeting of the Congress of the United States, and within every subsequent Term of ten Years, in such Manner as they shall by Law direct. The Number of Representatives shall not exceed one for every thirty Thousand, but each State shall have at Least one Representative; and until such enumeration shall be made, the State of New Hampshire shall be entitled to chuse three, Massachusetts eight, Rhode-Island and Providence Plantations one, Connecticut five, New York six, New Jersey four, Pennsylvania eight, Delaware one, Maryland six, Virginia ten, North Carolina five, South Carolina five, and Georgia three.

When vacancies happen in the Representation from any state, the Executive Authority thereof shall issue Writs of Election to fill such Vacancies.

The House of Representatives shall chuse their Speaker and other Officers; and shall have the sole Power of Impeachment.

Section. 3. The Senate of the United States shall be composed of two Senators from each State, chosen by the legislature thereof, for six Years; and each Senator shall have one Vote.

Immediately after they shall be assembled in Consequence of the first Election, they shall be divided as equally as may be into three Classes. The Seats of the Senators of the first Class shall be vacated at the Expiration of the second Year, of the second Class at the Expiration of the fourth Year, and of the third Class at the Expiration of the sixth Year, so that one third may be chosen every second Year; and if Vacancies happen by Resignation, or otherwise, during the Recess of the Legislature of any State, the Executive thereof may make temporary Appointments until the next Meeting of the Legislature, which shall then fill such Vacancies.

No Person shall be a Senator who shall not have attained to the Age of thirty Years, and been nine Years a Citizen of the United States, and who shall not, when elected, be an Inhabitant of that State for which he shall be chosen.

The Vice President of the United States shall be President of the Senate, but shall have no Vote, unless they be equally divided.

The Senate shall chuse their other Officers, and also a President pro tempore, in the Absence of the Vice President, or when he shall exercise the Office of President of the United States.

The Senate shall have the sole Power to try all Impeachments. When sitting for that Purpose, they shall be on Oath or Affirmation. When the President of the United States is tried, the Chief Justice shall preside: And no Person shall be convicted without the Concurrence of two thirds of the Members present.

Judgment in Cases of Impeachment shall not extend further than to removal from Office, and disqualification to hold and enjoy any Office of honor, Trust or Profit under the United States: but the Party convicted shall nevertheless be liable and subject to Indictment, Trial, Judgment and Punishment, according to Law.

Section. 4. The Times, Places and Manner of holding Elections for Senators and Representatives, shall be prescribed in each State by the Legislature thereof; but the Congress may at any time by Law make or alter such Regulations, except as to the Places of chusing Senators.

The Congress shall assemble at least once in every Year, and such Meeting shall be on the first Monday in December, unless they shall by Law appoint a different Day.

Section. 5. Each House shall be the Judge of the Elections, Returns and Qualifications of its own Members, and a Majority of each shall constitute a Quorum to do Business; but a smaller Number may adjourn from day to day, and may be authorized to compel the Attendance of absent Members, in such Manner, and under such Penalties as each House may provide.

Each House may determine the Rules of its Proceedings, punish its Members for disorderly Behaviour, and, with the Concurrence of two thirds, expel a Member.

Each House shall keep a Journal of its Proceedings, and from time to time publish the same, excepting such Parts as may in their Judgment require Secrecy; and the Yeas and Nays of the Members of either House on any question shall, at the Desire of one fifth of those Present, be entered on the Journal.

Neither House, during the Session of Congress, shall, without the Consent of the other, adjourn for more than three days, not to any other Place than that in which the two Houses shall be sitting.

Section. 6. The Senators and Representatives shall receive a Compensation for their Services, to be ascertained by Law, and paid out of the Treasury of the United States. They shall in all Cases, except Treason, Felony and Breach of the Peace, be privileged from Arrest during their Attendance at the Session of their respective Houses, and in going to and returning from the same; and for any Speech or Debate in either House, they shall not be questioned in any other Place.

No Senator or Representative shall, during the Time for which he was elected, be appointed to any civil Office under the Authority of the United States, which shall have been created, or the Emoluments whereof shall have been encreased during such time; and no Person holding any Office under the United States, shall be a Member of either House during his Continuance in Office.

Section. 7. All Bills for raising Revenue shall originate in the House of Representatives; but the Senate may propose or concur with Amendments as on other Bills.

Every Bill which shall have passed the House of Representatives and the Senate shall, before it become a Law, be presented to the President of the United States; If he approve he shall sign it, but if not he shall return it, with his Objections to that House in which it shall have originated, who shall enter the Objections at large on their Journal, and proceed to reconsider it. If after such Reconsideration two thirds of that House shall agree to pass the Bill, it shall be sent, together with the Objections, to the other House, by which it shall likewise be reconsidered, and if approved by two thirds of that House, it shall become a Law. But in all such Cases the Votes of both Houses shall be determined by Yeas and Nays, and the Names of the Persons voting for and against the Bill shall be entered on the Journal of each House respectively. If any Bill shall not be returned by the President within ten Days (Sundays excepted) after it shall have been presented to him, the Same shall be a Law, in like Manner as if he had signed it, unless the Congress by their Adjournment prevent its Return, in which Case it shall not be a Law.

Every Order, Resolution, or Vote to which the Concurrence of the Senate and House of Representatives may be necessary (except on a question of Adjournment) shall be presented to the President of the United States; and before the Same shall take Effect, shall be approved by him, or being disapproved by him, shall be repassed by two thirds of the Senate and House of Representatives, according to the Rules and Limitations prescribed in the Case of a Bill.

Section. 8. The Congress shall have Power To lay and collect Taxes, Duties, Imposts and Excises, to pay the Debts and provide for the common Defence and general Welfare of the United States; but all Duties, Imposts and Excises shall be uniform throughout the United States;

To borrow Money on the credit of the United States;

To regulate Commerce with foreign Nations, and among the several States, and with the Indian Tribes;

To establish an uniform Rule of Naturalization, and uniform Laws on the subject of Bankruptcies throughout the United States;

To coin Money, regulate the Value thereof, and of foreign Coin, and fix the Standard of Weights and Measures;

To provide for the Punishment of counterfeiting the Securities and current Coin of the United States;

To establish Post Offices and Post Roads;

To promote the Progress of Science and useful Arts, by securing for limited Times to Authors and Inventors the exclusive Right to their respective Writings and Discoveries;

To constitute Tribunals inferior to the supreme Court;

To define and punish Piracies and Felonies committed on the high Seas, and Offences against the Law of Nations;

To declare War, grant Letters of Marque and Reprisal, and make Rules concerning Captures on Land and Water;

To raise and support Armies, but no Appropriation of Money to that Use shall be for a longer Term than two Years;

To provide and maintain a Navy;

To make Rules for the Government and Regulation of the land and naval Forces;

To provide for calling forth the Militia to execute the Laws of the Union, suppress Insurrections and repel Invasions;

To provide for organizing, arming, and disciplining, the Militia, and for governing such Part of them as may be employed in the Service of the United States, reserving to the States respectively, the Appointment of the Officers, and the Authority of training the Militia according to the discipline prescribed by Congress;

To exercise exclusive Legislation in all Cases whatsoever, over such District (not exceeding ten Miles square) as may, by Cession of Particular States, and the Acceptance of Congress, become the Seat of the Government of the United States, and to exercise like Authority over all Places purchased by the Consent of the Legislature of the State in which the Same shall be, for the Erection of Forts, Magazines, Arsenals, dock-Yards, and other needful Buildings;—And

To make all Laws which shall be necessary and proper for carrying into Execution the foregoing Powers, and all other Powers vested by this Constitution in the Government of the United States, or in any Department or Officer thereof.

Section. 9. The Migration or Importation of such Persons as any of the States now existing shall think proper to admit, shall not be prohibited by the Congress prior to the Year one thousand eight hundred and eight, but a Tax or duty may be imposed on such Importation, not exceeding ten dollars for each Person.

The Privilege of the Writ of Habeas Corpus shall not be suspended, unless when in Cases of Rebellion or Invasion the public Safety may require it.

No Bill of Attainder or ex post facto Law shall be passed.

No Capitation, or other direct, Tax shall be laid, unless in Proportion to the Census or Enumeration herein before directed to be taken.

No Tax or Duty shall be laid on Articles exported from any State.

No Preference shall be given by any Regulation of Commerce or Revenue to the Ports of one State over those of another: nor shall Vessels bound to, or from, one State, be obliged to enter, clear, or pay Duties in another.

No Money shall be drawn from the Treasury, but in Consequence of Appropriations made by Law; and a regular Statement and Account of the Receipts and Expenditures of all public Money shall be published from time to time.

No Title of Nobility shall be granted by the United States: And no Person holding any Office of Profit or Trust under them, shall, without the Consent of the Congress, accept of any present, Emolument, Office, or Title, of any kind whatever, from any King, Prince, or foreign State.

Section. 10. No State shall enter into any Treaty, Alliance, or Confederation; grant Letters of Marque and Reprisal; coin Money; emit Bills of Credit; make any Thing but gold and silver Coin a Tender in Payment of Debts; pass any Bill of Attainder, ex post facto Law, or Law impairing the Obligation of Contracts, or grant any Title of Nobility.

No State shall, without the Consent of the Congress, lay any Imposts or Duties on Imports or Exports, except what may be absolutely necessary for executing its inspection Laws: and the net Produce of all Duties and Imposts, laid by any State on Imports or Exports, shall be for the Use of the Treasury of the United States; and all such Laws shall be subject to the Revision and Controul of the Congress.

No State shall, without the Consent of Congress, lay any Duty of Tonnage, keep Troops, or Ships of War in time of Peace, enter into any Agreement or Compact with another State, or with a foreign Power, or engage in War, unless actually invaded, or in such imminent Danger as will not admit of delay.

ARTICLE. II.

Section. 1. The executive Power shall be vested in a President of the United States of America. He shall hold his Office during the term of four Years, and, together with the Vice President, chosen for the same Term, be elected, as follows:

Each State shall appoint, in such Manner as the Legislature thereof may direct, a Number of Electors, equal to the whole Number of Senators and Representatives to which the State may be entitled in the Congress: but no Senator or Representative, or Person holding an Office of Trust or Profit under the United States, shall be appointed an Elector.

The Electors shall meet in their respective States, and vote by Ballot for two Persons, of whom one at least shall not be an Inhabitant of the same State with themselves. And they shall make a List of all the Persons voted for, and of the Number of Votes for each; which List they shall sign and certify, and transmit sealed to the Seat of the Government of the United States, directed to the President of the Senate. The President of the Senate shall, in the Presence of the Senate and House of Representatives, open all the Certificates, and the Votes shall then be counted. The Person having the greatest Number of Votes shall be the President, if such Number be a Majority of the whole Number of Electors appointed; and if there be more than one who have such Majority, and have an equal Number of Votes, then the House of Representatives shall immediately chuse by Ballot one of them for President; and if no Person have a Majority, then from the five highest on the List the said House shall in like Manner chuse the President. But in chusing the President, the Votes shall be taken by States, the Representation from each State having one Vote; A quorum for this Purpose shall consist of a Member or Members from two thirds of the States, and a Majority of all the States shall be necessary to a Choice. In every Case, after the Choice of the President, the Person having the greatest Number of Votes of the Electors shall be the Vice President. But if there should remain two or more who have equal Votes, the Senate shall chuse from them by Ballot the Vice President.

The Congress may determine the Time of chusing the Electors, and the Day on which they shall give their Votes; which Day shall be the same throughout the United States.

No Person except a natural born Citizen, or a Citizen of the United States, at the time of the Adoption of this Constitution, shall be eligible to the Office of President; neither shall any Person be eligible to that Office who shall not have attained to the Age of thirty five Years, and been fourteen Years a Resident within the United States.

In Case of the Removal of the President from Office, or of his Death, Resignation, or Inability to discharge the Powers and Duties of the said Office, the Same shall devolve on the Vice President, and the Congress may by Law provide for the Case of Removal, Death, Resignation or Inability, both of the President and Vice President, declaring what Officer shall then act as President, and such Officer shall act accordingly, until the Disability be removed, or a President shall be elected.

The President shall, at stated Times, receive for his Services, a Compensation, which shall neither be encreased or diminished during the Period for which he shall have been elected, and he shall not receive within that Period any other Emolument from the United States, or any of them.

Before he enters on the Execution of his Office, he shall take the following Oath or Affirmation:—"I do solemnly swear (or affirm) that I will faithfully execute the Office of President of the United States, and will to the best of my Ability, preserve, protect and defend the Constitution of the United States."

Section. 2. The President shall be Commander in Chief of the Army and Navy of the United States, and of the Militia of the several States, when called into the actual Service of the United States; he may require the Opinion, in writing, of the principal Officer in each of the executive Departments, upon any Subject relating to the Duties of their respective Offices, and he shall have Power to grant Reprieves and Pardons for Offences against the United States, except in Cases of Impeachment.

He shall have Power, by and with the Advice and Consent of the Senate, to make Treaties, provided two thirds of the Senators present concur; and he shall nominate, and by and with the Advice and Consent of the Senate, shall appoint Ambassadors, other public Ministers and Consuls, Judges of the supreme Court, and all other Officers of the United States, whose Appointments are not herein otherwise provided for, and which shall be established by Law; but the Congress may by Law vest the Appointment of such inferior Officers, as they think proper, in the President alone, in the Courts of Law, or in the Heads of Departments.

The President shall have Power to fill up all Vacancies that may happen during the Recess of the Senate, by granting Commissions which shall expire at the End of their next Session.

Section. 3. He shall from time to time give to the Congress Information of the State of the Union, and recommend to their Consideration such Measures as he shall judge necessary and expedient; he may, on extraordinary Occasions, convene both Houses, or either of them, and in Case of Disagreement between them, with Respect to the Time of Adjournment, he may adjourn them to such Time as he shall think proper; he shall receive Ambassadors and other public Ministers; he shall take Care that the Laws be faithfully executed, and shall Commission all the Officers of the United States.

Section. 4. The President, Vice President and all civil Officers of the United States, shall be removed from Office on Impeachment for, and Conviction of, Treason, Bribery, or other high Crimes and Misdemeanors.

ARTICLE. III.

Section. 1. The judicial Power of the United States, shall be vested in one supreme Court, and in such inferior Courts as the Congress may from time to time ordain and establish. The Judges, both of the supreme and inferior Courts, shall hold their Offices during good Behavior, and shall, at stated Times, receive for their Services, a Compensation, which shall not be diminished during their Continuance in Office.

Section. 2. The judicial Power shall extend to all Cases, in Law and Equity, arising under this Constitution, the Laws of the United States, and Treaties made, or which shall be made, under their Authority;—to all Cases affecting Ambassadors, other public Ministers and Consuls;—to all Cases of admiralty and maritime Jurisdiction;—the Controversies to which the United States shall be a Party;—to Controversies between two or more States;—between a State and Citizens of another State;—between Citizens of different States;—between Citizens of the same State claiming Lands under Grants of different States, and between a State, or the Citizens thereof, and foreign States, Citizens or Subjects.

In all cases affecting Ambassadors, other public Ministers and Consuls, and those in which a State shall be Party, the supreme Court shall have original Jurisdiction. In all the other Cases before mentioned, the supreme Court shall have appellate Jurisdiction, both as to Law and Fact, with such Exceptions, and under such Regulations as the Congress shall make.

The Trial of all Crimes, except in Cases of Impeachment, shall be by Jury; and such Trial shall be held in the State where the said Crimes shall have been committed; but when not committed within any State, the Trial shall be at such Place or Places as the Congress may by Law have directed.

Section. 3. Treason against the United States, shall consist only in levying War against them, or in adhering to their Enemies, giving them Aid and Comfort. No Person shall be convicted of Treason unless on the Testimony of two Witnesses to the same overt Act, or on Confession in open Court.

The Congress shall have Power to declare the Punishment of Treason, but no Attainder of Treason shall work Corruption of Blood, or Forfeiture except during the Life of the Person attainted.

ARTICLE. IV.

Section. 1. Full Faith and Credit shall be given in each State to the public Acts, Records, and judicial Proceedings of every other State. And the Congress may by general Laws prescribe the Manner in which such Acts, Records and Proceedings shall be proved, and the Effect thereof.

Section. 2. The Citizens of each State shall be entitled to all Privileges and Immunities of Citizens in the several States.

A Person charged in any State with Treason, Felony, or other Crime, who shall flee from Justice, and be found in another State, shall on Demand of the executive Authority of the State from which he fled, be delivered up, to be removed to the State having Jurisdiction of the Crime.

No Person held to Service or Labour in one State, under the Laws thereof, escaping into another, shall, in Consequence of any Law or Regulation therein, be discharged from such Service or Labour, but shall be delivered up on Claim of the Party to whom such Service or Labour may be due.

Section. 3. New States may be admitted by the Congress into this Union; but no new State shall be formed or erected within the Jurisdiction of any other State; nor any State be formed by the Junction of two or more States, or Parts of States, without the consent of the Legislatures of the States concerned as well as of the Congress.

The Congress shall have Power to dispose of and make all needful Rules and Regulations respecting the Territory or other Property belonging to the United States; and nothing in this Constitution shall be so construed as to Prejudice any Claims of the United States, or of any particular States.

Section. 4. The United States shall guarantee to every State in this Union a Republican Form of Government, and shall protect each of them against Invasion; and on Application of the Legislature, or of the Executive (when the Legislature cannot be convened) against domestic Violence.

ARTICLE. V.

The Congress, whenever two thirds of both Houses shall deem it necessary, shall propose Amendments to this Constitution, or, on the Application of the Legislatures of two thirds of the several States, shall call a Convention for proposing Amendments, which, in either Case, shall be valid to all Intents and Purposes, as Part of this Constitution, when ratified by the Legislatures of three fourths of the several States, or by Conventions in three fourths thereof, as the one or the other Mode of Ratification may be proposed by the Congress; Provided that no Amendment which may be made prior to the Year One thousand eight hundred and eight shall in any Manner affect the first and fourth Clauses in the Ninth Section of the first Article; and that no State, without its Consent, shall be deprived of its equal Suffrage in the Senate.

ARTICLE. VI.

All Debts contracted and Engagements entered into, before the Adoption of this Constitution, shall be as valid against the United States under this Constitution, as under the Confederation.

This Constitution, and the Laws of the United States which shall be made in Pursuance thereof; and all Treaties made, or which shall be made, under the Authority of the United States, shall be the supreme Law of the Land; and the Judges in every State shall be bound thereby, any Thing in the Constitution or Laws of any State to the Contrary notwithstanding.

The Senators and Representatives before mentioned, and the Members of the several State Legislatures, and all executive and judicial Officers, both of the United States and of the several States, shall be bound by Oath or Affirmation, to support this Constitution; but no religious Test shall ever be required as a Qualification to any Office or public Trust under the United States.

ARTICLE. VII.

The Ratification of the Conventions of nine States, shall be sufficient for the Establishment of this Constitution between the States so ratifying the Same.

Done in Convention by the Unanimous Consent of the States present the Seventeenth Day of September in the Year of our Lord one thousand seven hundred and Eighty seven and of the Independence of the United States of America the Twelfth. In witness thereof We have hereunto subscribed our Names,

G⁰. WASHINGTON—Presdᵗ.
and deputy from Virginia

NEW HAMPSHIRE
John Langdon
Nicholas Gilman

MASSACHUSETTS
Nathaniel Gorham
Rufus King

CONNECTICUT
Wᵐ Samˡ Johnson
Roger Sherman

NEW YORK
Alexander Hamilton

NEW JERSEY
Wil: Livingston
David A. Brearley
Wᵐ Paterson
Jona: Dayton

PENNSYLVANIA
B Franklin
Thomas Mifflin
Robᵗ Morris
Geo. Clymer
Thoˢ FitzSimons
Jared Ingersoll
James Wilson
Gouv Morris

DELAWARE
Geo: Read
Gunning Bedford jun
John Dickinson
Richard Bassett
Jaco: Broom

MARYLAND
James McHenry
Dan of Sᵗ Thoˢ Jenifer
Danˡ Carroll

VIRGINIA
John Blair—
James Madison Jr.

NORTH CAROLINA
Wᵐ Blount
Richᵈ Dobbs Spaight
Hu Williamson

SOUTH CAROLINA
J. Rutledge
*Charles Cotesworth
Pinckney*
Charles Pinckney
Pierce Butler

GEORGIA
William Few
Abr Baldwin

AMENDMENTS TO THE CONSTITUTION

Articles in addition to, and Amendment of the Constitution of the United States of America, proposed by Congress, and ratified by the Legislatures of the several States, pursuant to the fifth Article of the original Constitution.

AMENDMENT I.*

Congress shall make no law respecting an establishment of religion, or prohibiting the free exercise thereof; or abridging the freedom of speech, or of the press; or the right of the people peaceably to assemble, and to petition the Government for a redress of grievances.

AMENDMENT II.

A well regulated Militia, being necessary to the security of a free State, the right of the people to keep and bear Arms, shall not be infringed.

AMENDMENT III.

No Soldier shall, in time of peace be quartered in any house, without the consent of the Owner, nor in time of war, but in a manner to be prescribed by law.

AMENDMENT IV.

The right of the people to be secure in their persons, houses, papers, and effects, against unreasonable searches and seizures, shall not be violated, and no Warrants shall issue, but upon probable cause, supported by Oath or affirmation, and particularly describing the place to be searched, and the persons or things to be seized.

AMENDMENT V.

No person shall be held to answer for a capital, or otherwise infamous crime, unless on a presentment or indictment of a Grand Jury, except in cases arising in the land or naval forces, or in the Militia, when in actual service in time of War or public danger; nor shall any person be subject for the same offence to be twice put in jeopardy of life or limb; nor shall be compelled in any criminal case to be a witness against himself, nor be deprived of life, liberty, or property, without due process of law; nor shall private property be taken for public use, without just compensation.

AMENDMENT VI.

In all criminal prosecutions, the accused shall enjoy the right to a speedy and public trial, by an impartial jury of the State and district wherein the crime shall have been committed, which district shall have been previously ascertained by law, and to be informed of the nature and cause of the accusation; to be confronted with the witnesses against him; to have compulsory process for obtaining witnesses in his favor, and to have the Assistance of Counsel for his defence.

AMENDMENT VII.

In Suits at common law, where the value in controversy shall exceed twenty dollars, the right of trial by jury shall be preserved, and no fact tried by a jury, shall be otherwise re-examined in any Court of the United States, than according to the rules of the common law.

AMENDMENT VIII.

Excessive bail shall not be required, nor excessive fines imposed, nor cruel and unusual punishments inflicted.

AMENDMENT IX.

The enumeration in the Constitution, of certain rights, shall not be construed to deny or disparage others retained by the people.

AMENDMENT X.

The powers not delegated to the United States by the Constitution, nor prohibited by it to the States, are reserved to the States respectively, or to the people.

AMENDMENT XI.

The Judicial power of the United States shall not be construed to extend to any suit in law or equity, commenced or prosecuted against one of the United States by Citizens of another State, or by Citizens or Subjects of any Foreign State. [January 8, 1798]

AMENDMENT XII.

The Electors shall meet in their respective states, and vote by ballot for President and Vice-President, one of whom, at least, shall not be an inhabitant of the same state with themselves; they shall name in their ballots the person voted for as President, and in distinct ballots the person voted for as Vice-President, and they shall make distinct lists of all persons voted for as President, and of all persons voted for as Vice President, and of the number of votes for each, which lists they shall sign and certify, and transmit sealed to the seat of the government of the United States, directed to the President of the Senate;—The President of the Senate shall, in the presence of the Senate and

*The first ten Amendments (the Bill of Rights) were ratified in 1791.

House of Representatives, open all the certificates and the votes shall then be counted;—The person having the greatest number of votes for President, shall be the President, if such number be a majority of the whole number of Electors appointed; and if no person have such majority, then from the persons having the highest numbers not exceeding three on the list of those voted for as President, the House of Representatives shall choose immediately, by ballot, the President. But in choosing the President, the votes shall be taken by states, the representation from each state having one vote; a quorum for this purpose shall consist of a member or members from two-thirds of the states, and a majority of all the states shall be necessary to a choice. And if the House of Representatives shall not choose a President whenever the right of choice shall devolve upon them, before the fourth day of March next following, then the Vice-President shall act as President, as in the case of the death or other constitutional disability of the President.—The person having the greatest number of votes as Vice-President, shall be the Vice-President, if such number be a majority of the whole number of Electors appointed, and if no person have a majority, then from the two highest numbers on the list, the Senate shall choose the Vice-President; a quorum for the purpose shall consist of two-thirds of the whole number of Senators, and a majority of the whole number shall be necessary to a choice. But no person constitutionally ineligible to the office of President shall be eligible to that of Vice-President of the United States. [September 25, 1804]

Amendment XIII.

Section 1. Neither slavery nor involuntary servitude, except as a punishment for crime whereof the party shall have been duly convicted, shall exist within the United States, or any place subject to their jurisdiction.

Section 2. Congress shall have power to enforce this article by appropriate legislation. [December 18, 1865]

Amendment XIV.

Section 1. All persons born or naturalized in the United States, and subject to the jurisdiction thereof, are citizens of the United States and of the State wherein they reside. No State shall make or enforce any law which shall abridge the privileges or immunities of citizens of the United States; nor shall any State deprive any person of life, liberty, or property, without due process of law; nor deny to any person within its jurisdiction the equal protection of the laws.

Section 2. Representatives shall be apportioned among the several States according to their respective numbers, counting the whole number of persons in each State, excluding Indians not taxed. But when the right to vote at any election for the choice of electors for President and Vice President of the United States, Representatives in Congress, the Executive and Judicial officers of a State, or the members of the Legislature thereof, is denied to any of the male inhabitants of such State, being twenty-one years of age, and citizens of the United States, or in any way abridged, except for participation in rebellion, or other crime, the basis of representation therein shall be reduced in the proportion which the number of such male citizens shall bear to the whole number of male citizens twenty-one years of age in such State.

Section 3. No person shall be a Senator or Representative in Congress, or elector of President and Vice President, or hold any office, civil or military, under the United States, or under any State, who, having previously taken an oath, as a member of Congress, or as an officer of the United States, or as a member of any State legislature, or as an executive or judicial officer of any State, to support the Constitution of the United States, shall have engaged in insurrection or rebellion against the same, or given aid or comfort to the enemies thereof. But Congress may by a vote of two-thirds of each House, remove such disability.

Section 4. The validity of the public debt of the United States, authorized by law, including debts incurred for payment of pensions and bounties for services in suppressing insurrection or rebellion, shall not be questioned. But neither the United States nor any State shall assume or pay any debt or obligation incurred in aid of insurrection or rebellion against the United States, or any claim for the loss or emancipation of any slave; but all such debts, obligations and claims shall be held illegal and void.

Section 5. The Congress shall have power to enforce, by appropriate legislation, the provisions of this article. [July 28, 1868]

Amendment XV.

Section 1. The right of citizens of the United States to vote shall not be denied or abridged by the United States or by any State on account of race, color, or previous condition of servitude—

Section 2. The Congress shall have power to enforce this article by appropriate legislation. [March 30, 1870]

Amendment XVI.

The Congress shall have power to lay and collect taxes on incomes, from whatever source derived, without apportionment among the several States, and without regard to any census or enumeration. [February 25, 1913]

Amendment XVII.

The Senate of the United States shall be composed of two senators from each State, elected by the people thereof, for six years; and each Senator shall have one vote. The electors in each State shall have the qualifications requisite for electors of the most numerous branch of the State legislatures.

When vacancies happen in the representation of any State in the Senate, the executive authority of such State shall issue writs of election to fill such vacancies: *Provided,* That the legislature of any State may empower the executive thereof to make temporary appointments until the people fill the vacancies by election as the legislature may direct.

This amendment shall not be so construed as to affect the election or term of any senator chosen before it becomes valid as part of the Constitution. [May 31, 1913]

Amendment XVIII.

After one year from the ratification of this article, the manufacture, sale, or transportation of intoxicating liquors within, the importation thereof into, or the exportation thereof from the United States and all territory subject to the jurisdiction thereof for beverage purposes is hereby prohibited.

The Congress and the several States shall have concurrent power to enforce this article by appropriate legislation.

This article shall be inoperative unless it shall have been ratified as an amendment to the Constitution by the legislatures of the several States, as provided in the Constitution, within seven years from the date of the submission thereof to the States by Congress. [January 29, 1919]

Amendment XIX.

The right of citizens of the United States to vote shall not be denied or abridged by the United States or by any State on account of sex.

The Congress shall have power by appropriate legislation to enforce the provisions of this article. [August 26, 1920]

Amendment XX.

Section 1. The terms of the President and Vice-President shall end at noon on the twentieth day of January, and the terms of Senators and Representatives at noon on the third day of January, of the years in which such terms would have ended if this article had not been ratified; and the terms of their successors shall then begin.

Section 2. The Congress shall assemble at least once in every year, and such meeting shall begin at noon on the third day of January, unless they shall by law appoint a different day.

Section 3. If, at the time fixed for the beginning of the term of the President, the President-elect shall have died, the Vice-President-elect shall become President. If a President shall not have been chosen before the time fixed for the beginning of his term, or if the President-elect shall have failed to qualify,

then the Vice-President-elect shall act as President until a President shall have qualified; and the Congress may by law provide for the case wherein neither a President-elect nor a Vice-President-elect shall have qualified, declaring who shall then act as President, or the manner in which one who is to act shall be selected, and such person shall act accordingly until a President or Vice-President shall have qualified.

Section 4. The Congress may by law provide for the case of the death of any of the persons from whom the House of Representatives may choose a President whenever the right of choice shall have devolved upon them, and for the case of the death of any of the persons from whom the Senate may choose a Vice-President whenever the right of choice shall have devolved upon them.

Section 5. Sections 1 and 2 shall take effect on the 15th day of October following the ratification of this article.

Section 6. This article shall be inoperative unless it shall have been ratified as an amendment to the Constitution by the legislatures of three-fourths of the several States within seven years from the date of its submission. [February 6, 1933]

Amendment XXI.

Section 1. The eighteenth article of amendment to the Constitution of the United States is hereby repealed.

Section 2. The transportation or importation into any State, Territory or possession of the United States for delivery or use therein of intoxicating liquors, in violation of the laws thereof, is hereby prohibited.

Section 3. This article shall be inoperative unless it shall have been ratified as an amendment to the Constitution by convention in the several States, as provided in the Constitution, within seven years from the date of the submission thereof to the States by the Congress. [December 5, 1933]

Amendment XXII.

Section 1. No person shall be elected to the office of the President more than twice, and no person who has held the office of President, or acted as President, for more than two years of a term to which some other person was elected President shall be elected to the office of the President more than once. But this Article shall not apply to any person holding the office of President when this Article was proposed by the Congress, and shall not prevent any person who may be holding the office of President, or acting as President, during the term within which this Article becomes operative from holding the office of President or acting as President during the remainder of such term.

Section 2. This article shall be inoperative unless it shall have been ratified as an amendment to the Constitution by the legislatures of three-fourths of the several States within seven years from the date of its submission to the States by the Congress. [February 27, 1951]

AMENDMENT XXIII.

Section 1. The District constituting the seat of government of the United States shall appoint in such manner as the Congress may direct:

A number of electors of President and Vice-President equal to the whole number of Senators and Representatives in Congress to which the District would be entitled if it were a State, but in no event more than the least populous State; they shall be in addition to those appointed by the States, but they shall be considered, for the purposes of the election of President and Vice-President, to be electors appointed by a State; and they shall meet in the District and perform such duties as provided by the twelfth article of amendment.

Section 2. The Congress shall have the power to enforce this article by appropriate legislation. [March 29, 1961]

AMENDMENT XXIV.

Section 1. The right of citizens of the United States to vote in any primary or other election for President or Vice President, for electors for President or Vice President, or for Senator or Representative in Congress, shall not be denied or abridged by the United States or any State by reason of failure to pay any poll tax or other tax.

Section 2. The Congress shall have power to enforce this article by appropriate legislation. [January 23, 1964]

AMENDMENT XXV.

Section 1. In case of the removal of the President from office or of his death or resignation, the Vice President shall become President.

Section 2. Whenever there is a vacancy in the office of Vice President, the President shall nominate a Vice President who shall take office upon confirmation by a majority vote of both Houses of Congress.

Section 3. Whenever the President transmits to the President pro tempore of the Senate and the Speaker of the House of Representatives his written declaration that he is unable to discharge the powers and duties of his office, and until he transmits to them a written declaration to the contrary, such powers and duties shall be discharged by the Vice President as Acting President.

Section 4. Whenever the Vice President and a majority of either the principal officers of the executive departments or of such other body as Congress may by law provide, transmit to the President pro tempore of the Senate and the Speaker of the House of Representatives their written declaration that the President is unable to discharge the powers and duties of his office, the Vice President shall immediately assume the powers and duties of the office as Acting President.

Thereafter, when the President transmits to the President pro tempore of the Senate and the Speaker of the House of Representatives his written declaration that no inability exists, he shall resume the powers and duties of his office unless the Vice President and a majority of either the principal officers of the executive departments or of such other body as Congress may by law provide, transmit within four days to the President pro tempore of the Senate and the Speaker of the House of Representatives their written declaration that the President is unable to discharge the powers and duties of his office. Thereupon Congress shall decide the issue, assembling within forty-eight hours for that purpose if not in session. If the Congress, within twenty-one days after receipt of the latter written declaration, or, if Congress is not in session, within twenty-one days after Congress is required to assemble, determines by two-thirds vote of both Houses that the President is unable to discharge the powers and duties of his office, the Vice President shall continue to discharge the same as Acting President; otherwise, the President shall resume the powers and duties of his office. [February 10, 1967]

AMENDMENT XXVI.

Section 1. The right of citizens of the United States, who are eighteen years of age or older, to vote shall not be denied or abridged by the United States or by any State on account of age.

Section 2. The Congress shall have power to enforce this article by appropriate legislation. [June 30, 1971]

AMENDMENT XXVII.

No law, varying the compensation for the services of the Senators and Representatives shall take effect, until an election of Representatives shall have intervened. [May 8, 1992]

FROM GEORGE WASHINGTON'S FAREWELL ADDRESS (1796)

Friends and Citizens:

The period for a new election of a citizen to administer the executive government of the United States being not far distant, and the time actually arrived when your thoughts must be employed in designating the person who is to be clothed with that important trust, it appears to me proper, especially as it may conduce to a more distinct expression of the public voice, that I should now apprise you of the resolution I have formed, to decline being considered among the number of those out of whom a choice is to be made.

* * *

In looking forward to the moment which is intended to terminate the career of my public life, my feelings do not permit me to suspend the deep acknowledgment of that debt of gratitude which I owe to my beloved country for the many honors it has conferred upon me; still more for the steadfast confidence with which it has supported me; and for the opportunities I have thence enjoyed of manifesting my inviolable attachment, by services faithful and persevering, though in usefulness unequal to my zeal. If benefits have resulted to our country from these services, let it always be remembered to your praise, and as an instructive example in our annals, that under circumstances in which the passions, agitated in every direction, were liable to mislead, amidst appearances sometimes dubious, vicissitudes of fortune often discouraging, in situations in which not unfrequently want of success has countenanced the spirit of criticism, the constancy of your support was the essential prop of the efforts, and a guarantee of the plans by which they were effected. Profoundly penetrated with this idea, I shall carry it with me to my grave, as a strong incitement to unceasing vows that heaven may continue to you the choicest tokens of its beneficence; that your union and brotherly affection may be perpetual; that the free Constitution, which is the work of your hands, may be sacredly maintained; that its administration in every department may be stamped with wisdom and virtue; that, in fine, the happiness of the people of these States, under the auspices of liberty, may be made complete by so careful a preservation and so prudent a use of this blessing as will acquire to them the glory of recommending it to the applause, the affection, and adoption of every nation which is yet a stranger to it.

Here, perhaps, I ought to stop. But a solicitude for your welfare, which cannot end but with my life, and the apprehension of danger, natural to that solicitude, urge me, on an occasion like the present, to offer to your solemn contemplation, and to recommend to your frequent review, some sentiments which are the result of much reflection, of no inconsiderable observation, and which appear to me all-important to the permanency of your felicity as a people. These will be offered to you with the more freedom, as you can only see in them the disinterested warnings of a parting friend, who can possibly have no personal motive to bias his counsel. Nor can I forget, as an encouragement to it, your indulgent reception of my sentiments on a former and not dissimilar occasion.

Interwoven as is the love of liberty with every ligament of your hearts, no recommendation of mine is necessary to fortify or confirm the attachment.

The unity of government which constitutes you one people is also now dear to you. It is justly so, for it is a main pillar in the edifice of your real independence, the support of your tranquility at home, your peace abroad; of your safety; of your prosperity; of that very liberty which you so highly prize. But as it is easy to foresee that, from different causes and from different quarters, much pains will be taken, many artifices employed to weaken in your minds the conviction of this truth; as this is the point in your political fortress against which the batteries of internal and external enemies will be most constantly and actively (though often covertly and insidiously) directed, it is of infinite moment that you should properly estimate the immense value of your national union to your collective and individual happiness; that you should cherish a cordial, habitual, and immovable attachment to it; accustoming yourselves to think and speak of it as of the palladium of your political safety and prosperity; watching for its preservation with jealous anxiety; discountenancing whatever may suggest even a suspicion that it can in any event be abandoned; and indignantly frowning upon the first dawning of every attempt to alienate any portion of our country from the rest, or to enfeeble the sacred ties which now link together the various parts.

For this you have every inducement of sympathy and interest. Citizens, by birth or choice, of a common country, that country has a right to concentrate your affections. The name of American, which belongs to you in your national capacity, must always exalt the just pride of patriotism more than any appellation derived from local discriminations. With slight shades of difference, you have the same religion, manners, habits, and political principles. You have in a common cause fought and triumphed together; the independence and liberty you possess are the work of joint counsels, and joint efforts of common dangers, sufferings, and successes.

But these considerations, however powerfully they address themselves to your sensibility, are greatly outweighed by those which apply more immediately to your interest. Here every portion of our country finds the most commanding motives for carefully guarding and preserving the union of the whole.

The North, in an unrestrained intercourse with the South, protected by the equal laws of a common government, finds in the productions of the latter great additional resources of maritime and commercial enterprise and precious materials of manufacturing industry. The South, in the same intercourse, benefiting by the agency of the North, sees its agriculture grow and its commerce expand. Turning partly into its own channels the seamen of the North, it finds its particular navigation invigorated; and, while it contributes, in different ways, to nourish and increase the general mass of the national navigation, it looks forward to the protection of a maritime strength, to which itself is unequally adapted. The East, in a like intercourse with the West, already finds, and in the progressive improvement of interior communications by land and water, will more and more find a valuable vent for the commodities which it brings from abroad, or manufactures at home. The West derives from the East supplies requisite to its growth and comfort, and, what is perhaps of still greater consequence, it must of necessity owe the secure enjoyment of indispensable outlets for its own productions to the weight, influence, and the future maritime strength of the Atlantic side of the Union, directed by an indissoluble community of interest as one nation. Any other tenure by which the West can hold this essential advantage, whether derived from its own separate strength, or from an apostate and unnatural connection with any foreign power, must be intrinsically precarious.

While, then, every part of our country thus feels an immediate and particular interest in union, all the parts combined cannot fail to find in the united mass of means and efforts greater strength, greater resource, proportionably greater security from external danger, a less frequent interruption of their peace by foreign nations; and, what is of inestimable value, they must derive from union an exemption from those broils and wars between themselves, which so frequently afflict neighboring countries not tied together by the same governments, which their own rival ships alone would be sufficient to produce, but which opposite foreign alliances, attachments, and intrigues would stimulate and embitter. Hence, likewise, they will avoid the necessity of those overgrown military establishments which, under any form of government, are inauspicious to liberty, and which are to be regarded as particularly hostile to republican liberty. In this sense it is that your union ought to be considered as a main prop of your liberty, and that the love of the one ought to endear to you the preservation of the other.

These considerations speak a persuasive language to every reflecting and virtuous mind, and exhibit the continuance of the Union as a primary object of patriotic desire. Is there a doubt whether a common government can embrace so large a sphere? Let experience solve it. To listen to mere speculation in such a case were criminal. We are authorized to hope that a proper organization of the whole with the auxiliary agency of governments for the respective subdivisions, will afford a happy issue to the experiment. It is well worth a fair and full experiment. With such powerful and obvious motives to union, affecting all parts of our country, while experience

shall not have demonstrated its impracticability, there will always be reason to distrust the patriotism of those who in any quarter may endeavor to weaken its bands.

* * *

To the efficacy and permanency of your Union, a government for the whole is indispensable. No alliance, however strict, between the parts can be an adequate substitute; they must inevitably experience the infractions and interruptions which all alliances in all times have experienced. Sensible of this momentous truth, you have improved upon your first essay, by the adoption of a constitution of government better calculated than your former for an intimate union, and for the efficacious management of your common concerns. This government, the offspring of our own choice, uninfluenced and unawed, adopted upon full investigation and mature deliberation, completely free in its principles, in the distribution of its powers, uniting security with energy, and containing within itself a provision for its own amendment, has a just claim to your confidence and your support. Respect for its authority, compliance with its laws, acquiescence in its measures, are duties enjoined by the fundamental maxims of true liberty. The basis of our political systems is the right of the people to make and to alter their constitutions of government. But the Constitution which at any time exists, till changed by an explicit and authentic act of the whole people, is sacredly obligatory upon all. The very idea of the power and the right of the people to establish government presupposes the duty of every individual to obey the established government.

* * *

I have already intimated to you the danger of parties in the State, with particular reference to the founding of them on geographical discriminations. Let me now take a more comprehensive view, and warn you in the most solemn manner against the baneful effects of the spirit of party generally.

This spirit, unfortunately, is inseparable from our nature, having its root in the strongest passions of the human mind. It exists under different shapes in all governments, more or less stifled, controlled, or repressed; but, in those of the popular form, it is seen in its greatest rankness, and is truly their worst enemy.

The alternate domination of one faction over another, sharpened by the spirit of revenge, natural to party dissension, which in different ages and countries has perpetrated the most horrid enormities, is itself a frightful despotism. But this leads at length to a more formal and permanent despotism. The disorders and miseries which result gradually incline the minds of men to seek security and repose in the absolute power of an individual; and sooner or later the chief of some prevailing faction, more able or more fortunate than his competitors, turns this disposition to the purposes of his own elevation, on the ruins of public liberty.

Without looking forward to an extremity of this kind (which nevertheless ought not to be entirely out of sight), the common and continual mischiefs of the spirit of party are sufficient to make it the interest and duty of a wise people to discourage and restrain it.

It serves always to distract the public councils and enfeeble the public administration. It agitates the community with ill-founded jealousies and false alarms, kindles the animosity of one part against another, foments occasionally riot and insurrection. It opens the door to foreign influence and corruption, which finds a facilitated access to the government itself through the channels of party passions. Thus the policy and the will of one country are subjected to the policy and will of another.

There is an opinion that parties in free countries are useful checks upon the administration of the government and serve to keep alive the spirit of liberty. This within certain limits is probably true; and in governments of a monarchical cast, patriotism may look with indulgence, if not with favor, upon the spirit of party. But in those of the popular character, in governments purely elective, it is a spirit not to be encouraged. From their natural tendency, it is certain there will always be enough of that spirit for every salutary purpose. And there being constant danger of excess, the effort ought to be by force of public opinion, to mitigate and assuage it. A fire not to be quenched, it demands a uniform vigilance to prevent its bursting into a flame, lest, instead of warming, it should consume.

It is important, likewise, that the habits of thinking in a free country should inspire caution in those entrusted with its administration, to confine themselves within their respective constitutional spheres, avoiding in the exercise of the powers of one department to encroach upon another. The spirit of encroachment tends to consolidate the powers of all the departments in one, and thus to create, whatever the form of government, a real despotism. A just estimate of that love of power, and proneness to abuse it, which predominates in the human heart, is sufficient to satisfy us of the truth of this position. The necessity of reciprocal checks in the exercise of political power, by dividing and distributing it into different depositaries, and constituting each the guardian of the public weal against invasions by the others, has been evinced by experiments ancient and modern; some of them in our country and under our own eyes. To preserve them must be as necessary as to institute them. If, in the opinion of the people, the distribution or modification of the constitutional powers be in any particular wrong, let it be corrected by an amendment in the way which the Constitution designates. But let there be no change by usurpation; for though this, in one instance, may be the instrument of good, it is the customary weapon by which free governments are destroyed. The precedent must always greatly overbalance in permanent evil any partial or transient benefit, which the use can at any time yield.

* * *

Observe good faith and justice towards all nations; cultivate peace and harmony with all. Religion and morality enjoin this conduct; and can it be, that good policy does not equally enjoin it? It will be worthy of a free, enlightened, and at no dis-

tant period, a great nation, to give to mankind the magnanimous and too novel example of a people always guided by an exalted justice and benevolence. Who can doubt that, in the course of time and things, the fruits of such a plan would richly repay any temporary advantages which might be lost by a steady adherence to it? Can it be that Providence has not connected the permanent felicity of a nation with its virtue? The experiment, at least, is recommended by every sentiment which ennobles human nature. Alas! is it rendered impossible by its vices?

In the execution of such a plan, nothing is more essential than that permanent, inveterate antipathies against particular nations, and passionate attachments for others, should be excluded; and that, in place of them, just and amicable feelings towards all should be cultivated. The nation which indulges towards another a habitual hatred or a habitual fondness is in some degree a slave. It is a slave to its animosity or to its affection, either of which is sufficient to lead it astray from its duty and its interest. Antipathy in one nation against another disposes each more readily to offer insult and injury, to lay hold of slight causes of umbrage, and to be haughty and intractable, when accidental or trifling occasions of dispute occur. Hence, frequent collisions, obstinate, envenomed, and bloody contests. The nation, prompted by ill-will and resentment, sometimes impels to war the government, contrary to the best calculations of policy. The government sometimes participates in the national propensity, and adopts through passion what reason would reject; at other times it makes the animosity of the nation subservient to projects of hostility instigated by pride, ambition, and other sinister and pernicious motives. The peace often, sometimes perhaps the liberty, of nations, has been the victim.

* * *

The great rule of conduct for us in regard to foreign nations is in extending our commercial relations, to have with them as little political connection as possible. So far as we have already formed engagements, let them be fulfilled with perfect good faith. Here let us stop. Europe has a set of primary interests which to us have none; or a very remote relation. Hence she must be engaged in frequent controversies, the causes of which are essentially foreign to our concerns. Hence, therefore, it must be unwise in us to implicate ourselves by artificial ties in the ordinary vicissitudes of her politics, or the ordinary combinations and collisions of her friendships or enmities.

Our detached and distant situation invites and enables us to pursue a different course. If we remain one people under an efficient government, the period is not far off when we may defy material injury from external annoyance; when we may take such an attitude as will cause the neutrality we may at any time resolve upon to be scrupulously respected; when belligerent nations, under the impossibility of making acquisitions upon us, will not lightly hazard the giving us provocation; when we may choose peace or war, as our interest, guided by justice, shall counsel.

Why forego the advantages of so peculiar a situation? Why quit our own to stand upon foreign ground? Why, by interweaving our destiny with that of any part of Europe, entangle our peace and prosperity in the toils of European ambition, rivalship, interest, humor or caprice?

It is our true policy to steer clear of permanent alliances with any portion of the foreign world; so far, I mean, as we are now at liberty to do it; for let me not be understood as capable of patronizing infidelity to existing engagements. I hold the maxim no less applicable to public than to private affairs, that honesty is always the best policy. I repeat it, therefore, let those engagements be observed in their genuine sense. But, in my opinion, it is unnecessary and would be unwise to extend them.

Taking care always to keep ourselves by suitable establishments on a respectable defensive posture, we may safely trust to temporary alliances for extraordinary emergencies.

Harmony, liberal intercourse with all nations, are recommended by policy, humanity, and interest. But even our commercial policy should hold an equal and impartial hand; neither seeking nor granting exclusive favors or preferences; consulting the natural course of things; diffusing and diversifying by gentle means the streams of commerce, but forcing nothing; establishing (with powers so disposed, in order to give trade a stable course, to define the rights of our merchants, and to enable the government to support them) conventional rules of intercourse, the best that present circumstances and mutual opinion will permit, but temporary, and liable to be from time to time abandoned or varied, as experience and circumstances shall dictate; constantly keeping in view that it is folly in one nation to look for disinterested favors from another; that it must pay with a portion of its independence for whatever it may accept under that character; that, by such acceptance, it may place itself in the condition of having given equivalents for nominal favors, and yet of being reproached with ingratitude for not giving more.

* * *

Relying on its kindness in this as in other things, and actuated by that fervent love towards it, which is so natural to a man who views in it the native soil of himself and his progenitors for several generations, I anticipate with pleasing expectation that retreat in which I promise myself to realize, without alloy, the sweet enjoyment of partaking, in the midst of my fellow-citizens, the benign influence of good laws under a free government, the ever-favorite object of my heart, and the happy reward, as I trust, of our mutual cares, labors, and dangers.

Geo. Washington

The Seneca Falls Declaration of Sentiments and Resolutions (1848)

1. Declaration of Sentiments

When, in the course of human events, it becomes necessary for one portion of the family of man to assume among the people of the earth a position different from that which they have hitherto occupied, but one to which the laws of nature and of nature's God entitle them, a decent respect to the opinions of mankind requires that they should declare the causes that impel them to such a course.

We hold these truths to be self-evident: that all men and women are created equal; that they are endowed by their Creator with certain inalienable rights; that among these are life, liberty, and the pursuit of happiness; that to secure these rights governments are instituted, deriving their just powers from the consent of the governed. Whenever any form of government becomes destructive of these ends, it is the right of those who suffer from it to refuse allegiance to it, and to insist upon the institution of a new government, laying its foundation on such principles, and organizing its powers in such form, as to them shall seem most likely to effect their safety and happiness. Prudence, indeed, will dictate that governments long established should not be changed for light and transient causes; and accordingly all experience hath shown that mankind are more disposed to suffer, while evils are sufferable, than to right themselves by abolishing the forms to which they are accustomed. But when a long train of abuses and usurpations, pursuing invariably the same object, evinces a design to reduce them under absolute despotism, it is their duty to throw off such government, and to provide new guards for their future security. Such has been the patient sufferance of the women under this government, and such is now the necessity which constrains them to demand the equal station to which they are entitled. The history of mankind is a history of repeated injuries and usurpations on the part of man toward woman, having in direct object the establishment of an absolute tyranny over her. To prove this, let facts be submitted to a candid world.

He has never permitted her to exercise her inalienable right to the elective franchise.

He has compelled her to submit to laws, in the formation of which she had no voice.

He has withheld from her rights which are given to the most ignorant and degraded men—both natives and foreigners.

Having deprived her of this first right of a citizen, the elective franchise, thereby leaving her without representation in the halls of legislation, he has oppressed her on all sides.

He has made her, if married, in the eye of the law, civilly dead. He has taken from her all right in property, even to the wages she earns.

He has made her, morally, an irresponsible being, as she can commit many crimes with impunity, provided they be done in the presence of her husband.

In the covenant of marriage, she is compelled to promise obedience to her husband, he becoming, to all intents and purposes, her master—the law giving him power to deprive her of her liberty, and to administer chastisement.

He has so framed the laws of divorce, as to what shall be the proper causes, and in case of separation, to whom the guardianship of the children shall be given, as to be wholly regardless of the happiness of women—the law, in all cases, going upon a false supposition of the supremacy of man, and giving all power into his hands.

After depriving her of all rights as a married woman, if single, and the owner of property, he has taxed her to support a government which recognizes her only when her property can be made profitable to it.

He has monopolized nearly all the profitable employments, and from those she is permitted to follow, she receives but a scanty remuneration. He closes against her all the avenues to wealth and distinction which he considers most honorable to himself. As a teacher of theology, medicine, or law, she is not known.

He has denied her the facilities for obtaining a thorough education, all colleges being closed against her.

He allows her in Church, as well as State, but a subordinate position, claiming Apostolic authority for her exclusion from the ministry, and, with some exceptions, from any public participation in the affairs of the Church.

He has created a false public sentiment by giving to the world a different code of morals for men and women, by which moral delinquencies which exclude women from society, are not only tolerated, but deemed of little account in man.

He has usurped the prerogative of Jehovah himself, claiming it as his right to assign for her a sphere of action, when that belongs to her conscience and to her God.

He has endeavored, in every way that he could, to destroy her confidence in her own powers, to lessen her self-respect and to make her willing to lead a dependent and abject life.

Now, in view of this entire disfranchisement of one-half the people of this country, their social and religious degradation—in view of the unjust laws above mentioned, and because women do feel themselves aggrieved, oppressed, and fraudulently deprived of their most sacred rights, we insist that they have immediate admission to all the rights and privileges which belong to them as citizens of the United States.

In entering upon the great work before us, we anticipate no small amount of misconception, misrepresentation, and ridicule; but we shall use every instrumentality within our power to effect our object. We shall employ agents, circulate tracts, petition the State and National legislatures, and endeavor to enlist the pulpit and the press in our behalf. We hope this Convention will be followed by a series of Conventions embracing every part of the country.

2. RESOLUTIONS

WHEREAS, The great precept of nature is conceded to be, that "man shall pursue his own true and substantial happiness." Blackstone in his Commentaries remarks, that this law of Nature being coeval with mankind, and dictated by God himself, is of course superior in obligation to any other. It is binding over all the globe, in all countries and at all times; no human laws are of any validity if contrary to this, and such of them as are valid, derive all their force, and all their validity, and all their authority, mediately and immediately, from this original; therefore,

Resolved, That such laws as conflict, in any way, with the true and substantial happiness of woman, are contrary to the great precept of nature and of no validity, for this is "superior in obligation to any other."

Resolved, That all laws which prevent woman from occupying such a station in society as her conscience shall dictate, or which place her in a position inferior to that of man, are contrary to the great precept of nature, and therefore of no force or authority.

Resolved, That woman is man's equal—was intended to be so by the Creator, and the highest good of the race demands that she should be recognized as such.

Resolved, That the women of this country ought to be enlightened in regard to the laws under which they live, that they may no longer publish their degradation by declaring themselves satisfied with their present position, nor their ignorance, by asserting that they have all the rights they want.

Resolved, That inasmuch as man, while claiming for himself intellectual superiority, does accord to woman moral superiority, it is pre-eminently his duty to encourage her to speak and teach, as she has an opportunity, in all religious assemblies.

Resolved, That the same amount of virtue, delicacy, and refinement of behavior that is required of woman in the social state, should also be required of man, and the same transgressions should be visited with equal severity on both man and woman.

Resolved, That the objection of indelicacy and impropriety, which is so often brought against woman when she addresses a public audience, comes with a very ill-grace from those who encourage, by their attendance, her appearance on the stage, in the concert. Or in feats of the circus.

Resolved, That woman has too long rested satisfied in the circumscribed limits which corrupt customs and a perverted application of the Scriptures have marked out for her, and that it is time she should move in the enlarged sphere which her great Creator has assigned her.

Resolved, That it is the duty of the women of this country to secure to themselves their sacred right to the elective franchise.

Resolved, That the equality of human rights results necessarily from the fact of the identity of the race in capabilities and responsibilities.

Resolved, therefore, That, being invested by the Creator with the same capabilities, and the same consciousness of responsibility for their exercise, it is demonstrably the right and duty of woman, equally with man, to promote every righteous cause by every righteous means; and especially in regard to the great subjects of morals and religion, it is self-evidently her right to participate with her brother in teaching them, both in private and in public, by writing and by speaking, by any instrumentalities proper to be used, and in any assemblies proper to be held; and this being a self-evident truth growing out of the divinely implanted principles of human nature, any custom or authority adverse to it, whether modern or wearing the hoary sanction of antiquity, is to be regarded as a self-evident falsehood, and at war with mankind.

Resolved, That the speedy success of our cause depends upon the zealous and untiring efforts of both men and women, for the overthrow of the monopoly of the pulpit, and for the securing to women an equal participation with men in the various trades, professions, and commerce.

from Frederick Douglass's "What, to the Slave, Is the Fourth of July?" Speech (1852)

* * *

This, for the purpose of this celebration, is the Fourth of July. It is the birthday of your National Independence, and of your political freedom. This, to you, is what the Passover was to the emancipated people of God. It carries your minds back to the day, and to the act of your great deliverance; and to the signs and to the wonders associated with that act and that day. This celebration also marks the beginning of another year of your national life; and reminds you that the Republic of America is now seventy-six years old. I am glad, fellow citizens, that your nation is so young. Seventy-six years, though a good old age for a man, is but a mere speck in the life of a nation. Three score years and ten is the allotted time for individual men; but nations number their years by thousands. According to this fact, you are, even now, only in the beginning of your national career, still lingering in the period of childhood. I repeat, I am glad this is so. There is hope in the thought, and hope is much needed, under the dark clouds which lower above the horizon. The eye of the reformer is met with angry flashes, portending disastrous times; but his heart may well beat lighter at the thought that America is young, and that she is still in the impressible stage of her existence. May he not hope that high lessons of wisdom, of justice and of truth, will yet give direction to her destiny? Were the nation older, the patriot's heart might be sadder and the reformer's brow heavier. Its future might be shrouded in gloom and the hope of its prophets go out in sorrow. There is consolation in the thought that America is young. Great streams are not easily turned from channels worn deep in the course of ages. They may sometimes rise in quiet and stately majesty, and inundate the land, refreshing and fertilizing the earth with their mysterious properties. They may also rise in wrath and fury, and bear away on their angry waves the accumulated wealth of years of toil and hardship. They, however, gradually flow back to the same old channel and flow on as serenely as ever. But, while the river may not be turned aside, it may dry up and leave nothing behind but the withered branch and the unsightly rock, to howl in the abyss-sweeping wind, the sad tale of departed glory. As with rivers, so with nations.

Fellow citizens, I shall not presume to dwell at length on the associations that cluster about this day. The simple story of it is, that seventy-six years ago the people of this country were British subjects. The style and title of your "sovereign people" (in which you now glory) was not then born. You were under the British Crown. Your fathers esteemed the English government as the home government, and England as the fatherland. This home government, you know, although a considerable distance from your home, did, in the exercise of its parental prerogatives, impose upon its colonial children such restraints, burdens and limitations as, in its mature judgment, it deemed wise, right and proper.

* * *

Feeling themselves harshly and unjustly treated by the home government, your fathers, like men of honesty and men of spirit, earnestly sought redress. They petitioned and remonstrated, they did so in a decorous, respectful and loyal manner. Their conduct was wholly unexceptionable. This, however, did not answer the purpose. They saw themselves treated with sovereign indifference, coldness and scorn. Yet they persevered. They were not the men to look back.

* * *

Citizens, your fathers . . . succeeded; and today you reap the fruits of their success. The freedom gained is yours; and you, therefore, may properly celebrate this anniversary. The Fourth of July is the first great fact in your nation's history—the very ringbolt in the chain of your yet undeveloped destiny.

Pride and patriotism, not less than gratitude, prompt you to celebrate and to hold it in perpetual remembrance. I have said that the Declaration of Independence is the ringbolt to the chain of your nation's destiny; so, indeed, I regard it. The principles contained in that instrument are saving principles. Stand by those principles, be true to them on all occasions, in all places, against all foes, and at whatever cost.

* * *

[The fathers of this republic] were peace men, but they preferred revolution to peaceful submission to bondage. They were quiet men; but they did not shrink from agitating against oppression. They showed forbearance, but that they knew its limits. They believed in order, but not in the order of tyranny. With them, nothing was "settled" that was not right. With them, justice, liberty and humanity were "final," not slavery and oppression. You may well cherish the memory of such men. They were great in their day and generation. Their solid manhood stands out the more as we contrast it with these degenerate times.

* * *

Fellow citizens, pardon me, allow me to ask, why am I called upon to speak here today? What have I, or those I represent, to do with your national independence? Are the great principles of political freedom and of natural justice, embodied in that Declaration of Independence, extended to us? and am I, therefore, called upon to bring our humble offering to the national altar and to confess the benefits and express devout gratitude for the blessings resulting from your independence to us?

* * *

But such is not the state of the case. I say it with a sad sense of the disparity between us. I am not included within the pale of this glorious anniversary! Your high independence only reveals the immeasurable distance between us. The blessings in which you, this day, rejoice, are not enjoyed in common. The rich inheritance of justice, liberty, prosperity and independence, bequeathed by your fathers, is shared by you, not by me. The sunlight that brought light and healing to you, has brought stripes and death to me. This Fourth of July is *yours*, not *mine*. *You* may rejoice, *I* must mourn.

* * *

Fellow citizens, above your national, tumultuous joy I hear the mournful wail of millions! whose chains, heavy and grievous yesterday, are today rendered more intolerable by the jubilee shouts that reach them. If I do forget, if I do not faithfully remember those bleeding children of sorrow this day, "may my right hand forget her cunning, and may my tongue cleave to the roof of my mouth!" To forget them, to pass lightly over their wrongs and to chime in with the popular theme would be treason most scandalous and shocking and would make me a reproach before God and the world. My subject, then, fellow citizens, is American slavery. I shall see this day and its popular characteristics from the slave's point of view. Standing there identified with the American bondman, making his wrongs mine, I do not hesitate to declare, with all my soul, that the character and conduct of this nation never looked blacker to me than on this Fourth of July. Whether we turn to the declarations of the past or to the professions of the present, the conduct of the nation seems equally hideous and revolting. America is false to the past, false to the present, and solemnly binds herself to be false to the future.

* * *

For the present, it is enough to affirm the equal manhood of the Negro race. It is not astonishing that, while we are plowing, planting and reaping, using all kinds of mechanical tools, erecting houses, constructing bridges, building ships, working in metals of brass, iron, copper, silver and gold; that, while we are reading, writing and ciphering, acting as clerks, merchants and secretaries, having among us lawyers, doctors, ministers, poets, authors, editors, orators and teachers; that, while we are engaged in all manner of enterprises common to other men, digging gold in California, capturing the whale in the Pacific, feeding sheep and cattle on the hillside, living, moving, acting, thinking, planning, living in families as husbands, wives and children, and, above all, confessing and worshiping the Christian's God and looking hopefully for life and immortality beyond the grave, we are called upon to prove that we are men!

Would you have me argue that man is entitled to liberty? that he is the rightful owner of his own body? You have already declared it. Must I argue the wrongfulness of slavery?

Is that a question for republicans? Is it to be settled by the rules of logic and argumentation, as a matter beset with great difficulty, involving a doubtful application of the principle of justice, hard to be understood? How should I look today, in the presence of Americans, dividing and subdividing a discourse, to show that men have a natural right to freedom, speaking of it relatively and positively, negatively and affirmatively? To do so would be to make myself ridiculous and to offer an insult to your understanding. There is not a man beneath the canopy of heaven that does not know that slavery is wrong *for him*.

* * *

What, to the American slave, is your Fourth of July? I answer: a day that reveals to him, more than all other days in the year, the gross injustice and cruelty to which he is the constant victim. To him, your celebration is a sham; your boasted liberty an unholy license; your national greatness swelling vanity; your sounds of rejoicing are empty and heartless; your denunciation of tyrants brass-fronted impudence; your shouts of liberty and equality hollow mockery; your prayers and hymns, your sermons and thanksgivings, with all your religious parade and solemnity, are to Him mere bombast, fraud, deception, impiety and hypocrisy—a thin veil to cover up crimes which would disgrace a nation of savages. There is not a nation on the earth guilty of practices more shocking and bloody than are the people of the United States at this very hour.

Go where you may, search where you will, roam through all the monarchies and despotisms of the Old World, travel through South America, search out every abuse, and when you have found the last, lay your facts by the side of the everyday practices of this nation, and you will say with me, that, for revolting barbarity and shameless hypocrisy, America reigns without a rival.

* * *

Americans! your republican politics, not less than your republican religion, are flagrantly inconsistent. You boast of your love of liberty, your superior civilization and your pure Christianity, while the whole political power of the nation (as embodied in the two great political parties) is solemnly pledged to support and perpetuate the enslavement of three millions of your countrymen. You hurl your anathemas at the crowned-headed tyrants of Russia and Austria and pride yourselves on your democratic institutions, while you yourselves consent to be the mere *tools* and *bodyguards* of the tyrants of Virginia and Carolina. You invite to your shores fugitives of oppression from abroad, honor them with banquets, greet them with ovations, cheer them, toast them, salute them, protect them, and pour out your money to them like water; but the fugitives from your own land you advertise, hunt, arrest, shoot and kill. You glory in your refinement and your universal education; yet you maintain a system as barbarous and dreadful as ever stained the character of a nation—a system begun in avarice, supported in pride, and perpetuated in cruelty. You shed tears over fallen Hungary, and make the sad story of her wrongs the theme of your poets, statesmen and orators, till your gallant sons are ready to fly to arms to vindicate her cause against the oppressor;* but, in regard to the ten thousand wrongs of the American slave, you would enforce the strictest silence and would hail him as an enemy of the nation who dares to make those wrongs the subject of public discourse! You are all on fire at the mention of liberty for France or for Ireland, but are as cold as an iceberg at the thought of liberty for the enslaved of America. You discourse eloquently on the dignity of labor; yet, you sustain a system which, in its very essence, casts a stigma upon labor. You can bare your bosom to the storm of British artillery to throw off a three-penny tax on tea, and yet wring the last hard-earned farthing from the grasp of the black laborers of your country. You profess to believe "that of one blood God made all nations of men to dwell on the face of all the earth"† and hath commanded all men, everywhere, to love one another; yet you notoriously hate (and glory in your hatred) all men whose skins are not colored like your own. You declare before the world, and are understood by the world to declare, that you "*hold these truths to be self-evident, that all men are created equal;*

*The fledgling Hungarian republic was invaded by Austria and Russia in 1849.
†Acts 17:26.

and are endowed by their Creator with certain unalienable rights; and that among these are, life, liberty and the pursuit of happiness"; and yet, you hold securely, in a bondage which, according to your own Thomas Jefferson, "*is worse than ages of that which your fathers rose in rebellion to oppose,*" a seventh part of the inhabitants of your country.

Fellow citizens, I will not enlarge further on your national inconsistencies. The existence of slavery in this country brands your republicanism as a sham, your humanity as a base pretense, and your Christianity as a lie. It destroys your moral power abroad; it corrupts your politicians at home. It saps the foundation of religion; it makes your name a hissing and a byword to a mocking earth. It is the antagonistic force in your government, the only thing that seriously disturbs and endangers your union. It fetters your progress; it is the enemy of improvement; the deadly foe of education; it fosters pride; it breeds insolence; it promotes vice; it shelters crime; it is a curse to the earth that supports it; and yet you cling to it as if it were the sheet anchor of all your hopes.

* * *

Allow me to say, in conclusion, notwithstanding the dark picture I have this day presented, of the state of the nation, I do not despair of this country. There are forces in operation which must inevitably work the downfall of slavery.

* * *

The Gettysburg Address (1863)

Four score and seven years ago our fathers brought forth on this continent, a new nation, conceived in Liberty, and dedicated to the proposition that all men are created equal.

Now we are engaged in a great civil war, testing whether that nation, or any nation so conceived and so dedicated, can long endure. We are met on a great battle field of that war. We have come to dedicate a portion of that field, as a final resting place for those who here gave their lives that that nation might live. It is altogether fitting and proper that we should do this.

But, in a larger sense, we can not dedicate—we can not consecrate—we can not hallow—this ground. The brave men, living and dead, who struggled here, have consecrated it, far above our poor power to add or detract. The world will little note, nor long remember what we say here, but it can never forget what they did here. It is for us the living, rather, to be dedicated here to the unfinished work which they who fought here have thus far so nobly advanced. It is rather for us to be here dedicated to the great task remaining before us—that from these honored dead we take increased devotion to that cause for which they gave the last full measure of devotion—that we here highly resolve that these dead shall not have died in vain—that this nation, under God, shall have a new birth of freedom—and that government of the people, by the people, for the people, shall not perish from the earth.

Abraham Lincoln
November 19, 1863

ABRAHAM LINCOLN'S SECOND INAUGURAL ADDRESS (1865)

Fellow Countrymen:

At this second appearing to take the oath of the presidential office, there is less occasion for an extended address than there was at the first. Then a statement, somewhat in detail, of a course to be pursued, seemed fitting and proper. Now, at the expiration of four years, during which public declarations have been constantly called forth on every point and phase of the great contest which still absorbs the attention, and engrosses the energies of the nation, little that is new could be presented. The progress of our arms, upon which all else chiefly depends, is as well known to the public as to myself; and it is, I trust, reasonably satisfactory and encouraging to all. With high hope for the future, no prediction in regard to it is ventured.

On the occasion corresponding to this four years ago, all thoughts were anxiously directed to an impending civil war. All dreaded it—all sought to avert it. While the inaugural address was being delivered from this place, devoted altogether to *saving* the Union without war, insurgent agents were in the city seeking to *destroy* it without war—seeking to dissolve the Union, and divide effects, by negotiation. Both parties deprecated war; but one of them would *make* war rather than let the nation survive; and the other would *accept* war rather than let it perish. And the war came.

One eighth of the whole population were colored slaves, not distributed generally over the Union, but localized in the southern part of it. These slaves constituted a peculiar and powerful interest. All knew that this interest was, somehow, the cause of the war. To strengthen, perpetuate, and extend this interest was the object for which the insurgents would rend the Union, even by war; while the government claimed no right to do more than to restrict the territorial enlargement of it. Neither party expected for the war, the magnitude, or the duration, which it has already attained. Neither anticipated that the *cause* of the conflict might cease with, or even before, the conflict itself should cease. Each looked for an easier triumph, and a result less fundamental and astounding. Both read the same Bible, and pray to the same God; and each invokes His aid against the other. It may seem strange that any men should dare to ask a just God's assistance in wringing their bread from the sweat of other men's faces; but let us judge not that we be not judged. The prayers of both could not be answered; that of neither has been answered fully. The Almighty has His own purposes. "Woe unto the world because of offences! for it must needs be that offences come; but woe to that man by whom the offence cometh." If we shall suppose that American slavery is one of those offences which, in the providence of God, must needs come, but which, having continued through His appointed time, He now wills to remove, and that He gives to both North and South, this terrible war, as the woe due to those by whom the offence came, shall we discern therein any departure from those divine attributes which the believers in a living God always ascribe to Him? Fondly do we hope, fervently do we pray—that this mighty scourge of war may speedily pass away. Yet, if God wills that it continue until all the wealth piled by the bondsman's two hundred and fifty years of unrequited toil shall be sunk, and until every drop of blood drawn with the lash shall be paid by another drawn with the sword, as was said three thousand years ago, so still it must be said "the judgments of the Lord are true and righteous altogether."

With malice toward none; with charity for all; with firmness in the right as God gives us to see the right, let us strive on to finish the work we are in; to bind up the nation's wounds; to care for him who shall have borne the battle and for his widow and his orphan, to do all which may achieve and cherish a just and a lasting peace, among ourselves and with all nations.

The Populist Platform of 1892

Assembled upon the 116th anniversary of the Declaration of Independence, the People's Party of America, in their first national convention, invoking upon their action the blessing of Almighty God, puts forth in the name and on behalf of the people of this country, the following preamble and declaration of principles:

Preamble

The conditions which surround us best justify our co-operation; we meet in the midst of a nation brought to the verge of moral, political, and material ruin. Corruption dominates the ballot-box, the Legislatures, the Congress, and touches even the ermine of the bench. The people are demoralized; most of the States have been compelled to isolate the voters at the polling places to prevent universal intimidation and bribery. The newspapers are largely subsidized or muzzled, public opinion silenced, business prostrated, homes covered with mortgages, labor impoverished, and the land concentrating in the hands of the capitalists. The urban workmen are denied the right to organize for self-protection, imported pauperized labor beats down their wages, a hireling standing army, unrecognized by our laws, is established to shoot them down, and they are rapidly degenerating into European conditions. The fruits of the toil of millions are boldly stolen to build up the fortunes for a few, unprecedented in the history of mankind; and the possessors of these, in turn, despise the Republic and endanger liberty. From the same prolific womb of governmental injustice we breed the two great classes—tramps and millionaires.

The national power to create money is appropriated to enrich bondholders; a vast public debt, payable in legal tender currency, has been funded into gold-bearing bonds, thereby adding millions to the burdens of the people. Silver, which has been accepted as coin since the dawn of history, has been demonetized to add to the purchasing power of gold by decreasing the value of all forms of property as well as human labor, and the supply of currency is purposely abridged to fatten usurers, bankrupt enterprise, and enslave industry. A vast conspiracy against mankind has been organized on two continents, and it is rapidly taking possession of the world. If not met and overthrown at once it forebodes terrible social convulsions, the destruction of civilization, or the establishment of an absolute despotism.

We have witnessed for more than a quarter of a century the struggles of the two great political parties for power and plunder, while grievous wrongs have been inflicted upon the suffering people. We charge that the controlling influences dominating both these parties have permitted the existing dreadful conditions to develop without serious effort to prevent or restrain them. Neither do they now promise us any substantial reform. They have agreed together to ignore in the coming campaign every issue but one. They propose to drown the outcries of a plundered people with the uproar of a sham battle over the tariff, so that capitalists, corporations, national banks, rings, trusts, watered stock, the demonetization of silver, and the oppressions of the usurers may all be lost sight of. They propose to sacrifice our homes, lives, and children on the altar of mammon; to destroy the multitude in order to secure corruption funds from the millionaires.

Assembled on the anniversary of the birthday of the nation, and filled with the spirit of the grand general and chief who established our independence, we seek to restore the government of the Republic to the hands of "the plain people," with which class it originated. We assert our purpose to be identical with the purposes of the National Constitution, "to form a more perfect union and establish justice, insure domestic tranquility, provide for the common defense, promote the general welfare, and secure the blessings of liberty for ourselves and our posterity." We declare that this Republic can only endure as a free government while built upon the love of the whole people for each other and for the nation; that it cannot be pinned together by bayonets; that the civil war is over, and that every passion and resentment which grew out of it must die with it; and that we must be in fact, as we are in name, one united brotherhood of free men.

Our country finds itself confronted by conditions for which there is no precedent in the history of the world; our annual agricultural productions amount to billions of dollars in value, which must, within a few weeks or months, be exchanged for billions of dollars of commodities consumed in their production; the existing currency supply is wholly inadequate to make this exchange; the results are falling prices, the formation of combines and rings, the impoverishment of the producing class. We pledge ourselves, if given power, we will labor to correct these evils by wise and reasonable legislation, in accordance with the terms of our platform. We believe that the power of government—in other words, of the people—should be expanded (as in the case of the postal service) as rapidly and as far as the good sense of an intelligent people and the teaching of experience shall justify, to the end that oppression, injustice, and poverty shall eventually cease in the land.

While our sympathies as a party of reform are naturally upon the side of every proposition which will tend to make men intelligent, virtuous, and temperate, we nevertheless regard these questions—important as they are—as secondary to the great issues now pressing for solution, and upon which not only our individual prosperity but the very existence of free institutions depend; and we ask all men to first help us to determine whether we are to have a republic to administer before we differ as to the conditions upon which it is to be administered, believing that the forces of reform this day organized will never cease to move forward until every wrong is remedied, and equal rights and equal privileges securely established for all the men and women of this country.

PLATFORM

We declare, therefore—

First.—That the union of the labor forces of the United States this day consummated shall be permanent and perpetual; may its spirit enter into all hearts for the salvation of the Republic and the uplifting of mankind!

Second.—Wealth belongs to him who creates it, and every dollar taken from industry without an equivalent is robbery. "If any will not work, neither shall he eat." The interests of rural and civic labor are the same; their enemies are identical.

Third.—We believe that the time has come when the railroad corporations will either own the people or the people must own the railroads; and, should the government enter upon the work of owning and managing all railroads, we should favor an amendment to the Constitution by which all persons engaged in the government service shall be placed under a civil-service regulation of the most rigid character, so as to prevent the increase of the power of the national administration by the use of such additional government employees.

FINANCE.—We demand a national currency, safe, sound, and flexible, issued by the general government only, a full legal tender for all debts, public and private, and that without the use of banking corporations, a just, equitable, and efficient means of distribution direct to the people, at a tax not to exceed two per cent per annum, to be provided as set forth in the sub-treasury plan of the Farmers' Alliance, or a better system; also by payments in discharge of its obligations for public improvements.

1. We demand free and unlimited coinage of silver and gold at the present legal ratio of 16 to 1.

2. We demand that the amount of circulating medium be speedily increased to not less than $50 per capita.

3. We demand a graduated income tax.

4. We believe that the money of the country should be kept as much as possible in the hands of the people, and hence we demand that all State and national revenues shall be limited to the necessary expenses of the government, economically and honestly administered.

5. We demand that postal savings banks be established by the government for the safe deposit of the earnings of the people and to facilitate exchange.

TRANSPORTATION.—Transportation being a means of exchange and a public necessity, the government should own and operate the railroads in the interest of the people. The telegraph and telephone, like the post-office system, being a necessity for the transmission of news, should be owned and operated by the government in the interest of the people.

LAND.—The land, including all the natural sources of wealth, is the heritage of the people, and should not be monopolized for speculative purposes, and alien ownership of land should be prohibited. All land now held by railroads and other corporations in excess of their actual needs, and all lands now owned by aliens should be reclaimed by the government and held for actual settlers only.

EXPRESSION OF SENTIMENTS

Your committee on Platform and Resolutions beg leave unanimously to report the following:

Whereas, Other questions have been presented for our consideration, we hereby submit the following, not as a part of the Platform of the People's Party, but as resolutions expressive of the sentiment of this Convention:

1. *Resolved*, That we demand a free ballot and a fair count in all elections, and pledge ourselves to secure it to every legal voter without federal intervention, through the adoption by the States of the unperverted Australian or secret ballot system.

2. *Resolved*, That the revenue derived from a graduated income tax should be applied to the reduction of the burden of taxation now levied upon the domestic industries of this country.

3. *Resolved*, That we pledge our support to fair and liberal pensions to ex-Union soldiers and sailors.

4. *Resolved*, That we condemn the fallacy of protecting American labor under the present system, which opens our ports to the pauper and criminal classes of the world, and crowds out our wage-earners; and we denounce the present ineffective laws against contract labor, and demand the further restriction of undesirable emigration.

5. *Resolved*, that we cordially sympathize with the efforts of organized workingmen to shorten the hours of labor, and demand a rigid enforcement of the existing eight-hour law on Government work, and ask that a penalty clause be added to the said law.

6. *Resolved*, That we regard the maintenance of a large standing army of mercenaries, known as the Pinkerton system, as a menace to our liberties, and we demand its abolition; and we condemn the recent invasion of the Territory of Wyoming by the hired assassins of plutocracy, assisted by federal officers.

7. *Resolved*, That we commend to the favorable consideration of the people and the reform press the legislative system known as the initiative and referendum.

8. *Resolved*, That we favor a constitutional provision limiting the office of President and Vice-President to one term, and providing for the election of Senators of the United States by a direct vote of the people.

9. *Resolved*, That we oppose any subsidy or national aid to any private corporation for any purpose.

10. *Resolved*, That this convention sympathizes with the Knights of Labor and their righteous contest with the tyrannical combine of clothing manufacturers of Rochester, and declare it to be the duty of all who hate tyranny and oppression to refuse to purchase the goods made by the said manufacturers, or to patronize any merchants who sell such goods.

Franklin D. Roosevelt's First Inaugural Address (1933)

I am certain that my fellow Americans expect that on my induction into the Presidency I will address them with a candor and a decision which the present situation of our Nation impels. This is preeminently the time to speak the truth, the whole truth, frankly and boldly. Nor need we shrink from honestly facing conditions in our country today. This great Nation will endure as it has endured, will revive and will prosper. So, first of all, let me assert my firm belief that the only thing we have to fear is fear itself—nameless, unreasoning, unjustified terror which paralyzes needed efforts to convert retreat into advance. In every dark hour of our national life a leadership of frankness and vigor has met with that understanding and support of the people themselves which is essential to victory. I am convinced that you will again give that support to leadership in these critical days.

In such a spirit on my part and on yours we face our common difficulties. They concern, thank God, only material things. Values have shrunken to fantastic levels; taxes have risen; our ability to pay has fallen; government of all kinds is faced by serious curtailment of income; the means of exchange are frozen in the currents of trade; the withered leaves of industrial enterprise lie on every side; farmers find no markets for their produce; the savings of many years in thousands of families are gone.

More important, a host of unemployed citizens face the grim problem of existence, and an equally great number toil with little return. Only a foolish optimist can deny the dark realities of the moment.

Yet our distress comes from no failure of substance. We are stricken by no plague of locusts. Compared with the perils which our forefathers conquered because they believed and were not afraid, we have still much to be thankful for. Nature still offers her bounty and human efforts have multiplied it. Plenty is at our doorstep, but a generous use of it languishes in the very sight of the supply. Primarily this is because the rulers of the exchange of mankind's goods have failed, through their own stubbornness and their own incompetence, have admitted their failure, and abdicated. Practices of the unscrupulous money changers stand indicted in the court of public opinion, rejected by the hearts and minds of men.

True they have tried, but their efforts have been cast in the pattern of an outworn tradition. Faced by failure of credit they have proposed only the lending of more money. Stripped of the lure of profit by which to induce our people to follow their false leadership, they have resorted to exhortations, pleading tearfully for restored confidence. They know only the rules of a generation of self-seekers. They have no vision, and when there is no vision the people perish.

The money changers have fled from their high seats in the temple of our civilization. We may now restore that temple to the ancient truths. The measure of the restoration lies in the extent to which we apply social values more noble than mere monetary profit.

Happiness lies not in the mere possession of money; it lies in the joy of achievement, in the thrill of creative effort. The joy and moral stimulation of work no longer must be forgotten in the mad chase of evanescent profits. These dark days will be worth all they cost us if they teach us that our true destiny is not to be ministered unto but to minister to ourselves and to our fellow men.

Recognition of the falsity of material wealth as the standard of success goes hand in hand with the abandonment of the false belief that public office and high political position are to be valued only by the standards of pride of place and personal profit; and there must be an end to a conduct in banking and in business which too often has given to a sacred trust the likeness of callous and selfish wrongdoing. Small wonder that confidence languishes, for it thrives only on honesty, on honor, on the sacredness of obligations, on faithful protection, on unselfish performance; without them it cannot live.

Restoration calls, however, not for changes in ethics alone. This Nation asks for action, and action now.

Our greatest primary task is to put people to work. This is no unsolvable problem if we face it wisely and courageously. It can be accomplished in part by direct recruiting by the Government itself, treating the task as we would treat the emergency of a war, but at the same time, through this employment, accomplishing greatly needed projects to stimulate and reorganize the use of our natural resources.

Hand in hand with this we must frankly recognize the overbalance of population in our industrial centers and, by engaging on a national scale in a redistribution, endeavor to provide a better use of the land for those best fitted for the land. The task can be helped by definite efforts to raise the values of agricultural products and with this the power to purchase the output of our cities. It can be helped by preventing realistically the tragedy of the growing loss through foreclosure of our small homes and our farms. It can be helped by insistence that the Federal, State, and local governments act forthwith on the demand that their cost be drastically reduced. It can be helped by the unifying of relief activities which today are often scattered, uneconomical, and unequal. It can be helped by national planning for and supervision of all forms of transportation and of communications and other utilities which have a definitely public character. There are many ways in which it can be helped, but it can never be helped merely by talking about it. We must act and act quickly.

Finally, in our progress toward a resumption of work we require two safeguards against a return of the evils of the old order; there must be a strict supervision of all banking and credits and investments; there must be an end to speculation with other people's money, and there must be provision for an adequate but sound currency.

There are the lines of attack. I shall presently urge upon a new Congress, in special session, detailed measures for their fulfillment, and I shall seek the immediate assistance of the several States.

Through this program of action we address ourselves to putting our own national house in order and making income balance outgo. Our international trade relations, though vastly important, are in point of time and necessity secondary to the establishment of a sound national economy. I favor as a practical policy the putting of first things first. I shall spare no effort to restore world trade by international economic readjustment, but the emergency at home cannot wait on that accomplishment.

The basic thought that guides these specific means of national recovery is not narrowly nationalistic. It is the insistence, as a first consideration, upon the interdependence of the various elements in all parts of the United States—a recognition of the old and permanently important manifestation of the American spirit of the pioneer. It is the way to recovery. It is the immediate way. It is the strongest assurance that the recovery will endure.

In the field of world policy I would dedicate this Nation to the policy of the good neighbor—the neighbor who resolutely respects himself and, because he does so, respects the rights of others—the neighbor who respects his obligations and respects the sanctity of his agreements in and with a world of neighbors.

If I read the temper of our people correctly, we now realize as we have never realized before our interdependence on each other; that we cannot merely take but we must give as well; that if we are to go forward, we must move as a trained and loyal army willing to sacrifice for the good of a common discipline, because without such discipline no progress is made, no leadership becomes effective. We are, I know, ready and willing to submit our lives and property to such discipline, because it makes possible a leadership which aims at a larger good. This I propose to offer, pledging that the larger purposes will bind upon us all as a sacred obligation with a unity of duty hitherto evoked only in time of armed strife.

With this pledge taken, I assume unhesitatingly the leadership of this great army of our people dedicated to a disciplined attack upon our common problems.

Action in this image and to this end is feasible under the form of government which we have inherited from our ancestors. Our Constitution is so simple and practical that it is possible always to meet extraordinary needs by changes in emphasis and arrangement without loss of essential form. That is why our constitutional system has proved itself the most superbly enduring political mechanism the modern world has produced. It has met every stress of vast expansion of territory, of foreign wars, of bitter internal strife, of world relations.

It is to be hoped that the normal balance of executive and legislative authority may be wholly adequate to meet the unprecedented task before us. But it may be that an unprecedented demand and need for undelayed action may call for temporary departure from that normal balance of public procedure.

I am prepared under my constitutional duty to recommend the measures that a stricken nation in the midst of a stricken world may require. These measures, or such other measures as the Congress may build out of its experience and wisdom, I shall seek, within my constitutional authority, to bring to speedy adoption.

But in the event that the Congress shall fail to take one of these two courses, and in the event that the national emergency is still critical, I shall not evade the clear course of duty that will then confront me. I shall ask the Congress for the one remaining instrument to meet the crisis—broad Executive power to wage a war against the emergency, as great as the power that would be given to me if we were in fact invaded by a foreign foe.

For the trust reposed in me I will return the courage and the devotion that befit the time. I can do no less.

We face the arduous days that lie before us in the warm courage of national unity; with the clear consciousness of seeking old and precious moral values; with the clean satisfaction that comes from the stern performance of duty by old and young alike. We aim at the assurance of a rounded and permanent national life.

We do not distrust the future of essential democracy. The people of the United States have not failed. In their need they have registered a mandate that they want direct, vigorous action. They have asked for discipline and direction under leadership. They have made me the present instrument of their wishes. In the spirit of the gift I take it.

In this dedication of a Nation we humbly ask the blessing of God. May He protect each and every one of us. May He guide me in the days to come.

Martin Luther King Jr.'s, "I Have a Dream" Speech (1963)

I am happy to join with you today in what will go down in history as the greatest demonstration for freedom in the history of our nation.

Five score years ago, a great American, in whose symbolic shadow we stand today, signed the Emancipation Proclamation. This momentous decree came as a great beacon light of hope to millions of Negro slaves who had been seared in the flames of withering injustice. It came as a joyous daybreak to end the long night of captivity.

But one hundred years later, the Negro still is not free. One hundred years later, the life of the Negro is still sadly crippled by the manacles of segregation and the chains of discrimination. One hundred years later, the Negro is still languishing in the corners of American society and finds himself an exile in his own land. And so we've come here today to dramatize a shameful condition.

In a sense we have come to our nation's capital to cash a check. When the architects of our republic wrote the magnificent words of the Constitution and the Declaration of Independence, they were signing a promissory note to which every American was to fall heir. This note was a promise that all men, yes black men as well as white men, would be guaranteed the "unalienable Rights of Life, Liberty, and the pursuit of Happiness." It is obvious today that America has defaulted on this promissory note insofar as her citizens of color are concerned. Instead of honoring this sacred obligation, America has given the Negro people a bad check,—a check which has come back marked "insufficient funds."

But we refuse to believe that the bank of justice is bankrupt. We refuse to believe that there are insufficient funds in the great vaults of opportunity of this nation. And so we've come to cash this check,—a check that will give us upon demand the riches of freedom and the security of justice.

We have also come to this hallowed spot to remind America of the fierce urgency of now. This is no time to engage in the luxury of cooling off or to take the tranquilizing drug of gradualism. Now is the time to make real the promises of democracy. Now is the time to rise from the dark and desolate valley of segregation to the sunlit path of racial justice. Now is the time to lift our nation from the quicksands of racial injustice to the solid rock of brotherhood. Now is the time to make justice a reality for all of God's children.

It would be fatal for the nation to overlook the urgency of the moment. This sweltering summer of the Negro's legitimate discontent will not pass until there is an invigorating autumn of freedom and equality. Nineteen sixty-three is not an end, but a beginning. And those who hope that the Negro needed to blow off steam and will now be content will have a rude awakening if the nation returns to business as usual. There will be neither rest nor tranquility in America until the Negro is granted his citizenship rights. The whirlwinds of revolt will continue to shake the foundation of our nation until the bright day of justice emerges.

But there is something that I must say to my people, who stand on the warm threshold which leads into the palace of justice: In the process of gaining our rightful place, we must not be guilty of wrongful deeds. Let us not seek to satisfy our thirst for freedom by drinking from the cup of bitterness and hatred. We must forever conduct our struggle on the high plane of dignity and discipline. We must not allow our creative protest to degenerate into physical violence. Again and again, we must rise to the majestic heights of meeting physical force with soul force. The marvelous new militancy which has engulfed the Negro community must not lead us to a distrust of all white people, for many of our white brothers, as evidenced by their presence here today, have come to realize that their destiny is tied up with our destiny. And they have come to realize that their freedom is inextricably bound to our freedom. We cannot walk alone.

And as we walk, we must make the pledge that we shall march ahead. We cannot turn back. There are those who are asking the devotees of civil rights, "When will you be satisfied?"

We can never be satisfied as long as the Negro is the victim of unspeakable horrors of police brutality. We can never be satisfied as long as our bodies, heavy with the fatigue of travel, cannot gain lodging in the motels of the highways and the hotels of the cities. We cannot be satisfied as long as the Negro's basic mobility is from a smaller ghetto to a larger one. We can never be satisfied as long as our children are stripped of their selfhood and robbed of their dignity by signs stating "for whites only." We cannot be satisfied as long as a Negro in Mississippi cannot vote and a Negro in New York believes he has nothing for which to vote. No, no, we are not satisfied, and we will not be satisfied until, "justice rolls down like waters and righteousness like a mighty stream."

I am not unmindful that some of you have come here out of great trials and tribulations. Some of you have come fresh from narrow jail cells. Some of you have come from areas where your quest for freedom left you battered by the storms of persecution and staggered by the winds of police brutality. You have been the veterans of creative suffering. Continue to work with the faith that unearned suffering is redemptive.

Go back to Mississippi, go back to Alabama, go back to South Carolina, go back to Georgia, go back to Louisiana, go back to the slums and ghettos of our northern cities, knowing that somehow this situation can and will be changed. Let us not wallow in the valley of despair.

I say to you today, my friends, so even though we face the difficulties of today and tomorrow, I still have a dream. It is a dream deeply rooted in the American dream.

I have a dream that one day this nation will rise up and live out the true meaning of its creed: "We hold these truths to be self-evident, that all men are created equal."

I have a dream that one day on the red hills of Georgia, the sons of former slaves and the sons of former slave owners will be able to sit down together at the table of brotherhood.

I have a dream that one day even the state of Mississippi, a state sweltering with the heat of injustice, sweltering with the heat of oppression, will be transformed into an oasis of freedom and justice.

I have a dream that my four little children will one day live in a nation where they will not be judged by the color of their skin but by the content of their character. I have a dream today.

I have a dream that one day down in Alabama, with its vicious racists, with its governor having his lips dripping with the words of "interposition" and "nullification," one day right there in Alabama little black boys and black girls will be able to join hands with little white boys and white girls as sisters and brothers. I have a dream today.

I have a dream that one day "every valley shall be exalted, and every hill and mountain shall be made low; the rough places will be made plain, and the crooked places will be made straight; and the glory of the Lord shall be revealed, and all flesh shall see it together."

This is our hope. This is the faith that I go back to the South with. With this faith we will be able to hew out of the mountain of despair a stone of hope. With this faith will be able to transform the jangling discords of our nation into a beautiful symphony of brotherhood. With this faith we will be able to work together, to pray together, to struggle together, to go to jail together, to stand up for freedom together, knowing that we will be free one day. This will be the day, this will be the day when all of God's children will be able to sing with a new meaning:

My country, 'tis of thee, sweet land of liberty, of thee I sing.
Land where my fathers died, land of the pilgrim's pride,
From every mountainside, let freedom ring.

And if America is to be a great nation this must become true.

And so let freedom ring from the prodigious hilltops of New Hampshire.

Let freedom ring from the mighty mountains of New York.

Let freedom ring from the heightening Alleghenies of Pennsylvania.

Let freedom ring from the snowcapped Rockies of Colorado.

Let freedom ring from the curvaceous peaks of California.

But not only that: let freedom ring from Stone Mountain of Georgia.

Let freedom ring from Lookout Mountain of Tennessee.

Let freedom ring from every hill and molehill of Mississippi. From every mountainside, let freedom ring.

And when this happens, when we allow freedom to ring, when we let it ring from every village and every hamlet, from every state and every city, we will be able to speed up that day when all of God's children, black men and white men, Jews and Gentiles, Protestants and Catholics, will be able to join hands and sing in the words of the old Negro spiritual:

Free at last! Free at last!
Thank God Almighty, we are free at last!

RONALD REAGAN'S FIRST INAUGURAL ADDRESS (1981)

WEST FRONT OF THE U.S. CAPITOL
JANUARY 20, 1981

Senator Hatfield, Mr. Chief Justice, Mr. President, Vice President Bush, Vice President Mondale, Senator Baker, Speaker O'Neill, Reverend Moomaw, and my fellow citizens.

To a few of us here today this is a solemn and most momentous occasion, and yet in the history of our nation it is a commonplace occurrence. The orderly transfer of authority as called for in the Constitution routinely takes place, as it has for almost two centuries, and few of us stop to think how unique we really are. In the eyes of many in the world, this every-four-year ceremony we accept as normal is nothing less than a miracle.

Mr. President, I want our fellow citizens to know how much you did to carry on this tradition. By your gracious cooperation in the transition process, you have shown a watching world that we are a united people pledged to maintaining a political system which guarantees individual liberty to a greater degree than any other, and I thank you and your people for all your help in maintaining the continuity which is the bulwark of our republic. The business of our nation goes forward. These United States are confronted with an economic affliction of great proportions. We suffer from the longest and one of the worst sustained inflations in our national history. It distorts our economic decisions, penalizes thrift, and crushes the struggling young and the fixed-income elderly alike. It threatens to shatter the lives of millions of our people.

Idle industries have cast workers into unemployment, human misery, and personal indignity. Those who do work are denied a fair return for their labor by a tax system which penalizes successful achievement and keeps us from maintaining full productivity. But great as our tax burden is, it has not kept pace with public spending. For decades we have piled deficit upon deficit, mortgaging our future and our children's future for the temporary convenience of the present. To continue this long trend is to guarantee tremendous social, cultural, political, and economic upheavals.

You and I, as individuals, can, by borrowing, live beyond our means, but for only a limited period of time. Why, then, should we think that collectively, as a nation, we're not bound by that same limitation? We must act today in order to preserve tomorrow. And let there be no misunderstanding: We are going to begin to act, beginning today. The economic ills we suffer have come upon us over several decades. They will not go away in days, weeks, or months, but they will go away. They will go away because we as Americans have the capacity now, as we've had in the past, to do whatever needs to be done to preserve this last and greatest bastion of freedom.

In this present crisis, government is not the solution to our problem; government is the problem. From time to time we've been tempted to believe that society has become too complex to be managed by self-rule, that government by an elite group is superior to government for, by, and of the people. Well, if no one among us is capable of governing himself, then who among us has the capacity to govern someone else? All of us together, in and out of government, must bear the burden. The solutions we seek must be equitable, with no one group singled out to pay a higher price.

We hear much of special interest groups. Well, our concern must be for a special interest group that has been too long neglected. It knows no sectional boundaries or ethnic and racial divisions, and it crosses political party lines. It is made up of men and women who raise our food, patrol our streets, man our mines and factories, teach our children, keep our homes, and heal us when we're sick—professionals, industrialists, shopkeepers, clerks, cabbies, and truck drivers. They are, in short, "we the people," this breed called Americans.

Well, this administration's objective will be a healthy, vigorous, growing economy that provides equal opportunities for all Americans, with no barriers born of bigotry or discrimination. Putting America back to work means putting all Americans back to work. Ending inflation means freeing all Americans from the terror of runaway living costs. All must share in the productive work of this "new beginning," and all must share in the bounty of a revived economy. With the idealism and fair play which are the core of our system and our strength, we can have a strong and prosperous America, at peace with itself and the world.

So, as we begin, let us take inventory. We are a nation that has a government—not the other way around. And this makes us special among the nations of the Earth. Our government has no power except that granted it by the people. It is time to check and reverse the growth of government, which shows signs of having grown beyond the consent of the governed.

It is my intention to curb the size and influence of the federal establishment and to demand recognition of the distinction between the powers granted to the federal government and those reserved to the states or to the people. All of us need to be reminded that the federal government did not create the states; the states created the federal government.

Now, so there will be no misunderstanding, it's not my intention to do away with government. It is rather to make it work—work with us, not over us; to stand by our side, not ride on our back. Government can and must provide opportunity, not smother it; foster productivity, not stifle it.

If we look to the answer as to why for so many years we achieved so much, prospered as no other people on earth, it was because here in this land we unleashed the energy and individual genius of man to a greater extent than has ever been done before. Freedom and the dignity of the individual have been more available and assured here than in any other place on earth. The price for this freedom at times has been high, but we have never been unwilling to pay the price.

It is no coincidence that our present troubles parallel and are proportionate to the intervention and intrusion in our lives that result from unnecessary and excessive growth of government. It is time for us to realize that we're too great a nation to limit ourselves to small dreams. We're not, as some would have us believe, doomed to an inevitable decline. I do not believe in a fate that will fall on us no matter what we do. I do believe in a fate that will fall on us if we do nothing. So, with all the creative energy at our command, let us begin an era of national renewal. Let us renew our determination, our courage, and our strength. And let us renew our faith and our hope.

We have every right to dream heroic dreams. Those who say that we're in a time when there are no heroes, they just don't know where to look. You can see heroes every day going in and out of factory gates. Others, a handful in number, produce enough food to feed all of us and then the world beyond. You meet heroes across a counter, and they're on both sides of that counter. There are entrepreneurs with faith in themselves and faith in an idea who create new jobs, new wealth and opportunity. They're individuals and families whose taxes support the government and whose voluntary gifts support church, charity, culture, art, and education. Their patri-

otism is quiet, but deep. Their values sustain our national life.

Now, I have used the words "they" and "their" in speaking of these heroes. I could say "you" and "your," because I'm addressing the heroes of whom I speak—you, the citizens of this blessed land. Your dreams, your hopes, your goals are going to be the dreams, the hopes, and the goals of this administration, so help me God.

We shall reflect the compassion that is so much a part of your makeup. How can we love our country and not love our countrymen; and loving them, reach out a hand when they fall, heal them when they're sick, and provide opportunity to make them self-sufficient so they will be equal in fact and not just in theory?

Can we solve the problems confronting us? Well, the answer is an unequivocal and emphatic "yes." To paraphrase Winston Churchill, I did not take the oath I've just taken with the intention of presiding over the dissolution of the world's strongest economy.

In the days ahead I will propose removing the roadblocks that have slowed our economy and reduced productivity. Steps will be taken aimed at restoring the balance between the various levels of government. Progress may be slow, measured in inches and feet, not miles, but we will progress. It is time to reawaken this industrial giant, to get government back within its means, and to lighten our punitive tax burden. And these will be our first priorities, and on these principles there will be no compromise.

On the eve of our struggle for independence a man who might have been one of the greatest among the Founding Fathers, Dr. Joseph Warren, president of the Massachusetts Congress, said to his fellow Americans, "Our country is in danger, but not to be despaired of . . . On you depend the fortunes of America. You are to decide the important questions upon which rests the happiness and the liberty of millions yet unborn. Act worthy of yourselves." Well, I believe we, the Americans of today, are ready to act worthy of ourselves, ready to do what must be done to ensure happiness and liberty for ourselves, our children, and our children's children. And as we renew ourselves here in our own land, we will be seen as having greater strength throughout the world. We will again be the exemplar of freedom and a beacon of hope for those who do not now have freedom.

To those neighbors and allies who share our freedom, we will strengthen our historic ties and assure them of our support and firm commitment. We will match loyalty with loyalty. We will strive for mutually beneficial relations. We will not use our friendship to impose on their sovereignty, for our own sovereignty is not for sale. As for the enemies of freedom, those who are potential adversaries, they will be reminded that peace is the highest aspiration of the American people. We will negotiate for it, sacrifice for it; we will not surrender for it, now or ever.

Our forbearance should never be misunderstood. Our reluctance for conflict should not be misjudged as a failure of will. When action is required to preserve our national security, we will act. We will maintain sufficient strength to prevail if need be, knowing that if we do so we have the best chance of never having to use that strength. Above all, we must realize that no arsenal or no weapon in the arsenals of the world is so formidable as the will and moral courage of free men and women. It is a weapon our adversaries in today's world do not have. It is a weapon that we as Americans do have. Let that be understood by those who practice terrorism and prey upon their neighbors. I'm told that tens of thousands of prayer meetings are being held on this day, and for that I'm deeply grateful. We are a nation under God, and I believe God intended for us to be free. It would be fitting and good, I think, if on each Inaugural Day in future years it should be declared a day of prayer.

This is the first time in our history that this ceremony has been held, as you've been told, on the West Front of the Capitol. Standing here, one faces a magnificent vista, opening up on the city's special beauty and history. At the end of this open mall are those shrines to the giants on whose shoulders we stand.

Directly in front of me, the monument to a monumental man, George Washington, father of our country. A man of humility who came to greatness reluctantly. He led Americans out of revolutionary victory into infant nationhood. Off to one side, the stately memorial to Thomas Jefferson. The Declaration of Independence flames with his eloquence. And then, beyond the Reflecting Pool, the dignified columns of the Lincoln Memorial. Whoever would understand in his heart the meaning of America will find it in the life of Abraham Lincoln.

Beyond those monuments to heroism is the Potomac River, and on the far shore the sloping hills of Arlington National Cemetery, with its row upon row of simple white markers bearing crosses and Stars of David. They add up to only a tiny fraction of the price that has been paid for our freedom. Each one of those markers is a monument to the kind of hero I spoke of earlier. Their lives ended in places called Belleau Wood, the Argonne, Omaha Beach, Salerno, and halfway around the world on Guadalcanal, Tarawa, Pork Chop Hill, the Chosin Reservoir, and in a hundred rice paddies and jungles of a place called Vietnam.

Under one such marker lies a young man, Martin Treptow, who left his job in a small town barbershop in 1917 to go to France with the famed Rainbow Division. There, on the western front, he was killed trying to carry a message between battalions under heavy artillery fire.

We're told that on his body was found a diary. On the flyleaf under the heading "My Pledge," he had written these words: "America must win this war. Therefore I will work, I will save, I will sacrifice, I will endure, I will fight cheerfully and do my utmost, as if the issue of the whole struggle depended on me alone."

The crisis we are facing today does not require of us the kind of sacrifice that Martin Treptow and so many thousands of others were called upon to make. It does require, however, our best effort and our willingness to believe in ourselves and to believe in our capacity to perform great deeds, to believe that together with God's help we can and will resolve the problems which now confront us.

And after all, why shouldn't we believe that? We are Americans.

God bless you, and thank you.

Barack Obama's Inaugural Address (2009)

My fellow citizens: I stand here today humbled by the task before us, grateful for the trust you've bestowed, mindful of the sacrifices borne by our ancestors.

I thank President Bush for his service to our nation—(*applause*)—as well as the generosity and cooperation he has shown throughout this transition.

Forty-four Americans have now taken the presidential oath. The words have been spoken during rising tides of prosperity and the still waters of peace. Yet, every so often, the oath is taken amidst gathering clouds and raging storms. At these moments, America has carried on not simply because of the skill or vision of those in high office, but because we, the people, have remained faithful to the ideals of our forebears and true to our founding documents.

So it has been: so it must be with this generation of Americans.

That we are in the midst of crisis is now well understood. Our nation is at war against a far-reaching network of violence and hatred. Our economy is badly weakened, a consequence of greed and irresponsibility on the part of some, but also our collective failure to make hard choices and prepare the nation for a new age. Homes have been lost, jobs shed, businesses shuttered. Our health care is too costly, our schools fail too many—and each day brings further evidence that the ways we use energy strengthen our adversaries and threaten our planet.

These are the indicators of crisis, subject to data and statistics. Less measurable, but no less profound, is a sapping of confidence across our land; a nagging fear that America's decline is inevitable, that the next generation must lower its sights.

Today I say to you that the challenges we face are real. They are serious and they are many. They will not be met easily or in a short span of time. But know this America: They will be met. (*Applause*)

On this day, we gather because we have chosen hope over fear, unity of purpose over conflict and discord. On this day, we come to proclaim an end to the petty grievances and false promises, the recriminations and worn-out dogmas that for far too long have strangled our politics. We remain a young nation. But in the words of Scripture, the time has come to set aside childish things. The time has come to reaffirm our enduring spirit; to choose our better history; to carry forward that precious gift, that noble idea passed on from generation to generation; the God-given promise that all are equal, all are free, and all deserve a chance to pursue their full measure of happiness. (*Applause*)

In reaffirming the greatness of our nation we understand that greatness is never a given. It must be earned. Our journey has never been one of short-cuts or settling for less. It has not been the path for the faint-hearted, for those that prefer leisure over work, or seek only the pleasures of riches and fame. Rather, it has been the risk-takers, the doers, the makers of things—some celebrated, but more often men and women obscure in their labor—who have carried us up the long rugged path towards prosperity and freedom.

For us, they packed up their few worldly possessions and traveled across oceans in search of a new life. For us, they toiled in sweatshops, and settled the West, endured the lash of the whip, and plowed the hard earth. For us, they fought and died in places like Concord and Gettysburg, Normandy and Khe Sahn.

Time and again these men and women struggled and sacrificed and worked till their hands were raw so that we might live a better life. They saw America as bigger than the sum of our individual ambitions, greater than all the differences of birth or wealth or faction.

This is the journey we continue today. We remain the most prosperous, powerful nation on Earth. Our workers are no less productive than when this crisis began. Our minds are no less inventive, our goods and services no less needed than they were last week, or last month, or last year. Our capacity remains undiminished. But our time of standing pat, of protecting narrow interests and putting off unpleasant decisions—that time has surely passed. Starting today, we must pick ourselves up, dust ourselves off, and begin again the work of remaking America. (*Applause*)

For everywhere we look, there is work to be done. The state of our economy calls for action, bold and swift. And we will act, not only to create new jobs, but to lay a new foundation for growth. We will build the roads and bridges, the electric grids and digital lines that feed our commerce and bind us together. We'll restore science to its rightful place, and wield technology's wonders to raise health care's quality and lower its cost. We will harness the sun and the winds and the soil to fuel our cars and run our factories. And we will transform our schools and colleges and universities to meet the demands of a new age. All this we can do. All this we will do.

Now, there are some who question the scale of our ambitions, who suggest that our system cannot tolerate too many big plans. Their memories are short, for they have forgotten what this country has already done, what free men and women can achieve when imagination is joined to common purpose, and necessity to courage. What the cynics fail to understand is that the ground has shifted beneath them, that the stale political arguments that have consumed us for so long no longer apply.

The question we ask today is not whether our government is too big or too small, but whether it works—whether it helps families find jobs at a decent wage, care they can afford, a retirement that is dignified. Where the answer is yes, we intend to move forward. Where the answer is no, programs will end. And those of us who manage the public's dollars will be held to account, to spend wisely, reform bad habits, and do our business in the light of day, because only then can we restore the vital trust between a people and their government.

Nor is the question before us whether the market is a force for good or ill. Its power to generate wealth and expand freedom is unmatched. But this crisis has reminded us that without a watchful eye, the market can spin out of control. The nation cannot prosper long when it favors only the prosperous. The success of our economy has always depended not just on the size of our gross domestic product, but on the reach of our prosperity, on the ability to extend opportunity to every willing heart—not out of charity, but because it is the surest route to our common good. (*Applause*)

As for our common defense, we reject as false the choice between our safety and our ideals. Our Founding Fathers— (*applause*)—our Founding Fathers, faced with perils that we can scarcely imagine, drafted a charter to assure the rule of law and the rights of man—a charter expanded by the blood of generations. Those ideals still light the world, and we will not give them up for expedience sake. (*Applause*)

And so, to all the other peoples and governments who are watching today, from the grandest capitals to the small village where my father was born, know that America is a friend of each nation, and every man, woman and child who seeks a future of peace and dignity. And we are ready to lead once more. (*Applause*)

Recall that earlier generations faced down fascism and communism not just with missiles and tanks, but with the sturdy alliances and enduring convictions. They understood that our power alone cannot protect us, nor does it entitle us to do as we please. Instead they knew that our power grows through its prudent use; our security emanates from the justness of our cause, the force of our example, the tempering qualities of humility and restraint.

We are the keepers of this legacy. Guided by these principles once more we can meet those new threats that demand even greater effort, even greater cooperation and understanding between nations. We will begin to responsibly leave Iraq to its people and forge a hard-earned peace in Afghanistan. With old friends and former foes, we'll work tirelessly to lessen the nuclear threat, and roll back the specter of a warming planet.

We will not apologize for our way of life, nor will we waver in its defense. And for those who seek to advance their aims by inducing terror and slaughtering innocents, we say to you now that our spirit is stronger and cannot be broken—you cannot outlast us, and we will defeat you. (*Applause*)

For we know that our patchwork heritage is a strength, not a weakness. We are a nation of Christians and Muslims, Jews and Hindus, and non-believers. We are shaped by every language and culture, drawn from every end of this Earth: and because we have tasted the bitter swill of civil war and segregation, and emerged from that dark chapter stronger and more united, we cannot help but believe that the old hatreds shall someday pass; that the lines of tribe shall soon dissolve; that as the world grows smaller, our common humanity shall reveal itself; and that America must play its role in ushering in a new era of peace.

To the Muslim world, we seek a new way forward, based on mutual interest and mutual respect. To those leaders around the globe who seek to sow conflict, or blame their society's ills on the West, know that your people will judge you on what you can build, not what you destroy. (*Applause*)

To those who cling to power through corruption and deceit and the silencing of dissent, know that you are on the wrong side of history, but that we will extend a hand if you are willing to unclench your fist. (*Applause*)

To the people of poor nations, we pledge to work alongside you to make your farms flourish and let clean waters flow; to nourish starved bodies and feed hungry minds. And to those nations like ours that enjoy relative plenty, we say we can no longer afford indifference to the suffering outside our borders, nor can we consume the world's resources without regard to effect. For the world has changed, and we must change with it.

As we consider the role that unfolds before us, we remember with humble gratitude those brave Americans who at this very hour patrol far-off deserts and distant mountains. They have something to tell us, just as the fallen heroes who lie in Arlington whisper through the ages.

We honor them not only because they are the guardians of our liberty, but because they embody the spirit of service—a willingness to find meaning in something greater than themselves.

And yet at this moment, a moment that will define a generation, it is precisely this spirit that must inhabit us all. For as much as government can do, and must do, it is ultimately the faith and determination of the American people upon which this nation relies. It is the kindness to take in a stranger when the levees break, the selflessness of workers who would rather cut their hours than see a friend lose their job which sees us through our darkest hours. It is the firefighter's courage to storm a stairway filled with smoke, but also a parent's willingness to nurture a child that finally decides our fate.

Our challenges may be new. The instruments with which we meet them may be new. But those values upon which our success depends—honesty and hard work, courage and fair play, tolerance and curiosity, loyalty and patriotism—these things are old. These things are true. They have been the quiet force of progress throughout our history.

What is demanded, then, is a return to these truths. What is required of us now is a new era of responsibility—a recognition on the part of every American that we have duties to ourselves, our nation and the world; duties that we do not grudgingly accept, but rather seize gladly, firm in the knowledge that there is nothing so satisfying to the spirit, so defining of our character than giving our all to a difficult task.

This is the price and the promise of citizenship. This is the source of our confidence—the knowledge that God calls on us to shape an uncertain destiny. This is the meaning of our liberty and our creed, why men and women and children of every race and every faith can join in celebration across this magnificent mall; and why a man whose father less than 60 years ago might not have been served in a local restaurant can now stand before you to take a most sacred oath. (*Applause*)

So let us mark this day with remembrance of who we are and how far we have traveled. In the year of America's birth, in the coldest of months, a small band of patriots huddled by dying campfires on the shores of an icy river. The capital was abandoned. The enemy was advancing. The snow was stained with blood. At the moment when the outcome of our revolution was most in doubt, the father of our nation ordered these words to be read to the people:

"Let it be told to the future world . . . that in the depth of winter, when nothing but hope and virtue could survive . . . that the city and the country, alarmed at one common danger, came forth to meet [it]."

America: In the face of our common dangers, in this winter of our hardship, let us remember these timeless words. With hope and virtue, let us brave once more the icy currents, and endure what storms may come. Let it be said by our children's children that when we were tested we refused to let this journey end, that we did not turn back nor did we falter; and with eyes fixed on the horizon and God's grace upon us, we carried forth that great gift of freedom and delivered it safely to future generations.

Thank you. God bless you. And God bless the United States of America. (*Applause*)

Year	Number of States	Candidates	Parties	Popular Vote	% of Popular Vote	Electoral Vote	% Voter Participation
1789	11	**GEORGE WASHINGTON** John Adams Other candidates	NO PARTY DESIGNATIONS			69 34 35	
1792	15	**GEORGE WASHINGTON** John Adams George Clinton Other candidates	NO PARTY DESIGNATIONS			132 77 50 5	
1796	16	**JOHN ADAMS** Thomas Jefferson Thomas Pinckney Aaron Burr Other candidates	FEDERALIST Republican Federalist Republican			71 68 59 30 48	
1800	16	**THOMAS JEFFERSON** Aaron Burr John Adams Charles C. Pinckney John Jay	REPUBLICAN Republican Federalist Federalist Federalist			73 73 65 64 1	
1804	17	**THOMAS JEFFERSON** Charles C. Pinckney	REPUBLICAN Federalist			162 14	
1808	17	**JAMES MADISON** Charles C. Pinckney George Clinton	REPUBLICAN Federalist Republican			122 47 6	
1812	18	**JAMES MADISON** DeWitt Clinton	REPUBLICAN Federalist			128 89	

Year	Number of States	Candidates	Parties	Popular Vote	% of Popular Vote	Electoral Vote	% Voter Participation
1816	19	JAMES MONROE Rufus King	REPUBLICAN Federalist			183 34	
1820	24	JAMES MONROE John Quincy Adams	REPUBLICAN Independent			231 1	
1824	24	JOHN QUINCY ADAMS Andrew Jackson William H. Crawford Henry Clay	NO PARTY DESIGNATIONS	108,740 153,544 46,618 47,136	31.0 43.0 13.0 13.0	84 99 41 37	26.9
1828	24	ANDREW JACKSON John Quincy Adams	DEMOCRAT National Republican	647,286 508,064	56.0 44.0	178 83	57.6
1832	24	ANDREW JACKSON Henry Clay William Wirt John Floyd	DEMOCRAT National Republican Anti-Masonic Democrat	687,502 530,189 101,051	54.5 37.5 8.0	219 49 7 11	55.4
1836	26	MARTIN VAN BUREN William H. Harrison Hugh L. White Daniel Webster William P. Mangum	DEMOCRAT Whig Whig Whig Whig	765,483 739,795	51.0 49.0	170 73 26 14 11	57.8
1840	26	WILLIAM H. HARRISON Martin Van Buren	WHIG Democrat	1,274,624 1,127,781	53.0 47.0	234 60	80.2

Year	Number of States	Candidates	Parties	Popular Vote	% of Popular Vote	Electoral Vote	% Voter Participation
1844	26	JAMES K. POLK	DEMOCRAT	1,338,464	50.0	170	78.9
		Henry Clay	Whig	1,300,097	48.0	105	
		James G. Birney	Liberty	62,300	2.0		
1848	30	ZACHARY TAYLOR	WHIG	1,360,967	47.5	163	72.7
		Lewis Cass	Democrat	1,222,342	42.5	127	
		Martin Van Buren	Free Soil	291,263	10.0		
1852	31	FRANKLIN PIERCE	DEMOCRAT	1,601,117	51.0	254	69.6
		Winfield Scott	Whig	1,385,453	44.0	42	
		John P. Hale	Free Soil	155,825	5.0		
1856	31	JAMES BUCHANAN	DEMOCRAT	1,832,955	45.0	174	78.9
		John C. Frémont	Republican	1,339,932	33.0	114	
		Millard Fillmore	American	871,731	22.0	8	
1860	33	ABRAHAM LINCOLN	REPUBLICAN	1,865,593	40.0	180	81.2
		Stephen A. Douglas	Northern Democrat	1,382,713	29.0	12	
		John C. Breckinridge	Southern Democrat	848,356	18.0	72	
		John Bell	Constitutional Union	592,906	13.0	39	
1864	36	ABRAHAM LINCOLN	REPUBLICAN	2,206,938	55.0	212	73.8
		George B. McClellan	Democrat	1,803,787	45.0	21	
1868	37	ULYSSES S. GRANT	REPUBLICAN	3,013,421	53.0	214	78.1
		Horatio Seymour	Democrat	2,706,829	47.0	80	

Year	Number of States	Candidates	Parties	Popular Vote	% of Popular Vote	Electoral Vote	% Voter Participation
1872	37	ULYSSES S. GRANT	REPUBLICAN	3,596,745	55.6	286	71.3
		Horace Greeley	Democrat	2,843,446	43.9	66	
1876	38	RUTHERFORD B. HAYES	REPUBLICAN	4,036,572	48.0	185	81.8
		Samuel J. Tilden	Democrat	4,284,020	51.0	184	
1880	38	JAMES A. GARFIELD	REPUBLICAN	4,453,295	48.4	214	79.4
		Winfield S. Hancock	Democrat	4,414,082	48.3	155	
		James B. Weaver	Greenback-Labor	308,578	3.5		
1884	38	GROVER CLEVELAND	DEMOCRAT	4,879,507	48.5	219	77.5
		James G. Blaine	Republican	4,850,293	48.2	182	
		Benjamin F. Butler	Greenback-Labor	175,370	1.8		
		John P. St. John	Prohibition	150,369	1.5		
1888	38	BENJAMIN HARRISON	REPUBLICAN	5,447,129	47.9	233	79.3
		Grover Cleveland	Democrat	5,537,857	48.6	168	
		Clinton B. Fisk	Prohibition	249,506	2.2		
		Anson J. Streeter	Union Labor	146,935	1.3		
1892	44	GROVER CLEVELAND	DEMOCRAT	5,555,426	46.1	277	74.7
		Benjamin Harrison	Republican	5,182,690	43.0	145	
		James B. Weaver	People's	1,029,846	8.5	22	
		John Bidwell	Prohibition	264,133	2.2		
1896	45	WILLIAM McKINLEY	REPUBLICAN	7,102,246	51.0	271	79.3
		William J. Bryan	Democrat	6,492,559	47.0	176	

Year	Number of States	Candidates	Parties	Popular Vote	% of Popular Vote	Electoral Vote	% Voter Participation
1900	45	**WILLIAM McKINLEY**	REPUBLICAN	7,218,491	52.0	292	73.2
		William J. Bryan	Democrat; Populist	6,356,734	46.0	155	
		John C. Wooley	Prohibition	208,914	1.5		
1904	45	**THEODORE ROOSEVELT**	REPUBLICAN	7,628,461	56.4	336	65.2
		Alton B. Parker	Democrat	5,084,223	37.6	140	
		Eugene V. Debs	Socialist	402,283	3.0		
		Silas C. Swallow	Prohibition	258,536	1.9		
1908	46	**WILLIAM H. TAFT**	REPUBLICAN	7,675,320	52.0	321	65.4
		William J. Bryan	Democrat	6,412,294	43.4	162	
		Eugene V. Debs	Socialist	420,793	2.8		
		Eugene W. Chafin	Prohibition	253,840	1.7		
1912	48	**WOODROW WILSON**	DEMOCRAT	6,296,547	41.9	435	58.8
		Theodore Roosevelt	Progressive	4,118,571	27.4	88	
		William H. Taft	Republican	3,486,720	23.2	8	
		Eugene V. Debs	Socialist	900,672	6.0		
		Eugene W. Chafin	Prohibition	206,275	1.4		
1916	48	**WOODROW WILSON**	DEMOCRAT	9,127,695	49.4	277	61.6
		Charles E. Hughes	Republican	8,533,507	46.2	254	
		A. L. Benson	Socialist	585,113	3.2		
		J. Frank Hanly	Prohibition	220,506	1.2		
1920	48	**WARREN G. HARDING**	REPUBLICAN	16,153,115	60.6	404	49.2
		James M. Cox	Democrat	9,133,092	34.3	127	
		Eugene V. Debs	Socialist	915,490	3.4		
		P. P. Christensen	Farmer-Labor	265,229	1.0		
1924	48	**CALVIN COOLIDGE**	REPUBLICAN	15,719,921	54.0	382	48.9
		John W. Davis	Democrat	8,386,704	29.0	136	
		Robert M. La Follette	Progressive	4,832,532	16.5	13	

Year	Number of States	Candidates	Parties	Popular Vote	% of Popular Vote	Electoral Vote	% Voter Participation
1928	48	HERBERT C. HOOVER Alfred E. Smith	REPUBLICAN Democrat	21,437,277 15,007,698	58.2 40.9	444 87	56.9
1932	48	FRANKLIN D. ROOSEVELT Herbert C. Hoover Norman Thomas	DEMOCRAT Republican Socialist	22,829,501 15,760,684 884,649	57.7 39.8 2.2	472 59	56.9
1936	48	FRANKLIN D. ROOSEVELT Alfred M. Landon William Lemke	DEMOCRAT Republican Union	27,757,333 16,684,231 892,267	60.8 36.6 2.0	523 8	61.0
1940	48	FRANKLIN D. ROOSEVELT Wendell L. Willkie	DEMOCRAT Republican	27,313,041 22,348,480	54.9 44.9	449 82	62.5
1944	48	FRANKLIN D. ROOSEVELT Thomas E. Dewey	DEMOCRAT Republican	25,612,610 22,017,617	53.5 46.0	432 99	55.9
1948	48	HARRY S. TRUMAN Thomas E. Dewey J. Strom Thurmond Henry A. Wallace	DEMOCRAT Republican States' Rights Progressive	24,179,345 21,991,291 1,176,125 1,157,326	49.7 45.3 2.4 2.4	303 189 39	53.0
1952	48	DWIGHT D. EISENHOWER Adlai E. Stevenson	REPUBLICAN Democrat	33,936,234 27,314,992	55.1 44.4	442 89	63.3

Year	Number of States	Candidates	Parties	Popular Vote	% of Popular Vote	Electoral Vote	% Voter Participation
1956	48	DWIGHT D. EISENHOWER Adlai E. Stevenson	REPUBLICAN Democrat	35,590,472 26,022,752	57.6 42.1	457 73	60.6
1960	50	JOHN F. KENNEDY Richard M. Nixon	DEMOCRAT Republican	34,226,731 34,108,157	49.7 49.6	303 219	62.8
1964	50	LYNDON B. JOHNSON Barry M. Goldwater	DEMOCRAT Republican	43,129,566 27,178,188	61.0 38.4	486 52	61.9
1968	50	RICHARD M. NIXON Hubert H. Humphrey George C. Wallace	REPUBLICAN Democrat American Independent	31,785,480 31,275,166 9,906,473	43.2 42.6 12.9	301 191 46	60.9
1972	50	RICHARD M. NIXON George S. McGovern John G. Schmitz	REPUBLICAN Democrat American	47,169,911 29,170,383 1,099,482	60.7 37.5 1.4	520 17	55.2
1976	50	JIMMY CARTER Gerald R. Ford	DEMOCRAT Republican	40,830,763 39,147,793	50.0 48.0	297 240	53.5
1980	50	RONALD REAGAN Jimmy Carter John B. Anderson Ed Clark	REPUBLICAN Democrat Independent Libertarian	43,904,153 35,483,883 5,720,060 921,299	50.9 41.1 6.6 1.1	489 49	52.6

Year	Number of States	Candidates	Parties	Popular Vote	% of Popular Vote	Electoral Vote	% Voter Participation
1984	50	**RONALD REAGAN**	REPUBLICAN	54,455,075	58.8	525	53.1
		Walter F. Mondale	Democrat	37,577,185	40.5	13	
1988	50	**GEORGE H. BUSH**	REPUBLICAN	48,886,097	53.4	426	50.1
		Michael Dukakis	Democrat	41,809,074	45.6	111	
1992	50	**BILL CLINTON**	DEMOCRAT	44,909,326	42.9	370	55.0
		George H. Bush	Republican	39,103,882	37.4	168	
		H. Ross Perot	Independent	19,741,657	18.9		
1996	50	**BILL CLINTON**	DEMOCRAT	47,402,357	49.2	379	49.0
		Bob Dole	Republican	39,198,755	40.7	159	
		H. Ross Perot	Reform Party	8,085,402	8.4		
2000	50	**GEORGE W. BUSH**	REPUBLICAN	50,455,156	47.9	271	50.4
		Albert Gore	Democrat	50,992,335	48.4	266	
		Ralph Nader	Green Party	2,882,738	2.7		
2004	50	**GEORGE W. BUSH**	REPUBLICAN	62,040,610	50.7	286	56.2
		John F. Kerry	Democrat	59,028,111	48.3	251	
2008	50	**BARACK H. OBAMA**	DEMOCRAT	66,882,230	53%	365	56.8
		John S. McCain	Republican	58,343,671	46%	173	

Candidates receiving less than 1 percent of the popular vote have been omitted. Thus, the percentage of popular vote given for any election year may not total 100 percent. Before the passage of the Twelfth Amendment in 1804, the electoral college voted for two presidential candidates; the runner-up became vice president.

Admission of States

Order of Admission	State	Date of Admission	Order of Admission	State	Date of Admission
1	Delaware	December 7, 1787	26	Michigan	January 26, 1837
2	Pennsylvania	December 12, 1787	27	Florida	March 3, 1845
3	New Jersey	December 18, 1787	28	Texas	December 29, 1845
4	Georgia	January 2, 1788	29	Iowa	December 28, 1846
5	Connecticut	January 9, 1788	30	Wisconsin	May 29, 1848
6	Massachusetts	February 7, 1788	31	California	September 9, 1850
7	Maryland	April 28, 1788	32	Minnesota	May 11, 1858
8	South Carolina	May 23, 1788	33	Oregon	February 14, 1859
9	New Hampshire	June 21, 1788	34	Kansas	January 29, 1861
10	Virginia	June 25, 1788	35	West Virginia	June 30, 1863
11	New York	July 26, 1788	36	Nevada	October 31, 1864
12	North Carolina	November 21, 1789	37	Nebraska	March 1, 1867
13	Rhode Island	May 29, 1790	38	Colorado	August 1, 1876
14	Vermont	March 4, 1791	39	North Dakota	November 2, 1889
15	Kentucky	June 1, 1792	40	South Dakota	November 2, 1889
16	Tennessee	June 1, 1796	41	Montana	November 8, 1889
17	Ohio	March 1, 1803	42	Washington	November 11, 1889
18	Louisiana	April 30, 1812	43	Idaho	July 3, 1890
19	Indiana	December 11, 1816	44	Wyoming	July 10, 1890
20	Mississippi	December 10, 1817	45	Utah	January 4, 1896
21	Illinois	December 3, 1818	46	Oklahoma	November 16, 1907
22	Alabama	December 14, 1819	47	New Mexico	January 6, 1912
23	Maine	March 15, 1820	48	Arizona	February 14, 1912
24	Missouri	August 10, 1821	49	Alaska	January 3, 1959
25	Arkansas	June 15, 1836	50	Hawaii	August 21, 1959

POPULATION OF THE UNITED STATES

Year	Number of States	Population	% Increase	Population per Square Mile
1790	13	3,929,214		4.5
1800	16	5,308,483	35.1	6.1
1810	17	7,239,881	36.4	4.3
1820	23	9,638,453	33.1	5.5
1830	24	12,866,020	33.5	7.4
1840	26	17,069,453	32.7	9.8
1850	31	23,191,876	35.9	7.9
1860	33	31,443,321	35.6	10.6
1870	37	39,818,449	26.6	13.4
1880	38	50,155,783	26.0	16.9
1890	44	62,947,714	25.5	21.1
1900	45	75,994,575	20.7	25.6
1910	46	91,972,266	21.0	31.0
1920	48	105,710,620	14.9	35.6
1930	48	122,775,046	16.1	41.2
1940	48	131,669,275	7.2	44.2
1950	48	150,697,361	14.5	50.7
1960	50	179,323,175	19.0	50.6
1970	50	203,235,298	13.3	57.5
1980	50	226,504,825	11.4	64.0
1985	50	237,839,000	5.0	67.2
1990	50	250,122,000	5.2	70.6
1995	50	263,411,707	5.3	74.4
2000	50	281,421,906	6.8	77.0
2005	50	296,410,404	5.3	81.7

HISTORICAL STATISTICS OF THE UNITED STATES

LABOR FORCE—SELECTED CHARACTERISTICS EXPRESSED AS A PERCENTAGE OF THE LABOR FORCE: 1800–2000

Year	Agriculture	Manufacturing	Domestic service	Clerical, sales, and service	Professions	Slave	Nonwhite	Foreign-born	Female
1800	74.4	—	2.4	—	—	30.2	32.6	—	21.4
1860	55.8	13.8	5.4	4.8[1]	3.0[1]	21.7	23.6	24.5[1]	19.6
1910	30.7	20.8	5.5	14.1	4.7	—	13.4	22.0	20.8
1950	12.0	26.4	2.5	27.3	8.9	—	10.0	8.7	27.9
2000	2.4	14.7	0.6	38.0[2]	15.6	—	16.5	10.3[2]	46.6

[1] Values for 1870 are presented here because the available data for 1860 exclude slaves.
[2] 1990.
Note: "Clerical, sales, and service" excludes domestic service.

IMMIGRATION, BY ORIGIN (in thousands)

Period	Europe	Americas	Asia
1820–30	106	12	—
1831–40	496	33	—
1841–50	1,597	62	—
1851–60	2,453	75	42
1861–70	2,065	167	65
1871–80	2,272	404	70
1881–90	4,735	427	70
1891–1900	3,555	39	75
1901–10	8,065	362	324
1911–20	4,322	1,144	247
1921–30	2,463	1,517	112
1931–40	348	160	16
1941–50	621	355	32
1951–60	1,326	997	150
1961–70	1,123	1,716	590
1971–80	800	1,983	1,588
1981–90	762	3,616	2,738
1991–2000	1,100	3,800	2,200

UNEMPLOYMENT RATE, 1890–2010

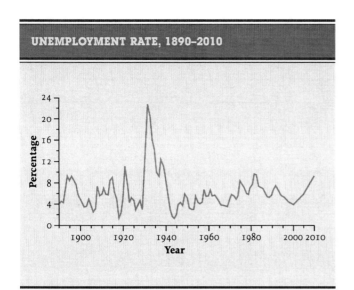

VOTER PARTICIPATION IN PRESIDENTIAL ELECTIONS, 1824–2008

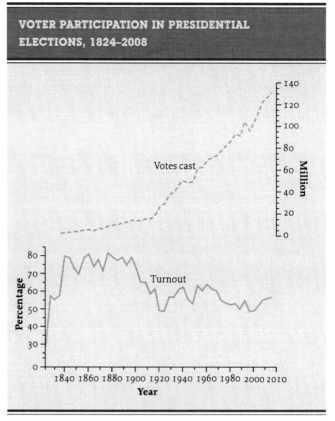

UNION MEMBERSHIP AS A PERCENTAGE OF NONAGRICULTURAL EMPLOYMENT, 1880–2009

BIRTHRATE, 1820–2009

Abolitionism Social movement of the pre–Civil War era that advocated the immediate emancipation of the slaves and their incorporation into American society as equal citizens.

Agricultural Adjustment Act (1933) New Deal legislation that established the Agricultural Adjustment Administration (AAA) to improve agricultural prices by limiting market supplies; declared unconstitutional in *United States v. Butler* (1936).

Aid to Families with Dependent Children Federal program, also known as "welfare," of financial assistance to needy American families; created in 1935 as part of the Social Security Act; abolished in 1996.

Alamo, Battle of the Siege in the Texas War for Independence, 1836, in which the San Antonio mission fell to the Mexicans.

Alien and Sedition Acts (1798) Four measures passed during the undeclared war with France that limited the freedoms of speech and press and restricted the liberty of noncitizens.

America First Committee Largely midwestern isolationist organization supported by many prominent citizens, 1940–1941.

American Civil Liberties Union Organization founded during World War I to protest the suppression of freedom of expression in wartime; played a major role in court cases that achieved judicial recognition of Americans' civil liberties.

American Colonization Society Organized in 1816 to encourage colonization of free blacks to Africa; West African nation of Liberia founded in 1822 to serve as a homeland for them.

American Federation of Labor Founded in 1881 as a federation of trade unions composed mostly of skilled, white, native-born workers; its long-term president was Samuel Gompers.

American System Program of internal improvements and protective tariffs promoted by Speaker of the House Henry Clay in his presidential campaign of 1824; his proposals formed the core of Whig ideology in the 1830s and 1840s.

Amistad Ship that transported slaves from one port in Cuba to another, seized by the slaves in 1839. They made their way northward to the United States, where the status of the slaves became the subject of a celebrated court case; eventually most were able to return to Africa.

Anarchism Belief that all institutions that exercise power over individuals, especially government, are illegitimate; it flourished among certain native-born individualists in the nineteenth century and radical immigrants in the early twentieth century.

Antietam, Battle of One of the bloodiest battles of the Civil War, fought to a standoff on September 17, 1862, in western Maryland.

Antifederalists Opponents of the Constitution who saw it as a limitation on individual and states' rights; their demands led to the addition of a Bill of Rights to the document.

Appomattox Courthouse, Virginia Site of the surrender of Confederate general Robert E. Lee to Union general Ulysses S. Grant on April 9, 1865, marking the end of the Civil War.

Army-McCarthy hearings Televised U.S. Senate hearings in 1954 on Senator Joseph McCarthy's charges of disloyalty in the army; his tactics contributed to his censure by the Senate.

Articles of Confederation First frame of government for the United States; in effect from 1781 to 1788, it provided for a weak central authority and was soon replaced by the Constitution.

Atlanta Compromise Speech to the Cotton States and International Exposition in 1895 by educator Booker T. Washington, the leading black spokesman of the day; black scholar W. E. B. Du Bois gave the speech its derisive name and criticized Washington for encouraging blacks to accommodate segregation and disenfranchisement.

Atlantic Charter Issued August 12, 1941, following meetings in Newfoundland between President Franklin D. Roosevelt and British prime minister Winston Churchill, the charter signaled the Allies' cooperation and stated their war aims.

Atomic Energy Commission Created in 1946 to supervise peacetime uses of atomic energy.

Axis powers In World War II, the nations of Germany, Italy, and Japan.

Aztec Mesoamerican people who were conquered by the Spanish under Hernán Cortés, 1519–1528.

Baby boom Markedly higher birthrate in the years following World War II; led to the biggest demographic "bubble" in American history.

Bacon's Rebellion Unsuccessful 1676 revolt led by planter Nathaniel Bacon against Virginia governor William Berkeley's administration because of governmental corruption and because Berkeley had failed to protect settlers from Indian raids and did not allow them to occupy Indian lands.

Baker v. Carr **(1962)** U.S. Supreme Court decision that established the principle of "one man, one vote," that is, that legislative districts must be equal in population.

Bakke v. Regents of the University of California **(1978)** Case in which the U.S. Supreme Court ruled against the California university system's use of racial quotas in admissions but allowed the use of race as one factor in admissions decisions.

Balance of trade Ratio of imports to exports.

Bank of the United States Proposed by the first secretary of the treasury, Alexander Hamilton, the bank opened in 1791 and operated until 1811 to issue a uniform currency, make business loans, and collect tax monies. The Second Bank of the United States was chartered in 1816 but President Andrew Jackson vetoed the recharter bill in 1832.

Barbary pirates Plundering pirates off the Mediterranean coast of Africa; President Thomas Jefferson's refusal to pay them tribute to protect American ships sparked an undeclared naval war with North African nations, 1801–1805.

Barbed wire First practical fencing material for the Great Plains was invented in 1873 and rapidly spelled the end of the open range.

Bay of Pigs invasion Hoping to inspire a revolt against Fidel Castro, the CIA sent 1,500 Cuban exiles to invade their homeland on April 17, 1961, but the mission was a spectacular failure.

Bill of Rights First ten amendments to the U.S. Constitution, adopted in 1791 to guarantee individual rights against infringement by the federal government.

Black Codes (1865–1866) Laws passed in southern states to restrict the rights of former slaves; to nullify the codes, Congress passed the Civil Rights Act of 1866 and the Fourteenth Amendment.

Black Legend Idea that the Spanish New World empire was more oppressive toward the Indians than other European empires; was used as a justification for English imperial expansion.

Black Power Post-1966 rallying cry of a more militant civil rights movement.

Bland-Allison Act (1878) Passed over President Rutherford B. Hayes's veto, the inflationary measure authorized the purchase each month of 2 to 4 million dollars' worth of silver for coinage.

"Bleeding Kansas" Violence between pro- and antislavery settlers in the Kansas Territory, 1856.

Boston Massacre Clash between British soldiers and a Boston mob, March 5, 1770, in which five colonists were killed.

Boston Tea Party On December 16, 1773, the Sons of Liberty, dressed as Indians, dumped hundreds of chests of tea into Boston Harbor to protest the Tea Act of 1773, under which the British exported to the colonies millions of pounds of cheap—but still taxed—tea, thereby undercutting the price of smuggled tea and forcing payment of the tea duty.

Boxer Rebellion Chinese nationalist protest against Western commercial domination and cultural influence, 1900; a coalition of American, European, and Japanese forces put down the rebellion and reclaimed captured embassies in Peking (Beijing) within the year.

Bracero **program** System agreed to by Mexican and American governments in 1942 under which tens of thousands of Mexicans entered the United States to work temporarily in agricultural jobs in the Southwest; lasted until 1964 and inhibited labor organization among farm workers since *braceros* could be deported at any time.

Brains trust Group of advisers—many of them academics—assembled by Franklin D. Roosevelt to recommend New Deal policies during the early months of his presidency.

Bretton Woods Town in New Hampshire and site of international agreement in 1944 by which the American dollar replaced the British pound as the most important international currency, and the World Bank and International Monetary Fund were created to promote rebuilding after World War II and to ensure that countries did not devalue their currencies.

Brook Farm Transcendentalist commune in West Roxbury, Massachusetts, populated from 1841 to 1847 principally by writers (Nathaniel Hawthorne, for one) and other intellectuals.

Brown v. Board of Education of Topeka (1954) U.S. Supreme Court decision that struck down racial segregation in public education and declared "separate but equal" unconstitutional.

Bull Run, Battles of (First and Second Manassas) First land engagement of the Civil War took place on July 21, 1861, at Manassas Junction, Virginia, at which Union troops quickly retreated; one year later, on August 29–30, Confederates captured the federal supply depot and forced Union troops back to Washington.

Bunker Hill, Battle of First major battle of the Revolutionary War; it actually took place at nearby Breed's Hill, Massachusetts, on June 17, 1775.

"Burned-over district" Area of western New York strongly influenced by the revivalist fervor of the Second Great Awakening; Disciples of Christ and Mormons are among the many sects that trace their roots to the phenomenon.

Bush v. Gore (2000) U.S. Supreme Court case that determined the winner of the disputed 2000 presidential election.

Calvinism Doctrine of predestination expounded by Swiss theologian John Calvin in 1536; influenced the Puritan, Presbyterian, German and Dutch Reformed, and Huguenot churches in the colonies.

Camp David accords Peace agreement between the leaders of Israel and Egypt, brokered by President Jimmy Carter in 1978.

Carpetbaggers Derisive term for northern emigrants who participated in the Republican governments of the Reconstruction South.

Chancellorsville, Battle of Confederate general Robert E. Lee won his last major victory and General "Stonewall" Jackson died in this Civil War battle in northern Virginia on May 1–4, 1863.

Chinese Exclusion Act (1882) Halted Chinese immigration to the United States.

Civil Rights Act of 1866 Along with the Fourteenth Amendment, guaranteed the rights of citizenship to former slaves.

Civil Rights Act of 1957 First federal civil rights law since Reconstruction; established the Civil Rights Commission and the Civil Rights Division of the Department of Justice.

Civil Rights Act of 1964 Outlawed discrimination in public accommodations and employment.

Closed shop Hiring requirement that all workers in a business must be union members.

Coercive Acts/Intolerable Acts (1774) Four parliamentary measures in reaction to the Boston Tea Party that forced payment for the tea, disallowed colonial trials of British soldiers, forced their quartering in private homes, and reduced the number of elected officials in Massachusetts.

Cold War Term for tensions, 1945–1989, between the Soviet Union and the United States, the two major world powers after World War II.

Commonwealth v. Hunt (1842) Landmark ruling of the Massachusetts Supreme Court establishing the legality of labor unions.

Communitarianism Social reform movement of the nineteenth century driven by the belief that by establishing small communities based on common ownership of property, a less competitive and individualistic society could be developed.

Compromise of 1850 Complex compromise devised by Senator Henry Clay that admitted California as a free state, included a stronger fugitive slave law, and delayed determination of the slave status of the New Mexico and Utah territories.

Compromise of 1877 Deal made by a Republican and Democratic special congressional commission to resolve the disputed presidential election of 1876; Republican Rutherford B. Hayes, who had lost the popular vote, was declared the winner in exchange for the withdrawal of federal troops from involvement in politics in the South, marking the end of Reconstruction.

Congress of Industrial Organizations (CIO) Umbrella organization of semiskilled industrial unions, formed in 1935 as the Committee for Industrial Organization and renamed in 1938.

Congress of Racial Equality (CORE) Civil rights organization started in 1942 and best known for its Freedom Rides, bus journeys challenging racial segregation in the South in 1961.

Conspicuous consumption Phrase referring to extravagant spending to raise social standing, coined by Thorstein Veblen in *The Theory of the Leisure Class* (1899).

Constitutional Convention Meeting in Philadelphia, May 25–September 17, 1787, of representatives from twelve colonies—excepting Rhode Island—to revise the existing Articles of Confederation; convention soon resolved to produce an entirely new constitution.

Containment General U.S. strategy in the Cold War that called for containing Soviet expansion; originally devised by U.S. diplomat George F. Kennan.

Continental army Army authorized by the Continental Congress in 1775 to fight the British; commanded by General George Washington.

Continental Congress Representatives of the colonies met first in Philadelphia in 1774 to formulate actions against British policies; the Second Continental Congress (1775–1789) conducted the war and adopted the Declaration of Independence and the Articles of Confederation.

Convict leasing System developed in the post–Civil War South that generated income for the states and satisfied planters' need for cheap labor by renting prisoners out; the convicts were often treated poorly.

Copperheads Republican term for northerners opposed to the Civil War; it derived from the name of a poisonous snake.

Coral Sea, Battle of the Fought on May 7–8, 1942, near the eastern coast of Australia, it was the first U.S. naval victory over Japan in World War II.

Cotton gin Invented by Eli Whitney in 1793, the machine separated cotton seed from cotton fiber, speeding cotton processing and making profitable the cultivation of the more hardy, but difficult to clean, short-staple cotton; led directly to the dramatic nineteenth-century expansion of slavery in the South.

Counterculture "Hippie" youth culture of the 1960s, which rejected the values of the dominant culture in favor of illicit drugs, communes, free sex, and rock music.

Court-packing plan President Franklin D. Roosevelt's failed 1937 attempt to increase the number of U.S. Supreme Court justices from nine to fifteen in order to save his Second New Deal programs from constitutional challenges.

Coverture Principle in English and American law that a married woman lost her legal identity, which became "covered" by that of her husband, who therefore controlled her person and the family's economic resources.

Crédit Mobilier scandal Millions of dollars in overcharges for building the Union Pacific Railroad were exposed; high officials of the Ulysses S. Grant administration were implicated but never charged.

Creoles (*Criollos* in Spanish) Persons born in the New World of European ancestry.

Cuban missile crisis Caused when the United States discovered Soviet offensive missile sites in Cuba in October 1962; the U.S.-Soviet confrontation was the Cold War's closest brush with nuclear war.

Crop-lien system Merchants extended credit to tenants based on their future crops, but high interest rates and the uncertainties of farming often led to inescapable debts.

D-Day June 6, 1944, when an Allied amphibious assault landed on the Normandy coast and established a foothold in Europe, leading to the liberation of France from German occupation.

***Dartmouth College v. Woodward* (1819)** U.S. Supreme Court upheld the original charter of the college against New Hampshire's attempt to alter the board of trustees; set precedent of support of contracts against state interference.

Dawes Act Law passed in 1887 meant to encourage adoption of white norms among Indians; broke up tribal holdings into small farms for Indian families, with the remainder sold to white purchasers.

Declaration of Independence Document adopted on July 4, 1776, that made the break with Britain official; drafted by a committee of the Second Continental Congress, including principal writer Thomas Jefferson.

Deindustrialization Term describing decline of manufacturing in old industrial areas in the late twentieth century as companies shifted production to low-wage centers in the South and West or in other countries.

Deism Enlightenment thought applied to religion; emphasized reason, morality, and natural law.

Democratic-Republican Societies Organizations created in the mid-1790s by opponents of the policies of the Washington administration and supporters of the French Revolution.

Department of Homeland Security Created to coordinate federal antiterrorist activity following the 2001 terrorist attacks on the World Trade Center and Pentagon.

Depression Period in which economic output declines sharply and unemployment rises; it applied especially to the Great Depression of the 1930s.

Depression of 1893 Worst depression of the nineteenth century, set off by a railroad failure, too much speculation on Wall Street, and low agricultural prices.

Disenfranchise To deprive of the right to vote; in the United States, exclusionary policies were used to deny groups, especially African-Americans and women, their voting rights.

Division of Powers The division of political power between the state and federal governments under the U.S. Constitution (also known as federalism).

Dixiecrats Deep South delegates who walked out of the 1948 Democratic National Convention in protest of the party's support for civil rights legislation and later formed the States' Rights Democratic (Dixiecrat) Party, which nominated Strom Thurmond of South Carolina for president.

Dominion of New England Consolidation into a single colony of the New England colonies—and later New York and New Jersey—by royal governor Edmund Andros in 1686; dominion reverted to individual colonial governments three years later.

***Dred Scott v. Sandford* (1857)** U.S. Supreme Court decision in which Chief Justice Roger B. Taney ruled that Congress could not prohibit slavery in the territories, on the grounds that such a prohibition would violate the Fifth Amendment rights of slaveholders, and that no black person could be a citizen of the United States.

Due-process clause Clause in the Fifth and the Fourteenth Amendments to the U.S. Constitution guaranteeing that states could not "deprive any person of life, liberty, or property, without due process of law."

Dust Bowl Great Plains counties where millions of tons of topsoil were blown away from parched farmland in the 1930s; massive migration of farm families followed.

Eighteenth Amendment (1919) Prohibition amendment that made illegal the manufacture, sale, or transportation of alcoholic beverages; repealed in 1933.

Ellis Island Reception center in New York Harbor through which most European immigrants to America were processed from 1892 to 1954.

Emancipation Proclamation (1863) President Abraham Lincoln issued a preliminary proclamation on September 22, 1862, freeing the slaves in areas under Confederate control as of January 1, 1863, the date of the final proclamation, which also authorized the enrollment of black soldiers into the Union army.

Embargo Act of 1807 Attempt to exert economic pressure by prohibiting all exports from the United States, instead of waging war in reaction to continued British impressment of American sailors; smugglers easily circumvented the embargo, and it was repealed two years later.

Emergency Banking Relief Act (1933) First New Deal measure that provided for reopening the banks under strict conditions and took the United States off the gold standard.

Emergency Immigration Act of 1921 Limited U.S. immigration to 3 percent of each foreign-born nationality in the 1910 census; three years later, Congress restricted immigration even further.

Encomienda System under which officers of the Spanish conquistadores gained ownership of Indian land.

Enlightenment Revolution in thought in the eighteenth century that emphasized reason and science over the authority of traditional religion.

Environmental Protection Agency (EPA) Created in 1970 during the first administration of President Richard M. Nixon to oversee federal pollution control efforts.

Equal Rights Amendment Amendment to guarantee equal rights for women, introduced in 1923 but not passed by Congress until 1972; it failed to be ratified by the states.

Era of Good Feelings Contemporary characterization of the administration of popular Republican president James Monroe, 1817–1825.

Erie Canal Most important and profitable of the canals of the 1820s and 1830s; stretched from Buffalo to Albany, New York, connecting the Great Lakes to the East Coast and making New York City the nation's largest port.

Espionage and Sedition Acts (1917–1918) Limited criticism of government leaders and policies by imposing fines and prison terms on those who opposed American participation in the First World War.

Eugenics "Science" of improving the human race by regulating who can bear children; flourished in early twentieth century and led to laws for involuntary sterilization of the "feeble-minded."

Fair Deal Domestic reform proposals of the Truman administration; included civil rights legislation, national health insurance, and repeal of the Taft-Hartley Act, but only extensions of some New Deal programs were enacted.

Fair Employment Practices Commission Created in 1941 by executive order, the FEPC sought to eliminate racial discrimination in jobs; it possessed little power but represented a step toward civil rights for African-Americans.

Family wage Idea that male workers should earn a wage sufficient to enable them to support their entire family without their wives having to work outside the home.

Federal Trade Commission Act (1914) Established the Federal Trade Commission to enforce existing antitrust laws that prohibited business combinations in restraint of trade.

The Federalist Collection of eighty-five essays that appeared in the New York press in 1787–1788 in support of the Constitution; written by Alexander Hamilton, James Madison, and John Jay and published under the pseudonym "Publius."

Federalist Party One of the two first national political parties; led by George Washington, John Adams, and Alexander Hamilton, it favored a strong central government.

Feminism Term that entered the lexicon in the early twentieth century to describe the movement for full equality for women, in political, social, and personal life.

Fifteenth Amendment Constitutional Amendment ratified in 1870, which prohibited states from discriminating in voting privileges on the basis of race.

"Fifty-four forty or fight" Democratic campaign slogan in the presidential election of 1844, urging that the northern border of Oregon be fixed at 54°40' north latitude.

Filibuster In the nineteenth century, invasions of Central American countries launched privately by groups of Americans seeking to establish personal rule and spread slavery; in the twentieth century, term for the practice of members of the U.S. Senate delivering interminable speeches in order to prevent voting on legislation.

Fletcher v. Peck (1810) U.S. Supreme Court decision in which Chief Justice John Marshall upheld the initial fraudulent sale contracts in the Yazoo Fraud cases; it upheld the principle of sanctity of a contract.

Fordism Early twentieth-century term describing the economic system pioneered by Ford Motor Company based on high wages and mass consumption.

Fort McHenry Fort in Baltimore Harbor unsuccessfully bombarded by the British in September 1814; Francis Scott Key, a witness to the battle, was moved to write the words to "The Star-Spangled Banner."

Fort Sumter First battle of the Civil War, in which the federal fort in Charleston (South Carolina) Harbor was captured by the Confederates on April 14, 1861, after two days of shelling.

Fourteen Points President Woodrow Wilson's 1918 plan for peace after World War I; at the Versailles peace conference, however, he failed to incorporate all of the points into the treaty.

Fourteenth Amendment (1868) Guaranteed rights of citizenship to former slaves, in words similar to those of the Civil Rights Act of 1866.

Franchise The right to vote.

"Free person of color" Negro or mulatto person not held in slavery; immediately before the Civil War, there were nearly a half million in the United States, split almost evenly between North and South.

Free Soil Party Formed in 1848 to oppose slavery in the territory acquired in the Mexican War; nominated Martin Van Buren for president in 1848. By 1854 most of the party's members had joined the Republican Party.

Free Speech Movement Founded in 1964 at the University of California at Berkeley by student radicals protesting restrictions on their right to distribute political publications.

Freedmen's Bureau Reconstruction agency established in 1865 to protect the legal rights of former slaves and to assist with their education, jobs, health care, and landowning.

French and Indian War Known in Europe as the Seven Years' War, the last (1755–1763) of four colonial wars fought between England and France for control of North America east of the Mississippi River.

Fugitive Slave Act of 1850 Gave federal government authority in cases involving runaway slaves; aroused considerable opposition in the North.

Fundamentalism Anti-modernist Protestant movement started in the early twentieth century that proclaimed the literal truth of the Bible; the name came from *The Fundamentals*, published by conservative leaders.

Gadsden Purchase (1853) Thirty thousand square miles in present-day Arizona and New Mexico bought by Congress from Mexico primarily for the Southern Pacific Railroad's transcontinental route.

Gag Rule Rule adopted by House of Representatives in 1836 prohibiting consideration of abolitionist petitions; opposition, led by former president John Quincy Adams, succeeded in having it repealed in 1844.

Gentlemen's Agreement (1907) The United States would not exclude Japanese immigrants if Japan would voluntarily limit the number of immigrants coming to the United States.

Gettysburg, Battle of Fought in southern Pennsylvania, July 1–3, 1863; the Confederate defeat and the simultaneous loss at Vicksburg marked the military turning point of the Civil War.

Gibbons v. Ogden (1824) U.S. Supreme Court decision reinforcing the "commerce clause" (the federal government's right to regulate interstate commerce) of the Constitution; Chief Justice John Marshall ruled against the State of New York's granting of steamboat monopolies.

Gideon v. Wainwright **(1963)** U.S. Supreme Court decision guaranteeing legal counsel for indigent felony defendants.

The Gilded Age Mark Twain and Charles Dudley Warner's 1873 novel, the title of which became the popular name for the period from the end of the Civil War to the turn of the century.

Glass-Steagall Act (Banking Act of 1933) Established the Federal Deposit Insurance Corporation and included banking reforms, some designed to control speculation. Repealed in 1999, opening the door to scandals involving banks and stock investment companies.

Globalization Term that became prominent in the 1990s to describe the rapid acceleration of international flows of commerce, financial resources, labor, and cultural products.

Gold standard Policy at various points in American history by which the value of a dollar is set at a fixed price in terms of gold (in the post–World War II era, for example, $35 per ounce of gold).

Good Neighbor Policy Proclaimed by President Franklin D. Roosevelt in his first inaugural address in 1933, it sought improved diplomatic relations between the United States and its Latin American neighbors.

Grandfather clause Loophole created by southern disfranchising legislatures of the 1890s for illiterate white males whose grandfathers had been eligible to vote in 1867.

Granger movement Political movement that grew out of the Patrons of Husbandry, an educational and social organization for farmers founded in 1867; the Grange had its greatest success in the Midwest of the 1870s, lobbying for government control of railroad and grain elevator rates and establishing farmers' cooperatives.

Great Awakening Fervent religious revival movement in the 1720s through the 1740s that was spread throughout the colonies by ministers like New England Congregationalist Jonathan Edwards and English revivalist George Whitefield.

Great Compromise (Connecticut Compromise) Settled the differences between the New Jersey and Virginia delegations to the Constitutional Convention by providing for a bicameral legislature, the upper house of which would have equal representation for each state and the lower house of which would be apportioned by population.

Great Depression Worst economic depression in American history; it was spurred by the stock market crash of 1929 and lasted until World War II.

Great Migration Large-scale migration of southern blacks during and after World War I to the North, where jobs had become available during the labor shortage of the war years.

Great Society Term coined by President Lyndon B. Johnson in his 1965 State of the Union address, in which he proposed legislation to address problems of voting rights, poverty, diseases, education, immigration, and the environment.

Greenback-Labor Party Formed in 1876 in reaction to economic depression, the party favored issuance of unsecured paper money to help farmers repay debts; the movement for free coinage of silver took the place of the greenback movement by the 1880s.

Griswold v. Connecticut **(1965)** Supreme Court decision that, in overturning Connecticut law prohibiting the use of contraceptives, established a constitutional right to privacy.

Gulf War Military action in 1991 in which an international coalition led by the United States drove Iraq from Kuwait, which it had occupied the previous year.

Habeas corpus, Writ of An essential component of English common law and of the U.S. Constitution that guarantees that citizens may not be imprisoned without due process of law; literally means, "you may have the body"; suspended by President Lincoln during the Civil War and limited by President Bush after the attacks of September 11, 2001.

Hacienda Large-scale farm in the Spanish New World empire worked by Indian laborers.

Harlem Renaissance African-American literary and artistic movement of the 1920s centered in New York City's Harlem neighborhood; writers Langston Hughes, Jean Toomer, Zora Neale Hurston, and Countee Cullen were among those active in the movement.

Harpers Ferry, Virginia Site of abolitionist John Brown's failed raid on the federal arsenal, October 16–17, 1859; Brown became a martyr to his cause after his capture and execution.

Hart-Celler Act (1965) Eliminated the national origins quota system for immigration established by laws in 1921 and 1924; led to radical change in the origins of immigrants to the United States, with Asians and Latin Americans outnumbering Europeans.

Hartford Convention Meeting of New England Federalists on December 15, 1814, to protest the War of 1812; proposed seven constitutional amendments (limiting embargoes and changing requirements for officeholding, declaration of war, and admission of new states), but the war ended before Congress could respond.

Hawley-Smoot Tariff Act (1930) Raised tariffs to an unprecedented level and worsened the Great Depression by raising prices and discouraging foreign trade.

Haymarket affair Violence during an anarchist protest at Haymarket Square in Chicago on May 4, 1886; the deaths of eight, including seven policemen, led to the trial of eight anarchist leaders for conspiracy to commit murder.

Hessians German soldiers, most from Hesse-Cassel principality (hence, the name), paid to fight for the British in the Revolutionary War.

Holding company Investment company that holds controlling interest in the securities of other companies.

Homestead Act (1862) Authorized Congress to grant 160 acres of public land to a western settler, who had to live on the land for five years to establish title.

Homestead Strike Violent strike at the Carnegie Steel Company near Pittsburgh in 1892 that culminated in the defeat of the Amalgamated Association of Iron and Steel Workers, the first steelworkers' union.

House Un-American Activities Committee (HUAC) Formed in 1938 to investigate subversives in the government and holders of radical ideas more generally; best-known investigations were of Hollywood notables and of former State Department official Alger Hiss, who was accused in 1948 of espionage and Communist Party membership. Abolished in 1975.

Hundred Days Extraordinarily productive first three months of President Franklin D. Roosevelt's administration in which a special session of Congress enacted fifteen of his New Deal proposals.

Impeachment Bringing charges against a public official; for example, the House of Representatives can impeach a president for "treason, bribery, or other high crimes and misdemeanors" by majority vote, and after the trial the Senate can remove the president by a vote of two-thirds. Two presidents, Andrew Johnson and Bill Clinton, have been impeached and tried before the Senate; neither was convicted.

Implied powers Federal powers beyond those specifically enumerated in the U.S. Constitution; based on the "elastic clause" of Article I, Section 8, of the Constitution that allows Congress to enact laws that promote the "general welfare."

"In God We Trust" Phrase placed on all new U.S. currency as of 1954.

Indentured servant Settler who signed on for a temporary period of servitude to a master in exchange for passage to the New World; Virginia and Pennsylvania were largely peopled in the seventeenth and eighteenth centuries by English and German indentured servants.

Indian Removal Act (1830) Signed by President Andrew Jackson, the law permitted the negotiation of treaties to obtain the Indians' lands in exchange for their relocation to what would become Oklahoma.

Individualism Term that entered the language in the 1820s to describe the increasing emphasis on the pursuit of personal advancement and private fulfillment free of outside interference.

Industrial Workers of the World Radical union organized in Chicago in 1905 and nicknamed the Wobblies; its opposition to World War I led to its destruction by the federal government under the Espionage Act.

Inflation An economic condition in which prices rise continuously.

Insular Cases Series of cases between 1901 and 1904 in which the Supreme Court ruled that constitutional protection of individual rights did not fully apply to residents of "insular" territories acquired by the United States in the Spanish-American War, such as Puerto Rico and the Philippines.

Interstate Commerce Commission Reacting to the U.S. Supreme Court's ruling in *Wabash Railroad v. Illinois* (1886), Congress established the ICC to curb abuses in the railroad industry by regulating rates.

Iran-Contra affair Scandal of the second Reagan administration involving sales of arms to Iran in partial exchange for release of hostages in Lebanon and use of the arms money to aid the Contras in Nicaragua, which had been expressly forbidden by Congress.

Iraq War Military campaign in 2003 in which the United States, unable to gain approval by the United Nations, unilaterally occupied Iraq and removed dictator Saddam Hussein from power.

Iron Curtain Term coined by Winston Churchill to describe the Cold War divide between western Europe and the Soviet Union's eastern European satellites.

Jamestown, Virginia Site in 1607 of the first permanent English settlement in the New World.

Japanese-American internment Policy adopted by the Roosevelt administration in 1942 under which 110,000 persons of Japanese descent, most of them American citizens, were removed from the West Coast and forced to spend most of World War II in internment camps; it was the largest violation of American civil liberties in the twentieth century.

Jay's Treaty Treaty with Britain negotiated in 1794 by Chief Justice John Jay; Britain agreed to vacate forts in the Northwest Territories, and festering disagreements (border with Canada, prewar debts, shipping claims) would be settled by commission.

Jim Crow Minstrel show character whose name became synonymous with racial segregation.

Kansas-Nebraska Act (1854) Law sponsored by Illinois senator Stephen A. Douglas to allow settlers in newly organized territories north of the Missouri border to decide the slavery issue for themselves; fury over the resulting repeal of the Missouri Compromise of 1820 led to violence in Kansas and to the formation of the Republican Party.

Kellogg-Briand Pact Representatives of sixty-two nations in 1928 signed the pact (also called the Pact of Paris) to outlaw war.

Keynesianism Economic theory derived from the writings of British economist John Maynard Keynes, which rejected the laissez-faire approach in favor of public spending to stimulate economic growth, even at the cost of federal deficits; dominated economic policies of administrations from the 1940s to the mid-1970s.

Knights of Labor Founded in 1869, the first national union lasted, under the leadership of Terence V. Powderly, only into the 1890s; supplanted by the American Federation of Labor.

Know-Nothing (American) Party Nativist, anti-Catholic third party organized in 1854 in reaction to large-scale German and Irish immigration; the party's only presidential candidate was Millard Fillmore in 1856.

Korean War Conflict touched off in 1950 when Communist North Korea invaded South Korea; fighting, largely by U.S. forces, continued until 1953.

Ku Klux Klan Organized in Pulaski, Tennessee, in 1866 to terrorize former slaves who voted and held political offices during Reconstruction; a revived organization in the 1910s and 1920s stressed white, Anglo-Saxon, fundamentalist Protestant supremacy; the Klan revived a third time to fight the civil rights movement of the 1950s and 1960s in the South.

Laissez-faire Term adopted from French, meaning "let people do as they choose," describing opposition to government action to regulate economic or personal behavior.

Land Ordinance of 1785 Directed surveying of the Northwest Territory into townships of thirty-six sections (square miles) each, the sale of the sixteenth section of which was to be used to finance public education.

League of Nations Organization of nations to mediate disputes and avoid war established after World War I as part of the Treaty of Versailles; President Woodrow Wilson's "Fourteen Points" speech to Congress in 1918 proposed the formation of the league, which the United States never joined.

Lend-Lease Act (1941) Permitted the United States to lend or lease arms and other supplies to the Allies, signifying increasing likelihood of American involvement in World War II.

Levittown Low-cost, mass-produced developments of suburban tract housing built by William Levitt after World War II on Long Island and elsewhere.

Lexington and Concord, Battle of The first shots fired in the Revolutionary War, on April 19, 1775, near Boston; approximately 100 minutemen and 250 British soldiers were killed.

Leyte Gulf, Battle of Largest sea battle in history, fought on October 25, 1944, and won by the United States off the Philippine island of Leyte; Japanese losses were so great that they could not rebound.

Liberalism Originally, political philosophy that emphasized the protection of liberty by limiting the power of government to interfere with the natural rights of citizens; in the twentieth century, belief in an activist government promoting greater social and economic equality.

Liberty Party Abolitionist political party that nominated James G. Birney for president in 1840 and 1844; merged with the Free Soil Party in 1848.

Lincoln-Douglas debates Series of senatorial campaign debates in 1858 focusing on the issue of slavery in the territories; held in Illinois between Republican Abraham Lincoln, who made a national reputation for himself, and incumbent Democratic senator Stephen A. Douglas, who managed to hold onto his seat.

Little Bighorn, Battle of Most famous battle of the Great Sioux War took place in 1876 in the Montana Territory; combined Sioux and Cheyenne warriors massacred a vastly outnumbered U.S. Cavalry commanded by Lieutenant Colonel George Armstrong Custer.

Lochner v. New York (1905) Decision by Supreme Court overturning a New York law establishing a limit on the number of hours per week bakers could be compelled to work; "Lochnerism" became a way of describing the liberty of contract jurisprudence, which opposed all governmental intervention in the economy.

Louisiana Purchase President Thomas Jefferson's 1803 purchase from France of the important port of New Orleans and 828,000 square miles west of the Mississippi River to the Rocky Mountains; it more than doubled the territory of the United States at a cost of only $15 million.

Loyalists Colonists who remained loyal to Great Britain during the War of Independence.

Lusitania British passenger liner sunk by a German U-boat, May 7, 1915, creating a diplomatic crisis and public outrage at the loss of 128 Americans (roughly 10 percent of the total aboard); Germany agreed to pay reparations, and the United States waited two more years to enter World War I.

Lyceum movement Founded in 1826, the movement promoted adult public education through lectures and performances.

Lynching Practice, particularly widespread in the South between 1890 and 1940, in which persons (usually black) accused of a crime were murdered by mobs before standing trial. Lynchings often took place before large crowds, with law enforcement authorities not intervening.

Manhattan Project Secret American program during World War II to develop an atomic bomb; J. Robert Oppenheimer led the team of physicists at Los Alamos, New Mexico.

Manifest Destiny Phrase first used in 1845 to urge annexation of Texas; used thereafter to encourage American settlement of European colonial and Indian lands in the Great Plains and the West and, more generally, as a justification for American empire.

Marbury v. Madison (1803) First U.S. Supreme Court decision to declare a federal law—the Judiciary Act of 1801—unconstitutional.

March on Washington Civil rights demonstration on August 28, 1963, where the Reverend Martin Luther King Jr.,

gave his "I Have a Dream" speech on the steps of the Lincoln Memorial.

Marshall Plan U.S. program for the reconstruction of post–World War II Europe through massive aid to former enemy nations as well as allies; proposed by General George C. Marshall in 1947.

Massive resistance In reaction to the *Brown* decision of 1954, effort by southern states to defy federally mandated school integration.

Maya Pre-Columbian society in Mesoamerica before about A.D. 900.

Mayflower Compact Signed in 1620 aboard the *Mayflower* before the Pilgrims landed at Plymouth, the document committed the group to majority-rule government.

McCarran Internal Security Act (1950) Passed over President Harry S. Truman's veto, the law required registration of American Communist Party members, denied them passports, and allowed them to be detained as suspected subversives.

McCarthyism Post–World War II Red Scare focused on the fear of Communists in U.S. government positions; peaked during the Korean War; most closely associated with Joseph McCarthy, a major instigator of the hysteria.

McCulloch v. Maryland (1819) U.S. Supreme Court decision in which Chief Justice John Marshall, holding that Maryland could not tax the Second Bank of the United States, supported the authority of the federal government versus the states.

McNary-Haugen bill Vetoed by President Calvin Coolidge in 1927 and 1928, the bill to aid farmers would have artificially raised agricultural prices by selling surpluses overseas for low prices and selling the reduced supply in the United States for higher prices.

Meat Inspection Act (1906) Passed largely in reaction to Upton Sinclair's *The Jungle*, the law set strict standards of cleanliness in the meatpacking industry.

Medicaid Great Society program established in 1965 that provided free medical care to the poor.

Medicare Key component of Great Society of Lyndon B. Johnson; government program created in 1965 to pay medical costs of elderly and disabled Americans.

Mercantilism Policy of Great Britain and other imperial powers of regulating the economies of colonies to benefit the mother country.

Mestizo Spanish word for person of mixed Native American and European ancestry.

Mexican War Controversial war with Mexico for control of California and New Mexico, 1846–1848; the Treaty of Guadalupe Hidalgo fixed the border at the Rio Grande and extended the United States to the Pacific coast, annexing more than a half-million square miles of Mexican territory.

Midway, Battle of Decisive American victory near Midway Island in the South Pacific on June 4, 1942; the Japanese navy never recovered its superiority over the U.S. navy.

Minstrel show Blackface vaudeville entertainment popular in the decades surrounding the Civil War.

Miranda v. Arizona (1966) U.S. Supreme Court decision required police to advise persons in custody of their rights to legal counsel and against self-incrimination.

Missouri Compromise Deal proposed by Kentucky senator Henry Clay in 1820 to resolve the slave/free imbalance in Congress that would result from Missouri's admission as a slave state; Maine's admission as a free state offset Missouri, and slavery was prohibited in the remainder of the Louisiana Territory north of the southern border of Missouri.

Molly Maguires Secret organization of Irish coal miners that used violence to intimidate mine officials in the 1870s.

Monitor and Merrimac, Battle of the First engagement between ironclad ships; fought at Hampton Roads, Virginia, on March 9, 1862.

Monroe Doctrine President James Monroe's declaration to Congress on December 2, 1823, that the American continents would be thenceforth closed to European colonization, and that the United States would not interfere in European affairs.

Montgomery bus boycott Sparked by Rosa Parks's arrest on December 1, 1955, for refusing to surrender her seat to a white passenger, a successful year-long boycott protesting segregation on city buses; led by the Reverend Martin Luther King Jr.

Moral Majority Televangelist Jerry Falwell's political lobbying organization, the name of which became synonymous with the Religious Right—conservative evangelical Protestants who helped ensure President Ronald Reagan's 1980 victory.

Mormons Founded in 1830 by Joseph Smith, the sect (officially, the Church of Jesus Christ of Latter-day Saints) was a product of the intense revivalism of the "burned-over district" of New York; Smith's successor Brigham Young led 15,000 followers to Utah in 1847 to escape persecution.

Muckrakers Writers who exposed corruption and abuses in politics, business, meatpacking, child labor, and more, primarily in the first decade of the twentieth century; their popular books and magazine articles spurred public interest in reform.

Mugwumps Reform wing of the Republican Party that supported Democrat Grover Cleveland for president in 1884 over Republican James G. Blaine, whose influence peddling had been revealed in the Mulligan letters of 1876.

Multiculturalism Term that became prominent in the 1990s to describe a growing emphasis on group racial and ethnic identity and demands that jobs, education, and politics reflect the increasingly diverse nature of American society.

Munn v. Illinois (1877) U.S. Supreme Court ruling that upheld a Granger law allowing the state to regulate grain elevators.

NAFTA Approved in 1993, the North American Free Trade Agreement with Canada and Mexico allowed goods to travel across their borders free of tariffs; critics argued that American workers would lose their jobs to cheaper Mexican labor.

Nat Turner Rebellion Most important slave uprising in nineteenth-century America, led by a slave preacher who, with his followers, killed about sixty white persons in Southampton County, Virginia, in 1831.

National Association for the Advancement of Colored People (NAACP) Founded in 1910, this civil rights organization brought lawsuits against discriminatory practices and published *The Crisis*, a journal edited by African-American scholar W. E. B. Du Bois.

National Defense Education Act (1958) Passed in reaction to America's perceived inferiority in the space race; encouraged education in science and modern languages through student loans, university research grants, and aid to public schools.

National Industrial Recovery Act (1933) Passed on the last of the Hundred Days, it created public-works jobs through the Federal Emergency Relief Administration and established a system of self-regulation for industry through the National Recovery Administration, which was ruled unconstitutional in 1935.

National Organization for Women Founded in 1966 by writer Betty Friedan and other feminists, NOW pushed for abortion rights, nondiscrimination in the workplace, and other forms of equality for women.

National Road First federal interstate road, built between 1811 and 1838 and stretching from Cumberland, Maryland, to Vandalia, Illinois.

National Security Act (1947) Authorized the reorganization of government to coordinate military branches and security agencies; created the National Security Council, the Central Intelligence Agency, and the National Military Establishment (later renamed the Department of Defense).

National Youth Administration Created in 1935 as part of the Works Progress Administration, it employed millions of youths who had left school.

Nativism Anti-immigrant and anti-Catholic feeling especially prominent in the 1830s through the 1850s; the largest group was New York's Order of the Star-Spangled Banner, which expanded into the American (Know-Nothing) Party in 1854.

Naval stores Tar, pitch, and turpentine made from pine resin and used in shipbuilding; an important industry in the southern colonies, especially North Carolina.

Navigation Acts Passed by the English Parliament to control colonial trade and bolster the mercantile system, 1650–1775; enforcement of the acts led to growing resentment by colonists.

Neutrality Acts Series of laws passed between 1935 and 1939 to keep the United States from becoming involved in war by prohibiting American trade and travel to warring nations.

New Deal Franklin D. Roosevelt's campaign promise, in his speech to the Democratic National Convention of 1932, to combat the Great Depression with a "new deal for the American people"; the phrase became a catchword for his ambitious plan of economic programs.

New Freedom Democrat Woodrow Wilson's political slogan in the presidential campaign of 1912; Wilson wanted to improve the banking system, lower tariffs, and, by breaking up monopolies, give small businesses freedom to compete.

New Frontier John F. Kennedy's program, stymied by a Republican Congress and his abbreviated term; his successor Lyndon B. Johnson had greater success with many of the same concepts.

New Harmony Founded in Indiana by British industrialist Robert Owen in 1825, the short-lived New Harmony Community of Equality was one of the few nineteenth-century communal experiments not based on religious ideology.

New Left Radical youth protest movement of the 1960s, named by leader Tom Hayden to distinguish it from the Old (Marxist-Leninist) Left of the 1930s.

New Nationalism Platform of the Progressive Party and slogan of former president Theodore Roosevelt in the presidential campaign of 1912; stressed government activism, including regulation of trusts, conservation, and recall of state court decisions that had nullified progressive programs.

New Orleans, Battle of Last battle of the War of 1812, fought on January 8, 1815, weeks after the peace treaty was signed but prior to the news reaching America; General Andrew Jackson led the victorious American troops.

New South *Atlanta Constitution* editor Henry W. Grady's 1886 term for the prosperous post–Civil War South he envisioned: democratic, industrial, urban, and free of nostalgia for the defeated plantation South.

Nineteenth Amendment (1920) Granted women the right to vote.

Nisei Japanese-Americans; literally, "second generation."

Normalcy Word coined by future president Warren G. Harding as part of a 1920 campaign speech—"not nostrums, but normalcy"—signifying public weariness with Woodrow Wilson's internationalism and domestic reforms.

North Atlantic Treaty Organization (NATO) Alliance founded in 1949 by ten western European nations, the United States, and Canada to deter Soviet expansion in Europe.

Northwest Ordinance of 1787 Created the Northwest Territory (area north of the Ohio River and west of Pennsylvania), established conditions for self-government and statehood, included a Bill of Rights, and permanently prohibited slavery.

Nullification Concept of invalidation of a federal law within the borders of a state; first expounded in Thomas Jefferson's draft of Kentucky resolution against Alien and Sedition Acts (1798); cited by South Carolina in its Ordinance of Nullification (1832) of the Tariff of Abominations, used by southern states to explain their secession from the Union (1861), and cited again by southern states to oppose the *Brown v. Board of Education* decision (1954).

Office of Price Administration Created in 1941 to control wartime inflation and price fixing resulting from shortages of many consumer goods, the OPA imposed wage and price freezes and administered a rationing system.

Okies Displaced farm families from the Oklahoma dust bowl who migrated to California during the 1930s in search of jobs.

Oneida Community Utopian community founded in 1848; the Perfectionist religious group practiced "complex marriage" under leader John Humphrey Noyes.

OPEC Organization of Petroleum Exporting Countries.

Open Door Policy In hopes of protecting the Chinese market for U.S. exports, Secretary of State John Hay demanded in 1899 that Chinese trade be open to all nations.

Open shop Situation in which union membership is not a condition of employment in a factory or other business.

Operation Dixie CIO's largely ineffective post–World War II campaign to unionize southern workers.

Oregon Trail Route of wagon trains bearing settlers from Independence, Missouri, to the Oregon Country in the 1840s through the 1860s.

Ostend Manifesto Memorandum written in 1854 from Ostend, Belgium, by the U.S. ministers to England, France, and Spain recommending purchase or seizure of Cuba in order to increase the United States' slaveholding territory.

Panic of 1819 Financial collapse brought on by sharply falling cotton prices, declining demand for American exports, and reckless western land speculation.

Panic of 1837 Beginning of major economic depression lasting about six years; touched off by a British financial crisis and made worse by falling cotton prices, credit and currency problems, and speculation in land, canals, and railroads.

Panic of 1857 Beginning of economic depression lasting about two years and brought on by falling grain prices and a weak financial system; the South was largely protected by international demand for its cotton.

Panic of 1873 Onset of severe six-year depression marked by bank failures and railroad and insurance bankruptcies.

Peace of Paris Signed on September 3, 1783, the treaty ending the Revolutionary War and recognizing American independence from Britain also established the border between Canada and the United States, fixed the western border at the Mississippi River, and ceded Florida to Spain.

Pendleton Civil Service Act (1883) Established the Civil Service Commission and marked the end of the spoils system.

Pentagon Papers Informal name for the Defense Department's secret history of the Vietnam conflict; leaked to the press by former official Daniel Ellsberg and published in the *New York Times* in 1971.

Philippine War American military campaign that suppressed the movement for Philippine independence after the Spanish-American War; America's death toll was over 4,000 and the Philippines' was far higher.

Pilgrims Puritan Separatists who broke completely with the Church of England and sailed to the New World aboard the *Mayflower*, founding Plymouth Colony on Cape Cod in 1620.

Pinckney's Treaty Treaty with Spain negotiated by Thomas Pinckney in 1795; established United States boundaries at the Mississippi River and the thirty-first parallel and allowed open transportation on the Mississippi.

Plantation An early word for a colony, a settlement "planted" from abroad among an alien population in Ireland or the New World. Later, a large agricultural enterprise that used unfree labor to produce a crop for the world market.

Planter In the antebellum South, the owner of a large farm worked by twenty or more slaves.

Platt Amendment (1901) Amendment to Cuban constitution that reserved the United States' right to intervene in Cuban affairs and forced newly independent Cuba to host American naval bases on the island.

Plessy v. Ferguson **(1896)** U.S. Supreme Court decision supporting the legality of Jim Crow laws that permitted or required "separate but equal" facilities for blacks and whites.

Poll tax Tax that must be paid in order to be eligible to vote; used as an effective means of disenfranchising black citizens after Reconstruction, since they often could not afford even a modest fee.

Popular sovereignty Allowed settlers in a disputed territory to decide the slavery issue for themselves; program most closely associated with Senator Stephen A. Douglas of Illinois.

Populist Party Founded in 1892, it advocated a variety of reform issues, including free coinage of silver, income tax, postal savings, regulation of railroads, and direct election of U.S. senators.

Potsdam Conference Last meeting of the major Allied powers, the conference took place outside Berlin from July 17 to August 2, 1945; United States president Harry Truman, Soviet dictator Joseph Stalin, and British prime minister Clement Attlee finalized plans begun at Yalta.

Proclamation of Amnesty and Reconstruction President Lincoln's proposal for reconstruction, issued in 1863, allowed southern states to rejoin the Union if 10 percent of the 1860 electorate signed loyalty pledges, accepted emancipation, and had received presidential pardons.

Proclamation of 1763 Royal directive issued after the French and Indian War prohibiting settlement, surveys, and land grants west of the Appalachian Mountains; caused considerable resentment among colonists hoping to move west.

Progressive Party Created when former president Theodore Roosevelt broke away from the Republican Party to run for president again in 1912; the party supported progressive reforms similar to the Democrats but stopped short of seeking to eliminate trusts. Also the name of party backing Robert La Follette for president in 1924.

Progressivism Broad-based reform movement, 1900–1917, that sought governmental action in solving problems in many areas of American life, including education, public health, the economy, the environment, labor, transportation, and politics.

Proposition 13 Measure approved by California voters in 1978 prohibiting future increases in property taxes; marked beginning of "tax revolt" as major political impulse.

Public sphere The world of political organization and debate in private associations and publications outside the control of government.

Pueblo Revolt Uprising in 1680 in which Pueblo Indians temporarily drove Spanish colonists out of modern-day New Mexico.

Pullman Strike Strike against the Pullman Palace Car Company in the company town of Pullman, Illinois, on May 11, 1894, by the American Railway Union under Eugene V. Debs; the strike was crushed by court injunctions and federal troops two months later.

Pure Food and Drug Act (1906) First law to regulate manufacturing of food and medicines; prohibited dangerous additives and inaccurate labeling.

Puritans English religious group that sought to purify the Church of England; founded the Massachusetts Bay Colony under John Winthrop in 1630.

Quakers (Society of Friends) Religious group in England and America whose members believed all persons possessed the "inner light" or spirit of God; they were early proponents of abolition of slavery and equal rights for women.

Radical Republicans Group within the Republican Party in the 1850s and 1860s that advocated strong resistance to the expansion of slavery, opposition to compromise with the South in the secession crisis of 1860–1861, emancipation and arming of black soldiers during the Civil War, and equal civil and political rights for blacks during Reconstruction.

Railroad Strike of 1877 Interstate strike, crushed by federal troops, which resulted in extensive property damage and many deaths.

Reaganomics Popular name for President Ronald Reagan's philosophy of "supply side" economics, which combined tax cuts with an unregulated marketplace.

Reconstruction Act (1867) Established temporary military governments in ten Confederate states—excepting Tennessee—and required that the states ratify the Fourteenth Amendment and permit freedmen to vote.

Reconstruction Finance Corporation Federal program established in 1932 under President Herbert Hoover to loan money to banks and other institutions to help them avert bankruptcy.

Red Scare Fear among many Americans after World War I of Communists in particular and noncitizens in general, a reaction to the Russian Revolution, mail bombs, strikes, and riots.

Redeemers Conservative white Democrats, many of them planters or businessmen, who reclaimed control of the South following the end of Reconstruction.

Regulators Groups of backcountry Carolina settlers who protested colonial policies.

Republican Party Organized in 1854 by antislavery Whigs, Democrats, and Free Soilers in response to the passage of the Kansas-Nebraska Act; nominated John C. Frémont for president in 1856 and Abraham Lincoln in 1860; also the name of the party formed by Thomas Jefferson and James Madison in the 1790s.

Republicanism Political theory in eighteenth-century England and America that celebrated active participation in public life by economically independent citizens as central to freedom.

Revolution of 1800 First time that an American political party surrendered power to the opposition party; Jefferson, a Republican, had defeated incumbent Adams, a Federalist, for president.

Right-to-work State laws enacted to prevent imposition of the closed shop; any worker, whether or not a union member, could be hired.

Roe v. Wade (1973) U.S. Supreme Court decision requiring states to permit first-trimester abortions.

Roosevelt Corollary (1904) President Theodore Roosevelt announced in what was essentially a corollary to the Monroe

Doctrine that the United States could intervene militarily to prevent interference from European powers in the Western Hemisphere.

Rough Riders The first U.S. Volunteer Cavalry, led in battle in the Spanish-American War by Theodore Roosevelt; they were victorious in their only battle near Santiago, Cuba, and Roosevelt used the notoriety to aid his political career.

Santa Fe Trail Beginning in the 1820s, a major trade route from St. Louis, Missouri, to Santa Fe, New Mexico Territory.

Saratoga, Battle of Major defeat of British general John Burgoyne and more than 5,000 British troops at Saratoga, New York, on October 17, 1777.

Scalawags Southern white Republicans—some former Unionists—who supported Reconstruction governments.

***Schenck v. U.S.* (1919)** U.S. Supreme Court decision upholding the wartime Espionage and Sedition Acts; in the opinion he wrote for the case, Justice Oliver Wendell Holmes set the now-familiar "clear and present danger" standard.

Scientific management Management campaign to improve worker efficiency using measurements like "time and motion" studies to achieve greater productivity; introduced by Frederick Winslow Taylor in 1911.

Scopes trial (1925) Trial of John Scopes, Tennessee teacher accused of violating state law prohibiting teaching of the theory of evolution; it became a nationally celebrated confrontation between religious fundamentalism and civil liberties.

Scottsboro case (1931) In overturning verdicts against nine black youths accused of raping two white women, the U.S. Supreme Court established precedents in *Powell v. Alabama* (1932), that adequate counsel must be appointed in capital cases, and in *Norris v. Alabama* (1935), that African-Americans cannot be excluded from juries.

Second Great Awakening Religious revival movement of the early decades of the nineteenth century, in reaction to the growth of secularism and rationalist religion; began the predominance of the Baptist and Methodist churches.

Segregation Policy of separating persons on the basis of race in schools, transportation, and other public facilities; *de facto* segregation refers to social customs that accomplish this, *de jure* segregation to laws requiring it.

Seneca Falls Convention First women's rights meeting and the genesis of the women's suffrage movement; held in July 1848 in a church in Seneca Falls, New York, organized by Elizabeth Cady Stanton and Lucretia Coffin Mott.

"Separate but equal" Principle underlying legal racial segregation, upheld in *Plessy v. Ferguson* (1896) and struck down in *Brown v. Board of Education* (1954).

Separation of Powers Feature of the U.S. Constitution, sometimes called "checks and balances," in which power is divided between executive, legislative, and judicial branches of the national government so that no one can dominate the other two and endanger citizens' liberties.

Servicemen's Readjustment Act (1944) The "GI Bill of Rights" provided money for education and other benefits to military personnel returning from World War II.

Settlement houses Late-nineteenth-century movement to offer a broad array of social services in urban immigrant neighborhoods; Chicago's Hull House was one of hundreds of settlement houses that operated by the early twentieth century.

Seventeenth Amendment (1913) Progressive reform that required U.S. senators to be elected directly by voters; previously, senators were chosen by state legislatures.

Shakers Founded by Mother Ann Lee in England, the United Society of Believers in Christ's Second Appearing settled in Watervliet, New York, in 1774 and subsequently established eighteen additional communes in the Northeast, Indiana, and Kentucky.

Sharecropping Type of farm tenancy that developed after the Civil War in which landless workers—often former slaves—farmed land in exchange for farm supplies and a share of the crop.

Shays's Rebellion (1787) Massachusetts farmer Daniel Shays and 1,200 compatriots, seeking debt relief through issuance of paper currency and lower taxes, attempted to prevent courts from seizing property from indebted farmers.

Sherman Antitrust Act (1890) First law to restrict monopolistic trusts and business combinations; extended by the Clayton Antitrust Act of 1914.

Sherman Silver Purchase Act (1890) In replacing and extending the provisions of the Bland-Allison Act of 1878, it increased the amount of silver periodically bought for coinage.

Single tax Concept of taxing only landowners as a remedy for poverty, promulgated by Henry George in *Progress and Poverty* (1879).

Sit-down strikes Tactic adopted by labor unions in the mid- and late 1930s, whereby striking workers refused to leave factories, making production impossible; proved highly effective in the organizing drive of the Congress of Industrial Organizations.

Sit-ins Tactic adopted by young civil rights activists, beginning in 1960, of demanding service at lunch counters or public accommodations and refusing to leave if denied access; marked the beginning of the most militant phase of the civil rights struggle.

Sixteenth Amendment (1913) Legalized the federal income tax.

Smith v. Allwright (1944) U.S. Supreme Court decision that outlawed all-white Democratic Party primaries in Texas.

Social Darwinism Application of Charles Darwin's theory of natural selection to society; used the concept of the "survival of the fittest" to justify class distinctions and to explain poverty.

Social Gospel Preached by liberal Protestant clergymen in the late nineteenth and early twentieth centuries; advocated the application of Christian principles to social problems generated by industrialization.

Social Security Act (1935) Created the Social Security system with provisions for a retirement pension, unemployment insurance, disability insurance, and public assistance (welfare).

Socialist Party Political party demanding public ownership of major economic enterprises in the United States as well as reforms like recognition of labor unions and women's suffrage; reached peak of influence in 1912 when presidential candidate Eugene V. Debs received over 900,000 votes.

Sons of Liberty Organizations formed by Samuel Adams, John Hancock, and other radicals in response to the Stamp Act.

South Carolina Exposition and Protest Written in 1828 by Vice-President John C. Calhoun of South Carolina to protest the so-called Tariff of Abominations, which seemed to favor northern industry; introduced the concept of state interposition and became the basis for South Carolina's Nullification Doctrine of 1833.

Southeast Asia Treaty Organization (SEATO) Pact among mostly Western nations signed in 1954; designed to deter Communist expansion and cited as a justification for U.S. involvement in Vietnam.

Southern Christian Leadership Conference (SCLC) Civil rights organization founded in 1957 by the Reverend Martin Luther King Jr., and other civil rights leaders.

Spoils system The term—meaning the filling of federal government jobs with persons loyal to the party of the president—originated in Andrew Jackson's first term.

Sputnik First artificial satellite to orbit the earth; launched October 4, 1957, by the Soviet Union.

Stalwarts Conservative Republican Party faction during the presidency of Rutherford B. Hayes, 1877–1881; led by Senator Roscoe B. Conkling of New York, Stalwarts opposed civil service reform and favored a third term for President Ulysses S. Grant.

Stamp Act (1765) Parliament required that revenue stamps be affixed to all colonial printed matter, documents, and playing cards; the Stamp Act Congress met to formulate a response, and the act was repealed the following year.

Standard Oil Company Founded in 1870 by John D. Rockefeller in Cleveland, Ohio, it soon grew into the nation's first industry-dominating trust; the Sherman Antitrust Act (1890) was enacted in part to combat abuses by Standard Oil.

Staple crop Important cash crop, for example, cotton or tobacco.

Steamboats Paddlewheelers that could travel both up- and down-river in deep or shallow waters; they became commercially viable early in the nineteenth century and soon developed into America's first inland freight and passenger service network.

Strategic Defense Initiative ("Star Wars") Defense Department's plan during the Reagan administration to build a system to destroy incoming missiles in space.

Student Nonviolent Coordinating Committee (SNCC) Founded in 1960 to coordinate civil rights sit-ins and other forms of grassroots protest.

Students for a Democratic Society (SDS) Major organization of the New Left, founded at the University of Michigan in 1960 by Tom Hayden and Al Haber.

Sugar Act (Revenue Act of 1764) Parliament's tax on refined sugar and many other colonial products.

Taft-Hartley Act (1947) Passed over President Harry Truman's veto, the law contained a number of provisions to weaken labor unions, including the banning of closed shops.

Tariff Federal tax on imported goods.

Tariff of Abominations (Tariff of 1828) Taxed imported goods at a very high rate; aroused strong opposition in the South.

Tariff of 1816 First true protective tariff, intended to protect certain American goods against foreign competition.

Tax Reform Act (1986) Lowered federal income tax rates to 1920s levels and eliminated many loopholes.

Teapot Dome Harding administration scandal in which Secretary of the Interior Albert B. Fall profited from secret leasing to private oil companies of government oil reserves at Teapot Dome, Wyoming, and Elk Hills, California.

Tennessee Valley Authority Created in 1933 to control flooding in the Tennessee River valley, provide work for the region's unemployed, and produce inexpensive electric power for the region.

Tenure of Office Act (1867) Required the president to obtain Senate approval to remove any official whose appointment had also required Senate approval; President Andrew Johnson's violation of the law by firing Secretary of War Edwin Stanton led to Johnson's impeachment.

Tet Offensive Surprise attack by the Viet Cong and North Vietnamese during the Vietnamese New Year of 1968; turned American public opinion strongly against the war in Vietnam.

Thirteenth Amendment Constitutional amendment adopted in 1865 that irrevocably abolished slavery throughout the United States.

Three Mile Island Nuclear power plant near Harrisburg, Pennsylvania, site of 1979 accident that released radioactive steam into the air; public reaction ended the nuclear power industry's expansion.

Title IX Part of the Educational Amendments Act of 1972 that banned gender discrimination in higher education.

Tonkin Gulf Resolution (1964) Passed by Congress in reaction to supposedly unprovoked attacks on American warships off the coast of North Vietnam; it gave the president unlimited authority to defend U.S. forces and members of SEATO.

Townshend Acts (1767) Parliamentary measures (named for the chancellor of the Exchequer) that taxed tea and other commodities, and established a Board of Customs Commissioners and colonial vice-admiralty courts.

Trail of Tears Cherokees' own term for their forced removal, 1838–1839, from the Southeast to Indian lands (later Oklahoma); of 15,000 forced to march, 4,000 died on the way.

Transcendentalism Philosophy of a small group of mid-nineteenth-century New England writers and thinkers, including Ralph Waldo Emerson, Henry David Thoreau, and Margaret Fuller; they stressed personal and intellectual self-reliance.

Transcontinental railroad First line across the continent from Omaha, Nebraska, to Sacramento, California, established in 1869 with the linkage of the Union Pacific and Central Pacific railroads at Promontory, Utah.

Truman Doctrine President Harry S. Truman's program announced in 1947 of aid to European countries—particularly Greece and Turkey—threatened by communism.

Trust Companies combined to limit competition.

Twenty-first Amendment (1933) Repealed the prohibition of the manufacture, sale, and transportation of alcoholic beverages, effectively nullifying the Eighteenth Amendment.

Twenty-second Amendment (1951) Limited presidents to two full terms of office or two terms plus two years of an assumed term; passed in reaction to President Franklin D. Roosevelt's unprecedented four elected terms.

Twenty-sixth Amendment (1971) Lowered the voting age from twenty-one to eighteen.

U.S.S. *Maine* Battleship that exploded in Havana Harbor on February 15, 1898, resulting in 266 deaths; the American public, assuming that the Spanish had mined the ship, clamored for war, and the Spanish-American War was declared two months later.

Uncle Tom's Cabin Harriet Beecher Stowe's 1852 antislavery novel popularized the abolitionist position.

Underground Railroad Operating in the decades before the Civil War, the "railroad" was a clandestine system of routes and safehouses through which slaves were led to freedom in the North.

Understanding clause Added to southern state constitutions in the late nineteenth century, it allowed illiterate whites to circumvent literacy tests for voting by demonstrating that they understood a passage in the Constitution; black citizens would be judged by white registrars to have failed.

Unitarianism Late-eighteenth-century liberal offshoot of the New England Congregationalist Church; rejecting the Trinity, Unitarianism professed the oneness of God and the goodness of rational man.

United Farm Workers Union for the predominantly Mexican-American migrant laborers of the Southwest, organized by César Chavez in 1962.

United Nations Organization of nations to maintain world peace, established in 1945 and headquartered in New York.

Universal Negro Improvement Association Black nationalist movement active in the United States from 1916 to 1923, led by Marcus Garvey.

V-E Day May 8, 1945, the day World War II officially ended in Europe.

Vertical integration Company's avoidance of middlemen by producing its own supplies and providing for distribution of its product.

Veto President's constitutional power to reject legislation passed by Congress; a two-thirds vote in both houses of Congress can override a veto.

Vicksburg, Battle of The fall of Vicksburg, Mississippi, to General Ulysses S. Grant's army on July 4, 1863, after two months of siege was a turning point in the war because it gave the Union control of the Mississippi River.

Vietnam War Longest war in which the United States has been involved; began with giving American financial assistance to France, who sought to maintain control over Vietnam colony; moved to dispatching advisers to bolster the government of South Vietnam; and finally sent over 500,000 American soldiers by the mid-1960s; resulted in massive antiwar movement, eventual American withdrawal, and communist victory in 1975; only war the United States has lost.

Virginia and Kentucky Resolutions (1798–1799) Passed by the Virginia and the Kentucky legislatures; written by James Madison and Thomas Jefferson in response to the Alien and Sedition Acts, the resolutions advanced the state-compact theory of the Constitution. Virginia's resolution called on the federal courts to protect free speech. Jefferson's draft for Kentucky stated that a state could nullify federal law, but this was deleted.

Virginia and New Jersey Plans Differing opinions of delegations to the Constitutional Convention: New Jersey wanted one legislative body with equal representation for each state; Virginia's plan called for a strong central government and a two-house legislature apportioned by population.

Volstead Act (1919) Enforced the Prohibition amendment, beginning January 1920.

Voting Rights Act of 1965 Passed in the wake of Martin Luther King Jr.'s, Selma to Montgomery March, it authorized federal protection of the right to vote and permitted federal enforcement of minority voting rights in individual counties, mostly in the South.

Wabash Railroad v. Illinois (1886) Reversing the U.S. Supreme Court's ruling in *Munn v. Illinois*, the decision disallowed state regulation of interstate commerce.

Wade-Davis bill (1864) Radical Republicans' plan for reconstruction that required loyalty oaths, abolition of slavery, repudiation of war debts, and denial of political rights to high-ranking Confederate officials; President Lincoln refused to sign the bill.

Wagner Act (National Labor Relations Act of 1935) Established the National Labor Relations Board and facilitated unionization by regulating employment and bargaining practices.

War Industries Board Run by financier Bernard Baruch, the board planned production and allocation of war materiel, supervised purchasing, and fixed prices, 1917–1919.

War of 1812 Fought with Britain, 1812–1814, over issues that included impressment of American sailors, interference with shipping, and collusion with Northwest Territory Indians; settled by the Treaty of Ghent in 1814.

War on Poverty Announced by President Lyndon B. Johnson in his 1964 State of the Union address; under the Economic Opportunity Bill signed later that year, Head Start, VISTA, and the Jobs Corps were created, and programs were created for students, farmers, and businesses in efforts to eliminate poverty.

War Powers Act Law passed in 1973, reflecting growing opposition to American involvement in Vietnam War; required congressional approval before president sent troops abroad.

War Production Board Created in 1942 to coordinate industrial efforts in World War II; similar to the War Industries Board in World War I.

Warren Court The U.S. Supreme Court under Chief Justice Earl Warren, 1953–1969, decided such landmark cases as *Brown v. Board of Education* (school desegregation), *Baker v. Carr* (legislative redistricting), and *Gideon v. Wainwright* and *Miranda v. Arizona* (rights of criminal defendants).

Washington Armaments Conference Leaders of nine world powers met in 1921–1922 to discuss the naval race; resulting treaties limited to a specific ratio the carrier and battleship tonnage of each nation (Five-Power Naval Treaty), formally ratified the Open Door to China (Nine-Power Treaty), and agreed to respect each other's Pacific territories (Four-Power Treaty).

Watergate Washington office and apartment complex that lent its name to the 1972–1974 scandal of the Nixon administration; when his knowledge of the break-in at the Watergate and subsequent coverup was revealed, Nixon resigned the presidency under threat of impeachment.

Webster-Hayne debate U.S. Senate debate of January 1830 between Daniel Webster of Massachusetts and Robert Hayne of South Carolina over nullification and states' rights.

Whig Party Founded in 1834 to unite factions opposed to President Andrew Jackson, the party favored federal responsibility for internal improvements; the party ceased to exist by the late 1850s, when party members divided over the slavery issue.

Whiskey Rebellion Violent protest by western Pennsylvania farmers against the federal excise tax on whiskey, 1794.

Wilmot Proviso Proposal to prohibit slavery in any land acquired in the Mexican War, but southern senators, led by John C. Calhoun of South Carolina, defeated the measure in 1846 and 1847.

Women's Christian Temperance Union Largest female reform society of the late nineteenth century; it moved from opposing sale of liquor to demanding the right to vote for women.

Works Progress Administration (WPA) Part of the Second New Deal, it provided jobs for millions of the unemployed on construction and arts projects.

Wounded Knee, Battle of Last incident of the Indian Wars took place in 1890 in the Dakota Territory, where the U.S. Cavalry killed over 200 Sioux men, women, and children.

Writs of assistance One of the colonies' main complaints against Britain, the writs allowed unlimited search warrants without cause to look for evidence of smuggling.

XYZ affair French foreign minister Tallyrand's three anonymous agents demanded payments to stop French plundering of American ships in 1797; refusal to pay the bribe was followed by two years of undeclared sea war with France (1798–1800).

Yalta conference Meeting of Franklin D. Roosevelt, Winston Churchill, and Joseph Stalin at a Crimean resort to discuss the postwar world on February 4–11, 1945; Joseph Stalin claimed large areas in eastern Europe for Soviet domination.

Yellow journalism Sensationalism in newspaper publishing that reached a peak in the circulation war between Joseph Pulitzer's *New York World* and William Randolph Hearst's *New York Journal* in the 1890s; the papers' accounts of events in Havana Harbor in 1898 led directly to the Spanish-American War.

Yeoman farmers Small landowners (the majority of white families in the Old South) who farmed their own land and usually did not own slaves.

Yick Wo v. Hopkins Supreme Court decision in 1886 overturning San Francisco law that, as enforced, discriminated against Chinese-owned laundries; established principle that equal protection of the law embodied in Fourteenth Amendment applied to all Americans, not just former slaves.

Yorktown, Battle of Last battle of the Revolutionary War; General Lord Charles Cornwallis along with over 7,000 British troops surrendered at Yorktown, Virginia, on October 17, 1781.

Young Americans for Freedom Organization of conservative students founded in 1960; played major role in 1964 presidential campaign of Barry Goldwater and in rebirth of conservatism in the 1960s.

Zimmermann Telegram From the German foreign secretary to the German minister in Mexico, February 1917, instructing him to offer to recover Texas, New Mexico, and Arizona for Mexico if it would fight the United States to divert attention from Germany in the event that the United States joined the war.

PHOTOS

Author Photo: © Flynn Larsen

2 (left) The John Carter Library at Brown University; **2 (right)** Library of Congress; **3 (top)** Corbis; **3 (bottom right)** Unidentified artist, British, 18th century or first quarter 19th century; *Quaker Meeting*; Oil on canvas; 64.1 × 76.2cm (25 1/4 × 30in.); Museum of Fine Arts, Boston; Bequest of Maxim Karolik; 64.456; **4–5** Bridgeman Art Library; **7** Cliché Bibliothèque nationale de France, Paris; **10** Photo Courtesy of Edward E. Ayer Collection, The Newberry Library, Chicago; **11 (top)** National Park Service, Chaco Culture National Historic Park, Chaco Archive neg. no. 25462; **11 (bottom)** Timothy O'Sullivan, *Ancient Ruins in the Canon de Chelle, N. M. in a Niche 50 Feet above Present Canon Bed*, albumen silver print, 1873; Amon Carter Museum, Fort Worth, Texas P1982.27.38; **12** The London Art Archive/Alamy; **15** British National Archives; **16** Bridgeman Art Library; **17 (top)** Library of Congress; **17 (bottom)** Courtesy Lilly Library, Indiana University, Bloomington, IN; **22** The Mariners' Museum, Newport News, VA; **23** Biblioteca Estense Universitaria, Modena; **24** By permission of the British Library; **26** Florence, Library Medicea Laurenziana, ms. Med. Palat. 220. By permission of the Ministero per I Beni e le Attivita' Culturali; **27** Granger Collection; **28** William L. Clements Library, University of Michigan; **29** Courtesy of the Library of Congress, *Huexotzinco Codex*, Painting V, Manuscript 1531; **30** Museo de America, Madrid, 1980.03.01, .02, .09; **31** Instituto Nacional de Antropologia e Historia, Chapultepec Castle, Mexico City; **32** Rare Books Division, The New York Public Library, Astor, Lenox, and Tilden Foundations; **33** Library of Congress; **34** Museo Naval, Madrid; **37** Library of Congress, Prints & Photographs Division, Edward S. Curtis Collection; **40** Abby Aldrich Rockefeller Folk Art Museum, Colonial Williamsburg Foundation, Williamsburg, VA; **41** History Collection, Nova Scotia Library; **43** Collection du monastère des Ursulines de Québec, Museé des Ursulines de Québec (1997.1017); **44** Bettmann/Corbis; **46** Alamy; **47** Museum of the City of New York/Bridgeman Art Library; **48** The Colonial Williamsburg Foundation; **52–53** Woburn Abbey, Bedfordshire, UK/The Bridgeman Art Library; **55** The London Art Archive/Alamy; **57** The John Carter Brown Library at Brown University; **58** The Library Company of Philadelphia; **59** Henry E. Huntington Library #3373; **60** GLC 4110. Document signed: contracts relating to the indenture of James Mahony, 31 March 1773. (The Gilder Lehrman Collection, courtesy of the Gilder Lehrman Institute of American

History, New York.); **61** Bridgeman Art Library; **62** Museum of Art, Rhode Island School of Design. Gift of Robert Winthrop. Photography by Erik Gould; **64 (top)** Corbis; **64 (bottom)** National Portrait Gallery, Smithsonian Institution/Art Resource, NY; **65** Library of Congress; **66** Library of Congress; **66** George Arents Collection, New York Public Library; **67** Corbis; **69** Library of Congress; **70** Courtesy, American Antiquarian Society; **71** Courtesy of the John Carter Brown Library at Brown University; **72** Granger Collection; **73** Courtesy of the Massachusetts Archives; **74** Worcester Art Museum, Worcester, Massachusetts, Gift of William A. Savage; **75** Massachussetts Historical Society; **81** Annenberg Rare Book and Manuscript Library, Van Pelt-Dietrich Library Center, U Penn; **82** Library of Congress; **83** *Self-Portrait*, by Thomas Smith, 1948.19, Worcester Art Museum, Worcester, Massachusetts; **84** *Mrs. Elizabeth Freake and Baby Mary*, unknown artist, 1963.134, Worcester Art Museum, Worcester, Massachusetts; **85** Historical Picture Archive/Corbis; **86 (top)** Private Collection/Bridgeman Art Library; **86 (bottom)** © National Portrait Gallery, London; **87** By permission of the British Library; **88** The Cromwell Museum, Huntingdon; **92–93** The Colonial Williamsburg Foundation; **94** The John Carter Brown Library at Brown University; **98** Library of Congress; **100** Germantown Historical Society, Philadelphia, PA; **101** Unidentified artist, British, 18th century or first quarter 19th century; *Quaker Meeting*; Oil on canvas; 64.1 × 76.2cm (25 1/4 × 30in.); Museum of Fine Arts, Boston; Bequest of Maxim Karolik; 64.456; **103** British Library 1786.c.9; **104** Courtesy of the John Carter Brown Library at Brown University; **105** Colonial Williamsburg Foundation; **107** National Maritime Museum, London; **109** Springhill, County Londonderry, Northern Ireland, National Trust Photographic Library/Derrick E. Witty/Bridgeman Art Library; **112** Courtesy of the Peabody Essex Museum; **116** National Archives; **117** The Historical Society of Pennsylvania; **121** Benjamin West, Pennsylvania Academy of the Fine Arts; Joseph and Sarah Harrison Collection; **122** The Library Company of Philadelphia; **123 (top)** Winterthur Museum; **123 (bottom)** Courtesy of the Maryland Historical Society 1900.5.1; **124** Photograph © 2010 Museum of Fine Arts, Boston; **125** Geoffrey Clements/Corbis; **126** Colonial Williamsburg Foundation; **129** Fenimore Art Museum, Cooperstown, New York; **130** Gift of Edgar William and Bernice Chrysler Garbisch, Image © 2006 Board of Trustees, National Gallery of Art, Washington; **134–35**: Abby Aldrich Rockefeller Folk Art Museum, Colonial Williamsburg Foundation, Williamsburg, VA; **137** Library of Congress; **138** The John Carter Library at Brown University; **141** Library of Congress; **142 (top)** Courtesy of the

Maryland Historical Society; **142 (bottom)** Colonial Williamsburg Foundation; 143 Courtesy of the Maryland Historical Society, **145** Granger Collection; **146** Newport Historical Society (53.3); **149** Charleston Library Society; **151** By Courtesy of the National Portrait Gallery, London; **152** Chicago Historical Society; **153** By courtesy of the Trustees of Sir John Soane's Museum; **154 (top)** Library of Congress; **154 (bottom)** © National Portrait Gallery, London; **155** Library of Congress; **158** This item is reproduced by permission of The Huntington Library, San Marino, California; **159** Bettmann/Corbis; **161** Wikimedia; **162** National Portrait Gallery, London; **163** Library of Congress; **165** Courtesy of the Bancroft Library, University of California, Berkeley; **166** Courtesy of Tulane University; **167** Granger Collection; **168** Library of Congress; **174** Library of Congress; **179 (top)** Corbis; **179 (bottom)** MPI/Getty Images; **180 (top)** Courtesy of the Beineke Rare Book and Manuscript Library, Yale University; **180 (bottom)** © New Bedford Whaling Museum; **181 (top)** Print Collection, Miriam and Ira D. Wallach Division of Art, Prints, and Photographs, The New York Public Library; Astor, Lenox, and Tilden Foundations; **181 (bottom)** The Saint Louis Art Museum; **182–83** The Colonial Williamsburg Foundation; **185** By permission of the Houghton Library, Harvard University; **186** © copyright the Trustees of The British Museum; **187 (top)** Corbis; **187 (bottom)** The Colonial Williamsburg Foundation; **188** Granger Collection; **189** Kunhardt/Picture History; **193** Library of Congress; **194 (top)** Michael Nicholson/Corbis; **194 (bottom)** Library of Congress; **195** Library of Congress; **197** Miriam and Ira D. Wallach Division of Art, Prints and Photographs, New York Public Library; **198** Chicago Historical Society; **199 (top)** National Portrait Gallery, London; **199 (bottom)** American Philosophical Society; **203** Library of Congress; **204** American Antiquarian Society; **205** Sid Lapidus Collection. Rare Books Division. Department of Rare Books and Special Collections. Princeton University Library; **206** Library of Congress; **207** Anne S. K. Brown Military Collection, Brown University; **208** Morristown National Historic Park; **212** Library of Congress; **214** Library of Congress Prints and Photographs Division; **218–19** York County Historical Society/The Bridgeman Art Library; **221** National Gallery of Art, Washington, Gift of Mrs. Robert Homans; **222** Cliché Bibliothèque nationale de France, Paris; **224** Historical Society of Pennsylvania; **226** Courtesy of the New-York Historical Society; **228** Granger Collection; **229** Courtesy of the Beineke Rare Book and Manuscript Library, Yale University; **230** American Antiquarian Society; **231** Bettmann/Corbis; **232** The Library

TEXT, TABLES, AND FIGURES

Page numbers in *italics* refer to illustrations.